# A MAN'S REACH

treasures, and among the many here included is his classic on the case of the *U.S.* v. *Roth*, probably the most cogent view of censorship and obscenity ever presented.

Justice William O. Douglas, in a Foreword, writes that Judge Frank had "a remarkable mind, a vital spirit, universal interests, and a capacity for warm personal relations." All these attributes are radiantly present in this book, which both lawyers and the intelligent general reader will find warmly rewarding.

Barbara Frank Kristein is Judge Jerome Frank's daughter. A freelance writer, she is the co-author of Judge Frank's last book, *Not Guilty*, completed the day before he died. She lives on Long Island with her husband, who is an economist.

୶ THE PHILOSOPHY OF JUDGE JEROME FRANK

# A MAN'S REACH

EDITED BY BARBARA FRANK KRISTEIN ੭०

---

Ah, but a man's reach should exceed his grasp,
Or what's a heaven for?

ROBERT BROWNING ੭०

---

THE MACMILLAN COMPANY, NEW YORK
COLLIER-MACMILLAN LIMITED, LONDON

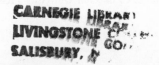

Second Printing

The Macmillan Company, New York
Collier-Macmillan Canada Ltd., Toronto, Ontario

Library of Congress catalog card number: 63–16104

Printed in the United States of America

DESIGNED BY RONALD FARBER

Acknowledgment is gratefully given to the following people and publications for permission to reprint copyrighted material:

The Foreword by William O. Douglas is reprinted by personal permission of Mr. Justice Douglas.

"The Place of the Expert in a Democratic Society" is reprinted by permission of the editor of the Philosophy of Science. Copyright 1949 by the Philosophy of Science Association.

"The Speech of Judges: A Dissenting Opinion" is reprinted by permission of the editor of the Virginia Law Review. Copyright 1943 by the University of Virginia.

"Judge Learned Hand," excerpts from a manuscript based on lectures delivered at Yale Law School, 1955: "Judge Learned Hand" originally appeared in the University of Chicago Law Review in a different version. Permission to reprint is from the University of Chicago Press. Copyright © 1957 by the University of Chicago.

Selections from If Men Were Angels by Jerome N. Frank, Harper & Brothers. Copyright 1930, 1938, 1942 by Jerome N. Frank. Reprinted by arrangement with Barbara Frank Kristein.

Book review of George Calhoun's Introduction to Greek Legal Science, reprinted by permission of the editor of the Harvard Law Review. Copyright 1944 by the Harvard Law Review Association.

Selections from Law and the Modern Mind by Jerome Frank, copyright 1930, 1933, 1949 by Coward McCann, Inc., copyright 1930 by Brentano's, Inc., are from Anchor Books edition, 1963. Copyright renewed in 1958 by Florence K. Frank. Reprinted by arrangement with Barbara Frank Kristein.

Selections from Not Guilty by Judge Jerome Frank and Barbara Frank. Copyright © 1957 by Barbara Frank. Reprinted by permission of Doubleday & Company, Inc.

Selections from Courts on Trial by Jerome Frank. Copyright 1949 by Jerome Frank. Reprinted by permission of Princeton University Press.

**EDITOR'S NOTE** ✌︎§ Although the author's works contain voluminous foot-notes, for reasons of purely personal taste I have omitted them as such. Those which I have included I have incorporated, in parentheses, in the body of the text. Deletions originally made by the author I have indicated by the use of three asterisks; all other deletions are the editor's. Because the writings in this book have been taken from various sources, minor editorial changes have been made to ensure uniformity of style. Readers who wish to consult the original works will find, in the back of the book, a bibliography of materials used. ৪◟

B. F. K.

# CONTENTS ε∾

# INTRODUCTION ॐ

IN THIS VOLUME a devoted daughter presents a rich anthology of Jerome Frank's essays, books, and judicial opinions. If you knew him during his lifetime, you can listen to him here again and invoke the magic of his personality. If you did not know him, here is your chance to meet one of the brightest spirits of the century. Though the man was vastly more than his writings, one door after another opens in this book, and through each of them Jerome Frank comes to visit.

It would be violating his own principles if I purported to give you anything like a biography, for, as he avowed in lecturing on Judge Learned Hand (page 48), there is an "unexplorable lonesomeness," "unique privacy," and "no-other-man's land" in a human being where it is impossible for anyone else to penetrate. He frequently called history "twistory," and would probably have called biography "lie-ography." Let me just list some of the main public facts of his career.

One paragraph will suffice. Born in New York in 1889, he practiced law in Chicago and New York for a number of years, created a sensation in 1930 when he published the controversial *Law and the Modern Mind*, became one of the most creative figures in President Roosevelt's New Deal, held important posts in the AAA and SEC, and in 1941 became a judge of the United States Court of Appeals for the Second Circuit where he served until his death in 1957. Meanwhile, besides lecturing at Yale Law School and writing several books, the most important of which was *Courts on Trial* (1949), Judge Frank played a ubiquitous role as leader in libertarian and humanitarian causes. Since he surpassed all other jurists in getting the findings of the behavioral sciences and the techniques of law under one hat, Justice Hugo L. Black wrote on his death: "I rate him as one of the great judges. No judge that I know had so great a knowledge of the history and development of human societies."

There is no use in trying to describe Jerome Frank impersonally. Some will picture his warm sympathy, some his intellectual radiance, some his delightful irreverence; everyone who knew him at all will remember how exuberant and zestful he was, for his psyche never grew middle-aged. Felix Frankfurter and Learned Hand rank among the grand conversationalists of the period, but Jerome Frank excelled both of them. He was supremely interesting for the simple reason that he was supremely interested.

The door opens now, and he comes to join us. With a long, narrow head, high, intellectual forehead, and sallow complexion which may remind some of a Spanish Jesuit, he brings the spark and crackle of electricity. He is Search personified; his brilliant eyes and sensitive mouth seem made for inquiries. Who knows, they keep suggesting, perhaps we are the very ones who may hand him the key? He is eager and curious, and does not want the world to deceive him. As soon as he enters, we sense his animation and feel more alive. He does not dominate the room; he peoples it.

In the years of his practice, he was exceedingly a tough and ingenious adversary to take on. When the stakes were down in court, legislature, or administrative agency, it was not comfortable to be on the opposite side. Like Pliny in ancient Rome, he was a superb advocate, and he subscribed to Pliny's policy of using every available proof and argument because no one could tell which among a score of points might sway the mind of an arbiter. It was this lawyerlike habit that Jerome Frank retained when he wrote for the general public. He believed that readers' minds were at least as varied as judges' and that an author who respected their right to be different should show his respect by multiplying his arguments.

But when he comes to visit, he does not confuse a social conversation with a case in court. If you disagree with him, you may get a laugh, a sigh, a change of subject, a sly question that probes your motives, and often an acknowledgment that, yes, you are right. If you indulge in some logical in- consistencies, they do not bother him, for he knows that where the consis- tency of logic is thin, the consistency of life is rich, promiscuous, and thick. He is convinced that truth is a wild species that we can seek and hunt and even feed upon but that, whatever we do, we are not going to domesticate it.

That is why almost every item he wrote was spangled with elaborate footnotes. Seeing so many side issues as he did, recognizing so many tangents and bypaths, sensing so many undiscovered connections, he needed a whole panoply of footnotes to hold his main text intact. Footnotes were not mere lists of authorities; they were points where his thought poked through the seams. Though omitted for the most part in this volume, they have a special claim to attention; they show the profuseness of Judge Frank's synapses. They also show what a variegated and leaky kind of universe he felt he was inhabiting. In some instances—for example, the Rosenberg case that we shall soon mention—he used footnotes to intimate more than he thought the text could bear. Justices Black and Douglas, among others on the United States Supreme Court, never overlooked Frank's footnotes.

Jerome Frank (to use a collective name for a fascinating multiplicity of selves) is not to be caught in any single formula that may be offered to explain him. He often inveighed against the psychologists' concept of "an integrated personality," which he regarded as not only misleading but impertinent. Agreeing with him as I do, I cannot attempt to explain him here. What I can attempt is something much more modest, yet, I think, quite intriguing: that is, to elaborate what he had in mind when he dubbed himself a "trimmer" (page 3). He may have shocked some people and confused others by using such a word about himself, and possibly he took a certain delight in administering the shock, though scarcely in creating the confusion. What is a "trimmer," and was Jerome Frank really one?

## Trimming Against the World

Like Lord Halifax who wrote a famous essay on the subject, Jerome Frank used the words "to trim," "trimming," and "trimmer" in a strictly nautical sense, as when one trims a boat to restore its equilibrium. In this usage, "trimming" rarely means taking a position midway between the sides; on the contrary, it usually means taking a fairly extreme position on one side or the other. The need for trimming does not ordinarily arise unless equilibrium has been lost and the boat put in danger. Hence a trimmer is not usually the man of the middle; he is the man who risks a wetting in order to give balance and safety to thoughtless persons or misplaced cargo on the other side. It is not a posture of compromise but of unpopularity, singularity, and deliberate risk.

In this sense almost all great men have been trimmers, setting themselves in extreme opposition to the majority of their time and seeking to counterpoise the majority's exaggerations and distortions. The great trimmers have been like the aristocrat in classical Hellas who, when he was making a speech and the crowd applauded, turned to his friend and asked, "Have I said something foolish?" What we call new wisdom in any era is very likely to consist in trimming against the old wisdom.

This creates a special problem of interpretation, for how are we to distinguish between the positions a man takes spontaneously and the positions he takes for the sake of trimming? I suggest that we may safely take a great trimmer's denials at their face value but need to proceed cautiously when we consider his affirmations. Often what looks like an affirmation is essentially no more than a denial or the elaboration of a denial. For example, with Jerome Frank we are safe in construing his philosophy of fact-skepticism precisely as he expressed it, but when he goes on to propose subjecting judges to psychoanalysis, we may interpret this rather as a criticism of unstable judges than as an affirmation of faith in psychoanalysis. An intelligent trimmer may occupy an extreme position because he accepts its merits or because he sees too many people leaning rashly on the opposite rail.

Judge Frank was a paragon of trimmers. Turn where you will in his writings, and you find him almost invariably in opposition to the intellectual fads of the day. To make his trimming more effective, he watched to see when the intellectual crowd was ready to rush to his side of the boat, and when they did they found him firmly planted on the side they had just left—though, of course, in a much more sophisticated posture. In the 1920's when the mass of judges and lawyers did not dream that Sigmund Freud's insights could apply to the judicial process, Frank pushed the Freudian program and displayed its utility in *Law and the Modern Mind* (1930). By 1945, when Freud had become familiar fare that even lawyers were swallowing, Frank wrote *Fate and Freedom* to demonstrate the dangers that inhered in Freud's deterministic psychology. In the same book, he assailed Hegelianism, Marxism, and natural-law doctrines as jeopardizing individual freedom and moral responsibility.

He established a similar sequence in his treatment of the social sciences, which, because he saw so little of scientific method in them, he always called "social studies." Like other liberals, but with infinitely more knowledge than most, he fought hard and long to convince courts and legislatures that they ought to consider the findings and opinions of the social scientists. By the time he came to write *Courts on Trial* (1949), the battle for an attitude of receptivity had been largely won and a new danger had begun to loom: the general weakness of social-science methods and the general credulity of judges and lawyers. Uniquely equipped as he was in both disciplines, Judge Frank kept admonishing the social scientists to improve their methods and the men of law to remain receptive but become critical.

During the 1920's Jerome Frank was an outstanding leader among the "legal realists," all of whom may be regarded as trimmers insofar as they attempted to counterbalance the stodgy conservatism and mechanical conceptualism of legal thinking in their era. Yet as soon as they began to make substantial headway and convince the brighter lawyers that rules were not eternal verities but implements of economic, social, and psychological interests, Frank moved away from the others. He believed that realists like

Karl Llewellyn and Felix Cohen were fighting the battle of the 1920's long after the adversary had left the field and that their continued preoccupation with rule-skepticism was not only redundant but actually dangerous. For while theorists kept their eyes glued on the permutations of legal rules, no one was doing anything about the law's seriously defective machinery for finding the *facts*. As he saw them, his fellow realists were defaulting in their obligation to shift the campaign from rule-skepticism to fact-skepticism.

To him, fact-skepticism was a moral faith. When he insisted that judicial methods of determining the facts of a past incident were pervasively unreliable and uncertain, he was always serving two highly constructive purposes: (a) to reduce the errors and uncertainties as far as procedural reforms could possibly reduce them; and (b) to warn us against relying on jury verdicts and other determinations of fact to a greater extent than they deserve. For example, he warned against relying on them to inflict capital punishment.

Trimmers can hardly expect popularity, and Jerome Frank was never a favorite with the bar associations. Everything he said seemed alien and disturbing to the majority of his profession. How could they feel at ease with a man of such deep and extensive culture who opposed injustice with deadly seriousness and kept insisting that in fact-finding, the law's most elementary process there was no ground for certitude? The average man may live for a while with a doubt as long as he expects relief in the form of an answer. But only superior minds can acknowledge doubts that are inherent and irremediable, analyze them with equanimity, and use them to draw practical and moral inferences. No wonder that Jerome Frank, for all his sparkle and wit, was often left to cut a lonely figure.

There is another side to Frank as trimmer. He trimmed not only against the excesses, imbalances, and popular fallacies of his world; he also trimmed against himself.

## Trimming Against Oneself

As we have seen, in Jerome Frank's acceptation of the word, trimming had nothing to do with wavering or compromising. It meant rather that one took thought, surveyed the scene, and chose deliberately to restore equilibrium by serving as a counterpoise. To him trimming was a species of discipline and self-restraint, not essentially different from the discipline that an artist might impose on himself in order to channel the force of his genius. "The free artist," Camus has told us, "is the one who, with great effort, creates his own order. The more undisciplined what he must put in order, the stricter will be his rule and the more he will assert his freedom. . . . Art lives only on the constraints it imposes on itself; it dies of all others."

This phenomenon—the pursuit of freedom through conscious self-limitation—appears just as characteristically among great judges as among painters, sculptors, composers, poets, and dramatists. The more powerful a jurist's mind and will, the more consciously we may find him attaching himself to some external form or tradition or authority that can sanction his decisions and keep them within bounds. Brandeis, for example, checked the drive of his will by seeking to restrict the Supreme Court's functions; Learned Hand sought limits by consulting the enigmatic "community conscience"; and Justice Hugo Black confines his desires tightly within the text of the Constitution. All these are techniques of self-discipline, that is, of trimming against one's own weight and force.

Jerome Frank likewise trimmed against himself, and in a variety of ways. Some of them his friends deprecated, for they seemed too restrictive and severe; but whether out of natural modesty or some strong inner need for self-limitation, he held to them nonetheless. Like other stars, he coruscated in his own style, and if you wanted to enjoy the light, you had to accept the bounds.

Take his habit of piling quotation on quotation. Frank was, of course, one of the most voracious readers on the face of the earth; it may be, as some have said, that he read more books than any other living person. Certainly he read more than any other lawyer. But he never took the slightest pride in this gargantuan bibliophagy; to him it was just a part of his persistent search for the truth. Why, then, did he think it necessary to spatter his books and articles with numberless quotations and multiply them in footnotes and appendixes?

In doing this, he was striving to trim against himself, against his own radical iconoclasm and disconcerting skepticism. Often we find him quoting an unimpressive or obscure source in support of some proposition that he might just as well have advanced out of his own experience. Quite often the style of the excerpt is not nearly so attractive as his own statement. Why, then, quote it at all? Because, he would say in effect, what I have to tell the lawyers is so contrary to their accepted slogans, so hostile to popular shibboleths, and so disturbing to some people's psychological security that I simply cannot rely on my own authority. Look, he would add, at bar-association presidents and suchlike types who are ready to dogmatize at will on any question under the sun. When all the smug ones declare that the emperor's new robe is magnificent, and my eyes tell me that the emperor is completely nude, who am I to contradict them without quoting corroborating witnesses?

Then, too, he would occasionally trim against himself on the bench—as, for instance, in the dreadful case of Julius and Ethel Rosenberg who were condemned to death in the early 1950's for espionage (page 291). Thoroughly convinced though he was that the Rosenbergs were guilty, and satisfied (as some of us were not) that their trial had met minimum standards of fairness, Judge Frank looked with horror on the death sentences—the first ever imposed by an American civil court for the crime of espionage. Although he had resolved to dissent and vote for a new and separate trial in the companion appeal of codefendant Morton Sobell, Judge Frank undertook the repulsive chore of preparing the Court's opinion which was to affirm the three convictions. Why did he? Why invite misunderstanding and bitter criticism?

Because he knew that if composed by either of his colleagues, the opinion would be merely a terse, cold statement of affirmance, whereas, in his ingenious hands, it could be salted with so many doubts and larded with so many unresolved questions of statutory and constitutional law that the Supreme Court might feel compelled to reexamine the entire legal and factual background of the death sentences. With this purpose, he drafted the text (and the footnotes) of the opinion in the hope that it would serve as a sort of oblique petition for certiorari to the Supreme Court. His colleagues went along with what he wrote—but, as the opinion shows, only a part of the way.

Alas, the Supreme Court under Chief Justice Vinson failed to perform its duty to the nation, and never considered most of the legal questions that Frank had raised. The trial judge's sentences were carried out. Nevertheless, Judge Frank's brilliant effort, extended not so much on the Rosenberg's behalf as on ours, deserves enduring acclaim. If ever a judge trimmed against himself in the cause of humane justice, it was Jerome Frank in the Rosenberg case.

For another example, we can take his so-called concurring opinions in two obscenity cases. In 1949 (*Roth v. Goldman*, 172 F.2d 788), when two very able colleagues of his tersely affirmed a decision upholding an order of the Postmaster General that excluded certain books from the mails, Judge Frank wrote at length to show that this kind of power in a mere administrator was incompatible with a free press and a free society. But then, instead of dissenting from the disposition as one would expect, he went on to concur in it—because he felt he ought to yield to his colleagues' greater experience with obscenity prosecutions until the Supreme Court, as he hoped, might undertake to review the entire question. In response, the Supreme Court did nothing.

During the last year of his life, Judge Frank repeated the pattern and elaborated it further (*United States v. Roth*, page 112). In this case, his court reviewed, not an administrative order, but a criminal conviction for mailing obscene books and photographs. Again two of the three judges found no difficulty in affirming; again Judge Frank concluded that the obscenity statutes ought to be held unconstitutional; and again he concurred in the outcome of the case—because, he said, it conformed to existing judicial precedents.

This time, after preparing a most impressive exposition he vacillated for days between publishing and suppressing it. Of course, publish it he eventually did, but nothing could persuade him to call it what it really was: a dissent. Although a majority of the Supreme Court affirmed the conviction, Judge Frank's magistral opinion will steadily influence the future movement of the law. True, respect for other judges and for previous holdings made him trim against his convictions and say that he concurred; but if what he wrote was a "concurrence," so too were the shots fired at Lexington in 1775.

Every thinker, we suppose, must express his own temperament and follow his own instincts in choosing just where and how to trim against the weight of the crowd and the pressure of inner impulsions. Trimming against oneself somewhere and somehow seems indispensable if a powerful mind is to escape the danger of arrogance, the sin of hubris, and—as in Nietzsche's instance— the risk of insanity.

Yet, as we saw at the beginning, there are certain postures that a trimmer assumes not merely to balance the public boat of the day but also to express his own most fundamental principles. There were aspects of Jerome Frank that no pressure or vicissitude could alter. Quicksilver in thought and conversation, in honor he was steel, in integrity ancient rock. The best of him will surely endure:

First, his original and creative philosophy of fact-skepticism;

Second, his sensitive humaneness that never turned aside, never grew weary, and never confused one human being's sorrow with another's; and

Third, his tireless pursuit of truth, in which anyone joining can find him again—inquisitive as ever, young, vernal, and bright with hope.

EDMOND CAHN
New York University

# FOREWORD ॐ

JUDGE CLARK, friends of Jerome Frank, my first memory of Judge Frank goes back to the fall of 1934 when I went to Washington, D.C., to head up a new bureau or division in the recently created Securities and Exchange Commission. I was anxious to assemble a good staff, and the man I wanted to head it was Abe Fortas who worked for Jerome Frank, then general counsel to the Agricultural Adjustment Administration.

I asked for an appointment with Mr. Frank and when I saw him in his office, he was most antagonistic. He figuratively tore me limb from limb. I realized as he talked that he had no animus toward me but only a zealous protective attitude toward his staff. They were friends in whom he had a great emotional investment. So I exploited that weakness by asking him, "Why do you stand in the way of your junior's professional advancement?" His attitude completely changed. He melted and at once became gentle and soft-spoken. And before I left, he was eager to help me find the best staff possible.

Soon I became a member of that small group toward whom Jerry Frank had a fatherly, protective attitude. It came to pass that, in his eyes, I was one who could do no wrong; and such virtues that I may have had became magnified out of all proportion. He was always quick to defend his friends whatever the criticism. He could never see faults in those he loved. Vivid memories of his expressions of affection for me and his seemingly unqualified confidence in me came flooding back when, in preparation for this occasion, I pored through my thick correspondence files that contain all his chits and letters. The reliving of our many experiences made it obvious that I could never be objective about this warmhearted, generous, witty, lovable, brilliant man. He had my heart—and to a great degree my mind. I mention my deep attachment to him in the interests of the principle of full disclosure —a principle to which I have given some years of my life.

This does not mean that he and I always saw eye to eye. We often disagreed. One of our disagreements concerned the institution of the jury trial. He was quite critical of the jury. One can find this criticism running through his writings. One of his last statements concerning it is contained in the June 1952 issue of the *Missouri Law Review* where he wrote, "More than anything else in the judicial system, the jury, I think, blocks the road to bettering the ways of finding the facts and applying to those facts the correct legal rules."

I have felt that, imperfect as the jury system is, it is better than any other fact-finding machinery we have evolved. And the longer I serve as a judge, the more I am convinced that fact-finding by juries is much less procrustean than fact-finding by judges.

Judge Frank assailed the inadequacy of the general verdict. He presented his views in a powerful way in *Skidmore v. Baltimore & Ohio R. Co.* 167 F(2d) 54. Why, he asked, were judges and lawyers suspicious of the fact verdict? ". . . the profession, which would smile the superior smile of derision at the suggestion of a trial by battle of bodies, accepts trial by battle of wits" (*idem*, 63). He would endorse the special-verdict procedure in vogue in some of the states. Yet I have concluded that the special verdict is apt to be a trap for the jury—confusing and misleading.

This is not the place to explore the differences in those two points of view. I mention them only to indicate that on some fundamentals Jerry Frank and I were opposed.

For several years Jerry Frank and I walked together along common paths. These were the heady days of the New Deal when Washington, D.C., teemed with brave dreams and bold experiments. Though I was at the SEC and he at Agriculture and though we were busy into the nights, we kept close together. I knew the mounting tensions within Agriculture. Jerry Frank spearheaded the drive to protect consumers in the restoration of agricultural conditions. He did not want all the benefits syphoned off to meatpackers and processors. There were increasing reverberations of the battle going on inside his department. The matter came to a head with his legal opinion that under the cotton-benefit contracts, the sharecroppers were to have some protection. That legal opinion cost him his job. He and some of his subordinates were discharged. The story has been quite faithfully told by Fisher in *The Harvest Labor Market in California* (1953), page 140: "When, in the early days of the New Deal, a group of government officials continued to insist that benefit payments to cotton growers be divided with sharecroppers, the famous purge of the Agricultural Adjustment Administration took place.

Even the overwhelming Democratic majorities of the first two Roosevelt administrations could not or would not extend the protections of the State to agricultural workers."

I was with him the night when he was discharged and felt the deep dark despair that filled his heart. He was one of those who had great enthusiasms and who felt, when a cause was lost, that all was lost. The universe seemed to hang in balance that night. But Jerome Frank was a wise man with a mature personality. By the next day he had regained his perspective and knew that the universe would still sing on, even though sharecroppers were harshly treated in America.

For a brief spell Jerry Frank went to the Reconstruction Finance Corporation as a special counsel. After a short stay there he moved to the Public Works Administration, where he became heavily embroiled in litigation that involved Roosevelt's public power program. At Agriculture, he was largely engaged in administrative, policy-making work. At PWA he was back in the courtroom; and that, I think, he loved more than anything else. I never saw him try a case. But I can vouch for his ability as an appellate lawyer. Perhaps his greatest victory was in *Alabama Power Co. v. Ickes*, 302 U.S. 464. Whether he won or lost, each opponent of Jerry Frank knew he had met the master advocate. Jerry Frank knew the art of orchestration of oral argument as no one else. He had the knack of reducing complicated records to simple terms and of finding the essential kernels in involved factual problems.

In many ways I think his months with PWA were his most rewarding. But financial pressures made him return to private practice in 1937 when I asked him to join me as a Commissioner at the Securities and Exchange Commission. His nostalgia for the public service was too strong to resist, and overrode his instinct for financial security. Roosevelt named him Commissioner and he returned to Washington, D.C., at a great monetary loss. But that sacrifice was forgotten as he got caught up in two exciting projects —(1) the reorganization of the New York Stock Exchange and (2) the launching of the reorganization programs for public utility holding companies under the 1935 Act.

Those were crowded, happy days for both of us. And we worked closely as a team. Those were days when the Commission was in session for eight or ten hours at a stretch, week after week, fashioning policy on a myriad of problems presented by the staff. It was in those two years that I came to know Jerry Frank best. I saw his brilliance make dull problems sparkle. I felt his ebullient spirit lift dreary conferences to the level of exciting discourse. I saw him time after time go swiftly through a sheaf of letters and yet know their contents intimately. He, like Charles Evans Hughes and George

Wharton Pepper, had the ability to take in a page almost at a glance and to retain the memory of it in his mind.

When I left the Securities and Exchange Commission for the Court, I urged Roosevelt to name Jerry Frank as my successor in the Chairmanship. He did so; and Frank served there energetically for two years, until he was named to the Court of Appeals for the Second Circuit in the spring of 1941.

He had not been on the court long when a contemporary wrote him: "I wish you were more shy as a judge and less shy as an essayist. In plain English, why don't you keep your two great endowments apart? Why must you fuse the two? Why not write essays qua essays and opinions qua opinions?"

Jerry Frank replied to this scolding: "You are dogmatic about the rightness of recent innovations. I am following the good old tradition. I suggest that you reread Mr. Justice Wilson's opinion in Chisholm v. Georgia (2 Dall. 419). There you'll find a quote from the Scotch philosopher Reid, an essay on semantics, a disquisition on sovereignty, an excerpt from Frederick the Great, a vignette of the Grand Monarch, a passage about Greece, etc."

He submitted this controversy to me for my opinion. I encouraged him in his essay-like opinions. Certainly they were refreshing. As one lawyer wrote him, "You certainly have a unique gift for perceiving the wider jurisprudential aspects of a seemingly humdrum controversy." Others referred to them as "gems." Many found them, as I did, inspiring exceptions to the dull literature which the courts turn out.

Jerry Frank once defended them as follows:

My aims, so far as I can articulate them, in writing opinions, when they are "essayistic," are these: (a) To stimulate the bar into some reflective thinking about the history of legal doctrines, so that they will go beyond the citator perspective of doctrinal evolution: (b) To induce them to reflect on the techniques of legal reasoning (e.g., to consider the nature and value of stare decisis, or the use and value and limitations on the proper employment of fictions); (c) To recognize that the judicial process is inescapably human, necessarily never flawless, but capable of improvement; (d) To perceive the diverse "forces" operative in decision-making, and the limited function of the courts as part of government.

And, underlying it all, is a strong desire, not easily curbed, to be pedagogic— not in a didactic manner but in a way that will provoke intelligent questioning as to the worth of accepted practices in the interest of bettering these practices. * * * In my clumsy way, I've tried to indicate the limited utility of generalization uttered by me in my opinions. I doubt whether I've given birth to many dicta.

I think Judge Frank's opinions are literary treasures. Perhaps it is good that all judges do not write essays around their opinions. Certainly not everyone could. But students and lawyers will, I think, bless Frank through the years for having endowed the reports with exciting literature.

One need only sample at random to be greatly rewarded.

A concurring opinion in *United States* v. *Roth*, 237 F(2d) 796, 801–827, covers the problem of obscenity in a characteristic way. Legal precedents, sociology, juvenile delinquency, history, arts and literature, the First Amendment, the Great Books—all are discussed in a fascinating analysis of an ancient and perplexing problem. One of his asides was a statement, by the late Mayor Walker, that he had never heard of a woman who had been seduced by a book.

Judge Frank went on to say, "New Mexico has never had an obscenity statute; and there is no evidence that, in that state, sexual misconduct is proportionately greater than elsewhere" (*idem*, 812). One can search the reports and not find a more interesting and profound canvass of an important legal problem than this one on obscenity. It will, I think, remain a classic.

*In re J. P. Linahan Inc.* (1943), 138 F(2d) 650, dealt with the seemingly cut-and-dried question whether a special master in a bankruptcy proceeding had been shown to be biased. Speaking for the Court, Judge Frank held that bias had not been shown. But he reached that conclusion only after he had explored the obligation of the judge, sitting as a trier of fact, to be "disinterested." Drawing on authorities which ranged from Aristotle to Wigmore, he discussed the human element in the judicial process, and the judge's obligation to recognize his predilections for what they are. But "disinterestedness does not mean child-like innocence" (*idem*, 654), for the judge has the duty, as trier of fact, to decide which witnesses are to be believed. "As a fact finder, he is himself a witness—a witness of witnesses" (*idem*, 653).

In *United States* v. *Grunewald* (1956), 233 F(2d) 556, he expressed disagreement with the majority's interpretation of the privilege against self-incrimination. His dissent is an articulate exposition of the reasons which underlie the criminal defendant's right to refuse to take the stand. For him, the Fifth Amendment was not a procedural bar to the development of relevant information in the courtroom. It protects the citizen's "right of privacy, a right to a private enclave where he may lead a private life. That right is the hallmark of our democracy. The totalitarian regimes scornfully reject that right. . . . They boast of the resulting efficiency in obtaining all the evidence in criminal prosecutions. We should know by now that their vaunted efficiency too often yields unjust, cruel decisions, based upon unreliable evidence procured at the sacrifice of privacy" (*idem*, pp. 581–582). The scholar in him prompted the addition of two appendices. The English and American authorities who defended the right of the accused to stand mute are marshaled in one appendix. The second compares the practices in the legal systems of the other countries of Western Europe.

I think Judge Frank was right in maintaining that his essay-like opinions were not likely to spawn dicta. The epigrammatic style of Holmes did have that effect; and his choice phrases often ended in noxious doctrine.

The contribution of Frank was unique in another way. His exploration of a legal problem left a treasure house for the lawyer. His mind led even the prosaic student into fields quite new and often startling to him. Frank opened wide vistas that lawyers did not often explore. He was at home in most fields of literature. Psychoanalysis and psychiatry were fascinating tools for him. His mastery of philosophy placed at his fingertips the wisdom of the ages. The allied field of mathematics helped him discover new worlds. His interest in the humanities and in social sciences often put him in possession of data, statistics, and surveys which illuminated shadowy areas of the law. One who comes to these essay-like opinions in search of knowledge discovers more leads to answers to legal problems than he ever dreamed existed.

We can only be grateful that Judge Frank explored a problem ahead of us. For his search usually left the clues to the answers we seek. Beyond that, he unveiled the true meaning of a case for future generations by letting light into the operation of the judicial mind.

Writing books was another outlet for his wide interests. In his middle years he produced *Law and the Modern Mind*, which I think will remain a classic. It substituted American pragmatism for Hegelian philosophy, and dealt decisively with the bugaboo of certainty in the law.

*Save America First* was a challenge to the economics of Marxism and an appeal to isolationism. Jerry Frank outgrew his isolationism but never, of course, his repulsion for the Communist creed.

*If Men Were Angels* was a treatise on government.

*Fate and Freedom* was his excursion into philosophy and history.

*Courts on Trial* was an incisive criticism of our trial system.

*Not Guilty*, on which his daughter collaborated, is a collection of instances where justice went astray and resulted in the conviction of innocent people.

If his articles for the periodicals and for the law reviews were added, the list would be a long one. And it would have to include an article called *The Speech of Judges: A Dissenting Opinion*, 29 Va. L. Rev. 625, which he published under the name Anon Y. Mous.

Throughout most of his writings (both on and off the bench) there are several common threads. First, the treacherous nature of the fact-finding process in the law. The trial of an issue of fact was to him a combination of human fallibility and conscious partianship. These made fact-finding the most hazardous process in the law—one that made impossible a fair prediction of what courts will do in a given instance.

In an issue of the *Rutgers Law Review* in 1954 he showed how the Holmes prediction theory of the law was applicable only to upper-court decisions, that facts are too "unruly" to make prediction provident at the trial court level.

Second, the problem of changing the nature of legal education. In 1941 he said at Yale:

Practicing law is an art—and a fairly difficult one. Training lawyers is no cinch at best. The Langdell method has increased the difficulties, has made the task of the teacher as complicated as possible. Even the teacher who is a genius cannot overcome the obstacles. * * * University law teaching today is * * * supposed to teach men what they are to do in courtrooms and law offices. But it stays as far away as possible from courtrooms and law offices. What the student sees is a reflection in a badly-made mirror of another reflection in a badly-made mirror, of what is going on in courtrooms and law offices. Why not smash the mirror? Why not have the students directly observe the subject matter of their study, the teachers acting as enlightened interpreters of what is thus observed?

Third, the problem of reconciling freedom from government. The law to him was not merely "a mannerless conflict over often sordid interests." It was rather an instrument through which individual freedom might be assured within the disciplines of democratic institutions.

Fourth, his concern that evenhanded justice be done not only to those who are influential, but to the lowly, the indigent, and the despised. This appears in his repeated denunciations of the use of the third degree by the police. He wrote in *United States v. Murphy*, 222 F(2d) 698, 706, "The test of the moral quality of a civilization is its treatment of the weak and powerless." His dissent in *United States v. Johnson*, 238 F(2d) 565, 567, called for a liberal construction of the *in forma pauperis* statute so that an indigent defendant with a meritorious case would not suffer a penalty "because he is guilty of the crime of being poor" (*idem*, p. 568)—a plea that did not go unnoticed. See *Johnson v. United States*, 352 U.S. 565. A like concern is mirrored in his attitude on entrapment. Dissenting in *United States v. Masciale*, 236 F(2d) 601, 604, 605, he urged that " . . . the police have not caught a criminal; they have taught a man how to become a criminal." It is seen again when he concluded that a trial judge had participated too actively in a criminal trial. . . . "I have the highest respect for the trial judge. Accordingly, I would hesitate to criticize him, were nothing more involved that judicial etiquette. But here the liberty of another human being is at stake." *United States v. Giallo*, 206 F(2d) 207, 211, 213. And, again, when he disagreed with the majority's application of the doctrine of harmless error in an appeal from a criminal conviction:

Perhaps I am old-fashioned in saying that I believe that the doctrine of "harmless error" does not dispense with the necessity of a fair trial of a defendant whom the appellate judges believe to be guilty [*United States* v. *Liss*, 137 F(2d) 999, 1001].

I never knew such an avid reader of books as Jerry Frank. I am sure he read at least one new book a day, even if it were only a detective story with which he unwound his mind before sleep. Books were the inexhaustible quarries from which he took materials for his thinking. He absorbed them quickly, digesting their contents and retaining them at the tip of his tongue for years after the event. To him reading a book was as vital and vivid as a plunge into the swirling sea or the ascent of an Alpine Peak. His learning was an experience in itself; and through it he came to know the world.

I often urged him to travel, especially to Asia where great revolutions are under way, where new societies are being constructed, where new schools of thought are being born. I felt that this adventure would open up new worlds for him. I was certain he would instantly be at home with the great intellects of Asia—men like Myint Thein, Narayan, Radhakrishnan, Sjahrir, and Tanaka.

But Jerry Frank never crossed the Pacific. He did, however, travel the world in his library. And he was completely at home in the world of ideas, whether they were Asian or American, contemporary or ancient.

Ideas did not lie quietly in his mind. They whirled there, multiplying in rapid fashion. The intense activity which produced them necessarily brought forth too many for all to be of equal value. None knew better than he that they needed editing. And he had no hesitation at a later date to say that he had blundered. He had no resentment of criticism which could justify itself by reason.

He had a passion for what William James called the "wild fact"—the obstinate rock on which brittle theories break. He had a truly skeptical mind that does not scoff but questions. He questioned accepted fact for the reason that its general acceptance indicated that it had not been recently reviewed. Nothing was true merely because it had been repeated through the centuries. Moreover, he felt that the only thing constant in this world was change; that all authority had to prove its continuing validity and constantly renew its franchise, or accept the penalties of obsolescence.

Jerome Frank was a many-sided man whom a stranger could not possibly know merely by reading what he wrote. It took personal acquaintance and long association to get the measure of the man in his many diverse phases.

He was witty, warmhearted, and ebullient, whether he was playing charades on a Saturday night or designing an opinion so that he could add Leonard Lyons to a footnote. The former he did brilliantly; and the latter he achieved with delight in *Katz* v. *Horni Signal Mfg. Co.*, 145 F(2d) 961, 963 where he said, "Leonard Lyons reports that Marconi said of the radio he invented, 'Only one thing bothers me: why do you suppose this thing really works?' "

Judge Frank knew the world of ideas as few have known it. He was a joy to be with, for each conversation was an exciting adventure. He was always conscious of his own dignity and of the dignity of others. His mind was too eager to be pompous, too skeptical to be arrogant. Some men require others to bow to them and to cater to their ego, if they are to be accepted in the inner circle. Jerome Frank liked friends; but he was too mature to want anyone to make an idol of him. He loved argument yet never felt rancor. He could laugh at himself, yet dare to match his mind and heart against the great and universal ideas. He was critical of voices accepted as prophetic, yet he cultivated the company of the masters of the ages.

He was an emotionally mature man who had no need for arrogance, who need not hammer other men down to be big himself, who need not perform antics on the bench to feed his ego, to impress the world with his importance. He was not a little man in an important position.

He was a man of humility whose greatness had depth and integrity. His ideas and accomplishments were the natural flowering of a remarkable mind, a vital spirit, universal interests, and a capacity for warm personal relations.

WILLIAM O. DOUGLAS

*Memorial address delivered in New York City on May 23, 1957*

# PREFACE 🦆

IN THIS ANTHOLOGY I have endeavored to present the most representative views of the author, my late father. In reply to those who, familiar with his work, will inevitably question certain omissions or inclusions: My choice has been governed by a desire to select those writings in which the author expressed himself with the greatest clarity and force.

Those readers unfamiliar with his work will be struck by the author's oft-repeated themes and melodies. He himself explained his method thus: "I have deliberately used a technique which . . . is reminiscent of the following: Mr. Smith of Denver was introduced to Mr. Jones at a dinner party in Chicago. 'Oh,' said Jones, 'do you know my friend, Mr. Schnicklefritz, who lives in Denver?' 'No,' answered Smith. Later in the evening, when Smith referred to Denver, Jones again asked whether Smith was acquainted with Schnicklefritz, and again received a negative reply. As the dinner party broke up, Smith remarked that he was leaving that night for Denver, and Jones once again inquired whether Smith knew Schnicklefritz. 'Really,' came the answer, 'his name sounds quite familiar.'"

I wish to thank those who have, in various ways, greatly assisted in this undertaking: Edmond Cahn, who first conceived the idea of the book, whose encouragement along the way has been incomparably helpful, and who, in the manuscript's final phase, gave most generously of his time and counsel; Harriet Pilpel, who obtained a publisher for the book and, together with John A. Pope, Jr., then of The Macmillan Company, arranged for my editorship; Roy Mersky, who made available to me the resources of the Yale Law Library and his own invaluable bibliography of my father's writings; Boris I. Bittker, Helen Silving Ryu, Julius Cohen, and Fowler Harper, whose advice I solicited and, to my great enlightenment, received; my husband, Marvin Kristein, who spent too much time away from his own writings to assist me, most importantly with creative suggestions regarding many fundamental aspects of the book; A. L. Hart, Jr., of The Macmillan Company, whose patience despite delays in the completion of the manuscript have been much appreciated and on whose sage editorial advice I have placed much reliance. Final responsibility for the contents of the book, however, rests entirely with me.

BARBARA FRANK KRISTEIN

Stony Brook, New York

Judge Jerome Frank

# PART 1 ❧ The Democratic Spirit

EDITOR'S NOTE ❧ The four pieces in this first section reflect the views of the author, my late father, about the democratic spirit, without which no democratic form of government can survive. "On Holding Abe Lincoln's Hat" is a speech delivered before a lawyers' group in 1953. "The Place of The Expert in a Democratic Society," a paper read before the Brandeis Lawyers' Society in 1944, was later printed in the *Philosophy of Science*. In publishing "The Speech of Judges: A Dissenting Opinion" (which appeared in the *Virginia Law Review* in 1944) the author signed himself "Anon Y. Mous." A reading of this wittily irreverent piece will reveal the motive for anonymity. "Judge Learned Hand" consists of excerpts from a manuscript based on lectures delivered at the Yale Law School in 1955. A different version appeared in the *University of Chicago Law Review* in 1957, after Judge Frank's death.

The speech "On Holding Abe Lincoln's Hat" addresses itself to the anti-democratic spirit of intolerance generated by the "McCarthyism" of the early 1950's. But the author's comments regarding political extremism remain apt: Extremists, the real enemies of liberty, traduce the democratic process.

In "The Place of the Expert" Judge Frank gives voice to his fundamental philosophy, which he himself called "fact-skepticism." Incessantly engaged in questioning that which tradition holds to be self-evident, sometimes for the sheer joy of doing so, he had a more compelling motive. As Sidney Davis has remarked, "Precisely because [Judge Frank] took nothing for granted, he discovered much that was hidden. He did not break idols solely for the fun of it; he did it to open the way to truth." In 1945 Judge Frank published a

[ 1 ]

book entitled *Fate and Freedom* dealing with free will versus determinism, in which the interested reader will find elaborations of points made in this article.

"The Speech of Judges" I include partly because it makes delightful reading. In it, however, the author states some important views—for example, about the need for clarity in legal writing. I hope the reader shares my enjoyment of this piece.

Judge Learned Hand, with whom Jerome Frank served on the bench, aroused in him an intense admiration and personal devotion. Asked by the Yale Law School to deliver a lecture on the subject of "Great Judges," Judge Frank took that opportunity to pay public tribute to Judge Hand and to Hand's dedication to the preservation of the democratic process. To him, Judge Frank once wrote: "You are, par excellence, the democratic aristocrat." About him, he said, "He opposed, vehemently, the idea that any eternal principles of justice exist. He does, also vehemently, insist that every society has fundamental attitudes. Those which our society has evolved, he treasures. . . . And today sometimes he apprehends that they may vanish, blown away in the hurricane of social indifference." "A true liberal, he is no dogmatist. . . . He believes in government by discussion, agreeing with Pericles about the virtues of Athenian democracy. . . ."

The reader will find the pages which follow infused with that democratic spirit which is antidogmatic, antideterministic, and which asserts that "the impossibility of reaching perfection does not justify indifference to the aim of constantly bettering man's lot." ❧

# ON HOLDING ABE LINCOLN'S HAT ह्₂

ATTACKED AS A TRIMMER, George Saville, Lord Halifax, in a famous tract published in 1684, replied that he delighted in that label. "This innocent term Trimmer," he wrote, "signifieth no more than this: If men are together in a boat, and one part of the company would weigh it down on one side, and another would make it lean as much to the contrary, it happeneth there is a third opinion of those who conceive it would do as well if the boat went even, without endangering the passengers."

Halifax's definition of a Trimmer satisfies, in large measure, my definition of a true liberal. Liberals, I think, should be proud to be tagged as Trimmers, in that sense. But they should know that the way of the liberal is hard. Often he will be denounced as a coward, a timeserver, a shameless appeaser. Seldom will he be backed up by a militant crowd. The apparent reason is that, as the Bible reports, men do not follow an uncertain call into battle.

Yet the spirit of the liberal is the spirit of American democracy, which has enabled us, again and again, to escape spasms of loathsome bigotry, and to emerge, recurrently, to increased tolerance. I ask you to recall that in 1789, the year in which we adopted our National Constitution, Catholics had the right to vote in but three states; and that not until 1844 in New Jersey and 1867 in New Hampshire could Catholics or Jews hold office. I ask you particularly to remember that in 1854 the "Native American" or "Know-Nothing" Party—charging a Catholic plot against American democracy and employing slander, hatred, and fear—elected nine state governors, eight United States senators, and 44 percent of the House of Representatives. Yet we outlived that disgrace.

We live now in a period of crisis, of daily dilemmas, trilemmas, or polylemmas, being confronted constantly with perplexing circumstances. External

[3]

foes threaten not only our institutions but our very existence. And so in terror, and out of frustration in the face of baffling perplexities, some misguided Americans turn to absurdly oversimplified solutions. Angered and bewildered, they seek scapegoats. They resort to extreme measures based on mere suspicions. They strike not alone at those among us who actually endanger our security but, informed by flimsy rumors only, they accuse of disloyalty, and thus sorely injure, some innocent persons and intimidate others. As Mrs. Dwight F. Davis—aroused by the case of Mrs. Mildred McAfee Horton—said just the other day: "A sickness has gripped this country—a sickness of fear, of mutual suspicion, of unhealthy credulity. Only a sick nation is willing to believe the worst about its best."

This is reminiscent of an ancient Greek state in trouble, as described by Thucydides centuries ago: "Prudent hesitation came to be considered specious cowardice; moderation was held to be a cloak for unmanliness; ability to see all sides of a question, inaptness to act on any. * * * The advocate of extreme measures was * * * trustworthy; his opponent a man to be suspected."

Someone has mentioned the "paradise of the imagination." But the imagination also has its hell. In that hell are conceived, these days, unfounded calumnies. Without opportunity to prove their innocence, without a court trial conducted according to our Constitution and our traditions of fair play, men, on the basis of such calumnies, are pronounced guilty of grave misconduct. No court enters judgments against them, but the consequences are often penalties stiffer than a court would exact after a trial—dismissals from jobs, the loss of the means of earning a living in occupations for which they were trained. A drop of acid gossip suffices to curdle a reputation irrevocably.

Guilt is imputed to any man who, unknown to him, employed another, later revealed as a spy—as if to say that George Washington should have been suspected of treason because the traitor Benedict Arnold was one of his trusted generals.

Our democracy, we had thought until now, prized a high degree of privacy for the ordinary man, afforded him some shelter from public scrutiny, some insulated enclosure, some enclave, some inviolate place as his castle. Unless we call a halt, such castles may soon be obsolete. Those who speak up for civil liberties are often now regarded as impractical visionaries—or worse.

One thinks of these lines from Ben Jonson's drama of tyranny, *Sejanus*: "What danger is't to dream? Talk in one's sleep or cough? * * * May I shake my head without a comment? * * * These are now the things whereon men's fortune, yea their fate, depends. Nothing hath privilege against the violent ear."

Our wisest judge, Learned Hand, who recently decried the current "spirit of general suspicion and distrust, which accepts rumor and gossip * * *," warned that it "may in the end subject us to a despotism as evil as any we dread. * * *"

America, however, has, before this, experienced crises in which our extremists acted not altogether dissimilarly when fear of a foreign menace stalked our land. I refer to 1798, when the hotheads among the Federalists—against the counsels of John Adams, Alexander Hamilton, and John Marshall—exploited the Sedition law to persecute, and even to jail, many an innocent Anti-Federalist. I refer also to 1920 when the infamous "Palmer raids" occurred.

The liberal, thinking of the present when surveying those past periods, will emphatically voice his indignation at the persecutory methods then used. And he will be eager to join those who want to devise practical means for protecting our citizens from such methods today.

But—and this I believe equally important—he will not fail also to note that, in each of those past periods, there was some objective justification for the fear which prompted those methods, there were then some persons who deserved not persecution but prosecution and conviction after a fair trial. So in our revulsion against contemporary despicable, fear-stimulated conduct, let us not lose sight of the frightening dangers that warrant some real apprehensions, of the fact that the totalitarian regime, which deems us the enemy, does have some active but secret agents in our midst. Since our "days are danger-ridden" indeed, little wonder that, for some of us, "the nightmare rides upon sleep."

Consider the notorious Titus Oates, a vile perjurer who, in seventeenth century England, by his lies swore innocent men to death. Macaulay writes of Oates: "His success proved that no romance is too wild to be received with faith by understandings which fear and hatred have disordered. His slanders were monstrous, but they were well timed. He spoke to a people made credulous by their passions." But, let me add, those passions gripped them because there were then in England some conspiratorial men who, if they could, would have carried out the sort of plot Oates described.

The American liberal must now fight on two fronts: First, against those who pooh-pooh all talk of real internal dangers; second, against those who would engulf our people in a panic fear in which they acquiesce in the most dangerous methods of meeting the dangers. At this moment, the hazard on the second front is by far the more ominous; there the liberal must throw in most of his forces. The extremists on that front are like those who would amputate a man's foot to cure a corn; shoot up a whole city to catch some sneak thieves; throw out with the bath water not only the baby and the nurse, but the parents—indeed, tear up the plumbing.

Extremists on one side breed extremists on the other. The liberal will be wary of both. His function, however, is to acknowledge that often the extremists on each side have a point, but one that is exaggeratedly stated; to perceive that these exaggerations foster undesirable ways by which each side pursues its aims; and, if possible, to discover some resolution of the differences which allows for whatever is sound in the respective polar positions. Thus it's dangerously absurd to burn down the house to eliminate rats. But when there are rats in the house, it's also absurd—although not to the same degree—not to apply a rat exterminator, making sure, however, that it won't poison the family.

I am not, you'll note, saying that, when presented with extremes, we must always reason that each must be partly right and partly wrong, that truth and wisdom invariably lie in the middle. One extreme—or both—may be entirely in error. As Thouless suggests, there is no sense in adopting the idea that two and two make five—as mean between the "extreme" view that they make four and the other "extreme" view that they make six. Sometimes a so-called compromise is stupid or a craven appeasement. The liberal does not part his mind in the middle or, like the Duke in Chesterton's play, try to show a balanced judgment by subscribing equal sums of money to both sides of every cause.

Yet compromise often does represent the wisest course. A sagacious French legal philosopher has remarked that the "contradictory elements found in problems * * * throw us into a regime of concession. * * * Thus we reach that middle ground which is all we can hope for in this world." Nor, I submit, should that distress us, since something of the sort is the very essence of living. Walking is a compromise between falling down and standing up; sleep a compromise between full vitality and death. The absolutists sneer at this attitude, for as Morley noted, "The disciples of the relative may afford to compromise. The disciples of the absolute, never."

In that spirit, the liberal approaches underdogs in trouble: He will battle for their civilized treatment. He will oppose any tendency to deal unjustly with members of unpopular minorities; and, when they are on trial, he will strive to ensure the fairness of the trial. On the other hand, he will not rush to conclude that there is an almost irrebuttable presumption that any member of such a minority who is convicted has been unfairly tried and must be innocent.

In short, the true liberal is no dogmatist. He does not (to borrow a phrase from Paul Freund) blow but one horn of a dilemma. He distrusts the one-eyed men. His own vision is bifocal. Himself dwelling in a temperate zone of attitudes, he has doubts about those who prefer the intemperate zones—the excessively hot or excessively cold. He believes in government by discussion, agreeing with Pericles about the virtues of Athenian democracy when he said: "Instead of looking on discussion as a stumbling block in the way of action, we think it an indispensable preliminary to any wise action at all." The liberal has no list of fixed particularized ideas on which he insists as always wholly right or wholly wrong. He does not, phonograph-like, rattle off, with an air of infallibility, a long series of do's and don't's applicable in all circumstances. He is no slogan addict. He looks upon liberalism as a mood, not as a system or a catalogue of precise commands. Nor will he forget that irrational extralegal restraints may tyrannically do more than the edicts of government to narrow liberty; that, among such extralegal restraints, are the irrational stereotypes of private groups, including the orthodox heresies and conformity-demanding taboos of rigid-minded pseudoliberals; and that with leaders of such groups—whether "right" or "left"—not alone power corrupts, but influence as well.

Thus the fashion in pseudoliberal circles dictates severe criticism of the FBI. But here is a force, held by its chief to the best police standards, abjuring the third degree, trained to respect civil liberties. Like any other investigatory body (the SEC, for instance), the FBI collects, as it must, all kinds of confidential information—often gossip—to serve as leads or clues. True liberals will not mistakenly confuse the FBI with those who obtain and misuse the data so collected.

Global problems torment us. At home, dramatic political trials fascinate us. Partly on that account, yet unforgivably I think, too few liberals interest themselves in the undramatic plight of obscure men on trial in nonpolitical criminal cases. In all too many such trials, the prosecutors utilize unjust techniques to obtain convictions of men who may be innocent. Sometimes the unjust practices constitute more or less hidden deviations from the conventional procedures. More frequently, the conventional practices are themselves unjust, and badly need reform. To disregard courthouse injustices to the humble, obscure man is to disregard that which renders a democratic society distinctive, antitotalitarian: its devotion to the worth of each person as a unique, unduplicatable, individual. William James's carpenter put it well: "There is very little difference between one man and another; but what little there is, is very important." Democracy ceases to exist when it ignores that difference.

Liberals at the bar need to speak up. As someone has said, no one assumes that a lawyer who defends a thief is a thief-lover; or a prostitute, a whoremaster; yet the pernicious doctrine is now abroad that a lawyer who defends a Communist believes in Communism. Surely the legal profession dare not allow that doctrine to prevail.

Look, for a moment, at the role of the judge, these troubled days. He must have courage to withstand the onslaughts of the extremists. He must not be intimidated when—enforcing the statutes enacted by the government whose laws he solemnly swore to enforce—he receives angry letters from one group of extremists because he and his colleagues, on account of major trial errors, reverse a conviction of a person tried for espionage. Nor must he be intimidated when, after he and his colleagues sustain a jury's conviction of another person tried for the same offense—because the alleged errors urged on appeal lacked substance—abuse is heaped upon him by the opposing extremist group. He must not be dismayed because many nonlawyers fallaciously assume that, in enforcing, or upholding the constitutionality of, a statute, he expresses his approval of it.

I remarked that, as the liberal often will be considered, by many, a softy or coward, the way of the liberal is hard. But it entails an even tougher difficulty. Each man has some unquenchable yearning for certainty and perfection, although the wise man learns that scarcely anything human can attain those qualities. The liberal, above all men, must reconcile himself to the unavoidably contingent and flawful nature of his contrivances, knowing with William James that "not a victory is gained, not a deed * * * of courage is done, except upon a maybe. * * *" Indeed, he must develop a kind of courage seldom described—the courage to endure some incurable defects in the solutions of most human problems. This fact should not daunt him, soften him into a flabby defeatist or harden him into a crusty cynic. For—as I've often said elsewhere—he will grow stronger by accepting this paradox: Insofar as we are aware of man's limitations and are mindful that life must be less perfect than we might like, we grow more circumspect and thus more likely to approach somewhat nearer to perfection. The impossibility of ever reaching complete perfection does not at all justify indifference to the aim of constantly bettering a man's lot, and increasing his freedom.

At the outset, I remarked that seldom will the liberal be backed up by a militant crowd, because usually men do not follow an uncertain call into battle. Nevertheless, the call of the liberal, since it is a call to exercise unusual courage and for the highest stakes, can be a challenge that wins wide response. Especially today, the liberals can lead a crusade beckoning others onward, a crusade to rescue our democracy.

Halifax ended his famous essay thus: "Our Trimmer * * * thinketh fit to conclude with these assertions: That * * * our laws are Trimmers between the excesses of unbounded power and the extravagance of liberty not enough restrained; that true Virtue hath ever been thought a Trimmer, and in the middle between the two extremes; that even God Almighty Himself is divided between His two great attributes, His Mercy and His Justice. In such company, our Trimmer is not ashamed of his name, and willingly leaveth to bolder champions of either extreme, the honour of contending with no less adversaries than nature, religion, liberty, prudence, humanity and common sense."

In many respects, seventeenth century Halifax anticipated Mr. Justice Holmes. Like Halifax, Holmes was no Pollyanna fatalist. I trust you did not think I was one when I told how America had emerged heretofore from periods enveloped in smogs of vile suspicions and terror. I am one with Holmes who thought it folly to believe that "we have nothing to do but sit still and let time run over us," and who said that "The mode in which the inevitable comes to pass is through effort."

If, then, we are to get out of the present poisonous miasma, if we are to save innocent men—and the spirit of our civilization—from ruin through the misuse of rumors, and, at the same time, not discourage the detection and conviction of the guilty, we dare not trust to luck. We must will to do so. We must summon our best liberal minds to invent sage techniques to surmount these difficulties, and we must energetically put those techniques to work.

Let me close with a picture of a great American liberal. Stephen Douglas, as you know, spent years of effort, opposing the hotheads in North and South, to prevent an American Civil War. Defeated for the presidency by Lincoln, Douglas at once urged the South not to secede. Then, at Lincoln's first inaugural, he appeared on the platform. When Lincoln awkwardly tried to dispose of his hat, Douglas seized it—and held it while Lincoln took the oath. I give you Abe Lincoln's hat in Douglas's hands as a symbol of liberalism.

*Talk before the Lawyers' Division,*
*Joint Defense Appeal, New York City, June, 1953*

# THE PLACE OF THE EXPERT IN
# A DEMOCRATIC SOCIETY ॐ

IN THEIR ADVERSELY CRITICAL ATTITUDE toward administrative agencies, many lawyers and judges disclose a distrust of the expert, the specialist. That distrust is curious, for the position of our profession in society rests on the fact that we ourselves are specialists.

In the famous colloquy (perhaps partly apocryphal) which is said to have occurred about three hundred years ago between King James I and Judge Coke, the king remarked that if "law was founded upon reason, he and others could reason as well as the judges," and Coke loftily replied that lawsuits "are not to be decided by natural reason, but by the artificial reason and judgement of the law, which law is an art that requires long study and experience before than a man can attain to the cognizance of it." The king, an intelligent amateur, was angered, for doubtless he saw that, as McIlwain observes, "if * * * the law was to be supreme, at the same time a mystery open only to the initiated, it is clear that, if the claim of the lawyers were to be admitted, the supreme authority would be their exclusive possession." Demos, now king, sometimes echoes James's anger at the idea of a government of lawyers, not of men.

Yet, within limits, Coke was justified: The "trained intuition of the judge," resulting from his education and experience, does and should give him, in his own field, an advantage over the layman. But lawyers and judges, as experts, disclose weaknesses common to all groups of specialists—weaknesses which present a democratic society with a difficult problem.

For expert groups usually become cults. Generally they create closed guilds which, resenting what they consider uninformed criticism from without, often also develop something like tyranny within. The very respect which their skills win for them from the public tends to make them smugly authoritarian toward the public. The specialist group evolves its own routines which, grown semisacred, are guarded by its leaders against significant change. One who, within the guild, seeks to break up any of those routines, is likely to be regarded as a silly ass or a dangerous disturber of the intellectual peace. Unless and until he receives the blessing of the guild's leaders, he will not be accorded a fair hearing. And if he does receive the blessing, in all probability he, in turn, will come to insist that his new truths are beyond question. His new ideas, supplanting the dogmas he attacked, become themselves dogmas. He now has a prestige-monopoly, a vested interest, which he will fiercely defend against other innovators. Yesterday's rebel, as you know, becomes, often, today's stuffed shirt.

On the ways of experts, fashion serves as a powerful compulsive. The eminent judge, says Tourtoulon, sacrifices more to fashion than does his wife, however worldly she may be. For many decades, Chief Justice Marshall set the style for decisions on constitutional issues. It took an unusually strong-minded man to deviate from that fashion. Recently, Justice Holmes's views have become the vogue.

But the foibles of the legal profession, while they need far more public exposure than as yet they have received, are moderately well known. I suggest that, in order to detect the inherent weaknesses of all specialist groups, we should observe the ways of the physicists, since they are supposed to be the most dispassionate, the most objective, of experts.

If we watch the physicists closely, we perceive that fashion helps to shape the very "laws of nature" which are their peculiar province. Schroedinger, the great physicist, one of the winners of the Nobel Prize, has told us that physics, at any particular time, is "dependent * * * on the fashionable frame of mind of the epoch of which it is part." In support of that statement he points to the following: The natural laws of physics are based upon experiments. As, however, the number of possible experiments is almost unlimited, the relatively few experiments that have been actually made to date have resulted from the choices of the physicists. But those choices, says Schroedinger, are induced by nonscientific considerations. "A certain group of ideas becomes dominant at a certain juncture" as a reflection of "the spirit of the age." At any given moment, "in all branches of civilization, there is one general world outlook dominant and there are numerous lines of activity which are attractive because they are the fashion of the age, whether in politics or in art or in science. These also make themselves felt in the 'exact' science of physics." The physicist, as a child of his age "cannot shuffle off his mundane coil when he enters his laboratory." The physicists, accordingly, conduct merely the "fashionable" experiments—those which, according to the current fashion, are interesting and important. So fashion has determined the choices which yield "the raw materials" from which "the whole texture of physical science is woven."

For instance, says Schroedinger, Grimaldi, in the seventeenth century, conducted an experiment with light waves; his observations attracted, at that time, little or no attention; "they were regarded as pointing to a phenomenon which had no general interest for science as such, and for the following one hundred and fifty years no similar experiments were carried out, though this could have been done with the simplest and cheapest material." Why? Because Grimaldi's observations were not in step with Newton's theory of light which accorded with the regnant fashion; "thus the general interest was carried along a different path" from Grimaldi's. Only in 1927, after the fashion had changed, did physicists note Grimaldi's experiment. So too with the idea of evolution. It was repugnant to many early nineteenth century thinkers. Then, as the style of thought changed, Darwin's theory of origins became the vogue. Recently the astronomers have applied the idea of evolution even in their field, some of them advancing the hypothesis that "the universe on the whole is not in a stationary stage, but that, at a definite time, which is relatively not very long ago, it changed from a quite different condition into a steadily expansive stage. * * *" Had that hypothesis been put forward in an earlier age, it "certainly would have been regarded as nonsensical." We "do not consider this hypothesis as merely empty phantasy," writes Schroedinger, "because we have grown accustomed to the evolutionary idea." I shall later criticize the Zeitgeist, or Time Spirit, thesis as it is usually presented and as Schroedinger presents it. But I do, within limits, acquiesce in his view that fashions are powerful.

Another eminent scientist, G. N. Lewis, says that scientists often suppress some part of the evidence for new theories which they advance, because such evidence cannot be presented with the formality which the fashion of the day dictates. Sometimes, in order to satisfy the current style in ideas, a scientist even introduces irrelevant proofs of his theory. Lewis refers to John Ray who, in 1630, first clearly enunciated the law of conservation of mass; Lewis queries whether Ray could himself have been convinced by the arguments that he offered to the public. "This learned physician was furnishing the sort of proof which was in vogue in his day. If we accept his conclusions," says Lewis, "without accepting his demonstration, it would be a precedent which we may often follow profitably with respect to the many demonstrations which follow the fashions of our own age."

As you know, Newton, in his greatest scientific endeavors, used a new mathematical method which he had invented—the infinitesimal calculus. He acquainted his close friends with this technique. But in publishing his results, he concealed that technique because he feared that its novelty would arouse opposition. Instead, he laboriously translated his work into "the well-known geometrical methods of the ancients" which would clothe "his work in a garb which would appear less strange and uncouth to those not familiar with the new method." And he concealed it from the general public for almost twenty years.

Fashion affects not merely scientific theories but the very facts whence those theories derive. A fact reflects, or results from, a human motive, interest, or purpose, in dealing with experience. "Pure observation" or "pure description" of experience never occurs. Looking and reporting are always motivated. Observation is selective, programmatic. A "descriptive statement," a so-called "statement of fact," often represents but a prediction of future experience in which the observer is interested.

The very origin of the word "fact" is illuminating. It derives from a word meaning "to make" or "to do." In English, indeed, one meaning of fact is "a thing done, a deed, an act." The word "feat" comes from the same root. In part, at least, men make their facts. Facts, at least partially, are human achievements, inventions, human feats.

We hear much talk of "hard facts." But facts are softer than they appear to the average person. Mankind, of course, does not create the totality of experience. Some phases of experience are, indeed, stubborn, tough. The "objects of perception" have hard cores which are independent of human responses to those objects. Those stubbornnesses, Justice Holmes called "Can't Helps"; Barry refers to them as "coercive" or "compulsive"; and Kenneth Burke, as the "recalcitrance of the materials." These Can't Helps, of course, do not come to us in the raw, for they are transformed for us by our sense organs. As our sense organs are not of our own making, the reports of our senses constitute, for us, part of the stubbornness of the Can't Helps.

We do not, however, mechanically accept those reports. We construct many of the interpretations which we call "facts." When we speak of "brute" or "hard" facts, we mean simply those "cores" which no man makes, which all men "have to take." But, since so large a part of our facts was originally man-made and can be changed by man, it is proper to say that every fact is "subjective" in this sense—that it involves a selection made by human beings, and human beings are so constitutionally limited in their perceptions that they cannot possibily know all that is going on in the universe. Any individual man's facts are subjective in another sense: They must, to "become objective," be acceptable to a sufficient number of other men.

"Facts" resemble "theories." For a theory, like a fact, is purposively selective. Indeed, a "fact" is a theory about some fragment of experience. There occurs, as Vaihinger has made clear, a constant shifting, to and fro, between what we call "fictions," "hypotheses," "theories," "laws," and "facts." Those names are but labels for different stages in the life of an idea. That the earth is round, not flat, is now a fact. Once it was merely some man's guess or theory. It was a fact to medieval chemists that mercury and other metals could be converted into gold; later, new evidence discredited that fact; in the nineteenth century it was a scientific fact that no chemical element could be transmuted into another; but today that is no longer a scientific fact.

I must disgress for a moment. Disputations about "subjectivity" and "objectivity" are never ending. I cannot here discuss that subject at length, but I make these tentative and elliptical suggestions: Man encounters at least five kinds of "subjectivities": (1) Those which inhere in the finite, limited capacities of all men. (2) Those which derive from the unique ("private") attitudes of individual persons. (3) Those which stem from the grammatical structures of particular languages. (4) Those due to the divers social heritages of social groups. (5) Those arising from location (Russell calls them "physical" subjectivities). The first are hopelessly ineradicable; the second are but partly surmountable; the third and fourth (which are related) can be overcome to some extent, but probably not entirely; the fifth, in part, have been successfully eliminated by modern physicists (Einstein, et al.). To acknowledge that some human "subjectivities" are inescapable does not compel the conclusion that men's way of interpreting experience lack "reality." Men are "real." They are part of "reality." At a minimum, in that sense, their interpretations of experience are "real." The valid "reality" of those interpretations includes human "feelings," the so-called "secondary qualities," and human values and ideals.

Many of the "objective" facts of the past are today considered illusions or superstitions. Without doubt, many of our facts and scientific laws will some day cease to be "objective" and will be regarded as illusions. Just as what we now consider falsities were once taken as true, so some of our truths will, in the future, be transformed into falsities. So in the familiar case of witchcraft. In 1484, when Pope Innocent VIII issued a Bull on that subject, and in 1486, when, with his approval, the famous *Witch Hammer* was published, witchcraft constituted a fact. To doubt the reality of witches was then both a heresy and a crime punishable by the civil arm. Certain kinds of conduct "proved" that a man or woman was a witch. Such evidence no longer convinces most of us. It is now the fashion that conduct once accepted as proof of demoniacal possession "proves" the existence of a neurosis or psychosis.

The intellectuals have created the fashion of speaking of the dominance of certain ideas in any given period as the *Zeitgeist*, or Time Spirit. Recently they have made it the fashion to substitute for the Time Spirit the now hackneyed phrase "the climate of opinion." The very history of that phrase is illuminating. It was coined by a remarkable seventeenth century skeptic, Joseph Glanvill, who wrote a treatise, *The Vanity of Dogmatizing*, in which he analyzed what today we call stereotypes—the preconceptions that distort human judgments. He urged, as the first condition of knowledge, a total abnegation of opinions received by education. And yet, himself influenced by the "climate of opinion" in which he lived, he later published a spirited defense of the belief in witchcraft.

Facts, then, insofar as they are interpretations of experience, are not immortal. They are made by mortals and may be changed by other mortals. Because a fact represents a selection, embodying an attitude or motive, it follows that in the contriving of every fact some aspects of experience have been suppressed or disregarded. Someone may, some day, bob up with what was disregarded and, liberating the suppressed material, may remake (refashion) any fact. Undeniably, there are fashions in facts and in approaches to facts.

Interestingly enough, the word "fact" is the parent of the word "fashion." We should perhaps, therefore, not be too surprised to discover factional—partisan—attitudes toward facts. One faction find repugnant the notion I have been discussing—that there is a human element in the making of facts, theories, and scientific "laws." That repugnance carries that faction to great lengths. They even refuse to recognize that many human laws for the governance of a society—legal rules—are made by the human beings called judges. When a judge decides a case according to a new legal rule which he announces and, when, in so doing, he overrules a former "precedent," this faction objects to saying that the abandoned legal rule was once the "law" and has now been changed. They insist that it never was the "law," but was merely a mistaken version of it; that the "Law" is eternal, immutable, and preexists all man-made formulations of it; that it is merely discovered by judges as Columbus discovered America; that a judge no more "makes law" than Columbus made or invented America; that an abandoned legal rule was a false map of the "Law," resembling a pre-Columbian map of the world.

Bell notes a similar attitude in some mathematicians: Some say, "We can choose a number less than $n$ and greater than $n - z$," but others say, "There exists such a number." The "we can choose" men, remarks Bell, recognize the creative human factor in mathematics, while the "there exists" men believe that "we" come upon the "eternal truths" of mathematics in our journey through life. When the physicist Boltzmann concluded a lecture on molecules, the sagacious Mach said, "You don't know that molecules exist," to which Boltzmann replied, "I know that there are molecules."

It is sometimes said, however, that such things as molecules are "theories," not "facts," and that disagreements about theories must be distinguished from differences about facts. Thus Jevons, in a well-known passage, said that "false facts in science * * * are more mischievous than false theories, since * * * a false theory is open to everyone's criticism, and is ever liable to be judged by its accordance with the facts," while "a false or grossly erroneous assertion of a fact often stands in the way of science for a long time because it may be extremely difficult * * * to prove the falsity of what has once been recorded." There is much truth in that comment; but it ignores the point that facts embody theories, that the observer does not blindly gather facts but selects them for a purpose, and that his theory, which guides his selection, tends to lead him to overlook matters which will frustrate his theory. The case of Darwin is illustrative. When at work gathering material bearing on his theory of natural selection, he made an unusually conscientious effort to note everything discrepant with that theory. Yet, although he and Mendel experimented with the same species of plants, Darwin, intent on his own hypothesis, overlooked those implications of what he observed which impressed Mendel, who had a different hypothesis. As a consequence, Darwin often failed to record "data" in which Mendel constructed his theory, a theory which scientists regard as importantly modifying Darwin's. Thus Darwin's "false" theory produced "false" facts. Another illustration: Some Protestant sociologists, collecting statistics about persons in a certain country, reported that Catholics in prison greatly outnumbered Protestants. From these facts they inferred a peculiar Catholic proclivity to crime. A later investigation, however, disclosed this flaw in the "data": Many Protestant prisoners, wishing to vary their monotonous diet, had registered as Catholics in order to obtain fish on Friday. Such instances suggest that many accepted scientific "facts" concerning physical as well as human nature derive from prejudiced theories.

Let us not be deceived by the apparent "dispassionateness" of science. True, science seems singularly free of human frailties. Someone has said, "The true man of science worships but one god—truth. He despises the ecclesiastic for teaching half-truths for the sake of moral influences; the politician for dressing up truth in a partisan guise; and the business man for subordinating truth to personal gain." But "candid camera shots" of scientists spoil that impression of serene selfless "objectivity." Bell, writing of the lives of the great mathematicians, says that there has been among them "enough dishonesty to discount the superstition that the pursuit of truth necessarily makes a man truthful," that envy is frequently present in scientific undertakings, that "narrow nationalisms and international jealousies, even in impersonal pure mathematics, have marred the history of discovery and invention to such an extent that it is almost impossible in some important instances to get at the facts or to form a just estimate of the significance of a particular man's work for modern thought." Newton, early in the eighteenth century, lent himself to a disgracefully dishonest campaign to prove that Leibnitz, his great German contemporary, had stolen from him the idea of the calculus which, in fact, Leibnitz had independently invented. The ensuing international feud largely cut English mathematicians off from contact with Continental mathematicians for almost a century, during which the latter forged far ahead—to the grave disadvantage of English science. Dalton, the early nineteenth century English chemist, became bitterly jealous when the Frenchman Guy-Lussac confirmed Dalton's theory, and when the Swede Berzelius improved the Daltonian techniques. Joule and Helmholtz, outstanding scientists, for years jealously refused to recognize Robert Mayer as the pioneer in formulating the modern theory of heat and of the conservation of energy, and themselves claimed priority until Tyndall compelled acknowledgment of Mayer's claims. Where, asks Trattman, "is that marvelous abstraction the 'true man of science'? Science is part of the universal biography of man and shares too often, alas, the crude anthropomorphism of his life. How else can one account for the petty hostility of Helmholtz, who sat in the seats of the mighty * * * begrudging Mayer recognition."

Occasionally, an unusually candid scientist tells tales out of school of how "facts" may be fudged in order to preserve "true" scientific doctrine. "I have heard," said William James, "of the lecturer on physics who had taken over the apparatus of the previous incumbent consulting him about a certain machine intended to show that, however the peripheral parts of it might be agitated, its center of gravity remained immovable. 'Well,' said the predecessor apologetically, 'whenever I used the machine, I found it advisable to drive a nail through the center of gravity.'" And James related that, when himself a young instructor, he was assisting a lecturer on the physiology of the heart. The lecturer employed a turtle's heart, supporting an index-straw which threw a greatly enlarged moving shadow upon a screen while the heart pulsated. To James's consternation, the turtle's heart refused to function according to the lecturer's prediction. "There was no time for deliberation," James continues, "so with my forefinger under a part of the straw that cast no shadow, I found myself impulsively and automatically imitating the rhythmical movements which my colleagues had prophesied the heart would undergo. I kept the experiment from failing * * * and established in the audience the true view of the subject."

Such deliberate deceptions in the interest "of the larger truth" will be regarded as dishonest by many scientists. But what of the observations and queries of scientists which they shove to one side and conceal as not compatible with the current fashions in science? Peirce spoke of the "moral terrorism" of respectable ideas which constrain the nonconformist who has a tabooed belief; "the greatest intellectual benefactors of mankind have never dared, and dare not now, utter the whole truth of their thought," Peirce said. "Singularly enough, the persecution does not all come from without; but a man torments himself and is oftentimes most distressed at finding himself believing propositions which he has been brought up to regard with aversion," and "finds it hard to resist the temptation to submit his opinions to authority." The pressure of reputability in ideas is immense. For that reason, the scientist often suppresses the ideas, unpopular with his fellow scientists, which have occurred to him, or the all-to-human mental processes by which he arrived at his published theories.

Planck, the great physicist, writes that it would be interesting to try to discover the combinations of thoughts to which significant scientific hypotheses owed their origin, but that the task is difficult, "because, generally speaking, creative master minds have felt a personal aversion to the idea of unfolding before the public gaze the delicate threads of thought out of which their productive hypotheses were woven, and the myriad other threads which failed to be interwoven into any final pattern." We may surmise that, if there were no such aversion, some quaint conceits would be unfolded before the public gaze. We have learned of a few. Buchanan notes that Descartes was directed by an angel to work out analytic geometry, Kepler was fascinated by sun worship, Faraday transferred a religious symbol to the magnetic field, Newton shot imaginary cannonballs around the earth to rival the moon, "and the idea of the carbon ring came out of the lurid imagery of a morning after a party."

The nabobs of the scientific group may easily frighten into silence the young scientist who has a fresh idea, or who made a novel observation of "facts," prompted by some unorthodox stimulus and out of step with accepted scientific thinking. Conformity is easy, and if the young scientist is not robust, he may, for fear of ridicule, fall in line with the reputable scientific thought-ways. Those thought-ways then straitjacket him. Kepler spent almost his entire life freeing himself from the traditional idea that a circle was the only possible orbit for a planet. No one knows how many fruitful ideas and observations of "facts" have been suppressed for fear of giving offense to the noted men of science. The concepts precious to the high priests of science are likely to escape outspoken criticism and, absent that criticism, may long act as contraceptives to seminal notions.

Truth crushed to earth may be prostrate for decades, even centuries. When an Einstein pontificates that the idea of "such a thing as free will in nature" is "of course preposterous," few scientists except a Nobel Prize winner like a Schroedinger or a Langmuir have the hardihood to express a belief in it. Many a theory, later to be discarded, has remained "true" for decades because the scientific pontiffs were ready to shout "preposterous" at those who opposed it. Sometimes a courageous young man breaks up some of the dogmas of the scientific elders. That is precisely what Einstein himself, when a youngster, succeeded in doing; he dared to attack the accepted gravitation theory of Newton. Fortunately for Einstein—and for the advance of "science"—a few eminent older scientists refused to join in general "scientific" sneers at his theory, and gave him a hearing.

Of course, I am not denying the existence of the "external world." I am (merely!) asserting that man cannot ever be aware of all its aspects. But we humans are reluctant so to admit. Men, confronted with a puzzling universe, about which they can obtain but a limited amount (and kind) of information, have always invented "just-so stories," some of which are more plausible or useful than others. But no such man-made interpretations will ever accurately describe, or cope with, all that goes on in the universe (or multiverse). Inescapable, we are confined in our "private" human world, our subuniverse. Conceivably, we might be able to merge the "private" worlds of individual men, or groups of men, into a "public" human world. Perhaps some day we can thus achieve such a "public" world to this extent: that men everywhere on this planet will confront experience with the combined understanding of our ablest scientists and our wisest philosophers and poets. But it is not conceivable that we can ever rid ourselves of all our human limitations. The ultimate perfection of our capacities would still have us provincials.

The ordinary man's view of "nature" derives largely (at second hand or third hand) from what we call "natural science." But "natural science," what does it mean? Merely the current set of scientific theories, the current "just-so stories," which receive the approval of those scientists who have prestige. Those of us who are not scientists perforce accept their judgments on matters of science. The scientists concede that many of their scientific explanations of nature are sure to change, at least in some respect, as "science progresses"; most scientists, however, say or imply that the explanations now accepted by them are not only the best and most accurate available at present but also that they came about inevitably.

But such a statement obscures the part that accident plays in both the birth and the acceptance of scientific theories. First there is the way in which a scientist accidentally stumbles on a new fact which pokes a hole in an old theory. Let us recall a well-known instance of such a stumbling, with amazing consequences, which might be captioned *From Frog Legs to Dynamos*: Galvani, a physician and anatomist, in 1780, having dissected a frog, happened to lay one of the frog's legs near the conductor of a charged electric machine; by sheer accident, his scalpel, while touching an exposed nerve in the leg, came in contact with the machine; a spark passed and the leg twitched convulsively. He thus discovered the electric current. Even Einstein (who seems to maintain that, generally, scientific progress is an inevitable, objectively determined, advance) admits that, in that one instance, "accident seemed to play an essential role" in scientific growth. There "is no doubt," he says, "that Galvani's accidental discovery led Volta, at the end of the eighteenth century, to the construction of what is known as the voltaic battery"; and Einstein goes on to describe how the resulting experiments of Volta and others brought about the "discovery of the electric current" and thus the "tremendous development of electricity as a branch of science and technique." That development included not only the use of electric power, which transformed our industries and our civilization, but also yielded a revolution, through Maxwell's formulations, in the basic theories of physics.

Accident plays a large part in science in even more profound ways, as will appear from the following: Any scientific theory, in order to gain recognition among those men of science who possess prestige, must usually be more than a minor, or relatively minor, correction of some theory which they previously recognized. A new theory is, therefore, usually linked up with an older accepted theory, for a theory wholly unrelated to the way in which the dominant scientific clique has been thinking about nature will seem so outlandish to them that they will generally snub it. The theory of Ptolemy, the theory of Newton, each in its day, became an accepted way of thinking; the same is true of Einstein's "relativity" theories in our times. Each of these theories was, in its origin, a "happy thought" of a great mind, a very effective "just-so story." Succeeding scientists grow up so accustomed to those stories that any new story has to be in line with the old. Einstein admits that sometimes a decision between two theories may be "more a matter of taste than of scientific conviction." The history of science shows that, often, "scientific taste" and "scientific conviction" are one and the same thing. Scientists, like mortals, are prone to adhere to their preconceived explanations. They are not altogether unlike the movie director who, Stefansson tells, insisted that his Eskimo actors, in Nanook of the North, catch their fish by spearing them through the ice—a method unknown to those Eskimos, but correct in fiction and the movies.

Always, says Swan, a scientific theory has in it something "artificial," something not clearly understood, and a new theory usually explains what was not clearly theretofore understood by adding something else which, also, is not altogether understood. (Swan calls this process the "unification of ignorance.") When a new theory departs too abruptly from the old, the scientific nabobs usually damn it as "unscientific." They have certain criteria, more or less "private," by which they judge a novel theory. Those criteria usually derive from the points of view (I would call them the "just-so stories") to which the members of the ruling clique are accustomed. They forget, says Swan, that those points of view "were themselves built up by analogy with the behavior of circumstances and things which had become familiar to them in their youth and which had become ingrained in their consciousness as natural before they reached the age at which they might question them." Words, be it noted, are potent in creating this feeling of "naturalness" or familiarity; what a scientist takes for granted in nature is in part a product of the way in which he was taught to talk about it (which, in turn, stems partly from the grammatical structure of his native language).

Here, again, accident enters: The accidents of fashion help to decide which of the scientists possess prestige. The accidents of fashion also help to decide which of these older theories are familiar to them and, accordingly, which of the advances in science the prestige will endorse. Had there been different scientific fashions in the past, a set of different scientific explanations might exist today; and those explanations might have been more accurate and effective than those now existing. What "nature" is like, according to "natural science," is, therefore, to no small extent a product of accident. For a suppressed idea, if it had been developed by its inventor and published, might radically have changed the structure of science. New ideas, if put to work, often proliferate, breed other ideas of value; the birth control of ideas may, then, kill off a potentially huge family of ideas. Moseley's conception of atomic numbers is said by Millikan to be one of the most brilliant and important in the history of science. Now, Moseley died in battle at Gallipoli in 1915 at the age of twenty-six. Suppose that he had thought his conception too daring and had secreted it. Einstein's relativity theories, Planck's quantum theory, have revolutionized physics. What if those men had never dared to make their theories public? They did dare, and their efforts created new patterns of scientific thought. Those patterns are, discernibly, man-made. They relate to nature and therefore constitute partial views of nature. When later modified—as of course they will be—the scientific view of nature will change. That is but another way of saying that "natural laws" and the "facts" about nature will change as new, daring, and inventive men come along. So that, if Moseley, Einstein, and Planck had been intimidated into suppressing their theories, our natural laws would not be what they now are. Perhaps no one else would ever have invented those theories, in which case there never would have been any such natural laws known to man. And, as such natural laws yield practical accomplishments based thereon, leading to man-made changes in the real world—machines and other means employed to alter nature—the suppression of those theories would have substantially retarded changes in nature itself.

The suppression of scientific ideas through the overawing dogmas of the smugly arrogant scientific elders thus accidentally affects the very character of nature—both in mankind's knowledge of the "facts" concerning nature and in mankind's transformations of nature. Here, then, we find one of the "scandals" of science about which most scientists preserve a hush policy: *Science is an all-too-human enterprise, not an aloof, calmly detached, body of objective laws and facts. In part, it is a function of the pride and prejudice of the scientific tycoons.*

Science, says Cooley, is knowledge that can be established to the satisfaction of an expert group. But that group may err. For "it is with science as elsewhere; the premises of thought, being common to a group, escape scrutiny, and so, by the most rigorous methods, the common error may be propagated indefinitely. No group is a trustworthy critic of its own premises. * * * Scientific men are almost as eager to believe as the religious. It * * * all comes back to the verdict of the expert group, which is the best guide we have, but not infallible * * *. The group disciplines its members, but who disciplines the group?" Many "professed men of science are no less partisans, propagandists, followers of fads than other people."

I trust that you will not gather that I share with certain misguided persons an antipathy to science and scientists. Science, properly exploited, is an indispensable instrument in the quest of a decent civilization. And that civilization will not be achieved unless the "scientific spirit" is extended far beyond its present confines—extended, for instance, so far that scientists will cease to be dogmatic philosophers and will examine their own basic assumptions with a critical, scientific, undogmatic, non-Euclidian, eye. The danger is not, as some persons say, that science is antiauthoritarian, but that scientists may be too authoritarian, not sufficiently scientific toward science.

Parenthetically, it is amusing to hear the chatter of those who, emphasizing the obvious, maintain that ideals are facts. Of course they are. When a group stubbornly sticks to an ideal, that ideal can be the hardest kind of hard fact. What is more to the point, facts are ideals; they symbolize hopes, aspirations, aims, goals. Still more important, there is nothing inherently noble about an ideal. Your ideal may be anathema to me, or mine to you. The Nazis are idealists, fiercely so. To us, their ideals are detestable, so detestable that we have been obliged to resort to killing in order to obliterate those ideals.

I hope that you will not infer that I accept uncritically the fashionable thesis of the "Spirit of the Age"—popularized by Hegel and accepted even by so wise a person as Schroedinger—with its dogmatic assertion that powerful fashions always irresistibly shape the thoughts and emotional attitudes of all those who live in any given age. I haven't time here to enlarge on my criticism of what I consider to be a silly thesis. Suffice it to say this: There is no one single Spirit in any age. The Time Spirits in any period are multiple. They often strive with one another for mastery. Discrepant Spirits, however, may co-exist—at different levels. What seems to be a single, uniform Zeitgeist may be merely the point of view of the highly vocal men, the articulate individuals, the highbrows.

Moreover, at bottom, every fashion—like every so-called "folk song"— has its origin in the thought and effort of some particular individual. That is surely true in the field of women's apparel, their hats and clothes, a field where all too clearly fashion exerts tremendous power. Individual enterprise helps to make fashions and to destroy them, whether as to clothes or ideas. The essence of a true democracy—as distinguished from societies, of the kind dear to Plato and all subsequent authoritarians—is that it encourages individuals to compete in contriving and popularizing new fashions. In truth, modern democracy itself was once but a suggested fashion. Jefferson and Lincoln were among its creative designers.

Now, if what I've said of the scientists is true, it must be even more true of other specialists. Stick-in-the-mud-ism is rife in every specialist group. As the top military clique court-martialed General Billy Mitchell, so the leading telephone engineers did their best to suppress the automatic telephone. The history of medicine is a story of unending warfare of medical theology with medical heretics. There is need for something like a Sherman Antitrust Act in the realm of ideas.

Although I have said much in criticism of inertia, I do not believe that there is any inherent virtue in mere change, that every change is praise-worthy. The new is not necessarily desirable, of course. Boredom, the tedium of the usual, and neurotic as well as healthy-minded impulses, often account for the pressure of novelty. Laymen are often more eager for change than the specialist. They may long for change for the mere sake of change. That longing sometimes needs to be resisted. And susceptibility to change may be but a fashion. The fashion of change is more popular in America than, until recently, it was in most other countries.

Now turn to another group of specialists who, although they deal with facts far "softer" than the physicists', seldom admit as much to the public. I refer to the historians.

Roman augurs, engaged in hoodwinking the populace with prophecies based upon examination of animals' entrails, would, so the story runs, wink at one another. Similarly, now and again, able historians—in what may be called "off-the-record" writings, not intended for the high school or college student or for the general reader, but for other historians—have confessed to the dismaying inadequacy of their raw materials. The historian Nevins, in such an "off-the-record" book, recently said that, while some historical facts—constituting "merely the skeleton of history"—are virtually indisputable, facts of that kind are surprisingly few. "It is," he added, "only on the most limited and precise topics that a 'definitive' history is possible." No historian, he admits, can answer with any high degree of finality such questions as, for example, why Carthage entered the First Punic War, why the Roman Empire disintegrated, why General Howe did not go to the rescue of Burgoyne, why the Southern Confederacy collapsed in 1865, why Napoleon III embarked on the Franco-Prussian War, or why President McKinley decided that America should fight Spain in 1898. One could compile a list a mile long of unanswerable questions concerning any century of Egyptian, Greek, Roman, European, or American history.

Many reasons exist for the inability of the historian to answer such questions. In the first place, he must depend on much dubious "data." There is much room for suspicion that many historical records, including many now regarded by most historians as authentic and accurate, may not be reliable. For instance, in the following and numerous other instances, as Nevins makes clear, historical narratives, once accepted as beyond question, have later proved false or misleading. Thus James Madison, the "father of the Constitution" and our fourth President, in his papers published after his death, gave detailed accounts, purporting to be notes, made contemporaneously, of the doings of the Constitutional Convention; they were accepted for many years as entirely accurate; however, Farrand has proved that long after the convention, Madison altered these notes in important ways. *Appleton's Cyclopedia of American Biography* contains forty-seven "lives" of men who never lived; many historians relied upon those false biographies during the several years before their exposure. Historians at one time regarded as a storehouse of valuable information the famous diary of Gideon Welles, which, while a Cabinet officer, he kept during the Lincoln and Johnson administrations; we now know that Welles altered his diary entries in the light of events which later occurred in order to blacken the reputations of men whom he had come to dislike. In 1873, Charles Francis Adams, at one time Lincoln's minister to England, published a book which gave a wealth of detail apparently demonstrating that the wise counsels of Seward accounted for Lincoln's success as President; but later writings of others, thoroughly familiar with the facts, made evident the inaccurate and biased character of Adams' book.

In those and many other instances, falsities and inaccuracies, for a time not noted, were afterward detected. If the errors had never been disclosed, our views of the past would have been seriously wrong. If, for example, no one had ever published contradictions of Adams' narrative, our current estimates of Lincoln would probably be incorrect.

Unfortunately, concerning many an important historical incident the only discoverable evidence consists of the narrative of a single person. For instance, the Roman historian Suetonius, as secretary to the Emperor Hadrian, had access to important documents in the Imperial Archives when he was writing his *Lives of the Twelve Caesars*; he is, as to many of those documents, long ago destroyed, our sole source of information. But most historians, regarding him as a biased and careless reporter, hold that he should not be trusted. Here, then, is a dilemma: Historians must either rely on the unreliable Suetonius or acknowledge that no one can know many crucial facts of Roman history. An equally disturbing but less often recognized dilemma confronts historians when there are no data indicating anything, one way or the other, about the truthworthiness of the sole narrator of an event. In such circumstances, historians frequently accept his narrative as true, although, for all they know, it may be wholly false.

Important facts of the past, both deeds and attitudes, may never have been written down, and are therefore now unknown and unknowable. Palmerston, the English Prime Minister, said of the Schleswig-Holstein question: "Only two men really understood it. One of them is dead. I am the other, and I have forgotten all about it." An event nowhere recorded, no matter how important it may have been, does not, of course, exist for the historian. In the nature of things, there must be many thousands of such unreported events. Yet historians usually treat the nonexistence of data about past occurrences as the equivalent of the nonexistence of those occurrences; they often write their histories as if they know all about what happened at a particular time, although in fact no one possesses such knowledge.

Is it not presumptuous for historians to suggest, as many of them do, that history is or can be a science and that there are precise "laws" of history which historians can learn and teach? The methods used by the physicist and the chemist in getting at their facts are not available to the historian. He cannot experiment with his materials or have firsthand acquaintance with them. He cannot make the Roman legions march again or see with his own eyes what went on in seventeenth century England.

The historian, admitting that he cannot employ the methods of the natural scientist, uses, he says, the scientific methods of the law courts. (God save the mark!) How scientific are the courts in their fact-finding techniques? True, a trial judge, before giving a decision in a lawsuit, must, as well as he can, ascertain the facts; and, in so doing, he must, like the historian, deal with past events. The judge, in that sense, becomes a historian, for the actual events in litigation have already happened in the past, before the lawsuit began. These past occurrences do not walk into the courtroom or reproduce themselves for the judge's inspection. All that the judge can do is to attempt to learn what actually happened—by listening to witnesses who saw or know the events and who tell their stories in his presence. They are under oath, and may go to jail if they perjure themselves, and if they are caught at it. Even so, some witnesses lie so skillfully that they are believed. Too, honest witnesses often observe the same facts in flatly contradictory ways. The unconscious prejudices of witnesses affect their testimony in remembering and narrating what they saw. No one has invented any scientific method for determining which witnesses (if any) are both truthful and accurate, or contrived any scale for "weighing" conflicting testimony. There is no such thing as a science of proof. Moreover, as there may be missing witnesses or missing papers, all the pertinent evidence may not be brought out. For all these reasons, the "facts" as "found" by the judge are, at best, conjectures— guesses. (I omit mention of jury trials where guessing is notoriously loose.) The judge cannot be sure his guesses are right. (When several judges hear the same evidence, not infrequently their guesses differ.) Judicial fact-finding is far from perfect; it is, indeed, the weakest part of the judicial process. Certainly it is not "scientific" in the sense of being an exact science, and shows little sign of ever becoming so.

When the historian attempts to imitate the nonscientific methods of the courts, he uses techniques which are even less adequate than theirs. Since the evidence he considers is often conflicting, his "facts" too are, for the most part, guesses—but guesses that usually have a much shakier foundation than those of the judge. The historian, let us say, desires to know what went on in the days of Oliver Cromwell, what all sorts and conditions of men were then doing, thinking, dreaming, hoping, taking for granted. The historian cannot, like a judge, order living witnesses to appear before him to testify under oath, to be examined and cross-examined. Usually, the historian's witnesses are in their graves. His evidence, therefore, consists largely of the unsworn writings of various dead men, none of whom can be interrogated. In their narratives of their times these dead men often differed among themselves. Most of them did not see or hear what they reported; most of them were—like the historians—guessers, dealers in second- or third- or fourth-hand information. Even as to the actual eyewitnesses and auditors of the past, how can the historian tell to what extent they were mistaken in their observations, or lying or prejudiced in their written accounts?

Obviously, then, the historian, in arriving at his facts, cannot use the methods of the natural scientist, and cannot even imitate successfully the nonscientific techniques of the law courts. Many of his "facts" are uncertain guesses based on evidence which is both untrustworthy and admittedly incomplete. As to many matters he is somewhat like the boy who said he could remember all the dates of history but couldn't say what they stood for.

The historian, wrote two eminent French historians, Langlois and Seignobos in an "off-the-record" book, "is in the situation of a chemist who should know a series of experiments only from the report of his laboratory boy * * *. In nearly every document the majority of the statements do not come from the author at first hand, but are reproductions of the statements of others. * * * The observations often "remain anonymous" so that "we are confronted with facts, observed we know not by whom or how, recorded we do not know when nor how. No other science accepts facts in such a condition, without possibility of verification, subject to incalculable chances of error."

The historian who wants to make a science of history runs into real trouble when he undertakes to formulate the "laws" of history—that is, to state what, over long stretches of time, constituted the real causes of historic change. The facts of the past, even assuming that all of them were accurately known, are so numerous that a mere narration of them would yield no "laws." The historian is like a detective with too many clues. In his effort to contrive historical laws, he must "interpret" the facts. This he tries to do by selecting those which are "significant," ignoring the others. But what makes any particular historical fact "significant"? Merely that some historian chooses it and so labels it. The difficulty is that historians do not at all agree in their choices of the significant facts. There exists no scientific method of choice. The peculiar interests, personalities, and prejudices of the several historians affect their selections. The historian Pirenne openly states that every history book is a "conjectural reconstruction of the past" and that, because of the differences among historians, "history is a conjectural science, or, in other words, a subjective science." A strange "science" indeed—one which consists of numerous discrepant, prejudiced guesses of individual historians. Nevins remarks that no important history book has yet appeared which did not reveal some bias. Jameson said of Bancroft's volumes on American history that every volume voted for Andrew Jackson.

Often it is said by historians that we cannot properly understand our own times, that we are too close to them, that not until the present becomes part of the past can it be adequately comprehended. So we are told that Lincoln's true significance could not be learned by men of his own day and that the "real meaning" of the New Deal must await the judgment of the future. When historians talk in that manner, what do they have in mind? One suspects that sometimes they mean merely this: When things are happening, there are so many of them that their interrelations are excessively complex and baffling. If, for instance, someone now could and did gather all the information at present available about the New Deal, there would be too much data; but, in future days, much of the evidence concerning the New Deal will be more manageable and an analysis of that movement will seem to be simpler—precisely because many of the important but complicated facts, now known by some persons who will not record them, will then have been forgotten and will then be undiscoverable. In other words, as a period recedes into the past, its "significance" appears to grow more obvious due to increasing ignorance of the facts of that period.

That is not the historian's usual explanation. Usually it is said that, when the present merges into the past, events will be seen in "better perspective." But whose perspective? That of men with a different viewpoint, an altered orientation, in the light of the problems of their own day. Their angle on the occurrences we are now experiencing will be a new angle. Will that aid them the better to understand our times? Of course not. The best proof of that fact is that an era, like the so-called Middle Ages, which is many centuries in the past, has taken on differing perspectives for each succeeding century: The Middle Ages did not look the same to Walter Scott in the nineteenth century as it had to Voltaire in the eighteenth; it does not look the same to most of us in the twentieth century as it did to either Scott or Voltaire. And the differing perspectives are not primarily due to increases in the amount of information about the Middle Ages. They are ascribable principally to variations in the outlooks, and therefore in the back-looks, of the lookers.

To some extent, the variations flow from the fact that, as time goes on, more things happen which can be said to result from the past. In 1944, one can purport to trace relations between the French Revolution and the Russian Revolution and Nazism—as one could not have done in 1850 or 1900 before there was a Russian Revolution and a Nazi movement. Consequently, it is possible in 1944 to give a new "significance" to the French Revolution. Every decade there is a revised version of Alexander, Julius Caesar, Charlemagne, George Washington, and Abraham Lincoln—because in each decade the events of the immediately preceding decade reconstruct those historic personages. The past, in that sense, is a present fact—a present reflection of our present hopes, frustrations, and despairs. The past is not, for us, what it was when it occurred; it is what we now make it.

The failure to note that fact is partly due to a confusion of two meanings of the word "history": It means events as they actually happened; it also means what is said and thought about those events at a later time. In truth, it is only history according to the second meaning that makes sense when we talk of the past. The nature of history, so understood, is clarified by considering the following: Even if we now knew every precise detailed fact about a past period—say, the English Revolution of 1688—and if we passed that complete information on to posterity, that past period would constantly alter as time elapsed and as human society changed its attitudes. Whether Magna Carta was a splendid or a reactionary document, whether the northern Abolitionists were heroes or scoundrels or fools, whether Cromwell was a great man or a bloody tyrant—will time tell? Yes, it will. But what will it tell? It will tell, at any particular future time, what sort of men the tellers are. A biography, it is said, is largely the autobiography of the writer, and so is a history. When someone asks, "Here is a lesson from the past," we should ask, "Whose past? What is the character and the program of the man who is interpreting it?"

It is amusing to note how easily one historian finds bias in the writings of another. Hear Macaulay on Hume's history of England: "Hume is an accomplished advocate. Without positively asserting much more than he can prove, he gives prominence to the circumstances which support his case [the virtues of the English Tories]. He glides lightly over those unfavorable to it * * *. Everything that is offered on the other side is scrutinized with the utmost severity; every suspicious circumstance is ground for argument and invective * * *; concessions even are sometimes made, but this insidious candor only increases the effect of the vast mass of sophistry." Now turn to Mark Pattison's comment on Macaulay's history of England. After noting that Macaulay was a Whig statesman, he says that "in writing of the history of the rise and triumphs of the Whig principles in the latter half of the 17th century, he identified himself with the cause [of the Whigs] * * *. When he is describing the merits of friends and the faults of enemies, his pen knows no moderation * * *. Macaulay's was the mind of the advocate, not of the philosopher * * *. Macaulay was, as he himself said of Bishop Burnet, 'a strong party man on the right side.'"

No wonder, then, that even those historians who believe that precise laws of history govern mankind do not agree with one another as to what those laws are. Many of them admit how guessy their facts are. Their attitude, then, boils down to this: "We historians, through no fault of our own, are failures in adequately discovering the true facts of history. Therefore you should trust us to discover 'laws' relating to those relatively little known facts. We can't tell you much of what actually happened, but we can tell you why it happened. As to most of what occurred in the past, we are very uncertain. But we are completely certain that whatever occurred was inevitable."

In the face of the insurmountable difficulties which conform them, the manner in which most historians write their histories surpasses belief. If there ever was an art calling for humility on the part of its practitioners, it is history-writing. The first sentence of almost every history book should read, "What follows consists of a series of guesses most of which are based on highly doubtful evidence, so doubtful that the reader is warned to take little of this book very seriously." Seldom, however, do historians insert any such warning anywhere in their history books.

The value of recognizing the imperfections in our knowledge of the past is that it undermines the belief that any accounts of the allegedly "true" causes of social change are substantially trustworthy. Thus we can learn that there are discoverable no inexorable laws which bind our future, that usually those laws are simply interpretations which wishful thinkers have contrived.

We should not, however, be snobs about the past. In its reservoir are ideas unwisely discarded, hopes and plans frustrated and abandoned, our information concerning which, although inadequate, may supply us with a few valuable suggestions for our present and future. Thus the unity which the Roman Empire gave Europe had its evil side, but some of the values it created may well be heeded today. History, too, liberates us from the fetters of the present, for it suggests that there were other ways of doing things than those we now employ.

The intelligent reading of history can and should serve as a liberator. It shows the past, not as a command to us but, at most, as a reservoir from which we can draw a few of the materials we now need. Of course, we cannot completely escape the habits which the past has implanted in us. But we owe it no obligations. The dead men whom we regard as great we should venerate; but we are living our lives and have no duty to live them as they lived theirs. It is to ourselves and to the future that our society owes a duty. From history we can obtain some hints; it will suggest a few do's and a few don't's. There is, said Mr. Justice Holmes, "a peculiar logical pleasure in making manifest the continuity between what we are doing and what has been done before. But the present has a right to govern itself so far as it can; and it ought always to be remembered that historic continuity with the past is not a duty, it is only a necessity." History is "the first step toward an enlightened scepticism, that is, towards a deliberate reconsideration of the worth" of old ways of conduct. It "encourages scepticism when one sees" how an old mode of behavior "has grown up or when one notices the naivete with which special prejudices are taken for eternal principles."

If we do not ask too much of historians, and if we content ourselves with relatively short-range looks ahead, the annals of the past can be of some help. Thus, in 1790, Burke, in his *Reflections on the Revolution in France*, on the basis of his study of history, predicted that the lax relations of the French government with the French Army, would lead to the rise of a "popular general" who would be a military dictator. When Alexander Hamilton wanted to show that the loose League of thirteen independent American states—under the Articles of Confederation—would not work, he went to history to show that such schemes of government, lacking any effective overall sovereignty, had always failed.

Despite the obstacles, some social planning for the future, guided by some knowledge of the past, is necessary, desirable, and possible. Men often forget that not to plan is a kind of planning—a plan to accept whatever happens, or a plan to abide by the uncorrected results of the past when meeting the future. Precise blueprints of the future are absurd. But men can do much to control their destiny, if their efforts are cautiously tentative and their plans are executed with a weather eye constantly open for signs that factors of importance have been overlooked or that new factors are emerging which compel revisions of their plans. We should not plot a course, take our ease, and sail blithely along, sure that there is nothing we have ignored and that we need never reckon with unanticipated hurricanes, fogs, or icebergs. We can, in the light of past experience—including past mistakes —see to it that our ship is as seaworthy as possible, and use the best educated guesses we are able to make as to what lies ahead. Our chief safeguard against shipwreck is a knowledge that we know little and a rejection of the cocksure illusion that anyone can foreknow with precision all the adventures yet to be encountered. We should beware of soothsayers, no matter how erudite or self-assured; we want, not soothsayers, but careful mariners.

We must not try to guide the future inflexibly. The future, when it becomes the present, is sure to bring new unanticipated problems. There is much wisdom in Valéry's reference to the "anachronism of the future." Still more important, we ought not shirk the present aspects of today's problems in order to indulge in too much tinkering with tomorrow's. The future, unless we are careful, can become as perniciously tyrannical over us as the past. Excessive posterity worship can be as bad as blind ancestor worship. And sometimes what passes for devotion to future generations is but a desire rigidly to control posterity; too cockily we often believe that, while our forefathers' ideas are outmoded for us, ours are sure never to grow stale; we hope that we, as future ancestors, will be worshiped.

Anatole France said that, as man needs to be amused by stories, we should not deprive him of history, the finest form of intellectual amusement. "I know as well as you that history is false," he wrote, "that all the historians * * * are narrators of fables. But that does not disturb me. I am quite willing that an Herodotus should deceive me in an agreeable manner; * * * I would even regret if it history were exact. I willingly say with Voltaire: reduce it to truth and you ruin it. * * *" History, he added, is "a sort of romance designed for those who have sagacious and curious minds. * * *"

Few historians, however, hold themselves out as fictionists. Most of

them purport to tell in detail exactly what actually happened. These specialists invite the rest of us to guide our present and future conduct by their
reports of the past, to depend on what they tell, to assume that they know
what they are talking about. There they sin. Their pretenses of accuracy
are false pretenses. A wag might suggest that, if there were some governmental agency which functioned with reference to historians as does the
SEC with respect to sellers of stocks and bonds, most—not all—history
books would be barred from the mails on the ground that they contain
seriously false and misleading information on which their purchasers are
solicited to rely; and no such book could lawfully be sold unless it was
labeled not "History" but "Twistory," or unless it fully had fairly disclosed
that the author did not vouch for the accuracy of most of its contents.

It is true that the "exact" science of physics is showing up today as far
less exact than has heretofore been supposed. It might then be argued that
the difference between physics, on the one hand, and the so-called "social
sciences," including history, on the other, is merely one of degree. But the
difference in degree is so great as to constitute a difference in kind. That
does not mean that social studies are utterly useless or that an effort should
not be made to reduce their uncertainties. No one but a fool rejects the possibility of reducing uncertainty as far as is practicable because it cannot be
completely eliminated—just as no sane man will turn his back on all
physicians merely because the flesh is heir to many diseases for which no
cure has been, and probably never will be, discovered by the medical profession. Perfection is not attainable. The insane asylum is the place for the
perfectionist, for those who demand complete freedom from uncertainties.
We are but mortal, and contingency and uncertainty are the essence of
mortality; only in the womb and the grave do we escape them. Nevertheless,
although history and the other so-called social sciences can become less
inexact, we should never forget their peculiarly inherent uncertainty.

With such an attitude, we will rescue ourselves from the two greatest
human fallacies: the fallacy of determinism, of denying the reality of all
human freedom, of seeking irresponsibility through recourse to Nature or
Providence which we expect to dictate our every move; and the opposed
fallacy of arrogantly assuming that mankind can ever be wholly free to guide
its own course, infallibly, to perfection. We can neither escape the flux and
variety of life nor our own finiteness. The only absolute knowledge on which
we can count is that human knowledge will always be relative and limited.
That awareness, however, will not enable us to elude our limitations. Thus
we come to the paradox of the American faith: Humility in the face of our
inescapable limitations but faith that the human will can—I say can, not
must—move us forward on the road to the good life. The impossibility of

reaching perfection does not justify indifference to the aim of constantly bettering man's lot.

Our problem vis-à-vis specialists is like that of the young lady to whom Shaw's Bishop said that she would be making a mistake if she married but a worse mistake if she didn't. We must have specialists. But we must democratize them. We must see to it that they do not, in an authoritarian manner, repel novelties. We must, too, subject the experts to constant criticism by the laity. We must, therefore, demand that the experts translate their esoteric formulations into terms easily comprehensible by non-experts. (Incidentally, I more than suspect that such translation will often bring to the experts themselves a nicer understanding of their own formulations.)

Take, for instance, the cult of experts, or specialists, to which, at least titularly, I belong. Seagle, in his recent book *The Quest for Law*, has described at length (with perhaps excessive hostility) the inertia-loving ways of lawyers and their devotion to needless mystery-mongering about matters legal. Certainly most judges have not sufficiently acquainted the public with the methods by which they arrive at their decisions. They have inadequately revealed to nonlawyers—indeed, often even to lawyers—the true springs of their actions. Moreover, encouraged by most lawyers, many judges wall off their routines from desirable innovations.

In particular, they have been backward and inefficient in what I regard as the most important part of their work—the ascertainment of the past facts on which specific judicial decisions turn. The law schools devote most of their time to improving legal rules and modes of using such rules. Such improvement is possible and needed. But courthouse finding of facts has been of little interest to the experts in legal education. I do not refer to those "background" facts—concerning economics and other social problems—which the famous "Brandeis briefs" illuminated. Today, most American courts welcome light on such problems. I refer, rather, to the inefficient judicial techniques for learning, so far as it is practical to do so (it is often impossible to do so completely), the actual past facts of the specific controversies which come before the courts for decision.

In part, the immense growth of commissions, administrative agencies, was a response to that judicial deficiency. Having been a member of such a commission and being now a member of the judiciary, I say, with some considerable assurance, that many commissions are far better equipped for that kind of fact-finding than are most courts today.

Largely unobserved by students of government, there began, in 1938, a novelty in so-called "administrative law." I have in mind the manner in which the SEC now functions in a case of corporate reorganization. The commission does not first pass on such a case which is then appealed to and reviewed by a court largely bound by the commission's findings of fact. On the contrary, the case, at every stage, is conducted by the judge. The SEC serves merely as the judge's assistant. Using its staff of experts—engineers, accountants, and the like—the commission gathers a multitude of data concerning the case and presents that data to the judge. Other parties are free to dispute the evidence presented by the SEC, and the judge is free to deal with the SEC's evidence, in the traditional judicial manner, in reaching his decision. But the court, with the aid of persons who specialize in a certain kind of fact-gathering, is thus far better able than it otherwise would be to approximate the facts and arrive at a fairly just conclusion.

I suggest that here is an importantly new departure, one which preserves the essential judicial techniques but introduces expertness where it is most needed in the judicial process. I believe that had that devise been invented fifty years ago, we would not have had the vast growth of that sort of administrative activity which has given rise to much recent irritation and angry discussion.

That new technique is capable of extensive application in the work of the courts. Its great virtue is that it tends to diminish the routineering and esotericism to which all expert groups are susceptible. It discloses one effective way of democratizing experts.

In closing, I call your attention to the fact that the present majority of the United States Supreme Court is bent on democratizing the judiciary. In the Bridges case, it denied to a judge the power to jail his critics for contempt of court unless those critics caused an actual disturbance in the courtroom. That decision went far to dissipate the legend that there is a divinity that doth hedge a judge.

Moreover, the present majority of the Supreme Court has been franker with the public than its predecessors. While from its earliest days the Supreme Court has, on many occasions, explicitly overruled some of its former decisions, the usual practice was to kill off precedents by indirection. The Court would usually not say, "Our decision in Black v. White was wrong," but would declare, "The Black-White decision has been misunderstood. It applies only to the peculiar facts of that case," those facts being so idiosyncratic that never again would that decision serve as a guide. To use lawyers' jargon, precedents were thus "distinguished." But in thus "distinguishing" them, the Court, in truth, "extinguished" them—without saying so. Today the Supreme Court is more candid, more frequently lets the public in on what it is doing. It now freely confesses that judges are human—and therefore fallible.

Let other experts go and do likewise.

*Philosophy of Science* (1949)

# THE SPEECH OF JUDGES:
## A DISSENTING OPINION &

IT IS, or should be, I believe, the inalienable right of any man in a democracy to prefer steak to veal, asparagus to spinach, Scotch to Rye, Conrad Aiken to Wordsworth, Shaw to Shakespeare, Dewey to Plato, Dashiell Hammett to Galsworthy. The canons of taste are not part of the law of the land or the law of nature. To my mind, taste, whether gustatory or literary, is inherently personal and subjective. It is in taste that individual initiative can and should have freest play. Men, it has been said, may be divided into two classes: those who don't know what is art but know what they like, and those who don't know what they like but profess to know what is art. I belong to the first class.

Confessing to such doubts as to the existence of objective literary standards, it may seem ridiculous that I should waste good ink and paper making comments on the literary style of the judiciary. But the subject deserves attention for this reason: The style of one of our greatest American judges, Mr. Justice Cardozo, recently deceased and properly venerated, has been praised without published dissent. It has lately been said, with almost tiring repetition, that he wrote "a singularly facile and lucid English," that he had "a liquid style that sparkles." Already that praise has induced some other judges to attempt to imitate him; and his imitators are beginning to breed their imitators. Unaware that there are many unable to subscribe to that praise but unwilling or too lazy to make public their dissents, the oncoming generation of lawyers may feel constrained to accept that so-called "singularly facile and lucid English" as the ideal pattern, and to esteem lightly the manner in which certain other American judges express themselves. That would be a misfortune, for it would retard the effect on legal writing of that healthy development, occurring elsewhere, of an unapologetic American style. And such a style has its importance.

First it makes for clearer understanding by American lawyers and laymen of what American courts are doing; I shall return to that point later.

Second, it is bad medicine for America that, too long, its literature, legal or other, has been written in English. We Americans are not English. And our speech—what we talk—is not English, but American. Our talk, to be sure, resembles our writing. But the two are importantly different. And the difference hampers, seriously, American written expression and, as a consequence, American thinking.

I remember, more than a decade ago, visiting an English appellate court. A case had just been argued and the three judges huddled together for some ten minutes after which the presiding judge uttered the court's opinion. The utterance was delivered without any preparation or the assistance of a single written note. I was amazed at its literary excellence. I could think of no American judge who could match that performance. What an inferior lot our judges are, I reflected.

But as I wandered about England I came to doubt the wisdom of that reflection. For, on all sides, I heard men and women speaking what seemed to me like English literature. The most mediocre or commonplace of moderately well-educated Englishmen could, without effort, talk in a manner that few Americans of genius equal in their best and most carefully prepared writings. Why? Because *Englishmen both talk and write English. But Americans try to write English, but talk American.*

There is no reason for perpetuating that divorce between our two languages, the spoken and the written. Once upon a time, all Europeans made that error. In those days no cultured Frenchman wrote in French; he spoke French and wrote Latin. The shift to the use of French as a literary medium was revolutionary. To write in French, it was thought, was to write in slang ("patois"). It was asserted that no masterpiece could be written in a modern language. The literary revolution was in its height when Du Bellay wrote (in French) of "the foolish arrogance and temerity * * * of some learned men who think our vernacular incapable of all good literature, and erudition." The vestiges of that old tradition are buried in the phrase "romance languages."

We are, in a sense, to the English what the French were to the Romans. Our speech is, in that sense, like a romance language. It is in large part derived from English. But English itself is a derived language—a composite of French, German, Scandinavian, Greek, Latin, and a dozen other tongues.

There's a key: *a language, at its core, is a tongue.* And the tongue, as we need no physiologist to tell us, is used (some of the time) for speaking. A written language should, therefore, be directly related to the tongue—to speech. And since American speech is not English, no more should American writing be.

It is no accident that we use, almost interchangeably, the words "language," "tongue," "speech." For the basic appeal of language is to the ear. "Language," says Sapir, "is primarily an auditory system of symbols. In normal individuals the impulse to speak, first takes effect in the sphere of auditory imagery. * * * Hence the cycle of speech * * * is a matter of sounds and of movements intended to produce these sounds. Written language is * * * a point to point equivalence to its spoken counterpart. The written forms are secondary symbols of the spoken ones—symbols of symbols." Although the written symbols may "in the actual practice of certain eye-readers, and possibly in certain types of thinking, be entirely substituted for the spoken ones, yet the auditory-motor associations are probably always latent."

*It would seem clear that good writing is speech heightened in tone and polished in form.* But heighten and polish up American speech, as you will, it is still not English. Yet, under the lash of tradition, we try to make it so. And we fail signally.

I repeat that it is bad medicine for Americans to speak American and try to write English. For one thinks in language. Our thought grooves and our language grooves are inseparable. So that Americans should think in American, in their native tongue. To force ourselves, as we do, to think in an alien tongue, in English, is to clog our thinking.

Mr. Justice Holmes once said, and profoundly, that we need "to think things instead of words, or at least we must constantly translate our words into the things for which they stand." But we think by means of our words. And we should use those words in a way which will bring them, with least effort, closest to the things about which we are thinking, else there will be loose connecting rods in our thoughts. So that it is unwise for Americans, when thinking of American things, to use words after the manner of Englishmen.

It is possible that it would be easier for us to learn to think in some language which we could not fail to recognize as foreign, such as French or Latin or German. The very fact that English is not obviously alien—that the difference between American and English are subtle, so that we are not aware of the task we impose on ourselves—may make that task the greater. How subtle are the differences and how difficult it is to discern them is easily shown by observing the reverse of the usual process: note how Bernard Shaw falls down when, in *Blanco Posnet,* he tries to write American.

Let me add that nothing I have said is to be taken as expressing distaste for the English or English style. I do not mean for a moment that Americans are better than Englishmen or American speech better than English. I do mean that Americans are not Englishmen and that American is not English. Nor am I expressing any disdain for the "classics," English or Latin or Greek. Of the classics, I say, with Du Bellay, "Devour them not in order to imitate but to turn them into blood and nutriment"; and I recall Hobbes, who said that "it is an argument of indigestion when Greek and Latin sentences come up again unchanged."

I have been told of a student at the University of Chicago who, as a native of China, had learned English in Barcelona, Spain. In Chicago he listened to a professor, talking American, and recorded what he heard in English learned from a Spanish teacher. In just what language he thought during that process, I do not know. His job was complicated. That of the American, trying to write and think in English, is but a trifle less so.

Thanks to Mencken, many Americans have become conscious of that needless difficulty. There were pre-Menckenites who sensed it. Veblen did, as I shall presently point out. And the writings of Thoreau or Mr. Justice Holmes are full of native idioms; are made of the American speech of their day, heightened and polished. Is it not possible that Holmes's clarity of thought owes much to that fact?

"Cardozo's style," writes one of his admirers, "flows with excitement across the printed page," adding that "here is an essayist rare enough to rank with * * * Lamb."

I shall doubtless be chided for questioning that judgment. I do so with no deviation from the deepest admiration for his greatness as a judge, a philosopher, or a scholar. That he was a great judge, that he advanced the progress of keen thinking about the purposes and workings of the courts, is beyond question. That he was a great person, too, is undeniable. Holmes called him "A beautiful spirit." And all who knew him have paid him similar tributes: they speak of him as "a unique personality"; of his "spiritual nature"; of his "nobility of character"; of his "simplicity." He was "reserved, unassuming, retiring, gracious to high and low," and "serene." It is said that "his every thought and action were mellowed by gentleness and humility." Yet "with the simplicity, modesty and gentleness of his character, there was a driving spirit to right the wrongs of the world." Surely here was a wise and good man, entitled to veneration.

But he was neither an immortal nor a mortal god. Being human, he escaped perfection.

The dogma that one should speak nothing but good of the dead surely needs to be discarded. It is plainly absurd as to rascals: there is every reason why, when an Insull dies, we should point out his vices. But it is almost as absurd that there should be silence as to the faults of great men. No man is great in all his aspects. Diderot observed that "everything, even among the greatest of all the sons of men, is incomplete, mixed, relative; everything is possible in the way of contradictions and limits; every virtue neighbors elements of uncongenial alloy; all heroism may hide points of littleness; all genius has its days of shortened vision." Unmitigated or monolithic praise of the great departed often encourages imitation of their errors and weaknesses.

I do not depart from these views when I venture to reproach Cardozo's style. If it should be said that it is presumptuous for so unaccomplished a person to criticize the style of one so great as Cardozo, my answer will be this: It is a prized democratic maxim that even an alley cat may look at a king; it was an untutored boy who saw the true nature of the emperor's clothes.

Cardozo was a contradictory personality: although he was a recluse, a retiring man, he devoted most of his life to public service and was therefore constantly making a public appearance. Deeply hurt, in his youth, by a certain bitter personal experience, he withdrew from the manner of living followed by most of his fellow men. Yet he did not seek refuge in morbid introspection or in an ivory tower. He did indeed retreat from twentieth century living. But he reentered it. And—here is the point—he reentered it disguised as an eighteenth century scholar and gentleman. His observations of the contemporary scene were keen, but they were not quite the observations of a contemporary. He wanted, at one and the same time, to be in and yet out of what was happening in the America of his time.

He achieved a compromise. And that compromise expresses itself in his style. It is neither twentieth century nor American. It is imitative of eighteenth century English: he wrote of twentieth century America not in the American idiom of today but in a style that employed the obsolescent "King's English" of two hundred years ago.

The result was by no means ugly. His writings have grace. But it is an alien grace. Significantly, in his essay on *Law and Literature*, Cardozo, in citing instances of literary excellence among judges, passes freely from English to American opinions without noting any need for differentiation.

He was not wholly indifferent to current American speech. I am told that one evening, when someone described the "principle of polarity" as expounded in Morris Cohen's *Reason and Nature*, Cardozo remarked, "Ah, Professor Cohen dignifies wobbling." But, when Cardozo wrote, such street language disappeared. His wit then took another and more "elegant" form. So, in a dissenting opinion, he said: "A Commission which is without coercive powers, which cannot arrest or amerce or imprison though a crime has been uncovered, or even punish for contempt, but can only inquire and report, the propriety of every question in the course of the inquiry being subject to the supervision of the ordinary courts of justice, is likened with denunciatory fervor to the Star Chamber of the Stuarts. *Historians may find hyperbole in the sanguinary simile.*" Contrast that pedantic judicial witticism with Holmes who wrote to Pollock on April 26, 1924: "I was amused by a question of taste yesterday. In one of my opinions I give a short account of a statute and say that there are amplifications 'to stop rat holes' that need not be stated as the plaintiffs admit that they are within the statute. The C. J. [Chief Justice Taft] criticized. I said our reports were so dull because we had the notion that judicial dignity required solemn fluffy speech, as, when I grew up, everybody wore black frock coats and black cravats (I didn't say that to them). I didn't care for the phrase but do for the principle."

It would be unfair to suggest that Cardozo usually thought in American and translated into semiarchaic English. One feels that he had used a private time machine to transport himself back into eighteenth century England. *He had, that is, translated himself into a past alien speech environment.* The style became the man. So that those who adulate his style do not compare him with contemporary Americans; they say that he was an "essayist rare enough to rank with Lamb."

All of us have some "guiding fictions," some images of a self or selves which we try to live up to. The word "person" derives from the Greek theatrical word for an actor's mask through which the actor talked. There is buried truth in that word history: every person is, in a sense, a mask, and we all have a set of masks. It may be surmised that one of Cardozo's selves or persons, one of the masks through which he talked, was that of an educated Englishman engaging in imaginary conversations with Charles Lamb or Dr. Johnson or Goldsmith.

Any translated style is likely to be awkward. As Sapir says, "A great style incorporates the basic form patterns of the language; * * * it builds on them. * * * It does with ease and economy what the language is always trying to do. Carlylese, though individual and vigorous, is yet not style; it is Teutonic mannerism. Nor is the prose of Milton and his contemporaries strictly English; it is semi-Latin done into magnificent English words." So Coleridge said of Milton that his prose style was better in Latin. James Russell Lowell remarked that one might almost learn Latin by reading Milton's prose; it might be said of Cardozo that one can almost learn English (not American) by reading his opinions. But Milton was translating into his native tongue and could therefore produce ruddy English stuff, sometimes too strong for Lowell—as, for instance, in such a phrase as "that queasy temper of luke-warmness that gives a vomit to God himself."

It was Lowell, by no stretch of the imagination a radical innovator, who, in 1889, explaining the history of the resistance to the use of living languages to produce living literatures, said that "as the knowledge of Greek and Latin was the exclusive privilege of a class, that class naturally made an obstinate defense of its vested right." Ten years later, Veblen exploited a somewhat similar thesis. Proficiency in the use of archaisms, he maintained, is a badge of membership in the leisure class, because it is a display of "conspicuous waste." So, he said, colleges insist that students must spend a number of years in acquiring the ability to use and understand certain of the dead languages of southern Europe because the possession of such "substantially useless information" signifies a conspicuous waste of time and effort and "hence the pecuniary strength necessary in order to afford this waste." The "classics," he maintained, "serve the decorative ends of leisure-class learning better than any other kinds of knowledge, and hence they are an effective means of reputability." But Latin and Greek are not, he said, the sole means of manifesting reputable "archaism and waste." The word "classic" also denotes "the obsolete and obsolescent forms of thought and diction in the living language. * * * The archaic idiom of the English language is spoken of as 'classic English.' * * * The newest form of diction is never used in writing; the sense of that leisure-class propriety which requires archaism in speech is present even in the most illiterate or sensational writers in sufficient force to prevent such a lapse. * * * Elegant diction, whether in writing or speaking, is an effective means of reputability. * * *. . . . It thereby goes to show his leisure-class antecedents." And Veblen goes on to describe—in a manner distinctively relevant to a discussion of judicial style—the arguments of those who defend "the conventional usages of archaism and waste." It is contended, he says, "that a punctilious use of ancient and accredited locutions will serve to convey thought more adequately and precisely than would the straightforward" use of the latest speech forms, although "it is notorious that the ideas of today are effectively expressed in the slang of today." . . . And he notes that, in this country, "leisure-class tastes are to some extent shaped on usages and habits which prevail, or are apprehended to prevail, among the leisure class of Great Britain, * * * the English leisure class being, for purposes of reputable usage, the upper leisure class of this country, and so the exemplar for the lower grades."

I confess that Veblen's thesis seems to me to be altogether too unqualified. The compulsion of leisure-class attitudes is more unconscious than he indicates; and there are, I believe, other reasons for pleasure in archaisms than those he suggests. (These views of mine are perhaps biased because I am a creature of those compulsions which he described, and so enslaved by tradition that, as the reader can easily observe, I tend to express myself in pseudo-English rather than in authentic American speech forms.) But it is difficult to deny that there is a large element of truth in Veblen's analysis. Making all due allowances, then, it can perhaps be said that Cardozo's style is highly esteemed, in part, because it shuns racy American speech, because it is caviar to the general, because John Q. Citizen finds it difficult to understand what Cardozo is saying, because some of those who admire his mode of writing can flatter themselves that they are sharing in English upper-class virtues, and because many of those who do not understand it do enjoy the snobbism of saluting the ways of those who seem to them to compose a superior caste.

I have said that Cardozo translated himself into an alien speech environment. But his translation was not a complete success. Graceful as is his writing at times, it is not always the equal of the best English writing. It is sometimes ornate, baroque, rococo. Emulated by those with lesser gifts, it is likely to produce writing which is reminiscent of the State, War and Navy building in Washington. (Here I catch myself [such is the power of tradition] traducing my own principles, asserting, impliedly, that one style of architecture is, objectively, more beautiful than another.) For sometimes Cardozo's ornaments are annoyingly functionless. "Eloquence," wrote Pascal, "is a painting of thought; and thus those who, after having painted it, add something more, make a picture instead of a portrait. * * * Nothing makes us understand better the ridiculousness of a false sonnet than * * * to imagine a woman or a house made according to that standard. * * * Whoever imagines a woman made after this model, which consists of *saying little things in big words*, will see a pretty girl adorned with mirrors and chains, at whom he will smile. * * *"

Cardozo delighted in elaborate metaphors. One of his admirers—an Australian be it noted—after saying that "his style was attractive, often picturesque," goes on, somewhat apologetically, to remark that "even the tendency towards metaphor, *seldom promoting lucidity*, was justified in his case as a reasonable means of persuading the less imaginative." Was it? One wonders. Would he have been less persuasive if less indirect?

Being a lawyer, I turn to citations. And so I must cite illustrative instances of Cardozo's style. Here are a few: "A trustee is held to something stricter than the morals of the market place. Not honesty alone, but a *punctilio of honor* the most sensitive, is then the standard of behavior." (Why not "a punctilio of the most sensitive honor?" And why, after all, use "punctilio?") "To foil the plans of knaves intent upon obscuring or suppressing a knowledge of their knavery * * *" "The sport of clever knaves. * * *" (Would it not have been refreshing to speak of "crooks" and "crookedness"? "Delicate enough and subtle is the inquiry. * * *" "Room for doubt is there none. * * *" "Fundamental hitherto has been the rule. * * *"

"Different, also would be the question of * * *." "No answer is it to say that * * *." "Contract in the true sense there is none * * *." "At the threshold is met the evidence * * *." "Error of judgment there may have been * * *." "For answer to all this the thrust will not avail * * *." "One may take leave to deny * * *." "So the concept be not abjuring * * *." "The subject the most lowly * * *." "An officer must not pause to parley." "The risk of rescue, if it be not wanton, is born of the occasion. The emergency begets the man." "Writ large in this style or title was the name of a living man who had done nothing by word or act to give the name a reality or a significance external to himself." "The dealer was indeed the one person of whom it might be said with some approach to certainty that by him the car would not be used." "There is here no seismic innovation." "Due process is a growth too sturdy to succumb to the infection of the least ingredient of error." "No doubt the income thus accrued derived sustenance and value from the soil of past events. We do not identify the seed with the fruit that it will yield. Income within the meaning of the Sixteenth Amendment is the fruit that is born of capital, not the potency of fruition."

In his essay on the style of judges, Cardozo remarks, "Form is not something added to substance as a mere protuberant adornment." Consider the form of that very sentence. Would it have been less effective if less decorative? One is reminded of Barney McGee who was "full of phrases of length and latinity such as honorificibilitudinity." Was Cardozo's style indeed intended to persuade? Was it not, sometimes, perhaps designed rather—no matter how unconsciously—to arouse that admiration for English leisure-class virtues which Veblen describes? (I do not mean to suggest that there is not a virtue in leisure. If we are intelligent in our uses of modern science, every American will have a good share of leisure in the days of peace.)

Cardozo was opposing the natural genius of the language. For as Toynbee says, in the history of costume, as in the history of writing, simplification is, generally, the path of progress. The trend is apparent in the development of costume in any civilization: in the dress of Queen Elizabeth there was "a profusion and extravagance of ornament * * *." There has been a tendency to the use of plainer materials—and even more markedly—towards a simpler cut, which aims at following and setting off the natural lines of the human body instead of contradicting or correcting them." And so with the American style of speaking: it, too, tends to the use of plainer materials and toward a simpler cut; it aims at following lines of the body of American thought instead of contradicting or correcting them.

That Englishmen may praise Cardozo's style is no answer to any part of my comments. For it flatters them that he tried to ape the English. And his use of obsolescent English locutions might well make it welcome to them:

they may find in it the pleasure of visiting what Toynbee calls a "living museum"—a living museum of departed English usages. (As Toynbee notes, the top hat orginated in England, was imported into America by the Puritans and Quakers, and was then reimported into and adopted in England where it had long been discarded.)

Cardozo's style is of the type which he himself classified "as the refined or artificial, smelling a little of the lamp," a style which "has its dangers, for unless kept well in hand, it verges at times on preciosity and euphuism." There is often a feeling of strain when one reads Cardozo. Heaven knows, there should be no criticism of a writer because he has worked hard, has written and rewritten. Anatole France, it is said, sometimes worked over a passage for weeks. But the reader ought not have to share in the writer's effort: Anatole France's patient efforts yielded a simplicity that made his prose seem effortless. But Cardozo's prose is all too patently worked-over. One thinks of Ransom's comment on Lycidas: "It was written smooth and rewritten rough; which was treason."

Cardozo attained eminence as a thinker not because but in spite of his style. To force himself to think in a foreign tongue must have cost him much effort. That with such a handicap he thought clearly is a tribute to his genius.

Yet the indirection of his style may sometimes have served a deliberate purpose. "Those of us whose lives have been spent on the bench," he admitted, "have learned caution and reticence, perhaps even in excess. We know the value of the veiled phrase, the blurred edge, the uncertain line." One of his most adulatory biographers says of him that he preferred "to make changes [in the law] not openly but through a skillful manipulation of precedents." Cardozo tells us that, as a young lawyer, he had a "blind faith" that the courts would follow precedents "inexorably to the limit of its logic." He confesses that, as he grew older, he learned the vast amount of legal uncertainty. But he could never bring himself, emotionally, to accept that uncertainty as an unavoidable fact. He indulged in what he called "laments" that the law is not an exact science. He acknowledged its inescapable lack of mathematical exactness but looked upon that inexactness as an "evil against which the intellect rebels." He wrote of "the curse of this fluidity," of "an ever shifting approximation" as a curse "that the law must bear." Reluctantly he was "content with many a makeshift compromise, with many a truth that is approximate and relative"; but, he conceded, he was "yearning for the absolute." That struggle between a yearning for the absolute in law and a recognition that it was unattainable was doubtless an important cause of his fondness for inverted expressions, negative constructions, sinuous turns of phrases, elaborated metaphors. They signify reluctant doubt.

Cardozo's mannerisms are sometimes an unmitigated nuisance to the lawyer who must, in a workaday world, make use of his judicial opinions. (He thinks of Gilbert's lines about a motto: " 'Though fools may tread upon a twig, / Wise men fear a bandit,' / All of which was very clever, but I did not understand it.") They sometimes obscure where there is need for clarity. Cardozo's ideas were unusually clear. He was a nice analyst with a zest, not always exercised, for following up all the implications of his ideas. But the clarity was in his thinking. His was not a lucid style.

And lucidity is the basic quality of good judicial opinions. As Cardozo himself put it, "There can be little doubt that the sovereign virtue for the judge is clearness." That lawyers, at least, should be able quickly to understand what a judge is saying is so obviously desirable as to need no argument. It is wise, too, that laymen should as far as possible comprehend what the judiciary means.

Cardozo once voiced that attitude in a case in which he reversed a judgment of a lower court because of remarks by a trial judge which confused the jury: "It is not enough to show that by the test of error of law there is no flaw in the instructions. What concerns us more profoundly is whether there is justice in the verdict. *Justice is not there unless there is also understanding.*"

To be sure, as Cardozo noted in one of his essays, lucidity need not be the exclusive attribute of judges' language. Clarity is not enough; if it were, then judges should be urged to reduce their opinions to algebraic equations or to employ the chill, emotionless symbols of logistics which make so forbidding many of the pages of Michael and Adler's interesting treatise on evidence. Hogben, in an essay in his volume *Dangerous Thoughts*, shows that the teaching of mathematics has been needlessly difficult because of the prosaic verbiage of most mathematical writers. He refers to Leacock's suggestion that journalism should enliven Euclid, so that for the statement that "a perpendicular is made to fall on a line, bisecting it at a point C" there would be substituted this:

"AWFUL CATASTROPHE
Perpendicular Falls Headlong on a Line
Line at Cincinnati Completely Cut
President of the Line Makes Statement."

Literary skill, if it promotes clarity, is a blessing in a judge. Lively, provocative, and graceful writing is not only not improper but is welcome in judicial opinions. As Cardozo asserted, "Clearness, though the sovereign quality, is not the only one to be pursued, and even if it were, may be gained through many avenues of approach. The opinion will need persuasive force, or the impressive virtue of sincerity and fire, or the mnemonic power of alliteration and antithesis, or the terseness and tang of the proverb and the maxim. Neglect the help of these allies and it may never win its way." But although clarity is not enough, although it is not a sufficient condition, it is necessary, indispensable, in the utterances of judges. "Those who make antitheses by forcing words are like those who make false windows for symmetry," says Pascal. "Their rule is not to speak accurately, but to make apt figures of speech." Sheer amusement or sheer beauty has its place—as in Jabberwocky or in much of Swinburne's poetry—but not in the opinions of judges. An obscurely worded pronouncement by a court, no matter how "literary," is, to use the American language, a pain in the neck. To avoid obscurity, to achieve a clarity which is essential, American judges should write good American.

When, in certain situations, the defendant's lawyer contends that the plaintiff's lawyer has brought the wrong kind of suit, the courts say that the defendant must give the plaintiff "a better writ," point out a proper way to bring the suit. And, here, I shall try to do the equivalent—to point to some judges whose style should serve as a better model than Cardozo's.

I nominate three—Mr. Justice Black, Mr. Justice Douglas, and Mr. Justice Jackson. They write much as they talk, as their fellow Americans talk. Unlike Cardozo, they express the ideas of today in the American idiom of today. They employ direct and forcible American speech. They do not shun the straightforward use of the current forms of spoken American. There is a racy and contemporary timbre in the way they write. They achieve simplicity and clarity. The American reader knows exactly what they mean. He has no sense of strain. He sees through their words as through a well-polished pane of glass. One recalls a line of Lowell's: "If this be not style, there is something better than style." The style of Black or Douglas or Jackson is of the earth . . . . And it is of the American earth.

I may be told that Cardozo (although he sounds as if he were striving to talk in the past) was writing for posterity ("What," someone once asked, "has posterity done for me, that I should think of posterity?"), and that Black, Douglas, and Jackson are writing ephemerally, for men of their own time and place. I count that in their favor. It is, indeed, a paradox that most of the writers whose posterity has cherished them are men who, like Shakespeare and Montaigne, gave little heed to what men in future times or in other lands would think of them; they wrote for their contemporaries. The "greatest—or shall we say the most satisfying—literary artists," says Sapir, "are those who have known subconsciously to fit or trim the deeper intuition to the provincial accents of their daily speech," for "style is not an absolute, a something to be imposed on the language * * * but merely the language itself, running in its natural grooves, and with enough of an individual accent to allow the artist's personality to be felt as a presence, not as an acrobat." Black, Douglas, and Jackson use the provincial accents of their daily speech; one feels, in the writings of each of them, the personality of the writer as a presence, not as an acrobat. Their now-ness is not a blemish but its outstanding virtue.

Hobbes, smarting under criticism of his own preoccupation with problems of his own time, said wisely: "Though I reverence these men of ancient time, that either have written truth perspicuously, or set us in a better way to find it out ourselves; yet to the antiquity itself I think nothing due. For if we reverence the age, the present is the oldest. If the antiquity of the writer, I am not sure that generally they to whom such honor is given were more ancient when they wrote than I am that am writing. But if it be well considered, the praise of ancient authors proceeds not from reverence of the dead, but from the competition and mutual envy of the living."

Black, Douglas, and Jackson write in their native tongue. Of Cardozo one might say this: He admitted that, at times, he wrote with his tongue in his cheek. And, frequently, it was not even his native tongue.

ANON Y. MOUS.
*Virginia Law Review* (1943)

# JUDGE LEARNED HAND 🦢

I WAS ASKED, originally, to speak of Great Judges. I objected. What, I queried, does one mean by "great"? I remembered my dispute with Sam Thorne and Justice Frankfurter about Lord Coke, once Chief Justice of England. I said Coke was a nasty, narrow-minded, greedy, cruel, arrogant, insensitive man, a timeserving politician and a liar who, by his adulation of some crabbed medieval legal doctrines, had retarded English and American legal development for centuries. Thorne and Frankfurter replied that I proved their case, that the duration of his influence, no matter whether good or bad, made him a great judge. I think I lost the argument. But if that be the test, then we must put on our list of "greats" such men as Attila, Robespierre, and Hitler, although most of us consider them evil. And so as to the great among legal thinkers, lawyers and judges. Consider Tribonian who contributed importantly to the Justinian codification of Roman law, which mightily affected the legal systems of the Western world. Who was Tribonian? A brilliant scholar but a corrupt judge.

I concede, indeed I insist, that great men, good or evil, have often helped to shape history. Carlyle's theory of history—that all history results from the deeds or thoughts of great men—is nonsense, of course. But I think equally nonsensical what I call the No-Man Theory of history, according to which men are but puppets of "social forces," or economics or geography or the "spirit of the times"—in short, nonhuman or unindividual factors which wholly account, deterministically, for all human events. I shan't here enlarge on that theme. I wrote a book about it in 1945 (*Fate and Freedom*). There I did by no means exclude accidents, but I included great men among the accidents.

The theme, "Great Judges," is then vast and important. Conceivably, one could write much of legal history—as Campbell, Pound, and Seagle have tried to do—through writing the biographies of great judges. But that would be a horrendous undertaking.

Were I to accept the theme originally allotted to me, I would at least confine it to some of the great judges whose influence has been beneficent. Even so, how decide what judges deserve inclusion in that category? Obviously, no objective yardstick exists; estimates of such greatness differ; it all depends on one's notion of the desirable.

So I've decided to restrict myself principally to one judge I consider great, Judge Learned Hand. I shall not, however, attempt even a short biography. For one thing, all biographies are full of gaps. "No man is an island," said John Donne. That's a half-truth, a misleading metaphor, because of what it omits. True, no man can be wholly apart from his fellows. But, if each of us is a promontory, yet the promontory reaches out beyond the social mainland to a point where others cannot intrude. Beyond that point lies an unexplorable lonesomeness, a unique privacy. It is a no-other-man's land, for others can't penetrate it, can't communicate with it.

If this be true of men generally, it is emphatically true of judges. The private life, the inner environment, of a judge, his deeper motivations, usually become extraordinarily opaque, hidden from public gaze, after he ascends the bench. No judge has had a Boswell, and none has ever left behind him a detailed, intimate diary like Pepys's. Sometimes, after his death, we can read a judge's private letters. But as Howarth said of Pepys's letters, with them, as distinguished from his diary, we are not "inside the man, looking through the window he made of himself on the world," we are only "peering through a curtained window from without." We see not his "private face," only his "public face." As another writer observed, "Behind the formal reserve of a high official a great deal more often goes on than most people suspect."

The Roman lawyers, affected by the etymology of the word "person," thought of a person, for legal purposes, as a mask, and recognized that legally one man may contain several different persons, having different masks or roles, or personalities, or (as we would say) selves. That pluralistic notion is not to be confined to legal thinking. We are all various persons; and most of the persons constituting a judge are exceptionally well hidden. As no biography, I think, can pretend to adequacy unless it includes a psycho-biography, a judicial biography must be inordinately incomplete. And glib psychological analyses of men, exciting or amusing as they may be, are terribly misleading.

Not long ago, some writers remarked that, since we entrust to "the judicial conscience" the interpretation and enforcement of our laws and constitutions, significant and accurate data about the occupants of the bench should be of major importance, yet few such data have been assembled. "We do not even have available any reliable indices of the intelligence of judges, to say nothing of measures of their psychiatric traits." Until the time when, the writers added, "we can reduce temperament, wisdom and probity to a scientific formula, many will say that any study of judicial personnel is merely touching the fringes of the problem." That time is surely not here.

To write a competent biography of Learned Hand would be singularly perplexing. For he is an exquisitely complex person, or, rather, a complex multitude of persons. As Whicher said of Emerson, "He can be summed up in a formula only by those who know their own minds better than his"; he is "impenetrable, for all his forty-odd volumes." Moreover, for all that Judge Hand is gregarious—a lifelong friend says that "he is a man of moods, and does not like to be alone"—he keeps inviolate, more than most of us, an enclave of reticent privacy which no one must enter.

Now and then, one comes on a man who has made of his life a work of art, like a novel written by himself. Such a man is Learned Hand. His long life—he is now eighty-three—has enabled him to round out that novel. It is replete with poetry, contains many delightful chapters and interludes. But some portions of that novel he alone has read and will never publish. If it be true that "nothing, except everything, can 'explain' anything," I can't possibly explain Learned Hand. Although I have worked with him for fourteen years, I wouldn't dare to say I have even begun thoroughly to know him. For that matter, who thoroughly knows any man, himself or any other? "Who," asked old Fuller, "hath sailed about the world of his own heart, sounded each creek, surveyed each corner, but that there still remains much terra incognita in himself?"

My principal aim, therefore, will be to give you merely some glimpses of Learned Hand's approach to his work as a judge; to suggest the genesis, the background, of that approach; and to compare with him some other great judges.

In all honesty, in order that you can make allowance for my partiality, I must begin by saying that no man do I esteem more highly. As I wrote him early this year: "No one else I've ever known has excited in me such admiration and affection. You are my model as a judge. More, you have influenced my attitudes in incalculable ways towards all sorts of matters, intellectual and others. For your eminence lies not alone in the singular nature of your mind, but in the manner in which you infuse your ideas with emotions, both noble and humorous. You are, par excellence, the democratic aristocrat." I am unabashed in my admiration. It is not unique. Repeatedly, and within the past few weeks, I have seen men leave his presence with a feeling of exaltation, lifted out of themselves to a vision of new horizons.

All who have written of Learned Hand have lamented the fact that he did not become a Supreme Court Justice, a post for which no one has ever been as well fitted. Yet I wonder. I think of Cervantes's advice: "Try to win the second prize. For the first is always by favor. The second goes for pure merit." The praises of Judge Hand he has earned, not by occupying the highest bench, but by pure merit. Nor has he sought these praises. So much the better, since, as the Scriptures say, "For men to search out their own glory is not glory."

The praises are still being earned, through Judge Hand's unflagging efforts in still producing matchless opinions, despite his years. This should, perhaps, not surprise. For Benjamin Franklin signed the Constitution at eighty; Gladstone was Prime Minister at eighty-five; Michelangelo designed the great dome of St. Peter's at eighty-seven; and Holmes continued his splendid work on the bench until over ninety.

Judge Hand's years have not abated his keenness or deprived him of a youthful resilience. In nowise does he resemble Kipling's old men who say, "And whatever we do, we shall fold our hands * * *, and think well of it. Yes, we shall be perfectly pleased with our work, and that is the perfectest Hell of it." Judge Hand's legendary fame has not made him arrogant. "A man," says the Bible, "is tried by his praise." Judge Hand has stood that trial well. Nor does he exploit the trappings of office to afford him any factitious dignity. He chuckled when recently I quoted to him Montaigne's lines: "Sitting on the loftiest throne in the world, we are still sitting on our behinds." He treats bright young men with warm generosity, and enjoys it when they disagree with him. He invites a colleague who differs from one of his opinions to write a dissenting opinion. He wants no slavish disciples, no hero worship. His way of life recalls Plutarch's report of the Athenians' welcome to Pompey: "So far may you be deemed a God as you confess yourself a man." This trait of humility, of self-skepticism, is fortunate in one who has such wide influence. Lord Acton's famous statement, "Power tends to corrupt and absolute power corrupts absolutely," did not end there. Acton added, "Great men are always bad men, even when they exercise influence and not authority * * *." I think Acton's aphorism absurdly sweeping. But it does highlight the fact that great influence is great power, and therefore may be corruptly wielded. Learned Hand's influence, if he can help it, will never corrupt.

When younger, he took Justice Holmes as one of his most important mentors. Like Holmes, he delights in contriving generalizations while recognizing their pernicious character if not constantly in gear with particulars;

or, to paraphrase Kant, he knows that generalizations without particulars are empty and particulars without generalizations are blind. Both men are skeptical of neat, closed, systems; like William James, they are on the lookout for "wild facts" that escape any system.

Often Judge Hand is compared with Holmes. Although Holmes is one of my heroes, I think that, in the comparison, Hand gets the better rating. For Hand is more generous, more outgoing, more easily accessible to others, always interested in the events of the day, while Holmes led an essentially cloistered life, and boasted of not reading the newspapers. Hand, too, has been more willing to admit he made mistakes.

Holmes once said that in writing judicial opinions, "one has to strike at the jugular and let the rest go"; and, in his later years, many of his opinions disclose a lack of interest in all but the jugular. Not so Judge Hand. Always as a young judge, and increasingly as he grows older, he has delved into the many legal niceties of a case, frequently to the dismay of his brother judges. Judge Hand wrote of Cardozo's "anguish which * * * preceded decision, for again and again, he had to wrestle with the angel all through the night; he wrote his opinions with his very blood. But once his mind came to rest, he was as inflexible as he had been uncertain before." Learned Hand has experienced that same anguish. But often it does not cease when the opinion has been uttered. I have known him to brood over, disquietingly, decisions he rendered several years earlier.

## Judge Hand on the Subject of Judicial Legislation

Once upon a time, and not so very long ago, most American judges and lawyers denied that judges ever legislated. The judges and lawyers exploited, and themselves largely believed, the following myth: In the creation of the huge body of common-law legal rules, not enacted by any legislature, the judges had played no part. Judges never have made and never will make legal rules. These rules preexisted all court decisions. The judges merely find or discover these preexisting rules—just as Columbus discovered America. The courts no more invent new rules than Columbus invented the "new world" when he found it. If a rule announced in a former case is later rejected by a court, it is an error to say that a new rule has been contrived by that court. To speak correctly, one must say that the old, abandoned, rule was a sort of false map of the "Law"—just as a pre-Columbian map was false. The judge who announced the erroneous rule in the former decision must have had bad eyesight, for he had made a mistake in trying to find the "Law." Calvin Coolidge was talking in terms of the myth when he wrote: "Men do not make laws. They do but discover them. * * * That state is most fortunate in its form of government which has the aptest instrument for the discovering of laws."

This myth, criticized in nineteenth century England, had a peculiarly strong and more tenacious hold in this country because, in theory, our constitutions give our legislatures the exclusive power to legislate. If the judges acknowledged that they made new rules, they would apparently be admitting that they were violating the principle of separation of governmental powers. The myth, if believed, absolved the judges from a charge of unconstitutionally usurping power. The myth did deceive the public. But it also induced the judges to deceive themselves.

When Learned Hand, aged twenty-two, entered Harvard Law School as a student in 1894, the myth still largely prevailed. However, in 1891, Professor James Bradley Thayer of Harvard, one of Hand's most influential law teachers, had published an article, entitled "Judicial Legislation," in which, with unusual boldness for an American lawyer, he dealt the myth a grave blow. In another article, in the same year, he said, "It is impossible to exercise the judicial function without incidental legislation." But he cautioned that, in lawmaking, judges should act "with great caution." Before that, Holmes, in 1881, had written that the "growth of the law," through judicial decisions, "is legislative * * *. It is legislative in its grounds," based on "considerations of what is expedient for the community * * *"; and he had suggested that, in the present, judges "should openly discuss the legislative considerations," or policies, "upon which their decisions must always rest."

When I was a law student, it was still heretical to agree openly with Thayer and Holmes. But today the myth has dissipated. Judges of our day candidly admit that past judges invented many rules and that present judges do the same. Even *Corpus Juris* states: "The courts * * * legislate * * * by decisions which modify the existing law. . . ."

Since the final interment of the myth in the 1920's, some law teachers and many law students have entertained a false notion. They believe that a judge can, and usually a judge does, contrive rules about as he pleases, without restraint. That is wicked nonsense. It represents a gross exaggeration of a partial truth. Judicial legislation, as Holmes put it, is "interstitial." Most legislation is legislative legislation, not judicial.

Repeatedly Judge Hand has discussed this question. No one is better equipped to do so. No one knows better than he that judges do legislate. For no other single judge has invented as many new rules, modified as many old ones. In every legal province—contracts, torts, equity, conflict of laws, criminal law, evidence, admiralty, patents, copyrights, trade names, taxation, statutory interpretation—he has shaped or reshaped the important doctrines. Everywhere in the judicial domain you can trace his handiwork. With his creative insights, his penetrating intellect, his imaginative experience, he has enlarged the legal universe, made it different from what it was before his advent. Of course, as a member of what we call an "inferior court," he obeys the Supreme Court's decisions. But many of those decisions have been based on rules of his making. When he whistles a Supreme Court tune, frequently it is really his own. Even the English House of Lords has followed him at times.

What, then, has this unusually creative judge said about the limits on judicial creativeness? As Judge Hand sees it, the judge faces a dilemma, being both bound and free. In 1939, he wrote of the self-contradiction "at the basis of a judge's work." For on the one hand, "his authority and his immunity depend upon the assumption that he speaks with the mouths of others: the momentum of his utterances must be greater than any which his personal reputation and character can command, if it is to do the work assigned to it—if it is to stand against the passionate resentments arising out of the interests he must frustrate" by his decisions. So the judge voices, not his own views, but the "dictates * * * of a communion which reaches" into the past "far beyond the memory of any now living * * *." But then, Judge Hand continued, one encounters this paradox: The common-law doctrines have grown. The judges, successively, have contributed to its growth, not merely repeating what their predecessors said, not always speaking with the "mouths of others." So a judge "must manage to escape both horns of this dilemma: he must preserve his authority by cloaking himself in the majesty of an over-shadowing past; but he must discover some composition with the dominant trends of his time * * *."

Judge Hand had considered this dilemma as early, at least, as 1916, when he said that a judge may not properly decide cases according to his own idea of what will best serve the common good, or of what he thinks will represent democratic aspirations not articulated in some legitimate matter. The judge must not thus give rein to his "personal notion" of the desirable; he must bow to "the social will" when clearly set forth in "written words." However, when the language of a statute or a precedent is ambiguous, the judge should not "frustrate his free power, by interpretation, to manifest the half-framed purposes of his time." If he does, he "misconceives the historical significance of his position and will in the end" become "incompetent to perform the very duties upon which it lays so much emphasis."

In greater detail, Judge Hand discussed this dilemma in a more or less popular radio talk, in 1933, entitled "How Far Is a Judge Free in Rendering a Decision?" Because this talk is so discerning and so balanced, and because it will help you law students immensely as you study the judicial process, I shall quote from it at some length.

He began by saying that there are two extreme views of a judge's role: Some think he ought to look solely "to his conscience, to follow its dictates," that he should not be bound by "what they call technical rules, having no relation to natural right or wrong." Others "wish him to observe strictly what they consider the law, reading it as though it were all to be found in written words, and never departing from the literal meaning." They are correct to this extent: A judge "ought not to usurp the power of government." And they believe that it would be "just such usurpation" were he to "exercise his own judgment as to the justice of the cause." Judge Hand disagrees with both these views.

Understanding of the problem requires a definition of "law," he says. Some persons think it "includes the customs or usages generally current in a society." Judge Hand prefers, with reference to a civilized modern society, a definition of law "as those rules which will be enforced by the government" —"the conduct which the government * * * will compel individuals to conform to, or to which it will at least provide forcible means to secure conformity." So defined, "the law is the command of the government, and it must be ascertainable in some form if it is to be enforced at all."

Its commands are put in words; and in our kind of society "they are always written," whether in statutes or in "books which report what has been decided before by judges whom the government gave power to decide." The judges have "the duty of saying what the law means, what the government has in fact commanded."

The government's commands cannot be put in precise terms like those of mathematics. To be understood by the persons who must obey, these commands must be stated in "terms of common speech." Nor can the commands be nicely precise, for no one can "provide for all situations which might come up," nobody can "divine all possible human events in advance and prescribe the rule for each." The law thus uses "vague commands" which the courts—judges or juries—apply in respect of "all the circumstances of the particular case."

"The judge must therefore find out the will of the government from words * * *." How does he in fact proceed? He takes "the language before him, whether it be from a statute or from the decision of another judge." He "tries to find out what the government, or his predecessor, would have done, if the case before him had been before them. This he calls finding the intent of the statute or of the doctrine." The men who used the language, however, did not have any intent at all about the case; it had not occurred to their minds. Strictly speaking, it is impossible to know what they would have said about it, if it had. All they have done is to write down certain words which they mean to apply generally to situations of that kind. "To apply these literally may either pervert what was plainly their general meaning, or leave undisposed of what there is every reason to suppose they meant to provide for.

"Thus it is not enough for the judge just to use a dictionary. If he should do no more, he might come out with a result which every sensible man would recognize to be quite the opposite of what was really intended; which would contradict or leave unfulfilled its plain purpose.

"Thus, on the one hand, he cannot go beyond what has been said, because he is bound to enforce existing commands and only those; on the other, he cannot suppose that what has been said should clearly frustrate or leave unexecuted the purpose. This is his frequent position in cases that are not very plain; that is to say, in the greater number that arise."

Here Judge Hand returns to a description of "two extreme schools, neither of which is really willing to apply its theory consistently, only applying it when its interest lies along the path it advocates: One school says the judge must follow the letter of the law absolutely. I call this the dictionary school. No matter what the result is, [the judge] must read the words in their usual meaning and stop where they stop * * *.

"The other school would give [the judge] almost complete latitude. They argue that a judge should not regard the law; that this has never really been done in the past, and that to attempt it is an illusion. He must conform his decision to what honest men think right, and it is better for him to look to his own heart to find out what that is."

Judge Hand grants that "* * * some such process is inevitable when one is interpreting any written words. When a judge tries to find out what the government would have intended which it did not say, he puts into its mouth what he thinks it ought to have said, and that is very close to substituting what he himself thinks right.

"Let him beware, however, or he will usurp the office of government * * *. In our country, we have always been extremely jealous of mixing the different processes of government, especially that of making law, with that of saying what it is after it is made. This distinction cannot be rigidly enforced but * * * it has a very sound basis as a guide, provided one does not make it an absolute rule."

The men who framed our Constitution "wanted to have a government by the people," and believed this could be done only "by giving the power to make laws to assemblies which the people chose * * *. They believed that such assemblies would express the common will of the people who were to rule * * *. They might have made the judge the mouthpiece of the common will, finding it out by his contact with people generally. But he would then have been ruler * * *.

"Still, they had to leave him scope in which he, in a limited sense, does act as if he were the government, because he cannot otherwise do what he is required to do. So far, they had to confuse law-making with law-interpreting.

"But the judge must always remember that he should go no further than he is sure the government would have gone, had it been faced with the case before him * * *. For he cannot tell that the conflicting interests in the society for which he speaks would have come to a just result even though he is sure that he knows what the result should be. He is not to substitute his will for theirs; otherwise it would not be the common will which prevails, and to that extent the people would not govern.

"So you will see that a judge is in a contradictory position; he is pulled by two opposite forces. On the one hand, he must not enforce whatever he thinks best; he must leave that to the common will expressed by the government. On the other, he must try as best he can to put into concrete form what that will is, not by slavishly following the words, but by trying honestly to say what was the underlying purpose expressed. Nobody does this exactly right; great judges do it better than the rest of us. It is necessary that someone shall do it, if we are to realize the hope that we can collectively rule ourselves."

I have several comments on Judge Hand's exposition in this paper:

1. Discarding the myth—that is, the Columbus-law-discovery myth—Judge Hand recognized that judges have considerable latitude for creativeness. A judge, like Learned Hand, no longer can deceive himself into believing that he never makes rules.

Judge Hand's discussion raises these questions: Did the self-deceiving myth actually restrain judicial creativeness? Does the destruction of the myth mean that the judges now create more freely, that we have come nearer to judicial despotism? I think the answer to both questions is No. On the contrary, the old judicial self-deception often led the judges to engage in extensive legislation.

2. Judge Hand maintains that, when a judge is called on to legislate, he must seek to balance competing social interests (that is, "desires and values"). Judge Hand concedes that such "desires and values are not quantitatively measurable, for," as he said in 1952, "they seldom have any common constituents, and without these they cannot be objectively compared." Many who have espoused this notion of adjusting such interests—in Europe, the members of the "jurisprudence-of-interests" school; in this country Pound and others—have not been as wise as Judge Hand in perceiving that it yields no panacea, no quick and easy solution of legal conundrums. At best, this idea brings home to the judge the nature of his task, prompts him to an

awareness of interests he might otherwise neglect. But that awareness merely creates a problem; does not solve it.

3. In this 1933 paper, Judge Hand is discussing the judge's function with respect to legal rules, principles, doctrines, legal generalizations. He is not discussing the way trial courts find facts, and the much wider scope of their power in that respect. To that subject I'll return in my next talk.

4. With particular reference to statutes, Judge Hand has in mind the separation-of-powers doctrine: He stresses "government by the people," the making of laws by the people's chosen representatives in legislatures which "express the common will."

This last theme suffuses his thinking. I think it fairly clear that he derived it from Thayer. In all Thayer's teaching—whether on judicial legislation or evidence or constitutional law—Thayer underscored this democratic idea.

## Judge Hand's Internal Balance

Thayer's insistence on the limited role of the judiciary in a democracy had a lasting impact on Learned Hand. You'll recall that, in his 1933 paper, Judge Hand said much of the "common will," of the respect a judge owes to the people's attitudes expressed in legislation enacted by the people's chosen delegates. In the closing passage of that paper, he spoke of the democratic "hope that we can collectively rule ourselves," the very hope which Thayer had encouraged. As I've suggested, this attitude has evoked in Judge Hand a fear lest, in deciding cases, he should set up his own personal beliefs of right or justice. For a judge to do so is, he thinks, a major judicial sin.

It would be a mistake, however, to ascribe this sense of sin to Thayer's influence alone. I think the explanation is deeper-lying. Although as I said, I'm suspicious of glib psychological analyses, I shall here venture this guess: Learned Hand, as a judge, fears his own self-assertive tendencies. He knows he is the intellectual superior of most men. He has, too, immense creative and critical powers. The impulse to impose his own brilliant views on others is necessarily strong. But he feels the dangers of his own will to power. Opposing his self-assertiveness is his strong sense of the community. There struggle within him two opposing drives—a desire for mastery and, in opposition, a social impulse—toward an identification with the group—ties of social sentiment, of social unity.

All men have some such struggle within themselves. Each of us works out some amalgam of his contending tendencies. If a man is what we call "normal," he achieves a dynamic balance or compromise of his internal conflicting pressures—just as a healthy society achieves a compromise between conflicting factions or interests or pressure groups. Since, as I earlier remarked, every man is a multitude of persons or selves, the image of duality, of but two opposing tendencies, is too limiting, and it would be more accurate to say, pluralistically, that the problem for each man is how far he can "collectively rule" his several selves.

Such an adjustment, with most "normal" men, is largely unconscious. In the case of Judge Hand—an exceptionally "normal" person—it is, in some considerable measure, conscious and deliberate, for he is singularly introspective and reflective. Consciously or unconsciously, he has struck a remarkable internal balance. In his internal policy, as in his social policy, he is a Trimmer: Because his self-assertive pressures are unusually powerful and he has unusual gifts for expressing them, just on that account he has felt the need for, and has exerted, an unusual self-control, in order to afford his social impulses a proper outlet. I surmise that his insistence on this sort of balance receives reinforcement from a felt need to curb his anger; for he confesses to having a tendency to violent rages which usually he successfully restrains. So he has, consciously and unconsciously, erected an interior wall to prevent his self-assertiveness from too easily breaking out.

I have mentioned his effective use of metaphors. One might say that he handles himself like a metaphor. For, as Pickrel suggests, "a metaphor is a yoking of opposites, as the soul of man is a yoking of opposites" (although, once more, I think this too dualistic a notion of a metaphor or of a man).

We should not ignore the religious background of Judge Hand's forebears. They were protestants, protesters, dissenters. Dissenters, too, politically, a small minority of Jacksonian Democrats living in a part of the country dominated by zealous Republicans. Paradoxically, they were rugged individualists, a minority with a fighting faith in popular, majority rule, a faith much like that of Thayer.

Hand's religious background naturally fostered an interest in that masterful man Martin Luther. His attitude toward such crusaders and agitators is significantly dual, ambivalent. They excite his admiration, yet he mistrusts the results of their aggressive leadership, their missionary zeal, their one-eyed vision, their refusal to listen to what he has called "the cold voice of doubt." He early resolved, I think, to suppress the Martin Luther dwelling inside Learned Hand.

Out of all these components comes Judge Hand, the democratic aristocrat, with his explicit antipathy to setting up his personal convictions against those of the people. This antipathy sometimes he expresses, when he says to me that it is not a judge's business to concern himself with justice. Very likely, he remembers Holmes's rejoinder to him when, many years past, he drove with Holmes on his way to the Supreme Court. As Holmes left his carriage and strode off, Hand called to him, "Do justice, sir!" Holmes replied:

"Young feller! I am not here to do justice. I am here to play the game according to the rules." Or he remembers what Holmes, in 1929, wrote to Wu, then a young Chinese law student: "I have said to my brethren many times that I hate justice, which means that I know if a man begins to talk about that, for one reason or another he is shirking thinking in legal terms."

Like Holmes, Judge Hand detests pretentiousness by wordy do-gooders, the perennially self-righteous. Like Jesus, he prefers publicans and sinners. In 1944, he told a college graduating class, "More cant, I fancy, is poured out to youthful ears in the name of serving mankind . . .;" and he spoke his dislike of "visionaries who are never content with less than the City of God," and who "decry all compromises as treason." So, to Judge Hand, a man who freely mouths the word "justice" is suspect. (One recalls Emerson's comment when Daniel Webster defended the Fugitive Slave Law as a gesture toward liberty: "The word 'liberty' in the mouth of Mr. Webster is like the word 'love' in the mouth of a whore.") Holmes once said, "Long ago I decided I was not God." That is also Hand's self-judgment.

In truth, however, for all his protests, Judge Hand, within the allowable limits as he sees them, untiringly tries to do justice more eagerly and painstakingly than most judges. On what he deems his lawful occasions, he innovates for the sake of being just.

He does not yield in such cases to the arguments against novelty, described by Cornford as the Wedge Argument and the Principle of the Dangerous Precedent. The first runs: Do not act "justly now for fear of raising expectations that you may act still more justly in the future—expectations which you are afraid you will not have the courage to satisfy." The second runs: Nothing "should ever be done for the first time. You should not now do an admittedly right action for fear you, or your equally timid successors, should not have the courage to do right in some future case; which, ex hypothesi, is essentially different, but superficially resembles the present one."

Nevertheless, Judge Hand, for fear that he may, undemocratically, import his own standards, endeavors, in some instances, to enforce the "common will" even if it falls short of what he considers just. This most compassionate man, out of dread of being undemocratic—that is, too deviant from what he believes the standards of the community—has sometimes rejected his own compassionate notions of justice. But I must postpone discussion of that matter until my next talk.

Tolerance in a judge, Judge Hand believes, breeds dispassionateness, detachment, essential to good judging. In a singularly insightful passage, stirred perhaps by the writings of the psychoanalysts, he wrote: "There are those who insist that detachment is an illusion; that our conclusions, when their bases are sifted, always reveal a passional foundation. Even so; though they be creatures of past emotional experience, it does not follow that that experience can never predispose us to impartiality. A bias against bias may be as likely a result of some buried crisis, as any other bias."

Paul Freund rejoined that some men have a bias against that sort of bias—a bias against bias against bias. Such men Judge Hand rates low. I share with him a bias against the bias which is adverse to the bias against bias.

He knows, however, that no man can always successfully control his deepest prejudices. So he is constantly watchful of, on guard against, his own. As nearly as any mortal can be, he is passionately dispassionate.

He opposes, vehemently, the idea that any eternal principles of justice exist. He does, also vehemently, insist that every society has fundamental attitudes. Those which our society has evolved, he treasures. Should they vanish, we will be in sad straits, he thinks. And today sometimes he apprehends that they may vanish, blown away in the current hurricanes of social intolerance. Nevertheless, it is one of his deepest convictions that judges cannot, and must not try—as judges—to save our people from their follies.

He has not, as a judge, always consistently rejected his own judgments of what is right in favor of lower popular evaluations. I could point to many cases in which he has set his sights higher than the crowd's. In 1952, after expressing his scorn for the sort of judge who, disregarding the established legal rules, acts as a crusader for righteousness, Judge Hand confessed that sometimes he had "brought about * * * desirable results at the expense of the rules, however flexibly one might interpret them."

## Judge Hand and Constitutionality

If elsewhere Judge Hand has sometimes steered by his own personal notions of justice, unquestionably, when it came to questions of constitutionality, he has been unwaveringly faithful to his creed about the limited role of judges in a democracy. I'll now trace the way in which he developed and articulated that creed in the constitutional area.

The undemocratic judicial destruction of social legislation, via unconstitutionality, criticized by Thayer in 1891, did not abate after Learned Hand became a lawyer. The courts, state and federal, largely regarded themselves as uncontrollable superlegislatures or, as Mr. Justice Clifford, protesting, had put it in a dissenting opinion in 1874, "sovereign over both the Constitution and the people," converting "the government into a judicial despotism."

The courts, Holmes said in 1894, were responding to the fear of Socialism on the part of the "comfortable classes of the community" who no longer hoped "to control the legislatures" but looked "to the courts as expounders of the Constitution"; in "some courts," Holmes added, "new principles have been discovered," outside the Constitution, which might be "generalized into acceptance of economic ideas which prevailed about fifty years ago, and a wholesale prohibition of what a tribunal of lawyers does not think * * * right."

Holmes's analysis was justified. In 1889, Peckham, then on the highest New York court, and later to become a Supreme Court Justice, said that a statute fixing the rates of elevators was "vicious in its nature and communistic in its tendencies." That statement echoed the sentiments of Tiedeman who, in an influential constitutional treatise published in 1886, wrote that Socialism and Communism were "rampant throughout the civilized world"; that the "conservative classes" in America were threatened by an "absolutism more tyrannical * * * than any before experienced by men, the absolutism of a democratic majority"; and that the Constitution was opposed to such "democratic absolutism." In 1894, the Supreme Court, with the plaudits of most leaders of the bar, destroyed the federal income-tax law; some of the Justices deemed it communistic; a dissenting Justice said that this decision involved "a surrender of the taxing power to the moneyed class." In 1905, in the famous Lochner case, the Supreme Court (per Justice Peckham) vetoed a state statute limiting the working hours of employees in bakeries.

In 1908, aged thirty-six, a year before he became a district judge, and after some twelve years at the bar, Learned Hand, in an article on the constitutionality of state eight-hours-of-labor statutes, boldly followed Thayer, and perhaps went even further. He agreed with what Shattuck (Thayer's former law partner) had written in 1891, that is, that the courts had usurped power when they construed "liberty" in the due-process clauses of the Fifth and Fourteenth Amendments to include "liberty of contract." Learned Hand said that the Supreme Court at one time had held that the "legislature might act as it thought best" in legislation on matters which actually affected the "public good" or "public welfare," and that the Court would interfere only if it was obvious that the legislature had acted but colorably (that is, dishonestly). He clearly indicated that, in his opinion, such was the proper outer limit of judicial review under the due-process clause as to social legislation. He pointed out, however, that the Court later had held that it could and would examine the expediency of a statute. He thought such a standard unjustified. But, if one assumed its propriety, then (following Thayer) he urged that the Court should use the analogy of a judge reviewing a jury's "verdict on the facts": "Only in those cases in which it is obvious beyond peradventure that the statute was the result, either of passion or of ignorance of folly, can the Court say that it was not due process of law." Then (perhaps here going beyond Thayer), he questioned whether even such judicial power —that is, to veto legislation "with whose economic or political expediency" the Court "totally disagrees"—"can endure in a democratic state"; "in the end," he said prophetically, the exercise of such a judicial veto "may demand some change, either in the Court or the Constitution." But until then, he declared, the Court should sustain as constitutional a statute limiting work to eight hours, unless the Court could not see "any reasonable relation to any purpose which reasonable men may think desirable for the public welfare"; it "must be shown that . . . no one could reasonably believe it expedient, in other words, that it was either absurd or oppressive." The Court ought not "step out of the role of interpreter of the Constitution and . . . decide" the question "as another legislature." Consequently, the wisdom of an eight-hour law ought to be for the legislature, not for the courts. The validity of such a statute ought not depend on "the individual opinions upon political and economic questions of the persons who compose" the Court. Pretty plainly, Learned Hand then believed that, concerning due process as to social and economic legislation, our courts should accept, substantially, the English principle of legislative supremacy. Remember that he thinks and writes in English (not American) and that English ways charm him.

Criticism of decisions in this area continued to mount. In 1911, Goodnow spoke for many when he wrote that the Supreme Court's attitude, if not modified, would create "permanent constitutional obstacles to reform in the United States," reform essential to meet changed economic and social conditions. We were intolerably governed, he said, "by the personal predilections" of the judges. Should this state of affairs not be rectified, he warned, "we may easily be tied up so tight in the bonds of constitutional limitation that either development will cease, and political death ensue, or these bonds will be broken by a shock that may at the same time threaten the foundations not merely of our political but even our social system."

The Supreme Court's decisions aroused the ire of ex-President Theodore Roosevelt. In 1912, he angrily complained that the judiciary had virtually closed "the path to industrial, economic and social reform." In the Bull Moose campaign of that year, in which he ran as a third-party candidate for the presidency against President Taft and Woodrow Wilson, Roosevelt came out for the "recall of decisions," an idea once suggested by John Marshall, that is, the Constitution should be amended to provide, in effect, that, if the Supreme Court nullified a statute, then, if Congress reenacted it, the statute would become valid despite the Court. In advancing this proposal, Roosevelt referred to Thayer's writings.

Although appointed a federal district judge by President Taft in 1909, Learned Hand lined up with Roosevelt. He had sent Roosevelt, while the latter was abroad, a copy of Herbert Croly's book *The Promise of American Life*, which became the basis of much of the Bull Moose political platform. Judge Hand supported Roosevelt in the 1912 campaign, and was, I think, then in favor of the "recall of decisions." In 1913, Judge Hand himself ran (unsuccessfully) on the Bull Moose ticket for the post of Chief Judge of the New York Court of Appeals.

Three years later, in 1916, still a federal judge, he again expressed his indignation at undemocratic decisions, in a remarkable article, "The Speech of Justice." He warned the judges and lawyers to discontinue thwarting the will of those not possessed of "property," by adhering always to old precedents and by narrow interpretations of new statutes favorable to labor. Here Judge Hand, aged forty-four, once more disclosed himself as an eager advocate of the lesson he had learned from Thayer.

He never forgot that lesson. It was underscored when, in the 1920's and the early 1930's, the Supreme Court demolished statute after statute which obviously had wide public approval, some of them apparently indispensable to the very economic existence of the country.

## Judge Hand on Procedural and Substantive Provisions of the Bill of Rights

Judge Hand, however, has been a doughty defender of the procedural provisions of the Constitution, whether contained in the Bill of Rights or elsewhere. Read, for instance, his dissenting opinion in the second Remington perjury case. In particular, he has, in his decisions, enforced rigorously the Fourth Amendment's prohibition of unreasonable searches and seizures; our kind of society, he believes, cannot survive unless the courts prevent such incursions on the individual's privacy.

But, thanks to Thayer's teaching, Judge Hand has, I think, never except once—and then only because he felt bound by Supreme Court decisions— held unconstitutional any federal statute not dealing with procedure. He has used his considerable ingenuity to avoid such a result.

Repeatedly, he has said that, except in its procedural provisions, our Bill of Rights, and in its "imprecise" provisions, such as the First Amendment, contains no more than "moral adjurations," mere "counsels of moderation," sententious phrases, not like laws which courts can or should enforce. In 1930, in a judicial opinion, he described these provisions as representing "a mood rather than a command, that sense of moderation, of fair play, without which states become the prey of faction." Eloquently, he has spoken against the hope that courts, in anything they do, can be the saviors of democracy. You hear echoes of Thayer in his assertion, in 1942, that a "society so riven that the spirit of moderation is gone, no court can save; that a society where that spirit flourishes no court need save; that in a society which evades its responsibility by thrusting on the courts the nurture of that spirit, that spirit in the end will perish." The "spirit of moderation" entails, he declaimed, a "faith in the sacredness of the individual." It "is idle to seek shelter" for that spirit and that faith "in a court room." They "cannot be imposed; . . . decisions will not maintain them." Again, in 1944, he said, "I often wonder whether we do not rest our hopes too much upon constitutions * * * and upon courts. They are false hopes; believe me, these are false hopes. Liberty lies in the hearts of men and women; when it dies there, no constitution, no court can save it; no constitution, * * * no court can even do much to help it."

## The Dennis Case

This brings me to the Dennis case. As you know, it involved the conviction of some Communist Party leaders, under the Smith Act, for willfully conspiring to "teach and advocate the overthrow and destruction" of the government "by force and violence," and "the duty" of so doing. In 1950, Judge Hand, on the appeal from this conviction, held, for the Court of Appeals, that the statute did not violate the First Amendment. As an "inferior" judge, he had to deal with the "clear and present danger" test, a test contrived by Holmes and which the Supreme Court had adopted in many decisions. Judge Hand interpreted this test to mean that, "In each case [courts] must ask whether the gravity of the 'evil,' discounted by its improbability, justifies such invasion of free speech as is necessary to avoid the danger."

I shan't discuss this interpretation of "clear and present danger." But I do again emphasize the fact of Judge Hand's belief, previously and subsequently expressed with vigor, that the courts should never treat nonprocedural provisions of the Bill of Rights as judicially enforcible commands. Possessed of that belief, it was pretty much a foregone conclusion that, if he possibly could, he would sustain the constitutionality of any federal statute interfering with free speech, no matter how undesirable he thought that interference.

In 1951, the Supreme Court affirmed Judge Hand's decision. Frankfurter wrote a concurring opinion. In effect, he rejected the "clear and present danger" test. Instead, he relied 100 percent on his version of the Thayer doctrine. "The Smith Act and this conviction under it," he said, "no doubt restrict the exercise of free speech and assembly." He conceded that, "coupled with" the defendants' forbidden advocacy of the overthrow of the government by force, were the defendants' other criticisms, not forbidden by the statute, "of defects in our society" and the defendants' lawful suggestions for reforms. He admitted that "criticism is the spur to reform" and that "a healthy society must reform in order to conserve." He went further and, with obvious misgivings, conceded that, "Suppressing advocacy of the overthrow [of the government by force] inevitably will also silence critics who do not advocate overthrow but fear that their criticism may be so construed." It "is self-delusion to think that we can punish [the defendants] for their advocacy without adding to the risks run by loyal citizens who honestly believe in some of the reforms these defendants advance. It is a sobering fact that in sustaining the conviction before us we can hardly escape restriction on the interchange of ideas. We must not overlook," he went on, "the value of that interchange." The "liberty of man to search for truth ought not to be fettered, no matter what orthodoxies he may challenge. Liberty of thought shrivels without freedom of expression. Nor can truth be pursued in an atmosphere hostile to the endeavor or under dangers which are hazarded only by heroes. * * * Without open minds there can be no open society. And if society be not open, the spirit of man is mutilated and becomes enslaved."

Yet, in spite of these real dangers which he regarded as flowing from the statute, he concluded that the Court, acting democratically, could not declare it invalid. He described what, to him, was an inescapable paradox: The Court, "by recognizing the right of Congress to put some limitation upon expression," was seeking to "maintain and further" our democratic civilization, although "freedom of expression is the well-spring" of that civilization and although the Smith Act would undoubtedly, by creating fears, seriously impede free expression by non-Communists not at all guilty of violating that statute. Nevertheless, he asserted, "The democratic process * * * is not impaired or restricted" by the Smith Act.

For he believed the Court was bound by his version of the Thayer principle. The Court, he said (quoting Brandeis and Holmes, dissenting in a case unrelated to free speech or the like), must not become a "superlegislature." Courts, he continued, "are not representative bodies. They are not designed to be a good reflex of a democratic society. * * * Primary responsibility for adjusting the interests which compete in the situation before us of necessity belongs to Congress." The Court can properly set aside the legislative judgment "only if there is no reasonable basis for it." Most explicitly he rejected Stone's view, theretofore accepted by a majority of the Court in decisions he cited, "that our function in reviewing statutes restricting freedom of expression differs sharply from our normal duty in sitting in judgment on legislation."

Frankfurter's paradox might be stated somewhat differently, thus: The legislature, in the Smith Act, aimed to prevent the Communists from using speech to subvert democratic rule by the people; but the legislature, acting democratically as the people's representatives, had enacted that statute which might well undermine the basis of popular rule. Stone's formula would have avoided that paradox.

Let me now bring you back for a moment to Stone's dissent in the first flag-salute case. There he observed that, in several previous cases, the Court had vetoed statutes restricting freedom of speech or worship where there were "other ways," other "alternatives," to "secure the legitimate state end without infringing the asserted immunity." Douglas, dissenting in the Dennis case, followed this lead. The government had argued, and the majority opinion made much of the argument, that the Communists had been guilty of "seditious conduct," of actions that were unlawful. Said Douglas, "There is a statute which makes seditious conspiracy unlawful," citing a statute which provides that it is a crime to "conspire to overthrow, put down, or destroy by force the Government of the United States." Had the defendants been convicted under that alternative statute, none of the fears inspired in other innocent citizens, as described by Frankfurter, would have ensued. The vice of the Smith Act, Douglas maintained, was that it criminalized advocacy —teaching, speech—not conduct.

Well, there you have markedly divergent judicial views about the meaning of the Thayer principle. Learned Hand and Frankfurter construe it one way; Stone, Black, Douglas, and others construe it another way.

I shall not express my own view of the Dennis decision. But I do say that it is absurd to say, as some have said, that only Communist sympathizers will disagree with that decision or with the rationale Frankfurter there employed. Surely Justices Black and Douglas cannot be so characterized.

I point also to three sagacious lawyers who have criticized the Dennis decision. None of them is, by any stretch of the imagination, a radical or subversive. Each detests, and is alive to, the real internal threat of, the purposes and conduct of, the American Communist leaders; each believes that such conduct deserves severe punishment, but each regards the Smith Act as an unfortunate method of accomplishing that end.

In 1952, a year after the Supreme Court uttered the Dennis decision, Eugene Rostow took his stand with Stone. He deplored the notion that the judicial power to nullify legislation is undemocratic, that it has a "tainted" character. On the contrary, he asserted, the Supreme Court, in the exercise of this power, can have the "effect not of inhibiting but of releasing the dominantly democratic forces of American life." Had the Court reversed the conviction in Dennis, Dean Rostow maintained, it would have "forced the executive to prosecute the communists on the direct charge of a conspiracy to subvert the state" under another plainly valid statute. The Smith Act, which provided punishment not for so conspiring but for "teaching and advocating" subversion, embodied, Rostow observed, a principle which would have "jailed Calhoun" and "perhaps Thoreau." It would have jailed, too, "the participants in the Hartford convention" of the Federalists opposed to our 1812 war with England.

Professor Paul Freund in 1953 criticized Dennis, à la Stone's and Douglas's suggestions about alternative remedies. "The law," he wrote, "must be viewed in the light of the availability of less drastic means. * * * No one doubts that the leaders of a party which disciplines its members in espionage, sabotage and perjury, to say nothing of instruction in techniques of violence, can be punished for such activity. But the Smith Act was not so framed." Congress, he suggested, had inserted "the knife" too "far from the seat of the disturbance." The statute was "an excessively drastic curb on freedom of expression in order to reach an evil which could be attacked more directly. * * * What is disquieting is that the question of choice of means received such scant notice, and that the decision may support other restrictions on expression which would be unsupportable if subjected to a properly rigorous line of inquiry. * * * Indeed, for all that appears, it would seem that open advocacy of violent revolution, so far from producing the dangers apprehended, was rather a weakening factor in the life of the Party because of its repelling effect." Then Freund added a point which Morris Ernst has often urged, that is, that "secrecy was the real threat." When speech is "covert," the "countercheck of the forum of ideas is by hypothesis lacking," wherefore "restrictions on such speech need not be subjected to a test * * * designed to foster open trading in ideas."

This year, Fred Rodell, in his coruscating book *Nine Men*, more bluntly stated: "The importance of the Dennis case did not lie in the front-paged fact that a few communist leaders * * * were jailed; it lay in the fact that the Supreme Court, without renouncing its self-proclaimed power and duty to uphold the Constitution even against Acts of Congress, gave its ultimate benediction * * * to a law that flatly violated the free-speech guaranty of the First Amendment."

In holding the Smith Act valid, Judge Hand, of course, did not remotely intimate that he deeded it desirable legislation. The truth is that he intensely disliked the popular mood which induced the enactment of that Act. In so saying, I do not rely on private conversations with me. I can point to several articles he published since Dennis.

## Does History Support Judge Hand?

In 1952, Judge Hand admitted that the Constitution would not have been ratified, had it not been promised at the time that the Constitution would be amended promptly to include the Bill of Rights, and had it not then been believed that, as Judge Hand himself phrased it, all its provisions would be "mandates" against which "no statute should prevail." There is every reason to think that statement historically accurate: Much popular opposition to the Constitution yielded only because of that promise and that belief. Moreover, such prominent men as Jefferson and Sam Adams abandoned their grave doubts about ratification on the assurance that the courts would enforce the provisions of all the Amendments. Madison, when, in the First Congress, he advocated the first Ten Amendments, said that "independent tribunals of justice will consider themselves in a peculiar manner the guardians of those rights; they will be an impenetrable bulwark against every assumption of power in the Legislative or Executive; they will be naturally led to resist every encroachment upon rights stipulated for in the Constitution by the declaration of rights."

Why, then, one may ask, should not the courts respect that history which discloses that the First Amendment was intended to be a legal "mandate" and not solely a "moral adjuration"?

## Can the Courts Save Democracy?

As I've reported, Judge Hand thinks it folly to believe that the courts can save democracy. Of course they cannot. But it seems to me that here, most uncharacteristically, Judge Hand indulges in a judgment far too sweeping, one which rests on a too sharp either-or, all-or-nothing dichotomy. In a posthumously published book, Justice Jackson similarly objected to the idea "that the Court can * * * supply some clear bulwark against all dangers and evils that beset us internally," that the "protection of civil liberties" should be left "wholly to the judiciary."

Obviously, the courts cannot do the whole job. But, just as obviously, they can sometimes help to arrest evil popular trends in their inception. Not only are the Supreme Court's opinions educational in a general way; they have also had discernible practical effects in stopping undemocratic tendencies. See, for instance, the Hague decision in 1939.

In an address delivered in September of this year, Frankfurter, after quoting Judge Hand, noted, with marked pleasure, that no other English-speaking country has adopted anything like what Judge Hand calls the "imprecise" provisions of our Bill of Rights. Here Frankfurter virtually repeated something he had said in an article published in 1924, that is, that, without such provisions, "life, liberty and property were amply protected" in those countries, including South Africa. McWhinney pointedly comments, "There is today a special irony in the reference to South Africa." Just the other day, at the Yale Law School, we heard from a brilliant South African lawyer how, absent a Bill of Rights in that unhappy land, each time its courts had interpreted a statute to protect legal equality, the legislature had at once enacted legislation to wipe out the democratic decision. When our Supreme Court, acting pursuant to our Bill of Rights, invalidates such a discriminatory statute, our legislatures cannot validly emasculate the decision. Whether, if supported by a Bill of Rights like ours, the South African court's decisions would have withstood the onslaughts of the regnant majority in the legislature, no one can say with certainty. But who can tell that such decisions would not have done much to stem the terrifying growth of tyranny in that troubled country, a growth which, so many intelligent observers believe, may issue, before long, in a devastating civil war?

For a number of reasons, my own strong inclination is to disagree with Judge Hand's position that the First Amendment represents merely a "moral adjuration" addressed solely to the people and their elected representatives. However, so profound is my respect for his wisdom in general that my disagreement with him on this subject disturbs me. I warn you therefore not to make up your minds without much reflection.

## Conclusion

A great man, such as Learned Hand, we should prize. Yet—as I'm sure he would tell you—you should beware lest you do him an ill-service by so venerating him that he will stand in the way of those who come after him, paralyzing them through awe of his achievements. Some men, wrote seventeenth century John Donne, "do not fill the place they are raised to"; but a man may "over-fill his place. He may bring so much justice, so much integrity, to fill the place as shall * * * burthen the place * * *" and so become "a burthen upon his successor to proceed by example * * *"

Learned Hand would be the last to claim perfection. Being human, he has his faults, of course. But no other judge has contributed as much of enduring value to his civilization. To borrow the words of Anatole France, "We owe him the gratitude due to minds that have fought against prejudices. * * * Men are rare who are free from the prejudices of their period, and look squarely at what the crowd dares not face." Judge Hand has a kind of courage seldom described and too seldom manifested—the courage to accept the fact that, as man is but a finite creature, there are some incurable defects in the solution of most human problems and that life presents to us challenging uncertainties. This fact does not daunt him, soften him into a flabby defeatist, or harden him into a crusty cynic. A true liberal, he is no dogmatist. Himself dwelling in a temperate zone of attitudes, he has doubts about those who prefer the intemperate zones. He believes in government by discussion, agreeing with Pericles about the virtues of Athenian democracy when he said: "Instead of looking on discussion as a stumbling block in the way of action, we think it an indispensable preliminary to any wise action at all." Such a liberal has no list of fixed particularized ideas on which he insists as always wholly right or wholly wrong. He does not, phonograph-like, rattle off, with an air of infallibility, a long series of do's and don't's applicable in all circumstances. He is no slogan addict. He looks upon liberalism as a mood, not as a system or a catalogue of precise commands. Nor will he forget that irrational extralegal restraints may tyrannically do more than the edicts of government to narrow liberty; that, among such extralegal restraints, are the irrational, biased stereotypes of private groups, including the orthodox heresies and conformity-demanding taboos of rigid-minded pseudoliberals.

Some persons denounce one who, like Learned Hand, accepts the fact of life's uncertainties, who fearlessly confronts man's limitations as finite, mortal being. Themselves unable courageously to look at life as a drama full of contingencies, they resent it that any other can live without any assurance of absolute cosmic guaranties.

This brings me, once more, to Judge Hand's rejection of the idea of eternal principles of justice or morality. In this, he resembles Holmes. Since Holmes has been berated, on that account, as dangerously immoral, as an exponent of a cynical, skeptical philosophy which leads to totalitarianism, doubtless, ere long, Judge Hand will be similarly assaulted.

I shall not here defend his repudiation of any form of natural law. I shall, however, question the suggestion that such a repudiation necessarily yields immoral, unjust, undemocratic conclusions.

I might begin with a countersuggestion, by asking: Does adherence to a natural-law philosophy ensure morality, justice, devotion to democracy? Certainly not. Judge Manton adhered to that philosophy, and Judge Manton went to jail for taking bribes. The Italian philosopher Del Vecchio preached a version of natural-law—and became a sponsor of Mussolini. Thomas Aquinas, the leading Catholic natural-law philosopher, approved submission to despots. The lands which, in our times, succumbed to dictatorship were those where antirelativism was far more popular than in those lands which resisted the dictators; for example, America, in which flourished the pragmatism of William James, the arch-advocate of democracy and the dignity of the individual.

I grant at once the unfairness of such an argument. I advance it merely to show the unfairness of those who severely criticize men like Holmes or Hand because they do not espouse natural law, except perhaps what has been labeled a "natural law with a changing content," a relativistic natural law. Holmes and Hand believe only in relative or temporary absolutes, cultural absolutes. Their critics, reversing the anthropologists' notion of the relativity of obscenity, assert what amounts to the obscenity of relativity.

It can be demonstrated, I think, that moral relativism neither implies nor induces cynicism or moral indifference. "Why," asks Oppenheim, "should an ethical relativist who has adopted the credo of democracy necessarily be a less enthusiastic defender of his convictions than a philosophic absolutist who claims these convictions correspond to absolute truth? In Europe, the most ardent defenders of the democratic principle of individual dignity against the attacks by absolute monarchy, and subsequently by totalitarianism of the Right and Left, have come from the ranks of the liberal movements" whose "background has been traditionally one . . . of ethical relativism." To "hold that value judgments cannot be *validated*, does not preclude anyone from *making* them," or mean that to utter them is meaningless.

Chesterton said that a man's philosophy is the most important fact about him. Once I endorsed that statement. I have come to doubt its wisdom, unless most carefully interpreted. For one should, I think, distinguish a man's formal philosophy from his actual working creed. Influenced by their social heritage, or their teachers, men adopt, and express loyalty to, some particular system of ethics or metaphysics or ontology or epistemology. Yet many a man, in the actual conduct of his life, negates the system to which he avows adherence. He takes over the language of some philosophic school, yet his verbal loyalty does not signify his acceptance of its spirit. He adjusts the system to his own unique inner needs, the product of his peculiar makeup, and of his singular reactions to his experience. An ideal, become institutionalized, has many adherents who, while appearing, even to themselves, to accept it, inwardly dissent in varying degrees. We all know men who talk like absolutists and act like relativists, or talk relativism but act on what they deem unalterable dogmas. For example, as I've tried to show elsewhere, Aristotle was a better legal pragmatist than John Dewey. It is notable that the "right wing" of a philosophic school is often closer to the "left wing" of an opposing school than to its own "left wing."

In short, when looking to a man's philosophy as a key to his character, you should search beneath his formal, spoken, avowals to discover, if you can, his living philosophy.

I ask, then, whether any of Judge Hand's judicial decisions would have been one whit different had he talked in terms of natural law, had he declared a belief in eternal principles of morality or justice? I can think of none. In this respect, at least, any sensible person should be a pragmatist. For pragmatism, wrote C. S. Peirce, "is only an application of the sole principle of logic which was recommended by Jesus: 'Ye may know them by their fruits.' "

Horace Walpole said that "life is a comedy for those who think and a tragedy for those who feel." Learned Hand, who both thinks deeply and feels deeply, sees life as a marvelous comic-tragedy. He is not one who "despises men tenderly." He has a love for and an understanding of his fellow creatures, like him, humanly fallible. I commend him to you as a great man and as our wisest judge.

*Excerpts from a manuscript based on lectures delivered at Yale Law School, November, 1955. A different version was published in the* University of Chicago Law Review *in 1957*

PART 2 &ε The Conflict

Between Freedom

and Authority

EDITOR'S NOTE  ᵉᵍ The ubiquitous problem of maintaining individual freedom within the framework of democratic governmental authority is the subject of the section which follows. The group I call "Government Is Human" consists of five chapters from the book *If Men Were Angels*. In "Censorship: The First Amendment" the reader will find the now classic *United States* v. *Roth*, a concurring opinion in a case involving the mailing of "obscene" literature. "The Fallacy of Universal Law," although it reads like an essay, is, in fact, a book review of George Calhoun's *Introduction to Greek Legal Science* which appeared in the *Harvard Law Review* in 1944.

The chapters from *If Men Were Angels* represent the author's views about the importance of the kind of men who, in a democratic government, administer its laws. In 1941, Jerome Frank resigned as Chairman of the Securities and Exchange Commission to become a judge of the United States Court of Appeals for the Second Circuit. The book, published the year following, was intended to rebut the current violent arguments centering around the SEC and other New Deal regulatory agencies. *If Men Were Angels* concerns itself with the concept of "a government of laws." The author believes that "[W]hat we, in a democracy, must insist upon is a *government of laws well administered by the right kind of men.*" Dated in respect to occasional references, these chapters nevertheless bear directly on contemporary governmental problems.

[ 75 ]

In *Roth*, Judge Frank says, "As a judge of an inferior court, I am constrained by opinions of the Supreme Court concerning the obscenity statute to hold that legislation valid." However, he was clearly asking the Court to reconsider the question of the constitutionality of that legislation. On the basis of the searching questions raised in his opinion, the Supreme Court did review the case; however, the Court affirmed the judgment of the court below. About *Roth*, Harriet Pilpel writes: "In the 'good old days' we burned witches because of the supposed harm they would do if permitted at large. Today . . . we ban 'obscene' publications . . . because of the supposed harm they would do if permitted to circulate. But would they do such harm, and even if they would, would they do as much harm as the attempt to suppress them? These are fundamental inquiries and they have been posed by one of our most thoughtful judges. . . ." The opinion is also generally regarded as a fascinating example of a fusion of social studies and judicial logic. Thurman Arnold says, "[Judge Frank's] success in making this fusion [in *Roth*] may be his most enduring monument."

Judge Frank used the book review of Calhoun's *Introduction to Greek Legal Science* as a device to express his opinions about the concept of "natural law" as applied to the democratic process, as well as to reiterate his views about the meaning of Aristotle's contributions to legal and political thought. The interested reader will find a chapter in Judge Frank's *Courts on Trial* devoted to the former subject, as well as a section of the Preface to the sixth printing of the author's first book, *Law and the Modern Mind*.

Without the courage to face up to the dilemma inherent in the democratic process, we run the risk of anarchy or tyranny. In the pages which follow, the reader will find the author probing this problem, central to a democratic form of government: How to reconcile individual freedom with the regulation of society, on which this freedom rests. ৡৠ

# GOVERNMENT IS HUMAN ❧

We DIFFERENTIATE—and properly—between the obligations of men engaged in administering business and men engaged in administering government. Freer play is given to John Q. Smith as officer of the Zenith Corporation than to John Q. Smith when he gives up his corporate job, moves from New York or Des Moines to Washington, and becomes a federal official. The "law" as it relates to corporate-officer Smith embodies merely minimum moral standards. The "law" relating to government-officer Smith necessarily embodies higher moral standards. And that is as it should be. For Smith, when in the government, is the public's servant, representing the public generally; and, too, the powers which he exercises are, usually, more compelling.

The differentiation, at times, finds expression in the formula "a government of laws, and not of men," an ancient formula having a variety of connotations, but disclosing fundamentally a desire to avoid, as far as practicable, the intrusion of the "personal" element in government. It means that government officers are the public's servants, and must not follow their own caprices. We may spell out the formula in this way: A public servant, a government official, should, as to the scope of his duties, be restricted by the orders issued by his master, the public; he and his master should know, as well as may be, the limits within which the servant can properly act; the servant must stay within those limits. The public's orders to the public's servants are what, in this context, we call "law" or "legal standards." The public's servants should, then, not be allowed to draw freely on their imaginations, to exercise their initiative to the same extent as if they were private individuals. The "laws" set forth the confines of their conduct, canalize their legitimate activities.

Officers of private corporations must also comply with "legal standards." But we want them to use a more flexible judgment than government officers, to be at liberty to use their imaginations within a less restricted area. Yet there are certain similarities between the obligations of such private and public officers. Even a corporation's officers cannot lawfully do just as they please. They, too, are servants, corporate servants, the servants of those who invest in the corporation.

But what, on occasions, we astonishingly fail to note are these more important resemblances: We know, of course, that corporate officials are human beings. Those who invest in a corporation are investing in its management; the personalities and characters of corporate officials often are, therefore, matters of vast importance. If those officials are crooks or knaves, the corporation will get into trouble. *Everyone recognizes that a private corporation is not and cannot be managed by machines. What is too often ignored is the obvious fact that the same is true of government.* As already noted, the scope for the legitimate play of the personalities and characters of government officials, under our form of government, is narrower than in the case of private officials. That is what we often mean when we say that we have "a government of laws, and not of men." But we dare not push the literal meaning of that phrase too far. If we do, we lose sight of the fact that *government, too, must, unavoidably, be administered by human beings. Government is not and cannot be made into a piece of automatic machinery.*

Within the limits of their lawful powers, the characters, personalities, integrity, and the intelligence of government officers affect, and most importantly, the way the government is run. If government officials are stupid or ill-informed or uneducable or careless or corrupt, then, as long as they hold office, the government will be badly managed.

That is a truth of which all of us are—at times—aware. It was stressed in 1931 by the so-called Wickersham Committee appointed by President Hoover. Even so conservative a lawyer as Mr. Frank Hogan, recently President of the American Bar Association, made that point, in 1938, with respect to judges. He quoted with approval from an earlier report of the Bar Association, in which it was said (somewhat exaggeratedly): "In the last analysis justice depends upon the judge. Given a judge of sound judgment, learned, courageous and independent, and justice will be well administered under almost any system of laws. Given a judge unlearned, timid, and whose horizon is the next election, and justice will be poorly administered under the best system of laws." If that is essentially true of judges, of course it must be true of all other government officers.

Yet, curiously, it often happens that the very men who one day stress that truth the next day help to obscure it, by distorting the real truth contained in the phrase "a government of laws, and not of men." As a consequence, sometimes, hyponotized by those words, we picture as an existing reality—or at least at a completely achievable ideal—a government so contrived that it matters not at all what men, at any given moment, constitute the government. Such an idea is a narcotic. It is bad medicine. It does not protect us from bad government. On the contrary, it invites bad government. It can be used, and it has been used, by bunglers or crooks in government, to cloak their ineptness or their crookedness.

The strange notion that government is not or need not be administered by human beings has no place in a democracy. In a democracy the people can and should hold their public officials to account. They can and should be vigilant in scrutinizing what their public servants are doing. They have a right to say that Official White is a fool, or Official Black is a knave. If White or Black is an elected official, they can oust him at the polls. If he is an appointed official, they can demand his removal. That is one of the signal virtues of a democracy. It is only in a dictatorship that public officials are not thus accountable. There they are above public criticism. Their infallibility is a dogma, never to be doubted. To question their infinite wisdom is treason. To assert their humanness means the concentration camp or the firing squad.

*It is imperative that in a democracy it should never be forgotten that public office is, of necessity, held by mere men, who, of course, have human frailties.* It is only where government officials are deemed to be semidivine that people have any excuse for ignoring the unavoidable personal factor in government. It is for that reason that *the belief that government can ever consist of perfect creatures is alien to a democracy. That false belief is the core of the philosophy of dictatorship; it is the basis of "personal government" in its most extreme and pernicious form.* For, where "personal government" is at its maximum, the effects on government of the all-too-human personalities of government officials is least open to discussion.

But there is a paradox from which we, in a democracy, suffer: Out of a legitimate desire to restrict, within proper limits, the effects of the personalities of our public officials—to avoid the "personal governments" adulated in an autocracy—we posit the ideal of a government of laws, and not of men. And then corrupt and tyrannical men in government hide behind a false interpretation of that ideal. They employ it to obstruct their true aims, their real purposes. They use it to convince us that their own characters are not a proper subject of inquiry. They sometimes make us believe that (according to a distorted theory of "a government of laws") laws are or can be self-operative, that the personalities of the men who administer those laws is immaterial. It is often, although not invariably, true that those public officials who too frequently announce, and with fervor, that ours is "a government of laws, and not of men," are those who most need watching. To illustrate:

We have all, unfortunately, known of judges who have turned out to be corrupt. Experience discloses that those corrupt judges make the greatest pretense of the purely mechanical workings of the courts, in the application of the laws, when they decide cases. In their opinions and speeches, they never concede for an instant that judges are human, that the personality of the judge, his prejudices, predilections, and passions, have any effect on his decisions. In their judicial opinions, delivered from the bench, there is a magnificent appearance of complete objectivity. Each of their judgments is made to appear to be the product of a mere logic machine, of purely logical reasoning in which the conclusion was reached by applying a precise rule of "law," as to which there can be no question, to definite "facts," as to which there can be do doubt. And yet, when the real character of such a judge is exposed, then, behind that front—of dispassionate logic working on indubitable legal rules and a definite state of facts—we find gross dishonesty. Then we see that the judging process, in the case of his decisions, actually began with conclusions which were bought and paid for, and that the legal precedents and the facts were deliberately chosen by him so as dishonestly to justify that predetermined, purchased, decision.

Surely, then, it makes a difference whether our judges are honest, intelligent, conscientious, decent, and just men. It is folly to ignore or obscure that truth. To do so is to aid the crook or tyrant on the bench. The character and personal makeup of our judges we dare not overlook.

In all this there is nothing new or startling. President Hoover's so-called Wickersham Commission in 1931 published a "Report on Lawlessness in Law Enforcement," the second portion of which, dealing with unfairness in prosecutions by prosecutors and judges, concluded thus:

Specific changes in the machinery of criminal prosecutions, such as have been suggested, will help lessen unfairness by defining limits which must not be overstepped and providing the accused with a more efficient legal remedy if there is transgression. But changes in machinery are not sufficient to prevent unfairness. Much more depends upon the men that operate the machinery. And whatever limits are imposed by statute, prosecuting officials and trial judges must necessarily be left with great powers and wide discretion. The most important safeguards of a fair trial are that these officials want it to be fair and are active in making it so. As Mr. Wigmore has said: "All the rules in the world will not get us substantial justice if the judges and the counsel have not the correct living moral attitude toward substantial justice."

And, to repeat, what is true of judges is true of all public officials. To cover up the effects of their personalities leads to the operation of their personalities in the most sinister and damaging form. It develops *concealed* personal government. It *yields a government of men at their worst*—of men pretending to give us nothing but a government of self-operating laws. Here we arrive at another paradox: *The thorough awareness that there is an un-avoidable personal factor in government is the best way to reduce to a minimum the bad effects of that personal factor.*

There are some men who, because they would like to have a government in which the personal factor is entirely absent, grow angry when their attention is directed to the unavoidable presence of some of that personal factor. They are the kind of men who dislike being told any of the facts of life which they consider unpleasant. They apply, literally, and therefore mistakenly, the adage that "what you don't know won't hurt you." They belong to the Ancient Order of Self-Deluding Ostriches. (The reference here is to the ostrich of literature. As Stefansson has shown, the real ostrich never buries his head in the sand.) Their password is "Hush." They act on the principle that silence concerning disturbing facts somehow destroys or prevents the existence of such facts; they identify such silence with the non-existence of those facts. They share with primitive man a belief in word magic, a belief that to name something is to evoke it or create it.

And so they denounce anyone who speaks of any unlovely or undesirable aspects of life as if, by speaking of them, he was giving them vitality or applauding them. They assume that to say, "This is so" is the same as to say, "I'm delighted that this is so," or "This ought to be so." If one were to apply their notions to medicine and kindred arts, he would assert that a physician who studies and writes of diseases of the liver is in favor of diseased livers and wants to perpetuate them; that mortality tables are compiled by men who hate mankind and relish the harsh reality of death.

Such worshipers of ignorance, such devotees of silence, are kin to those who, several centuries ago, wanted to burn Vesalius at the stake because, ignoring the traditional learning based on Galen's teachings (derived from a study solely of the insides of monkeys), he first dissected the human body and learned and taught how it was constructed. Vesalius, by dissipating prior ignorance about it, enabled physicians to increase human health. The hush-mongers think that public ignorance is golden, and try to bludgeon into inactivity those who think that knowledge is power. They are particularly active in their efforts to hush up any talk about the unpleasant facts of social and political life. They are opposed to any careful dissection of the body politic, made in the interest of improving it. They regard any contemporary political Vesalius as a "dirty muckraker" who revels in the filth he reveals. One of them once said to the writer that it was improper for lawyers ever to assert publicly that some judges are corrupt; he actually preferred to have corrupt judges rather than to expose and get rid of them. That kind of bullying Pollyana-ism recalls the deceased President of whom it is said that he resented the restraints on the power of the nation's Chief Executive contained in the provisions of the Constitution and transferred his animosity against those provisions to anyone who called them to his attention.

Such a desire to obtain mental comfort through enforced ignorance is, often, not merely cowardly and stupid, but socially dangerous. It may perhaps be a philosophic truth that we need to live by illusions as to the possibility of achieving our ultimate ideals. Whether or not that be true, illusions about events in the workaday world are most unwise. An engineer who has illusions about the soundness of the bridges he builds is a dangerous man. He should be fully aware of the unavoidable weaknesses in the steel, cement, and the wood he uses. He can build strong bridges only if he knows those weaknesses.

Another way to put the matter is to repeat the ancient wisdom that it is important to differentiate between the possible and he desirable. Many things which would be desirable are impossible. To assume the contrary, to assume that the way you think things ought to be, so they are, is often to invite disaster. Strangely enough, frequently it is the knowledge that existing facts are not as they want them, that makes it possible for men to better them.

Just as an engineer cannot build sound bridges unless he knows the inherent and unavoidable weaknesses of the materials which he uses, so we cannot have a capable, decent government, mindful of the rights of citizens, if we ignore the fact that unavoidably it consists of men, and if we then disregard the inherent imperfections of all men, whether engaged in government or other activities.

To pretend, then, that government, in any of its phases, is a machine; that it is not a human affair; that the language of statutes—if only they are adequately worded—plus appeals to the upper courts, will, alone, do away with the effect of human weaknesses in government officials is to worship illusion. And it is a dangerous illusion.

Properly interpreted, the phrase "a government of laws, and not of men" is of inestimable value. Thus interpreted, it means that the personal prejudices and predilections of government officers should be reduced, by statutory provisions and other means, to as narrow confines as is possible, having due regard to the practical workings of the governmental functions involved.

But to that end, legal machinery is not enough. This, too, is needed: The men who operate that machinery must be men keenly alive to their own prejudices, to their own human weaknesses, and, armed with that self-knowledge, must discharge their obligations to our citizens. And the citizens, also, must be watchful of the behavior of those officers. They must not go to sleep on the phrase about a government of laws. Let it be said again: They should be warned to be most watchful of those government officers who, day in and day out, mouth that phrase.

It would be comforting to know what we could contrive a government in which the weaknesses and mistakes of men played no part. But we must admit that that is not possible, however desirable it would be. Let us strive to come as near such a government as we can. Let us have as much of a government of laws as it is humanly attainable. But be careful of those who say we can have it in its full literalness.

At times, every man wishes that there were some way of automatically operating government like a mass-production factory. But it is dangerous to substitute one's wishes for reality. Now, wishful thinking, properly employed, is not to be derided: Civilization is based upon wishes—wishes which could be and have been realized. It used to be said that, if wishes were horses, beggars would ride. Well, certain inventors did have the right kind of wish, found it could be realized, and, as a result, many men who were once beggars can ride—in automobiles—today. The proper use of a wish is to see whether and how far it is possible to change existing reality to conform to the wish. The wish we are here discussing can be realized thus far: To the extent that statutory and constitutional provisions unavoidably leave personal factors operative in government, awareness of the operation of those personal factors can help, substantially, to reduce their consequences. But one should not hope to go further. When Margaret Fuller said, "I accept the universe," Carlyle wisely remarked, "Begad, she'd better."

Let these remarks not be misunderstood. When the writer asserts that decent government requires that government officials be decent men—that governmental powers, since they are necessarily vested in men, can be abused and that, to avoid such abuses, we must have public officials who are honest, conscientious, liberty-loving, intelligent, informed, God-fearing men—he is not saying for a moment that that is all we need for competent and adequate government. He is talking of but one ingredient of good government. There are other ingredients, of course. If it is said that no man can live without water, that is not the same as saying that any man can live by water alone; water is a necessary factor for the sustenance of human life, but it is not an all-sufficient factor. Adequately worded statutes limiting discretion, proper rules of procedure, sufficient subjection to judicial correction—those are among the indispensable elements of any proper government. But public officials of the right kind are also essential. Not to see that is to invite personal government at its worst.

"If men were angels," it was said long ago in The Federalist, "no government would be necessary. If angels were to govern men, neither external nor internal controls on government would be necessary. In framing a government *which is to be administered by men over men,* the great difficulty lies in this: You must first enable the government to control the governed and in the next place oblige it to control itself. A dependence on the people is, no doubt, the primary control on the government; but experience has taught mankind the necessity of auxiliary precautions."

See where we have arrived: (1) To insist that we can have a pure "government of laws"—one in which a question as to the kind of men who compose the government is irrelevant—is likely to lead to concealed and, therefore, corrupt or tyrannical "personal government." For government must, of necessity, be "administered by men over men." (2) To insist that, if we have a government made up of "good men," we need not bother about legal restraints on their activities is to ensure unconcealed "personal government" —dictatorship. (3) What we, in a democracy, must insist upon is *a government of laws well administered by the right kind of men.*

* * * * *

Because our federal and our early state constitutions were modeled somewhat on the American colonial charters which, in turn, were actually—or were analogous to—corporation charters, an atmosphere of corporateness pervades our public laws. An invalid act of a public officer has, indeed, occasionally been described by the Supreme Court as *ultra vires,* a phrase ordinarily applied to acts of private corporate officers which means that they are acting outside their authority. A variety of circumstances has led the courts to be more stringent in their application of the *ultra vires* doctrine to governmental than to private corporate officers. The fact, however, that "the law of public officers" and "the law of private officers" are related is not without significance. It serves to underscore the thesis . . . that many of our great private corporations, possessed as they are of immense coercive powers over millions of our citizens, are, realistically regarded, a kind of government. The way in which a great corporation is managed affects the lives of its shareholders, bondholders, and other creditors, its host of employees, the numerous persons interested in the concerns from whom it buys its raw materials, the multitude to whom it sells its products, and its competitors. The conduct of such giant corporations is more important than the conduct of many a state or city. The responsibilities of their officers are therefore public in their nature. They are, although in varying degrees, trustees for all the groups of persons whose lives their actions affect.

Of those who conduct such corporate government, no less than those whom we call public officers, we should say: They must be the right kind of men, and they must obey the commands—the laws—of the persons for whom they act as corporate servants. There is, to be sure, a difference in emphasis when we talk of corporate officials, since they must have a wider discretion than public officials. The "laws" must give them a freer rein—more snaffle and less curb; there can and should be more "personal government" than in the case of public officials. For the demand on the former is more for efficiency and initiative. As a consequence, however, the character and personalities of corporate officers may be more important.

Like a governmental power, corporate power can be abused. And we must find how, so far as possible, to stop abuses of that kind of power. The Insull affair, the Krueger affair, the Hopson affair, and the recent Coster (or McKesson & Robbins) affair have brought to the fore that kind of thinking about the duties of directors. It is manifested, in part, by current proposals for the appointment of so-called "professional directors." But that is only one manifestation of the fact that we are becoming more aware of the public character of the great corporation and therefore of its officials. In the past few years the writer has had many talks with one of America's leading industrialists who never tires of saying that his corporation is now so large that it is no longer private; he acknowledges that officers of his company are at the focal point where vast public interests converge; he is sensitive to the fact that his corporation is a kind of government.

The differences between such private government and public government are narrowing. That is not to say that the differences have been or will be or should be obliterated. Nor are we here taking the legalistic approach and saying that every corporation is a creature of the state, exercising a franchise or privilege conferred on it by government. We are, rather, trying to focus attention on the consequences of the giant corporation's power over the welfare of our citizens.

The business executive who comes into government is sometimes unaware of the difference. In 1933, such a transplanted executive was shocked to learn from the writer that government licenses could not be revoked without hearings. "Why," he said impatiently, "when I was with the X Company, when a dealer wasn't acting right, we just sent him a telegram telling him we had canceled his 'franchise.' "

The writer recalls that, a short time ago, the president of such a corporation said that one of his most troublesome problems was what to do with his stockholders. They were, often, he said, a considerable nuisance, because it was difficult to make them intelligently comprehend the business problems of his company. In discussing the question with him, the writer recollected this story: It was anticipated that, at the annual meeting of a corporation, a certain stockholder would appear and raise valid but annoying questions. The stenographer who made the transcripts of the meeting happened to have particularly acute hearing, and, when the troublesome stockholder arose, she caught for the record the whispered comment of the company's president: "Cripes! Here it comes!"

The writer told that story to his friend who was bothered about his stockholders, adding: "You see, a government officer in a democracy has the same kind of trouble. His stockholders, so to speak, are the voters. And any voter has the right to ask him, at any time, one of those 'Cripes-here-it-comes' questions. But that's what democracy means. That is its best feature. It compels every government officer to watch his step. He has to be ready for any kind of question. Some of the questions, of course, are foolish. But many of them are much to the point. An officer of a corporation like yours is facing the same difficulty. He is engaged in a sort of democratic government. His voters are his stockholders. The possibility that they will ask him embarrassing questions will keep him on his toes."

Which adds up to this: There is need to recognize that the equivalent of something like purely "personal government" of our giant corporations—the kind of government of industry we got from Insull or Coster—is no longer in order, that it will often yield not efficiency but its opposite, that it will often help to wreck public confidence and may undermine our economy. The governance of our great corporations by their directors and the administration of public government must, as we have said, be made to resemble one another to a great extent. Be it noted again that this does not mean that the two kinds of government should be idential. The difference is one of degree—and differences of degree are unquestionably important. But the directors of great enterprises must be honest, capable men, with a sense of public responsibility. And they, too, must conform to higher standards than have heretofore been imposed upon them, and must not exercise their powers as if those powers were their personal property. We want, then, with respect to private corporate government, something not altogether different from a government of laws administered by the right kind of men.

Recently the writer met Mr. Robert Barlow, managing director of one of England's leading industrial corporations. He advanced the interesting idea that there should be a sort of school for directors: All prospective directors should be obliged to take a course in the duties and functions of directors. They should, at a minimum, he said, have some clear notion of their obligations under the law and they should have some adequate notion of accounting principles and techniques. That is an idea worth considering. It moves in the direction we have been indicating.

There is another feature of corporate and public government that deserves much discussion. Business, we hear it said, must stress efficiency; but, it is asserted, since government in a democracy must allow for freedom, that means a loss of efficiency which can be attained, at its maximum, only under dictatorship. In other words, it is implied that an autocratic government is more efficient than a democracy.

That is an illusion. In the long run, the methods of the brutalitarian state will blot out inventiveness. The freedom of the individual citizen to think and speak new ideas, to criticize, unrestrainedly, the existing ways in which either government or business is operated, to devise and experiment with new techniques—such freedoms, which are the essential features of our democracy, have brought us our national wealth. To destroy these freedoms is to obstruct the emergence of novelties; such novelties often add to our long-range well-being and more than offset the temporary wastes which might be eliminated by a dictator-bossed society. Dictatorship, since it crushes all new ideas not sanctioned by the dictator and his handful of satellites, leads to immense losses of inventiveness and thus brings not national wealth but national illth.

To the freedoms inherent in a real democracy most of the men in our national government are devoted. And that signifies that they are devoted to those efficiencies which go with such a democracy. And when they say that they want our democratic government to be made up of decent, honest, God-fearing men to whom absolutism is nauseating, they are surely not to be charged with a secret or open hankering for "personal government" or with advocacy of the autocracy of the Nazis or the Fascists.

Yet many of them have recently been denigrated in just that way. And such charges have, with particular vehemence, been leveled at the members of the federal commissions and so-called administrative agencies.

\* \* \* \* \*

. . . It has been suggested by some persons—who not only dislike the delegation of discretion to administrative agencies, but who also are opposed to the fitfulness of enforcement by prosecuting officers—that all "delegation of discretionary power" can be avoided, and all uncertainty in enforcement eliminated, through merely incorporating regulatory prohibitions in corporate charters as in corporation laws. But delegation would then still be involved: Statutes are not self-executing—until such time as the minimum moral standards which they embody become a part of established customs with which the bulk of the community habitually and almost unconsciously complies. Presumably, therefore, the suggestion implies that such prohibitions are to be enforced at the suit of stockholders—which means "delegation," to them, of "discretionary enforcing power." But experience shows that enforcement by stockholders is not only, in most cases, ineffective, but also unusually sporadic, thus giving rise to that very state of uncertainty for the corporate executives which the suggested device is supposed to remove.

Conflicting attitudes concerning such a device were disclosed in the following colloquy before the Temporary National Economic Committee (TNEC) on March 3, 1939:

SENATOR O'MAHONEY: The thought that comes to my mind—and this without any intention at all to reflect upon the Federal Trade Commission—that the Federal Trade Commission from 1914 to 1921 was one sort of a Commission, but from 1921 down to 1933 it was an utterly different sort of a Federal Trade Commission; and though these gentlemen who are testifying here today in most instances were on the staff of that Commission throughout that period, their activity was controlled by the policy-making power of the members of the Commission whose point of view and whose purposes changed with the administration.

MR. FRANK: Certainly; that same thing is true of any prosecutor's enforcement of any statute, even if the prosecution is not vested in an administrative body. The personal perspective, background, characteristic outlook or whatever you choose to call it—we can pick many words out of the thesaurus to describe what we are getting at—those same factors are found in the Department of Justice.

SENATOR O'MAHONEY: Exactly.

MR. FRANK: Under one administration minded to enforce the antitrust laws vigorously, you may find enforcement; under another administration minded not to enforce them, the Department of Justice would go into court, begin a proceeding and agree to a consent decree which would give a complete wholesale exemption to any affected industry. There is no way I have been able to discover by which the vicissitudes of human nature can be controlled by legislation. Government officials having such powers must be impressed by their own inward restrictions and by the outward pressure of public opinion.

SENATOR O'MAHONEY: I think we might agree on that. I have repeatedly stated that the success or failure of the antitrust laws as we have had them has depended too much upon the diligence and the point of view of those who happen temporarily to be in the Department of Justice. If we happen to have a vigorous and active head of an antitrust division, we have a certain type of enforcement. If, on the other hand, we have a head of the antitrust division who is not so vigorous, we have an utterly different sort of enforcement.

That, I feel, is largely due to the fact that our antitrust laws to date have either by their interpretation by the court or by express language, lodged discretionary power in the courts or in the commission. That is the specific fact which has led me to the conclusion that the satisfactory way of solving this problem of preventing restraints of trade is to do it by means of the charters of the corporations which carry on the trade. *I don't believe that you are ever going to succeed by personal government, by personal power, by personal enforcement of particular personal desires, and that the only possible success can be attained by clearly writing into the charters of these corporations—that is to say into their contracts with the people—the powers which they shall have. And by these charters to withdraw from corporations the corporate power to commit the abuses which the entire experience of the American people has proven be-*

yond any possibility of contradiction are bad upon the economic affairs of the entire people.

MR. FRANK: Senator * * * I find this difficulty: Whether the inhibitions be put in charters, statutes, criminal laws or whether their enforcement be sought through civil penalties, some human being has to see that there is no violation of the matters that are prohibited.

Now, putting prohibitions in a charter will not prevent violations of the provisions of that charter unless somebody, whether he be a private person or a public agency, or a prosecuting officer, designated by statute, sees to it that those provisions are not violated. The books are full (sometimes the law books, sometimes the court reports, sometimes reports of investigatory bodies) of instances where plain unmistakable provisions of State laws are violated. Only a very small fraction of the instances of violation are brought to judgment before some court which either redressed the wrong by damages or prevents the wrong by injunction. It seems clear to me that *someone, somewhere, has to have the power to enforce statutes—unless we turn men into angels* so that the mere fact that there is an inhibition in a statute will mean that men, by their own impulses, will comply with it.

It matters not whether the person who enforces the statute is a Government officer or a stockholder or officer of a corporation, someone has got to see to it that infraction of prohibitions in a statute are vindicated. I find it difficult to see how you can avoid vesting that power in some human being. And once you recognize that fact, you must also recognize that if that human being does not exercise that power, violations of the statute will result.

There is necessarily involved a delegation of authority to someone. We call it "delegation" when the enforcing authority is given to administrative agencies; we do not use the word "delegation" when we give that authority to a prosecuting attorney or to a stockholder; but, nevertheless, there is a delegation no matter what words we use. For the decision as to when and whether to enforce the statute has to be made by someone, whether that someone be a Department of Justice, a prosecuting attorney, or a stockholder. The statute won't enforce itself, if men are minded not to comply. Someone, somewhere, has to have the discretion to enforce laws; whether the penalties be civil, criminal, or injunctive, that is true. We do not usually use the word "discretion" in that context; but yet it is discretion, because there has to be a decision by some person as to whether and when the statute is to be enforced.

SENATOR O'MAHONEY: Of course, that isn't entirely correct. It has not been the theory upon which our law has been built up at all. As a matter of fact, the fundamental principle which is taught in every elementary law school with respect to criminal law, for example, is this, that it is better to allow nine guilty persons to escape than to punish one innocent person. That is our fundamental principle. Our economic system has become so complicated that we have been endeavoring to escape from that fundamental, and somehow or other to clothe some government authority with the power to take every violator by the back of the neck and rub his nose in the sand, regardless of the effect upon the innocent, and it is because the innocent have been compelled to suffer along with those who have violated it, that we find such a fear among many businessmen of what they call government regulation. I feel that we have got to find the way to do as you suggested a moment ago, to make men a little more like angels, but I would express that rather in this way, to say to get a better understanding among a larger proportion of business leaders of the abuses that ought to be abolished.

I fear, in other words, that there is always the danger of creating more abuses by vesting discretionary power in any government than there is from permitting things to govern themselves as far as possible.

Set up your standards for the masses of the people and that is the most you can hope to do, because when all is said and done, law is the crystallization of public opinion, and you can no more enforce the antitrust law upon the business community without an understanding upon the part of the business community of what ought to be abandoned, than you could enforce prohibition among the masses of the people. Unless the people want a law enforced, it won't be enforced, no matter how large a government machinery you establish to carry it out.

MR. FRANK: Senator, I most heartily agree with you as to that last point. I think any governmental arrangement or economic institution cannot be effective and persist unless it is founded upon the habits of the community. Those habits can be changed to some extent by law, but in the last analysis any law must have a foundation in a favorable community attitude. But, unless we proceed on the hypothesis (which none of us would be willing to accept in toto) that all laws should be abolished, or that laws should merely be hortatory and never enforced in courts of law, we must rely upon someone to enforce them. Now to enact into a statute a provision that something has to be done, is not sufficient, unless there be somebody who can enforce it either, as I say, by way of damages, by way of injunction, or by way of penalties.

I am heartily in accord with you on this point: I don't know anyone who could feel more strongly than I that in this day of all days we need to guard against the abuse of the innocent, the terrorizing of the innocent by the threat of the use of state force against them without the preservation of their civil liberties. If anything, we should throw more safeguards about the innocent to prevent the abuse of criminal enforcing powers in the hands of prosecutors. But, whether it be by criminal law, civil law, equity or common law, statute or otherwise, merely writing or having something in a law, or merely putting something in a charter, saying "This shall" or "This shall not be done," isn't sufficient, because it won't work automatically. Somebody has got to have, whatever you want to call it—"discretion," "judgment," or the like—as to whether or not, and when, the statute shall be enforced.

We have on the books of most States thousands of laws. All of them cannot be enforced, some of them are obsolete, some of them are inadequately drafted, some of them are just plain foolish. The enforcing officer, the prosecuting officer, having to do with these criminal laws, has to make a selection. He has to determine which statutes to enforce and which of the numerous suspected violators to enforce them against. We are not accustomed to calling the power to make that selection "discretion." But we can't enforce all laws against all violators or, as you said, half the people in the United States (I should say three-fourths of the people in the United States) would be engaged in enforcing law. Whether you call it "discretion" or not, somebody has to make a choice.

SENATOR O'MAHONEY: Let me give you an example of what I mean. In the bill which Senator Borah and I have introduced from time to time for the establishing of Federal licensing or a Federal franchise system, it is provided among other things that no person who has himself loaned money to a corporation, or who is a director of an institution which has loaned money to a corporation, may be a director of that corporation. Now I want to ask you, as a lawyer, whether you think that any lawyer would advise the director of a bank to allow himself to be elected director of a corporation which was borrowing from that bank, or whether the corporation which was borrowing it would permit the director of a bank to continue to serve as director. Would it be necessary to clothe anybody with discretion to enforce a provision of that kind?

MR. FRANK: Senator, I can answer that best by saying that similar statutes have been on the books and have been violated, or have been allowed to go into desuetude. I think the history of "corporation law" shows that clients in those instances either do not go to their lawyer, or go to a foolish lawyer, or a crooked lawyer, and also that they find all kinds of devices for apparently complying so that they can salve their consciences or their lawyer's conscience, or meet his high or low standard of intelligence sufficiently so that they are willing to do what you or I would consider a violation of statute. I just can't think of any law that some people haven't violated, and unfortunately, some people who ought to know better.

Senator O'Mahoney's generalization as to the vice of granting discretionary powers to administrative bodies or officials is typical. It expresses the age-old longing that all laws should be self-operative. . . .

At times, the attack on administrative regulation, instead of using the angel argument, employs what might be called the devil thesis: "You can't make men honest by law or regulation," it is said, "so what's the use of trying?" That devil thesis is based on what we have called negative perfectionism, a demand that, if a statute is not sure to be 100 percent effective, then it ought not to be enacted. Such a position is bottomed on a sort of diabolic anarchism. And the answer is obvious: Of course, laws and regulations cannot make all men honest. But that does not mean that one must go to the other extreme and abolish all laws prescribing standards of honesty. There are thieves and murderers in the world despite the fact that there are laws against theft and murder; but no one in his senses would want to repeal those laws. Many laws have their effects, partly because fear of punishment for their violation acts as a deterrent; partly, because, as already indicated, after a long period of enforcement by governments, the existence of the standards that the laws embody creates habits so strong that most men will not even contemplate breaking those laws but come to accept them as they do the air they breathe. When, however, laws deal with a complicated subject matter, different considerations apply. "I think," said Judge Hucheson, "it would be very foolish for us to expect, as to a great many of our laws, that they will be self-operating. Consider the oil business. We could not simply pass a law saying that nobody can produce more than so much oil, out of his well, nobody can produce more than so much gas, nobody can drill a well or equip or operate it except in a certain way, and then for enforcement of it look only to a criminal proceeding against the violators. That was for a long time the idea of law enforcement; pass the law; if somebody violates it, bring him into court and punish him. But no one has that idea now. Except in regard to the simplest matter, the legislative body, which represents the people in passing laws, now appoints administrative boards or agencies for the purpose of administering the laws. These administrative agencies within the scope of the law, may and do make rules and regulations clarifying and applying the law, so that instead of going out on their own and taking the chance of being haled into court for having violated the law, the people look to the boards to blueprint the matter for them and advise them how to conform." Such bodies, he says, "are designed to teach people to obey law (not as we teach our dogs, and sometimes our people, by beating them when they disobey), but by teaching them as they should be taught, taking care that they know the law in advance, and are furnished with the information how, and the inclination, to obey it. . . .

And yet, daily, such useful and indispensable agencies are denounced as "bureaucracy." That is merely a "snarl word" for the "administration" essential in any large-scale enterprise, whether governmental or business. "The industrial revolution," says Riesman, "multiplied the division of labor in factory and office. It gave us technical skill and management, the Siamese twins bureaucracy binds together. * * * Mass armies, mass industries, mass cities—these brought bureaucracy about, and they in turn depend on it." . . .

Why is regulation of some businesses needed? The primary reason is complexity: The industrial and financial machinery of the nation has become so complicated that the average person has had to turn to the government to preserve certain of his rights and individual liberties. Various parts of the business community, because of this increasing complexity, have asked government for protection against other parts of the business community. Thus we have, for instance, statutes against misrepresentation of products and unfair competitive practices.

Many of the statutes which some businessmen denounce as "hostile to business" were actually sponsored and are supported by a large portion of business itself. . . .

America can work out its destinies under a political democracy and inside the profit system. If it could not succeed in doing so, then our country would be in for the gravest kind of difficulties. Now, at the basis of the profit system are trust and confidence. And undermining of them tends to destroy that system. The Communists assert that it is an inherent and ineradicable vice of the profit system that it is unable to purge itself of improper practices in connection with such matters as transactions in the capital market. . . . The answer to the Communists' criticism must take the form, not of mere verbal denials, but of a demonstration that, with relatively minor exceptions, such misconduct will not and cannot occur. It is patent that past devices are insufficient to that end. The preservation of our kind of economy, therefore, necessitated the creation of new devices, designed to prevent such abuses of trust and confidence. And since the judiciary, for obvious reasons, cannot adequately be implemented to discharge that time-consuming function, it is imperative that that function be assigned to adequately staffed governmental administrative agencies. . . .

\* \* \* \* \*

. . . Adverse critics of the federal administrative agencies often jumble together a more or less disparate set of ideas: They say that such agencies violate the maxim of "a government of laws, and not of men," because those agencies exercise discretion in the application of delegated legislative power; this power they exercise, in combination with judicial and executive powers, in a way which is not in keeping with the doctrine of the "separation of power"; and thus they traduce the principle of "checks and balances." Are those ideas justifiably associated or should they be dissociated?

Let us first consider objections to the vesting of discretion in the federal administrative agencies, objections to giving them the power to apply general rules or standards, laid down by Congress, to a variety of particular circumstances—through making subordinate rules or regulations to specific cases. Such protests are frequently phrased thus: To grant such discretion, it is said, is to create a "government of men" and to offend against the principle of a "government of laws." Is that criticism well founded? Is such discretionary power inconsistent with the idea of "a government of laws"? We will be the better able to answer those questions if we see whence that idea came:

The first notable use in this country of the phrase, "a government of laws, and not of men," was in the Bill of Rights of the Massachusetts Constitution of 1780. (The provision reads: "In the government of this commonwealth, the legislative department shall never exercise the executive and judicial powers, or either of them: the executive shall never exercise the legislative and judicial powers, or either of them: the judicial shall never exercise the legislative and executive powers, or either of them; to the end it may be a government of laws and not of men.") That instrument was drafted by John Adams, who later became our second President. He was much influenced by Harrington's *Oceana*, published in 1656 and dedicated to Oliver Cromwell.

That book had popularized the "government of laws" phrase in English-speaking countries.

Harrington was a curious mixture: He comforted Charles the First in his last days, yet he was opposed to monarchy. His treatise has been called "a singular blending of democratic and aristocratic principles." He endeavored to combine "such apparently contradictory tendencies as those derived from the democracy of English Puritanism and the oligarchy of Venice. In the Commonwealth which he proposed there was to be a written constitution, establishing a bicameral legislature (a Senate and an Assembly) and providing for elections to office by a secret ballot, and for rotation in office. But senators must be worth a hundred pounds a year. He believed that the government of the Commonwealth should and would be conducted by "a natural aristocracy"; it could only be carried on by "gentlemen." ("There is something, first in the making of a Commonwealth, then in the governing * * * which * * * seems to be peculiar to the Genius of a Gentleman." "A Nobility or Gentry in a popular government is not over-balancing, it is the very life and soul of it.") Says Levett, "For the small landowner Harrington showed little concern; he was an aristocratic republican with a strong belief in the 'genius of a gentleman.'" He believed that his Commonwealth should be a world empire, saying, "To ask whether it be lawful for a Commonwealth to aspire to the empire of the world, it is to ask whether it be lawful for it to do its duty, or to put the world in better condition than it was before." And that idea was coupled with the undemocratic thesis that it is not safe to give colonists full ownership of land, for to do so would be to give root to a liberty abroad that might be hostile to the mother state.

Gough reports that Harrington's "* * * doctrinaire mind was more concerned that a system should be correct than workable in practice." And Dwight remarks: "The prime feature of Harrington's scheme is that a government can be made to run forever, if there is only good machinery, well oiled, and of the most improved pattern." Many present-day Americans who speak of a government of laws, and not of men, still cherish that fatuous hope of contriving a mechanically perfect, human-proof, government. However, Harrington was not so simple-minded. His program was by no means without merit; otherwise it would not have impressed keen thinkers like John Adams and Daniel Webster.

Harrington's political thought, it has been said, "appears to owe much to Plato's *Laws*." It certainly owed much to Aristotle, for whom Plato's writings were a starting point. Indeed, Harrington admittedly derived the famous phrase from that great Greek political thinker; he avows his intention to answer Hobbes's comment that "it is another error of Aristotle's *Politics* that in a well ordered Commonwealth, not Men should govern, but the Laws." In our search for the meaning of the famous phrase, then, we should go back to Plato and Aristotle. It is to be noted that Plato did not have a high regard for democracy. Indeed, he has been referred to—and not altogether without reason—as a regimenting totalitarian, with little regard for free speech, and as an advocate of the use of concentration camps. Plato's student, Aristotle, was far less of a regimenter. But the state which he favored was not what today we consider a democracy. It was founded on slavery. His defense of that institution was one widely used by the slave party in the Old South in this country; also it could be quoted, with gusto, by Hitler today. Without knowledge of the facts, a case against Aristotle as a believer in Hitlerism might be made out on the basis that Alexander the Great, the imperialist, a sort of moderate Greek Hitler, was Aristotle's pupil. But the teacher had no admiration for, or interest in, imperialism, his major interest being in the Hellenic city-state; in that kind of city-state which he considered most desirable there was no room for dictatorship. Yet, like his own teacher, Plato, Aristotle seems, at times, to have had a sneaking admiration for the government of Sparta—which is an excellent model, on a small scale, for a totalitarian state.

To be sure, that an idea emanates from persons devoted to forms of government which are undemocratic or less democratic than ours does not necessarily deprive it of all value for those who are devoted to democracy. We would not reject discoveries in physics or medicine merely because they were imported from Nazi Germany. ("But why should we not use such parts of foreign contrivances as we want," asked Woodrow Wilson, "if they be in any way serviceable? We are in no danger of using them in a foreign way. We borrowed rice, but we do not eat it with chopsticks.") While, then, we should be cautious about accepting, too glibly, Aristotelian epigrams as slogans for contemporary American democracy, it would be folly to conclude that we cannot learn much about many aspects of government from the studies of Aristotle, one of the shrewdest observers of the ways of human beings.

But we must beware of misinterpreting writers of other times and climes. Ancient Greek glassware, buried in the soil and excavated after centuries, has an acquired iridescence not native to its original condition. Something not unlike that metamorphosis often affects ancient Greek texts. Simkhovitch has pointed out that "because we 'understand' things in our own way (i.e., in terms of our own general and specific attitudes), we imagine that we understand concepts, ideas or words that belong to a foreign culture or a different plane of thought. That is not the case. Our understanding is only 'our' understanding; the very words have only the meaning that our culture supplies." There is much wisdom in Anatole France's comment that it is the ingenious labor of gloss and super-gloss which alone perpetuates works of genius through the ages. The long life of a masterpiece is assured only at the price of quite pitiable intellectual hazards, in which the gabble of pedants reinforces the ingenious word-twisting of aesthetic souls. I am not afraid to say that, at the present day, we do not understand a single line of the *Iliad*, of the *Divine Comedy*, in the sense primitively attaching to it. To live is to change, and the posthumous life of our written-down thoughts is not free from the rule; they only continue to exist on condition that they become more and more different from what they were when they issued from our minds. Whatsoever in future may be admired in us, will have become altogether alien from us.

Accordingly, any current interpretation of Plato's or Aristotle's writings may well be something of a distortion. With such apologies, let us proceed.

Certainly, there is no excuse for an interpretation which consists of using phrases torn from their context. Yet that method has frequently been applied to Aristotle. When learned persons speak of "a government of laws" as incompatible with delegated discretion, they often refer to or quote, Aristotle's lines that "the law ought to be supreme over all"; that "he who bids the law rule, may be deemed to bid God and reason rule, but he who bids man rule adds an element of the beast"; that "whereas the law is passionless, passion must ever rule the hearts of men"; and that "the rule of law is preferable to that of any individual." But those lines are parts—lifted out of their explanatory context—or extended Aristotelian arguments in no manner directed against discretion in the application of general rules. Let us see what Aristotle was talking about when he used those famous phrases.

Aristotle's *Politics* is, in considerable measure, a reaction to, and criticism of, Plato's *Republic*, *Laws*, and the *Statesman*. Wherefore, to understand the *Politics*, it is necessary, in turn, briefly to note the character of those writings of Plato's:

The *Republic* was the product of Plato's younger days. There he depicted his ideal state. Such a state, in which the wise men would govern, cannot, he said, be established "until philosophers are kings, or the kings and princes * * * have the spirit and power of philosophy, and political greatness and wisdom meet in one * * *." Apparently he had hoped that in some state there would be "a tyrant who was young, temperate, quick at learning, having a good memory, courageous, and of a noble nature," "who would have as his contemporary" a great legislator, and that some happy chance "would bring them together." The "best government is produced from a tyranny and originates in a good law giver and an orderly tyrant, and most easily and readily passes out of such a tyranny into a perfect form of government * * *." And perhaps he thought that such a "happy chance" had occurred when he was invited to serve as a brain truster to a "tyrant" (a sort of benevolent despot) in Syracuse. But, alas, the experiment failed; he discovered that the Hitlers of this world are not amenable to philosophers. Made wiser and sadder by that experience, he wrote the *Laws* and the *Statesman* in which he dealt more with actual and possible governments as distinguished from the ideal.

Reviewing what he had written earlier, Plato (if we assume that Socrates is speaking for him in those dialogues) says in the *Statesman* that, in an ideal government, one or two or a few would govern, as a science, whether with or without law (that is, general rules). He states that "*the best thing of all is not that the law should govern, but that a man should rule,* supposing him to have wisdom and royal power." For the law "is like an obstinate and ignorant tyrant" who will not allow anything to be done contrary to commands he has once given, "not even in a sudden change of circumstances"; the law, he suggests, also resembles, a foolish physician who would prescribe inflexibly for his patient, regardless of changes in the patient's condition. The "best thing," says Plato, would be a government by the wisest man,

because the law does not perfectly comprehend what is best. The differences of men and actions, and the endless irregular movements of human things, do not admit of any universal and simple rule. And no art whatsoever can lay down a rule which will last for all time. * * * But the law is always striving to make one. * * * A perfectly simple principle can never be applied to a state of things which is the reverse of simple.

The law is unable "to provide exactly what is suitable for each particular case." The legislator "will lay down laws in general form for the majority, roughly meeting the cases of individuals. * * * For how can he sit at every man's side all through his life, prescribing for him the exact particulars of his duty?" (Putting that in verbiage of our day, Plato was saying that "individualization" of cases is impossible.) Since the best (that is, flexible government by a wise ruler with or without law) is not attainable, we must reluctantly fall back on the "second best"—"not to allow either the individual or the multitude to break the law in any respect," by providing that "no citizen shall do anything contrary to the laws." "*The nearest approach" to the ideal of "the true government of the one scientific ruler" is "to do nothing contrary to * * * written laws and national customs.*"

Here, as in the *Laws*, "he still casts longing eyes upon the ideal, which he acknowledges to be impossible in practice." The consequence is that, in his disappointment at the unattainability of his ideal, he tends to go to the other extreme and to shut out of his description of the "second best" the practicable means for avoiding the legal rigidities which he deplores.

Aristotle, in his *Politics*, replying to Plato, is, as always, impatient with an abstract discussion of the desirable—except to the extent that it is realizable in practice. Specifically referring to Plato, he says, "In framing an ideal we may assume what we wish, but should avoid impossibilities." And again:

For the best is often unattainable, and therefore the true legislator and states-man ought to be acquainted not only with that which is best in the abstract, but also with that which is best relatively to circumstances. * * * For political writers, although they have excellent ideas, are often impractical. We should consider not only what form of government is best, but also what is possible and what is easily attainable by all.

Accordingly, he describes the different forms of government, "relatively to given conditions, since a particular government may be preferable, but an-other form may be better for some people"; he aims "to consider what and what kind of government is suitable to what and what kind of men."

With that approach, he gives a somewhat revised emphasis to Plato's classification of the divers kinds of government. He classifies governments as those in which there is rule by (a) the one, or (b) the few, or (c) the many. He then subdivides each of those classifications into its true and its perverted form. The true forms are those in which government is conducted "with a view to the common interest; but governments which rule with a view to the private interest whether of the one, or the few, or the many, are perversions." So the true forms are (1) monarchy, (2) aristocracy, and (3) polity (a con-stitutional government). The respective perversions are (1) tyranny, (2) oligarchy, and (3) democracy. "For tyranny is a kind of monarchy which has in view the interest of the monarch only; oligarchy has in view the interest of the wealthy; democracy, of the needy; none of them the common good of all." (He says that, in an oligarchy, the principle of selection for office is wealth; in a democracy freedom or equality; in an aristocracy, merit. [A democracy exists when the authority is in the hands of the free and poor who are in the majority, and an oligarchy when it is in the hands of the propertied who are in the minority.] A polity [or constitutional government] results from a fusion of these principles of oligarchy and democracy; if the merit principle of aristocracy is added, then there is polity which most nearly approximates the ideal.) There are many types of each of the governmental forms; for instance, there are five kinds of democracy. He appraises the several forms and types of government by two touchstones: their stability, and their capacity to yield the good life for their citizens. On both scores he concludes that a considerable measure of popular participation in government is usually de-sirable. But there is a grave defect in ultrademocratic government.

And here we come to his treatment of the problem posed by Plato. Aristotle, with his common sense, and in the light of his extensive study of actual governments and his experience as a "practicing politician," rejects Plato's needlessly sharp antithesis between (1) an ideal government, flexibly administered by the best man or men, and (2) a government by rigid and invariable laws. It is possible, Aristotle saw, to reconcile the need for generality in laws and the need for adaptation of laws to particular circumstances. He restates the problem thus:

A "law" means a general rule. When there is government by one or a few (with no popular participation in government) then there is no differentiation between the functions of (a) enacting general rules and (b) issuing specific decrees or orders, each relating to a particular occasion or affecting a particular person or object. And the same, he says, is true in democracies when the populace acting in a legislative assembly, is not confined to the enactment of "laws," that is, general rules, but also makes specific decrees. The making of such specific decrees is not a proper legislative function. The application of the general rules—the laws—to particular cases should be left to the citizens acting in a different capacity as courts or left to other officials.

But in the application of any general rule, discretion is, he said, unavoidably involved, for a general rule—a law—cannot deal in detail with all particular cases. In that way he solved the problem left unsolved by Plato. Thus he writes of one kind of democracy

in which not the law, but the multitude, have the supreme power and supersede the law by their decrees. This is a state of affairs brought about by the demagogues. For in democracies which are subject to the law the best citizens hold the first place, and there are no demagogues; but where the laws are not supreme, there demagogues spring up. For the people becomes a monarch, and is many in one; and the many have the power in their hands, not as individuals, but collectively. * * * At all events, this sort of democracy, which is now a monarch * * * seeks to exercise monarchical sway and grows into a despot * * * ; this sort of democracy being relatively to other democracies what tyranny is to other forms of monarchy. The spirit of both is the same, and they alike exercise a despotic rule over the better citizens. *The decrees of the demos correspond to the edicts of the tyrant.* * * * *The demagogues make the decree of the people override the laws, by referring all things to the popular assembly.* * * * Such a democracy is fairly open to the objection that it is not a constitution at all; for where the laws have no authority, there is no constitution. *The law ought to be supreme over all, and the magistracies should judge of particulars, and only this should be considered a constitution. So that* * * * *the sort of system in which all things are regulated by decrees is clearly not even a democracy in the true sense of the word, for decrees relate only to particulars.*

In a passage in which (in connection with a discussion of the desirability of general participation in government) he remarks that "the rule of law is preferable to that of any individual," he also significantly says:

Nay, there may indeed be cases which the law seems unable to determine, but in such cases can a man? Nay, it will be replied, *the law trains officers for this express purpose, and appoints them to determine matters which are left un-*

*decided by it to the best of their judgment.* Further it permits them to make any amendment of the existing laws which experience suggests. *Therefore, he who bids the law rule, may be deemed to bid God and Reason alone rule, but he who bids man rule adds an element of the beast; for desire is a wild beast, and passion perverts the minds of rulers, even when they are the best of men. The law is reason unaffected by desire.* * * * And at this day there are some magistrates, for example judges, who have authority to decide matters which the law is unable to determine, since no one doubts that the law would command and decide in the best manner whatever it could. *But some things can, and other things cannot, be comprehended under the law, and this is the origin of the vexed question whether the best law or the best man should rule. For matters of detail about which men deliberate cannot be included in legislation. Nor does anyone deny that the decision of such matters must be left to man.* * * *

In other words, Aristotle was saying that, while no "law"—no general rule—can (to use modern jargon) "individualize" cases, yet it is feasible—through adequate ascertainment of the facts of specific cases to which the general rules are applied by officials—to achieve at least moderate "individualization." Thus Aristotle substituted "both-and" thinking for the "either-to" thinking of Plato.

And so, when we find set forth in American state instruments, such as the Massachusetts Bill of Rights, the slogan "a government of laws, and not of men," let us remember that its first author, Aristotle, was not talking of rigid, inflexible rules of law mechanically applied; he was referring to rules administered by trained officers appointed to "determine matters, which are left undecided by" general rules, and to determine them, "to the best of their judgment." Why? Because "the decision of such matters" in particular cases "must be left to man." And this was his conclusion, despite his awareness that men are fallible and despite his assertion that "passion must ever sway the heart of man."

Aristotle, in other writings, discussed "discretion" (which he called "equity") in what most persons would consider a strikingly "modern" fashion. He wrote

that all law is couched in general terms, but there are some cases upon which it is impossible to pronounce correctly in general terms. Accordingly, where a general statement is necessary, but such a statement cannot be correct, the law embraces the majority of cases, although it does not ignore the element of error. Nor is it the less correct on this account; for the error lies not in the law, nor in the legislature, but in the nature of the case. For it is plainly impossible to pronounce with complete accuracy upon such a subject matter as human action. Whenever then the terms of the law are general, but the particular case is an exception to the general law, it is right, where the legislator's rule is inadequate or erroneous in virtue of its generality, to rectify the defect which the legislator himself, if he were present, would admit, and had he known it, would have rectified in legislating. That which is equitable then is just, and better than one kind of justice, not indeed better than absolute justice, but better than the error of justice which arises from legal generality. This is in fact the nature of the equitable; it is rectification of law where it fails through generality. For the reason why things are not all determined by law is that there are some things about which it is impossible to lay down a law and for which a special decree is therefore necessary. For where the thing to be measured is indefinite the rule must be indefinite, like the leaden rule that is used in Lesbian architecture; for as the rule is not rigid but adapts itself to the shape of the stone, so does the decree to the circumstances of the case.

Elsewhere he said:

The equitable seems to be just, and equity is a kind of justice, but goes beyond the written law. This margin is left by legislators, sometimes voluntarily, sometimes involuntarily; involuntarily when the point escapes their notice, voluntarily when they are unable to frame a definition, and yet it is necessary to lay down an absolute rule; also in cases where inexperience makes it hard to define * * * ; *for life would not be long enough for a person who tried to enumerate the cases.*

And again he said: "As in other sciences, so in politics, it is impossible that all things should be precisely set down in writing; for enactments must be universal, but actions are concerned with particulars."

Thus Aristotle, the father of the phrase "a government of laws, and not of men," far from being an opponent, was a lucid advocate of the thesis that discretion and individualization of cases are desirable and necessary elements of any practicable system of government. . . .

Were Congress, which is concerned with enacting laws—statutes containing rules of wide general application—also to decide specific cases and to make specific decrees, then Aristotle would say that we had a "government of men." (Congressional "private bill" legislation has something of that character.) But he would not say that ours had ceased to be "a government of laws" merely because Congress delegates discretion to apply the general rules, made by it, through subordinate administrative rules and through specific orders in specific cases.

"There may be indeed cases which the law seems unable to determine, but in such cases, can a man? Nay, it will be answered, the law trains officers for this express purpose, and appoints them to determine matters which are left undecided by it, to the best of their judgment." Those words of Aristotle sound familiar to American lawyers: Aristotle was anticipating the verbiage in which the United States Supreme Court has justified the delegation of discretion to administrative officials. In *Buttfield* v. *Stranahan*, . . . the Court said: "Congress legislated on the subject as far as was reasonably practicable, and from the necessities of the case, was compelled to leave to executive officials the duty of bringing about the result pointed out by the statute." In *Panama Refining Co.* v. *Ryan* . . . it said:

Undoubtedly, legislation must often be adapted to complex conditions involving a host of details with which the national legislature cannot deal directly. The Constitution has never been regarded as denying to the Congress the necessary resources of flexibility and practicability. * * * Without capacity to give authorizations of that sort we should have the anomaly of a legislative power which, in many circumstances calling for its exertion, would be but a futility.

In those and other cases, the Supreme Court has held statutes constitutional which vested in administrative officers the discretionary power to make subordinate rules or regulations, and to make specific decisions or orders, applying the statute or such rules or regulations, to specific situations.

Aristotle, in arriving at his conclusion that delegation of discretion to apply laws did not given rise to a "government of men" as distinguished from a "government of laws," was not unmindful that the administration of justice, involved, inescapably, a personal element. For, in typical Greek trials, evidence was presented to, and cases were decided by, batches of from 201 to 1,001 jurors who, in deciding, *not only determined questions of fact but questions of "law."* Such popular courts are commended by Aristotle. And, in the Greek legal system, says Vinogradoff, so far as it is concerned with the application of equity,

*the subjective element is very prominent.* * * * The courts were influenced by * * * subjective considerations, which sounded plausible, and appealed to public opinion .* * * It is clear that the administration of law in Athens demanded wide discretion on the part of the Courts. In the first place, we are often told that the old laws—especially those of Solon, which in the fourth century were still recognized, as the foundation of existing law—were archaic and obscure. But the clumsiness and difficulty of the legislative process made it hard to introduce amendments in good time; consequently they mostly retained their archaic form, and the best course open for amendment was to use wide discretion in interpreting and applying them. *This is expressed in the oath taken by the Heliasts [jurors] in which they say that if there is a law covering the case, they will obey it, but if the application be doubtful they will judge "to the best of their belief."* * * * It is evident from the speeches that the range of "considerations of justice" was very extensive, and was not really restricted to cases where there were no laws.

(Our own jury system, although less openly, operates in much the same way. . . .)

Aristotle wrote in an era of handicraft industry, of a small city-state, which, he thought, would be too large if its population consisted, as Plato suggested, of 5,000 citizens (about 30,000 inhabitants) and which should be so small that it "can all be taken in at a single view." He had a strong bias against concentration of wealth and against those engaged in trade. He was opposed to interest-taking. And, as we have seen, he fully recognized the necessity of exercising discretion in the application of general laws to particular cases. He would, then, surely be aghast to discover his writings employed today—in a highly industrialized country, 3,000 miles wide, with a population of 130 millions—to criticize governmental regulation of "big business" by administrative agencies vested with discretion in applying general regulatory laws to particular business situations.

He would be surprised, as well, to find men like Pound still having difficulty in solving the problem which Aristotle, answering Plato, thought he had solved in the *Politics*, centuries ago. And, he would be surprised, too, to find a thinker like Pound unable to comprehend this fact: that one who admits that there is an ineradicable personal element in the administration and application of general legal rules is not, for that reason, to be accused of (1) espousing "a regime of unchecked administrative discretion," the governance, without rules, "by the wise leader of his people," an "administrative absolutism" which posits "ex-officio omniscience" and the "disappearance of law because it is superseded by an omnicompetent administration"; or (2) insisting that there is no choice except "between the logical extremes of anarchy or absolutism," that "the arbitral, personal, subjective element in magisterial behavior * * * is the reality" and that "accumulated experience" is a "mere shame"; or (3) urging that "the results achieved by long experience of administering justice according to law can be achieved by * * * the wisest of men acting on single cases with nothing but their personal judgment to guide them" (Pound, *Contemporary Juristic Theory*, . . .). Aristotle would say, if he read Pound's latest book: "This man, like Plato, is learned; but, like Plato, too, he is so eager for what he regards as an ideal state that he cannot content himself with what is practically achievable; as a consequence, he fails to observe with accuracy what actually does exist and what can exist."

This much we can surely say: For Aristotle, from whom Harrington derived the notion of a government of laws, and not of men, that notion was not expressive of hostility to what today we call administrative discretion. Nor did it have such a meaning for Harrington. (Because Harrington was more doctrinaire than Aristotle, he pays relatively little attention to the problems of administration with which Aristotle was much concerned when he discussed a government of laws.) With him it was tied into a concept of the relation of government to property. And here again we must note how Aristotle's thinking affected him:

Aristotle made much of what Beard has called "the economic basis of politics," maintaining that one of the prime problems of government is to arrange a stable balance between the interests of the major economic groups. After describing the various forms which government takes, he explained the factors which make for stability—the causes and means of preventing revolutions: "The legislator * * * should endeavor to have a firm foundation according to the principles * * * concerning the preservation and destruction of states. * * *" He must regard the relation between the status of the groups in the state and the governmental forms; the fundamental question is the respective participations of the several classes. "The reason why there are many forms of government is that every state contains many elements." "Now in all states there are three elements: one class is rich, another very poor, and a third in a mean" (that is, the middle class). The last "are most ready to follow rational principle (reason)."

Those who have too much of the goods of fortune, strength, wealth, friends, and the like, are neither willing nor able to submit to authority. * * * On the other hand, the very poor * * * are too degraded. So that the one class cannot obey, and can only rule despotically; the other knows not how to command and must be ruled like slaves. Thus arises a city, not of free-men, but of masters and slaves, the one despising, the other envying. But a city ought to be composed of equals and similars; and these are generally the middle classes.

The stabilizing element is that class. If they are absent, "the rich and poor quarrel with one another," and one side or the other tends to get the better, establishing, usually, only a temporary dominance. "Political revolutions" often "spring from a disproportionate increase in any part of the state" as when the number of poor increases. "When the rich grow numerous or properties increase, the form of government changes into an oligarchy or a government of families." "Revolutions also break out when opposite parties, e.g., the rich and the people, are equally balanced and there is little or no middle class. * * *

Thus it is manifest that the best political community is formed by citizens of the middle class, and that those states are likely to be well administered, in which the middle class is large, and stronger if possible than both the other classes, or at any rate than either singly; for the addition of the middle class turns the scale, and prevents either of the extremes from being dominant. Great then is the fortune of the state in which the citizens have a moderate and sufficient property; for where some possess much, and the others nothing, there may rise an extreme democracy, or a pure oligarchy; or a tyranny may grow out of either extreme—either out of the most rampant democracy, or out of an oligarchy; but it is not so likely to arise out of the middle constitutions (polities) or those akin to them. The mean condition of states is clearly the best, for no other is free from faction; and where the middle class is large, there are less likely to be factions and dissensions. For a similar reason large states are less liable to faction than small ones, because the middle class is large. And democracies are safer and more permanent than oligarchies, because they have a middle class which is more numerous and has a greater share in government; for when there is no middle class and the poor greatly exceed in number, trouble arises, and the state soon comes to an end. * * * The legislator should always include the middle class in his government; if he makes his laws oligarchical, to the middle class let him look; if he makes them democractic, he should equally by his laws try to attach this class to the state. * * *

The more perfect the admixture of the political elements, said Aristotle, the more lasting will be the constitution. "Many even of those who desire to form aristocratical governments make a mistake, not only in giving too much power to the rich, but in attempting to over-reach the people. There comes a time when out of a false good there arises a true evil, since the encroachments of the rich are more destructive to the constitution than those of the people." (Aristotle is not dogma-ridden: He does not overlook accidents as important factors in history. "In revolutions," he says, "the occasions may be trifling, but great interests are at stake." So he tells how "the Syracusan constitution was once changed by a love-quarrel of two young men, who were in the government." And once in Hestiaea, the occasion of a revolution was a quarrel about the division of an inheritance between two brothers, while, at Delphi, "a quarrel about a marriage was the beginning of all the troubles which followed." . . .) "Especially should the laws provide against anyone having too much power, whether derived from friends or money. * * * There ought to be a magistracy which will have an eye to those whose life is not in harmony with the government. And for a like reason an increase in prosperity of any part of the state should be watched." One way is "to increase the middle class." If would seem, then, that Aristotle had this in mind: If there was a proper balance of interests—and primarily a balance of economic interests—then government would function as it should; there would then be no capricious decrees uttered by legislative assemblies, and "laws" (general rules) would be applied by proper agencies of government in individual cases. An appropriate balance of interests would thus yield a government of laws and not a government of men.

The effect of the impact on Harrington of Aristotle's economic-political views was profound: Harrington proposed a Commonwealth based on a proper balancing of property interests. He said that his book was devoted to "the skill of raising such superstructures of government as are natural to the known foundations." And the foundations he found in the division of property among the citizens. (It should be noted that Karl Marx, who seemingly owes much to Harrington, frequently used that metaphor of "foundation" and "superstructure.") Harrington's discussion of "an empire of laws, and not of men," is directly connected with that economic thesis.

He begins his book by splitting the history of government into two periods, one (ending with the end of the Roman republic and the rise of the Caesars) which he calls the "empire of ancient prudence"; the second (beginning with "the arms of Caesar") which he calls "modern prudence." He then goes on thus: "Government (to define it [de jure] or according to ancient prudence) is an art whereby a civil society of men is instituted upon the foundation of common right or interest, or (to follow Aristotle and Livy) it is the empire of laws and not of men. And government (to define it [de facto] or according to modern prudence) is an art whereby some man, or some few men, subject a city or a nation, and rule it according unto his or their private interest; which, because the laws in such cases are made according to the interest of a man, or of some few families, may be said to be the empire of men, and not of laws."

He says that "domestic empire" is founded upon "dominion," and that dominion is property, real or personal. Land is, he notes, in most countries, far more important. "Such as is the proportion or balance of dominion or property in land, such is the nature of empire." (He recognized that where the economy was based on money or trade, as in Holland or Genoa, a balance could be based on that kind of property. . . .) Accordingly, if one man owns most of the land, there is a monarchy; and if a few, an aristocracy. "And if the whole people be landlords, or hold the lands so divided among them that no one man, or number of men * * * overbalance them, the Empire * * * is a commonwealth." The key to government is the "balance of power." He explained the course of English history, culminating in the beheading of Charles I, as due to economic causes: Henry VIII had divided the large estates of the nobility destroyed in the Wars of the Roses, among relatively small owners, and later, by breaking up the monasteries and dividing up their properties, dispossessed the greatest of English landlords, the Church. In that way, wealth was redistributed among a multitude of persons. As control of the land had passed into the hands of the middle class, they acquired the sources of political power; sooner or later government had to conform to the distribution of property. He reaches the conclusion that "equality of estates causeth equality of power, and equality of power is the liberty not only of the Commonwealth but of every man." Accordingly, to establish and maintain an "equal commonwealth," he proposes an "agrarian law" requiring the division of large estates among heirs so that no one could have an annual income of more than £2,000.

He poses this problem: "But seeing that they that make the laws in a commonwealth are but men, the main question seems to be, how a commonwealth comes to be an empire of laws, and not of men? Or how the debate or result of a commonwealth is sure to be according unto reason; seeing that they who debate, and they who resolve be but men." For men may be "against reason."

His answer is simple: "Reason is nothing but interest." And in his discussion shows he means property (or economic) interest. If, then, there are "divers interests," there will be "divers reason." Now there is "private reason" —which is the "interest of a private man." There is also "reason of State" which is the "interest of the ruler or rulers." And finally, there is "that reason which is the interest of mankind, or of the whole." If, says Harrington, "reason be nothing else but interest, and the interest of mankind be the right interest, then the reason of mankind must be right reason." But the "interest of popular governments comes the nearest unto the interest of mankind." So it follows that "the reason of popular government comes the nearest unto right reason."

Harrington wanted to create a stable society. Instructed by Aristotle, he, therefore, planned first to build a stable economic "foundation" through laws which would prevent concentration of wealth, which was land in England— and which would ensure an approximation of equality in its distribution— an equality of "interests." Then he sought to contrive a governmental "superstructure" compatible with this economic "foundation." It should consist of (1) a senate which proposes laws, (2) an assembly which resolves (without debate) whether the proposed laws should be enacted, and (3) an executive or magistracy which executes the laws.

And so Harrington, although not a rigid economic determinist, followed Aristotle in associating the notion of "a government of laws, and not of men" with a belief in the "economic basis of politics." He would avoid "a government of men" through an adequate balance of property interests.

Our own John Adams (who, as we noted, wrote the famous phrase, which he borrowed from Harrington, into the Massachusetts Bill of Rights) was deeply impressed by Harrington's views as to the relation between property and politics: "Harrington," he wrote, "has shown that power always follows property. This I believe to be as infallible a maxim in politics, as that action and reaction are equal, is in mechanics." In 1787, in his *Defense of the Constitution* Adams wrote:

It is agreed that "the end of all government is the good and ease of the people, in secure enjoyment, of their rights, without oppression"; but it must be remembered that the rich are people as well as the poor; that they have rights as well as others; that they have as clear and as sacred a right to their large property as others have to theirs which is smaller; that oppression to them is as possible and as wicked as to others. The rich, therefore, ought to have an effectual barrier in the constitution against being robbed, plundered, and murdered as well as the poor; and this can never be without an independent senate. The poor should have a bulwark against the same dangers and oppression; and this can never be without a house of representatives of the people. But neither the rich nor the poor can be defended by their respective guardians in the constitution, without an executive power, vested with a negative, equal to the other, to hold the balance even between them, and decide when they cannot agree.

To achieve a mean between tyranny and anarchy, between oligarchy and unrestrained democracy, he sought a system of balanced interests, in which the greater property interest must be held in due balance with the smaller, in which the selfishness of one group should be neutralized by the counter selfishness of other groups.

So that John Adams, too, with his stress on economic class interests as the foundation of government, could be said to have been a sort of forerunner of Karl Marx. Indeed, he seems to have fused the notions now ascribed to Marx and Freud when he said: "That the first want of every man is his dinner and the second his girl were truths well known * * * long before the great philosopher Malthus arose to think he enlightened the world by his discovery."

In *The Federalist*, No. 10, James Madison, "the father of the Constitution," set forth views which seemingly owe much to Harrington's as to the effects of property ownership and group interests on government: "From the protection of different and unequal faculties of acquiring property," he said, "*the possession of different degrees and kinds of property immediately results; and from the influence of these on the sentiments and views of the respective proprietors, ensues a division of the society into different interests and parties. The latent causes of faction are thus sown in the nature of man; and we see them everywhere brought into different degrees of activity, according to the different circumstances of civil society. * * * But the most common and durable, source of faction, has been the various and unequal distribution of property. Those who hold and those who are without property have ever formed distinct interests in society.* Those who are creditors, and those who are debtors, fall under a like discrimination. A landed interest, a manufacturing interest, a mercantile interest, a moneyed interest, with many lesser interests, grow up of necessity in civilized nations, and divide them into different classes, actuated by different sentiments and views. The regulation of these various and interfering interests forms the principal task of modern legislation, and involves the spirit of party and faction in the necessary and ordinary operations of the government."

Pound . . . makes much of the influence, on those who wrote the early American state constitutions and our federal constitution, of the English writings in the seventeenth century prior to 1688. But among those writings was Harrington's Oceana. And of that book and of the effects of its economic-political views, Pound makes no mention whatever. It may be that Parrington and Beard overemphasize those effects. Yet they cannot be ignored. And it is surprising to find Pound, in his recent book, thus disregarding the belief on the part of those who, like John Adams—influenced by Harrington—advocated a "government of laws, and not of men" in economics and class interests as the principal determinants of governmental action; especially as Pound ascribes a belief in "administrative absolutism" and a contempt for "a government of laws" to administrative officers—on the absurd ground that they are under the influence of so-called "juristic realists" who, in turn, he says, are exponents of some kind of economic determinism and class-struggle thesis, when, in fact, none of those so-called "realists" has anything like the belief in the "economic basis of politics" that was entertained by men like Aristotle, Harrington, Adams, or Madison.

\* \* \* \* \*

The concept of a government of laws and not of men was not originally identified with *laissez-faire*—the thesis that government should be nothing but a policeman—and a very inactive one at that. . . .

Although our "founding fathers" were not believers in rampant individualism, yet they were generally not in favor of much legislative activity. And so a "government of laws" came to be associated with legislative minimalism.

This attitude became transmuted into nineteenth century let-aloneism. And the resulting association of ideas, although accidental and not inherent, has this significance: To many who denounce "a government of men," all governmental regulation of business is distasteful. "A government of laws, and not of men" signifies complete *laissez-faire* to them. But such a regime, possible in an agrarian civilization, is no longer possible in our complicated industrial setup.

"More and more," says Lord MacMillan, "the main issue in political science has come to be—not whether the State should intervene at all in the regulation of our daily lives but where the frontier line ought most wisely to be drawn between the province of State activity and that of individual enterprise. On all hands it is now recognized that the policy of *laissez-faire*, which gave us no doubt our industrial and commercial supremacy but also gave us our slums and many other attendant evils, must give place to a new regime. \* \* \* The definition of the sphere of government has become the main preoccupation of the student of political science. . . . Merriam [says]:

The modern problem is that of a unified and intelligent action—a program in which delay may be the unpardonable sin, as fatal as ignorance or betrayal of the general interest. When government was regarded as an enemy, weakness was the strategy of the hour; but when government is the friend of the commonwealth, the reverse becomes the strategy of a new time. \* \* \* An aspect of democracy is confidence in the utility of government as a social organizer. . . . In various periods also government was identified with tyranny, and efforts were made to provide restrictions against government on the theory that whatever it did would be bad, and that the less done the better. In more recent times, however, it has been realized that government may be the friend of the community as well as its foe * * *. When governments have not acted vigorously and progressively in moments of distress, they have exposed themselves to danger of overthrow, as in Italy and Germany, where more vigorous political action might have averted revolution. The unpardonable sin of government is inaction in emergencies. To do nothing is to abdicate. The distrust of government as an alien force, which a century or so ago was characteristic of the Many who feared the encroachments of the Few, is now more characteristic of the Few who fear the encroachments of the Many upon their special set of values.

*There is danger, however, in overstressing that antithesis between the few and the many.* The economically powerful few in America, should they become the victims of fear of loss of the major portion of their power, may make a try for some sort of fascist government. The result, in all likelihood, would be civil war. And the few, even if they won in that civil war, would ultimately lose out, as the events in Germany under Hitler serve to show. *Intelligent compromises should make it possible to achieve the welfare of the many without a destruction of the major powers of the minority. Sagacious use of governmental powers can achieve that result, without destruction of our democracy, if the minority will cooperate, recognizing the social obligations that should accompany their power. . . .*

There is a middle road. Some checks we need, but not too many; the proper proportions cannot be fixed for all time in any static formula. An absence of all checks means despotism; too many checks means anarchy. Our Constitution, interpreted to meet changing demands, can give us the solution; for it does not, said Holmes, establish "fields of black and white," but each field terminates "in a penumbra shading gradually, from one extreme to another."

McIlwain, a sagacious and learned historian of government [says]: . . . *"The principle of the separation of powers * * * when extended too far into the spheres of legislation and administration becomes a menace and an open invitation to illegal usurpation or to actual revolution. * * * True constitutionalism * * * has never meant government enfeebled by divisions within itself; it has meant government limited by law."* And how shall that end be attained? By an independent judiciary, replies McIlwain. The principle of powers is *"valid and necessary if restricted so as to mean merely the independence of the judiciary."*

No friend of American democracy can fail to agree with McIlwain—as far as he goes. But here, once more, we encounter a fatuous belief, although in subtler form, in the efficacy of mere governmental machinery. Responsible and effective government—yes. A diminution of any extreme system of hampering checks and balances—yes. Legal limits on arbitrary use of governmental power—yes. An independent judiciary—of course. But will that be enough to preserve constitutionalism and democracy? One may doubt it. An independent judiciary can wisely enforce the constitutional limitations on the powers of the other branches of government. But the judiciary, as well as those other branches, consists not of angels but of human beings.

McIlwain's excessive reliance on an independent judiciary as the preserver of American democracy is perhaps to be explained by his tendency to be satisfied by form rather than substance, a tendency exemplified in his treatment of sovereignty. He insists that sovereignty should be regarded solely as a *legal* concept. Yet he freely acknowledges that the sovereign, thus conceived, "may be a fiction"; that it can "be squared with fact only by a liberal use of legal fictions." "In some cases it will itself tend to become little more than a legal fiction. It is true, of course, that many legal fictions "may be defended as useful and beneficent." But a legal fiction is likely to be dangerous in its consequences whenever it is not recognized as such. And it is never wise or useful to refuse, in proper circumstances, to peer behind any legal fiction to the realities. It is peculiarly unwise to refuse to take into account what one sees back of the fiction of the legal sovereign. McIlwain thus peers behind the English sovereign, and sees "public opinion" and "a dozen other non-legal forces" which are so potent that, factually, the sovereign is virtually "non-existent," being "controlled by" those "other and stronger forces outside itself." McIlwain says that those other "forces"—which at times are superior in fact to the *legal* sovereign—"belong to *the realm of the practical*."

They do indeed. And we dare not, if we are intelligent, become so legalistic as to ignore that "realm of the practical"—the realm in which men live. It is the realm of human beings, not angels. It can and, as McIlwain admits, often does control the acts of the legal sovereign. . . .

Legal forms are not to be laughed at. Legal machinery is not a joke. . . . The more independent the judiciary is made, the more important becomes the way in which it exercises its powers and, therefore, the more important the manner of men who constitute the judiciary. We must peer behind the words "independent judiciary" to the actual men who are the judges. And the same is true of our administrative agencies.

So we conclude where we began: We need efficient governmental machinery. But, in a democracy, we must also insist upon a government of laws well administered by the right kind of men. If we do not select such men, men who have both faith in democracy and the ability to make it efficient— at the same time avoiding the arbitrary use of power to invade those civil liberties which are the essence of democracy—may God help us. And let us not forget, that, usually, God helps them who are able and willing to help themselves.

*If Men Were Angels* (1942)

# CENSORSHIP: THE FIRST AMENDMENT ⮵

UNITED STATES V. ROTH ⮶§ In June, 1956, Samuel Roth, convicted under a federal statute of sending obscene literature through the mails, appealed his conviction in the United States Court of Appeals for the Second Circuit. Roth claimed that there had been errors in the conduct of his trial; and he attacked the constitutionality of the statute. In September of that year, with Judge Charles E. Clark writing the opinion, the court upheld Roth's conviction. Judge Clark said that "whatever our personal opinions," the court was following the view of a colleague, Judge Learned Hand who, in an earlier obscenity case, wrote, "If the question [of the constitutionality of the statute] is to be reopened, the Supreme Court must reopen it." Judge Clark added that even if the Court of Appeals were free to strike down the statute, such a step might be unwise in the absence of knowledge of the social consequences of the problem of obscenity, and refers to "strongly held views of those in the premises as to the very direct connection of this traffic [in obscenity] with the development of juvenile delinquency." As to the alleged errors in the trial, Judge Clark dismissed them. Judge Frank wrote a concurring opinion which appears below. ⮵

FRANK, Circuit Judge (concurring): The reference in Judge Clark's opinion to juvenile delinquency, might lead the casual reader to suppose that, under the statute, the test of what constitutes obscenity is its effect on minors, and that the defendant, Roth, has been convicted for mailing obscene writings to (or for sale to) children. This court, however, in United States v. Levine ... has held that the correct test is the effect on the sexual thoughts and desires, not of the "young" or "immature," but of average, normal, adult persons. The trial

[ 112 ]

judge here so instructed the jury. (He said: "The test is not whether it would arouse sexual desires or sexually impure thoughts in those comprising a particular segment of the community, the young, the immature or the highly prudish. * * * In other words, you must determine its impact upon the average person in the community.")

On the basis of that test, the jury could reasonably have found, beyond a reasonable doubt, that many of the books, periodicals, pamphlets and pictures which defendant mailed were obscene. Accordingly, I concur.

I do so although I have much difficulty in reconciling the validity of that statute with opinions of the Supreme Court, uttered within the past twenty-five years, relative to the First Amendment as applied to other kinds of legislation. The doctrine expressed in those opinions, as I understand it, may be summarized briefly as follows: Any statute authorizing governmental interference (whether by "prior restraint" or punishment) with free speech or free press runs counters to the First Amendment, except when the government can show that the statute strikes at words which are likely to incite to a breach of the peace, or with sufficient probability tend either to the overthrow of the government by illegal means or to some other overt antisocial conduct. (The judicial enforcement of private rights—as in suits, for example, for defamation, injury to business, fraud, or invasion of privacy —comes within the exception.)

The troublesome aspect of the federal obscenity statute—as I shall try to explain in the Appendix to this opinion—is that (a) no one can now show that, with any reasonable probability obscene publications tend to have any effects on the behavior of normal, average adults, and (b) that under that statute, as judicially interpreted, punishment is apparently inflicted for provoking, in such adults, undesirable sexual thoughts, feelings, or desires —not overt dangerous or antisocial conduct, either actual or probable.

Often the discussion of First Amendment exceptions has been couched in terms of a "clear and present danger." However, the meaning of that phrase has been somewhat watered down by *Dennis v. U.S.* . . . The test now involves probability: "In each case [courts] must ask," said Chief Justice Vinson in *Dennis*, "whether the gravity of the 'evil' discounted by its improbability, justifies such invasion of free speech as is necessary to avoid the danger." It has been suggested that the test now is this: "The more serious and threatened the evil, the lower the required degree of probability." It would seem to follow that the less clear the danger, the more imminent must it be. At any rate, it would seem that (1) the danger or evil must be clear (that is, identifiable) and substantial, and (2) that, since the statute renders words punishable, it is invalid unless those words tend, with a fairly high degree of probability, to incite to overt conduct which is obviously harmful. For, under the First Amendment, lawless or antisocial "acts are the main thing. Speech is not punishable for its own sake, but only because of its connection with those * * * acts. * * * But more than a remote connection is necessary * * *". . . .

. . . . As I read the Supreme Court's opinions, the government, in defending the constitutionality of a statute which curbs free expression, may not rely on the usual "presumption of validity." No matter how one may articulate the reasoning, it is now accepted doctrine that, when legislation affects free speech or free press, the government must show that the legislation comes within one of the exceptions described above. . . . Moreover, when legislation affects free expression, the void-for-vagueness doctrine has a peculiar importance; and the obscenity statute is exquisitely vague (See the Appendix, Point 9.)

True, the Supreme Court has said several times that the federal obscenity statute (or any such state statute) is constitutional. But the Court has not directly so decided; it has done so *sub silentio* in applying the federal statute, or has referred to the constitutionality of such legislation in dicta. The Court has not thoroughly canvassed the problem in any opinion, nor applied to it the doctrine (summarized above) concerning the First Amendment which the Court has evolved in recent years. I base that statement on the following analysis of the cases:

In *Ex parte Jackson*, . . . the Court held valid a statute relating to the mailing of letters, or circulars, concerning lotteries. Such letters or circulars might well induce the addressees to engage in the overt conduct of engaging in lotteries. The Court, only in passing, referred to the obscenity statute and said it, too, was valid.

In *Rosen v. U.S.*, . . . the issue was solely the sufficiency of an indictment under the obscenity statute, not the validity of that legislation, and the Court did not discuss its validity.

In *Van Swearingen v. U.S.*, . . . the Court reversed a conviction under the obscenity statute; it did not consider its constitutionality.

*Dunlop v. U.S.* . . . did not discuss the constitutionality of the statute; moreover, the opinion . . . shows that it dealt with advertisements soliciting improper sexual relations, that is, with probable conduct, not with mere thoughts or desires.

In *Public Clearing House v. Coyne*, . . . which did not involve the validity of the obscenity Act, the Court said in passing . . . that its constitutionality "has never been attacked."

In *U.S. v. Limehouse*, . . . the Court decided the correct interpretation of the word "filthy" in the statute, and did not consider the question of constitutionality. Moreover, there the defendant had mailed letters attacking the characters of the recipients who might well have been moved to conduct in breach of the peace.

In *Winters v. New York,* . . . the Court held void for vagueness a state statute making it a crime to distribute publications consisting principally of news or stories of criminal deeds of bloodshed or lust so massed as to become vehicles for inciting violent and depraved crimes. The Court said in passing . . . that legislation subjecting obscene publications to governmental control is valid.

In *Doubleday v. New York,* . . . the Court, by an evenly divided vote, without opinion affirmed a state court decision sustaining a state obscenity statute.

In *U.S. v. Alpers,* . . . the Court construed the statute as amended, and affirmed a conviction thereunder, but did not consider its constitutionality. . . .

I agree with my colleagues that, since ours is an inferior court, we should not hold invalid a statute which our superior has thus often said is constitutional (albeit without any full discussion). Yet I think it not improper to set forth, as I do in the Appendix, considerations concerning the obscenity statute's validity with which, up to now, I think the Supreme Court has not dealt in any of its opinions. I do not suggest the inevitability of the conclusion that the statute is unconstitutional. I do suggest that it is hard to avoid that conclusion, if one applies to that legislation the reasoning the Supreme Court has applied to other sorts of legislation. Perhaps I have overlooked conceivable compelling contrary arguments. If so, maybe my Appendix will evoke them.

To preclude misunderstanding of my purpose in stirring doubts about this statute, I think it well to add the following:

(a) As many of the publications mailed by defendant offend my personal taste, I would not cross a street to obtain them for nothing; I happen not to be interested in so-called "pornography"; and I think defendant's motives obnoxious. But if the statute were invalid, the merit of those publications would be irrelevant. . . . So, too, as to defendant's motives: "Although the defendant may be the worst of men * * * the rights of the best of men are secure only as the rights of the vilest and most abhorrent are protected."

(b) It is most doubtful (as explained in the Appendix) whether anyone can now demonstrate that children's reading or looking at obscene matter has a probable causal relation to the children's antisocial conduct. If, however, such a probable causal relation could be shown, there could be little doubt, I think, of the validity of a statute (if so worded as to avoid undue ambiguity) which specifically prohibits the distribution by mail of obscene publications for sale to young people. But discussion of such legislation is here irrelevant, since, to repeat, the existing federal statute is not thus restricted.

(c) Congress undoubtedly has wide power to protect public morals. But the First Amendment severely limits that power in the area of free speech and free press.

(d) It is argued that antiobscenity legislation is valid because, at the time of the adoption of the First Amendment, obscenity was a common law crime. Relying (*inter alia*) on *Bridges v. California* . . . and *Grosjean v. American Press*, . . . I have tried in the Appendix to answer that argument.

(e) The First Amendment, of course, does not prevent any private body or group (including any Church) from instructing, or seeking to persuade, its adherents or others not to read or distribute obscene (or other) publications. That constitutional provision—safeguarding a principle indispensable in a true democracy—leaves unhampered all non-governmental means of molding public opinion about not reading literature which some think undesirable; and, in that respect, experience teaches that democratically exercised censorship by public opinion has far more potency, and is far less easily evaded, than censorship by government. (Public opinion, by influencing social attitudes, may create a convention, with no governmental "sanction" behind it, far more coercive than any statute. . . . Notably is this true of conventions as to obscenity. . . .) The incessant struggle to influence public opinion is of the very essence of the democratic process. A basic purpose of the First Amendment is to keep that struggle alive, by not permitting the dominant public opinion of the present to become embodied in legislation which will prevent the formation of a different dominant public opinion in the future. (The results of the pressure of current public opinion may not always be happy. But our democracy accepts the postulate that, in the long run, the struggle to sway public opinion will produce the wisest policies. For further discussion of this theme, see the Appendix.)

(f) At first glance it may seem almost frivolous to raise any question about the constitutionality of the obscenity statute at a time when many seemingly graver First Amendment problems confront the courts. But (for reasons stated in more detail in the Appendix) governmental censorship of writings, merely because they may stimulate, in the reader, sexual thoughts the legislature deems undesirable, has more serious implications than appear at first glance: We have been warned by eminent thinkers of the easy path from any apparently mild governmental control of what adult citizens may read to governmental control of adults' political and religious reading. John Milton, Thomas Jefferson, James Madison, J. S. Mill and Tocqueville have pointed out that any paternalistic guardianship by government of the thoughts of grown-up citizens enervates their spirit, keeps them immature, all too ready to adopt towards government officers the attitude that, in general, "Papa knows best." If the government possesses the power to censor publications which arouse sexual thoughts, regardless of whether those thoughts tend probably to transform themselves into antisocial behavior, why may not the government censor political and religious publications regardless of any causal relation to probable dangerous deeds? And even if we confine attention to official censorship of publications tending to stimulate sexual thoughts, it should be asked why, at any moment, that censorship cannot be extended to advertisements and true reports or photographs, in our daily press, which, fully as much, may stimulate such thoughts?

(g) Assuming, arguendo, that a statute aims at an altogether desirable end, nevertheless its desirability does not render it constitutional. As the Supreme Court has said, "The good sought in unconstitutional legislation is an insidious feature because it leads citizens and legislatures of good purpose to promote it without thought of the serious break it will make in the ark of our covenant. * * *"

. . . [Elsewhere] I voiced puzzlement about the constitutionality of administrative prior restraint of obscene books. I then had little doubt about the validity of a purely punitive obscenity statute. But the next year, in Commonwealth v. Gordon, . . . Judge Curtis Bok, one of America's most reflective judges, directly attacked the validity of any such punitive legislation. His brilliant opinion, which states arguments that (so far as I know) have never been answered, nudged me into the skeptical views contained in this opinion and the Appendix.

APPENDIX ◆§ As a judge of an inferior court, I am constrained by opinions of the Supreme Court concerning the obscenity statute to hold that legislation valid. Since, however, I think (as indicated in the foregoing) that none of those opinions has carefully canvassed the problem in the light of the Supreme Court's interpretation of the First Amendment, especially as expressed by the Court in recent years, I deem it not improper to set forth, in the following, factors which I think deserve consideration in passing on the constitutionality of that statute.

Benjamin Franklin, in 1776 unanimously designated Postmaster General by the First Continental Congress, is appropriately known as the "father of the Post Office." Among his published writings are two—Letter of Advice to Young Men on the Proper Choosing of a Mistress and The Speech of Polly Baker—which a jury could reasonably find "obscene," according to the judge's instructions in the case at bar. On that basis, if tomorrow a man were to send those works of Franklin through the mails, he would be subject to prosecution and (if the jury found him guilty) to punishment under the federal obscenity statute.

That fact would surely have astonished Jefferson, who extolled Franklin as an American genius, called him "venerable and beloved" of his countrymen, and wrote approvingly of Franklin's *Polly Baker.* No less would it have astonished Madison, also an admirer of Franklin (whom he described as a man whose "genius" was "an ornament of human nature") and himself given to telling "Rabelaisian anecdotes." Nor was the taste of these men unique in the American Colonies: "Many a library of a colonial planter in Virginia or a colonial intellectual in New England boasted copies of *Tom Jones, Tristram Shandy,* Ovid's *Art of Love,* and Rabelais. * * *"

As, with Jefferson's encouragement, Madison, in the first session of Congress, introduced what became the First Amendment, it seems doubtful that the constitutional guaranty of free speech and free press could have been intended to allow Congress validly to enact the "obscenity" Act. That doubt receives reinforcement from the following:

In 1799, eight years after the adoption of the First Amendment, Madison, in an Address to the General Assembly of Virginia, said that the "truth of opinion" ought not to be subject to "imprisonment, to be inflicted by those of a different opinion"; he there also asserted that it would subvert the First Amendment to make a "distinction between the freedom and the licentiousness of the press." Previously, in 1792, he wrote that "a man has property in his opinions and free communication of them," and that a government which "violates the property which individuals have in their opinion * * * is not a pattern for the United States." Jefferson's proposed Constitution for Virginia (1776), provided: "Printing presses shall be free, except so far as by commission of private injury cause may be given of private action." In his Second Inaugural Address (1805), he said: "No inference is here intended that the laws provided by the State against false and defamatory publications should not be enforced. * * * The press, confined to truth, needs no other restraint * * *; and no other definite line can be drawn between the inestimable liberty of the press and demoralizing licentiousness. If there still be impropieties which this rule would not restrain, its supplement must be sought in the censorship of public opinion."

The broad phrase in the First Amendment, prohibiting legislation abridging "freedom of speech or of the press," includes the right to speak and write freely for the public concerning any subject. As the Amendment specifically refers "to the free exercise of religion" and to the right "of the people to assemble" and to "petition the government for a redress of grievances," it specifically includes the right freely to speak to and write for the public concerning government and religion; but it does not limit this right to those topics. Accordingly, the views of Jefferson and Madison about the freedom to speak and write concerning religion are relevant to a consideration of the constitutional freedom in respect of all other subjects. Consider, then, what those men said about freedom of religious discussion: Madison, in 1799, denouncing the distinction "between the freedom and the licentiousness of the press" said, "By its help, the judge as to what is licentious may escape through any constitutional restriction," and added, "Under it, Congress might denominate a religion to be heretical and licentious, and proceed to its suppression. * * * Remember * * * that it is to the press mankind are indebted for having dispelled the clouds which long encompassed religion. * * *" Jefferson, in 1798, quoting the First Amendment, said it guarded "in the same sentence, and under the same words, the freedom of religion, of speech, and of the press; insomuch, that whatever violates either, throws down the sanctuary which covers the others." In 1814, he wrote in a letter, "I am really mortified to be told that in the United States of America, a fact like this (the sale of a book) can become a subject of inquiry, and of criminal inquiry too, as an offense against religion; that (such) a question can be carried before the civil magistrate. Is this then our freedom of religion? And are we to have a censor whose imprimatur shall say what books may be sold and what we may buy? * * * Whose foot is to be the measure to which ours are all to be cut or stretched?"

Those utterances high-light this fact: Freedom to speak publicly and to publish has, as its inevitable and important correlative, the private rights to hear, to read, and to think and to feel about what one hears and reads. The First Amendment protects those private rights of hearers and readers.

We should not forget that, prompted by Jefferson, Madison (who at one time had doubted the wisdom of a Bill of Rights) when he urged in Congress the enactment of what became the first ten Amendments, declared, "If they are incorporated into the Constitution, independent tribunals of justice will consider themselves in a peculiar manner the guardian of those rights; they will be an impenetrable barrier against every assumption of power in the Legislative or Executive; they will be naturally led to resist every encroachment upon rights expressly stipulated for in the Constitution by the declaration of rights." In short, the Bill of Rights, including the First Amendment, was not designed merely as a set of admonitions to the legislature and the executive; its provisions were to be enforced by the courts.

Judicial enforcement necessarily entails judicial interpretation. The question therefore arises whether the courts, in enforcing the First Amendment, should interpret it in accord with the views prevalent among those who sponsored and adopted it or in accord with subsequently developed views which would sanction legislation more restrictive of free speech and free press.

So the following becomes pertinent: Some of those who in the twentieth century endorse legislation suppressing "obscene" literature have an attitude towards freedom of expression which does not match that of the framers of the First Amendment (adopted at the end of the eighteenth century) but does stem from an attitude, towards writings dealing with sex, which arose decades later, in the mid-nineteenth century, and is therefore labeled —doubtless too sweepingly—"Victorian." It was a dogma of "Victorian morality" that sexual misbehavior would be encouraged if one were to "acknowledge its existence or at any rate to present it vividly enough to form a lifelike image of it in the reader's mind"; this morality rested on a "faith that you could best conquer evil by shutting your eyes to its existence," and on a kind of word magic. The demands at that time for "decency" in published words did not comport with the actual sexual conduct of many of those who made those demands: "The Victorians, as a general rule, managed to conceal the 'coarser' side of their lives so thoroughly under a mask of respectability that we often fail to realize how 'coarse' it really was. * * * Could we have recourse to the vast unwritten literature of bawdry, we should be able to form a more veracious notion of life as it (then) really was." The respectables of those days often, "with unblushing license," held "high revels" in "night houses." Thanks to them, Mrs. Warren's profession flourished, but it was considered sinful to talk about it in books. (Paradoxically, this attitude apparently tends to "create" obscenity. For the foundation of obscenity seems to be secrecy and shame: "The secret becomes shameful because of its secrecy." See Kaplan, "Obscenity As An Esthetic Category" . . .) Such a prudish and purely verbal moral code, at odds (more or less hypocritically) with the actual conduct of its adherents was (as we have seen) not the moral code of those who framed the First Amendment. One would suppose, then, that the courts should interpret and enforce that Amendment according to the views of those framers, not according to the later "Victorian" code.

## The "founding fathers" did not accept the common law concerning freedom of expression

It has been argued that the federal obscenity statute is valid because obscenity was a common law crime at the time of the adoption of the First Amendment. Quite aside from the fact that, previous to the Amendment, there had been scant recognition of this crime, the short answer seems to be that the framers of the Amendment knowingly and deliberately intended to depart from the English common law as to freedom of speech and freedom of the press. . . .

Of course, the legislature has wide power to protect what it considers public morals. But the First Amendment severely circumscribes that power (and all other legislative powers) in the area of speech and free press.

## Subsequent punishment as, practically, prior restraint

For a long time, much was made of the distinction between a statute calling for "prior restraint" and one providing subsequent criminal punishment; the former alone, it was once said, raised any question of constitutionality vis-à-vis the First Amendment. Although it may still be true that more is required to justify legislation providing "preventive" than "punitive" censorship, this distinction has been substantially eroded. . . .

## The statute, as judicially interpreted, authorizes punishment for inducing mere thoughts, and feelings, or desires

For a time, American courts adopted the test of obscenity contrived in 1868 by Cockburn, L. J., in Queen v. Hicklin . . .: "I think the test of obscenity is this, whether the tendency of the matter charged as obscenity is to deprave and corrupt those whose minds are open to such immoral influences, and into whose hands a publication of this sort might fall." He added that the book there in question "would suggest * * * thoughts of a most impure and libidinous character."

The test in most federal courts has changed: They do not now speak of the thoughts of "those whose minds are open to * * * immoral influences" but, instead, of the thoughts of average adult normal men and women, determining what these thoughts are, not by proof at the trial, but by the standard of "the average conscience of the time," the current "social sense of what is right." . . . Yet the courts still define obscenity in terms of the assumed average normal adult reader's sexual thoughts or desires or impulses, without reference to any relation between those "subjective" reactions and his subsequent conduct. The judicial opinions use such key phrases as this: "suggesting lewd thoughts and exciting sensual desires"; "arouse the salacity of the reader," "allowing or implanting * * * obscene, lewd or lascivious thoughts or desires," "arouse sexual desires." The judge's charge in the instant case reads accordingly: "It must tend to stir sexual impulses and lead to sexually impure thoughts." Thus the statute, as the courts construe it, appears to provide criminal punishment for inducing no more than thoughts, feelings, desires.

## No adequate knowledge is available concerning the effects on the conduct of normal adults of reading or seeing the "obscene"

Suppose we assume, *arguendo*, that sexual thoughts or feelings, stirred by the "obscene," probably will often issue into overt conduct. Still it does not at all follow that that conduct will be antisocial. For no sane person can believe it socially harmful if sexual desires lead to normal sexual behavior, and not antisocial, since without such behavior the human race would soon disappear.

Doubtless, Congress could validly provide punishment for mailing any publications if there were some moderately substantial reliable data showing that reading or seeing those publications probably conduces to seriously harmful sexual conduct on the part of normal adult human beings. But we have no such data.

Suppose it argued that whatever excites sexual longings might *possibly* produce sexual misconduct. That cannot suffice: Notoriously, perfumes sometimes act as aphrodisiacs, yet no one will suggest that therefore Congress may constitutionally legislate punishment for mailing perfumes. It may be that among the stimuli to irregular sexual conduct, by normal men and women, may be almost anything—the odor of carnations or cheese, the sight of a cane or a candle or a shoe, the touch of silk or a gunnysack. For all anyone knows, stimuli of that sort may be far more provocative of such misconduct than reading obscene books or seeing obscene pictures. Said John Milton, "Evil manners are as perfectly learnt, without books, a thousand other ways that cannot be stopped."

## Effect of "obscenity" on adult conduct

To date there exist, I think, no thoroughgoing studies by competent persons which justify the conclusion that normal adults' reading or seeing of the "obscene" probably induces antisocial conduct. Such competent studies as have been made do conclude that so complex and numerous are the causes of sexual vice that it is impossible to assert with any assurance that "obscenity" represents a ponderable causal factor in sexually deviant adult behavior. "Although the whole subject of obscenity censorship hinges upon the unproved assumption that 'obscene' literature is a significant factor in causing sexual deviation from the community standard, no report can be found of a single effort at genuine research to test this assumption by singling out as a factor for study the effect of sex literature upon sexual behavior."

What little competent research has been done, points definitely in a direction precisely opposite to that assumption.

Alpert reports that, when, in the 1920's, 409 women college graduates were asked to state in writing what things stimulated them sexually, they answered thus: 218 said "Man"; 95 said books; 40 said drama; 29 said dancing; 18 said pictures; 9 said music. Of those who replied "that the source of their sex information came from books, not one specified a 'dirty' book as the source. Instead, the books listed were: The Bible, the dictionary, the encyclopedia, novels from Dickens to Henry James, circulars about venereal diseases, medical books, and Motley's *Rise of the Dutch Republic*." Macaulay, replying to advocates of the suppression of obscene books, said: "We find it difficult to believe that in a world so full of temptations as this, any gentleman whose life would have been virtuous if he had not read Aristophanes or Juvenal, will be vicious by reading them." Echoing Macaulay, "Jimmy" Walker remarked that he had never heard of a woman seduced by a book. New Mexico has never had an obscenity statute; there is no evidence that, in that state, sexual misconduct is proportionately greater than elsewhere.

## Effect on conduct of young people

Most federal courts (as above noted) now hold that the test of obscenity is the effect on the "mind" of the average normal adult, that effect being determined by the "average conscience of the time," the current "sense of what is right"; and that the statute does not intend "to reduce our treatment of sex to the standard of a child's library in the supposed interest of a salacious few"; *U.S.* v. *Kennerley*. . . .

However, there is much pressure for legislation, designed to prevent juvenile delinquency, which will single out children, that is, will prohibit the sale to young persons of "obscenity" or other designated matter. That problem does not present itself here, since the federal statute is not thus limited. The trial judge in his charge in the instant case told the jury that the "test" under that statute is not the effect of the mailed matter on "those comprising a particular segment of the community," the "young" or "the immature"; and see *U.S.* v. *Levine*. . . .

Therefore a discussion of such a children's protective statute is irrelevant here. But, since Judge Clark does discuss the alleged linkage of obscenity to juvenile delinquency, and since it may perhaps be thought that it has some bearing on the question of the effect of obscenity on adult conduct, I too shall discuss it.

The following is a recent summary of studies of that subject: "(1) Scientific studies of juvenile delinquency demonstrate that those who get into trouble, and are the greatest concern of the advocates of censorship, are far less inclined to read than those who do not become delinquent. The delinquents are generally the adventurous type, who have little use for reading and other nonactive entertainment. Thus, even assuming that reading sometimes has an adverse effect upon moral behavior, the effect is not likely to be substantial, for those who are susceptible seldom read. (2) Sheldon and Eleanor Glueck, who are among the country's leading authorities on the treatment and causes of juvenile delinquency, have recently published the results of a ten-year study of its causes. They exhaustively studied approximately 90 factors and influences that might lead to or explain juvenile delinquency; but the Gluecks gave no consideration to the type of reading material, if any were read by the delinquents. This is, of course, consistent with their finding that delinquents read very little. When those who know so much about the problem of delinquency among youth—the very group about whom the advocates of censorship are most concerned—conclude that what delinquents read has so little effect upon their conduct that it is not worth investigating in an exhaustive study of causes, there is good reason for serious doubts concerning the basic hypothesis on which obscenity censorship is dependent. (3) The many other influences in society that stimulate sexual desire are so much more frequent in their influence and so much more potent in their effect that the influence of reading is likely, at most, to be relatively insignificant in the composite of forces that lead an individual into conduct deviating from the community sex standards. * * * And the studies demonstrating that sex knowledge seldom results from reading indicate the relative unimportance of literature in sexual thoughts and behavior as compared with other factors in society." (Novick, Superintendent of the New York Training School for Girls, writes: "In the public eye today juvenile delinquency is alternately the direct result of progressive education, horror comics, T.V. programs, and other pet peeves of our present society. * * * This is not a new phenomenon. Each generation of adults has been concerned about the behavior of its children and has looked for a scapegoat on which to place the blame for its delinquency. At the same time, adults have always sought a panacea which would cure the problem. It is sufficient to note that delinquency has always risen during periods of stress and strain, and the era in which we are living is no exception. * * * Neither do restrictive measures such as * * * censorship of reading matter * * * prevent delinquency. They merely have an effect upon the manner in which the delinquency will be expressed." . . .

Judge Curtis Bok, perhaps remembering Lamb's remarks, said of the publications before him in *Commonwealth* v. *Gordon* . . . : "It will be asked whether one would care to have one's young daughter read these books. I suppose that by the time she is old enough to wish to read them she will have learned the biologic facts of life and the words that go with them. There is something seriously wrong at home if those facts have not been met and faced and sorted by then; it is not children so much as parents that should receive our concern about this. I should prefer that my own three daughters meet the facts of life and the literature of the world in my library than behind a neighbor's barn, for I can face the adversary there directly. If the young ladies are appalled by what they read, they can close the book at the bottom of page one; if they read further, they will learn what is in the world and in its people, and no parents who have been discerning with their children need fear the outcome. Nor can they hold it back, for life is a series of little battles and minor issues, and the burden of choice is on us all, every day, young and old. Our daughters must live in the world and decide what sort of women they are to be, and we should be willing to prefer their deliberate and informed choice of decency rather than an innocence that continues to spring from ignorance. If that choice be made in the open sunlight, it is more apt than when made in shadow to fall on the side of honorable behavior." . . .

Judge Clark, however, speaks of "the strongly held views of those with competence in the premises as to the very direct connection" of obscenity "with the development of juvenile delinquency." He cites and quotes from a recent opinion of the New York Court of Appeals and an article by Judge Vanderbilt, which in turn, cite the writings of persons thus described by Judge Clark as "those with competence in the premises." One of the cited writings is a report, by Dr. Jahoda and associates, entitled *The Impact of Literature: A Psychological Discussion of Some Assumptions in the Censorship Debate* (1954). I have read this report (which is a careful survey of all available studies and psychological theories). I think it expresses an attitude quite contrary to that indicated by Judge Clark. In order to avoid any possible bias in my interpretation of that report, I thought it well to ask Dr. Jahoda to write her own summary of it, which, with her permission, I shall quote. (In doing so, I am following the example of Mr. Justice Jackson who, in *Fed. Trade Commission v. Ruberoid* . . . acknowledged that he relied on "an unpublished treatise," that is, one not available to the parties. If that practice is proper, I think it similarly proper to quote an author's unpublished interpretation of a published treatise.) Dr. Jahoda's summary reads as follows:

Persons who argue for increased censorship of printed matter often operate on the assumption that reading about sexual matters or about violence and brutality leads to antisocial actions, particularly to juvenile delinquency. An examination of the pertinent psychological literature has led to the following conclusions:

1. There exists no research evidence either to prove or to disprove this assumption definitively.

2. In the absence of scientific proof two lines of psychological approach to the examination of the assumption are possible: (a) a review of what is known on the causes of juvenile delinquency; and (b) review of what is known about the effect of literature on the mind of the reader.

3. In the vast research literature on the causes of juvenile delinquency there is no evidence to justify the assumption that reading about sexual matters or about violence leads to delinquent acts. Experts on juvenile delinquency agree that it has no single cause. Most of them regard early childhood events, which precede the reading age, as a necessary condition for later delinquency. At a later age, the nature of personal relations is assumed to have much greater power in determining a delinquent career than the vicarious experiences provided by reading matter. Juvenile delinquents as a group read less, and less easily, than nondelinquents. Individual instances are reported in which so-called "good" books allegedly influenced a delinquent in the manner in which "bad" books are assumed to influence him.

Where childhood experiences and subsequent events have combined to make delinquency psychologically likely, reading could have one of two effects: it could serve a trigger function releasing the criminal act or it could provide for a substitute outlet of aggression in fantasy, dispensing with the need for criminal action. There is no empirical evidence in either direction.

4. With regard to the impact of literature on the mind of the reader, it must be pointed out that there is a vast overlap in content between all media of mass communication. The daily press, television, radio, movies, books and comics all present their share of so-called "bad" material, some with great realism as reports of actual events, some in clearly fictionalized form. It is virtually impossible to isolate the impact of one of these media on a population exposed to all of them. Some evidence suggests that the particular communications which arrest the attention of an individual are in good part a matter of choice. As a rule, people do not expose themselves to everything that is offered, but only to what agrees with their inclinations.

Children, who have often not yet crystallized their preferences and have more unspecific curiosity than many adults, are therefore perhaps more open to accidental influences from literature. This may present a danger to youngsters who are insecure or maladjusted who find in reading (of "bad" books as well as of "good" books) an escape from reality which they do not dare face. Needs which are not met in the real world are gratified in a fantasy world. It is likely, though not fully demonstrated, that excessive reading of comic books will intensify in children those qualities which drove them to the comic book world to begin with: an inability to face the world, apathy, a belief that the individual is hopelessly impotent and driven by uncontrollable forces and, hence, an acceptance of violence and brutality in the real world.

It should be noted that insofar as causal sequence is implied, insecurity and maladjustment in a child must precede this exposure to the written word in order to lead to these potential effects. Unfortunately, perhaps, the reading of Shakespeare's tragedies or of Andersen's and Grimm's fairy tales might do much the same.

Most of the current discussion of the relation between children's reading and juvenile delinquency has to do with so-called "comic books" which center on violence (sometimes coupled with sex) rather than mere obscenity. Judge Vanderbilt, in an article from which Judge Clark quotes, cites Feder, *Comic Book Regulation.* . . . Feder writes: "It has never been determined definitely whether or not comics portraying violence, crime and horror are a cause of juvenile delinquency."

Judge Vanderbilt, in the article from which Judge Clark quotes, also cites Wertham, *Seduction of the Innocent.* . . . Dr. Wertham is the foremost proponent of the view that "comic books" do contribute to juvenile delinquency. The Jahoda Report takes issue with Dr. Wertham, who relies much on a variety of the *post-hoc-ergo-propter-hoc* variety of argument, that is, youths who had read "comic books" became delinquents. The argument, at best, proves too much: Dr. Wertham points to the millions of young readers of such books; but only a fraction of these readers become delinquents. Many of the latter also chew gum, drink Coca-Cola, and wear soft-soled shoes. Moreover, Dr. Wertham specifically says . . . that he is little concerned with allegedly obscene publications designed for reading by adults, and . . . that the legislation which he advocates would do no more than forbid the sale or display of "comic books" to minors. As previously noted, the federal obscenity statute is not so restricted.

Maybe some day we will have enough reliable data to show that obscene books and pictures do tend to influence children's sexual conduct adversely. Then a federal statute could be enacted which would avoid constitutional defects by authorizing punishment for using the mails or interstate shipments in the sale of such books and pictures to children.

It is, however, not at all clear that children would be ignorant, in any considerable measure, of obscenity, if no obscene publications ever came into their hands. Youngsters get a vast deal of education in sexual smut from companions of their own age. A verbatim report of conversations among young teen-age boys (from average respectable homes) will disclose their amazing proficiency in obscene language, learned from other boys. Replying to the argument of the need for censorship to protect the young, Milton said: "Who shall regulate all the * * * conversation of our youth * * * appoint what shall be discussed * * *?" Most judges who reject that view are long past their youth and have probably forgotten the conversational ways of that period of life: "I remember when I was a little boy," said Mr. Dooley, "but I don't remember how I was a little boy."

## The obscenity statute and the reputable press

Let it be assumed, for the sake of the argument, that contemplation of published matter dealing with sex has a significant impact on children's conduct. On that assumption, we cannot overlook the fact that our most reputable newspapers and periodicals carry advertisements and photographs displaying women in what decidedly are sexually alluring postures, and at times emphasizing the importance of "sex appeal." That women are there shown scantily clad, increases "the mystery and allure of the bodies that are hidden," writes an eminent psychiatrist. "A leg covered by a silk stocking is much more attractive than a naked one; a bosom pushed into shape by a brassiere is more alluring than the pendant realities." (Myerson, *Speaking of Man.* . . . See also the well known chapter on clothes in Anatole France's *Penguin Island.*

Dr. Wertham discussing "comic books," makes much of the advertisements they carry. He speaks of their "breast ads," and also of their playing up of "glamour girls," their stress on the "sexy," their emphasis on women's "secondary sexual characteristics." Is not this also descriptive of the advertisements in our "best periodicals"?) Either, then, the statute must be sternly applied to prevent the mailing of many reputable newspapers and periodicals containing such ads and photographs, or else we must acknowledge that they have created a cultural atmosphere for children in which, at a maximum, only the most trifling additional effect can be imputed to children's perusal of the kind of matter mailed by the defendant.

## The obscenity statute and the newspapers

Because of the contrary views of many competent persons, one may well be skeptical about Dr. Wertham's thesis. However, let us see what, logically, his crusade would do to the daily press: After referring repeatedly to the descriptions, in "comic books" and other "mass media," of violence combined with sadistic sexual behavior, descriptions which he says contribute to juvenile delinquency, he writes, "Juvenile delinquency reflects the social values current in a society. Both adults and children absorb these social values in their daily lives, * * * and also in *all the communications through the mass media.* * * * Juvenile delinquency holds up a mirror to society. * * * It is self-understood that such a pattern in a mass medium does not come from nothing. * * * Comic books are not the disease, they are only a symptom. * * * The same social forces that made comic books make other social evils, and the same social forces that keep comic crime books keep the other social evils the way they are." (Emphasis added.)

Now the daily newspapers, especially those with immense circulations, constitute an important part of the "mass media"; and each copy of a news-paper sells for much less than a "comic book." Virtually all the sorts of descriptions, of sex mingled with violence, which Dr. Wertham finds in the "comic books," can be found, often accompanied by gruesome photographs, in those daily journals. Even a newspaper which is considered unusually re-spectable, published prominently on its first page, on August 26, 1956, a true story of a "badly decomposed body" of a twenty-four-year-old woman school teacher, found in a clump of trees. The story reported that police had quoted a twenty-nine-year-old salesman as saying that "he drove to the area" with the school teacher, that "the two had relations on the ground, and later got into an argument," after which he "struck her three times on the back of the head with a rock, and leaving her there, drove away." Although today no one can so prove, one may suspect that such stories of sex and violence in the daily press have more impact on young readers than do those in the "comic books," since the daily press reports reality while the "comic books" largely confine themselves to avowed fiction or fantasy. Yet Dr. Wertham, and most others who propose legislation to curb the sale of "comic books" to children, propose that it should not extend to newspapers. Why not?

The question is relevant in reference to the application of the obscenity statute: Are our prosecutors ready to prosecute reputable newspaper publishers under that Act? I think not. I do not at all urge such prosecutions. I do suggest that the validity of that statute has not been vigorously challenged because it has not been applied to important persons like those publishers but, instead, has been enforced principally against relatively inconspicuous men like the defendant here.

## Da Capo: Available data seem wholly insufficient to show that the obscenity statutes come within any exception to the First Amendment

I repeat that, because that statute is not restricted to obscene publica-tions mailed for sale to minors, its validity should be tested in terms of the evil effects of adult reading of obscenity on adult conduct. With the present lack of evidence that publications probably have such effects, how can the government discharge its burden of demonstrating sufficiently that the statute is within the narrow exceptions to the scope of the First Amendment? One would think that the mere possibility of a causal relation to misconduct ought surely not be enough.

Even if Congress had made an express legislative finding of the probable evil influence, on adult conduct, of adult reading or seeing obscene publications, the courts would not be bound by that finding, if it were not justified in fact. See, for example, *Chastleton Corp.* v. *Sinclair* . . . where the Court (per Holmes, J.) said of a statute (declaring the existence of an emergency) that "a Court is not at liberty to shut its eyes to an obvious mistake, when the validity of the law depends upon the truth of what is declared." And the Court there and elsewhere has held that the judiciary may use judicial notice in ascertaining the truth of such a legislative declaration.

*If the obscenity statute is valid, why may Congress not*
*validly provide punishment for mailing books which*
*will provoke thoughts it considers undesirable*
*about religion or politics?*

If the statute is valid, then, considering the foregoing, it would seem that its validity must rest on this ground: Congress, by statute, may constitutionally provide punishment for the mailing of books evoking mere thoughts or feelings about sex, if Congress considers them socially dangerous, even in the absence of any satisfactory evidence that those thoughts or feelings will tend to bring about socially harmful deeds. If that be correct, it is hard to understand why, similarly, Congress may not constitutionally provide punishment for such distribution of books evoking mere thoughts or feelings, about religion or politics, which Congress considers socially dangerous, even in the absence of any satisfactory evidence that those thoughts or feelings will tend to bring about socially dangerous deeds.

## The Judicial Exception of the "Classics"

As I have said, I have no doubt the jury could reasonably find, beyond a reasonable doubt, that many of the publications mailed by defendant were obscene within the current judicial definition of the term as explained by the trial judge in his charge to the jury. But so, too, are a multitude of recognized works of art found in public libraries. Compare, for instance, the books which are exhibits in this case with Montaigne's Essay on *Some Lines of Virgil* or with Chaucer. Or consider the many nude pictures which the defendant transmitted through the mails, and then turn to the reproductions in the articles on painting and sculpture in the *Encyclopædia Britannica* (14th edition): Some of the latter are no less "obscene" than those which led to the defendant's conviction. Yet these *Encyclopædia* volumes are readily accessible to everyone, young or old, and, without let or hindrance, are frequently mailed to all parts of the country. Catalogues, of famous art museums, almost equally accessible and also often mailed, contain reproductions of paintings and sculpture, by great masters, no less "obscene."

To the argument that such books (and such reproductions of famous paintings and works of sculpture) fall within the statutory ban, the courts have answered that they are "classics"—books of "literary distinction" or works which have "an accepted place in the arts," including, so this court has held, Ovid's *Art of Love* and Boccacio's *Decameron*. There is a "curious dilemma" involved in this answer that the statute condemns "only books which are dull and without merit," that in no event will the statute be applied to the "classics," that is, books "of literary distinction." ( . . . No one can argue with a straight face [1] that reading an obscene "classic" in a library has less harmful effects or [2] that, as the "classics" often are published in expensive volumes, they usually affect only persons who have large incomes, and that such persons' right to read is peculiarly privileged.) The courts have not explained how they escape that dilemma, but instead seem to have gone to sleep (although rather uncomfortably) on its horns.

This dilemma would seem to show up the basic constitutional flaw in the statute: No one can reconcile the currently accepted test of obscenity with the immunity of such "classics" as, for example, Aristophanes' *Lysistrata*, Chaucer's *Canterbury Tales*, Rabelais' *Gargantua and Pantagruel*, Shakespeare's *Venus and Adonis*, Fielding's *Tom Jones*, or Balzac's *Droll Stories*. For such "obscene" writings, just because of their greater artistry and charm, will presumably have far greater influence on readers than dull inartistic writings.

It will not do to differentiate a "classic," published in the past, on the ground that it comported with the average moral attitudes at the time and place of its original publication. Often this was not true. It was not true, for instance, of Balzac's *Droll Stories*, a "classic" now freely circulated by many public libraries, and which therefore must have been transported by mail (or in interstate commerce). More to the point, if the issue if whether a book meets the American common conscience of the present time, the question is how "average" Americans now regard the book, not how it was regarded when first published, here or abroad. Why should the age of an "obscene" book be relevant? After how many years—twenty-five or fifty or one hundred—does such a writing qualify as a "classic"?

The truth is that the courts have excepted the "classics" from the federal obscenity statute, since otherwise most Americans would be deprived of access to many masterpieces of literature and the pictorial arts, and a statute yielding such deprivation would not only be laughably absurd but would squarely oppose the intention of the cultivated men who framed and adopted the First Amendment.

This exception—nowhere to be found in the statute—is a judge-made device invented to avoid that absurdity. The fact that the judges have felt the necessity of seeking that avoidance, serves to suggest forcibly that the statute, in its attempt to control what our citizens may read and see, violates the First Amendment. For no one can rationally justify the judge-made exception. The contention would scarcely pass as rational that the "classics" will be read or seen solely by an intellectual or artistic elite; for, even ignoring the snobbish, undemocratic, nature of this contention, there is no evidence that the elite has a moral fortitude (an immunity from moral corruption) superior to that of the "masses." And if the exception, to make it rational, were taken as meaning that a contemporary book is exempt if it equates in "literary distinction" with the "classics," the result would be amazing: Judges would have to serve as literary critics; jurisprudence would merge with aesthetics; authors and publishers would consult the legal digests for legal-artistic precedents; we would some day have a Legal Restatement of the Canons of Literary Taste.

The exception of the "classics" is therefore irrational. Consequently, it would seem that we should interpret the statute rationally—that is, without that exception. If, however, the exception, as an exception, is irrational, then it would appear that, to render the statute valid, the standard applied to the "classics" should be applied to all books and pictures. The result would be that, in order to be constitutional, the statute must be wholly inefficacious.

## How Censorship Under the Statute Actually Operates

### (a) Prosecutors, as censors, actually exercise prior restraint

Fear of punishment serves as a powerful restraint on publication, and fear of punishment often means, practically, fear of prosecution. For most men dread indictment and prosecution; the publicity alone terrifies, and to defend a criminal action is expensive. If the definition of obscenity had a limited and fairly well-known scope, that fear might deter restricted sorts of publications only. But on account of the extremely vague judicial definition of the obscene, a person threatened with prosecution if he mails (or otherwise sends in interstate commerce) almost any book which deals in an unconventional, unorthodox manner with sex, may well apprehend that, should the threat be carried out, he will be punished. As a result, each prosecutor becomes a literary censor (that is, dictator) with immense unbridled power, a virtually uncontrolled discretion. A statute would be invalid which gave the Postmaster General the power, without reference to any standard, to close the mails to any publication he happened to dislike. Yet, a federal prosecutor, under the federal obscenity statute, approximates that position: Within wide limits, he can (on the advice of the Postmaster General or on no one's advice) exercise such a censorship by threat, without a trial, without any judicial supervision, capriciously and arbitrarily. Having no special qualifications for that task, nevertheless, he can, in large measure, determine at his will what those within his district may not read on sexual subjects. (It is, therefore, doubtful whether, as suggested by Emerson, . . . a statute calling for punishment involves very much less arbitrary conduct and very much less censorship than one calling for prior restraint. In actual fact, by his threats of prosecution, the prosecutor does exercise prior restraint. . . .) In that way, the statute brings about an actual prior restraint of free speech and free press which strikingly flouts the First Amendment.

### (b) Judges as censors

When a prosecution is instituted and a trial begins, much censorship power passes to the trial judge: If he sits without a jury, he must decide whether a book is obscene. If the trial is by jury, then, if he thinks the book plainly not obscene, he directs a verdict for the accused or, after a verdict of guilt, enters a judgment of acquittal. How does the judge determine whether a book is obscene? Not by way of evidence introduced at the trial, but by way of some sort of judicial notice. Whence come the judicial notice data to inform him?

Those whose views most judges know best are other lawyers. Judges can and should take judicial notice that, at many gatherings of lawyers at Bar Associations or of alumni of our leading law schools, tales are told fully as "obscene" as many of those distributed by men, like the defendant, convicted for violation of the obscenity statute. Should not judges, then, set aside such convictions? If they do not, are they not somewhat arrogantly concluding that lawyers are an exempt elite, unharmed by what will harm the multitude of other Americans? If lawyers are not such an elite then, since, in spite of the "obscene" tales lawyers frequently tell one another, data are lacking that lawyers as a group become singularly addicted to depraved sexual conduct, should not judges conclude that "obscenity" does not importantly contribute to such misconduct, and that therefore the statute is unconstitutional?

### (c) Jurors as censors

If, in a jury case, the trial judge does not direct a verdict or enter a judgment of acquittal, the jury exercises the censorship power. Courts have said that a jury has a peculiar aptitude as a censor of obscenity, since, representing a cross section of the community, it knows peculiarly well the "common conscience" of the time. Yet no statistician would conceivably accept the views of a jury—twelve persons chosen at random—as a fair sample of community attitudes on such a subject as obscenity. A particular jury may voice the "moral sentiments" of a generation ago, not of the present time.

Each jury verdict in an obscenity case has been sagely called "really a small bit of legislation ad hoc." So each jury constitutes a tiny autonomous legislature. Any one such tiny legislature, as experience teaches, may well differ from any other, in thus legislating as to obscenity. And, one may ask, was it the purpose of the First Amendment, to authorize hundreds of divers jury-legislatures, with discrepant beliefs, to decide whether or not to enact hundreds of divers statutes interfering with freedom of expression? (I shall note, infra, the vast difference between the applications by juries of the "reasonable man" standard and the "obscenity" standard.)

## The Dangerously Infectious Nature of Governmental Censorship of Books

Governmental control of ideas or personal preferences is alien to a democracy. And the yearning to use governmental censorship of any kind is infectious. It may spread insidiously. Commencing with the suppression of books as obscene, it is not unlikely to develop into official lust for the power of thought-control in the areas of religion, politics, and elsewhere. Milton observed that "licensing of books * * * necessarily pulls along with it so many other kinds of licensing." J. S. Mill noted that the "bounds of what may be called moral police" may easily extend "until it encroaches on the most unquestionably legitimate liberty of the individual." We should beware of a recrudescence of the undemocratic doctrine uttered in the 17th century by Berkeley, Governor of Virginia: "Thank God there are no free schools or preaching, for learning has brought disobedience into the world, and printing has divulged them. God keep us from both."

### The people as self-guardians: censorship by public opinion, not by government

Plato, who detested democracy, proposed to banish all poets; and his rulers were to serve as "guardians" of the people, telling lies for the people's good, vigorously suppressing writings these guardians thought dangerous. Governmental guardianship is repugnant to the basic tenet of our democracy: According to our ideals, our adult citizens are self-guardians, to act as their own fathers, and thus become self-dependent. When our governmental officials act towards our citizens on the thesis that "Papa knows best what's good for you," they enervate the spirit of the citizens: To treat grown men like infants is to make them infantile, dependent, immature.

So have sagacious men often insisted. Milton, in his *Areopagitica*, denounced such paternalism: "We censure them for a giddy, vicious and unguided people, in such sick and weak [a] state of faith and discretion as to be able to take down nothing but through the pipe of a licensor." "We both consider the people as our children," wrote Jefferson to Dupont de Nemours, "but you love them as infants whom you are afraid to trust without nurses, and I as adults whom I freely leave to self-government." Tocqueville sagely remarked: "No form or combination of social policy has yet been devised to make an energetic people of a community of pusillanimous and enfeebled citizens." "Man," warned Goethe, "is easily accustomed to slavery and learns quickly to be obedient when his freedom is taken from him." Said Carl Becker, "Self-government, and the spirit of freedom that sustains it, can be maintained only if the people have sufficient intelligence and honesty to maintain them with a minimum of legal compulsion. This heavy responsibility is the price of freedom." The "great art," according to Milton, "lies to discern in what the law is to bid restraint and punishment, and in what things persuasion only is to work." *So we come back, once more, to Jefferson's advice: The only completely democratic way to control publications which arouse mere thoughts or feelings is through non-governmental censorship by public opinion.*

## The Seeming Paradox of the First Amendment

Here we encounter an apparent paradox: The First Amendment, judicially enforced, curbs public opinion when translated into a statue which restricts freedom of expression (except that which will probably induce undesirable conduct). *The paradox is unreal: The Amendment ensures that public opinion—the "common conscience of the time"—shall not commit suicide through legislation which chokes off today the free expression of minority views which may become the majority public opinion of tomorrow.*

### Private persons or groups may validly try to influence public opinion

The First Amendment obviously has nothing to do with the way persons or groups, not a part of government, influence public opinion as to what constitutes "decency" or "obscenity." The Catholic Church, for example, has a constitutional right to persuade or instruct its adherents not to read designated books or kinds of books.

## The Fine Arts Are Within the First Amendment's Protection

"The framers of the First Amendment," writes Chafee, "must have had literature and art in mind, because our first national statement on the subject of 'freedom of the press,' the 1774 address of the Continental Congress to the inhabitants of Quebec, declared, 'The importance of this (freedom of the press) consists, beside the advancement of truth, science, morality and arts in general, in its diffusion of liberal sentiments on the administration of government"; 165 years later, President Franklin Roosevelt said, "The arts cannot thrive except where men are free to be themselves and to be in charge of the discipline of their own energies and ardors. The conditions for democracy and for art are one and the same. What we call liberty in politics results in freedom of the arts." The converse is also true.

In our industrial era when, perforce, economic pursuits must be, increasingly, governmentally regulated, it is especially important that the realm of art—the non-economic realm—should remain free, unregimented, the domain of free enterprise, of unhampered competition at its maximum. An individual's taste is his own, private, concern. De gustibus non disputandum represents a valued democratic maxim.

Milton wrote: "For though a licenser should happen to be judicious more than the ordinary, yet his very office * * * enjoins him to let pass nothing but what is vulgarly received already." He asked, "What a fine conformity would it starch us all into? * * * We may fall * * * into a gross conformity stupidly.* * *" In 1859, J. S. Mill, in his essay On Liberty, maintained that conformity in taste is not a virtue but a vice. "The danger," he wrote, "is not the excess but the deficiency of personal impulses and preferences. By dint of not following their own nature [men] have no nature to follow. * * * Individual spontaneity is entitled to free exercise. * * * That so few men dare to be eccentric marks the chief danger of the time." Pressed by the demand for conformity, a people degenerate into "the deep slumber of a decided opinion," yield a "dull and torpid consent" to the accustomed. "Mental despotism" ensues. For "whatever crushes individuality is despotism by whatever name it be called. * * * It is not by wearing down into uniformity all that is individual in themselves, but by cultivating it, and calling it forth, within the limits imposed by the rights and interests of others, that human beings become a noble and beautiful object of contemplation; and as the works partake the character of those who do them, by the same process human life also becomes rich, diversified, and animating. * * *

In proportion to the development of his individuality, each person becomes more valuable to himself, and is therefore capable of being more valuable to others. There is a greater fullness of life about his own existence, and when there is more life in the units there is more in the mass which is composed of them."

To vest a few fallible men—prosecutors, judges, jurors—with vast powers of literary or artistic censorship, to convert them into what J. S. Mill called a "moral police," is to make them despotic arbiters of literary products. If one day they ban mediocre books as obscene, another day they may do likewise to a work of genius. Originality, not too plentiful, should be cherished, not stifled. An author's imagination may be cramped if he must write with one eye on prosecutors or juries; authors must cope with publishers who, fearful about the judgments of governmental censors, may refuse to accept the manuscripts of contemporary Shelleys or Mark Twains or Whitmans. (Milton remarked that "not to count him fit to print his mind without a tutor or examiner, lest he should drop * * * something of corruption, is the greatest * * * indignity to a free and knowing spirit that can be put upon him.")

Some few men stubbornly fight for the right to write or publish or distribute books which the great majority at the time consider loathsome. If we jail those few, the community may appear to have suffered nothing. The appearance is deceptive. For the conviction and punishment of these few will terrify writers who are more sensitive, less eager for a fight. What, as a result, they do not write might have been major literary contributions. "Suppression," Spinoza said, "is paring down the state till it is too small to harbor men of talent."

## The Motive or Intention of the Author, Publisher or Distributor Cannot Be the Test

Some courts once held that the motive or intention of the author, painter, publisher or distributor constituted the test of obscenity. That test, the courts have abandoned: That a man who mails a book or picture believes it entirely "pure" is no defense if the court finds it obscene. . . . Nor, conversely, will he be criminally liable for mailing a "pure" publication—Stevenson's *Child's Garden of Verses* or a simple photograph of the Washington Monument—he mistakenly believes obscene. Most courts now look to the "objective" intention, which can only mean the effect on those who read the book or see the picture; the motive of the mailer is irrelevant because it cannot affect that effect.

## Judge Bok's Decision as to the Causal Relation
## to Antisocial Conduct

In Commonwealth v. Gordon . . . Judge Bok said: "A book, however sexually impure and pornographic * * * cannot be a present danger unless its reader closes it, lays it aside, and transmutes its erotic allurement into overt action. That such action must inevitably follow as a direct consequence of reading the book does not bear analysis, nor is it borne out by general human experience; too much can intervene and too many diversions take place. * * * The only clear and present danger * * * that will satisfy * * * the Constitution * * * is the commission or the imminence of the commission of criminal behavior resulting from the reading of a book. Publication alone can have no such automatic effect." The constitutional operation of "the statute," Judge Bok continued, thus "rests on narrow ground. * * * I hold that [the statute] may constitutionally be applied * * * only where there is a reasonable and demonstrable cause to believe that a crime or misdemeanor has been committed or is about to be committed as the perceptible result of the publication and distribution of the writing in question: the opinion of anyone that a tendency thereto exists or that such a result is self-evident is insufficient and irrelevant. The causal connection between the book and the criminal behavior must appear beyond a reasonable doubt."

I confess that I incline to agree with Judge Bok's opinion. But I think it should be modified in a few respects: (a) Because of the Supreme Court's opinion in the Dennis case . . . decided since Judge Bok wrote, I would stress the element of probability in speaking of a "clear danger." (b) I think the danger need not be that of probably inducing behavior which has already been made criminal at common law or by statute, but rather of probably inducing any seriously antisocial conduct (that is, conduct which, by statute, could validly be made a state or federal crime). (c) I think that the causal relation need not be between such antisocial conduct and a particular book involved in the case on trial, but rather between such conduct and a book of the kind or type involved in the case. (According to Judge Bok, an obscenity statute may be validly enforced when there is proof of a causal relation between a particular book and undesirable conduct. Almost surely, such proof cannot ever be adduced. In the instant case, the government did not attempt to prove it.)

## The Void-for-Vagueness Argument

There is another reason for doubting the constitutionality of the obscenity statute. The exquisite vagueness of the word "obscenity" is apparent from the way the judicial definition of that word has kept shifting: Once (as we saw) the courts held a work obscene if it would probably stimulate improper thoughts or desires in abnormal persons; now most courts consider only the assumed impact on the thoughts or desires of the adult "normal" or average human being. A standard so difficult for our ablest judges to interpret is hardly one which has a "well-settled" meaning, a meaning sufficient adequately to advise a man whether he is or is not committing a crime if he mails a book or picture. . . .

237 F2d 796 (1956)

*The case was reviewed by the Supreme Court which affirmed the lower court's decision.*

354 U.S. 476 (1957)

# THE FALLACY OF UNIVERSAL LAW &

M AITLAND's "seamless web" theory of history expresses but a half-truth; and half-truths notoriously mislead. In a fundamental sense, history is not unitary but full of disjunctions. The inquiring person carefully scrutinizing civilizations and their institutions perceives many seams. Every culture contains components acquired accidentally through causes external to the culture. Culture traits which in their native habitat were functionally associated may continue to be coupled in an alien culture where the reason for the coupling has ceased to exist. Important among the ingredients of our culture which have not been wholly integrated with others, we can discern many acquired from Greece. Through Rome, Greek legal ideas have had significant influences on our legal system. Scholars differ about the extent of those influences—for instance, as to the effect of Greek ideas of equity, via civil and canon law, on the Anglo-American concept of equity. Time was when English and American scholars heavily discounted the Greco-Roman factor, tracing most of our basic legal notions to Germanic sources. World War I, which made Germany our foe and Italy our ally, tended to bring more appreciation of Greco-Roman origins. Perhaps World War II, with both Germany and Italy ranged against us, will redress the balance, will yield a more impartial appraisal of origins.

But whatever historians may say of such questions of genetics, a study of Greek legal thinking has direct present value for us: the reflections of the wisest Greeks on the problems of government can aid us in facing similar problems today. For those problems are, in part, recurrent; and they, and some of their possible solutions, were brilliantly articulated by keen-minded men in ancient Greece.

Those of us who do not read Greek with ease can probably trust the translations made by experts. Adequate translation of texts, however, is not enough. Thorough understanding requires complete translation of the spirit of the ancient authors. And such translation is impossible. (See how difficult it is for us to understand the greatest English poet, dead but some three centuries. . . .) For many of the attitudes which color a man's thinking are those which he holds in common with men of his time; those attitudes he takes for granted, does not express. The taken-for-granted attitudes of the ancient Greeks no one can hope to recapture. But there are some aspects of the background of many texts, helpful to their understanding, which, while absent from the texts themselves, have been elsewhere preserved. A book like Calhoun's [Introduction to Greek Legal Science] supplies an invaluable key to knowledge of that background. (For example, he notes, the common error of referring to the popular courts of the fourth and fifth centuries B.C. as "juries," and to their members as "jurors"; and points out that the members of these courts were "as truly judges as any who wear the ermine today," and were "capable of deciding questions involving fundamental legal questions." . . .)

We learn that in Athens courts declared legislation unconstitutional and therefore void; "judicial supremacy" did not originate in England or America. We are told that in Greece men vainly sought legal certainty through codification, tried to make interpretation of their codes illegal, and believed that through written laws the common man could easily learn his legal rights; thus we see that the ideas of eighteenth and nineteenth century legal reformers, like Frederich the Great, Napoleon, Bentham, and Edward Livingston, were anticipated, as was also the idea of law revision commissions. As in modern times, attempts to arrest legal change by legislation paradoxically accelerated change, unwittingly fostered complexity and uncertainty. We discover that the Athenian democracy deliberately and knowingly rejected "representative" government in favor of direct participation of all citizens in government because (like our American democracy of the Jacksonian era) it believed that professional specialization was oligarchic, undemocratic. (Here we come upon the problem of how a democracy should deal with "experts," a problem that has recently provoked much angry discussion of administrative agencies and "bureaucrats." . . . )

Precisely because this little book supplies a valuable introduction to Greek attitudes toward legal and political affairs, it seems well to protest against the note on which it ends. The "most important element," says Calhoun, in Greek "philosophy of law" is "perhaps the continuity and tenacity of the doctrine of natural law. * * * The emphasis placed on this doctrine by the Stoics made it a factor of importance in the development of Roman Law." It is, he writes, "implicit in the Platonic dialogues in which the nature and authority of law are under consideration; it is specifically formulated by Aristotle and fundamental to his legal philosophy. In proof of this comment, Calhoun states that in Aristotle's *Rhetoric* "an underlying assumption throughout is the doctrine of natural law, the validity of an absolute standard of right, behind and above the particular statute or code; * * * the notion of equity * * * is connected by Aristotle with the unwritten common law which is in accordance with nature, and unlike written codes, always remains and never changes. So the doctrine of equity serves as * * * a theoretical link between the imperfection of human legislation and the perfection of the absolute unwritten law of nature."

Here Calhoun accepts unhesitatingly the traditional notion that the views of Aristotle on this question coincided substantially with those of Plato and led smoothly to the Stoic doctrine. As an amateur in this field, it may be presumptuous to criticize Calhoun, but when I read Aristotle, and particularly his *Rhetoric* on which Calhoun relies, I reach a very different conclusion. And a discussion of the reasons for my dissent may not be amiss: since study of Aristotle is being widely encouraged today, and since from him, via Harrington and John Adams, the concept of "a government of laws, and not of men" has become part of the American political and legal philosophy, Aristotle's attitude toward "law" has some contemporary importance.

We may begin by noting, Calhoun himself reminds us, that although the Athenians abhorred professionalism, professional teachers wrote handbooks, called *Rhetorics*, on the conduct of litigation in order to enable citizens to handle their own lawsuits. Aristotle's manual on that subject is apparently the earliest of such handbooks now extant. Let us, then, observe the character of his treatise to see whether it supports Calhoun's thesis concerning Aristotle's views of "natural law."

Defining rhetoric as "the art of persuasion," Aristotle remarks that it "exists to affect the giving of decisions" including those "in lawsuits." And persuasion must in every case be affected either by working on the emotions of the judges themselves, by giving them the right impression of the speakers' character, or by proving the truth of the statements made. For "the whole business of rhetoric" is "concerned with appearances." Since "people always think well of speeches adapted to and reflecting their own character," it is important to "compose our speeches so as to adapt them and ourselves to our audiences." So he analyzes "the various types of human character in relation to the emotions and moral qualities," showing how they correspond to "various ages." And Aristotle tells how "to excite prejudice," by aiming at the hearer's "good will, or at arousing his resentment, or sometimes at gaining his serious attention to the case, or even at distracting it—for gaining it is not always an advantage, and speakers will often for that reason try to make him laugh." He shows how to argue many questions in opposing ways: E.g., education leads to unpopularity which is bad, and to wisdom, which is good. Hence, you either argue, 'It is therefore not well to be educated, since it is not well to be unpopular'; or you answer, 'No, it is well to be educated, since it is well to be wise.'" Referring to a certain kind of argument, he says, "We are to make either such assumptions or their opposites, as suits us best." He writes, "Another line is to apply to the speaker what he has said against yourself. It is an excellent turn to give a debate. * * * The purpose is to discredit the prosecutor." "Even hackneyed and commonplace maxims are to be used, if they suit one's purpose: just because they are commonplace, everyone seems to agree with them, and therefore they are taken for truth." And the following passage gives the flavor of this entire treastise:

In dealing with the evidence of witnesses, the following are useful arguments. If you have no witnesses on your side, you will argue that the judges must decide from what is probable; that this is meant by "giving a verdict in accordance with one's honest opinion"; that probabilities cannot be bribed to mislead the court; and that probabilities are never convicted of perjury. If you *have* witnesses, and the other man has not, you will argue that probabilities cannot be put on their trial, and that we could do without the evidence of witnesses altogether if we need do no more than balance the pleas advanced on either side.

The evidence of witnesses may refer either to ourselves or to our opponent; and either to questions of fact or to questions of personal character: so, clearly, we need never be at a loss for useful evidence. For if we have no evidence of fact supporting our own case or telling against that of our opponent, at least we can always find evidence to prove our own worth or our opponent's worthlessness. Other arguments about a witness—that he is a friend or an enemy or neutral, or has a good, bad, or indifferent reputation, and any other such distinctions—we must construe upon the same general lines as we use for the regular rhetorical proofs.

It is in such a setting that twice, in the course of a few pages, he discusses "universal law." The first time he writes in a seemingly objective expository manner of "two kinds of law," that is, "particular and universal law." He there says, in the passage on which Calhoun and those who agree with him rely:

Particular law is that which each community lays down and applies to its own members: this is partly written and partly unwritten. Universal law is the law of nature. For there really is, as everyone to some extent divines, a natural justice and injustice that is binding on all men, even on those who have no association or covenant with each other. It is this that Sophocles' Antigone clearly means when she says that the burial of Polyneices was a just act in spite of the prohibition: she means that it was just by nature. . . .

However, in a passage which follows soon after, a passage which Calhoun and the traditionalists never mention, Aristotle writes:

First, then, let us take laws and see how they are to be used in persuasion and dissuasion, in accusation and defence. If the written law tells against our case, clearly we must appeal to the universal law, and insist on its greater equity and justice. We must argue that the juror's oath "I will give my verdict according to my honest opinion" means that one will simply follow the letter of the written law. We must urge that the principles of equity are permanent and changeless, and that the universal laws does not change either, for it is the law of nature, whereas written laws often do change. This is the bearing of the lines in Sophocles' Antigone, where Antigone pleads that in burying her brother she had broken Creon's law, but not the unwritten law: "Not of today or yester-day they are, But live eternal: none can date their birth. Not I would fear the wrath of any man, And brave Gods' vengeance for defying these." We shall argue that justice indeed is true and profitable, but that sham justice is not, and that consequently the written law is not, because it does not fulfil the true pur-pose of law. Or that justice is like silver, and must be assayed by the judges, if the genuine is to be distinguished from the counterfeit. Or that the better a man is, the more he will follow and abide by the unwritten law in preference to the written. Or perhaps that the law in question contradicts some other highly es-teemed law, or even contradicts itself. Thus it may be that one law will enact that all contracts must be held binding, while another forbids us ever to make illegal contracts. Or if a law is ambiguous, we shall turn it about and consider which construction best fits the interests of justice or utility, and then follow that way of looking at it. . . . If however the written law supports our case, we must urge that the oath "to give my verdict according to my honest opinion" is not meant to make the judges give a verdict that is contrary to the law, but to save them from the guilt of perjury if they misunderstand what the law really means. . . . Or that not to use the laws is as bad as to have no laws at all. . . . Or that trying to be cleverer than the laws is just what is forbidden by those codes of law that are accounted best. * * *

When we turn to Aristotle's other writings, skepticism increases as to his belief in eternal unchanging natural law. For, as with many Greek thinkers from the earliest days of Greek philosophizing, his views of nature (physics) and of human affairs interlace and interact. And here, as elsewhere, he deviated sharply from Plato. Plato, lovers of democracy should never forget, detested democracy, and was an ardent propagandist for the authoritarian, totalitarian state. "No one who does not know," he wrote satirically, an-ticipating Hitler, "would believe how much greater is the liberty which animals who are under the dominion of men have in a democracy than in any other State: for, truly the she-dogs, as the proverb says, are as good as their she-mistresses, and the horses and asses have a way of marching along with all the rights and dignities of free men; and they will run at anybody who comes in their way, if he does not leave the way clear for them, and all things are just ready to burst with liberty." A proper state, he said, must be a caste-state, one which regiments all thought through rigid control of education. Even play must be disciplined, for innovation in play might lead to innovations in serious affairs, and all departures from the established order involve grave risks to the health of society; accordingly, any novelty in music and poetry must be regarded as sacrilegious. In the interest of maintaining order, the rulers should "have the privilege of lying" for the public good. Recognizing that, despite all care, some men would dissent, Plato, who urged state regulation of religious beliefs, advised severe punishment for heretics. His conception of the ultimate character of reality, discerned behind what (to him) was the disturbing flux of circumstance, corresponded to and reflected Plato's ideal of the state: that of a fixed, virtually unchanging, order. The totalitarian Plato, not Aristotle, espouses the notion of a never-changing natural law.

This is not the place to appraise that concept or to point out in detail how ambiguities in the words "natural law" have made them a slogan usable and used not only by democrats and devoutly religious men but also by despots and atheists. But this much can here be said: Those who, in the interest of emphasizing the importance of ideals, urge us to read Plato, should warn us that he despised democracy, should remember, too, that some ideals are loathsome, that, for example, Nazidom has its ideals, its own vicious notions of "natural law" and justice. (All ideals, one might say, are not "ideal.")

It is perhaps not without significance that the great physicist Schroe-dinger, a refugee from the Nazi regime, has emphasized the inadequacy of scientific determinism and encouraged a belief in "acausalism." In the nine-teenth century, when most scientists were determinists and when determinism dominated much thinking about politics and economics, most students of Aristotle glossed over what seemed to them his scandalous idea of chance. For to him chance was not but a label for man's ignorance of causes; it was an inescapable part of reality. Some events, he maintained, came about without any determining cause of principle whatever, by "lawless" sporadic action incapable of being brought within the scope of tidy, undeviating, scientific laws. He entertained a correlative notion of human affairs: No society, he thought, could or should try to be air-tight, endeavor to blot out individuality, originality, novelty. The loose texture of democracy did not with him, as it did with Plato, invite derision. Since he saw unconquerable unruliness, spontaneous chance and change, as part of reality, his notion of "natural law" was not likely to be that of an "absolute standard," permanent and un-changing. Anti-Platonist, antitotalitarian, he was an exponent of a point of view which, once more, we today are formulating: That all the legal rules men encounter in actual experience are man-made, but that the ideal of justice is ever at work, demanding that, to meet new circumstances, those rules be constantly adjusted so that, in particular cases, they will respond to the community's sense of fairness. The word "justice," too, someone may reply, is vague and has many meanings. But it carries no false connotation of being a gift to mankind, something that men can attain effortlessly.

There have been persons bold enough deliberately to break away from the fashion of reasoning in terms of the "natural" about a desirable social order—of reasoning as if the desirable must grow naturally, or that what has grown naturally must be right. They have dared to say that men cannot find, ready-made, in nature any laws or rules which prescribe what is just, decent, humane; that observation of nature can merely inform us as to what we can and cannot do, and never what we ought or ought not to do. Civilization, they say, represents a human achievement resulting from man's changing what would otherwise have been the course of nature; in that sense, the values, the ideals, of civilized man are not "natural" but "artificial." Foremost among those daring souls was Thomas Huxley. He was outraged by the "social Darwinism" of his day, by Herbert Spencer's creed of acceptance of ruthless natural laws, by the uses to which the study of nature (which Huxley himself had done much to advance) were being put by those who said that, as in nature there is a relentless selfish struggle for existence, therefore crass individualistic egotism must be the basis of social morality. Huxley proclaimed:

Let us understand, once for all, that the ethical progress of society depends, not on imitating the cosmic process, still less in running away from it, but in combating it. It may seem an audacious proposal thus to pit the microcosm against the macrocosm and to set man to subdue nature to his higher ends; but I venture to think that the great intellectual difference between the ancient times * * * and our day, lies in the solid foundation we have acquired for the hope that such an enterprise may meet with a certain measure of success. The history of civilization details the steps by which men have succeeded in building up an artificial world within the cosmos. Fragile reed as he may be, man, as Pascal says, is a thinking reed: there lies within him a fund of energy, operating intelligently and so far akin to that which pervades the universe, that it is competent to influence and modify the cosmic process. In virtue of his intelligence, the dwarf bends the Titan to his will. * * * Laws and moral precepts are directed to the end of curbing the cosmic process and reminding the individual of his duty to the community, to the protection and influence of which he owes, if not existence itself, at least the life of something better than a brutal savage. * * * the practice of that which is ethically best—what we call goodness or virtue—involves a course of conduct which, in all respects, is opposed to that which leads to success in the cosmic struggle for existence. In place of ruthless self-assertion it demands self-restraint; in place of thrusting aside, or treading down, all competitors, it requires that the individual shall not merely respect, but shall help his fellows; its influence is directed, not so much to the survival of the fittest, as to the fitting of as many as possible to survive. It repudiates the gladiatorial theory of existence. * * * [C]osmic nature is not school of virtue, but the headquarters of the enemy of ethical nature. * * * The thief and the murderer follow nature just as much as the philanthropist * * * the cosmic process has no sort of relation to moral ends; * * * the imitation of it by man is inconsistent with the first principles of ethics. * * * [We have] command over the course of non-human nature greater than that once attributed to the magicians. * * * And much may be done to change the nature of man himself.

Surely that is sound thinking. One may today disagree with some of Huxley's science; one may find some of his theology wholly or partly un-acceptable; but such disagreement is no more a justification for disregarding his sagacious reflections on the relation between nature and ethics than for refusing to utilize a helpful mechanical invention because it was discovered by a Fascist. Aided by Huxley's analysis, we should agree with Fouillée that we ought not speak of "natural rights" but of "ideal rights," since "nature knows nothing of rights, which appear only in the thoughts of man." Nature is no copybook containing precepts for civilized man. Nor is human nature, unartificialized, a sound foundation for a beneficent social structure. Millions of Nazis today disclose what human nature can be. When Cicero said that justice is implanted in man's nature, he was wise enough to observe (even if parenthetically) that habits can deafen men to the call of such justice. Thomas Aquinas taught that there are men whose reason is so perverted that they fail to follow the dictates of "natural reason." The rules of civilized behavior cannot operate, of course, if they demand that which physical nature makes impossible, or that to which human nature cannot conform. But those rules are not the products of the unguided workings of nature, human or otherwise. They are not to be logically reasoned from principles found in nature. They constitute the glorious accomplishments of original, inventive, enterprising, noble-spirited, civilized men—godly men, if you please.

To say that is not to reject religion. Man is part of the universe, which, because of his finiteness, he cannot fully comprehend. His achievements, his ideals—both the good and the evil ones—are "natural" because he and they are parts of nature. (In that sense, if ideals which some men regard as noble are realized, they are "natural.") Man does not find his "oughts" spelled out for him in nature; he puts them there. Religion may perhaps be defined as faith that man's ideals are achievable and will be achieved, his hope that the universe, of which he can understand but a limited portion, will not prevent those ideals from being actualized and from, in some part, surviving. That is a sorry, sickly, religion which says that man can have what he wants for the mere asking, that his values, his achievements, are donations handed to him by nature. Men can attain what they consider the good life only by ener-getically striving for it, while recognizing that they will never reach perfec-tion. That is the traditional American faith. It does not accept the Stoic

Epictetus' defeatist belief, adopted by Hegel, that freedom consists of learning "to wish that everything may happen as it does."

Unless we guard ourselves against the traditional interpretation of Aristotle as essentially a Platonist, we lose the present value to us of many of Aristotle's wise insights. Thus, had Calhoun not succumbed to that tradition, he might have brought out the anti-Platonic character of Aristotle's idea of "a government of laws and not of men." . . . [S]agely, [Aristotle] noted that "there may indeed be cases in which the law seems unable to determine," and asked "but in such cases can a man?" He answered that "the law trains officers for this express purpose, and appoints them to determine matters which are left undecided by it, to the best of their judgment. Further it permits them to make any amendment of the existing laws which experience suggests. * * * And at this day there are magistrates, for example judges, who have authority to decide matters which the law is unable to determine. * * *" He added that "no one doubts that the law would command and decide in the best manner whenever it could. But some things can, and others cannot be comprehended under the law, and this is the origin of the vexed question whether the best law or the best man should rule. For matters of detail about which men deliberate cannot be included in legislation. Nor does anyone deny that the decisions of such matters must be left to man. * * *" By a "government of men" Aristotle apparently meant a government in which a specific judgment or decree affecting a specific person is rendered by the legislator or legislative body. Curiously, some of our Congressional "private bill" legislation would come within that criticized category. (Aristotle's point of view reappeared in a *New York Times* editorial: "It is the proper function of Congress to frame laws and general policies, to delegate powers wherever detailed control is necessary, and to see that laws are properly administered. But it is not the function of Congress itself to administer the law. It is not its business to meddle in specific decisions. Once it undertakes to do so, * * * [i]t will find itself overwhelmed with administrative details that it is not remotely organized to attend to. * * * Such detailed meddling can only * * * lead toward administrative chaos." *New York Times*, Dec. 15, 1943, p. 26, col. 2)

But if this little book by Calhoun has its defects, it has also many offsetting virtues. At a time when a war with Fascism has compelled us to reexamine carefully our first principles of government, it is worthwhile to have at hand a volume which brings to our attention the following gem from Xenophon's *Memorabilia*:

It is said that Alcibiades, before he was twenty, had a conversation on the subject of law with Pericles, his guardian and head of the government, somewhat as follows:

"Tell me, Pericles," he said, "could you explain to me what a law is?"

"Why of course," said Pericles.

"Then for Heaven's sake explain it," said Alcibiades. "For when I hear people being praised for being law-abiding I have the idea that a man couldn't rightly be accorded this praise if he didn't know what a law is."

"Well, what you want is nothing difficult, Alcibiades," said Pericles. "Why all these are laws which the people in assembly approve and enact, setting forth what is or is not to be done."

"With the idea that good is to be done, or bad?"

"Good, by Jove, my boy, and not bad!" said Pericles.

"But if it is not the people, but, as in an oligarchic state, a minority who assemble and enact what is or is not to be done, what is this?"

"Everything," said Pericles, "that the sovereign power in the state enacts with due deliberation, enjoining what is to be done, is termed a law."

"And if a despot, then, holding the sovereign power in the state, enacts rules for the citizens, enjoining what is to be done, is this, too, a law?"

"Yes, everything that a despot, as a ruler," said Pericles, "enacts, this, too, is termed a law."

"But force," said Alcibiades, "and lawlessness, what are they, Pericles? Is it not when a stronger compels a weaker to do his will, not by getting his consent but by force?"

"That is my idea," said Pericles.

"Then everything a despot compels the citizens to do by his enactments, without getting their consent, is lawlessness?"

"That is right," said Pericles. "I retract the statement that anything a despot enacts, without the consent of the citizens is law."

"But anything the minority enacts, not getting the consent of the majority but through superior power, shall we call this force or shall we not?"

"Anything, I think," said Pericles, "that anyone compels another to do without getting his consent, whether by enactment or otherwise, is force rather than law."

"Then anything that the whole people, by reason of being stronger than the well-to-do, enact without getting consent, would be force rather than law?"

"Let me tell you," said Pericles, "Alcibiades, when I was your age I was good at this sort of thing. For we used to practice just the sort of clever quibbling I think you are practicing now."

And Alcibiades said, "I should like to have met you in those days, Pericles, when you were at your best."

So should I. For there is many an Alcibiades abroad in the land today.

*Harvard Law Review* (book review of
*Introduction to Greek Legal Science* by George Calhoun, 1944)

# PART 3 ❧ What Courts Do in Fact

**EDITOR'S NOTE** ❧ Said Mr. Justice Holmes in 1897, "The prophecies of what the courts will do in fact, and nothing more pretentious, are what I mean by law." Thirty-four years later Jerome Frank wrote, "There are some words . . . which it might be well to abolish, if we could, because their vagueness provokes endless futile and sometimes rancorous disputation. . . . Suppose, then, that whenever a dispute arose as to the meaning of 'Law' . . . someone were to step in between the combatants and say, 'Why not, instead, discuss what courts do in fact?' " An analysis of what courts do in fact is the foundation of Jerome Frank's jurisprudence—referred to as "legal realism"—to which this section is devoted. The group which I call "Certainty: The Legal Myth" consists of five chapters from *Law and the Modern Mind*, the author's first book. In the sections "Facts Are Guesses," "Getting at the Facts," "The Jury's Verdict," and "Legal Education," I have grouped together six chapters from *Courts on Trial*; an excerpt from *Not Guilty*, which I co-authored and which was published after Judge Frank's death; and a judicial opinion, *Skidmore v. Baltimore & Ohio R. Co.*

In publishing *Law and the Modern Mind* in 1930, the author began his frontal attack on conventional, complacent theories about our judicial system. The book, since become a classic, at once found itself the subject of heated controversy. It attempts a Freudian explanation—which the author emphasizes is only a partial one—of the fact that lawyers cling to and, thus, seek to perpetuate the socially harmful myth of certainty and predictability in "law." With its publication the author took his place in the ranks of the so-called legal realists. Despite his obvious zeal for judical reform, his critics accused him of "anti-rationalism" and "anti-idealism." In his Preface to the Sixth Printing of the book, written in 1948, he answered thus: "To accomplish . . . reform . . . one needs to look at, not away from, the non-rational and non-idealistic elements at play now in courthouse government. . . . There can be no greater hindrance to the growth of rationality than the illusion that one is rational when one is the dupe of illusions. Man can invent no better way to balk any of his ideals than the delusion that they have already been achieved." At the end of this important Preface (reprinted in the Anchor Books edition) the author refers the reader to a list of his post-1930 publications which amplify some of the major themes found in *Law and the Modern Mind*. Only a small portion of this book is reprinted here because *Courts on Trial*, published in 1949, is a later, more complete statement of many of the same themes.

In "Facts Are Guesses," "Getting at the Facts, and "The Jury's Verdict" I have attempted to incorporate Judge Frank's most important, more recent writings dealing with his self-styled "fact-skepticism," his major philosophical concern. For he came to believe that, due in part to human fallibility and, in part, to prejudice in its various forms, "fact-finding is today the soft spot in the administration of justice." He tirelessly devoted himself to the elimination of judicial error, insofar as that achievement is humanly possible. In *Courts on Trial* (in my opinion, his most important book), the reader will find him preoccupied with these twin notions: That the trial court, where the "facts" are found, is at the heart of the judicial process, for, in most instances, it is there that the fate of the individual is determined; and that the just disposition of that individual's fate is the major consideration. From that point of view, the book critically asseses the procedures of our trial courts. Judge Frank's intense concern for the individual remained his core literally until the day he died. The imprisonment or execution of an innocent person, the ultimate horror of the wrong verdict, is the subject of *Not Guilty*, in which thirty-six such actual cases are narrated. In the comments accompanying the narrative the inquisitive reader will find Judge Frank's most significant views about our methods of trying criminal cases. The book, stimulated by Edwin Borchard's earlier *Convicting the Innocent*, attempts to bring the message of that work up to date, with a greater appeal to a lay audience. Our major purpose in writing it was to arouse the public to the human tragedy of judicial injustice. In *Skidmore*, the author states his views about the jury system, which he thought the most imperfect instrument man could have devised for arriving at a just verdict; as a partial, although dubious, remedy, he urges a "fact" rather than a "general" verdict, so as to separate out, to the extent that that is possible, the functions of judge (the application of the legal rules) from jury (the finding of the facts).

In "Legal Education" the author vigorously criticizes the currently popular trend in law schools, one which he believes helps to perpetuate the legal myth of certainty and, hence, that complacency which breeds injustice. Since most law schools are "library schools," their students, mainly engaged in studying upper-court decisions, turn their backs on the all-important trial courts. In Chapter XVI of *Courts on Trial*, the author refers the reader to his other writings on the subject.

In basic disagreement with many brilliant legal philosophers, Jerome Frank thought that "John Q. Citizen should be told of the flaws in the workings of the courts, and should be taught to become well-qualified to consider them—differentiating between inherent, ineradicable, difficulties in the administration of justice and those which are eradicable and should be eliminated. For, in a democracy, the courts belong not to the judges and the lawyers, but to the citizens." ⧽

# CERTAINTY: THE LEGAL MYTH 🐦

THE LAY ATTITUDE toward lawyers is a compound of contradictions, a mingling of respect and derision. Although lawyers occupy leading positions in government and industry, although the public looks to them for guidance in meeting its most vital problems, yet concurrently it sneers at them as tricksters and quibblers.

Respect for the bar is not difficult to explain. Justice, the protection of life, the sanctity of property, the direction of social control—these fundamentals are the business of the law and of its ministers, the lawyers. Inevitably the importance of such functions invests the legal profession with dignity.

But coupled with a deference toward their function there is cynical disdain of the lawyers themselves. "Good jurist, bad Christian," preached Martin Luther in the sixteenth century. Frederich the Great and Herbert Hoover, Rabelais and H. G. Wells have echoed that sentiment. In varying forms it is repeated daily. The layman, despite the fact that he constantly calls upon lawyers for advice on innumerous questions, public and domestic, regards lawyers as equivocators, artists in double-dealing, masters of chicane. . . .

Diatribes against lawyers contain such words and phrases as "duplicity," "equivocation," "evasions," "a vast system of deception," "juggling," "sleight of hand," "craft and circumvention," "the art of puzzling and confounding," "darken by elucidation," "the pettifoging, hypocritical, brigandage rampant under forms of law." Kipling expresses the feeling of many in his fling at the "tribe who describe with a gibe the perversions of Justice."

What is the source of these doubts of the lawyer's honesty and sincerity?

A false tradition "invented by twelfth-century priests and monks," replies Dean Roscoe Pound. "For the most part clerical jealousy of the rising profession of non-clerical lawyers was the determining element. * * * Naturally, the clergy did not relinquish the practice of law without a protest." What those priests began, says Pound, Luther developed, and since Luther's day the other learned professions have taken over. "Unless one perceives that a struggle of professions for leadership is involved," one cannot understand the distrust of the legal profession. . . .

An ingenious explanation, but patently superficial. (Pound's other writings indicate that he would admit as much. The explanation quoted in the text is perhaps what Llewellyn calls one of Pound's "bed-time stories for the tired bar.") Surely twentieth-century mistrust of lawyers is based on something more than a twelfth-century monkish invention embodied in a tradition kept alive principally because the physicians, the engineers, and the journalists have been jealous of the lawyers' prestige. Modern dispraise of the Bar is not to be explained as merely an outcropping of angry rivalry; obviously it is not confined to members of competing professions. That lawyers are scheming hairsplitters is a popular commonplace.

What lies back of this popular criticism? It appears to be founded on a belief that the lawyers complicate the law, and complicate it wantonly and unnecessarily, that, if the legal profession did not interpose its craftiness and guile, the law could be clear, exact, and certain. The layman thinks that it would be possible so to revise the lawbooks that they would become something like logarithm tables, that the lawyers could, if only they would, contrive some kind of legal slide rule for finding exact legal answers. . . .

But the law as we have it is uncertain, indefinite, subject to incalculable changes. This condition the public ascribes to the men of law; the average person considers either that lawyers are grossly negligent or that they are guilty of malpractice, venally obscuring simple legal truths in order to foment needless litigation, engaging in a guild conspiracy of distortion and obfuscation in the interest of larger fees.

Now it must be conceded that, if the law can be made certain and invariable, the lawyers are grievously at fault. For the layman is justified in his opinion that the coefficient of legal uncertainty is unquestionably large, that to predict the decisions of the courts on many a point is impossible. . . .

Yet the layman errs in his belief that this lack of precision and finality is to be ascribed to the lawyers. The truth of the matter is that the popular notion of the possibilities of legal exactness is based upon a misconception. The law always has been, is now, and will ever continue to be, largely vague and variable. And how could this well be otherwise? The law deals with human relations in their most complicated aspects. The whole confused, shifting helter-skelter of life parades before it—more confused than ever, in our kaleidoscopic age.

Even in a relatively static society, men have never been able to construct a comprehensive, eternized set of rules anticipating all possible legal disputes and settling them in advance. Even in such a social order no one can foresee all the future permutations and combinations of events; situations are bound to occur which were never contemplated when the original rules were made. How much less is such a frozen legal system possible in modern times. New instruments of production, new modes of travel and of dwelling, new credit and ownership devices, new concentrations of capital, new social customs, habits, aims, and ideals—all these factors of innovation make vain the hope that definitive legal rules can be drafted that will forever after solve all legal problems. When human relationships are transforming daily, legal relationships cannot be expressed in enduring form. The constant development of unprecedented problems requires a legal system capable of fluidity and pliancy. (Unheeded by most members of the bar, a minority group of brilliant critics of our legal system have demonstrated that anything like complete legal certainty cannot be realized. They have made clear that, in the very nature of things, not nearly as much rigidity in law exists or can be procured as laymen or most lawyers suppose. The law, they point out, can make only relative and temporary compromises between stability and indispensable adjustment to the constantly shifting factors of social life. "All thinking about law has struggled to reconcile the conflicting demands of the need of stability and the need of change." And this struggle has been incessant. Law, in attempting a harmony of these conflicting demands, is at best governed by "the logic of probabilities." This point the reader will find expounded by such writers as Maine, Holmes, Pound, Cohen, Cardozo, Cook, Demogue, Geny, Gmelin, Gray, Green, Coudert, Bingham, Yntema, Hutcheson, Radin, Llewellyn and Lehman.) Our society would be straightjacketed were not the courts, with the able assistance of the lawyers, constantly overhauling the law and adapting it to the realities of ever-changing social, industrial, and political conditions; although changes cannot be made lightly, yet law must be more or less impermanent, experimental, and therefore not nicely calculable. *Much of the uncertainty of law is not an unfortunate accident: it is of immense social value.* . . .

Since legal tentativeness is inevitable and often socially desirable, it should not be considered an avoidable evil. But the public learns little or nothing of this desirability of legal tentativeness from the learned gentlemen of the law. Why this concealment? Have the lawyers a sinister purpose in concealing the inherent uncertainty of law? Why, it may fairly be asked, do they keep alive the popular belief that legal rules can be made predictable?

If lawyers are not responsible for legal indefiniteness, are they not guilty, at any rate, of duping the public as to the essential character of law? Are they not a profession of clever hypocrites?

There is no denying that the bar appears to employ elaborate pretenses to foster the misguided notions of the populace. Lawyers do not merely sustain the vulgar notion that law is capable of being made entirely stable and unvarying; they seem bent on creating the impression that, on the whole, it is already established and certain. When a client indignantly exclaims, "A pretty state of affairs when I can't learn exactly what my rights are!" how does the lawyer usually respond? With assurances that the situation is exceptional, that generally speaking the law is clear enough, but that in the particular instance, for some reason or other the applicable rules cannot be definitely ascertained. Often the facts are the scapegoat: "If," says the lawyer, "the facts of your case were established and undisputed, the law could be categorically stated." When this explanation won't wash, because the pertinent facts do not happen to be in doubt, the client is told that the rules affecting his problem have become but temporarily unsettled: "Congress has just passed a badly worded statute," or "The judges who have recently tampered with the law of the subject are exceptionally stupid, or thoughtless, or weak, or radical, or what not." Implicit in these rejoinders is the view that, for the most part, legal rights and obligations are clear and indubitable, and that such small portion of the law as is not already certain can easily be made so.

Of course, such assurances are unwarranted. Each week the courts decide hundreds of cases which purport to turn not on disputed "questions of fact" but solely on "points of law." If the law is unambiguous and predictable, what excuses can be made by the lawyers who lose these cases? They should know in advance of the decisions that the rules of law are adverse to their contentions. Why, then, are these suits brought or defended? In some few instances, doubtless, because of ignorance or cupidity or an effort to procure delay, or because a stubbornly litigious client insists. But in many cases, honest and intelligent counsel on both sides of such controversies can conscientiously advise their respective clients to engage in the contest; they can do so because, prior to the decision, the law is sufficiently in doubt to justify such advice.

It would seem, then, that the legal practitioners must be aware of the unsettled condition of the law. Yet observe the arguments of counsel in addressing the courts, or the very opinions of the courts themselves: they are worded as if correct decisions were arrived at by logical deduction from a precise and preexisting body of legal rules. Seldom do judges disclose any contingent elements in their reasoning, any doubts or lack of wholehearted conviction. The judicial vocabulary contains few phrases expressive of uncertainty. . . .

Why these pretenses, why this professional hypocrisy? The answer is an arresting one: There is no hypocrisy. The lawyers' pretenses are not consciously deceptive. The lawyers, themselves, like the laymen, fail to recognize fully the essentially plastic and mutable character of law. Although it is the chiefest function of lawyers to make the legal rules viable and pliable, a large part of the profession believes, and therefore encourages the laity to believe, that those rules either are or can be made essentially immutable. And so you will find lawyers saying that "The judicial process in ascertaining or applying the law is essentially similar to the process by which we acquire our knowledge of geometry. * * * In the great majority of cases the solution of them [legal problems] is as certain and exact as an answer to a problem in mathematics."

Now, the true art of the lawyer is the art of legal modification, an art highly useful to the layman. For the layman's interests, although he does not realize it, would be poorly served by an immobile system of law. Especially is this so in the twentieth century. The emphasis of our era is on change. . . . [T]he layman's ordinary practical needs would be seriously thwarted by an inelastic legal arrangement. A body of undeviating legal principles he would find unbearably procrustean. Yet paradoxically he and his lawyers, when they express their notions of a desirable legal system, usually state that they want the law to be everlastingly settled.

Here we arrive at a curious problem: Why do men crave an undesirable and indeed unrealizable permanence and fixity in law? . . . Why do the generality of lawyers insist that law should and can be clearly knowable and precisely predictable although, by doing so, they justify a popular belief in an absurd standard of legal exactness? Why do lawyers, indeed, themselves recognize such an absurd standard, which makes their admirable and socially valuable achievement—keeping the law supple and flexible—seem bungling and harmful? Why do men of our time repeat the complaint made by Francis Bacon several hundred years since, that "our laws, as they now stand, are subject to great incertainties" and adhere to his conviction that such "incertainties" are pernicious and altogether avoidable? . . .

One keen thinker, Wurzel, has directed his attention to this question. . . . He finds the answer in what he terms a "social want" for a body of law which shall appear to be, what it can never be, an exhaustive list of commands, issued by the state, sufficient to settle every conceivable controversy which may arise. He maintains that the psychology of our administration of justice imperatively requires that this "social want" be satisfied by false appearances. This is scarcely a sufficient answer. It provokes the further questions,

What is back of this "social want"? Why must law seem to be, what it is not, a virtually complete set of commands? . . . Why this desire to be fooled? . . .

We shall . . . attempt a partial answer. . . . If it be true that greater legal certainty is sought than is practically required or attainable, then the demand for excessive legal stability does not arise from practical needs. It must have its roots not in reality but in a yearning for something unreal. Which is to say that the widespread notion that law either is or can be made approximately stationary and certain is irrational and should be classed as an illusion or a myth.

What is the source of this basic legal myth?

\* \* \* \* \*

We are on the trail of a stubborn illusion. Where better, then, to look for clues than in the direction of childhood? For in children's problems, and in children's modes of meeting their problems, are to be found the sources of most of the confirmed illusions of later years.

It is indeed true, however platitudinous, that the child is father to the man. With more or less awareness, educators have always applied that truth; they have known—and not those in the Catholic Church alone—that attitudes formed in early years persist and play important roles in the views and opinions of adult life. Yet it is but yesterday that psychiatrists began systematically to relate the bad habits of youth to the maladjustments of later life. And only today are psychologists noting that the behavior patterns of early childhood are the basis of many subsequent adaptations. At long last, they are using a genetic approach; the emotional handicaps of adult life, they now tell us, "represent almost invariably, if not always, the unsolved problems or the partially solved or badly solved problems of childhood."

For our purpose, then, of finding the cause of a vigorous illusion of grown men, we shall probably not go astray in observing some phases of child development.

The child at birth is literally forced from a small world of almost complete and effortless security into a new environment which at once sets up a series of demands. Strange sensations of light, sound, touch, and smell attack him. The nearly perfect prebirth harmony and serenity are over. The infant now must breathe and eat. His struggle for existence has begun. But his wants, at first, are few and are satisfied with a minimum of strain on his own part. The parents do their best to meet, almost instantly, the infant's desires. In this sense, he approximates omnipotence, because, relative to his askings, he achieves nearly complete obedience. His handwavings and cries magically command responses on the part of the environment.

As infancy recedes, his direct omnipotence diminishes. But that there is omnipotence somewhere the child does not doubt. Chance does not yet exist for him. . . . There is, he believes, no happening without a knowable reason. The contingent and the accidental are unthinkable. There must always be whys and wherefores. Chaos is beyond belief. . . .

As early childhood passes and consciousness grows keener, now and again the child becomes sharply aware of his incapacity for controlling the crushing, heedless, reluctant, and uncertain facts of the outer world. Recurrently, confusion descends upon him. Sudden experiences surprise him, crash in on his childish scheme of things, and temporarily overwhelm him. Fears beset him—fear of the vague things that stalk the darkness, fear of the unruly, the unseen, the horrible bogies of the unknown.

Then he rushes to his parents for help. They stand between him and the multitudinous cruelties and vagaries of life. They are all-powerful, all-knowing. . . . They hold sway over the outer world, they run things, they are rulers and protectors. . . . They know what is right and what is wrong. They bring order out of what seems to be chaos.

The child still possesses omnipotence—but now, vicariously. Through his dependence upon his parents' omnipotence he finds relief from unbearable uncertainty. His overestimation of the parental powers is an essential of his development.

It must not be overlooked that a significant division of parental functions takes place early in the life of the child. In all communities where the father is head of the family, the mother comes to "represent the nearer and more familiar influence, domestic tenderness, the help, the rest and the solace to which the child can always turn," writes Malinowski in a recent anthropological study. But "the father has to adopt the position of the final arbiter in force and authority. He has gradually to cast off the role of tender and protective friends, and to adopt the position of strict judge, and hard executor of law." And so, in the childish appraisal of the parents, the mother tends to become the embodiment of all that is protectively tender while the father personifies all that is certain, secure, infallible, and embodies exact lawmaking, law-pronouncing, and law-enforcing. The child, in his struggle for existence, makes vital use of his belief in an omniscient and omnipotent father, a father who lays down infallible and precise rules of conduct.

Then, slowly, repeated experiences erode this fictional overestimate. "Adam," said Mark Twain's Eve, "knows ever so many things, but, poor dear, most of them aren't so." To the child, parental wisdom now comes to seem like Adam's. There are many things Father doesn't know, things he can't do. Other humans successfully oppose him. And there are forces loose in the world beyond his control. One's own father is at times helpless, deficient; he is all too human. The child's lofty conception of fatherly dignity and infallibility crumbles before the cumulative evidence of disappointing paternal weakness and ignorance. (Edmund Gosse in his autobiography, *Father and Son*, relates the following: "I believed that my Father knew everything and saw everything. One morning in my sixth year, my Mother and I were alone in the morningroom, when my Father came in and announced some fact to us. I was standing on the rug, gazing at him, and when he made this statement, I remember turning quickly in embarrassment, and looking into the fire. The shock to me was as that of a thunderbolt, for what my Father had said *was not true*. My Mother and I, who had been present at the trifling incident, were aware that it had not happened exactly as it had been reported by him. My Mother gently told him so, and he accepted the correction. Nothing could possibly have been more trifling to my parents, but to me it meant an epoch. Here was the appalling discovery, never suspected before, that my Father was not as God, and did not know everything. The shock was not caused by any suspicion that he was not telling the truth, as it appeared to him, but by the awful proof that he was not, as I had supposed, omniscient.")

But the average child cannot completely accept this disillusionment. He has formed an irresistible need for an omniscient and omnipotent father who shall stand between him and life's uncertainties. The child's own sense of power and control vanished in early infancy. Now life seems to demand that he shall take a next step and abandon his reliance on the conviction that someone close to him possesses consummate wisdom. His attitudes and adaptations had been built upon his relations to his idealized, his incomparable father. The child is disoriented. Again panic fear attacks him. He is unwilling and largely unable to accept as realities the ungovernable, the unorderable aspects of life. Surely, he feels, somewhere there must be Someone who can control events, make the dark spots light, make the uncertain clear. Chance and contingency he will not submit to as finalities; the apparently fortuitous must be susceptible of subjection to the rule of some person—a person, too, like his father, whom the child can propitiate.

Many are the persons who become substitutes for the deposed father: the priest or pastor, the rulers and leaders of the group. They, too, turn out to be disappointing. But the demand for fatherly authority does not die. To be sure, as the child grows into manhood, this demand grows less and less vocal, more and more unconscious. The father-substitutes become less definite in form, more vague and impersonal. But the relation to the father has become a paradigm, a prototype of later relations. Concealed and submerged, there persists a longing to reproduce the father-child pattern, to escape uncertainty and confusion through the rediscovery of a father.

For although as we grow older we are compelled to some extent to acknowledge the existence of reasonless, limitless, and indeterminate aspects of life, yet most of us strive to blind our eyes to them. And then, at moments when chaos becomes too evident to be denied, we rush, fear-ridden, as if we were children, to some protective father-like authority. . . . Few are the persons able to relinquish the props of childhood and bravely admit that life is full of unavoidable hazards beyond the control, direct or indirect, of finite humans.

A book has been written with the witty title, *Were You Ever a Child?* That is a question well worth asking. It prompts the further question: To what extent is a grown man still a child? To the extent perhaps that he cannot stand the idea of pure and avoidless chance.

William James's career is suggestive. As a young man "a sense of the insecurity of life," a consciousness of a "pit of insecurity beneath the surface of life," so obsessed him that he was seized with that morbid melancholy "which takes the form of panic fear" and reached the point of suicidal mania. He might, he reports, have gone insane, if he had not clung to scripture-texts such as "The Eternal God is my refuge." Suddenly he was "cured." And the cure consisted in a sudden shift to a positive delight in the hazardous, incalculable character of life. Life's very insecurity became its most inviting aspect. He came to enjoy an attitude which "involves an element of active tension, of holding my own, as it were, and trusting outward things to perform their part so as to make it a full harmony, but without any *guaranty* that they will. Make it a guaranty—and the attitude immediately becomes to my consciousness stagnant and stingless. Take away the guaranty, and I feel * * * a sort of deep enthusiastic bliss, of utter willingness to do and suffer anything. * * *" This sudden shift from panic fear of insecurity to a deep enthusiastic bliss in the absence of security marked for James the advent of emotional adulthood. He then first began to play a man's part.

But there are few who reach such adult stature. Most men do not achieve, as James did, the courage to tolerate, much less to enjoy, the idea of ultimate and irreducible contingency; they retain a yearning for Someone or Something, qualitatively resembling Father, to aid them in dissipating the fear of chance and change.

That religion shows the effects of the childish desire to recapture a father-controlled world has been often observed. But the effect on the law of this childish desire has escaped attention. And yet it is obvious enough. To the child the father is the Infallible Judge, the Maker of definite rules of conduct. He knows precisely what is right and what is wrong and, as head of the family, sits in judgment and punishes misdeeds. The Law—a body of rules apparently devised for infallibly determining what is right and what is wrong and for deciding who should be punished for misdeeds—inevitably becomes a partial substitute for the Father-as-Infallible-Judge. That is, the desire persists in grown men to recapture, through a rediscovery of a father, a childish, completely controllable universe, and that desire seeks satisfaction in a partial unconscious, anthropomorphizing of Law, in ascribing to the Law some of the characteristics of the child's Father-Judge. That childish longing is an important element in the explanation of the absurdly unrealistic notion that law is, or can be made, entirely certain and definitely predictable.

This, then, is our partial explanation of the basic legal myth: The filial relation is clearly indicated as one important unconscious determinant of the ways of man in dealing with all his problems, including the problem of his attitude toward the law. The several components of this explanation may be summarized thus:

(1) The infant strives to retain something like prebirth serenity. Conversely, fear of the unknown, dread of chance and change, are vital factors in the life of the child.

(2) These factors manifest themselves in a childish appetite for complete peace, comfort, protection from the dangers of the unknown. The child, "unrealistically," craves a steadfast world which will be steady and controllable.

(3) The child satisfies that craving, in large measure, through his confidence in and reliance on his incomparable, omnipotent, infallible father.

(4) Despite advancing years, most men are at times the victims of the childish desire for complete serenity and the childish fear of irreducible chance. They then will to believe that they live in a world in which chance is only an appearance and not a reality, in which they can be free of the indefinite, the arbitrary, the capricious. When they find life distracting, unsettling, fatiguing, they long to rise above the struggle for existence; to be rid of all upsetting shifts and changes and novelties; to discover an uninterrupted connection between apparently disjunctive events; to rest in an environment that is fundamentally stable. They revert, that is, to childish longings, which they attempt to satisfy through "the rediscovery of father," through father-substitutes. Even where the fear factor is absent, the desire for father-substitutes may persist; father-dependence, originally a means of adaptation, has become an end-in-itself. (Father-dependence in adult years was once socially valuable—when the economic organization of society was patriarchal. The social code then reinforced that component of the individual's makeup which makes him seek to prolong his infantile dependence on his father. Floyd Dell . . . maintains that we have but recently advanced beyond patriarchalism economically and are therefore still largely controlled psychologically by mores, no longer appropriate to our times, which favor excessive reliance on the father.)

(5) The Law can easily be made to play an important part in the

attempted rediscovery of the father. For, functionally, the law apparently resembles the Father-as-Judge. (Law and Religion are, of course, not the only activities affected by the search for fatherly authority. Science, too, suffers when it is made to bear the burden of being a complete guarantor of cosmic certainty.

What is significant is that the law, which as we have seen, inherently is one of the least certain of human enterprises, is looked to for an absurdly disproportionate degree of certainty; more certainty is demanded in law than in biology, for instance. The fact that, more obviously than most other departments of life, the law seems to resemble the child's conception of the Father-as-Judge, will serve as a partial explanation of this paradox.)

(6) The child's Father-as-Judge was infallible. His judgments and commands appeared to bring order out of the chaos of conflicting views concerning right conduct. His law seemed absolutely certain and predictable. Grown men, when they strive to recapture the emotional satisfactions of the child's world, without being consciously aware of their motivation, seek in their legal systems the authoritativeness, certainty, and predictability which the child believed that he had found in the law laid down by the father.

(7) Hence the basic legal myth that law is, or can be made, unwavering, fixed, and settled.

Other explanations of the legal-certainty myth there are, to be sure. Some of them (such as the religious explanation) are based on the supposed effects of tendencies no longer operative except as "survivals" of past history. The particular cause we are isolating is no mere "survival"; it is as powerfully operative today as it was in the past. It could be said of any period of history as it can be said at this moment; society is made up of persons all of whom now are, or recently were, children. Our thesis rests on observations of current phenomena clear to the eye of any amateur anthropologist in any modern group.

We have used the phrases "one important determinant" and "an important element" in referring to the father-regarding attitude as an explanation of the basic illusion of complete legal predictability. For it is not pretended that we have isolated the sole cause of a reaction which, like most human reactions, is of course the product of a constellation of several forces. Yet, for the sake of emphasis, we shall in what follows treat a partial explanation as if it were the only one. We shall openly and avowedly take a part for the whole; we shall employ what has been aptly called a "neglective fiction."

With such qualifications we may now state succinctly our answer to the puzzling question: Why do men seek unrealizable certainty in law? Because, we reply, they have not yet relinquished the childish need for an authoritative father and unconsciously have tried to find in the law a substitute for those attributes of firmness, sureness, certainty, and infallibility ascribed in child-hood to the father. (We do not intend to assert that lawyers are "childish" nor to deny that lawyers are far less prone than laymen to be controlled in their thinking by illusory aims with respect to law. . . .)

\* \* \* \* \*

Have judges the right and power to make law and change law? Much good ink has been spilled in arguing that question. A brief survey of the controversy will illuminate our thesis.

The conventional view may be summarized thus:

Law is a complete body of rules existing from time immemorial, and unchangeable except to the limited extent that legislatures have changed the rules by enacted statutes. Legislatures are expressly empowered thus to change the law. But the judges are not to make or change the law but to apply it. The law, ready-made, preexists the judicial decisions.

Judges are simply "living oracles" of law. . . . Their function is purely passive. They are "but the mouth which pronounces the law." They no more make or invent new law than Columbus made or invented America. ("Men do not make laws," writes Calvin Coolidge. "They do but discover them. \* \* \* That state is more fortunate in its form of government which has the aptest instruments for the discovery of laws.") Judicial opinions are evidence of what the law is; the best evidence, but no more than that. When a former decision is overruled, we must not say that the rule announced in the earlier decision was once the law and has now been changed by the later decision. We must view the earlier decision as laying down an erroneous rule. It was a false map of the law just as a pre-Columbian map of the world was false. Emphatically, we must not refer to the new decision as making new law. It only seems to do so. It is merely a bit of revised legal cartography.

If a judge actually attempted to contrive a new rule, he would be guilty of usurpation of power, for the legislature alone has the authority to change the law. . . .

Such is the conventional notion. There is a contrary minority view, which any dispassionate observer must accept as obviously the correct view:

"No intelligent lawyer would in this day pretend that the decisions of the courts do not add to and alter the law," says Pollock (clearly in error: most lawyers deny the reality of judge-made law). . . . "Judge-made law is real law," writes Dicey, another famous legal commentator, "though made under the form of, and often described by judges no less than jurists, as the mere interpretation of law. \* \* \* The amount of such judge-made law is in England far more extensive than a student realizes. Nine-tenths, at least, of the law of contract, and the whole, or nearly the whole, of the law of torts are not to be discovered in any volume of the statutes. \* \* \* Whole branches, not of ancient but of every modern law, have been built up, developed or created by action of the courts."

Judges, then, do make and change law. The minority view is patently correct; the opposing arguments will not bear analysis. What, then, explains the belief so tenaciously held that the judiciary does not ever change the law or that, when it does, it is acting improperly? Why is it that judges adhere to what Morris Cohen has happily called "the phonographic theory of the judicial function"? What explains the recent remark of an eminent member of the bar: "The man who claims that under our system courts make law is asserting that the courts habitually act unconstitutionally"? . . .

We revert to our thesis: The essence of the basic legal myth or illusion is that law can be entirely predictable. Back of this illusion is the childish desire to have a fixed father-controlled universe, free of chance and error due to human fallibility.

In early stages of legal development this desire was more intense than now and there was what Sir Henry Maine has called "superstitious disrelish of change" which went to the extent of making men oppose any modification of existing law even by statutory legislation. We have partially overcome the superstitious antipathy to legal change so far as the change results from the action of legislative bodies, and no little part of law is modified each year by statutes enacted by state legislatures and by Congress.

But such statutory legislation, while it may alter the law, does so, ordinarily, only prospectively. It is the usual practice—to some extent it is required by constitutional prohibitions—that changes embodied in statutes enacted by legislative bodies should not be retroactive but should apply only to future conduct. Which is to say that, generally speaking, a legal novelty brought about through statutory legislation can be known *before* men do any acts which may be affected by the innovation. Insofar, a man can conduct himself in reliance upon the existing law, knowing, at the time he acts, that any changes thereafter made by a legislative body will not modify the law upon which he relied.

Consequently, absolute certainty and predictability are apparently not endangered by alterations of law made or adopted by legislatures.

But if it once recognized that a judge, in the course of deciding a case, can for the first time create the law applicable to that case, or can alter the rules which were supposed to exist before the case was decided, then it will also have to be recognized that the rights and obligations of the parties to that case may be decided retroactively. A change thus made by a judge, when passing upon a case, is a change in the law made with respect to past events—events which occurred before the law came into existence. Legal predictability is plainly impossible, if, at the time I do an act, I do so with reference to law which, should a lawsuit thereafter arise with reference to my act, may be changed by the judge who tries the case. For then the result is that my case is decided according to law which was not in existence when I acted and which I, therefore, could not have known, predicted, or relied on when I acted.

If, therefore, one has a powerful need to believe in the possibility of anything like exact legal predictability, he will find judicial lawmaking intolerable and seek to deny its existence.

Hence the myth that the judges have no power to change existing law or make new law: it is a direct outgrowth of a subjective need for believing in a stable, approximately unalterable legal world—in effect, a child's world.

This remark might be challenged on the ground that the desire to avoid legal retroactivity is not "subjective" but practical, because, it may be said, men cannot and will not engage in affairs without having in mind the pertinent law. Yet reflection reveals the fact that the supposed *practical* importance of avoiding legal retroactivity and uncertainty is much overrated, since most men act without regard to the legal consequences of their conduct, and, therefore, do not act in reliance upon any given preexisting law. . . .

[T]he factor of uncertainty in law has little bearing on practical affairs. Many men go on about their business with virtually no knowledge of, or attention paid to, the so-called legal rules, be those rules certain or uncertain. If the law but slightly affects what a man does, it is seldom that he can honestly maintain that he was disadvantaged by lack of legal stability. Although, then, judges have made law, vast quantities of law, and judge-made innovations, retroactively applied, are devised yearly; although frequently a man must act with no certainty as to what legal consequences the courts will later attach to his acts; although complete legal predictability and with it safety from slippery change are therefore by no means possible—yet retroactivity and the resulting unavoidable uncertainty are not as great practical evils as they are often assumed to be. The no judge-made law doctrine, it seems, is not, fundamentally, a response to practical needs. It appears rather to be due to a hunger and a craving for a nonexistent and unattainable legal finality—which, in turn, may be ascribed to a concealed but potent striving to recapture in the law the child's conception of the fatherly attributes.

But what of it? What harm in this myth? No harm, if the denial of judicial lawmaking were a mere pleasantry, in the category of what Austin and Morris Cohen refer to as polite or euphemistic fictions; that is, statements contrary to fact, but known by all to be such and comparable to the fibs of daily social intercourse.

But the denial of the fact of judge-made law is no mere fib. At times, indeed, it seems to resemble an outright benevolent lie, a professional false-hood designed actually to deceive the laity for their own good; Gray suggests that the misrepresentation derives in part from a belief of the legal profession that it is "important that judges should say, and that the people should believe, that the rules according to which the judges decide these cases had a previous existence." The lay public, that is, are to be duped.

Now, this dupery is not harmless. It leads, sooner or later, to a distrust of the judges, a disrespect for their opinions. For now and again the public becomes aware that in some actual cases the judges have made or changed the law. Then follow accusations of dishonesty, of corruption, of usurpation of authority, of revolutionary violation of the judicial oath of office, and the like. And it is difficult to reply to such accusations when the judges themselves deny that they have power to make law and yet go on (unavoidably and unmistakably) making it.

Why, then, do the judges deceive the public? Because they are themselves deceived. The doctrine of no judge-made law is not, generally speaking, a "lie"—for a lie is an affirmation of a fact contrary to the truth, made with knowledge of its falsity and with the intention of deceiving others. Nor is it a "fiction"—a false affirmation made with knowledge of its falsity but with no intention of deceiving others.

It is rather a myth—a false affirmation made without complete knowledge of its falsity. We are confronting a kind of deception which involves self-deception. The self-deception, of course, varies in degree; many judges and lawyers are half-aware that the denial of the existence of judicial legislation is what Gray has called "a form of words to hide the truth." And yet most of the profession insists that the judiciary cannot properly change the law, and more or less believes that myth. When judges and lawyers announce that judges can never validly make law, they are not engaged in fooling the public; they have successfully fooled themselves.

And this self-delusion has led to many unfortunate results. With their thinking processes hampered by this myth, the judges have been forced, as we have seen, to contrive circumlocutions in order to conceal from themselves and the laity the fact that the judiciary frequently changes the old legal rules. Those evasive phrases are then dealt with as if they were honest phrases, with consequent confusion and befuddlement of thought. Legal fictions are mistaken for objective legal truths, and clear legal thinking becomes an unnecessarily arduous task.

This is not the place to discuss at length the immense importance of valid fictions. Suffice it to say that valid fictions, whether in mathematics, physics, medicine, or law, are invaluable. But the correct and effective use of a fiction involves a constant recognition of its character. It is often desirable to treat A "as if" it were B. Mathematics, for instance, finds it useful to employ the fiction that a circle is a polygon; that is, to be dealt with, for certain purposes, as if it were a polygon. Medical thinking is aided by the fiction of the completely healthy man. So in law, it is helpful at times to treat a corporation as if, for certain purposes, it were a real citizen, distinct and apart from its flesh-and-blood stockholders, directors, officers, and agents.

But there are a vast number of so-called fictions which are really bastard fictions or semimyths, where the "as if" or "let's pretend" factor has, in some measure, been submerged. It is said, not that A is to be treated *for certain purposes* "as if" it were B, but instead it is said and believed, incorrectly, that A *is* B. While thinking is often advanced by a valid fiction, it is hindered when a fiction becomes a myth or semimyth; that is, when the artificial character of the fiction, its lack of literalness, it's basically metaphorical significance, are in whole or in part overlooked. (There can be no objection, in the interest of saving time, to the temporary verbal omission of the "as if" when using a fiction, provided the "as if" is not ignored. But such shorthand expressions are dangerous to clear thinking unless the fact that they are abbreviations is kept clearly in mind. . . .)

. . . One might almost say that the capacity for sustained valid "as if" thinking is the mark of the civilized man. . . . To the extent that fictions are recognized as such that their "as if" or "let's pretend" element is kept clear, that the omission of qualifications from such abbreviated or metaphorical statements is not taken to mean the permanent irrelevance of such qualifications—just to that extent fictional representations should be encouraged as invaluable thought-tools. Objection properly arises only when the partial, metaphorical, artificial character of the fiction is overlooked—when, that is, the fiction becomes a myth or semimyth. . . .

Valid fictions are defensible—more, they are indispensable. But what is significant for our purposes is the defense of the bastard fictions, the semimyths. To Blackstone, they were among the cherished beauties of the law. To Mitchell, it seems that the common law is largely indebted to these verbal mechanisms for its rapid development and its ability to follow closely social needs. Why this praise? Because, says Mitchell, these devices make "less noticeable, both to the world and to the judges themselves (and therefore more easy) the legislation that is being accomplished by the judges." Such judicial legislation he considers essential to the life of the law. But no less essential, he contends, is the necessity of concealing what is going on. Wherefore to him these misleading, inaccurate and troublemaking phrases are well worth the price of "the discredit which their apparent falsity brings upon the law."

Stated thus baldly, how childish is such a defense: Judges must continue to create law, but they and the public must be kept unaware of their accomplishment. Untruths must continue to be told to the laity about the essential function of law, and law must continue to be made by men befuddled by myths and only partially aware of what they are doing. And why? Because, apparently, many full-grown men, whether they be laymen or lawyers, cannot bear to learn the truth, and must be kept in a world of make-believe where they can continue to cherish the illusion that the law of an adult civilization is, in spirit, of a kind with the authoritative rules laid down for children by their father. (This is a "*partial* explanation." . . .)

The genealogy of legal myth-making may be traced as follows: Childish dread of uncertainty and unwillingness to face legal realities produce a basic legal myth that law is completely settled and defined. Thence springs the subsidiary myth that judges never make law. That myth, in turn, is the progenitor of a large brood of troublesome semimyths. One is reminded of Morley's comments with respect to a like development in Church history:

"Subordinate error was made necessary and invented, by reason of some pre-existent main stock of error, and to save the practice of the Church. Thus we are often referred to the consolation which this or that doctrine has brought to the human spirit. But what if the same system had produced the terror which made absence of consolation intolerable? How much of the necessity for expressing the enlarged humanity of the Church, in the doctrine of Purgatory, arose from the experience of the older, unsoftened doctrine of eternal hell?"

*     *     *     *     *

We have talked much of the law. But what is "the law"? A complete definition would be impossible and even a working definition would exhaust the patience of the reader. But it may not be amiss to inquire what, in a rough sense, the law means to the average man of our times when he consults his lawyer.

The Jones family owned the Blue & Gray Taxi Company, a corporation incorporated in Kentucky. That company made a contract with the A. & B. Railroad Company, also a Kentucky corporation, by which it was agreed that the Blue & Gray Taxi Company was to have the exclusive privilege of soliciting taxicab business on and adjacent to the railroad company's depot.

A rival taxicab company, owned by the Williams family, the Purple Taxi Company, began to ignore this contract; it solicited business and parked its taxicabs in places assigned by the railroad company to the Blue & Gray Company and sought in other ways to deprive the Blue & Gray Company of the benefits conferred on it by the agreement with the railroad.

The Jones family were angered; their profits derived from the Blue &

Gray stock, which they owned, were threatened. They consulted their lawyer, a Louisville practitioner, and this, we may conjecture, is about what he told them: "I'm afraid your contract is not legally valid. I've examined several decisions of the highest court of Kentucky and they pretty clearly indicate that you can't get away with that kind of an agreement in this state. The Kentucky court holds such a contract to be bad as creating an unlawful monopoly. But I'll think the matter over. You come back tomorrow and I'll try meanwhile to find some way out."

So, next day, the Joneses returned. And this time their lawyer said he thought he had discovered how to get the contract sustained: "You see, it's this way. In most courts, except those of Kentucky and of a few other states, an agreement like this is perfectly good. But, unfortunately, as things now stand, you'll have to go into the Kentucky courts.

"If we can manage to get our case tried in the federal court, there's a fair chance that we'll get a different result, because I think the federal court will follow the majority rule and not the Kentucky rule. I'm not sure of that, but it's worth trying.

"So this is what we'll do. We'll form a new Blue & Gray Company in Tennessee. And your Kentucky Blue & Gray Company will transfer all its assets to the new Tennessee Blue & Gray Company. Then we'll have the railroad company execute a new contract with the new Tennessee Blue & Gray Company, and at the same time cancel the old contract and, soon after, dissolve the old Kentucky Blue & Gray Company."

"But," interrupted one of the Joneses, "what good will all that monkey-business do?"

The lawyer smiled broadly. "Just this," he replied with pride in his cleverness: "The A. & B. Railroad Company is organized in Kentucky. So is the Purple Taxi which we want to get at. The federal court will treat these companies as if they were citizens of Kentucky. Now, a corporation which is a citizen of Kentucky can't bring this kind of suit in the federal court against other corporations which are also citizens of Kentucky. But if your company becomes a Tennessee corporation, it will be considered as if it were a citizen of Tennessee. Then your new Tennessee company can sue the other two in the federal court, because the suit will be held to be one between citizens of different states. And that kind of suit, based on what we lawyers call 'diversity of citizenship,' can be brought in the federal court by a corporation which organized in Tennessee against corporations which are citizens of another state, Kentucky. And the federal court, as I said, ought to sustain your contract."

"That sounds pretty slick," said one of the Joneses admiringly. "Are you sure it will work?"

"No," answered the lawyer. "You can't ever be absolutely sure about such a plan. I can't find any case completely holding our way on all these facts. But I'm satisfied that's the law and that that's the way the federal court ought to decide. I won't guarantee success. But I recommend trying out my suggestion."

His advice was followed. Shortly after the new Tennessee Blue & Gray Company was organized and had entered into the new contract, suit was brought by the Joneses' new Blue & Gray Corporation of Tennessee in the Federal District Court against the competing Purple Co. and the railroad company. In this suit, the Blue & Gray Taxi Company of Tennessee asked the court to prevent interference with the carrying out of its railroad contract.

As the Joneses' lawyer had hoped, the federal court held, against the protest of the Purple Company's lawyer, first, that such a suit could be brought in the federal court and, second, that the contract was valid. Accordingly the court enjoined the Purple Company from interfering with the depot business of the Joneses' Blue & Gray Company. The Joneses were elated, for now their profits seemed once more assured.

But not for long. The other side appealed the case to the Federal Circuit Court of Appeals. And the Joneses' lawyer was somewhat worried that that court might reverse the lower federal court. But it didn't, and the Joneses again were happy.

Still the Purple Company persisted. It took the case to the Supreme Court of the United States. That Court consists of nine judges. And the Joneses' lawyer couldn't be certain just how those judges would line up on all the questions involved. "Some new men on the bench, and you never can tell about Holmes and Brandeis. They're very erratic," was his comment.

When the United States Supreme Court gave its decision, it was found that six of the nine judges agreed with counsel for the Joneses. Three justices (Holmes, Brandeis, and Stone) were of the contrary opinion. But the majority governs in the United States Supreme Court, and the Joneses' prosperity was at last firmly established.

Now, what was "the law" for the Joneses' who owned the Blue & Gray Company, and the Williamses, who owned the Purple Company? The answer will depend on the date of the question. If asked before the new Tennessee Company acquired this contract, it might have been said that it was almost surely "the law" that the Joneses would lose; for any suit involving the validity of that contract could then have been brought only in the Kentucky state court and the prior decisions of that court seemed adverse to such an agreement.

After the suggestion of the Joneses' lawyer was carried out and the new Tennessee corporation owned the contract, "the law" was more doubtful. Many lawyers would have agreed with the Joneses' lawyer that there was a good chance that the Jones family would be victorious if suit were brought in the federal courts. But probably an equal number would have disagreed: they would have said that the formation of the new Tennessee company was a trick used to get out of the Kentucky courts and into the federal court, a trick of which the federal court would not approve. Or that, regardless of that question, the federal court would follow the well-settled Kentucky rule as to the invalidity of such contracts as creating unlawful monopolies (especially because the use of Kentucky real estate was involved) and that therefore the federal court would decide against the Joneses. "The law," at any time before the decision of the United States Supreme Court, was indeed unsettled. (That is, it was unsettled whether the Williamses had the energy, patience, and money to push an appeal. If not, then the decision of the lower federal court was the actual settled law for the Jones and Williams families.) No one could know what the court would decide. Would it follow the Kentucky cases? If so, the law was that no "rights" were conferred by the contract. Would it refuse to follow the Kentucky cases? If so, rights were conferred by the contract. To speak of settled law governing that controversy, or of the fixed legal rights of those parties, as antedating the decision of the Supreme Court, is mere verbiage. If two more judges on that bench had agreed with Justice Holmes, Brandeis, and Stone, the law and the rights of the parties would have been of a directly opposite kind.

After the decision, "the law" was fixed. There were no other courts to which an appeal could be directed. The judgment of the United States Supreme Court could not be disturbed and the legal "rights" of the Joneses and the Williamses were everlastingly established.

We may now venture a rough definition of law from the point of view of the average man: For any particular lay person, the law, with respect to any particular set of facts, is a decision of a court with respect to those facts so far as that decision affects that particular person. Until a court has passed on those facts no law on that subject is yet in existence. Prior to such a decision, the only law available is the opinion of lawyers as to the law relating to that person and to those facts. Such opinion is not actually law but only a guess as to what a court will decide. (The United States Supreme Court has wittily been called the "court of ultimate conjecture.")

Law, then, as to any given situation is either (a) actual law, that is, a specific past decision, as to that situation, or (b) probable law, that is, a guess as to a specific future decision.

Usually when a client consults his lawyer about "the law," his purpose is to ascertain not what courts have actually decided in the past but what the courts will probably decide in the future. He asks, "Have I a right, as a stockholder of the American Taffy Company of Indiana, to look at the corporate books?" Or, "Do I have to pay an inheritance tax to the State of New York on bonds left me by my deceased wife, if our residence was in Ohio, but the bonds, at the time of her death, were in a safety-deposit box in New York?" Or, "Is there a right of 'peaceful' picketing in a strike in the State of California?" Or, "If Jones sells me his Chicago shoe business and agrees not to compete for ten years, will the agreement be binding?" The answers (although they may run "There is such a right," "The law is that the property is not taxable," "Such picketing is unlawful," "The agreement is not legally binding") are in fact prophecies or predictions of judicial action. It is from this point of view that the practice of law has been aptly termed an art of prediction. . . .

\* \* \* \* \*

No intelligent person can question the wisdom of the revised attitude toward the law which our Pounds, Wurzels, Demogues, and Cardozos would have the lawyers and the laity adopt. They want our "courts to perceive what it is they are doing" and thus be "enabled to address themselves consciously to doing it in the best way." They want an effective, intelligent fusion of the two competing tendencies toward stability and change; a working principle of growth; a constant revision of the law's heritage of knowledge and thought; the frequent adaptation of the legal rules so as to relate them to the realities of contemporary social, industrial, and political conditions. They desire that traditional premises should be so shaped as to give effect to social interests, with reference not to the abstract claims of abstract individuals, but to the concrete situation; they picture law as continuously more efficacious social engineering, satisfying, through social control, as much as is possible of the whole body of human wants.

They urge that lawyers and judges should deal realistically with their materials and their technique, and that there should be an adult recognition, by the public generally, of the possibilities and limitations of the law with consequent improvement of its legitimate functioning.

All this is no easy task. Men in any of life's relations will never be completely free of delusions. But delusions can be diminished. And those who desire the healthy growth of the law will with courage seek to diminish legal delusions and, to that end, to comprehend the nature and sources of their own weaknesses, and of the powerful yearning in themselves as well as others for unrealities in law. (One recalls Gilbert's fairies who, chided for falling in love with mortals, exclaimed, "We know it's weakness, but the weakness is so strong.")

Just in so far as we ourselves are childish, do we want to keep our children from growing up. . . . This is the "snare of patronage," the great sin of parenthood: to obstruct the psychological freedom of the child. The prolongation of infancy is essential to the development of the human infant, but to prolong infancy unduly at the expense of the child's development is to violate the eleventh commandment.

A coming-of-age has its perils for the children and its pains for the parents. Yet, if our legal critics are to play the role of wise fathers, they must have the courage to let their "children" grow up. Myth-making and fatherly lies must be abandoned. . . . We must stop telling stork-fibs about how law is born and cease even hinting that perhaps there is still some truth in Peter Pan legends of a juristic happy hunting ground in a land of legal absolutes.

To the extent that lawyers, whether more or less consciously, join the conspiracy of silence about, or denial of, the ineradicable mutability of law, they do an injury to their fellows. For to that extent—and in one of the most important life activities—they are keeping men in subjection to a falsehood and, worse, to the debilitating irresponsibility arising from reliance on supposed safety-conferring external authority. Not only is there involved an injury to the maturation of law, but as well to the spirit of men generally. For, if what we have suggested is true, if something of a paralyzing father-worship is one of the hidden causes of men's belief in a body of infallible law, then the perpetuation of that belief means that everywhere the noxious thralldom to mere authority and tradition is strengthened. . . .

Increasing constructive doubt is the sign of advancing civilization. We must put question marks alongside many of our inherited legal dogmas, since they are dangerously out of line with social facts.

Indeed, we may throw some light on our problem by asking what, in general parlance, we mean by a "fact." Holmes has answered that it is something one can't help believing. "What gives it objectivity is that I find my fellow man to a greater or less extent (never wholly) subject to the same Can't Helps." Barry more recently has defined a fact as a "coercive" or "compulsory" experience "established by common agreement which is indicated by similar behavior with reference to it." And Eddington speaks of it as a "symposium" of presentations to individuals in all sorts of circumstances.

Now these common agreements as to "coercive experiences," these symposia with respect to the nature of Can't Helps, keep changing, even where the subject matter has reference to what we call the laws of nature. In other words, stubborn facts are, in a sense, not so stubborn as we are wont to suppose. In the natural sciences the rate of change in the accepted symposia is rapid because there the habit of constant questioning, of unremitting doubt, has come to be accepted, at least by the scientists, as a virtue. Even in those sciences, it took thousands of years to justify doubt. And outside of the sciences, most of our facts have remained unchanged for at least several hundred generations. A large part of our accepted or unquestioned "truths" are the "unverified world-pictures of vanished barbaric (prehistoric) peoples." The toughness of these facts is due—to what? To the vast power of the authority behind them. They have become sacred; they are protected from close scrutiny by terrifying taboos.

Primitive man could not endure the terrors that surrounded him. He made masks to conceal the menace they involved, so that now, says Shaw, "every mask requires a hero to tear it off." In each man's infancy, generation after generation, his father has taught him the eternal verity of these masking "truths." Wherefore he is coerced by them and treats them as if they were nature's irreducibles. And if the tendency to tear off the masks, to question man-made Can't Helps, has progressed far less rapidly in the law than in the natural sciences—if, that is, our "law facts" need to be brought in line with our "science facts"—this is no doubt because in the law father-authority has found a firmer lodgment.

This point is so important that we venture to state it once more in slightly variant terms. As we have often remarked in the foregoing pages, our legal abstractions can only be approximations. They are, by definition, drawn off—abstracted—from the facts. Hence, the results can never be precise, perfect. They must be inexact. If the "environment" were stable, the degree of inexactness could become more negligible and remain relatively fixed. But the economic, political, and social problems are ever-shifting. So that, in the very nature of the situation, the approximations must be revised frequently and can never be accepted as final in terms of satisfactory consequences. We must be content with modest probabilities, as Dewey puts it, and not foolishly pretend that our legal abstractions are mathematically accurate, for that pretense obstructs the will to modify and adjust these abstractions in the light of careful observation of their working results.

These abstractions, that is to say, are tools whose whole value is instrumental. They have been contrived to meet particular problems. As new problems arise, the old tools must be adapted to cope with them. But when the old tools have been authoritatively pronounced to be once-and-for-all perfect, when, that is, they have the father-sanction, then to question their everlasting sufficiency is difficult. Then the tools seem not human contrivances but a very part of the nature of things. The questioning, when it begins, has to be oblique, the adaptations surreptitious. Even the questioner, the adapter, must not let himself know that he is daring to depart from the accepted ways. Science made large strides when man began to treat the traditional formulations as no longer completely correct and definite knowledge of objective nature but as hypotheses or fictions; in other words, when men were ready to treat as tentative the guesses about the external world which had been handed down to them. Then only could they fearlessly observe the events, dispassionately consider new guesses about the character of these events.

All the guesses are human and, therefore, subject to question. But the old guesses come to us as the father's truths and are, therefore, sacrosanct. Humanity increases its chances of survival and of progress to the extent that it becomes able to question—neither blindly to accept nor violently to defy—the father's guesses, and to discontinue calling them self-evident truths. In the sciences this attitude has won out. Although the law is a more patently human construction than, say, physics, yet, in the calm reconsideration of the value of inherited truths, law is decades behind physics. Why? Because in law, the father is more deeply entrenched. The law is a near substitute for that father, a belief in whose infallibility is essential to the very life of the child. And in the life of the adult that authority now no longer usefully, but still potently, often holds sway. . . .

If we are to grow more civilized, we must arrive at a more adult attitude toward chance and change. And here a nice distinction must be made between the adult position with respect to danger and a less developed sentiment which falsely resembles it. . . .

The child is motivated not only by the desire to escape the terrors of the unknown; he has also within him a store of vital energy; he is a growing dynamic organism. His dynamic capacities constantly assert themselves; the child is never completely a mere creature of parental authority. In a certain sense, danger and risk, as well as safety and security, make their appeal to him. As sometimes he runs away from chance and change, so at other times he seeks them.

Now, the curious fact is that such childish courting of danger may be, in part, a product of father-authority. All children have a dual attitude toward the father. The child needs a belief in an all-powerful, all-wise parent. Yet that parent ever and again takes on the aspect of a harsh tyrant who cruelly and unfairly interferes with the child's aims and purposes. Even the most loving and obedient child feels occasional animosity toward the father and, at times, revolts against the father. His conduct, in such circumstances, may be in the direction of healthy growth, but, insofar as it is merely expressive of revolt, it is purely negative in meaning. The child, that is, may not be forging ahead, but only running away from a new terror—the terror of too strict fatherly authority. . . .

And so we must distinguish between that growth toward maturity which produces an acceptance of danger and that childish reaction against fatherly authority which takes on the appearance of adult courage. The constrained rebellion against paternalism is not a symptom of development but of prolonged infantilism. It is another form of slavish obedience. The person engaged in such rebellion is not free of paternal authority, but is still subjectively dependent upon it.

True growth involves healthy encouragement of the inherent spontaneity of the child, an encouragement of wakeful vitality and the discouragement of half-blind adherence to, or half-blind breaking away from, the traditional.

And so in law. If the search for the father-judge is ended, if the authority-ridden mode of regarding law is eliminated, if men see law as a human adjustment and not as a gift or mandate from some external source, no violent transformation need or will occur. The relief from fear of change need not result in the adoption of a policy of incessant, hectic change, but should lead to a policy of healthy and vital growth.

Today, excessive regard for certified stability yields to an excessive desire for modification, so that there is a constant unconscious struggle between these two impulses, a struggle unnecessarily violent. There is vacillation in the mind even of the average man between worship and denunciation of legal certainty. The demand for too much change is as little based on practicality as the demand for too much rigidity. Holmes has warned us that continuity with the past is not a duty. It is no less true that there is no obligation to effect discontinuity with the past. A recognition of those two truths, resulting from a thoroughly adult attitude toward fatherly authority, will produce a balanced, not an anarchic, attitude toward law. When men are free of childish compulsions away from or toward the traditional, it will be possible for them to have an open mind on the question of the advisability of radical alterations of law.

In other words, such a revised attitude will not entail constant inquiry into the sufficiency of all legal formulations. *It is unnecessary and undesirable to attack on all fronts at once.* Certain formulations must have been and will be at any given moment treated as, for the time being, fixed and settled while others are being investigated. But those "rules" that are thus, for the time being, taken for granted, will be only temporarily dealt with as permanent. They will be considered as *temporary absolutes.* Some of them will be accepted because repeated checkings show them still to be working well; others because the attention, at the moment, will be too occupied.

Modern civilization demands a mind free of father-governance. To remain father-governed in adult years is peculiarly the modern sin. *The modern mind is a mind free of childish emotional drags, a mature mind.* And law, if it is to meet the needs of modern civilization must adapt itself to the modern mind. It must cease to embody a philosophy opposed to change. It must become avowedly pragmatic. To this end there must be developed a recognition and elimination of the carryover of the childish dread of, and respect for, paternal omnipotence; that dread and respect are powerful strongholds of resistance to change. Until we become thoroughly cognizant of, and cease to be controlled by, the image of the father hidden away in the authority of the law, we shall not reach that first step in the civilized administration of justice, the recognition that man is not made for the law, but that law is made by and for men.

*Law and the Modern Mind* (1930)

# FACTS ARE GUESSES ⧓

IF YOU scrutinize a legal rule, you will see that it is a conditional statement referring to facts. Such a rule seems to say, in effect, "If such and such a fact exists, then this or that legal consequence should follow." It seems to say, for example, "If a trustee, for his own purposes, uses money he holds in trust, he must repay it." Or, "If a man, without provocation, kills another, the killer must be punished." In other words, a legal rule directs that (if properly asked to do so) a court should attach knowable consequences to certain facts, if and whenever there are such facts. That is what is meant by the conventional statement, used in describing the decisional process, that courts apply legal rules to the facts of law-suits. (I am here referring to so-called "substantive" rules, which state that certain sorts of out-of-court conduct will, in court, yield certain consequences. There is another kind of rules, rules of "procedure," which relate to the way cases in court should be commenced and tried . . . [U]pper courts, on appeals, deal not only with "substantive" rules, but also try to see that trial courts do not too widely depart from "procedural" rules.) For convenience, let us symbolize a legal rule by the letter R, the facts of a case by the letter F, and the court's decision of that case by the letter D. We can then crudely schematize the conventional theory of how courts operate by saying

$$R \times F = D$$

In other words, according to the conventional theory, a decision is a product of an R and an F. If, as to any lawsuit, you know the R and the F, you should, then, know what the D will be.

In a simple, stable, society, most of the R's are moderately well stabilized. Which legal rules that society will enforce it is not difficult for men—or at any rate, for the lawyer, the professional court-man—to know in advance of any trial. In such a society, the R—one of the two factors in the $R \times F = D$ formula—is usually fixed.

In our society, however, with the rapid changes brought about by modern life, many of the $R$'s have become unstable. Accordingly, in our times, legal uncertainty—uncertainty about future decisions and therefore about legal rights—is generally ascribed to the indefiniteness of the $R$'s. The increasing multiplicity of the rules, the conflicts between rules, and the flexibility of some of the rules, have arrested the attention of most legal thinkers. Those thinkers, perceiving the absence of rigidity in some rules, have assumed that the certainty or uncertainty of the $D$'s, in the $R \times F = D$ equation, stems principally from the certainty or uncertainty of the $R$'s.

That assumption leads to a grave miscomprehension of courthouse government and to the neglect by most legal scholars of the more difficult part of the courts' undertaking. I refer to the courts' task with respect to the other factor in the $R \times F = D$ formula, the $F$. The courts, as we saw, are supposed to ascertain the facts in the disputes which become lawsuits. That is, a court is supposed to determine the actual, objective acts of the parties, to find out just what they did or did not do, before the lawsuit began, so far as those facts bear on the compliance with, or the violation of, some legal rule. If there is uncertainty as to whether the court will find the true relevant facts—if it is uncertain whether the court's $F$ will match the real, objective $F$—then what? Then, since the decision, the $D$, is presumably the joint product of an $R$ and an $F$, the $D$ is bound to be uncertain. To put it differently: No matter how certain the legal rules may be, the decisions remain at the mercy of the courts' fact-finding. If there is doubt about what a court, in a lawsuit, will find were the facts, then there is at least equal doubt about its decision.

Go back now to Mr. Sensible and his lawyer. Suppose that the lawyer knows the pertinent $R$'s, and that they are as fixed as fixed can be, as precise as a table of logarithms. But, I ask again, how can the lawyer in 1946 prophesy what will be the $D$ in 1950, unless he also knows the $F$ that, in 1950, the trial judge (or jury) will use in the $R \times F = D$?

What is the $F$? Is it what actually happened between Sensible and Smart? Most emphatically not. At best, it is only what the trial court—the trial judge or jury—thinks happened. What the trial court thinks happened may, however, be hopelessly incorrect. But that does not matter—legally speaking. For court purposes, what the court thinks about the facts is all that matters. The actual events, the real objective acts and words of Sensible and Smart, happened in the past. They do not walk into court. The court usually learns about these real, objective, past facts only through the oral testimony of fallible witnesses. Accordingly, the court, from hearing the testimony, must guess at the actual, past facts. Judicially, the facts consist of the reaction of the judge or jury to the testimony. The F is merely a guess about the actual facts. There can be no assurance that that F, that guess, will coincide with those actual, past facts.

To be sure, this difficulty becomes of no importance when the parties to the suit do not dispute about the facts, when their sole difference concerns the proper R. Then the R will settle the court fight. In other words, if Smart agrees to the facts as Sensible tells them, then the only question for the court will be whether the R is as Sensible claims it to be. With reference to that sort of lawsuit, the trained lawyer, as a specialist in the R's, is frequently an excellent predicter of decisions. For often (although not always) the applicable R is fairly certain and knowable, or sufficiently so that a competent lawyer can foretell what the court will say it is.

But usually, when men "go to law," the facts are not admitted, and the testimony is oral and in conflict. For convenience, call such suits "contested" cases. It cannot be known in advance which cases will be "contested." To predict a decision in a suit not yet begun, about a dispute which has not yet occurred, requires then, the most extensive guessing. For whenever there is a question of the credibility of witnesses—of the believability, the reliability, of their testimony—then, unavoidably, the trial judge or jury must make a guess about the facts. The lawyer, accordingly, must make a guess about those guesses. The uncertainty of many "legal rights" corresponds to the correctness or incorrectness of such lawyer-guesses.

## 2

Let me bring out that point more sharply. When, in 1946, the Sensible-Smart contract is signed, no dispute has yet arisen. The lawyer, in making his guess at that time must attempt to take into account what may be the future acts of Sensible and Smart, the acts they may do in he interval between 1946 and the date of a future lawsuit. Patently, that contingency makes the guessing pretty difficult.

Suppose, however, that Sensible consults his lawyer in 1948, after a dispute has arisen, so that all the actual facts have already happened. It may seem to you that if the client, Sensible, accurately reports all those facts to his lawyer, the latter can undoubtedly tell his client just what a court will decide. I'm sorry to say you are wrong. The lawyer must still cope with many elusive, uncontrollable, wayward factors which may upset any prediction. Trials are often full of surprises. The adversary introduces unanticipated testimony. Witnesses, on whom the lawyer relied, change their stories when they take the witness stand. The facts as they appeared to the lawyer when, before a trial, he conferred with his client and his witnesses, frequently are not at all like the facts as they later show up in the courtroom.

But perhaps you believe that the trial judge or jury will surely learn the truth about the facts. If so, you are adopting an axiom, implied in the conventional theory of how courts decide cases, the "Truth-Will-Out axiom." But often that "axiom" does not jibe with reality. For reflect on the following: When a witness testifies, what is he doing? He is reporting his present memory of something he observed in the past, something he saw or heard. A witness is not a photographic plate or phonographic disc. Let us suppose that he is entirely honest. Nevertheless, note these sources of possible error:

(1) The witness may erroneously have observed the past event at the time it occurred. The rankest amateur in psychology knows how faulty observation is, knows that what a man thinks he observes may not accord with what actually happened. Human observation is obviously fallible, subjective. It is affected by defects of sight, or hearing, or by the observer's emotional state or physiological condition, and by his preconceived notions. "Men," say the courts, "often think they see when they did not see, * * * misinterpret what they hear." As hundreds of experiments have demonstrated, two observers of the same happening frequently disagree.

(2) But suppose a witness made no error in his original observation of an event. He may, nevertheless, erroneously remember that correct observation. The faulty, subjective, nature of human memory is notorious. Many a witness has an imaginative memory. "Even a conscientious person," said a court, "in trying to narrate a transaction which exists in his memory in a faded or fragmentary state, will, in his effort to make the reproduction seem complete and natural, substitute fancy for fact, or fabricate the missing or forgotten facts."

"When," writes Paton, "a witness makes a simple statement—'the prisoner is the man who drove the car after the robbery'—he is really asserting: (a) that he observed the car; (b) that the impression became fixed in his mind; (c) that the impression has not been confused or obliterated; (d) that the resemblance between the original impression and the prisoner is sufficient to base a judgment not of resemblance but of identity. Scientific research into the nature of the eye has shown how easy it is for vision to be mistaken; lack of observation and faulty memory add to the difficulties. Borchard, in discussing established cases of error in crinminal convictions, points out that many of those errors arose from faulty identification and that in eight of the cases there was not the slightest resemblance between the real criminal and the person who was falsely convicted."

(3) Now we come to the stage where the witness reports in the courtroom his present recollection of his original observation. Here, again, error may enter. The honest witness, due to a variety of causes, may inadvertently

misstate his recollection, may inaccurately report his story. Ram, writing of witnesses, notes that "it happens to all persons occasionally to use one word for another, making the sense very different from what was intended; unconsciously we say what we did not mean to say. * * *"

Sir William Eggleston, a noted lawyer, now Australian Ambassador to this country, expresses the opinion that "no witness can be expected to be more than 50% correct, even if perfectly honest and free from preconception." "In order to know what another person has seen and apprehended, we must first of all know what he thinks—and that is impossible," says Gross. "If we know, at least approximately, the kind of mental process of a person who is close to us in sex, age, culture, position and experience, we lose this knowledge with every step that leads to differences. * * * Suppose that in some case, several people of different degrees of education and intelligence have made observations. Suppose all want to tell the truth. Their testimonies, nevertheless, may be very different."

Thus far, I have posited an honest and unprejudiced witness. But many witnesses are neither. Some are downright liars. Aside from perjurers, there are the innumerable biased witnesses, whose narratives, although honest, have been markedly affected by their prejudices for or against one of the parties to the suit. A court has said that a biased witness, out of sympathy for a litigant he regards as having been wronged, "with entire innocence may recall things that have never occurred, or forget important instances that have occurred. * * * "Perhaps the most subtle and prolific of all the 'fallacies of testimony' arises out of unconscious partisanship," writes Wellman. "It is rare that one comes across a witness in court who is so candid and fair that he will testify as fully and favorably for the one side as the other. * * * Witnesses usually feel more or less complimented by the confidence that is placed in them by the party calling them to prove a certain state of facts, and it is human nature to prove worthy of this confidence." Miller, another experienced trial lawyer, says: "When a disinterested person is enlisted as a witness on one side of the case, his sympathies and desires naturally become involved with the person calling him; and when he discovers what things the litigant desires to prove, a witness, especially if the events are distant in time, is apt unconsciously to give a strong coloring to the facts and sometimes to remember things he did not see; and more often innocently to misrepresent things he did see. * * * That fact arises not from an intention deliberately to falsify but from the desire to be an important element in the case." "The liar * * * is far less dangerous than the honest but mistaken witness who draws upon his imagination," Moore remarks. It is difficult to "determine in the case of an honestly intentioned witness how much of his evidence should be discarded as unreliable, and how much accepted as true. * * *

Nothing is more deceitful than half the truth, and biased witnesses are much addicted to half-truths and coloring of facts. * * * Such a witness is more dangerous than one who commits a gross perjury. . . ."

A story is told of a trial judge who, after hearing the testimony and the lawyers' arguments, announced: "Gentlemen, if Humphrey, the deceased, said—in the light of these Missouri decisions—'Daughter, if you'll come and live with me, I'll give you this house,' then I'll decide for the plaintiff. Now just what was the testimony?" Unfortunately the court reporter had boggled his notes. The judge impatiently asked if the principal witness, the plaintiff's maid, was present, and, learning that she was in the courtroom, asked her again to take the stand and repeat her testimony. This is what she said: "I remember very well what happened. It was a cold and stormy night. We were all sitting around the fire. Old Mr. Humphrey said to Mrs. Quinn, 'In the light of these Missouri decisions, Daughter, if you'll come and live with me, I'll give you this house.' " Of course, in that case it was obvious enough to the judge that the witness had a convenient and partisan recollection. But there are hundreds of cases where that kind of memory and that kind of testimony are not exposed but believed.

The axiom or assumption that, in all or most trials, the truth will out, ignores, then, the several elements of subjectivity and chance. It ignores perjury and bias; ignores the false impression made on the judge or jury by the honest witness who seems untruthful because he is frightened in the courtroom or because he is irascible or overscrupulous or given to exaggeration. It ignores the mistaken witness who honestly and convincingly testifies that he remembers acts or conversations that happened quite differently than as he narrates them in court. It neglects, also, the dead or missing witness without whose testimony a crucial fact cannot be brought out, or an important opposing witness cannot be successfully contradicted. Finally it neglects the missing or destroyed letter, or receipt, or canceled check.

Nor is it true that trial courts will be sure to detect lies or mistakes in testimony. That is clearly not so when a jury tries a case. Many experienced persons believe that of all the possible ways that could be devised to get at the falsity or truth of testimony, none could be conceived that would be more ineffective than trial by jury.

Judges, too, when they try cases without juries, are often fallible in getting at the true facts of a "contested" case. Partly that is due to our faulty way of trying cases in which we hamstring the judge. But even with the best system that could be devised, there would be no way to ensure that the judge will know infallibly which witnesses are accurately reporting the facts. As yet we have no lie detector for which all responsible psychologists will vouch and which most courts will regard as reliable. But even a perfect lie detector will not reveal mistakes in a witness' original observation of the facts to which he testifies, and probably will not disclose his mistakes due to his unconscious prejudices.

Lacking any adequate mechanical means of detecting such mattters, the courts resort to a common-sense technique: All of us know that, in everyday life, the way a man behaves when he tells a story—his intonations; his fidgetings or composure, his yawns, the use of his eyes, his air of candor or of evasiveness—may furnish valuable clues to his reliability. Such clues are by no means impeccable guides, but they are often immensely helpful. So the courts have concluded. "The appearance and manner of a witness," many courts have said, "is often a complete antidote to what he testifies." The "witness' demeanor," notes Wigmore, "is always * * * in evidence."

Osborn has admirably explained the reasons for giving weight to witness demeanor: "Let us imagine that every spoken word in a trial is all correctly written out, and then all read by the jury, or read to the jury or the judge. Is there anyone so foolish as to say that a wrong decision would not be more likely in the absence of the living witnesses and speakers. * * * The most skillful official stenographer could not write down all of the varied influences that appeal to [the jury]. The witnesses speak and the lawyers speak but not by words alone. Many of these speakers are eloquent in other ways, sometimes to their detriment and sometimes to their advantage. Their faces and their changing expressions may be pictures that prove the truth of the ancient Chinese saying that a picture is equal to a thousand words. * * * Unconsciously we all tell about ourselves certain things by our actions and our general appearance. This language of others it becomes necessary for the juror to interpret. * * * The task of the juror therefore * * * is to interpret this language without words, as well as he can, and distinguish the true from the false. * * * An important phase of the study of this wordless language is no doubt a scrutiny of everything about a speaker that may indicate sincerity or insincerity. The steps down seem to be unnaturalness, uneasiness, nervousness, hesitation, affectation, concealment, and deceit, and the steps up seem to be outspokenness, naturalness, frankness, openness, and properly qualified statements." Osborn wrote about a jury trial, but what he said is true also of a judge trial.

3

Having in mind this significance properly attached to close observation of the witnesses, I now must emphasize an element in the decisional process which, curiously, has seldom been considered; trial judges and juries, in trying to get at the past facts through the witnesses, are themselves witnesses of what goes on in our courtrooms. They must determine the facts from what they see and hear, from the gestures and other conduct of the testifying witnesses as well as from their words. Now, as silent witnesses of the witnesses, the trial judges and juries suffer from the same human weaknesses as other witnesses. They, too, are not photographic plates or phonographic discs. If the testifying witnesses make errors of observation, are subject to lapses of memory, or contrive mistaken, imaginative reconstruction of events they observed, in the same way trial judges or juries are subject to defects in their apprehension and their recollection of what the witnesses said and how they behaved. (Suppose a trial judge is so deaf that he cannot hear what the witnesses say, or so nearsighted that he cannot see the facial expressions and other aspects of the witnesses' demeanor. . . .)

The facts as they actually happened are therefore twice refracted—first by the witnesses, and second by those who must "find" the facts. The reactions of trial judges or juries to the testimony are shot through with subjectivity. Thus we have subjectivity piled on subjectivity. It is surely proper, then, to say that the facts as "found" by a trial court are subjective.

When Jack Spratt, as a witness, testifies to a fact, he is merely stating his belief or opinion about that past fact. When he says, "I saw McCarthy hit Schmidt," he means, "I believe that is what happened." When a trial judge or jury, after hearing that testimony, finds as a fact that McCarthy hit Schmidt, the finding means no more than the judge's or jury's belief that the belief of the witness Spratt is an honest belief, and that his belief accurately reflects what actually happened. A trial court's findings of fact is, then, at best, its belief or opinion about someone else's belief or opinion.

This aspect of judging seems to have puzzled Plato, who tried to distinguish sharply between "knowledge" and "opinion." "When," he has Socrates say, "judges are justly persuaded about matters which you can only know by seeing them, and not in any other way, and when thus judging them from reports they attain a true opinion about them, they judge without knowledge, and yet are rightly persuaded, if they have judged well. * * * And yet, * * * if true opinion and knowledge are the same, the perfect judge could not have judged rightly without knowledge; and therefore I must infer that they are not the same." Jowett, commenting on this passage, writes, "The correctness of such an opinion will be purely accidental. * * * Plato would have done better if he had said that true opinion was a contradiction in terms."

## 4

And now I come to a major matter, one which most nonlawyers do not understand, and one which puts the trial courts at the heart of our judicial system: An upper court can seldom do anything to correct a trial court's mistaken belief about facts. Where, as happens in most cases, the testimony at the trial was oral, the upper court usually feels obliged to adopt the trial court's determination of the facts. Why? Because in such a case the trial court heard and saw the witnesses as they testified, but the upper court did not. The upper court has only a typewritten or printed record of the testimony. The trial court alone is in a position to interpret the demeanor clues, this "language without words." An upper court, to use Judge Kennison's phrase, "has to operate in the partial vacuum of the printed record." A "stenographic transcript," wrote Judge Ulman, "* * * fails to reproduce tones of voice and hesitations of speech that often make a sentence mean the reverse of what the mere words signify. The best and most accurate record [of oral testimony] is like a dehydrated peach; it has neither the substance nor the flavor of the peach before it was dried." That is why, when testimony is taken in a trial court, an upper court, on appeal, in most instances accepts the facts as found by the trial court, when those findings can be supported by reasonable inferences from some witness' testimony, even if it is flatly contradicted in the testimony of other witnesses.

Considering how a trial court reaches its determination as to the facts, it is most misleading to talk, as we lawyers do, of a trial court "finding" the facts. The trial court's facts are not "data," not something that is "given"; they are not waiting somewhere, ready made, for the court to discover, to "find." More accurately, they are processed by the trial court—are, so to speak, "made" by it, on the basis of its subjective reactions to the witnesses' stories. Most legal scholars fail to consider that subjectivity, because, when they think of courts, they think almost exclusively of upper courts and of their written opinions. For, in these opinions, the facts are largely "given" to the upper courts—given to those courts by the trial courts.

It should now be obvious that the conventional description of the decisional process needs alteration. For that description implies that the $F$, in the $R \times F = D$ equation, is an objective fact—what might be called an $OF$—so that, seemingly, $R \times OF = D$. But, as the $F$ is subjective—what might therefore be called an $SF$—the formula should read: $R \times SF = D$.

## 5

I can feel that at this moment some lawyer-critic, reading this book, is itching to reply: "Doubtless, decisions in 'contested' cases turn on the judge's or jury's belief, and that belief may be mistaken. Court orders may depend upon such beliefs of the trial judges or the juries who happen to try the cases. But a man's legal rights are what they are, even if a trial court, through an erroneous belief about the facts, decides against him."

That I deny. At any rate, I deny that the words "legal rights" have any practical meaning, if used as my critic uses them. If a court decides that Smart has, in fact, done no legal wrong to Sensible, then Sensible has no meaningful legal right against Smart. Not on this earth, not in this life. If a court, after listening to conflicting oral testimony, mistakes the facts and decides for Smart, and Sensible appeals, losing his appeal, that's all there is to Sensible's legal rights—there isn't any more. His legal rights, so far as the courts are concerned, consist precisely of what he can persuade a court to make Smart do. If Sensible wins the court fight, then he'll have a legal right; if he loses, he won't. There is no middle ground, no judicial Purgatory. If Sensible loses in court, I think it plain nonsense to say that nevertheless he still has a legal right against Smart, or that Smart owes him a legal duty. Please note that I say nothing of moral rights. Moral considerations should, and unquestionably do, play a part in many court decisions. But when a court, once and for all, holds that a man is without a legal right, his remaining moral rights are usually of no interest to the courts, for usually the courts will do nothing more for him.

See, then, the lawyers' difficulties: (1) Contested lawsuits turn on $F$'s. (2) No one knows whether lawsuits will arise or which of them will be contested. (3) The $F$'s of future contested lawsuits are not now knowable. (4) Legal rights and duties mean lawsuits lost or won. (5) Accordingly, legal rights and duties depend on the outcome of future lawsuits which turn on presently unknowable $F$'s. (6) Wherefore, no matter how well settled are the pertinent legal rules, a lawyer, before suit is begun, frequently cannot tell a man his legal rights. For the lawyer faces a multitude of variable factors which he cannot definitely ascertain.

A lawyer friend of mine once objected when he heard me express such views. He said that it is not difficult for a lawyer of experience to answer unequivocally most of the legal questions that confront him in his daily practice. If my friend meant that a lawyer can unequivocally answer a generalized question, such as whether a gift by a man who was insolvent when he made it can be set aside by the man's creditors, then, of course, my friend was correct. But the client usually is not interested in getting answers to merely general questions of that character. He doesn't want his lawyer to copy rules for him out of lawbooks. The client wants to know, for example, whether he can induce a court to set aside a gift of $50,000 made by a definite person, John Jones, so that the client can collect the $10,000 Jones owes him. (This brings up a matter which, although most important, I can but mention here: Ordinarily, a client does not merely want a decision. He wants a decision which will be enforced or with which the loser will voluntarily comply. A court's judgment against Jones for $10,000 will usually be of no value unless Jones is able to pay that judgment. Many a judgment is not paid because the losing party is insolvent or has successfully secreted his property. Legal rights should therefore be viewed from the angle of their actual enforcibility. . . .)

The ability to answer unequivocally many so-called legal questions does not, then, signify, by any manner of means, that a lawyer, however experienced, can unequivocally tell his client that which the client wants to know. Only a soothsayer, a prophet, or a person gifted with clairvoyance, can tell a man what are his enforceable rights arising out of any particular transaction, or against any other person, before a lawsuit with respect to that transaction or that person has arisen. For only a clairvoyant can foretell what evidence will be introduced and will be believed, and can foresee what will be the reaction of the trial judge or the jurors to such testimony as he or they believe.

I think the reader will now see that a lawyer's ability successfully to predict a decision varies with the stage at which he is asked for his opinions:

(1) When a client, having just signed a contract, asks what are his rights thereunder, at that time neither the client nor the other party to the contract has as yet taken any steps under the contract. The lawyer's prediction at this stage must include a hazardous guess as to what each of the parties will do or not do in the future. Frequently the prediction must be so full of if's as to be of little practical value.

(2) After events have occurred which give rise to threatened litigation, the client may inquire concerning the outcome of the suit, if one should be brought.

    a. Before the lawyer has interviewed prospective witnesses, his guess is on a shaky foundation.

    b. After interviewing them, his guess is somewhat less shaky. But, unless the facts are certain to be agreed upon, the guess is still dubious. For, if, as is usual, the witnesses are to testify orally and will disagree about what they saw and heard, seldom can anyone guess how the trial judge or jury will react to the testimony. Especially is the guessing wobbly if the lawyer does not know who the judge will be, should the trial be jury-less; it is still more so, if there may be a jury trial, since the lawyer cannot know what persons will compose the jury.

(3) After the trial, but before decision, the lawyer's prophecy may be better. For he is now estimating the reaction to the testimony of a known trial judge or a known jury, observed in action in the particular case. Yet, if the testimony was oral, that guessing is frequently not too easy.

(4) After trial and a decision by the trial court, the guess relates to the outcome of an appeal, should one be taken. It therefore usually relates solely to the rules the upper court will apply to the facts as already "found" by the

trial judge or jury. At this stage, a competent, trained lawyer can often (not always) predict with accuracy.

# 6

Let me summarize: Lawsuits are fights. They are legal battles fought in a courtroom. They are historically (and contemporaneously) substitutes for private gunfights and knife fights. Instead of using your knife or gun to make Robinson do what you want him to do, you fight in a courthouse with non-lethal weapons, with implements of persuasion, to induce a court to enter an order directing Robinson to do what you want—fight to produce a court order which will direct the sheriff, if necessary, to use his gun to make Robinson do what you want. And lawsuits alone—nothing else—ultimately fix tested legal rights. If Robinson, voluntarily—or because he is ashamed not to, or afraid not to—does what you want, you haven't tested out your legal rights against him, or his legal obligations to you. It is only if he doesn't do what you want, and if you try to get a court to order him to do so, that you really learn what those legal rights and duties are. Jones's tested legal rights against Smith on a mortgage, a lease, an employment contract, or because of an automobile accident, are unknown until Jones sues Smith and a court decides that suit.

We are all Smiths and Joneses. You can't really know your legal rights (your court-enforceable rights) against any other person, about anything, until you obtain an enforceable decision in a specific lawsuit brought against that other person. No lawsuits, no tested legal rights. Until there has been an enforceable courtorder in a specific lawsuit, there can be only guesses about any legal rights or duties. And those guesses—even if they are lawyers' guesses —are not always too good, especially before a lawsuit arises. For court decisions in lawsuits depend on at least two things (Rules and Facts), and one of those is peculiarly unguessable—namely, what the trial court (judge or jury) will believe were the facts. Guessing legal rights, before litigation occurs, is, then, guessing what judges or juries will guess were the facts, and that is by no means easy. Legal rights and duties are, then, often guessy, if-y.

See what this means: Most legal rights turn on the facts as "proved" in a future lawsuit, and proof of those facts, in "contested" cases, is at the mercy of such matters as mistaken witnesses, perjured witnesses, missing or dead witnesses, mistaken judges, inattentive judges, biased judges, inattentive juries, and biased juries. In short, a legal right is usually a bet, a wager, on the chancy outcome of a possible future lawsuit. (When I so state, and when I also state that potential force lies behind court decisions, of course I am not expressing a worship of force, or taking a neutral attitude toward morality and moral rights. I am describing the actualities of courthouse government—doing so indeed because I think that such a description will help to promote an understanding of both the avoidable and the unavoidable imperfections of our legal system. . . .)

## 7

I must now modify somewhat the distrubing picture I have painted. I turn to lawyers as preventers of litigation.

Lawyers do not confine themselves to trying lawsuits. Many of them spend all or most of their time in their offices advising clients. Many clients go to them to obtain assurance, confidence. For life is hazardous and among the hazards are the dangers of being sucked into litigation and being defeated in court. The lawyer thus often serves as a tranquillizer, as an allayer of the doubts of perplexed men. In that sense, one might say he acts as a psychiatrist, subduing his clients' fears, enabling them to act without undue apprehensions.

Some lawyers sometimes raise unnecessary doubts in the minds of their clients. To that extent, they are bad psychiatrists. However, the lawyer who too glibly gives assurances may be an equally bad psychiatrist. The competent psychiatrist, as I understand it, does not create illusions in his patients, but seeks to enable them, in adult fashion, to recognize and bravely cope with reality. He does not act as his patients' emotional wet nurse. No more should the lawyer with respect to his patients, his clients. He should deal with them as grown-up persons. He should not illusion them about their legal rights. He should, for his own sake and theirs, tell them the facts of life. And included in those facts is the inherent uncertainty of litigation—and therefore of legal rights.

The wise lawyer often tries to prevent litigation. For just as there is preventive medicine, so there is preventive legal practice. The lawyer often can and does keep people from litigating. Here we come to lawyers' paper work—the legal documents they prepare. In theory, that paper work is generally efficacious in preventing lawsuits, by so equipping one side with legal weapons that its easily foreseeable victory deters the other side from commencing court warfare. Let us examine into that theory.

A client has his lawyer draw his contract, or his mortagage, his lease, his deed. Then the client feels secure, for his lawyer presumably has safeguarded him against successful attack. And we lawyers, generally, seeing how little of our paper work is ever assailed, how few of our contracts or deeds are ever called into question, take pride in the efficacy of our handiwork as litigation-preventives. But is that pride always justified? When no litigation occurs, is it usually our draftsmanship that kept the parties from disputing? To what extent does the explanation of nonlitigation lie in the fact that most people are usually not litigious? Perhaps lawyers resemble Chanticleer who thought the sun could not rise without his crowing. Perhaps this lawyer-pride rests largely on the false principle of *post hoc ergo propter hoc*, nicely illustrated by the case of the savage rainmaker: He performs a ceremony. Two days later it rains. His reputation with his group is assured. They assume that, if A follows B in time, then B is caused by A. They imagine a causal relation where none exists.

Consider this fact: Any lawyer who examines many abstracts of title to real estate finds hundreds of instances of defective papers prepared by lawyers —defective deeds or wills or corporate resolutions, and the like—which were potential provocatives of litigation. Most of these defects are cured by mere lapse of time ("adverse possession"). In other words, such abstracts reveal lawyers' written contrivances which did not prevent litigation but which, on the contrary, created potential lawsuits that did not occur—thanks to other factors, including ignorance of the errors, or inertia.

One of my favorite lawyer stories is relevant. A lawyer friend of mine— call him Mr. Inquisitive—represented a corporation which was about to borrow a million dollars on mortgage bonds. One of the leading New York law firms—call them Messrs. Big, Keen & Snappy—represented the bankers. They sent Mr. Inquisitive a sixty-page printed draft of the mortgage trust deed for his client to sign. My friend, it happens, hadn't had much experience in such matters. So he read through the proposed document with exceeding care. Then he phoned Messrs. Big, Keen & Snappy.

"I can't," he said, "understand the meaning of pages 42 to 51. What is it all about?"

"Oh," they replied, patronizingly, "that is our usual form. We have used it just that way for the last four years. At least a billion dollars of bonds are issued and outstanding under similar instruments."

"All right," said Mr. Inquisitive, "I'll admit I am stupid. But, for my peace of mind, just write me a few lines telling me the meaning of those pages."

A day later, on the phone, he received this surprising answer from Big, Keen & Snappy: Two years before, in getting out a trust deed in a hurry, the printer had dropped three pages and spoiled the sense of some dozen other pages. The error, undetected, had been perpetuated ever since.

Well, there they were—about a billion dollars of bonds issued by divers corporations and sold to the public under defective instruments. Now how many lawsuits did that mistake occasion? Probably none. For most people don't go around looking for lawsuits. The absence of such litigation cannot

be said to be due to what was done by the lawyers who drafted those mortgages. It was in spite of their work that court fights did not occur.

How far the instruments drafted by lawyers act prophylactically we simply
do not know. To have such knowledge we would need, at the least, to learn
(1) the instances in which lawyers' mistakes were never found out, and (2)
the instances in which threatened litigation, growing out of such mistakes,
was settled out of court. We would need also to take into account the fact
that, in some areas of business, there would seem to be a peculiarly strong
social taboo against litigation. It would be interesting to know whether, in a
period of sharp business decline, lawsuits do not become more frequent even
in those business areas in which, in normal times, this litigation taboo
governs.

A paper carefully drafted by a lawyer does, undoubtedly sometimes prevent lawsuits. For the courts have evolved what is known as the "parol evidence" rule. Roughly speaking, that rule says that a court will not listen to
evidence which is at variance with, contradicts, a writing. Seemingly, that
means that most oral evidence will be shut out, and that therefore the
dangers of mistaken testimony will be absent. That rule, however, is subject
to so many exceptions that it resembles a swiss cheese with more holes than
cheese. That rule permits a man who wants to contest such a paper to
nullify it by introducing oral testimony which, if believed, will show, for
instance,

that his signature is a forgery; or

that he was induced by fraud to sign it; or

that both parties who signed it intended it to be a joke or a sham; or

that by mutual mistake it omitted important matter which gives it a
different meaning; or

that it was orally agreed that the paper was not to have any effect until something happened which has never happened; or

that, after it was signed, the other party and he orally agreed to cancel it.

(This last exception is not recognized by all courts.) If the court believes the witnesses who testify in support of any of those alleged facts, it does
not matter one iota whether such facts are true. What solely matters is the
trial court's belief in their truth. The written paper will be effective or not
according to that belief. Oral testimony may create fatal chinks in the paper
armor. For instance, in many a will contest, the will itself, carefully prepared,
contains no legal flaws, but the court sets it aside because the court believes
from some of the oral testimony that the making of the will was the result of
"undue influence."

But I must not exaggerate. In all probability, because of the parol evidence
rule, carefully prepared, lawyer-made documents not infrequently forestall

litigation. My good friend Professor Karl Llewellyn, in recent discussion with me, estimated that, in certain sorts of business situations, skillful documents mean that the chances of victory in a lawsuit become 3 out of 4, or 4 out of 5. Whether that figure is correct, no one knows. Doubtless, as to some kinds of transactions, skilled legal paper work often does the trick. Yet that belief cannot be verified statistically.

This, too, should be kept in mind. Many documents of the kind to which Llewellyn refers are used by economically powerful corporations. Suppose it could be proved that, in suits relating to such documents, their batting average was very high, and that, consequently, few persons venture to "go to law" with them concerning those documents. Even so, we would not have a "controlled experiment." For these giant institutions employ exceptionally competent trial lawyers, better on the average than those employed by their adversaries. And allowance must be made for the fact that many a man is unable to finance litigation with those giants, or, when able, is reluctant to do so, either because of the giants' prestige, or out of fear—often more imaginary than real—of indirect harm to himself, by way of retaliation, through loss of credit or supplies needed in his business.

We shall never, I think, obtain reliable information on these subjects. No one will ever know just how much more or less men would litigate if lawyers were to abandon their paper work. But this much one may say: The fact that, in general, there is a relatively small amount of litigation should almost surely not be ascribed principally to the preventive paper work of lawyers. The legal profession cannot reasonably claim most of the credit for whatever it is that makes folks more peaceable, less litigious, than they conceivably might be. Let lawyers, then, be modest in asserting the extent to which the words they dictate to their stenographers serve to prevent quarrels, in the courtroom or elsewhere. Above all, remember that only a small part of the human activities which become or might become lawsuits could be fully covered by lawyer-made instruments or be otherwise lawyer-guided. At most, the activities open to prophylaxis must be few.

## 8

Many nonlawyers and some lawyers, when they talk of "facts" in litigation, refer not to the kind of facts I have been considering (that is, whether Jones ran over young Tommy Smith), but to what might be called "background" or "social and economic" facts, often of a statistical character—the sort of facts presented to the courts in the famous "Brandeis briefs." Facts of that sort do not involve witnesses' credibility. But the great majority of actual lawsuits do involve some crucial fact issues which turn on determinations by the trial courts of orally testifying witnesses' credibility. There the trial court usually has the final say about the facts. There we have what Tourtoulon calls the "sovereignty of the trial court." With that in mind, Judge Olso recently suggested that lawsuits are misnamed: They should be called "fact suits." (Warning: Only where a trial court sees and hears witnesses, and thus is in a more advantageous position than the upper court to ascertain witness credibility, are its fact-findings usually accorded finality by the upper court. Where, then, no oral testimony is involved, no such finality necessarily exists. . . .)

Chief Justice Hughes—who distrusted administrative agencies, considering them far less entitled to respect than orthodox courts—once remarked: "An unscrupulous administrator might be tempted to say, 'Let me find the facts * * *, and I care little who lays down the general principles.' " The Chief Justice failed to note that his observation related also to fact-finding by trial courts—and not merely to fact-finding caused by unscrupulousness but, as well, to erroneous fact-finding caused by honest mistakes of trial judges and juries.

Hughes's remark serves to bring out the importance of trial-court fact-finding. For suppose that a trial court, in deciding a case, makes a mistake about the facts, and applies to those facts, mistakenly found, the correct legal rule, that is, the rule which it ought to have applied if those were the actual facts. Then injustice results fully as much as if the court had applied an incorrect rule to the actual facts. In other words, it is as unjust to apply the "right" rule to the wrong facts as to apply the "wrong" rule. Or, rather, no rule can be the "right" rule, the just rule, in any specific lawsuit, if applied to facts that did not occur, to unreal, spurious facts. Can it be said, for instance, that the court enforced a just rule when Mr. Campbell was sent to jail for a crime he had not committed? It is as if a surgeon, flawlessly following approved rules of surgery, mistakenly removed the gallbladder of a healthy man.

Indeed, in a case where a correct rule is misapplied by a court because applied to unreal facts, it is not really enforced, its enforcement becomes illusory. And that misapplication, that illusory application of a rule, means a frustration of the community ideal or policy embodied in that rule; for the misapplication of such an ideal or policy is at least the equivalent of its non-application. Mistaken findings of the facts render impotent such ideals or policies. You may perhaps think that, because I have stressed trial-court fact-finding, I consider the legal rules of little importance. Not at all. As I sit on an upper court which spends most of its time on legal rules, it should be obvious that I do not regard them lightly. Indeed, it is precisely because I think that the rules are of great importance that I am distressed when, due to unnecessarily defective fact-finding, they are frustrated by being applied to the wrong facts. Since, however, the specific applications of the rules depend on fact-finding, the upper courts, which function primarily as guardians of the rules, have far less importance in our legal system than the trial courts. In the first place, the overwhelming majority of cases are not appealed; probably 95 percent of all cases end in the trial courts. In the second place, since, in most of the few cases that are appealed, the upper courts accept the trial court's fact-findings, the trial courts decide the fate of, say, 98 percent of all cases.

## 9

Throughout this book, I shall continue to be critical of some courthouse ways. I must therefore take notice of a recently developed argument opposed to such criticism: American democracy, it is said, competes today in world affairs with Russian totalitarianism. Consequently, it is urged, we should observe a "hush" policy concerning any faults, eradicable or not, in the American economy or government, even if by so doing we diminish the possibility of removing some of those faults. For otherwise, so the argument goes, Soviet critics, taking advantage of the disclosures, will win away America's friends or potential friends.

Surely that cannot be sound policy. It tries to preserve democracy by negating it. It proposes that we should employ the very mode of undemocratic suppression of the truth for the use of which we often criticize totalitarianism. It asserts that democracy, in order to survive, must cease to be democratic. Such an argument, applied to proposed reforms, economic or governmental, is a cowardly counsel of despair. Only a robust, developing democracy, true to its own fundamental principles, can successfully compete with Sovietism for world influence.

That our judicial system is not as good as it could and should be does not mean, however, that, as it stands, it does not have many features deserving of high praise. I therefore agree with Bar Associations when, recurrently, they deplore reckless, uninformed, blanket denigrations of our courts. But, in part, those denigrations are invited by almost equally deplorable excessive praise of our courts sometimes uttered by some prominent members of Bar Associations. Significantly, in such utterances they often quote Cicero. That fascinating Roman, as a legal philosopher, eloquently maintained that any civilized legal system must be based on reason, grounded on universal, eternal, principles of justice, and on the ideal we today phrase as "equality before the law." Yet Cicero, as a practicing court lawyer, felt free to use a lawyer's wiles to pervert reason, and to render ineffective the doctrines, which he, as legal philosopher, purported to worship. In his nonphilosophic moments, he boasted of his prowess as a lawyer in winning lawsuits for clients which they should have lost, and would have lost but for his clever stratagems. Now if, à la the philosophic Cicero, a legal system approximates rationality and "equality before the law," then cases which are substantially the same should, at any given time, be identically decided. Insofar as suchlike cases are decided differently, solely because of inequalities in the skills in wiliness of lawyers, then just to that extent the legal ideals proclaimed by Cicero are traduced. Cicero did nothing to close the gap between those ideals and the judicial realities. He kept his noble principles in one pocket and his actual lawyer's practices in another. Since he never sought to actualize the high principles he mouthed, he could not have entertained them seriously. I suggest that you examine critically the mouthings of our modern Ciceros.

Recently I read a book written for laymen by a lawyer. The author says that, should you lose a lawsuit, because the court misapprehended the facts, and should you leave the courtroom complaining of injustice, you would be an unreasonable, small-minded critic. For, he explains, in every suit there must be a loser, and you must learn to appreciate that no legal system can be perfect.

That not uncommon patronizing lawyer's way of brushing off laymen leaves me indignant. Of course, no legal system can be perfect. But think of this: A man is accused of killing another man and is tried for murder. If the accused is convicted, the government will kill him. The government's killing is lawful and therefore not murder. But if the government's killing follows a conviction brought about by the trial court's mistaken belief about the facts, so that the government, although acting according to legal forms, kills an innocent man—what then? Then a shocking act of judicial injustice has occurred. Yet our author writes, "Such a contingency does not justify condemnation of a system which is necessarily subject to human judgment; and if this complacent view exasperates a victim who has been found guilty of a crime which he has never committed, it is an incontrovertible fact," it is inevitable, like an "Act of God," as when a stroke of lightning kills a man.

That defense of grave miscarriages of justice is legitimate only if they are inevitable—that is, only if everything practical has been done to avoid such injustices. But, often, everything practical has not been done. Thanks to avoidable courtroom errors, innocent men are convicted of crimes; and every week, for similar reasons, someone loses his life's savings, his livelihood, his job. Most of such injustices stem not from lack of justice in the legal rules but from mistakes in fact-finding. And a high percentage of those mistakes derive from needless defects in the courthouse methods of getting at the facts.

It is up to the nonlawyers to demand a reform of those methods. They should not, I repeat, demand perfection. Perfect justice lies beyond human reach. But the unattainability of the ideal is no excuse for shirking the effort to obtain the best available. . . . As the poet MacNeice puts it:

> And to the good who know how wide the gulf, how deep,
> Between Ideal and Real, who being good have felt
> The final temptation to withdraw, sit down and weep,
> We pray the power to take upon themselves the guilt
> Of human action, though still ready to confess
> The imperfection of what can and must be built. . . .

## 10

The legal profession, as a whole, however, should not be singularly blamed for the remediable faults of our legal system. Most of those who comprise any profession or trade tend to venerate almost all its traditions, to overlook its defects, and are unable to inspect with much detachment its customary ways. And many noted lawyers, including some leading members of that conservative lawyers' organization, the American Bar Association, have been conspicuous as constructive critics of legal and judicial practices, just as they have been foremost in other phases of American life. Nevertheless, I believe that, to achieve substantial reforms of our trial-court methods, it is necessary to enlist the assistance of the nonlawyers.

\* \* \* \* \*

I have discussed the invention of courts as a means of preserving the peace, and the substitution of courtroom fights, called lawsuits, for private peace-disturbing wars. In a later chapter I shall say more of that subject; I shall there try to show that the fighting method of judicially administering justice has been carried too far, and needs very substantial modification, if justice is to be well administered by the courts. But, as a preface to that discussion, I want to show . . . how and why many lawyers have obscured, to themselves and to the public, the fighting character of present-day trials, and some of the resultant uncertainties and injustices of courthouse government.

## 2

Since the actual facts of a case do not walk into court, but happened outside the courtroom, and always in the past, the task of the trial court is to reconstruct the past from what are at best second-hand reports of the facts. Thus the trial court acts as an historian, its job being much the same as the historian's. The historian, too, tries to reconstruct the past, but usually he relies on second-hand or third-or-fourth-hand reports of dead witnesses. Indeed, the historian has been called a judge of the dead.

Increasingly, competent historians—at least in books written for other historians—confess that theirs is not a science but a guessy art. They admit that, on many issues, their knowledge of the past is far from sure to be accurate, because of a variety of circumstances which include (1) the unavailability of important data, (2) disagreements among the witnesses on whom the historians must depend for information as to what happened, and (3) the errors, prejudices or mendacity of those witnesses. "The historian," wrote Pirenne, himself a noted Belgian history writer, "only rarely finds himself face-to-face with an authentic fragment of the past. * * * Even if we had observed all that had been written about an event, we could not pretend to have complete information. No account, detailed as it may be, ever exhausts its subject. * * * In spite of all his efforts, therefore, the historian cannot gain an adequate knowledge of what has been." Two famous French historians have said, "Facts which we do not see, described in language which does not permit us to represent them in our minds with exactness, form the data of history."

The historian's job, we are told, is to study "events not accessible to * * * observation, and to study those events inferentially, arguing to them from something else which is accessible * * * to observation * * * that is, the evidence. For he "is not an eyewitness of the facts he desires to know. * * * His "only possible knowledge is mediate or inferential or indirect, never empirical." He must endeavor to "re-enact the past in his own mind." In this endeavor, he performs two tasks: (1) He first critically examines the evidence, attempting to determine which (if any) of his witnesses made reliable reports. To discover the real meanings which lie behind a witness' words, the historian must try to identify himself with the witness, to relive the witness' life. The witness' "personality intervenes between" the historian and "the facts." This task leaves "a very large role to the tact, finesse, and intuition" of the historian, involves an evaluation of credibility which is largely "subjective." For the historian does not passively accept testimony but interprets it, and the criterion in his critical interpretation "is the historian himself." (2) Having evaluated the credibility of the testimony, the historian must construct a narrative of the past events. This narrative "is at once a synthesis and a hypothesis. It is a synthesis inasmuch as it combines the mass of known facts in an account of the whole; it is a hypothesis inasmuch as the relations that it establishes between the facts are neither evidence nor verifiable by themselves. * * * Everything then depends * * * upon the degree of the creative imagination of the historian and upon his general conception of human affairs." The historian "imagines the past." His picture of the past is a "web of imaginative construction stretched between certain fixed points" provided by his critical judgment of his witnesses' testimony. Here, obviously, subjectivity enters. "The human actions which [historians] study cannot appear the same to different historians. It needs only a moment of reflection to understand that two historians using the same material will not treat it in an identical fashion, primarily because the creative imagination which permits them to single the factors of movements out of chaos varies, but also because they do not have the same ideas as to the relative importance of the motives which determine men's conduct. They [divers historians] will inevitably write accounts which will contrast as do their personalities. * * * Thus, historical syntheses depend to a very large degree not only upon the personality of their authors but upon all the social, religious, or natural, environments which surround them. It follows, therefore, that each historian will establish . . . relationships determined by the convictions, the movements, and the prejudices, that have molded his point of view." These elements shape his peculiar "conjectural reconstruction of the past." (. . . Of course, the historian, like the trial judge, may have before him evidence the authenticity of which is indubitably clear. Thus he may have no possible doubt of the words of a particular treaty or that Lincoln issued his emancipation proclamation on a certain day. But, when it comes to a determination of the causal relations of any such facts to other facts, each historian must often draw on his "constructive imagination." Wherefore historians often disagree about such matters—just as two trial judges often disagree about the facts of a case.)

The franker historians, then, admit that learning the "facts" about the past involves "interpretations" of the available data; that those "interpretations" depend on selection of, and emphasis on, some of the data as "significant"; and that, unavoidably, historians differ in their choice of the "significant," with the result that we have sharply discrepant accounts in divers history books concerning, say, Nero, Cromwell, Napoleon, the American Revolution, or our Civil War. Since every history book is a "conjectural reconstruction of the past," Pirenne concludes that, due to the differences among historians, "history is a conjectural science, or in other words, a subjective science." "How," asked the English historian Froude, "can we talk of a science in things long past which come to us only in books?"

Froude's comment suggests that the historian, in one important way, is at a disadvantage as compared with the trial court: Usually, as all or most of the historian's witnesses are dead, he cannot examine and cross-examine them. But he has some marked advantages as compared with a court: He can take as much time as he wants to gather his evidence, and to reflect on it, while a trial in court cannot go on endlessly. Moreover, the historian is free to consider any kind of evidence; but, in court, some kinds of evidence, for wise or unsound reasons, are excluded.

If the honest historian confesses to the conjectural and subjective character of his products, surely lawyers should similarly confess the conjectural nature of the products of the judicial process. But the lawyers' resistance to so confessing is astonishingly persistent. There are many possible explanations of that resistance. I shall not here attempt to discuss, or even mention, all of them. But one explanation ought to be obvious: Many men fear the chanciness of life. The uncertainty of legal rights, due to their dependence on imperfect human fact-finding, therefore provokes terror. In the sixteenth century, Montaigne advised, "We must shun lawsuits," even at the cost of suffering "very manifest injustice." "No judge has yet, thank God," he exclaimed, "spoken to me as a judge in any cause whatsoever, whether my own or another's, whether criminal or civil. * * * I * * * will never, if I can help it, place myself in the power of a man who can dispose of my head, when my honor and life depend on the skill of a lawyer more than on my innocence. * * * How many innocent people we have known to be punished, I mean without the fault of the judges; and how many there are that we have not known of!"

That fear of litigation was uttered some three centuries ago in France. In this country, in the twentieth century, eagerness to escape that terror induces self-deluding denials that the source of that terror exists, to denials that litigation is extraordinarily chancy in its outcome. To be sure, Judge Learned Hand, after much experience as a trial judge, not long ago remarked, "I must say that, as a litigant, I should dread a lawsuit beyond almost anything else short of sickness and of death." But only occasionally does a modern American lawyer forthrightly make such a comment.

## 3

To support my suggestion that fear accounts for much of the unwillingness of many lawyers today to acknowledge the immense hazards of litigation and the guessiness of legal rights, I shall make a historical detour. I shall go back to the early day of the European legal systems from which our own system derived. In those days, men had recourse to a device designed, they thought, to avoid mistakes or lies in testimony, and to preclude human errors of judgment grounded upon such testimony. I refer to the ordeals. They were methods of fact-finding which have been used, not universally, but in many parts of the globe, in what we moderns are pleased to call "primitive" or "archaic" societies.

The ordeals have taken many forms. There was, for instance, the "trial by battle," a "judicial duel" fought under court supervision. This fight, although socially regulated, was still overt warfare, conducted with physical weapons, between the parties to the dispute or their agents. There was also the ordeal by fire, or hot water, or cold water, or the balanced ax, or the suspended sacred object, or by poison, or the morsel, or the scales. For example, a person accused was required to plunge his hand into boiling water; then the hand was bandaged for three nights; if, when the bandage was removed, the hand was uninjured, he was deemed innocent. In the ordeal of the morsel, the accused was compelled to try to swallow a piece of bread, or cheese, of a prescribed size. If he succeeded without difficulty, he was innocent. If he choked and grew black in the face, he was guilty. In the ordeal of the scales, the accused was weighed in the scales and then removed. The judge then adjured the scales, and the accused was again placed in the balance. If he increased in weight, he was guilty; if his weight was the same or less, his innocence was established. (In passing, recall the modern symbols of justice, the sword and the scales—the fight and the ordeal, shall we say?)

The pertinent rule, the R, was announced by the court, in advance of the trial. That pronouncement was not too difficult. The serious difficulty was with the facts, the F. The function of the ordeal was to ascertain that F. When it was once ascertained, the final decision followed.

Always, you see, in the ordeals, the F, and therefore the decision, turned on one or the other party to the dispute passing a perilous test. The court set him a task. If he performed it, he won the judicial fight. If he failed in his performance, he lost. "He whom the blazing fire burns not," runs the ancient Hindu code of Manu (about 300 B.C.), "whom the water forces not to come quickly up, who meets with no speedy misfortune, must be held innocent." The trial, as Radin suggests, was more literally a "trial"—a test—than is a trial as we conduct it.

Here we get a clue to the inner meaning of all ordeals. They were supernatural, apparently nonhuman, means for determining whether a man spoke the truth. He was put in peril. If he came through safely, that was a sign that he spoke truly. If he succumbed to the peril, it was a sign that he lied. Whence came this sign? It is usually said that it was deemed to come from heaven—from deity (the Gods or God)—that heaven decided the issue of fact. The ordeal is therefore often called *judicuum dei*, God's decision. But in some "primitive" communities, we find that the appeal was not to heaven but to a power residing in things—in fire, in water, in poison, and so on. Some anthropologists use the word *mana* to describe this latent power. *Mana* is supernatural, impersonal, nonhuman power. Belief in such a power and in the possibility of its use in human affairs was a belief in magic. The ordeals, then, represent one aspect of a magico-religious attitude.

I want here, for the moment, to stress the more strictly magical aspects of the ordeals. Let us, then, inquire how and why "primitive" or "archaic" societies utilize magic. In this necessarily brief discussion, I shall rely largely on the writings of Malinowski. His views need qualifications. For such qualifications, I refer you to Ruth Benedict. . . . I shall say a little something of her views later. But for my immediate purpose, Malinowski's portrayal of magic, slightly modified, will suffice. On that basis, I may summarize as follows:

Primitive man has a considerable amount of correct technical knowledge. He learns a great deal, from observation, about his environment and how, by rationally conceived techniques, to control it. Of the ways of domesticating plants and animals, of agriculture and husbandry, fishing, house-building, boat-making, he knows much. These techniques, for direct control of the environment, based upon observation, we might call "primitive science."

But there are forces at large that the so-called savage cannot thus control, evils that stalk him, perils which strike at his food supply, that capsize his boats, destroy his houses, take his life. There is "magic power" in things. That power, that mana, man feels he must learn to control. Not by the ordinary techniques; they fail him. And so, alongside "primitive science," we find the "savage" using magic. Where ignorance is thickest about the ways of things, where dangers are the greatest, where luck plays the largest part—there magic is employed.

Magic, then, appears to be primitive man's ways of dealing with specific practical problems when he is in peril or in need, and his strong desires are thwarted because his rational techniques, based upon observation, prove ineffective. "We do not," says Malinowski, "find magic wherever the pursuit is certain, reliable and under the control of rational methods and technological processes. * * * We do not find it wherever absolute safety eliminates any elements of foreboding." So, he continues, "in lagoon fishing, where man can rely completely upon his knowledge and skill, magic does not exist, while in the open-sea fishing, full of danger and uncertainty, there is extensive magical ritual to secure safety and good results."

When "primitive" man loses his way, when he reaches an impasse, when he is terrified by uncertainty, or baffled or trapped, he turns to magic. We can understand his mental and emotional processes if we observe similar conduct in some of those about us in our own society who seek to climb out of oppressing difficulties (such as economic problems, for instance) by the wish-route, or on what James called the faith-ladder, the rungs of which are: What I want might conceivably be true. It may be true. It must be true. It is true.

With "primitive" man, the wish-route to desired ends was overt, openly acknowledged, definitely crystallized and routinized. The words and gestures employed to evoke magical power were worked out in conventional patterns, prescribed by tradition. There was a fixation of beliefs in standardized spells, in elaborated rituals. To a considerable degree, magic came to be based on precedents, became a professional task, esoteric and unpracticed by the group at large.

Magic, then, was one of the ways of coping with practical problems. If we designate as "primitive science" the primitive arts of fishing, hunting, agriculture, and the like, so far as they are based on direct observation, then magic might be called "primitive pseudo-science." For magic, like science, is technological in a sense. It is, says Benedict, "essentially mechanistic," involving "a manipulation of the external world by techniques and formulae" that are assumed to "operate automatically." But, in its reliance on wishes, it departs from science. Primitive science, we are advised, "is founded on the conviction that experience, effort and reason are valid; magic on the belief that hope cannot fail, nor desire deceive." . . .

Thence the ordeal. What human contrivances are there, in litigation, for learning the truth about past events? How to ascertain whether men honestly tell what they know? What lie detectors are available? What man can look into the mind of his neighbor? Lives and possessions, wives and honor, hang on the determination of whether a claimant in the judicial contest and his witnesses are telling the truth. Since a trial's just outcome depends on truth-telling, and since the outcome may deprive a man of his life, or his dearest possessions, successful perjury is as grave a danger as drought, disease, lightning or the fierce claws of wild beast. Leave to the inadequate judgments of mere human judges the testing of the truth-telling of witnesses, when life or property are at stake? By no means. There the human techniques fail. Then call in magic, the mystic power of fire, water, poison, the scales—summon that invisible force, by appropriate spells, to find out the truth mechanically. Magic, and nothing else, is needed in the difficult and dangerous task of discovering the guilty, of getting at the truth.

"O Fire," runs the ritual, "thou seest, even as a witness, into each human being's heart. Thou alone knowest that which mortals alone cannot know." This, you observe, is an expression of confidence in a power inherent in the object employed. The supernatural supplies a perfect, infallible, decision. The magical power is charged with revealing the truth. It is clairvoyant, as man is not. It penetrates into the secret places of the heart. What is private and hidden is revealed by the supernatural, the superhuman. . . .

The oath may be considered a late form of the ordeal. What is an oath? It is an imprecation, a curse. If I curse you, I call down evil upon you. But an oath, used in "primitive" dispute-deciding, is a self-curse, conditionally made. The oath-taker says, in effect, "If I do not tell the truth, may destruction or torments be visited upon me." The oath is an ordeal in words, instead of acts. Supernatural power vouches or refuses to vouch for the oath-taker. If he tells his story and goes unharmed, he has told the truth. If he lies, he will be stricken by the supernatural.

So the early trials by oath of the party, or of the party and his oath-helpers, were not at all the kind of trial conducted today. The oath was *ipso facto* (mechanically) efficacious. No more than in the ordeal by water did the judge weigh the evidence, consider the testimony and determine the credibility of the witnesses. If a party's witnesses swore according to the formula, making no slips of the tongue, that party won. For it was presumed that no man, having taken an oath, would dare swear falsely and thus risk supernatural vengeance. Supernatural power was, in effect, the judge of the facts.

However, skepticism arises. Men begin to doubt the efficacy of the ordeals. It becomes obvious that these performances can be humanly manipulated, that there can be fraud and favoritism involved in their use. There grows up what lawyers call the "rational" mode of trial. The stories told by witnesses are heard by human beings who, on the basis of these stories, are to ascertain the past facts. The acceptance of this method was a gradual process. For a long time the magical and the "rational" modes of trial both continue to be used—the ordeals for those cases where someone is charged with an act committed in a solitary forest, or at night, or in the interior of a house. In such cases, God, the all-seeing, all-knowing, ever-present, is still called to judge the truth.

In England, the jury trial finally put the ordeals to rout. The early days of the English jury are of interest here. It was imported into England by the Norman dukes, and more or less forced by them on the people of England as a desirable method of trial. At first, it was vastly unpopular. Let Maitland tell the story: "Doubtless there was a very strong feeling that to try a man by a jury, when he had not submitted to be so tried, was thoroughly unjust," a feeling that the "mere oaths of * * * witnesses are not enough to fix a man with guilt, unless indeed he has voluntarily submitted his fate to this test; he ought to be allowed to demonstrate his innocence by supernatural means, by some such process as the ordeal. * * * God may be for him, though his neighbors be against him. * * *"

Putting the matter in our modern terminology, our ancestors were unwilling to rely in all cases on the subjective reactions of any human being, on the unknowable vagaries of the "personal" element in fact-finding. Only with reluctance did they wholly give up their dependence on the supernatural in deciding the $F$ in disputes. But in England, as on the Continent, trials before men, who determine the past facts, finally superseded the ordeals. The use of magic and the appeals to Heaven appear to have been abandoned. They lent themselves to trickery and chicane. They seem absurd, irrational, to us today.

Let us, however, note one last obvious vestige of these primitive ideas. The witness in court today raises his right hand, or puts his hand on the good book and says, "I swear to tell the truth, the whole truth and nothing but the truth, so help me God." Is that a mere form? Must the witness believe in God? The answer in this country was clear until recently. In the early nineteenth century the courts said that the testimony of a witness could not be received unless he not only took an oath but believed that his oath was a solemn invocation upon him of the vengeance of omniscient deity if he did not tell the truth. Accordingly, atheists were disqualified as witnesses. For, as the courts often said, on the belief in an avenging deity "rests all our institutions and especially the distribution of justice between man and man." But that attitude is virtually obsolete today. Generally, the oath now merely signifies a knowledge of the solemnity of testimony and of the liability to indictment and conviction for perjury if the witness deliberately lies.

It would be pleasant to end here, to say: "We are now thoroughly rational. The sword and the scales do not today signify the substitution of magical settlement of quarrels for private wars. Our attitude toward our legal system is thoroughly nonmagical." But I think that would be inaccurate reporting. Current views of the judicial process are, to a considerable extent, expressed in what appear to be highly sophisticated terms. But, as I shall try to show you, those views are still permeated with magic.

# 4

If you translate into our current speech forms the "primitive" attitude operative when men used the ordeals, you will see that what bothered them was the imperfection of the art of psychology. They would not thus have phrased the matter. We have progressed at least this far beyond our early predecessors: We have a label, "psychology," for a mass of difficult problems. But the inadequacy of the art of psychology, with respect to that problem which bothered "primitive" and "archaic" societies, is today almost as great as it was then. We are still usually unable to look into the minds of others, still frequently stumped when it comes to learning whether witnesses are lying or innocently mistaken. The road to the subjective remains obstructed.

Our ancestors faced this problem squarely. They tried to meet it—with magic. Most of us today do not face it squarely. Most of us look at it obliquely, meet it with evasions, and, I think, with a sort of sophisticated verbalized magic—which we refuse to recognize as such.

In our modern method of trial, as I told you, there are two factors which make subjectivity unavoidable. The first relates to the witnesses. They do not reproduce mechanically the events which they saw and heard. Their sight and hearing are often faulty, and so are their memories. More than that, they often err in telling their stories in court. So here is one element of subjectivity. There is another, which, as I said, is less frequently recognized and acknowledged: The trial judges or juries are fallible witnesses of the fallible witnesses.

Consider, first, cases in which the second factor is absent: Even in upper courts, where all the testimony is in writing, the ablest judges often differ with one another about the facts of a case. Said Mr. Justice Miller, "In my experience in the conference room of the Supreme Court of the United States, which consists of nine judges, I have been surprised to find how readily those judges came to an agreement upon questions of law, and how often they disagree in regard to questions of fact." That point is neatly illustrated in a case which arose in 1908, *United States v. Shipp*. Johnson, a Negro, was indicted in the Tennessee state court and convicted of rape. The United States Circuit Court denied his petition for habeas corpus. An appeal from this decision was allowed by the United States Supreme Court, which ordered the state sheriff to retain custody of Johnson, until the determination of the appeal. While the prisoner was in the custody of the sheriff, a mob seized the prisoner and lynched him. An original proceeding was begun in the Supreme Court, charging the sheriff with contempt, in that he had aided, abetted and conspired with the mob which lynched the prisoner. The Supreme Court appointed a commissioner merely to take and report the testimony; (that is, he was directed not to make any findings of fact of his own or to state any legal conclusions). Accordingly, he transmitted to the court a written record of the testimony. Briefs were filed, and the case was argued orally. The court split, five to three. Chief Justice Fuller wrote an opinion, concurred in by four other judges, holding the sheriff liable for contempt. One judge took no part. Mr. Justice Peckham filed a dissenting opinion which was concurred in by two other judges.

There was no disagreement as to any legal question (any R). The court divided solely on a question of fact. The majority opinion devoted seventeen pages to the discussion of the facts; the minority opinion, eight pages. The majority opinion stated: "Only one conclusion can be drawn from these facts, all of which are clearly established by the evidence—Shipp not only made the work of the mob easy, but in effect aided and abetted it." The minority opinion stated: "A careful consideration of the case leaves us with the conviction that there is not one particle of evidence that any conspiracy had ever been entered into or existed on the part of the sheriff, as charged against him."

This case illustrates how difficult it is to criticize a judge's statement of the facts, even when the testimony is entirely in writing. When a trial judge must find the facts from conflicting oral testimony of witnesses he heard, then criticism is far more difficult for anyone who has before him merely a printed or typewritten transcript. How, in such a case, is anyone to say that the trial judge's finding of facts is right or wrong? How can there be any objective means of testing the correctness of that finding? . . .

Let us approach the problem from a somewhat different angle. Is there any standard of belief a trial court can employ when trying to determine the facts? We talk of the "weight" of the evidence, of "weighing" evidence, of the "preponderance" of the evidence. But can conflicting evidence be weighed? Is there any accurate device for measuring which witnesses are worthy of belief? The courts and the great masters of evidence have said "No" to all these questions. "The reasons for believing particular witnesses or particular testimony in preference to others cannot be defined," said one court. "There is no standard for the sufficiency of evidence to induce belief," declared another court. The only standard, it has been said, is a "feeling of probability." But that feeling is subjective; it varies from man to man.

Wigmore has written a book—now in its third revised edition—on the Principles of Judicial Proof. That book, of over 1,000 pages, demonstrates that there are no principles of that kind, and probably never will be. For Wigmore confesses that the difficulty is that "belief is purely mental" (that is, subjective). Wigmore hoped to find scientific or logical "laws" for determining rationally "the net persuasive effect of a mixed mass of evidence." But, he tells us, there are no such "laws." There is, to use his phraseology, no scientific or logical "method of solving a complex mass of evidence in contentious litigation." He adds that such laws "will perhaps some day be discovered." He is not too sanguine in that hope. For "the data available from judicial annals * * * are almost always defective, in that the objective truth, necessary to test the correctness of any belief, can seldom be indubitably ascertained, as it often can be in the physical sciences. E.g., if we were to study one hundred murder trials, so as to ascertain some law of thought lurking in certain combinations of evidence, the very basis of that study, viz., the actual guilt or innocence of the accused, cannot usually be known to us, and our study is useless without that fact."

No means, then, have as yet been discovered, or are likely to be discovered, for ascertaining whether or to what extent the belief of the trial judge about the facts of a case corresponds to the objective facts as they actually occurred, when the witnesses disagree, and when some of the oral testimony, taken as true, will support the judge's conclusion. In other words, in such a case there is no objective measure of the accuracy of a judge's finding of the facts. There exists no yardstick for that purpose.

In a "contested" lawsuit, therefore, with the witnesses in disagreement, usually no one can adequately criticize the trial judge's fact-finding. If, at the end of the trial, the trial judge says that Jones hit Smith, or that Mrs. Moriarity called Mrs. Flannagan a liar, or that old widow Robinson was insane when she made her will, or that Wriggle used fraud in inducing Simple to sign a contract—the judge's word goes. And the same would be true if, in most of those instances, the trial judge had found exactly the opposite to be the facts.

Do you see where we have arrived? We are at last honestly confronting the problem which drove our ancestors to the ordeals—to magic or to God. The development of our legal system can indeed be described in terms of an increasing tolerance of the human element in judicial dispute-deciding. That human element is unavoidable. It was present but unrecognized even in the ordeals; after all, a human being had to decide whether the perilous test had been successfully passed. It enters more obviously, once the so-called "rational" mode of trial is introduced. For legal rights are then dependent on human guesses about the facts of cases. And usually, in such circumstances, no one can tell what another human being will guess. Primitive man could say that legal rights were on the knees of the gods. We must say that they are on the knees of men—of the trial judges or the juries. . . .

## 5

Many lawyers, I repeat, are reluctant to admit that state of affairs and its concomitant chanciness. Like "primitive" men, they consider that chanciness terrifying. "Primitive" man, to overcome his terror, used magic, openly and unashamed. Many modern lawyers use magic—without being aware of it. I mean that, in order to avoid facing up to disagreeable situations and difficulties in courthouse government, they have contrived a description, and a theory, of its workings which do not jibe with its observable realities.

This modern legal magic will be found in books, written by profound legal thinkers, books sometimes labeled with the high-sounding names "legal philosophy" or "jurisprudence." The legal theory of the pundits carries over to the less reflective lawyers. They, in turn, invoke that theory when explaining our courts' operations to nonlawyers. So that, if at the core of the pundits' legal theory we find magical notions, those magical notions will be likely to affect public attitudes toward, and beliefs about, our judicial system.

What, then, is the generally accepted legal theory? As I have said, it runs something like this: The basic component of court decisions consists of the legal rules. Insofar as those rules are crisp and definite, declares the theory, future court decisions usually are nicely forseeable. Some few of the rules, the R's, are indefinite, not finally fixed and settled. To that limited extent, prediction of future decisions is difficult. This lack of precision of some few of the R's is, the pundits declare, virtually the only impediment to precise predictions. So that, whatever little uncertainty there may be about how courts will deal with one's legal rights, it is, for the most part, a function of the uncertainty in a relatively few legal rules. So runs the theory. . . .

I could quote dozens of . . . remarks by eminent legal scholars and lawyers. Back of all such statements is the magical notion that uniformity in the use of precise legal rules must yield approximate uniformity in the decisions of specific cases, if only the judges conduct themselves properly. These legal thinkers say or imply that the only real leeway for the judges is in the rules: If the legal rules are tight and neat, then, if a judge is intelligent and behaves himself, his decision can be predicted; and, if he doesn't so behave himself, his misconduct will be glaringly obvious to third persons.

I hope that by now you perceive the fallacy of these notions. Remember the many cases, reported by Borchard, where innocent men were convicted of crimes. Here is Jones, charged with a theft, but innocent. He is acquitted. Here is Campbell, charged with the same crime, to which the very same legal rule applied. Although also guiltless, he was convicted. Why? Solely because the trial court mistook the facts. Such fact-mistakes are not confined to criminal cases. They can occur in any kind of lawsuit. And no legal rules can prevent them.

Legal rules, therefore, will not suffice to control the trial courts, even if those rules are applied conscientiously. You cannot control such courts unless you can also control their fact-finding. But that you usually can't do. For the process of fact-finding is altogether too subjective and, consequently, too elusive. It is "un-ruly." The refusal to recognize such unruliness constitutes modern legal magic. It stems from a "desire to be deceived."

*Courts on Trial* (1949)

\* \* \* \* \*

. . . "He lies like an eyewitness," you may hear a lawyer say. That statement is made in jest. But it does point up an important fact: Any witness, being human, may be fallible.

Eminent lawyers and judges have expressed awareness of this fact. A well-known judge said, "It has been profoundly observed, that of all the various sources of error, one of the most copious and fatal is an unreflecting faith in human testimony." Another judge wrote: "It must be admitted that at the present day the testimony of even a truthful witness is much overrated."

An experienced trial lawyer says, "Human testimony has been sweepingly condemned as being largely the product of distorted recollection, unsound inferences from inaccurate observation, and baseless conjecture. This stricture may be too severe, but such investigations as have been made support the view that the usual assumptions of the value of human testimony err on the side of generosity, and that the value ordinarily assigned to it in courts of law is exaggerated."

Such pessimistic remarks are sometimes addressed by judges and lawyers to other judges and lawyers, seldom to the general public. But it is the public that sorely needs to learn how fallible much testimony is and why. The following discussion of witnesses is directed to that end.

When an honest witness testifies to something he saw, what does he do? He represents under oath that he accurately saw or heard some past event; that now, in the courtroom, he accurately remembers what he saw or heard; and that he is now accurately reporting his memory. Into each of these three—his initial observation of the event, his memory of that observation, his communication of his memory in the courtroom—error can enter, and often does. Let us consider each of those sources of mistaken testimony.

When a witness says, "I saw" or "I heard," what he really means is, "I believe I saw," "It is my opinion that I heard." His testimony consists of nothing but a report of his beliefs. A witness's beliefs, which derive from his reaction to an event, do not necessarily jibe with the actual facts. For observation is not a mechanical process. An eyewitness is not a tape-recording machine or a photographic film. He does not necesarily reproduce sights and sounds accurately.

Behind you, you hear tires screech and a sound like crashing automobiles. Then you look around and see two wrecked cars. You did not see the collision. But if later you are questioned, you are not unlikely to say (and believe) that you did see just how it happened.

"We never get any impression from the world raw," says C. E. M. Joad. "It is always cooked; and from the culinary operations of the mind there is no escape." William James said much the same: "Whilst part of what we perceive comes from the object before us, another part (and it may be the larger part) always comes out of our mind."

Sights and sounds serve us as clues to an occurrence, clues we interpret in line with our own previous experiences. An eyewitness, according to Robert William Otto, "mixes art with observation * * * and in this work of art, items which had their counterpart in reality are not distinguished from those which had not."

A witness's observation of an event does not precisely mirror the event.

His mirror is imperfect; it distorts, to some extent, like the "funny" mirrors at a penny arcade. In the retina of the eye there is a "blind spot," but we ignore it, assuming that we see all there is to see. In the same way we fill in gaps in our observations of events. We "interpolate," with unconscious imagination, things we did not observe. We fill in what really is but bare outline, so as to meet what our past experience leads us to expect. We standardize most of our experiences, disregarding the unusual. An experienced hunter, out for deer, mistakenly shot a horse. He explained that he was all set to see an elk and, when the horse appeared, he assumed that it was an elk. Similarly, a witness's perception is frequently governed by his wishes. "Men," said a judge, "are prone to see what they want to see." An observer is, says W. J. Arnold, apt to see what he expects—or wishes, or fears—to see, and overlooks what he is inclined to disbelieve. His perceptions may be controlled by his preconceptions. He supplements what he observed with what he thinks should have occurred.

There is an amusing story about a destitute Moslem boy in the United States who, because he insisted that he was heir to a huge fortune in India, was taken to a psychiatric hospital. Just about the time when the psychiatrists had convinced him that his belief in his wealth was a delusion, a State Department representative informed them that in truth he had inherited a million dollars.

We select, organize, and add to any experience; and, so, in part, we make it. We mingle the objective facts with our subjective needs on which we base our impressions, our preconceptions. The great body of honest testimony, writes George Gardner, is "subjectively accurate but objectively false." We often "perceive what we expect to perceive rather than what actually occurs," so that we mistake "the moaning night-wind for a human cry, an innocent tramp for the escaped convict." Observations of happenings in the "outside world" are rarely pure, says the great criminal investigator Hans Gross; they are affected and transformed by imagination. Observing is a complex affair; it is mingled with inferences, judgments, interpretations. All observation, wrote James Sully, involves some unconscious inferences; consequently there is a thin line of distinction between observation and inference, and thus an "observation" often includes an "interpretative imagination."

An eyewitness is present when two men argue angrily in a bar. He sees one man raise his fist and the other fall to the floor. He thinks the first knocked down the second. In fact, if the truth were known, the blow was inflicted by a third man who came up in the rear, unobserved by this witness. But the truth may never be known.

You overhear two women talking. You think that you know the subject of their conversation. Unconsciously you fill in what you do not hear with what you think they said. "Much of the evidence introduced in court," says Gross, "concerning threats and other spoken words is the witness describing not the language which operated on his senses but the conclusions he formed from them in his own mind. Men often * * * misinterpret what they hear." Few of us have cultivated the art of accurate listening.

For the ordinary witness, then, it is not true that a fact is a fact is a fact.

A blind man can't see a burglary. But a man by no means blind may have poor vision. Many witnesses, because of bad eyesight, give inaccurate testimony about a crime or its perpetrator. Army and Navy tests, and tests for applicants for driver's licenses, disclose that a large number of Americans see inadequately. Defects in vision account for many auto fatalities. Among these defects are "night blindness" and "tunnel vision" (an inability to see objects that are not straight ahead). Acuity of vision usually grows less as men grow older. They become nearsighted or farsighted. A color-blind witness will mistake the color of a man's hair or his overcoat; and color-blindness is more common than we generally suppose.

A deaf man can't hear a shot. A man partly deaf may not hear it or, having heard it, may misjudge the direction from which it came. Faulty hearing is not uncommon. So also is an incapacity to measure the lapse of time correctly; and a witness's incorrect time estimate may forfeit the life of an innocent defendant.

Menninger says that human beings with "deficient perceptual machinery" resemble "radios with bad aerials." Many persons do not know, or are unwilling to admit to, their "bad aerials." If they appear as witnesses, their mistakes of observation may not be discovered.

The principal reason for many a witness's faulty observation of a criminal act is this: He was an observer of the crime by chance only, since for him it occurred unexpectedly. He saw it, so to speak, out of the corner of his eye; it was on the margin of his vision, out of focus.

Compare this happenstance observation with that of a scientific observer. A physicist, conducting an experiment in a laboratory, has carefully prepared himself to be a witness. He meticulously records what he sees, and records it the moment after he sees it. He employs precision instruments as an aid to his observation. He makes every effort to allow for the personal equation. Supplied with his written report of his observation, other physicists can repeat the experiment under almost exactly the same conditions. The witness of a robbery or a murder, however, engages in no carefully prepared observation. He is not equipped with instruments of precision. Usually he does not immediately record his observation. What he observed is not something that can be substantially repeated, so that others can have the same experience. In other words, unlike a scientist, the ordinary witness has not concentrated his attention on what happened.

Not always is his inattention caused solely by the fact that he did not plan to see the happening. Other factors explain his inattention. He may be fatigued, or suffering from a headache, or preoccupied with business problems. He may be badly frightened, and fright can severely diminish the capacity for accurate perception; if he were drunk, his observation would be faulty—and one can be drunk with fear.

An observer's interests and his training affect his attention. A hunter is exceptionally sensitive to the sound of a gun. An undertaker and a portrait painter will look differently at a dead man. A garage mechanic will detect things under the hood of a car that an ordinary driver does not notice. A poilceman's view of a burglarized house may differ from that of its owner.

Concentration of attention on some aspects of a situation will screen out other aspects; it confines our hearing and seeing to a limited part of an occurrence, and the rest, for us, is practically nonexistent.

One writer remarks on "the wonderful variety with which the details of a transaction are described by a variety of witnesses, each relating incidents which especially attracted his attention and omitting all others."

Akin to a witness's inadequate attention are his illusions of the senses that induce misinterpretations of things actually perceived. If two equally long lines are at right angles to one another, the vertical one looks longer; so testimony about a man's size may depend on whether the witness saw him lying on the ground or standing, and a witness tends to overestimate the height of a building or the distance up a hill. There is a tendency to think that small angles are right angles, to overestimate the size of an empty room or an empty lot, and to underestimate the size of a small person in the company of a large one. In a dark night a small man dressed in white looks tall. You are alone in the house, the stairs creak, you are sure someone has entered. Your collar is too tight and you think you are being stifled.

"Most human beings," says Arnold, "are from time to time subject to illusions; indeed, nobody is always sober and intelligent in all his perceptions * * *. The luminous center of our intelligent perception is wrapped in a cloudy half-shadow of illusion."

Related are hallucinations, when we seem to see or hear something real that in fact does not exist: A fever, or pronounced fatigue, or overeating, or hunger, or loss of blood, or "drugs," or fear, may cause such imaginings.

Witnesses' illusions and hallucinations poison their observations and produce false testimony that may jeopardize innocent men. As these witnesses are seldom aware that they were thus self-deceived, defense counsel may not know that they were, and thus may not even try to expose their perhaps dangerous mistakes.

Facts do not register impartially or identically with all observers. The facts they perceive are not, for them, objective, but are subjective. The outer world and their respective inner worlds combine, interwind, and in differing ways for each one. Each dwells partly in a world of his own, compounded uniquely of the internal and the external. He observes in terms of his unique needs, personality, temperament, emotions. According to Hans Gross, the individuality of the particular person makes his perception individual, and makes it almost the creature of the one who perceives. Each observer interprets what he observes in his own peculiar fashion. He "puts the stamp of his personality on the facts," says Wladimir G. Eliasberg. What he sees does not match objective reality except in part; it blends with his inner self.

The word "observation" is, indeed, too abstract and artificial. We should, instead, speak of different persons engaged in observing. " 'Tis with our judgment as our watches, none go just alike, yet each believes his own," said Alexander Pope. "Every experience," maintains psychologist Abraham Myerson, "is modified by the experiencer." The physiologist Roger Williams informs us that, physiologically, the uniformity of human beings is a myth; that the "average man," the "normal man," is a fiction; that different people live in different worlds "so far as their sensory reactions are concerned"; that sight sensations, hearing sensations, and smell sensations widely differ in different individuals; that "every human being has a pattern of existence which is distinctively different from all others and enormously different from many others"; that "no individual has a pattern that even remotely approaches what we may idealize as that of 'normal man' "; that "normal" individuals have their abnormalities, and "abnormal" individuals have their normalities. In sickness and in health their responses vary.

Shakespeare wrote, "Time travels in divers places with divers persons. I'll tell you who Time ambles withal, who Time trots withal, who Time gallops withal, and who he stands still withal." Unfortunately such individual differences in time perceptions, or in any other perceptions, cannot be easily discovered.

One's emotional attitude at the moment of observing makes a difference; an electrical engineer reports that even the color the eye sees depends on the mood of the observer. A witness's emotional condition may depend on a tiff he just had with his wife or on a hangover from a spree. His prejudices, too, influence his perceptions, and those prejudices may not be constant.

From all this it follows that one witness's reaction to an observed external, objective happening may be different from the reactions of another witness of that happening. "No two witnesses can have the same experiences when they observe the same event," says the psychologist J. S. Gray.

Since in a trial, all facts for the trial judge or jury are necessarily past facts—of which the judge or jury can learn only from witnesses' testimonies— the memories of witnesses become crucial.

But how reliable is anyone's memory? Can you tell accurately what you ate, and the conversation you had with two friends, at lunch a month ago?

We have already seen how unreliable a witness's observation of an event may be. Mistakes of memory are even greater. Seldom can one carry for any length of time his recollection of his past perceptions. Even if I correctly saw the goings-on in a street fight on January 10, 1955, my recollection in April 1957 of that fight may well be far less correct. In recollecting a past experience I do not repeat it. My recollection is a "new experience." Memory does not "mirror" the past; memory re-creates the past.

In that re-creating process memory often adds something the witness never saw. Many a witness remembers what pleased him, forgets the distasteful. His memory is colored by his likes and dislikes. Most of us put too much faith in our own and in other people's memory. We readily recognize that every man forgets most of the things he has experienced. We do not equally recognize that, when a man does recall a past experience, his recollection may easily misrepresent actualities of that experience.

Each of us has a store of "buried memories." What we consciously remember represents but a tiny fragment of that store. Hypnosis, the sight of an old hat, the smell of leather, the sound of a creaking hinge may provoke a recollection of a forgotten ten-year-old incident. Just how and why we remember, just how and why we forget, no one can completely explain. Although the workings of memory have been studied for centuries, they remain a good deal of a mystery.

The most frequent cause of a false memory, according to William James, consists of "the accounts we give others of our experience. Such accounts we almost always make both more simple and interesting than the truth. We quote what we should have said or done rather than what we really said or did; and in the first telling we may be fully aware of the distinction. But ere long the fiction expels the reality from our memory, and reigns in its stead alone." As another psychologist puts it, "Memory excited for the second time is partly a memory of the first attempt to remember. Often we are unable to distinguish one from the other. Then the first mistake becomes permanent."

Pride subtly contaminates memory. Writes Nietzsche, "'I have done that,' says my memory. 'I cannot have done that,' says my pride, and remains inexorable. Finally my memory yields."

Think of the angry differences between former President Truman and former Secretary of State Byrnes about what each said and wrote to the other with reference to Byrne's dealings with Russia. Or the dispute as to whether *The Forrestal Diaries* contained a correct report of a letter from Senator Taft to Truman about Taft's pleasure in the defeat of Dewey. The differing recollections were pretty plainly affected by pride.

Pride plays an even more important part in trials. Suppose that the police ask you about a case of purse-snatching that happened in your presence three months ago while you were waiting for a bus. Actually you were not very attentive at the time; you were thinking of your day at the office, or a date you had for that night, or your sore throat. But now, at the police station, you think that you remember the details of the purse-snatching. You identify the suspect as the man who did it. At his trial you so testify. On cross-examination defense counsel challenges your memory. This challenge makes you angry. For each of us has a singularly strong egotistic pride in his memory, feeling it a very part of his inner self. Major marital quarrels can develop when a wife differs from her husband's recollection of some trivial occurrence. As a witness you will resent any doubt about your memory as an assault on your basic integrity, a presumptuous intrusion on your personality. The more the lawyer cross-examines, the more stubbornly you stick to your story, more than ever sure that you are right. Your show of sincere righteous indignation may well persuade the jury. But an honest witness's belief in the accuracy of his memory is no guarantee that he is correct. "Many a man with a pure conscience," said a country editor, "has only a poor memory."

When a judge tries a case without a jury, he seeks to discern witnesses' errors of memory. So we have many court opinions in which judges have commented on the way an honest witness will unconsciously falsify his memory. Here are some examples of such judicial comments: Witnesses, "with ease, can persuade themselves that they remember by-gone circumstances" that never occurred. "It is a very common thing for an honest witness to confuse his recollection of what he actually observed with what he persuaded himself has happened." "There is a danger that, even a conscientious person, in trying to narrate a transaction which exists in his memory, in a faded or fragmentary state will, in his effort to make the reproduction complete and natural, substitute fancy for fact, or fabricate the missing or forgotten links." "We easily believe what we wish to believe." "Memories are much inclined to accord with desires." "It frequently happens that a person, by long dwelling on a subject, thinks that a thing may have happened, and he at last comes to believe that it actually did occur." "Witnesses who are perfectly honest are in danger of turning inference into recollection." "The effort of the memory often supplies circumstances harmonious with the general impression of a fact or event, but which are supplied only by the imagination."

These judicial utterances march with the views of many psychologists. They tell us that what is lost from memory is often replaced by products of the imagination; that, in memory, our wishes or our fears transform or transpose what really happened, so that, for instance, we change the time or the place of past observed incidents, and actions are omitted, substituted, or inserted in the series of observed events; that a witness may "remember what he imagined as if it were a real memory of an actual fact." The psychologists refer to "creative forgettery," "imaginative memory," to the way imagination "retouches the details" and fills in the gaps in memory. They say that imagination works with memory and "often does the larger part of the task," that it "tidies up" our recollections, giving them greater coherence than the remembered experience actually had, interpolating facts never perceived, and changing the emphasis on the component details; that the "end product of a recall process is often a memory illusion"; that we "corrupt" and partially falsify the past by a "confusion of fact and imagination"; that much "self-deception enters into the processes of memory"; that our minds are "refracting media," and the past reappears to us not as it actually appeared but in numerous ways altered and disguised by the intervening spaces of our conscious experience, so that what we seem to see in the act of recall is thus very different from reality. Just as the eye has a "blind spot" of which we take no account, so the eye of memory has its blind spots of which we are so unaware that in all honesty we recall things we did not observe. Using a somewhat like analogy, one psychologist mentions the color blindness of memory.

We have previously noted that each person's perception of an event is unique. So, too, is his memory. What a man remembers, how long he remembers, and the conditions that cause him to recall what he remembers, says the psychologist J. S. Gray, all depend on his own peculiar "internal factors." They include his unique inherited abilities; his unique aches and pains, hunger, thirst, fatigue, disease; his unique life experiences. Men differ in their memories of certain kinds of experience. Some have exceptional memories of sounds, others of color, of touch, or taste.

Memory and "forgettery" are inseparably related. Psychologists once thought that forgetting results from a passive "fading" or "decay" of memory owing to the lapse of time. Now they think that forgettery is a more active process, a result of the passage of time filled with new events, of lively interest to the rememberer, that interfere or inhibit or obliterate his recollection of the old. In this process the individual's unique interests loom large. Thus each man's individuality influences his rate of forgetting particular sorts of past incidents. "Is it any wonder," Gray sagely asks, "that a witness's report of something he saw at a distant date is different from that of another who observed the same event?"

The courts, then, agree with the psychologists about the treachery of memory. They agree that memory is the weakest element in testimony; that, because of the numerous unknown factors that affect it, a witness's memory is often not trustworthy as a proof of any fact in a trial.

The courts give counsel a wide latitude in cross-examining an adverse witness in an effort to show that he has a prejudice for the side that called him. So counsel for the accused is permitted to bring out the fact that a prosecution witness, for instance, has long been hostile to the accused because of an old business dispute or out of jealousy. For the judges well know that such a bias or prejudice colors a witness's observation or memory. Courts have said, "Even where witnesses are upright or honest, their belief is apt to be more or less warped by their partiality or prejudice for, or against, one of the parties. It is easy to reason ourselves into a belief in the existence of that which we desire to be true, whereas the facts testified to, and from which the witness deduces his conclusions, might produce a very different impression on the minds of others." "A witness may have a strong bias from what he conceives to be the justice of the case, so that with entire innocence he may recall things which have never occurred, or forget important instances which have occurred."

The trouble is that often an honest witness's prejudices are unconscious: Without himself being aware of it he may, for obscure reasons, be hostile to the accused. Usually any such unconscious, hidden bias cannot be exposed at the trial.

Yet such a concealed prejudice, unknown to the witness or anyone else, may be the cause of the gravest mistakes in his testimony. Because of his buried unconscious animosity toward the accused he may have distorted the facts of a robbery he saw, or may mistakenly identify the accused as the man charged with murder.

Other kinds of unconscious prejudice may perniciously influence memory: You see a fight between the police and union pickets. Your original impression was confused. If you are an ardent union sympathizer, you may later remember with clarity that the police brutally assaulted the pickets. "Honest" bias, says Gardner, may "be the deciding factor in filling in the gaps of memory."

A frequent cause of unconscious prejudice is a witness's partisanship owing to the fact that one side or the other called him as a witness. Here are some comments of some highly experienced lawyers: "Partisan witnesses," says Arthur Train, may "swear convincingly to facts of which they have no real knowledge, such as that they saw the defendant strike the complainant, exactly how he did it, the words he said, and that the complainant made no offer to strike the defendant. From allowing their minds to dwell on their own conception of what must have occurred they are soon convinced that it did occur in that way, and their account flows forth with a circumstantiality that carries with it an irresistible impression of veracity." "Perhaps," writes Francis Wellman, "witnesses usually feel more or less complimented by the confidence that is placed in them by the party calling them to prove a certain state of facts, and it is human nature to prove worthy of this confidence. That fact arises not from an intention deliberately to falsify but from the desire to be an important element in the case."

It is most important, therefore, to note this remark by another well-known lawyer: "Nothing is more deceitful than half the truth, and biased witnesses are much addicted to half truths. Such a witness is more dangerous than one who commits a gross perjury." "Unconscious bias," says Gardner, "is more dangerous than conscious bias. In everyone there is 'an empire of subconscious loyalties,' likes and dislikes, preferences and hatreds, some * * * unconscious * * * all entering into and affecting what we perceive, how we perceive it, and, most important of all, how we recall it."

No matter how accurate a witness's observation and memory, his testimony will mislead the jury if the jury misunderstands what he says. A trial is a process of communication between the witnesses and the jurors. It goes wrong if the witnesses do not communicate correctly.

If Antonelli, an Italian witness, does not speak English, he speaks to a translator, familiar with Italian and English, who translates for the jury what the witness says. A witness, not a foreigner, may so use our language that he conveys a wholly wrong impression. He may use words in his own peculiar and unusual way, according to a sort of private code or personal dictionary. Practically, he is speaking in a "foreign" language, that is, foreign to his listeners. But, as he seems to be speaking English, no one translates his words. Misunderstanding results.

A young child, telling his father about his geography lesson, said that he had learned that the equator "is a menagerie lion that goes around the earth." Adults make similar mistakes.

The written report of a U.N. debate on a Pakistan-India dispute showed a Pakistan delegate saying, "Six soldiers have raped thousands of Pakistan women." Actually the delegate had referred to "Sikh soldiers."

The meaning of a word, it has been said, is not in the word but in the person who uses it and persons who hear him. We too glibly assume that we always understand one another. There is frequently an illusion of communication, an erroneous assumption that we invariably know what others mean. Frequently we talk past one another.

In a criminal trial, breakdowns of the communications process between witnesses and the jury may spell disaster for the accused. Newman Levy tells this story: Cohen was on trial for assault. He had the habit, attributed to many Jews, of answering a question with a question. When, on the witness stand, he was asked, "Did you strike McGuire?" he indignantly replied, "*I* struck McGuire?" The jury found Cohen guilty. His lawyer then moved that the judge enter a judgment of acquittal for Cohen because the evidence was not sufficient to justify the verdict. The prosecutor, pointing to the typewritten transcript of the testimony, asserted that Cohen had admitted his guilt in saying, "I struck McGuire." The stenographer, in writing up the testimony, had omitted the question mark and substituted a period. Fortunately for Cohen, the judge was familiar with this Jewish trick of speech and remembered Cohen's answer. Cohen was set free. Unfortunately for many defendants, such misunderstandings may not be detected.

All of us, most of the time, judge the truth of what a man says to us by the way he says it. We remark, "He looked me square in the eye," or, "He had a shifty gaze." Similarly, the judges lay great stress on the "demeanor" of a witness while testifying in the courtroom—his gestures, grimaces, intonations, his straightforward or evasive manner, his facial expressions, his hesitations, his fluency. That is one reason why, in a criminal trial, most of the witnesses are required to testify in court rather than by written, sworn, typewritten statements: The accused is entitled to have the jury observe the witness's appearance and manner of testifying. The witness's demeanor has been called "language without words."

The courts say that this demeanor "is often a complete antidote to what he testifies." "A witness may convince all who hear him testify that he is disingenuous and untruthful, and yet his testimony, when read, may carry a most favorable impression." "Every person who has had experience in the trial of jury cases knows that the jury give close attention to the manner of witnesses while testifying, and are sometimes more strongly influenced by appearances than they are by the words of the witnesses. A juror can see as well as hear, and has the right to use his eyes and ears in making up his mind as to what weight, if any, shall be given to the evidence of a witness." Judge Joseph Ulman said that "a stenographic transcript correct in every detail fails to reproduce tones of voice and hesitations of speech that often make a sentence mean the reverse of what the mere words signify. The best and most accurate written record is like a dehydrated peach; it has neither the substance nor the flavor of the fruit before it was dried." "The right of the accused to have a witness subjected to the personal view of the jury is a valuable right, of which he should not be deprived * * * except by necessity."

However, although "demeanor evidence" (as it has been called) helps often to illuminate the truth or falsity of testimony, it may do just the opposite. Demeanor can be deceptive. An unscrupulous lying witness, well trained in perjury, may not betray himself by his manner. He may look the jury square in the eye; he may have an excellent "poker face." One may smile and smile and be a villain.

On the other hand, an honest witness may so behave as to arouse the jury's distrust. He may have an unpleasant, squeaky voice or a habit of twisting his fingers. He may be restless, peevish, or he may talk in a sneering manner. If he is nervous and timid, especially when fiercely cross-examined, he may seem furtive and evasive. For, it has been said, "his apprehensions and conjectures often work through his imagination on his memory, until without intending falsehood he omits or colors facts * * * irreconcilable with the truth. No sooner are his ideas uttered, however, than he becomes conscious of their errors. If he now attempts an explanation, it usually results in his entire discomfiture. If he persists in the misrepresentation or concealment, a new cause of embarrassment arises in the fear of subsequent exposure, and leads to still more harmful falsehoods and suppressions. Thus, with the best intentions at the outset * * * a nervous, apprehensive witness may retire suspected of the grossest perjury * * *" A distinguished lawyer, testifying in a recent case, was "so careful to qualify every statement and refine every bit of his evidence, that the jury took the word of a perjured loafer and streetwalker in preference." Said Arthur Train, a veteran of many criminal trials, "An assertive lie is of much more weight with a jury than an anemic statement of the truth * * *. Ofttimes a witness leads the jury to suspect that he is a liar because he has too strong a sense of the proprieties of his position [as a witness] vehemently to resent a suggestion of untruthfulness" when cross-examined.

It is tough enough for the innocent defendant when he faces adverse witnesses who are honestly mistaken but "normal." His dangers increase when those who testify against him are "abnormal" and their abnormalities are not obvious.

Maybe you think this seldom happens. But a ponderable percentage of our population is not "normal." The estimates vary. One physician declares that at least 30 percent of a general practitioner's patients require some psychiatric treatment. A psychiatrist says that about 8 percent of Americans have been inmates, at some time, of mental hospitals; the number of disturbed persons not hospitalized must be much larger. Another psychiatrist remarks that "any large family without some psychotics is quite an exception." Chronic alcoholics are numerous, with their number apparently on the increase. As men in prison often testify for the prosecution as alleged accomplices of a defendant, we cannot ignore the high percentage of prison inmates diagnosed as mentally defective or disordered; in Sing Sing, a few years back, some 11 percent were so diagnosed. How many Americans are seriously "neurotic" no one knows, but it seems safe to say that 15 percent are.

In varying degrees these "abnormals" have importantly distorted perceptions and memories. The alarming fact is that, when their abnormalities are unknown, many of them make an excellent showing on the witness stand. This is singularly true of the "psychopathic liar," the alcoholic, and the man with a so-called "psychopathic personality." The highly disturbed neurotic may appear a serene and accurate witness, at worst only an eccentric; but his hidden, subjective fears and anxieties, unrelated to the external situation, may markedly interfere with his capacity to perceive or recollect accurately. An aged witness, white-haired and dignified, may impress a jury. But he may suffer lapses of memory that he cleverly conceals, even from himself, filling in the gaps with falsities. To make matters worse, there are witnesses, young in years, afflicted with "premature senility," who have similar difficulties that they similarly conceal.

Said Hans Gross, "The numberless errors in perceptions derived from the senses, the faults of memory, the far-reaching differences in human beings as regards sex, nature, culture, moods of the moment, health, passionate excitement, environment, all these things have so great an effect that we scarcely ever receive two quite similar accounts of one thing; and between what people really experience and what they confidently assert, we find only error heaped on error." Gross, after noting that several witnesses, speaking of the same incident, will differently characterize it as "a very ordinary event" or "altogether a joke," or "quite disgusting," says, "Now is it possible to think that people who have so variously characterized the same event will give an identical description of the mere fact? They have seen the event in accordance with their attitude toward life. One has seen nothing; another this; another that; and, although the thing may have lasted only a very short time, it made such an impression that each has in mind a completely different picture which he now reproduces. One man overlooks half because he is looking at the wrong place; another substitutes his own inferences for objects; while another tends to observe the quality of objects and neglects their quantity; and still another divides what is to be united, and unites what is to be separated. If we keep in mind what profound differences may result in this way, we must recognize the source of the conflicting assertions by witnesses. * * * In order to know what another person has seen and apprehended, we must first of all know how he thinks, and that is impossible. If we know, at least approximately, the kind of mental process of a person who is as close as possible to us in sex, age, culture, position, experience, etc., we lose this knowledge with every step that leads to differences. We know well what great influence is exercised by the multiplicity of talents, superpositions, knowledge and apprehensions. * * * The individuality of the particular person makes [his] perception * * * individual, and makes it almost the creature of him who perceives."

A renowned English lawyer wrote: "The power to tell the truth, which implies accurate observation, knowledge of the relative importance of facts, and power of description * * * is much less common than people usually suppose it to be. * * * A man's power to speak the truth depends upon his knowledge and his power of expression. His knowledge depends partly on his accuracy of observation, partly on his memory, and partly on his presence of mind; his power of expression depends on an infinite number of circumstances. * * * A man's will to tell the truth depends on his education, his character, his courage, his sense of duty, his relation to the particular facts as to which he is to testify, his humour for the moment . . ."

"It would be correct, I think, to say," writes Sir Frederic Eggleston, a famous Australian trial lawyer, "that no witness can be expected to be more than 60% correct, even if perfectly honest and free from preconception." "From my experience as a man, a lawyer, a prosecuting attorney, and a judge," said a noted jurist, "I am compelled to say that the most uncertain thing I know of is human testimony." Mr. Justice Dixon of Australia once remarked that the ability to observe correctly "is an idiosyncrasy, and that the ability to give evidence in the witness-box in a clear, definite and convincing manner is also an idiosyncrasy, but that the two idiosyncrasies are not necessarily related."

The next time a dozen or so friends visit you, try something like this witness game: While they are conversing, arrange that two men, strangers to your guests, dash into the room. One of the two men will point at you, shouting, "Damned rascal." The other will burst an inflated paper bag. You will fall on the floor, groaning. The two men will run out of the house. Immediately afterward ask each guest to write a description of what happened. Almost certainly the descriptions will differ remarkably from one another. Dozens of experiments of this sort have so demonstrated.

Earlier we called attention to the way a stool pigeon's testimony may endanger the innocent. A similar danger attends the prosecutor's use of a related type of testimony—that of a man who confesses to a crime, turns state's evidence, and testifies that the accused was his accomplice. Strangely enough, often jurors are impressed by such testimony: They believe that the confessing accomplice tells the truth in order to clear his own conscience.

Actually the prosecution frequently assures an accomplice that he will not be prosecuted if he gives testimony against the accused. That assurance may put a premium on perjury. The same may be true when, without such an assurance, the accomplice has some reason to hope that he will not be indicted if he "cooperates" with the prosecutor. And the tendency to lie is also considerable when the witness has confessed, pleaded guilty, but has not yet been sentenced: He hopes that his "cooperation" will bring a light sentence.

In many states the judge will warn the jury to be wary of an accomplice's testimony. In some states, by statute, a man cannot be convicted on such testimony standing alone: it must be "corroborated." This would seem to mean that someone else must give supporting testimony. But several courts have held that it suffices if some other witness supports a part of the accomplice's testimony that has nothing at all directly to do with the crime. A noted legal authority writes: "Suppose the accomplice tells * * * of a murder and states in the course of his testimony, 'I had my shoes shined that morning at a shoeshine stand on Broadway.' Subsequently the prosecution introduces the shoeshine boy as a witness who testifies, 'Yes, I shined the shoes of Mr. Accomplice that morning.' Granted the truth of that insignificant fact, it in no manner connects the defendant with the commission of the offense. Yet such proof is poisonous. * * * The difficulty * * * is caused by a fallacious belief that, if the accomplice is telling the truth about one thing, he is telling the truth about all things."

Having in mind not only perjurious and psychologically "abnormal" witnesses but also the numerous errors of honest "normal" men and women who testify, we say again that many a mistaken witness for the prosecution may be a lethal weapon directed at the accused, endangering his life or liberty.

Little wonder that Learned Hand, our wisest judge, remarked after years of service as a trial judge, "I must say that, as a litigant, I should dread a lawsuit beyond almost anything short of sickness and death." He was speaking primarily of civil-law suits, but what he said applies in full to . . . a criminal trial.

*Not Guilty* (1957)

# GETTING AT THE FACTS 🐦

W HEN WE say that present-day trial methods are "rational," presumably we mean this: The men who compose our trial courts, judges and juries, in each law-suit conduct an intelligent inquiry into all the practically available evidence, in order to ascertain, as near as may be, the truth about the facts of that suit. That might be called the "investigatory" or "truth" method of trying cases. Such a method can yield no more than a guess, nevertheless an educated guess.

The success of such a method is conditioned by at least these two factors: (1) The judicial inquirers, trial judges or juries, may not obtain all the important evidence. (2) The judicial inquirers may not be competent to conduct such an inquiry. Let us, for the time being, assume that the second condition is met—i.e., that we have competent inquirers—and ask whether we so conduct trials as to satisfy the first condition, i.e., the procuring of all the practically available important evidence.

The answer to that question casts doubt on whether our trial courts do use the "investigatory" or "truth" method. Our mode of trials is commonly known as "contentious" or "adversary." It is based on what I would call the "fight" theory, a theory which derives from the origin of trials as substitutes for private out-of-court brawls.

Many lawyers maintain that the "fight" theory and the "truth" theory coincide. They think that the best way for a court to discover the facts in a suit is to have each side strive as hard as it can, in a keenly partisan spirit, to bring to the court's attention the evidence favorable to that side. Macaulay said that we obtain the fairest decision "when two men argue, as unfairly as possible, on opposite sides," for then "it is certain that no important consideration will altogether escape notice."

Unquestionably that view contains a core of good sense. The zealously partisan lawyers sometimes do bring into court evidence which, in a dispassionate inquiry, might be overlooked. Apart from the fact element of the case, the opposed lawyers also illuminate for the court niceties of the legal rules which the judge might otherwise not perceive. The "fight" theory, therefore, has invaluable qualities with which we cannot afford to dispense.

But frequently the partisanship of the opposing lawyers blocks the uncovering of vital evidence or leads to a presentation of vital testimony in a way that distorts it. I shall attempt to show you that we have allowed the fighting spirit to become dangerously excessive.

## 2

This is perhaps most obvious in the handling of witnesses. Suppose a trial were fundamentally a truth-inquiry. Then, recognizing the inherent fallibilities of witnesses, we would do all we could to remove the causes of their errors when testifying. Recognizing also the importance of witnesses' demeanor as clues to their reliability, we would do our best to make sure that they testify in circumstances most conducive to a revealing observation of that demeanor by the trial judge or jury. In our contentious trial practice, we do almost the exact opposite.

No businessman, before deciding to build a new plant, no general before launching an attack, would think of obtaining information on which to base his judgment by putting his informants through the bewildering experience of witnesses at a trial. "The novelty of the situation," wrote a judge, "the agitation and hurry which accompanies it, the cajolery or intimidation to which the witness may be subjected, the want of questions calculated to excite those recollections which might clear up every difficulty, and the confusion of cross-examination * * * may give rise to important errors and omissions." "In the court they stand as strangers," wrote another judge of witnesses, "surrounded with unfamiliar circumstances giving rise to an embarrassment known only to themselves."

In a book by Henry Taft (brother of Chief Justice Taft, and himself a distinguished lawyer) we are told: "Counsel and court find it necessary through examination and instruction to induce a witness to abandon for an hour or two his habitual method of thought and expression, and conform to the rigid ceremonialism of court procedure. It is not strange that frequently truthful witnesses are * * * misunderstood, that they nervously react in such a way as to create the impression that they are either evading or intentionally falsifying. It is interesting to account for some of the things that witnesses do under such circumstances. An honest witness testifies on direct examination.

He answers questions promptly and candidly and makes a good impression. On cross-examination, his attitude changes. He suspects that traps are being laid for him. He hesitates; he ponders the answer to a simple question; he seems to 'spar' for time by asking that questions be repeated; perhaps he protests that counsel is not fair; he may even appeal to the court for protection. Altogether the contrast with his attitude on direct examination is obvious; and he creates the impression that he is evading or withholding." Yet on testimony thus elicited courts every day reach decisions affecting the lives and fortunes of citizens.

What is the role of the lawyers in bringing the evidence before the trial court? As you may learn by reading any one of a dozen or more handbooks on how to try a law-suit, an experienced lawyer uses all sorts of stratagems to minimize the effect on the judge or jury of testimony disadvantageous to his client, even when the lawyer has no doubt of the accuracy and honesty of that testimony. The lawyer considers it his duty to create a false impression, if he can, of any witness who gives such testimony. If such a witness happens to be timid, frightened by the unfamiliarity of court-room ways, the lawyer, in his cross-examination, plays on that weakness, in order to confuse the witness and make it appear that he is concealing significant facts. Longenecker, in his book *Hints On The Trial of a Law Suit* (a book endorsed by the great Wigmore), in writing of the "truthful, honest, over-cautious" witness, tells how "a skilful advocate by a rapid cross-examination may ruin the testimony of such a witness." The author does not even hint any disapproval of that accomplishment. Longenecker's and other similar books recommend that a lawyer try to prod an irritable but honest "adverse" witness into displaying his undesirable characteristics in their most unpleasant form, in order to discredit him with the judge or jury. "You may," writes Harris, "sometimes destroy the effect of an adverse witness by making him appear more hostile than he really is. You may make him exaggerate or unsay something and say it again." Taft says that a clever cross-examiner, dealing with an honest but egotistic witness, will "deftly tempt the witness to indulge in his propensity for exaggeration, so as to make him 'hang himself.' And thus," adds Taft, "it may happen that not only is the value of his testimony lost, but the side which produces him suffers for seeking aid from such a source"—although, I would add, that may be the only source of evidence of a fact on which the decision will turn.

"An intimidating manner in putting questions," writes Wigmore, "may so coerce or disconcert the witness that his answers do not represent his actual knowledge on the subject. So also, questions which in form or subject cause embarrassment, shame or anger in the witness may unfairly lead him to such demeanor or utterances that the impression produced by his statements does not do justice to its real testimonial value." Anthony Trollope, in one of his novels, indignantly reacted to these methods. "One would naturally imagine," he said, "that an undisturbed thread of clear evidence would be best obtained from a man whose position was made easy and whose mind was not harassed; but this is not the fact; to turn a witness to good account, he must be badgered this way and that till he is nearly mad; he must be made a laughing-stock for the court; his very truths must be turned into falsehoods, so that he may be falsely shamed; he must be accused of all manner of villainy, threatened with all manner of punishment; he must be made to feel that he has no friend near him, that the world is all against him; he must be confounded till he forget his right hand from his left, till his mind be turned into chaos, and his heart into water; and then let him give his evidence. What will fall from his lips when in this wretched collapse must be of special value, for the best talents of practiced forensic heroes are daily used to bring it about; and no member of the Humane Society interferes to protect the wretch. Some sorts of torture are as it were tacitly allowed even among humane people. Eels are skinned alive, and witnesses are sacrificed, and no one's blood curdles at the sight, no soft heart is sickened at the cruelty." This may be a somewhat overdrawn picture. Yet, referring to this manner of handling witnesses, Sir Frederic Eggleston recently said that it prevents lawyers from inducing persons who know important facts from disclosing them to lawyers for litigants. He notes, too, that "the terrors of cross-examination are such that a party can often force a settlement by letting it be known that a certain * * * counsel has been retained."

The lawyer not only seeks to descredit adverse witnesses but also to hide the defects of witnesses who testify favorably to his client. If, when interviewing such a witness before trial, the lawyer notes that the witness has mannerisms, demeanor-traits, which might discredit him, the lawyer teaches him how to cover up those traits when testifying: He educates the irritable witness to conceal his irritability, the cocksure witness to subdue his cocksureness. In that way, the trial court is denied the benefit of observing the witness's actual normal demeanor, and thus prevented from sizing up the witness accurately.

Lawyers freely boast of their success with these tactics. They boast also of such devices as these: If an "adverse," honest witness, on cross-examination, makes seemingly inconsistent statements, the cross-examiner tries to keep the witness from explaining away the apparent inconsistencies. "When," writes Tracy, counseling trial lawyers, in a much-praised book, "by your cross-examination, you have caught the witness in an inconsistency, the next question that will immediately come to your lips is, 'Now, let's hear you explain.' Don't ask it, for he may explain and, if he does, you point will have been lost.

If you have conducted your cross-examination properly (which includes interestingly), the jury will have seen the inconsistency and it will have made the proper impression on their minds. If, on re-direct examination the witness does explain, the explanation will have come later in the case and at the request of the counsel who originally called the witness and the jury will be much more likely to look askance at the explanation than if it were made during your cross-examination." Tracy adds, "Be careful in your questions on cross-examination not to open a door that you have every reason to wish kept closed." That is, don't let in any reliable evidence, hurtful to your side, which would help the trial court to arrive at the truth.

"In cross-examination," writes Eggleston, "the main preoccupation of counsel is to avoid introducing evidence, or giving an opening to it, which will harm his case. The most painful thing for an experienced practitioner * * * is to hear a junior counsel laboriously bring out in cross-examination of a witness all the truth which the counsel who called him could not" bring out "and which it was the junior's duty as an advocate to conceal." A lawyer, if possible, will not ask a witness to testify who, on cross-examination, might testify to true facts helpful to his opponent.

Nor, usually, will a lawyer concede the existence of any facts if they are inimical to his client and he thinks they cannot be proved by his adversary. If, to the lawyer's knowledge, a witness has testified inaccurately but favorably to the lawyer's client, the lawyer will attempt to hinder cross-examination that would expose the inaccuracy. He puts in testimony which surprises his adversary who, caught unawares, has not time to seek out, interview, and summon witnesses who would rebut the surprise testimony. "Of course," said a trial lawyer in a bar association lecture in 1946, "surprise elements should be hoarded. Your opponent should not be educated as to matters concerning which you believe he is still in the dark. Obviously, the traps should not be uncovered. Indeed, you may cast a few more leaves over them so that your adversary will step more boldly on the low ground believing it is solid."

These, and other like techniques, you will find unashamedly described in the many manuals on trial tactics written by and for eminently reputable trial lawyers. The purpose of these tactics—often effective—is to prevent the trial judge or jury from correctly evaluating the trustworthiness of witnesses and to shut out evidence the trial court ought to receive in order to approximate the truth.

In short, the lawyer aims at victory, at winning in the fight, not at aiding the court to discover the facts. He does not want the trial court to reach a sound educated guess, if it is likely to be contrary to his client's interests. Our present trial method is thus the equivalent of throwing pepper in the eyes of a surgeon when he is performing an operation.

## 3

However unpleasant all this may appear, do not blame trial lawyers for using the techniques I have described. If there is to be criticism, it should be directed at the system that virtually compels their use, a system which treats a law-suit as a battle of wits and wiles. As a distinguished lawyer has said, these stratagems are "part of the maneuvering * * * to which [lawyers] are obliged to resort to win their cases. Some of them may appear to be tricky; they may seem to be taking undue advantage; but under the present system it is part of a lawyer's duty to employ them because his opponent is doing the same thing, and if he refrains from doing so, he is violating his duty to his client and giving his opponent an unquestionable advantage. * * *" These tricks of the trade are today the legitimate and accepted corollary of our fight theory.

However, some tactics, unfortunately too often used, are regarded as improper by decent members of the legal profession. We know, alas, that an immense amount of testimony is deliberately and knowingly false. Experienced lawyers say that, in large cities, scarcely a trial occurs, in which some witness does not lie. Perjured testimony often goes undetected by trial courts and therefore often wins cases. Judge Dawson of the Kansas Supreme Court found one of the "real and crying hindrances to a correct and efficient administration of justice * * * the widespread prevalence of perjury practiced with impunity by litigants and witnesses. * * *" A wag has it that courts decide cases according to the "preponderance of the perjury." Some—not all— of that lying testimony results from coaching of witnesses by dishonest lawyers.

But much inaccurate testimony, not to be classified as perjurious, results from a practice that is not dishonest: Every sensible lawyer, before a trial, interviews most of the witnesses. No matter how scrupulous the lawyer, a witness, when thus interviewed, often detects what the lawyer hopes to prove at the trial. If the witness desires to have the lawyer's client win the case, he will often, unconsciously, mold his story accordingly. Telling and re-telling it to the lawyer, he will honestly believe that his story, as he narrates it in court, is true, although it importantly deviates from what he orginally believed. So we have inadvertent but innocent witness-coaching. The line, however, between intentional and inadvertent grooming of witnesses cannot easily be drawn. Now, according to many lawyers of wide experience, the contentious method of trying cases augments the tendency of witness to mold their memories to assist one of the litigants, because the partisan nature of trials tends to make partisans of the witnesses. They come to regard themselves, not as aids in an investigation bent on discovering the truth, not as aids to the court, but as the "plaintiff's witnesses" or the "defendant's witnesses." They become soldiers in a war, cease to be neutrals.

"I do not think I am exaggerating," wrote Eggleston in 1947, after a résumé of the ways of trial lawyers and trial courts, "when I say that the evidence contains only kaleidoscopic fragments of the facts. It is as if a checker of light and dark patches were held over reality. All that gets down in the record is that seen through the light patches. It is quite clear," he continues, "that reality does not survive in the process of analysis to which" the contending lawyers "submit it from opposite poles. Cases are won by the exercise of the last degree of ingenuity, and this marginal utility makes the contest highly artificial."

In 1906, the French lawyer, De la Grasserie, said that, in a modern (civil) trial, "deceit" has "succeeded to * * * force, bringing with it almost the same disasters. It is * * * a conflict * * * which has been substituted for the primitive conflict of force. * * * Its wounds are often as deep, its risks as serious. * * * The battle of craft is enacted by the parties under the eyes of the judge. * * * Each [party] strives to conceal what is contrary to his interests and to take advantage of everything that helps his cause. * * * No doubt craft is preferable to violence from the point of view of the social order, but the risk that judgment is wrong is at times as great." An English lawyer, at about the same time, said that, in litigation, "one party or the other is always supremely interested in misrepresenting, exaggerating, or suppressing the truth"; and he spoke "of the characteristic dangers of deception * * * to which judicial tribunals are exposed. * * *" As applied to all contemporary American trials, these statements are excessive, misdescriptive. Yet one who visits many of our trial courts, or who reads the books and articles on practical trial techniques to which I have referred, will perhaps incline to believe that, in many cases, matters are not altogether different in this country today. The views of so competent a student of trials as Judge Learned Hand (whom I shall quote in a moment) tend to support such a depressing belief.

### 4

The effects of the contemporary American fighting or adversary method must sorely puzzle many a litigating citizen. The parties to a suit, remarks Eggleston, "know exactly what they are fighting about when the writ is issued, but find themselves fighting a very different case when the trial is actually launched. It is a wise litigant who knows his own quarrel when he sees it in court." "If," said Judge Learned Hand to the lawyer, "you lead your client into the courtroom with you * * *, you will, if you have the nerve to watch him, see in his face a baffled sense that there is going on some kind of game which, while its outcome may be tragic to him in its development, is incomprehensible." The legal profession should not take much pride in a system which evokes from Judge Hand the remark, "About trials hang a suspicion of trickery and a sense of result depending upon cajolery or worse." To Judge Hand's comments I would add that, were it impossible to contrive a better system, we lawyers could legitimately defend ourselves, saying, "We do the best we can." But I think such a defense not legitimate because I think we do not do the best we can, since an improved system can be contrived.

Mr. Justice Frankfurter recently observed that a criminal statute is not unconstitutional merely because in one trial under that statute a man goes scot-free while in another trial under the same statute another man is sent to jail for "similar conduct." Such "diversity in result * * * in different trials," said the Justice, is "unavoidable," because, in each trial, the ascertainment of the facts must be left to "fallible judges and juries." He concluded that "so long as the diversities are not designed consequences, they do not deprive persons of due process of law." This statement by Justice Frankfurter— which I think correctly states the judicial attitude towards trials—has such significance that I want the reader thoroughly to understand it. When, in that context, the Justice spoke of "due process of law," he meant a "fair trial," that is, one which meets the minimum test of fairness required by the Constitution. The Supreme Court holds that a trial is constitutionally "fair," if only it does not depart from the methods usually employed in our trial courts. I am not criticising the Supreme Court when I suggest that one imbued with a lively sense of justice will not be satisfied with that minimal constitutional test. A particular trial may be thus minimally "fair" when measured by the standard of our present usual trial practices. But the question remains whether those usual practices can be regarded as actually fair when, due to practically avoidable human errors, they deprive men of life or liberty in criminal proceedings, or of property or money in civil suits. I would answer, No. Our mode of trials is often most unfair. It will, I think, continue to be, until everything feasible has been done to prevent avoidable mistakes. Only avoidless mistakes should we accept among life's necessary dangers.

After careful scrutiny of the record of the famous Sacco-Vanzetti case, lawyers of experience have concluded that those men received an egregiously unfair trial, because obviously the trial judge was poisonously biased against the accused, and the prosecutors hit below the belt, restorting to measures which violated the Marquis of Queensbury rules governing courtroom bouts.

However, in the case of Campbell, and many others like it, innocent men have been convicted after trials from which such glaring defects were absent. Were those trials fair? Yes, in a constitutional sense. They would be pronounced technically fair by the lawyers who criticize the Sacco-Vanzetti decision. But forget the lawyer's perspective. In terms of common sense, how can we say that those trials were fair since, almost surely, in their course, the government lawyers utilized some of the legitimized lawyer-tactics which were likely to mislead the trial courts? Intelligent laymen should insist that it is not enough that a trial seems fair to many lawyers, who, indurated to the techniques of their trade, have become so calloused that they acquiesce in needless judicial injustices.

Take, for instance, a speech made last year, before a Bar Association, by a highly respected judge. He began by saying, "We start with the fundamental conception that a trial, under our procedure, is not a game or battle of wits but a painstaking, orderly inquiry for the discovery of the truth." Now that judge, I have no doubt, believed that statement—or, rather, believed that he believed it. Yet a few minutes later in his speech, he cautioned the lawyer never on cross-examination "thoughtlessly [to] ask the one question which will supply an omission in your opponent's case." He quoted, with approval, the remark of an expert cross-examiner that, if you put such a question, "you may find the witness has had time to think, and you will get an answer" that hurts your client. So here you have a judge who, after seriously depicting a trial as "an inquiry for the discovery of truth," goes on to encourage lawyers to avoid bringing out the truth. That bewildered judge—and alas there are too many like him—will make no serious effort to change a system which permits a lawyer to act as did Mr. Chaffanbrass in another of Trollope's novels: "Nothing would flurry this [witness he was cross-examining], force her to utter a word of which she herself did not know the meaning. The more he might persevere in such an attempt, the more dogged and steady she would become. He therefore soon gave that up * * * and resolved that, as he could not shake her, he would shake the confidence the jury might place in her. He could not make a fool of her, and therefore he would make her out a rogue. * * * As for himself, he knew well enough that she had spoken nothing but the truth. But he * * * so managed that the truth might be made to look like falsehood,—or at any rate to have a doubtful air."

I repeat that we ought not to blame the trial lawyers for employing such tactics. Yet the legal profession is somewhat responsible for the fact that non-lawyers do sometimes assess such blame. For lawyers and judges declare solemnly that every lawyer is an "officer of the court." So to designate the lawyer, said one court, "is by no means a figure of speech," since "it is his duty to help save the court from error and imposition, and to aid the court to a proper determination of the law and the facts. Theoretically, at least, it is counsel's first duty to see that the issue is justly decided, however his client is affected." His "office" is "indispensable to the administration of justice. * * *"" But these words mean only that a lawyer must not affirmatively mislead a court, must not introduce in evidence, at a trial, documents which he knows to be false, testimony which he knows to be perjured. Most courts do not effectively disapprove of the lawyers' wiles I have described. Little wonder, then, if laymen sometimes smile cynically when they hear lawyers called court "officers," think it a strange sort of judicial officer who is authorized ingeniously to obscure the facts from trial judges and juries.

The layman's bafflement at the workings of the judicial system has been remarkably described by Kafka, in his book, *The Trial*. There, too, he gives a layman's attitude towards the apathy of many lawyers concerning reforms of the system. Although "the pettiest Advocate," he writes, "might be to some extent capable of analysing the state of things in the Court, it never occurred to the Advocates that they should suggest or insist on any improvements in the system, while—and this was very characteristic—almost every accused man, even quite ordinary people among them, discovered from the earliest stages a passion for suggesting reforms which often wasted time and energy that [the Advocate's thought] could have been better employed in other directions. The only sensible thing [for an Advocate] was to adapt oneself to existing conditions. * * * One must lie low, no matter how much it went against the grain. Must try to understand that this great organization remained, so to speak, in a state of delicate balance, and that if someone took it upon himself to alter the disposition of things around him, * * * the organization would simply right itself by some compensating reaction in another part of its machinery—since everything interlocked—and remain unchanged, unless, indeed, which was very probable, it became still more rigid, more vigilant, more severe, and more ruthless."

Kafka's reaction is one of mild bitterness. Jonathan Swift was more vitriolic. He referred to lawyers as "a society of men * * * bred up from their youth in the art of proving by words, multiplied for the purpose"—and in "a jargon of their own that no other mortal can understand"—that "white is black, and black is white, according as they are paid." Kipling talks of "the tribe who describe with a jibe the perversions of justice"; and Soddy calls lawyers "charlatans" who aim to "mystify the public." Those strictures are altogether too severe; their analyses of lawyers' motivations are inaccurate. And such writers, being uninformed laymen, cannot be constructively critical. What we need today is the kind of vigorous, patient, reformist zeal of a knowing critic like Jeremy Bentham, whose untiring attacks (in the late 18th and early 19th centuries) on lawyers' complacency in the face of judicial injustice, led to the elimination of some of the worst features of judicial procedure.

## 5

Our contentious trial method, I have said, has its roots in the origin of court trials as substitutes for private brawls. But that does not altogether explain its survival. Wigmore (following up a suggestion made by Bentham) suggested that "the common law, originating in a community of sports and games, was permeated by the instinct of sportsmanship" which led to a "sporting theory of justice," a theory of "legalized gambling." This theory, although it had some desirable effects, "has contributed," said Wigmore, "to lower the system of administering justice and in particular of ascertaining truth in litigation, to the level of a mere game of skill or chance * * *," in which lawyers use evidence "as one plays a trump card, or draws to three aces, or holds back a good horse till the home-stretch. * * *"

Damon Runyon had much the same idea. "A big murder trial," he wrote, "possesses some of the elements of a sporting event. I find the same popular interest in a murder trial that I find * * * on the eve of a big football game, or a pugilistic encounter, or a baseball series. There is the same conversational speculation on the probable result, only more of it. * * * The trial is a sort of game, the players on the one side the attorneys for the defense, and on the other side the attorneys for the State. The defendant figures in it merely as the prize. * * * And the players must be men well-schooled in their play. They must be crafty men. * * * The game of murder trial is played according to very strict rules, with stern umpires, called judges, to prevent any deviations from these rules. * * *" The players "are supposed to be engaged in a sort of common cause, which is to determine the guilt or innocence of the defendant. * * * A player * * * for the State represents the people. His function, as I understand it," Runyon continued, "is to endeavor to convict any person who has transgressed the law. * * * It is inconceivable that he would wish to convict an innocent man. But it has been my observation that the player or attorney for the State is quick to take any advantage of the rules * * * that puts his side in front, and equally quick to forestall any moves by the other side."

This Wigmore-Runyon explanation may be partially sound, but it seems to me to over-emphasize sportsmanship. I suggest, as an additional partial explanation of the perpetuation of the excessive fighting method of trials, both civil and criminal, the belief in uncontrolled competition, of unbridled individualism. I suggest that the fighting theory of justice is not unrelated to, and not uninfluenced by, extreme laissez-faire in the economic field.

"Classical" laissez-faire economic theory assumed that, when each individual, as an "economic man," strives rationally, in the competitive economic struggle or "fight," to promote his own self-interest, we attain public welfare through the wisest use of resources and the most socially desirable distribution of economic goods. The "fight" theory of justice is a sort of legal laissez-faire. It assumes a "litigious man." It assumes that, in a law suit, each litigious man, in the courtroom competitive strife, will, through his lawyer, intelligently and energetically try to use the evidential resources to bring out the evidence favorable to him and unfavorable to his court-room competitor; that thereby the trial court will obtain all the available relevant evidence; and that thus, in a socially beneficial way, the court will apply the social policies embodied in the legal rules to the actual facts, avoiding the application of those rules to a mistaken version of the facts. Legal laissez-faire theory therefore assumes that the government can safely rely on the "individual enterprise" of individual litigants to ensure that court-orders will be grounded on all the practically attainable relevant facts.

Most of us have come to distrust, in the economic field, ultra let-alone-ism, the ultra laissez-faire theory with its anti-social concept of an "economic man." For observation of social realities has shown that the basic postulates of that theory, although in part correct, are inadequate as exclusive postulates. I think that, in like fashion, observation of court-room realities shows that the postulates of legal laissez-faire are insufficient as exclusive postulates. We should retain what there is of value in the fighting theory of justice, eliminating what is socially harmful. We should retain, I repeat, so much of "individual initiative" in the trial of cases as serves to bring out evidence that might be overlooked and the niceties of legal rules a court might otherwise ignore. (However, there may be aspects of the rules to which neither litigant will call the court's attention. As Demogue suggests, the "duellistic" nature of litigation may create a false "dualistic" attitude towards the pertinent legal rules . . .) But the fight should not so dominate a law-suit that it leads to the non-discovery of important evidence and the distortion of testimony.

## 6

The fighting theory has, in part, broken down. Time was when a litigant could refuse to disclose evidence in his possession to the adversary party before trial. But so-called "discovery" procedure has been developed which requires such disclosure in non-criminal cases. The federal courts are particularly energetic in compelling such "discovery." Thus far, at least, have we advanced towards effectuating the "truth" theory.

There have been other advances, such as increased insistence on the power and right of the trial judge to take a hand in examining witnesses, and even to summon witnesses of whom he is aware and whom neither litigant has called. I must add, however, that regrettably (as I see it) few judges avail themselves of that power. Judge Shientag, a learned and respected judge, recently said that "a litigant has the right to expect * * * that the judge will not interfere in the examination of witnesses, even though he believes he can do a better job than counsel, except to correct patent errors, misconceptions or misrepresentations. * * *" Some bolder trial judges disagree.

But even if the judge does "interfere," and even if "discovery" procedure is open, the trial court may fail to learn of crucial evidence. Partly this may be due to the incompetence of the lawyer for one side. For lack of means to retain an able lawyer, the impecunious litigant may here be singularly disadvantaged. To some extent we are overcoming that handicap, through Legal Aid Services, although much remains to be done before the legal profession catches up with the medical profession in assisting the indigent and the "white-collar" men.

Apart from failure to bring out the evidence, the mistakes of a man's lawyer may cause him to lose his case—a proper result under strict legal laissez-faire theory. But is it fair that a litigant should be punished because he retained an incompetent lawyer? When an error of a trial court, resulting from a lawyer's blunder, is egregious, the upper courts sometimes relieve the litigant. But there persists a reluctance to grant such relief. Maybe that reluctance is justified. I am not sure.

## 7

There is one most serious handicap in litigation that has received little attention: With the ablest lawyer in the world, a man may lose a suit he ought to win, if he has not the funds to pay for an investigation, before trial, of evidence necessary to sustain his case. I refer to evidence not in the files of the other party and therefore not obtainable by "discovery" procedure. What I mean is this: In order to prove his claim, or to defend against one, a man may need to hire detectives to scour the country—even sometimes foreign countries—in order to locate witnesses who alone may know of events that occurred years ago, or to unearth letters or other papers which may be in distant places. Or, again, he may need the services of an engineer, or a chemist, or an expert accountant, to make an extensive—and therefore expensive—investigation. Without the evidence which such an investigation would reveal, a man is often bound to be defeated. His winning or losing may therefore depend on his pocketbook. He is out of luck if his pocketbook is not well-lined with money. For neither his lawyer nor any legal-aid institution will supply the needed sums. For want of money, expendable for such purposes, many a suit has been lost, many a meritorious claim or defense has never even been asserted.

Let me illustrate. Fisher, in his recent excellent book, *The Art of Investigation*, writes: "The percentage of witnesses who cannot be found if enough effort is exerted is infinitesimal. A famous investigator once said that the man who could not be found is the man at the bottom of the sea, and even then he must be at the bottom at its points of greatest depth. Anyone alive can be found if enough effort is put forth." That statement may be exaggerated. But you get the point: Suppose there is one man, John Brown, who alone could testify to a crucial event—such as that Sam Jones was in New York City on June 12, 1948. Brown is missing. He may be in China, India or Peru. If he can be found, and if he testifies, the plaintiff will win his suit; otherwise he will lose it. If the plaintiff can afford to pay enough to investigators to scour the world for the missing witness, he may be located. If the plaintiff is a man of means, he will hire such investigators. But if he has little money, he can't do so—and will lose his case which may involve all his worldly goods.

That is not true justice, democratic justice. This defect in our judicial system makes a mockery of "equality before the law," which should be one of the first principles of a democracy. That equality, in such instances, depends on a person's financial condition. The tragedy of such a situation is etched in irony when a man's impoverished condition has resulted from a wrong done him by another whom he cannot successfully sue to redress the wrong. Many of our state constitutions contain a provision that "every person ought to obtain justice freely and without being obliged to purchase it." But, as things stand, this is too often a provision in words only. For the advantage in litigation is necessarily on the side of the party that can "purchase justice" by hiring private assistance in obtaining evidence when his adversary cannot. Unless we contrive some method to solve the problem I have posed, we must acknowledge that, in a very real sense, frequently we are "selling justice," denying it to many under-incomed persons. It should shock us that judicial justice is thus often an upper-bracket privilege. Here we have legal laissez-faire at its worst.

That brings me to a point which the fighting theory obscures. A court's decision is not a mere private affair. It culminates in a court order which is one of the most solemn of governmental acts. Not only is a court an agency of government, but remember that its order, if not voluntarily obeyed, will bring into action the police, the sheriff, even the army. What a court orders, then, is no light matter. The court represents the government, organized society, in action.

Such an order a court is not supposed to make unless there exist some facts which bring into operation a legal rule. Now any government officer, other than a judge, if authorized to do an act for the government only if certain facts exist, will be considered irresponsible if he so acts without a governmental investigation. For instance, if an official is empowered to pay money to a veteran suffering from some specified ailment, the official, if he does his duty, will not rely solely on the applicant's statement that he has such an ailment. The government officer insists on a governmental check-up of the evidence. Do courts so conduct themselves?

In criminal cases they seem to, after a fashion. In such cases, there is some recognition that so important a governmental act as a court decision against a defendant should not occur without someone, on behalf of the government itself, seeing to it that the decision is justified by the actual facts so far as they can be discovered with reasonable diligence. For, in theory at least, usually before a criminal action is begun, an official investigation has been conducted which reveals data sufficient to warrant bringing the defendant to trial. In some jurisdictions, indigent defendants charged with crime are represented by a publicly-paid official, a Public Defender—a highly important reform which should everywhere be adopted. And the responsibility of government for mistakes of fact in criminal cases, resulting in erroneous court judgments, is recognized in those jurisdictions in which the government compensates an innocent convicted person if it is subsequently shown that he was convicted through such a mistake.

In civil cases (non-criminal cases), on the whole a strikingly different attitude prevails. Although, no less than in a criminal suit, a court's order is a grave governmental act, yet, in civil cases, the government usually accepts no similar responsibilities, even in theory. Such a suit is still in the ancient tradition of "self help." The court usually relies almost entirely on such evidence as one or the other of the private parties to the suit is (a) able to, and (b) chooses to, offer. Lack of skill or diligence of the lawyer for one of those parties, or that party's want of enough funds to finance a pre-trial investigation necessary to obtain evidence, may have the result, as I explained, that crucial available evidence is not offered in court. No government official has the duty to discover, and bring to court, evidence, no matter how important, not offered by the parties.

In short, the theory is that, in most civil suits, the government, through its courts, should make orders which the government will enforce, although those court-orders may not be justified by the actual facts, and although, by reasonable diligence, the government, had it investigated, might have discovered evidence—at variance with the evidence presented—coming closer to the actual facts.

Yet the consequence of a court decision in a civil suit, based upon the

court's mistaken view of the actual facts, may be as grave as a criminal judgment which convicts an innocent person. If, because of such an erroneous
decision, a man loses his job or his savings and becomes utterly impoverished,
he may be in almost as serious a plight as if he had been jailed. His poverty
may make him a public charge. It may lead to the delinquency of his children, who may thus become criminals and go to jail. Yet in no jurisdiction
is a man compensated by the government for serious injury to him caused
by a judgment against him in a non-criminal case, even if later it is shown
that the judgment was founded upon perjured or mistaken testimony.

I suggest that there is something fundamentally wrong in our legal system
in this respect. If a man's pocket is picked, the government brings a criminal
suit, and accepts responsibility for its prosecution. If a man loses his life's
savings through a breach of a contract, the government accepts no such responsibility. Shouldn't the government perhaps assume some of the burden
of enforcing what we call "private rights"?

Some few moves have been made in the right direction. In an English
divorce court, an official, the King's Proctor, brings forward evidence, bearing on possible collusion, not offered by either contestant; some American
states provide that the public prosecutor shall do likewise in divorce actions.
In our own Domestic Relations Courts, government officers procure and
present most of the evidence. Lawyers for any of the parties may cross-examine
any witness, may offer additional evidence, and may argue about the applicable legal rules. The advantages of the adversary method are fully preserved, but the fighting spirit is much diminished. Under the Chandler Act,
enacted in 1938, in certain types of cases relating to corporate reorganization,
the SEC, at large public expense, uses its expert staff to obtain and present
to the court evidence which usually no private party could afford to procure;
the judge and the private parties may treat this evidence like any other evidence, and the parties may introduce further supplementary or conflicting
evidence.

Many of our administrative agencies have large and efficient staffs to conduct investigations in order to ferret out evidence put before those agencies
in their own administrative proceedings. I know, from personal experience,
that not much evidence escapes an agency like the SEC. Mr. Justice Jackson has said: "Such a tribunal is not as dependent as the ordinary court upon
the arguments of skilled counsel to get at the truth. Skilled advocacy is
neither so necessary to keep such a body informed nor is stupid or clever
advocacy so apt to blur the merits of a controversy."

I do not suggest that courts, like such administrative bodies, conduct
their own investigations through their own employees. I do suggest that we
should consider whether it is not feasible to provide impartial government

officials—who are not court employees, and who act on their own initiative —to dig up, and present to the courts, significant evidence which one or the other of the parties may overlook or be unable to procure. No court would be bound to accept that evidence as true. Nor would any of the parties be precluded from trying to show the unreliability of such evidence (by cross-examination or otherwise) or from introducing additional evidence. Trials would still remain adversary. As I concede that to use that device in all civil cases would lead to many complications, I do not urge that it be at once generally adopted. But I think experiments along those lines should now be made.

This proposal resembles somewhat the procedures long used in criminal cases on the European continent. Critics may oppose it on that ground, saying that we should not take over ideas from countries which have been less democratic than ours. To any such argument, Woodrow Wilson gave the answer: "But why should we not use such parts of foreign contrivances as we want if they may be in any way serviceable? We are in no danger of using them in a foreign way. We borrowed rice, but we do not eat it with chopsticks."

It will also be said that any such proposal is absurdly radical. Yet something of the sort was endorsed by President Taft, by no means a radical. More than thirty years ago he said: "Of all the questions * * * before the American people I regard no one as more important than this, the improvement of the administration of justice. We must make it so that the poor man will have as nearly as possible an opportunity in litigating as the rich man, and under present conditions, ashamed as we may be of it, this is not the fact." (Chief Justice Hughes, urging the need of "legal aid," said in 1920: "There is no more serious menace than the discontent which is fostered by a belief that one cannot enforce his legal rights because of poverty. To spread that notion is to open a broad road to Bolshevism.") Moreover, we now have public-utility commissions which, on behalf of private persons, bring rate-suits against utility companies. With that in mind, Willoughby wrote a book, published in 1927 by the conservative Brookings Institution, in which he proposed the appointment of a "public prosecutor of civil actions." If a complaint were made to the prosecutor, he would first try to settle the matter or to have the parties agree to submit the dispute to arbitration. Only if these efforts failed would he bring that suit. No one would be obliged to retain [that] prosecutor; his employment would be optional; and, if any action were brought on a person's behalf by the prosecutor, that person would be at liberty to retain a private lawyer to assist in the preparation for, and conduct of, the trial. That idea, I think, merits public discussion and consideration. Were it adopted, it should perhaps be supplemented to include a practice now adopted, in some states, by the Public Defender in criminal actions: That official is authorized to expend public funds to seek out and procure what he regards as essential evidence.

Statutes in some jurisdictions authorize the trial judge to call as a witness an expert selected by the judge. Judges might sometimes avail themselves of that power to help indigent or under-incomed litigants. But I believe that none of those statutes, as they now read, provides for payment by the government to judge-called experts in non-criminal suits. Moreover, those statutes will not meet the difficulties of a prospective litigant when making up his mind whether to bring or defend a suit. Nor do they permit expenditures for detectives and other investigators not regarded as "experts." Nevertheless, this expedient might be expanded so as partially to solve the problem I have presented.

None of these proposals, if adopted, would usher in the millennium. Official evidence gatherers, or public prosecutors of civil actions, will make mistakes, or become excessively partisan. The trial process is, and always will be, human, therefore fallible. It can never be a completely scientific investigation for the discovery of the true facts.

## 8

I said that, in theory, in criminal suits the government seems to take greater responsibility than in civil suits, that theoretically, in each criminal trial, the public prosecutor has made a pre-trial investigation and that he brings out, at the trial, the evidence he has uncovered. Actually, many prosecutors, infected badly by the fighting spirit, in partisan manner produce only the evidence they think will cause convictions. In most jurisdictions, "discovery" in criminal cases is denied; even where permitted it is narrowly limited. We should, I think, follow the practice now well settled in England where, before trial, the prosecutor must disclose to the accused all evidence the prosecutor intends to offer.

The "third degree" is widely employed by our police, too often with the tacit approval of prosecutors, to extort confessions which, obtained by physical or mental torture, are not infrequently untrue. To our shame be it said that the English, who do not tolerate the "third degree," call it the "American method." Competent American police—such as the FBI force—do not resort to that outrageous device. To rid ourselves of it, we must have a public demand for properly trained police forces. And to rid ourselves of unfair prosecutors, we should not permit any man to hold that office who has not been specially educated for that job and passed stiff written and oral examinations demonstrating his moral and intellectual fitness.

## 9

It has been suggested that trained psychologists, called by trial judges as the court's experts, be permitted to testify as "testimonial experts" concerning the witnesses. Such an expert, it is proposed, having interviewed and examined the witness out of court, would testify at the trial about the witness's capacity for hearing, seeing, touching, tasting, his capacity for attention and memory, and any "abnormal" tendencies (such as "pathological lying," for instance). (In some cities, applicants for drivers' licenses are examined to determine whether they are neurotic or psychotic, for such persons will be menaces if they drive cars. Yet we now allow men's lives and fortunes to be menaced by witnesses of that sort whose defects are undisclosed.) The expert would be subject to cross-examination, and his testimony about a witness would not be binding on the trial judge or jury.

Applied to every witness at every trial, this proposal (of which Wigmore approves) is open to the objection that it would make trials endless. Yet I think we ought to experiment with the idea. Aware that judges and juries lack competence in medicine, physics, chemistry, and a host of other subjects, we now use expert witnesses to guide our trial courts. Sizing up a witness from his statements and demeanor when on the witness-stand is a difficult task at best, and one at which juries and most judges are amateurs. Expert aid in the discharge of that task might do much to minimize mistakes in fact-finding.

## 10

Suppose that, in a crude "primitive" society, A claims that B took A's pig. If that is true, B violated a well-settled tribal rule. But B denies that he took the pig. A attacks B and kills him. Does A's killing of B prove that B was wrong about the facts? Does that killing constitute the enforcement of the tribal rule? Now suppose somewhat the same sort of dispute in the U.S.A. A sues B, claiming that, by fraud and deceit, B got A's pig. A legal rule says that if B did those acts, then A has a legal right to get back the pig or its money value. If A wins that suit, does the decision in his favor constitute the enforcement of that legal rule, even if A won through perjured testimony or because the trial court erroneously believed an honest but mistaken witness?

A lawyer friend of mine, to whom I put this question, replied, "Yes, in theory. In theory, the facts as found must be assumed to be true." His answer does not satisfy me. That we must accept the facts found by a trial court does not mean that a rule against fraud is really enforced when a court holds a man liable for a fraud he did not commit. My friend is saying, in effect, that, even were it true that the courts misfound the facts in 90% of all cases, still the courts would be enforcing the rules.

That conclusion does not bother the hardened cynic. "In the long run," one may imagine him saying, "what is the difference whether courts make many mistakes in fact-finding, and, as a result, render erroneous decisions—as long as the public generally doesn't learn of those mistakes? Take, for instance, all this to-do about 'convicting the innocent.' One of the important purposes of punishing a man for a crime is to deter others from becoming criminals. Conviction and punishment of the innocent serve just as effectively as if they were guilty to deter others from crime—provided only the errors are not, too frequently, later discovered and publicized. It's tough on the innocent; but we can afford to sacrifice them for the public good. In the same way, if a non-criminal legal rule is of a desirable kind—for instance, a rule concerning the duty of a trustee to the beneficiaries of a trust—why bother whether, in particular law-suits, the courts, through failure to discover the actual facts, apply it to persons who haven't violated it? Public respect for that rule, and its infiltration into community habits, will come just as well from its misapplications as from its correct applications—if only the public doesn't learn of its misapplications. If you call it injustice to punish the innocent or mistakenly to enter money judgments against men who have done no legal wrongs, then I answer that effectively concealed instances of injustice are not only harmless but socially beneficial. They serve as useful examples. Don't get squeamish about such mistakes." I doubt whether any reader will agree with the cynic.

## 11

No one can doubt that the invention of courts, which preserve the peace by settling disputes, marked a great step forward in human progress. But are we to be so satisfied with this forward step that we will rest content with it? Should not a modern civilized society ask more of its courts than that they stop peace-disrupting brawls? The basic aim of the courts in our society should, I think, be the just settlement of particular disputes, the just decision of specific law-suits.

The just settlement of disputes demands a legal system in which the courts can and do strive tirelessly to get as close as is humanly possible to the actual facts of specific court-room controversies. Courthouse justice is, I repeat, done at retail, not at wholesale. The trial court's job of fact-finding in each particular case therefore looms up as one of the most important jobs in modern courthouse government. With no lack of deep admiration and respect for our many able trial judges, I must say that that job is not as well done as it could and should be. No wonder it is not, when a leading law-teacher, Professor Morgan of Harvard, a close student of trials, can write that a law-suit, as most law-suits are now required to be conducted, is not "a proceeding for the discovery of truth," but "a game in which the contestants are not the litigants but the lawyers." Reviewing a book on trial techniques by an experienced trial lawyer, which revealed in detail the tactics of court-room fighting—tactics considered entirely legitimate, but which patently impede the discovery of the true facts, so far as they are practically discoverable—Morgan commented sadly, "If only a reviewer could assert that this book is a guide not to the palaces of justice but to the red-light districts of the law. But a decent respect for the truth compels the admission that [the author] has told his story truly."

A distinguished legal historian, Vinagradoff, has said that an "ancient trial" was little more than a "formally regulated struggle between the parties in which the judge acted more as an umpire or warden of order and fair play than as an investigator of truth." To continue that ancient tradition, unmodified, to treat a law-suit as, above all, a fight, surely cannot be the best way to discover the facts. Improvement in fact-finding will necessitate some considerable diminution of the martial spirit in litigation.

*  *  *  *  *

. . . Sometimes in connection with a decision, a trial judge publishes a statement, called an "opinion," in which he purports to explain why he decided as he did. In his "opinion," he reports the facts as he finds them (the F) and the legal rule (the R) he applied. Theoretically, one can then see whether his decision (his D) was correct, can favorably or unfavorably criticize his decision on the basis of his explanation.

To illustrate: There is a legal rule (an R) that an oral (unwritten) agreement for the sale of goods, if not to be performed within a year, is not binding unless in part confirmed in writing. Mr. Small sues Mr. Big for breach of contract. At the trial, Small testifies that Big orally offered to sell Small a thousand tons of coal, at $10 a ton to be delivered, on Small's orders, during the next two years; that Small promptly accepted that offer; but that Big refused to deliver any coal; and that Small, as a consequence, suffered a loss of $5,000. Small also testifies that he received a letter from Big, a few days after the oral agreement, confirming it. Big, however, testifies that he never made such an offer, that the signature to the letter is not his, and that he had not authorized anyone to write such a letter. The trial judge gives a $5,000 judgment for Small. In his published opinion, the judge states that there was such an oral agreement, that Big signed the letter, that he refused to deliver the coal, that Small's loss was $5,000, and that, applying the legal rule, Small is entitled to the decision. That decision seems unquestionably correct—just as it would seem unquestionably erroneous if the trial judge had said that Big neither signed nor authorized the letter. A moment's reflection shows that that criticism, favorable or unfavorable, of his decision has little meaning. For the judge's F (his "finding" of the facts) is at best but an SF; at best, it is only what the judge thinks were the facts, and that thought depends on his belief in the story of one witness rather than that of another. No one, reading the judge's opinion can effectively criticize his belief, can tell whether it was right or wrong. So that, if his reported F has a foundation in some of the conflicting testimony, one must accept his F; it is then beyond criticism. True, one can still partially criticize his decision, his D: One can say that he did or did not use the proper legal rule, or that if the R he used is proper, nevertheless his decision is or is not erroneous, in that he did or did not reach it by logically applying that R to the F he found. Such criticism is obviously limited in scope, and therefore not very satisfactory.

But even such partial criticism is often impossible. For, in many states at least in some kinds of cases, a trial judge is not required to report anything but a laconic D ("Judgment for defendant," or "Judgment for plantiff for $5,000"). He need not state what facts he found (his F) or the R he used. If he does not so state—and many a trial judge in such jurisdictions does not —usually, his decision is wholly beyond intelligent criticism by anyone but himself. It may be that, if he had reported his F, it would have appeared that (on the basis of that F) his decision was wrong, that is, that he used an improper R or illogically deduced his D from his F and the R he used. Thus, in the Small-Big case, if the judge had publicly reported that Big did not sign or authorize the letter, it would have been clear that his decision for Small was wrong, because he had used an incorrect R. But, without such a report, no one knows what witnesses he believed or disbelieved. Since no one knows even his SF, it follows that the R he applied is also undiscoverable. His decision, his D, is even more obscure than a jury's general verdict.

Yet, if any such decision is appealed, the upper court is asked to criticize it. What does the upper court do? Generally, it tries to sustain the decision. If the upper court can, it works out for itself some combination of a correct R and an assumed F which will logically justify the trial judge's D. It will assume that the judge found that F, if there is some oral testimony which will support it. In the Small-Big case, the judge may actually have believed Big's testimony; if so, according to the accepted legal rule, the decision should have been for Big and should be reversed. But, as the judge decided for Small, the upper court will assume he believed Small's testimony, that is, believed that Big and Small made the oral agreement and that the letter was signed or authorized by Big. Yet the upper court cannot possibly know whether the trial judge did so believe, and whether he grounded his decision on that belief. The real reasons for his decision are a mystery.

Such unexplained, inscrutable, general-verdict-like, trial-judge decisions have been deemed undesirable, because they put a burden on the upper courts, and for other reasons. Consequently, in some jurisdictions, published explanations by the trial judge have been made mandatory. For instance, in the federal courts, the Rules of Civil Procedure require the trial judges in most noncriminal cases to publish special findings of fact, and, separately, statements of the R's they used.

Significantly, many federal trial judges resent this requirement. The reason for that resentment was given in a recent comment by former Federal District Judge McLellan. He was discussing a new federal rule which provides that, if a defendant so requests, the trial judge must make special findings of fact in a criminal case tried without jury. Of that rule, Judge McLellan said: "We all know, don't we, that when we hear a criminal case tried, we get convinced of the guilt of the defendant or we don't; and isn't it enough if we say guilty or not guilty, without going through the form of making special findings of fact designed by the judge—unconsciously, of course—to support the conclusions at which he has arrived?" Judge McLellan there pithily expressed the conviction that a trial judge's published explanation does not disclose the actual basis of his decision so as to expose it to effective criticism.

Let us spell out Judge McLellan's position in terms of what I have been saying. The argument would then be as follows: The facts of a case are not the actual past facts as they happened in the past. At first glance they seem to be what the trial judge thinks happened. But that is a superficial analysis: When the judge publishes his findings, we can never be sure that they report what he thinks were the facts. Those findings report merely what he says he thinks the facts were. And seldom, if ever, can we learn whether what he says on the subject of what he thinks matches what, in truth, he does think. To discover what he thinks, it would be necessary to learn what "went on in his mind." But it is difficult to explore the mind of any man. In the case of a witness, cross-examination and other devices are available which may sometimes show, in part at least, what he is thinking while on the witness stand and what he had previously thought. But no one is permitted to cross-examine a judge or to use other methods applicable to witnesses. How, then, can one "investigate his secret thought * * *? He is the master of them, and what he says must be conclusive, as there is nothing to contradict or explain it."

The trial judge is therefore in this position: He can begin with the decision he considers desirable, and then, working backward, figure out and publish an $F$ and an $R$ which will make his decision appear to be logically sound, if only there is some oral testimony which is in accord with his reported $F$, and if he applied the proper $R$ to that reported $F$. If so, it does not matter whether actually he believed that testimony, that is, whether the facts he reports are the facts as he believes them to be. In other words, he can, without fear of challenge, "fudge" the facts he finds, and thus "force the balance." No one will ever be able to learn whether, in the interest of what he thought just, or for any other cause, he did thus misstate his belief.

I will never forget one of my experiences as a young lawyer. I participated in a lawsuit, lasting a week, tried by an able trial judge without a jury. During the course of the trial, on every doubtful question concerning the admission or exclusion of evidence, the judge, to my great indignation, ruled in favor of the other side. To my surprise, a few weeks after the trial ended, the judge decided the case in my client's favor, with strong findings of fact. A year later I met the judge, who referred to the case, saying: "You see, on the first day of the trial, I made up my mind that the defendant, your client, was a fine, hardworking woman who oughtn't to lose all her property to the plaintiff who had plenty of money. The plaintiff was urging a legal rule which you thought was wrong. I thought it was legally right, but very unjust, and I didn't want to apply it. So I made up my mind to lick the plaintiff on the facts. And by giving him every break on procedural points during the trial, and by using in my opinion the legal rule he urged, I made it impossible for him to reverse me on appeal, because, as the testimony was oral and in conflict, I knew the upper court would never upset my findings of fact." That judicial conduct was not commendable. But the judge's story did open my eyes to the way in which the power of a trial judge to find the facts can make his decision final, even if, had he correctly stated his honest notion of the facts, his decision would have been reversed for error in applying the wrong legal rule.

I recently said in an opinion that since, when a trial judge's decision turns on his view of the credibility of witnesses, "his 'finding' of 'facts,' responsive to [some of the] testimony, is inherently subjective (that is, what he believes to be the facts is hidden from scrutiny by others), his concealed disregard of evidence is always a possibility. An upper court must accept that possibility, and must recognize, too, that such hidden misconduct by a trial judge lies beyond its control." I doubt whether many trial judges thus deliberately "fudge" or "force the balance"; when this practice is employed, I think it is usually unconscious or only semiconscious. As, however, such findings are possible, and are certainly sometimes made, we can never be sure whether, when a trial judge publishes his findings, he is accurately reporting even his true SF. The upshot is this: In most lawsuits, the issues are solely issues of fact and the testimony oral; in those suits, the decisions, even if erroneous, are often exempt from criticism and from reversal by the upper courts.

There is a delightful World War I tale of General Pershing's first visit to the front. After he and his party had advanced some distance, he asked his aide how far they were from their goal. Down the line went the question and up the line came the answer, in a whisper, "Five miles," After a further advance, Pershing whispered the same question and received, in a whisper, the reply "Four miles." "Why in the devil," queried the general, "are we whispering? This question went down the line to a buck private who responded, "Because I have a sore throat." In our judicial system, most of the time, the trial judge plays the role of the private in the Pershing tale. . . .

## 2

I have probably amplified Judge McLellan's remarks to include more than he intended. Let me now adhere more literally to what he said. He voiced a sentiment often expressed by trial judges, but usually, in private conversations only. However, Judge Hutcheson, after years of service on the trial bench, published an article in which he stated that a trial judge "really decides by feeling, by hunching, and not by ratiocination," that the ratiocination appears only when he writes an opinion, which is but an apologia to "justify his decision to himself" and to "make it pass muster with his critics." This published justification (in the form of a reasoned $R \times F = D$) is ex post facto.

Is Judge Hutcheson's description wholly mistaken? And is Judge McLellan's use of it wholly without warrant? I believe not. Pertinent here is gestalt psychology, the main thesis of which is, roughly, this: All thinking is done in forms, pattern, configurations. A human response to a situation is "whole." It is not made up of little bricks of sight, sound, taste, and touch. It is an organized entity which is greater than, and different from, the sum of what, on analysis, appear to be its parts. The gestaltist's favorite illustration is a melody: A melody does not result from the summation of its parts; thus to analyze a melody is to destroy it. It is a basic, primary, unit. The melody, a pattern, determines the functions of the notes, its parts; the notes, the parts, do not determine the melody. Just so, say the gestaltists, no analysis of a pattern of thought, of a human response to a situation, can account for the pattern. Thus George, a natural scientist, asserts the need of "contrapuntal thinking," a type of mental activity like that of the artist who can "pay infinite attention to detail without losing sight of the whole."

I do not suggest that anyone swallow whole this notion of the "whole."

But it does illuminate, does tell us something of importance about, men's reactions to experience. In particular, it sheds light on a trial judge's "hunching." The trial judge, we may say, experiences a Gestalt. That is why he has difficulty in reporting his experience analytically. That is why, too, when he has heard oral testimony, his decision, even though accompanied by an "opinion," may defy intelligent criticism. One recalls Kipling's lines: "There are nine-and-sixty ways of constructing tribal lays, And every single one of them is right."

Some nineteen years ago, I wrote: "The decision of a judge after trying a case is the product of a unique experience." To justify that remark, I shall now approach the subject of judicial fact-finding from a slightly different angle. This approach involves a more probing consideration of logic as applied to trial-court decisions, of the assumption that, when a trial judge files a written opinion, or otherwise publishes his R and his F, he reveals the logic, or illogic, of his decision for observation by critics.

Relatively recent studies of logic have emphasized its inseparable connection with language. Perhaps the most perfect products of logic are the physical sciences, aided by mathematics—which is, itself a highly developed language, and which, in its "pure" form, is today generally regarded as another name for logic. Stressing language as the source of logic, certain thinkers, sometimes called "logical positivists" or "scientific positivists," maintain that, in effect, "What can I know?" means, "What can I intelligently ask?" They assert that the answer is this: I can intelligently ask whatever questions language clearly expresses; I can know (at least potentially, or in theory) what experiment—verification—will reply to such queries. Whatever under no circumstances could be thus stated and be thus verified or refuted, is a "pseudo-proposition." It is not true or false. It is unthinkable, "meaningless." Of course, say these "positivists," men do utter unthinkables; but those utterances are not "rational." They express "mere" emotions, feelings, like tears, laughter, or profanity. Feelings, therefore, have only subordinate importance, are but the irrational reactions of that pitiable creature, man.

Susanne Langer, in her stimulating book *Philosophy in a New Key*, criticizes the logical positivists. She points to an important defect of language: Words "have a linear, discrete, successive form; they are strung together like beads on a rosary; beyond the very limited meanings of inflections . . . we cannot talk in simultaneous bunches of names." This fact gives a peculiar character to logic, that is, "discursive" reasoning. . . . A language-bound theory of mind, therefore, rules it out of the domain of understanding and the sphere of knowledge."

Professor Langer maintains that the logical positivists go astray because they disregard this inherent weakness of language. On that account they mistakenly depict human rationality as a "tiny grammar-bound island in the middle of feeling expressed by sheer babble," and deny reality to feelings. . . .

Professor Langer (to sketch her views rapidly and skimpily) asserts that language, which inadequately communicates feelings, is not our only medium of articulation, not our sole means of symbolizing our responses to experience. Notable for this invention of nonlogical forms to symbolize feelings are the fine arts. They use "Wordless symbolism, which is nondiscursive and untranslatable, * * * and cannot directly convey generalities." Their "symbolic elements * * * are understood only through the meaning of the whole, through their relations within the total structure." Such symbolizing is as rational as that of language. Our feelings, which dwell "on the deeper level of insight," can be known through "wordless knowledge" expressed in "nondiscursive forms"—as, for instance, in music. As Victor Hugo said: "Music expresses that which cannot be said, and on which it is impossible to remain silent." . . .

Return now to the trial judge who has heard conflicting oral testimony on a pivotal issue, and you will perhaps the better understand his difficulty when he tries to articulate the bases of his "hunch," to state logically in words—that is, by "discursive" reasoning—why he decided as he did: His decisional process, like the artistic process, involves feelings that words cannot ensnare. A large component of a trial judge's reaction is "emotion." That is why we hear often of the judge's "intuition." Holmes, referring to the decision of an administrative agency, said it expressed "an intuition of experience which outruns analyses and sums up many unnamed and tangled impressions; impressions which may lie beneath consciousness without losing their worth." That comment applies as well to the decisions of a trial judge. He cannot, with entire adequacy, formulate in logical, lingual, form, his reaction to the conflicting testimony at a trial. His response to that testimony is, in part, "wordless knowledge." To be completely articulate, to communicate that response satisfactorily, he would be obliged—as a once-popular song put it —to "say it with music." For his emotion-toned experience is contrapuntal.

Since the trial judge is not, then, engaged in a wholly logical enterprise, the effort to squeeze his "hunch," his wordless rationality, into a logical verbal form must distort it, deform it. His ineffable intuition cannot be wholly set down in an R and an F. There are overtones inexpressible in words. He has come upon nonlogical truth. One may doubt whether, even if he resorted to music or poetry, he could make himself thoroughly understood by others, when one considers the many discrepant interpretations of artistic compositions and performances. When the trial judge tries really to express his composite response by a finding of fact (an F) and a legal rule (an R), he may well feel that the result is a misrepresentation of his actual experience in the decisional process. Accordingly, he may, not unreasonably, resent criticism of his decision, when that criticism rests on that misrepresentative analysis. . . .

Frequently (although without resort to the word "gestalt") something like the gestalt aspect of an artist's efforts has been stressed by those who declare the futility of criticism of artistic products. For instance, recently the novelist, E. M. Forster, writing "especially of music," asserted the existence of "a gulf between artist * * * and critic." When a critic approaches a work of art, "two universes have not even collided, they have [merely] been juxtaposed." For the critic to claim that he "actually entered into [the artist's] state" is "presumptuous." If a "critic comes along and tells [the artist] what is right and wrong" about "his product, [the artist] has a feeling of irrelevance." For there is "a basic difference between the critical and creative states of mind." Why? Because the artist "lets down as it were a bucket into his subconscious. * * * When the process is over, * * * looking back on it, he will wonder how on earth he did it. * * * There is * * * [a] connection between the subconscious and the conscious, which has to be effected before the work of art can be born, and there is the surprise of the creator at his own creation." It follows that "the critical state is grotesquely remote from the state responsible for the work it affects to expound. It does not let buckets down into the subconscious."

A trial judge's composite response to conflicting oral testimony has something of this opaque quality. For he, too, has "let down a bucket into his subconscious." Bok, one of our most gifted trial judges, recently said: "Each case [was] a work of art, so far as possible, and not an act of grace or a scientific demonstration. * * * It is here, at the point of the greatest judging, that the law can cease to be a matter of rule and compensation and reach the realm of the intangibles: gentleness of heart, with clarity of mind and the quiet salt of faith. * * * The Law suffers from being thought of as an intellectual profession. It is intellectual, of course. * * * But it is not scientific in the sense of a science whose rules are impersonal and beyond the reach of human emotions or behavior. Emotions and behavior are the raw materials from which the law is distilled in one way or another. * * * There is no plea to be made except to keep the law personal."

### 3

I revert to my statement that it oversimplifies to ascribe the difficulty met in predicting a trial judge's decision to the subjectivity of his fact-finding: the subjectivity is more complex; it inheres in his total reaction to the trial.

If the judge's own effort logically to explain his decision, after he reaches it, is so baffling because it results from an experience to which he cannot give complete expression in logical terms, it must also be true that any person other than the judge will seldom be able to know at all accurately, in advance, what the decision will be. For the judge's reaction is unique.

Probably, many of the experiences of every man are unique; even when an experience appears to recur, often it is with some slightly novel difference. "We do not fall in love twice in the same way," says Sullivan. "Even boredom has its shades." To criticize effectively a trial judge's decision, after he renders it, we should, then, in many cases have to relive his unique experience. To predict his decision we should have had to live it, as he did. That we cannot do. Nor will empathy carry us more than a part of the way into the emotional reactions of another person. . . .

The "sociological school," as we saw, wisely noted the effects of the social, economic, and political views of judges. But because that school primarily studied the legal rules, and, therefore, the published opinions of upper courts, it disregarded, for the most part, the less obvious components of judges' attitudes. Cardozo was less restricted. He wrote: "Deep below consciousness are other forces, the likes and dislikes, the predilections and the prejudices, the complex of instincts and emotions and habits and convictions, which make the man, whether he be litigant or judge." However, as Cardozo had little interest in trial-court fact-finding, because he believed it did not affect "jurisprudence," he never discussed the impact of such influences on trial judges' findings of fact. Yet the way those influences affect trial judges has far more significance for most litigants than the way they affect upper-court judges, because, for reasons previously canvassed, trial-court decisions usually have finality.

## 4

Spingarn regards as the sole function of the critic of poetry a critical understanding of the poet's aim; the critic should "re-dream the poet's dream," should ask, "What has the poet tried to express and how has he expressed it?" Assuming it to be possible to answer that question with respect to poetry, often it is not possible to answer a similar question with respect to the trial judge who decides a case involving a credibility issue: because of the inaccessibility of what the trial judge has tried to express, his critic cannot "re-dream" the judge's "dream." Although some persons contend that no objective aesthetic standards exist, that contention is too sweeping. There are minimal uniformities in human nature, and, in any given culture at any given time, minimal cultural uniformities; these uniformities yield an irreducible minimum of artistic norms. For similar reasons, there is an irreducible minimum of moral norms. These moral norms (group ideals and values) express themselves, to some extent, in the substantive legal rules. In that sense, we can attain objectivity in criticism of the R's which the courts employ, and therefore of upper-court opinions, which concern themselves chiefly with the R's. But similar objectivity is not possible in criticism of most trial-court decisions.

For most of those decisions, resulting from idiosyncratic reactions to orally testifying witnesses, express unique and hidden norms—individual, personal, norms—which, varying from judge to judge, lack uniformity and are therefore peculiarly subjective. It is this kind of subjectivity which has been ignored by the legal thinkers who minimize the difficulties of criticism and prediction of decisions. Such thinkers overlook the distinction between the more or less "objective" character of the norms embodied in the legal rules and the "subjective" character of the trial judge's response to oral testimony. They are thinking of upper-court opinions in cases in which those courts accept as their F the explicit findings of the trial courts. In any such upper-court decision, the F is given, and the critic therefore need ask merely whether the appellate court in its opinion (1) used a proper R and (2) logically applied to the given F. Subjectivity and the gestalt factor often have relatively little effect on the opinion accompanying such a decision.

In assuming that upper-court and trial-court decisions are equally susceptible of prediction and criticism, conventional legal thinking blunders egregiously. It forgets that a trial judge, faced with oral testimony, does not wholly differ from a jury. . . . The New Hampshire Supreme Court has said: "Judges are men, and their decisions upon complex facts must vary as those of jurors on the same facts. Calling one determination an opinion and the other a verdict does not * * * make that uniform and certain which from its nature must remain variable and uncertain."

## 5

It is true that a conscientious trial judge will pay more attention to the legal rules than a jury usually can or does. That means that, in a jury-less case, there may occur, in the trial judge's mental processes, interactions of the R's and the F which may be exquisitely complicated in many obscure ways. I shall here note but one of those ways.

As I previously stated, it is a wise and accepted principle that a trial judge's finding of the facts should be affected not merely by the words of the witness but by their manner of testifying. Suppose, then, that when listening to the testimony the judge thinks a particular formulation of a particular rule will govern the case. That rule will serve as his attention-guide, that is, it will focus his attention sharply on the testimony and demeanor of those witnesses who testify with respect to matters specifically germane to his version of that rule. But suppose that, when the trial is over, and the judge comes to his decision, he concludes that his earlier formulation of that rule was wrong. He cannot now vividly recall the demeanor of those witnesses whose testimony is relevant to what he now considers the correct formulation of the proper rule. As a result, he may well find the facts erroneously. Yet neither he nor any critic is able to know whether or not he did thus err.

## 6

The presence of what, by way of shorthand, I have labeled the gestalt factor is alone enough to expose the misleading oversimplification of the conventional theory that a trial judge's decision results from his "application" of a legal rule (or rules) to the "facts" of the case. For note the word "application," and consider the following: Suppose that a trial judge has a strong unconscious animus against, or liking for, Catholics or Negroes, and that such a predilection influences his attitude toward important witnesses who testify at a trial—and thus influences his decision. Would it be helpful to say that his decision resulted from his "application" of that bias? A more dispassionate description would be this: That bias was one among many stimuli which helped to bring about the decision. Similarly, one should say that the legal rule is but one of a multitude of such stimuli. . . .

The traditional formulation $(R \times F = D)$ being inadequate, especially with reference to trial courts, one might, then, for the benefit of those who like mathematical-looking formulas, suggest, as a substitute, $S \times P = D$, when $P$ represents the trial judge's "personality," and $S$ represents the stimuli that affect him (those which influence his belief as to the facts, and all other stimuli). But such a formula has little value for predictive and critical purposes. The "personality" of the judge denotes an exquisitely complicated mass of phenomena. Break down $P$, and you will find a mass of subjective, unascertainable factors. Break down $S$, and you will find a horde of conflicting stimuli, some of them being the so-called "social forces," some of them being the legal rules (the $R$'s), some of them being undiscoverable.

## 7

I suggested earlier that most legal thinking is two-dimensional, that consideration of trial-court processes in "finding" the "facts" demands three-dimensional legal thinking. Perhaps that suggestion should be amended:

The physicists now deem it artificial to separate space and time. Using the idea of space-time, they add space as a fourth dimension. In the same way, if we take into account the trial court's gestalt, we should perhaps regard it as adding a fourth dimension, and see the need of fourth-dimensional legal thinking, which requires not mere intellectual but also artistic insights.

## 8

Despite the futility of the attempt to use the written opinion as a basis for complete evaluation of trial-court fact-finding, I think it highly desirable to require trial judges to make special findings of fact. The usual argument for such a requirement—that it aids the appellate courts—seems to me to be far less cogent than the argument that the breaking down of his decisional process into two parts, the rule and the "facts," compels the trial judge carefully to examine his decision. For, as every judge knows, to set down in precise words the facts as he finds them is the best way to avoid carelessness in the discharge of that duty. Often a strong impression that, on the basis of the evidence, the facts are thus-and-so gives way when it comes to expressing that impression on paper. A trial judge, every now and then, thus discovering that his initially contemplated decision will not jell, is obliged to decide otherwise.

It is no sufficient rejoinder that the judge's decision has its roots in a nonlogical hunch. Logic need not be the enemy of hunching. Most of the conclusions men reach in their daily lives are similarly hunch products, originally arrived at in nonlogical ways; yet we do not deny that frequently the correctness of many of these conclusions can profitably be tested by logical analysis. That a conclusion is prior in time to the reasoning which logically justifies it may make that reasoning seem artificial, but does not necessarily make that reasoning fallacious or useless. Even physicists and mathematicians frequently use logically tested hunches. Of course, the mere fact that the reason given for an act or a judgment is *ex post facto* does not invalidate that reason. Jones may hit Smith, or make love to a girl, or explore the Arctic without reflecting on his conduct. When asked to justify his acts, he may give excellent reasons which are entirely satisfactory. That is, in spite of the fact that he did not act on the basis of logically tested reasoning, his conduct may, on subsequent analysis, show up as having been logically justifiable. When any man tries to determine whether his appraisal of persons or events is sound, he tests it by seeing whether it is a legitimate inference from his data and from some generally accepted principle or assumption.

So it may be with a trial judge's decision: He may first arrive at it intuitively and, then only, work backward to a major "rule" premise and a minor "fact" premise to see whether or not that decision is logically defective. In so working, the judge is doing nothing improper or unusual. (There is the story of the old lady, accused of being illogical, who, when told what "logic" was supposed to be, exlaimed: "Logic! What nonsense! How can I know what I think until I know what I say?") The chronological priority of the judge's hunch does not mean that his subsequent logical analysis is valueless. That analysis may have an artificial appearance. But such an appearance does not detract from the worth of such ex *post facto* analyses in other fields. If one chooses, loosely, to call that hunch-testing process "rationalization," then, in that sense, most logical rationality involves some "rationalization."

Logic, said Balfour, "never aids the work of thought; it only acts as its auditor and accountant general." That is too limited a statement of the role of logic. But even if logic's role were solely that of "auditing," it would be immensely valuable. As F. C. S. Schiller said, "To put an argument in syllogistic form is to strip it bare for logical inspection. We can then see where its weak point must lie, if it has any, and consider whether there is reason to believe that it is actually * * * weak at these points. We thereby learn where and for what the argument should be tested further." That a trial judge should make special findings of fact is therefore of importance, since his doing so is essential to his own logical assaying of his decision. In sum, because of the inescapable and un-get-at-able subjectivity of his reactions, and because of the gestalt factor, his published report will leave an unbridged gap between him and his critics; yet findings of fact will act as a partial check on that subjectivity.

Nevertheless, to require the trial judge to make and publish his findings of fact will yield no panacea where, because of a conflict in the oral testimony, the credibility of witnesses becomes crucial. Frustration of the purpose of the requirement occurs where, as too often happens, the judge uncritically adopts the findings drafted by the lawyer for the winning side. For then the judge may ostensibly make a finding of some facts of which—although they are based on some testimony—the judge never thought, and which, had he done his own job, he would not have included; in that event, his finding does not represent any real inference he drew from the evidence—does not reflect his own actual views concerning the witnesses' credibility. With conscientious trial judges, however, that difficulty is not insurmountable.

But a graver difficulty remains: the facts, as "found," can never be known to be the same as the actual past facts—as what (adapting Kant's phrase) may be termed the "facts in themselves." How closely the judge's "findings" approximate those actual facts he can never be sure—nor can anyone else.

*Courts on Trial* (1949)

# THE JURY'S VERDICT &

SKIDMORE V. BALTIMORE & OHIO R. CO. ✒️ In January, 1945, Buzzy Skidmore, a railroad worker on the Baltimore & Ohio, injured his back as a result of icy conditions under a coal car he was repairing. He sued the railroad on the grounds of negligence. The jury returned a verdict for the plaintiff in the amount of $30,000. The railroad appealed the verdict, saying that (a) the trial judge improperly denied them a directed verdict and, (b) the judge erred in denying their request for a "special" verdict. Although he wrote the opinion in which the judgment of the trial court was affirmed, Judge Frank used this occasion to voice his opinion about the desirability of the special as against the general verdict. ✒️

FRANK, Circuit Judge: . . . Undeniably, [this] verdict affords no satisfactory information about the jury's findings. But almost every general verdict sheds similar or even greater darkness. Such verdicts account for much (not all) of the criticism of the civil jury. Some revaluation of the jury system seems not unjustified in the light of the fact that ours is the only country in the world where it is still highly prized. Lauded as essential to individual liberty and democracy, and imported in the late eighteenth and early nineteenth centuries from England and the United States, trial by jury was adopted in criminal cases on the European continent but subsequently ceased there, in pre-Hitler days, to maintain its popularity. Nor can that attitude be explained as a symptom of decreased interest in democracy and individualism. For Scotland, surely long a land of liberty-loving individualists, having in the sixteenth century virtually rejected the civil jury, readopted it in 1815, and, still later, all but gave it up. In England, whence trial by jury came to us, it is now seldom employed in civil suits, has been abandoned in criminal prosecutions other than for major crimes, and even there is used decreasingly. In the United

States, the number of jury waivers indicates the jury's slowly waning popularity. But here, especially in the federal courts, the civil jury, in many cases, cannot be eliminated except by constitutional amendments. We must, then, as to some kind of cases, assume that it will long be with us. (Of course, in a very considerable number of cases, no right to trial by jury exists because of historically determined fortuities. Thus in a suit on a note, the right exists, but not in a suit to cancel the note; the same difference maintains between a suit for breach of contract for the sale of land and one for specific performance thereof. So, too, the right to a jury vanishes if, before suit is brought, the defendant goes into bankruptcy. Were jury trial as beneficent as its ardent devotees proclaim, such differences would be indefensibly irrational.)

But what many persons regard as its major defects can be mitigated. One device which will help to achieve that end is the special, or fact, verdict. Those who resent any reform which invades the jury's province should be reassured by the historians who teach that the special verdict is no new-fangled idea, but one almost as old as the jury itself, older indeed than the modern jury. In those early days, Morgan tells us, jurors often successfully insisted upon the right to render such verdicts against the desires of the judges who wanted general verdicts. To be sure, in this country, during the latter part of the eighteenth and the early part of the nineteenth centuries, the right to return a general verdict was highly esteemed as the jury's prerogative, especially in criminal cases; the judges then instructed the juries that they were to decide both "the law" and the facts, not being bound by the opinion of the trial judge. Most jurisdictions later repudiated that doctrine. The courts and legal writers declared that, if juries had the right to ignore the judges' instructions as to the applicable legal rules, the "law" would "become as variable as the prejudices, the inclinations and the passions of men"; "the parties would suffer from an arbitrary decision" "decisions would depend entirely upon juries uncontrolled by any settled, fixed, legal principle," and would be "according to what the jury in their own opinion suppose the law is or ought to be"; our "government" would "cease to be a government of laws and become a government of men"; "jurors would become not only judges but legislators as well"; the "law" would "be as fluctuating and uncertain as the diverse opinions of different juries in regard to it"; jurors would be "superior to the national legislature, and its laws * * * subject to their control" so that a "law of Congress" would "be in operation in one state and not in another."

Yet no amount of brave talk can do away with the fact that, when a jury returns an ordinary general verdict, it usually has the power utterly to ignore what the judge instructs it concerning the substantive legal rules, a power which, because generally it cannot be controlled, is indistinguishable for all practical purposes, from a "right." (. . . The trial judge, of course, can grant a new trial in any civil case, and in a criminal case where the verdict is against the defendant. But he thus exercises merely a temporary veto, since another jury, with like power, again hears the case. Except in unusual circumstances, there is a limit to the number of new trials which may be granted. . . .) Practically, then, for all we may say about the jury's duty when juries render general verdicts, we now do have the very conditions which we were warned would result if the jury had the right to decide legal propositions: cases are often decided "according to what the jury suppose the law is or ought to be"; the "law," when juries sit, is "as fluctuating and uncertain as the diverse opinion of different juries in regard to it"; and often jurors are "not only judges but legislators as well." Indeed, some devotees of the jury system praise it precisely because, they say, juries, by means of general verdicts, can and often do nullify those substantive legal rules they dislike, thus becoming ad hoc ephemeral (unelected) legislatures (a state of affairs singularly neglected by most writers on jurisprudence, who would do well to modify their ideas by recognizing what might be called "juriesprudence"). Surprisingly, that sort of defense of the general verdict is not seldom voiced by lawyers who, in the next breath, demand strict adherence to the legal precedents.

"Competent observers," writes Judge Rossman, "who have interviewed the jurors in scores of jury trials, declare that, in many cases where the general verdict was employed, principal issues received no consideration whatever from the jury." The general verdict, then, has some strange characteristics. As Sunderland puts it: "The peculiarity of the general verdict is the merger into a single indivisible residuum of all matters, however numerous, whether of law or fact. It is a compound made by the jury which is incapable of being broken up into its constituent parts. No judicial reagents exist for either a qualitative or a quantitative analysis. The law supplies the means for determining neither what facts were found, nor what principles of law were applied, nor how the application was made. There are therefore three unknown elements which enter into the general verdict; (a) the facts; (b) the law; (c) the application of the law to the facts. And it is clear that the verdict is liable to three sources of error, corresponding to these three elements. It is also clear that if error does occur in any of these matters it cannot be discovered, for the constituents of the compound cannot be ascertained. No one but the jurors can tell what was put into it and the jurors will not be heard to say. The general verdict is as inscrutable and essentially mysterious as the judgment which issued from the ancient oracle of Delphi. Both stand on the same foundation—a presumption of wisdom. The court protects the jury from all investigation and inquiry as fully as the temple authorities protected the priestess who spoke to the suppliant votary at the shrine. It is quite probable that the law is wise in not permitting jurors to testify as to how they compounded their verdict, for all stability would disappear if such inquiries were open. * * * As to the second element in the general verdict, the law, it is a matter upon which the jury is necessarily ignorant. The jurors are taken from the body of the county, and it is safe to say that the last man who would be called or allowed to sit would be a lawyer. They are secondhand dealers in law, and must get it from the judge. They can supply nothing themselves; they are a mere conduit pipe through which the court supplies the law that goes into the general verdict. But while the jury can contribute nothing of value so far as the law is concerned, it has infinite capacity for mischief, for twelve men can easily misunderstand more law in a minute than the judge can explain in an hour. Indeed, can anything be more fatuous than the expectation that the law which the judge so carefully, learnedly and laboriously expounds to the laymen in the jury box will become operative in their minds in its true form? One who has never studied a science cannot understand or appreciate its intricacies, and the law is no exception to this rule. The very theory of the jury and its general verdict is thus predicated upon a premise which makes practically certain an imperfect or erroneous view of the principles of law which are to be compounded into the verdict. The instructions upon the law given by the court to the jury are an effort to give, in the space of a few minutes, a legal education to twelve lawmen upon the branch of the law involved in the case. Law cannot be taught in any such way. As to this element, accordingly, the general verdict is almost necessarily a failure. As to the third element in the general verdict —the application of the law to the facts—we find the same difficulty as in the case of the first element—a merging of the law into the verdict in such a way that it is impossible to tell how or whether the jury applied the law. They may have applied it in a wholly wrong way, or they may have failed to apply it at all. No analysis of the verdict can be made which will throw any light on the process. Since the case can ordinarily go to the jury only if a verdict either way is legally possible, whatever the jury does is presumed to be right, and this presumption excludes any inquiry from the jurors themselves. Cases may arise where the verdict shows on its face a failure to properly apply the law, usually as relating to the measure of damages, but in the vast majority of cases the verdict is a complete mystery, throwing a mantle of impenetrable darkness over the operations of the jury. Whether the jurors deliberately and openly threw the law into the discard, and rendered a verdict out of their own heads, or whether they applied the law correctly as instructed by the court, or whether they tried to apply it properly but failed for lack of understanding—these are questions respecting which the verdict discloses nothing. So far, therefore, as the third element goes, the general verdict is an unkown and unknowable mystery, with the balance of probability against it. * * * We come, then, to this position, that the general verdict * * * confers on the jury a vast power to commit error and do mischief by loading it with technical burdens far beyond its ability to perform, by confusing it in aggregating instead of segregating the issues, and by shrouding in secrecy and mystery the actual results of its deliberations. * * * The record must be absolutely flawless, but such a result is possible only by concealing, not by excluding mistakes. This is the great technical merit of the general verdict. It covers up all the shortcomings which frail human nature is unable to eliminate from the trial of a case. In the abysmal abstraction of the general verdict concrete details are swallowed up, and the eye of the law, searching anxiously for the realization of logical perfection, is satisfied. In short, the general verdict is valued for what it does, not for what it is. It serves as the great procedural opiate, * * * draws the curtain upon human errors and soothes us with the assurance that we have attained the unattainable."

The general verdict enhances, to the maximum, the power of appeals to the biases and prejudices of the jurors, and usually converts into a futile ritual the stock phrases about dispassionateness almost always included in judges' charges. Many books on trial tactics, written by experienced trial lawyers, which give advice as to how to arouse juries' emotions, make the point that a jury tries the lawyers rather than the case, and that the lawyers, in jury trials, must recognize themselves as actors or stage managers engaged in theatrical performances. In a series of pamphlets on trial practice, recently published under the auspices of the American Bar Association, one author writes that "the advocate * * * must always recognize that the jury is judging the lawyer as well as the witnesses, quick to take sides because of the protagonists rather than their opinion of the testimony"; another says that the jurors' reaction to trial counsel "may be more important than the reaction to the client, for the client appears on the stand only during a relatively brief period, while the lawyer is before the jury all the time"; this same author gives detailed suggestions of means by which a lawyer may "ingratiate himself" with the jury. A court has solemnly decided that "tears have always been considered legitimate arguments before a jury," that such use of tears is "one of the natural rights of counsel which no court or constitution could take away," and that "indeed, if counsel has them at his command, it may be seriously questioned whether it is not his professional duty to shed them whenever proper occasion arises. * * *" Harris, in his well-known book on advocacy, says, "It may be that judgment is more easily deceived when the passions are aroused, but if so, you (the lawyers) are not responsible. Human nature was, I presume, intended to be what it is, and when it gets into the jury-box, it is the duty of the advocate to make the best use of it he fairly can in the interests of his client." This is no laughing matter. For prejudice has been called the thirteenth juror, and it has been noted that "Mr. Prejudice and Miss Sympathy are the names of witnesses whose testimony is never recorded but must nevertheless be reckoned with in trials by jury."

Small wonder that Thayer commented that jury trials are "a potent cause of demoralization to the bar," or that Morgan, well versed in trial tactics, in reviewing a book on jury trial techniques, recently wrote: "If only some lawyer could rise up and honestly denounce Mr. Goldstein as a defamer of his profession. * * * If only a reviewer could assert that this book is a guide not to the palaces of virtue but to the red-light districts of the law. But a decent respect for the truth compels the admission that Mr. Goldstein has told his story truly. He has told it calmly, without a pretense of shame and (God save us!) without the slightest suspicion of its shamefulness. He has shown by his own unperturbed frankness with what complaisance the profession, which would smile the superior smile of derision at the suggestion of a trial by battle of bodies, accepts trial by battle of wits. In all innocence, he has produced a volume which is a devastating commentary upon an important aspect of our administration of justice." Not that lawyers, trying to protect their clients, should be censured for employing the stratagems described in such a book—as long as we retain the general-verdict jury system. But, with the general verdict in operation, and those stratagems as its usual concomitants, it should not be surprising that one of the members of this court said, "I am by no means enamored of jury trials, at least in civil cases * * *" and that Mr. Justice Cardozo, speaking for the Supreme Court, remarked, "Few would be so narrow or provincial as to maintain that a fair and enlightened system of justice would be impossible without" trial by jury.

That is not to say that, by way of contrast with juries, all trial judges are free of all susceptibility to emotional appeals, or that—although most trial judges, because of experience, are more skilled in fact-finding than juries and better armored against the seductive wiles of lawyers—any trial judge can (or should) slough off all predilections. (Lord Bramwell observed, "One third of a judge is a common law juror if you get beneath his ermine"; and Mr. Justice Riddell added that "the other two thirds may not be far different.") Nor is it to say that, where constitutional or statutory provisions require jury trials, judges do not have the highest obligation to see that such trials are conducted in accordance with the basic principles which govern such proceedings. (The writer of this opinion has expressed his own views on this subject in a dissenting opinion in United States v. Antonelli Fireworks Co. . . . ) But, as reasonable modifications of the jury system are not thereby precluded, a vigorous revival of a traditional adjunct of that system, that is, the special verdict, represents no deviation from judicial obligations.

Perhaps the least desirable feature of the general verdict, a feature which the fact verdict wipes out, is this: The theory of the general verdict involves the assumption that the jury fully comprehends the judge's instructions concerning the applicable substantive legal rules. Yet, often the judge must state those rules to the jury with such niceties that many lawyers do not comprehend them, and it is impossible that the jury can. Judge Bok notes that "juries have the disadvantage * * * of being treated like children while the testimony is going on, but then being doused with a kettleful of law during the charge that would make a third-year law-student blanch." (. . . There are at least three theories of how the general-verdict-jury-system works: [1] According to a naïve theory, the judge conclusively determines the pertinent substantive legal rules, and the jury confines itself to finding the facts. [2] A more sophisticated theory runs thus: The judge has one function and the jury two. The judge announces authoritatively the pertinent rules of law. The jury [a] ascertain the facts and [b] apply to these facts the rules of law laid down by the judge and [c] thus arrive at their general verdict. The judge, that is, supplies the major premise, consisting of the abstract rules of law; the jury determine the minor premise from the evidence, and then work out the syllogism to its logical conclusion in the verdict which they report to the judge. Some of those who accept this theory assert that juries often circumvent the legal rules by misfinding the facts; the facts, it is said, are "found in order to reach the result." . . . That thesis assumes that the jurors, understanding what the judge told them about the substantive legal rules, proceed with consummate skill and cunning to devise the exact finding of facts which, when correlated with those rules, will logically compel the judgment the jurors desire. [3] A more realistic theory maintains that jurors often do not understand the judge's instructions and simply bring in an unexplained verdict for the party they favor. . . .) Nevertheless, the patently fictitious assumption that the jurors have more legal wisdom than third-year law students requires the upper court to reverse when a trial judge failed to state the pertinent substantive rules with sufficient particularity. Such faulty instructions, it has been said, "are the greatest single source of reversible error." Judge Rossman says: "The general verdict is responsible for the elaborate instructions given to the jury. * * * The necessity for (these) instructions creates pitfalls which may trap the trial judge and which in turn may result in new trials, appeals and reversals." (. . . These reversals appear to be at war with the thesis . . . that the great virtue of the jury system consists of the jury's power to disregard or nullify the substantive legal rules. Perhaps, however, a defender of that thesis believes that a jury ought to know the substantive rules before it nullifies them.

Since lawyers use the trial judge's instructions about the substantive rules [instructions often uninteligible to the jurors] as traps for the judge, it is manifest that the substantive rules in general-verdict jury cases often are in large part but procedural devices. . . .

It is a curious fact that many courts which refuse to reverse for [1] so-called "procedural" errors they call "harmless" nevertheless will be prompt to reverse for [2] errors in the charge to the jury about the substantive rules— although the first kind of errors—such as, for example, improper remarks of one of the lawyers—are often matters well within the comprehension of the jurors and may have influenced their verdict, while the second kind frequently are outside the jurors' comprehension and therefore could not have affected their judgment.) In many instances, such a reversal means merely another trial at which the judge will intone to another uncomprehending jury a revised version of those legal rules. There results an enormous waste of time and money. Indeed, the prospect of a prolonged new trial undoubtedly often induces a litigant of modest means to accept an unfair settlement. The fact verdict provides an obvious escape from these wasteful or unfair consequences of the general verdict.

The finding of facts, says Sunderland, "is much better done by means of the special verdict. Every advantage, which the jury is popularly supposed to have over the court as a trier of facts, is retained, with the very great additional advantage that the analysis and separation of the facts in the case which the court and the attorney must necessarily effect in employing the special verdict, materially reduces the chance of error. It is easy to make mistakes in dealing at large with aggregates of facts. The special verdict compels detailed consideration. But above all it enables the public, the parties and the court to see what the jury has really done. * * * The morale of the jury also is aided by throwing off the cloak of secrecy, for only through publicity is there developed the proper feeling of responsibility in public servants. So far, then, as the facts go, they can be much more effectively, conveniently and usefully tried by abandoning the general verdict and substituting the special verdict. * * * The special verdict is devised for the express purpose of escaping the sham of false appearances."

When using a special verdict, the judge need not—should not—give any charge about the substantive legal rules beyond what is reasonably necessary to enable the jury to answer intelligently the questions put to them. As, accordingly, the jury is less able to know whether its finding will favor one side or the other, the appeal to the jurors' cruder prejudices will frequently be less effective. "A perverse verdict may still be returned, granted a jury clever enough to appreciate the effect of its answers, and to shape them to harmonize with its general conclusions. But it is much more difficult * * * and by requiring the jury to return the naked facts only we may fairly expect to escape the results of sympathy, prejudice and passion." That may be too sanguine a hope; but the fact verdict may often reduce the more undesirable sway of emotions. It is suggested, too, that a special verdict "searches the conscience of the individual juror, as a general verdict does not," because "such are the contradictions in human nature that many a man who will unite in a general verdict for a large and unwarranted sum of money will shrink from a specific finding against his judgment and sense of right and wrong." Judge Rossman writes, "Bearing in mind that in the judge-jury relationship both members of the team are entitled to fair treatment, may we not ask ourselves: Is it fair to require a jury to employ a general verdict? Since recourse to the special verdict is available, is it right to demand that a juror swear that he will obey the instructions (which the lawyers frequently say they are not sure of until they have been transcribed) and return a general verdict in obedience thereto?"

True, the common-law type of special verdict, when utilized in this country, frequently caused so many complications that it fell into disrepute. But in three states, North Carolina, Wisconsin, and Texas, the special-verdict practice in civil cases was so modified as to avoid most of those complications. The Wisconsin and Texas procedures, apparently the most effective, seem to have been the model for Rule 49(a) of the Federal Civil Rules which authorizes the trial judge to dispense with a general verdict and, instead, to require the return of special written findings. Rule 49(b) also authorizes the judge to call for a general verdict accompanied by written interrogatories. But, unlike the Texas trial judge, the federal district judge, under the Rule, has full, uncontrolled discretion in the matter: He may still require merely the old-fashioned general verdict.

Accordingly, we cannot hold that a district judge errs when, as here, for any reason or no reason whatever, he refuses to demand a special verdict, although we deem such a verdict usually preferable to the opaque general verdict. Perhaps some day soon Rule 49 will be amended to make compulsory either special verdicts or written interrogatories in civil jury cases. Meanwhile, we can but hope that, in such cases, the district judges will require one or the other, on their own motion or when asked to do so.

The fact verdict will furnish no panacea. Among other things, as previously noted, it will still be true that, in a relatively simple case, the jury will still be able to foresee what answers to the questions will produce a judgment for the side it favors. There is this, too, to consider: Some persons oppose the requirement that trial judges in nonjury cases shall file special findings of fact. As such findings closely resemble a jury's special verdict, it is therefore pertinent here that some of those opponents suggest, in effect, that a trial judge's decision is a unique composite reaction to the oral testimony, a composite which ought not—or, rather, cannot without artificiality—be broken down into findings of fact and legal conclusions. Back of this suggestion there lurks something like the notions of gestalt psychology. A judge's reaction to the evidence at a trial is apparently considered a "whole" (a "gestalt" or "pattern") which cannot adequately be analyzed. Seperation of a decision into "law" and "fact" components, it seems to be asserted, will be "too logical," in the sense that it excludes the "intuition of experience which outruns analysis and sums up many unnamed and tangled impressions, impressions which may lie beneath consciousness without losing their worth." Some support for this position might be sought in recent writings to the effect that logic stems from language (the word "logic," of course, stems from the Greek word for "word") which, in turn, because of its inherent character, cannot fully express or symbolize "feeling," and that feelings have a rational validity, expressive of "wordless knowledge," which must not be disregarded. While, on net balance, however, a logical assaying by a trial judge of his decision has immense value, so that in a nonjury case special findings of fact by a trial judge are eminently desirable, the argument against special findings of fact by trial judges might perhaps be applied with somewhat greater effectiveness against fact verdicts by juries: It might be said that some one person or body, either a trial judge or a jury, should be entrusted in each case with reaching a composite reaction to the evidence, and that therefore a division of functions into explicit fact-finding by a jury and "law-finding" by a judge will yield an undesirable artificiality. Nonetheless, even assuming that that argument has some cogency, fact verdicts seem clearly better than general verdicts. . . .

*167 F.2d 54 (1948)*

# LEGAL EDUCATION ❧

THE difficulty of practicing an art is no excuse for practicing it stupidly, carelessly. To acquire absolutely reliable knowledge of the objective past facts of most lawsuits is undeniably beyond human power. Yet, although those facts can only be approximated, we should strive to have that approximation, as nearly as possible, asymptotic. Of course, we must rely on probabilities. But there are degrees of probability, as Bishop Butler remarked two hundred years ago. What he said of medicine has relevance here: "Is it not a poor thing for a physician to have so little knowledge in the cure of diseases as even the most eminent have? To act upon conjecture and guesses where the life of man is concerned? Undoubtedly it is," replied the Bishop to his own questions, "but not in comparison of having no skill at all in that useful art, and being obliged to act wholly in the dark." So as to the judicial art: The facts as "found" in trials are inherently guessy; but we need not be content with the present guessing-in-the-dark techniques of our trial courts. Everything feasible should be done so that the probability of accuracy in discovering the true facts of cases will be as high as is possible. That trial-court fact-finding can never be completely objective, that unavoidably it involves conjectures, that often it is but one element in a gestalt—all this does not at all compel the conclusion that the traditional fact-finding methods are not capable of marked improvement. Today, to a shocking and needless extent, they are tragically bad. I now turn to one of the main obstacles to their improvement.

## 2

In legal mythology, one of the most popular and most harmful myths is the upper-court myth, the myth that upper courts are the heart of courthouse government. This myth induces the false belief that it is of no importance whether or not trial judges are well trained for their job, fair-minded, conscientious in listening to testimony, and honest. In considerable part, this belief arises from the fallacious notion that the legal rules, supervised by the upper courts, control decisions. But the false belief about the unimportance of the trial judge's activities is also encouraged by another tenet of the upper-court myth, that is, that the upper courts on appeals can and will safeguard litigants against the trial judge's mistakes concerning the facts. I think that by now the reader knows how delusional that notion is, knows that, when the oral testimony is in conflict as to a pivotal issue of fact, and when some of that testimony supports the trial court's (express or implied) finding on that issue, then the upper court ordinarily has to accept that finding. Usually it can refuse to do so only if it appears in the written or printed record of the trial that the finding was the product of the trial judge's incompetence, unfairness or dishonesty. Such matters, however, show up in such a record in but the tiniest fraction of cases. Because of the inherent subjectivity of the trial judge's decisional process, his deliberate or unintentional disregard or misunderstanding of honest and truthworthy oral testimony is ordinarily hidden from the scrutiny of the upper court.

Since, however, the upper-court myth creates and perpetuates the illusory notion that upper courts can offset all the failings of the trial judges, the public puts too much reliance on, and gives too much kudos to, upper-court judges. Note the consequences: In states where judges are elected, the politicos, responsive to public opinion, usually nominate, for upper-court positions, lawyers of distinguished ability and integrity. But, as the public is not onto the far greater importance of the trial courts, the politicos often (not always) are much less careful about whom they nominate to sit on the trial-court bench. I do not mean that many elected trial judges are not men of competence, character and ability. I do mean that the public tends to give relatively little attention to their qualifications.

Yet the duties of trial judges demand far more ability than do those of "higher" court judges. Concerned as the latter are primarily with the legal rules, knowledge of those rules and skill in dealing with them constitute the chief requisites for the performance of their task. Many lawyers possess such knowledge and skill, which can be acquired by an intelligent man through an education in a law school and a few years in practice. But neither in the law schools—as legal education goes today—nor elsewhere can a lawyer obtain any systematic training necessary to give him the peculiar skills a trial judge should have.

Writing of trial judges, Professor Morgan recently said: "Of course, no rules prescribed by legislation or judicial decision can create character or competence [in a trial judge]." "But," he continued, "it is equally true that no system of administering justice can be satisfactory if constructed on the hypothesis that the trial judge will be crooked or incompetent." Then he went on to say, "Inevitably some trial judges will be slippery, prejudiced or otherwise unfit for office." Please mark the word "inevitably." I grant the inevitability of some such misfortunes. But what are we doing to reduce them to a minimum? If the number of ill-equipped trial judges is larger than is inevitable, then we have negligently provided ourselves with a system of administering justice bound to be unsatisfactory to an extent that is not inevitable but evitable. I think we have been astonishingly careless in our haphazard method of educating and selecting men to serve as trial judges. . . .

\* \* \* \* \*

The upper-court myth and legal rule magic are plainly related. For the perpetuation of that myth, and for the widespread dissemination of the belief in that magic, American legal education must take considerable blame. And if the addiction to such magic indicates a core of somewhat neurotic attitudes, the explanation of the faults of legal education in this respect are not far to seek. For contemporary law-school teaching got its basic mood at Harvard, some seventy years ago, from a brilliant neurotic, Christopher Columbus Langdell.

When Langdell was himself a law student he was almost constantly in the law library. He served for several years as an assistant librarian. He slept, at times, on the library table. One of his friends found him one day absorbed in an ancient lawbook. "As he drew near," we are told, "Langdell looked up and said, in a tone of mingled exhilaration and regret, and with an emphatic gesture, 'Oh, if only I could have lived in the time of the Plantagenets!' "

After graduation, he practiced as a lawyer in New York City for sixteen years. But he seldom tried a case or went into court. His clients were mostly other lawyers for whom, after much lucubration, he wrote briefs or prepared pleadings. He led a peculiarly secluded life. A biographer says of him, "In the almost inaccessible retirement of his office, and in the library of the Law Institute, he did the greater part of his work. He went little into company."

Is it any wonder that such a man had an obsessive and almost exclusive interest in books? The raw material of what he called "law," he devoutly believed, was to be discovered in a library and nowhere else; it consisted, as he himself said, solely of what could be found in print. Practicing law to Langdell meant chiefly the writing of briefs, examination of published "authorities." The lawyer-client relation, the numerous nonrational factors involved in a trial, the face-to-face appeals to the emotions of juries, the elements that go to make up what is loosely known as the "atmosphere" of a case—everything that is undisclosed in upper-court opinions—was virtually unknown (and was therefore all but meaningless) to Langdell. The greater part of the realities of the life of the average lawyer was unreal to him.

What was almost exclusively real to him he translated into the law-school curriculum when in 1870, at the age of forty-four, he became a teacher at Harvard Law School, and, soon after, its Dean. His pedagogic theory reflected the man. The actual varied experiences of the practicing lawyer were, to Langdell, improper materials for the teacher and the student. They must, he insisted, shut their eyes to such data. They must devote themselves exclusively to what was discoverable in the library. The essence of his teaching philosophy he expressed thus: "First that law is a science; second, that all the available materials of that science are contained in printed books." This second proposition, it is said, was "intended to exclude the traditional methods of learning law by work in a lawyer's office, or attendance upon the proceedings of courts of justice."

Langdell declared that "the library is to us what the laboratory is to the chemist or the physicist and what the museum is to the naturalist. * * * The most essential feature of the [Harvard Law] School, that which distinguishes it most widely from all other schools of which I have any knowledge, is the library. * * * Without the library the School would lose its most important characteristics, and indeed its identity." In the same vein, the President of Harvard commented, not long after, "The Corporation recognizes that the library is the very heart of the Law School." "What qualifies a person to teach law," wrote Langdell, "is not experience in the work of a lawyer's office, not experience in dealing with men, not experience in the trial or argument of causes, not experience, in short, in using law, but experience in learning law. * * * In The Centennial History of Harvard Law School (published in 1918), it was said, "If it be granted that law is to be taught as a science and in the scientific spirit, previous experience in practice becomes as unnecessary as is continuance in practice after teaching begins."

This philosophy of legal education was that of a man who cherished "inaccessible retirement." Inaccessibility, a nostalgia for the forgotten past, devotion to the hush and quiet of a library, the building of a pseudoscientific system based solely upon book materials—of these Langdell compounded the Langdell method.

The neurotic escapist character of Langdell soon stamped itself on the educational programs of our leading law schools. Unavoidably, their acceptance of the Langdell-Harvard method meant that most of the university law-school teachers were men who had never practiced or had practiced for only a brief interval. . . .

The Langdell spirit choked American legal education. It tended to compel even the experienced practitioner, turned teacher, to belittle his experience at the bar. It tended to force him to place primary emphasis on the library, to regard a collection of books as the heart of the school. A school with such a heart is what one may well imagine. The men who teach there, however interested some of them may once have been in the actualities of law offices and courtrooms, feel obliged to pay but subordinate regard to those actualities. The books are the thing. The words, not the deeds. Or only those deeds which become words.

Langdell invented, and our leading law-schools still employ, the so-called "case system." That is, the students are supposed to study cases. They do not. They study, almost entirely, upper-court opinions. Any such opinion, however, is not a case, but a small fraction of a case, its tail end. The law students are like future horticulturists studying solely cut flowers; or like future architects studying merely pictures of buildings. They resemble prospective dog breeders who never see anything but stuffed dogs. (Perhaps there is a correlation between such stuffed-dog legal education and the overproduction of stuffed shirts in my profession.)

In such a school, that which is not in books has become "unscientific"; it may perhaps have truth, but it is a lesser truth, relatively unreal; true reality is achieved by facts only when reported in books. To be sure, Dean Pound, many years ago, spoke of "law in action." That awakened hopes. But has Harvard been showing its students "law in action"? The students have had the opportunity to read in books and law-review articles about some very limited phases of "law" in action. But that, at most, is "law in action" in the library.

At Harvard's law school the students are given courses in evidence, practice, and pleading. Close by, courts are in action, and especially trial courts, where one can observe evidence in action, practice in action, pleading in action. Are the students urged to attend the courts frequently? Do they spend many days there? Are they accompanied there by their professors who comment thereafter on what has been observed? Are the students familiar with the development of cases in those courts? Are they asked to speculate on the next move to be made in a trial—at a time when the results of that move depend on foresight and skill, instead of hindsight? Are the procedural possibilities of a real lawsuit shown to the students by their professors, together with the so-called "substantive law" formulae—or are the two split up into separate courses? Do they make any effort to watch, describe and interpret courts in action? I mention Harvard. I could as well refer to almost any of the leading university law schools.

"Law in action" was a happy phrase. It contained, to be sure, that miserably ambiguous word "law." Yet it was a pointer or guidepost; it seemed to indicate a new direction. But what university law school has followed the pointer? The phrase "law in action" has remained largely a phrase; at any rate, so far as legal pedagogy is concerned, the function of the phrase, psychologically, has been principally to substitute a new verbal formula for revised conduct. The contents of the bottle remained much the same; the label was changed. One is reminded of the scene in the Gilbert and Sullivan opera where the policemen march around and around the stage, promising the distracted father that they will rescue his daughters from the pirates who have abducted them. "We go, we go," shout the policemen as they continue to march in circles. "But they don't go," exclaims the father despairingly. . . .

If it were not for a tradition which blinds us, would we not consider it ridiculous that, with litigation laboratories just around the corner, law schools confine their students to what they can learn about litigation in books? What would we say of a medical school where students were taught surgery solely from the printed page? No one, if he could do otherwise, would teach the art of playing golf by having the teacher talk about golf to the prospective player and having the latter read a book relating to the subject. The same holds for toe dancing, swimming, automobile-driving, haircutting, or cooking wild ducks. Is legal practice more simple? Why should law teachers and their students be more hampered than golf teachers and their students? Who would learn golf from a golf instructor, contenting himself with sitting in the locker room analyzing newspaper accounts of important golf matches that had been played by someone else several years before? Why should law teachers be like Tomlinson? " 'This I have read in a book,' he said, 'and that was told to me. And this I have thought that another man thought of a Prince of Muscovy.' "

Legal practice, I have said, is an art, a fairly difficult one. Why make its teaching more indirect, more roundabout, more baffling and difficult than teaching golf? But that is what the Langdell method has done. Legal teaching would be no "cinch" at best. The Langdell method has increased the difficulties, has made the task of the teacher as complicated as possible. Even the teacher who is a genius cannot overcome the obstacles. When I was at law school I sat next to a Chinese student who had learned his English in Spain. As a consequence, when he took his notes on what the American professors said, he took them in Spanish. On inquiry, I ascertained that he actually thought them in Chinese. University law teaching today is involved in a process not unlike that. It is supposed to teach men what they are to do in courtrooms and law offices. What the student sees is a reflection in a badly made mirror of a reflection in a badly made mirror of what is going on in the workaday life of lawyers. Why not smash the mirrors? Why not have the students directly observe the subject matter of their study, with the teachers acting as enlightened interpreters of what is thus observed?

As you will see in a moment, I am not advocating a plan for legal education which will produce mere legal technicians. It is imperative that lawyers be made who are considerably more than that. That "more" is alien to the Langdell spirit. That spirit, I grant, is somewhat weakened. The undiluted Langdell principles are nowhere in good repute today. But they are still the basic ingredient of legal pedagogy, so that, whatever else is mixed with them, the dominant flavor is still Langdellian. Our leading law schools are still library-law schools, book-law schools. They are not, as they should be, *lawyer-schools*.

The history of American legal education commenced with the apprentice system: The prospective lawyer "read law" in the office of a practicing lawyer. Daily he saw for himself what courts and lawyers were doing. Before his eyes, legal theories received constant tests in legal practice. Even if he did not always articulate the discrepancies between theory and practice, he felt them. The first American law school, founded by Judge Reeves in the 1780's, was merely the apprentice system on a group basis. The students were still in intimate daily contact with the courts and law offices.

To shorten a long story, legal apprenticeship, à la Reeves or otherwise, all but disappeared in the universities under the impact of Langdellism, as school after school quarantined its students in the library. Some twenty-five years ago, however, the university law schools began to have a troubled conscience. Why, they asked, does what we teach as "law" so little resemble "law" as practiced? The question and the troubled conscience yielded something labeled "sociological jurisprudence." Its watchword was that "law" is one of the "social sciences." All, then, would be well if legal education meshed with sociology, history, ethics, economics and political science. That became the great new dispensation.

It was all to the good, as far as it went. But it did not bring the schools back on the track from which they had fatefully strayed under Langdell's neurotic wizardry. If you want to go from New York to San Francisco, you're not likely to get there soon by voyaging to Rio de Janeiro. Maybe you should go to Rio, even if your ultimate destination is Frisco; for, when you arrive in Frisco, you'll be a wiser citizen, thanks to the knowledge gained on that detour. But if your final goal is Frisco, then Frisco ought to be somewhere on your itinerary. On the itinerary of most university law schools you'll find no mention of a trip, not even of a side-trip, to the courthouse or to real everyday lawyerdom. The student's travels consist almost entirely of detours.

The sole way for these law schools to get back on the main track is unequivocally to repudiate Langdell's morbid repudiation of actual legal practice, to bring the students into intimate contact with courts and lawyers. That simple, obvious step most university law schools have shunned as if such contact would infect the students with intellectual bubonic plague. These schools have been devising the most complicated ways to avoid taking that step; instead of marching straight up to lawyerdom, they have walked all around it. They have been like a man who reaches with his right hand around behind his neck to scratch his left ear.

I maintain that something of immense worth was lost when our leading law schools wholly abandoned the legal apprentice system. I do not for a moment suggest that we return to that old system in its old form. But is it not plain that, without giving up entirely the casebook method and without discarding the invaluable alliance with the so-called "social sciences," our law schools should once more bring themselves into close contact with what clients need and what courts and lawyers actually do? Should the schools not execute an about-face? Should they not now adopt Judge Reeves' eighteenth century apprentice-school method, modifying it in the light of the wisdom gained on the long detour?

Let me now be more specific. I present the following ideas for consideration:

*First:* A considerable proportion of teachers in any law school should be men with not less than five to ten years of varied experience in actual legal practice. They should have had work in trial courts, appellate courts, before administrative agencies, in office work, in dealing with clients, in negotiations, in arbitrations. Their practical experience should not have been confined chiefly to a short period of paper work in a law office. I do not mean that there are not some highly capable teachers with little or no such practical experience: some such teachers, who are brilliantly intuitive, partially make up for their deficiencies by imaginative insight. Nor do I say that mere experience in legal practice will make a man a good law teacher. By and large, teachers are born, not made.

There is room in any school for the mere book-teacher. Part of the job of the lawyers is to write briefs for appellate courts. Brief-writing in part does employ "library law." The exclusively book-lawyer is perhaps at his best in teaching such "library law." But the "library-law" teacher should cease to dominate the schools. More than that, some of the teaching of the art of "persuasive reasoning" in briefs might well be done by men who have written many real briefs for real courts.

Unfortunately, attempted reform of legal pedagogy is frequently in the hands of the "library-law" teacher. With the best will in the world, such a teacher often finds it almost impossible to warp over the old so-called case system so as to adapt it to the needs of the future practicing lawyer. So long as teachers who know little or nothing except what they learned from books under that case system control a law school, the actualities of the lawyer's life are there likely to be considered peripheral and as of secondary importance. A medical school dominated by teachers who had seldom seen a patient, or diagnosed the ailments of flesh-and-blood human beings, or actually performed surgical operations, would not be likely to turn out doctors equipped with a fourth part of what doctors ought to know. But our law schools are not doing for their students even the equivalent of that shoddy job. Many of those schools are so staffed that they are best fitted, not to train lawyers, but to graduate men able to become book-law teachers who can educate still other students to become book-law teachers—and so on ad infinitum, world without end. They are, in large part, excellent book-law-teacher schools. Because many law-school professors have cut themselves off from the realities of a lawyer's life, because viewing these realities from too great a distance, they are classroom lawyers, one might say that they teach what they call law "through a class darkly."

As I have already intimated, the spirit of Langdell so dominates many a university law school that even the practitioner who becomes a teacher in such a school often succumbs to that spirit and forgets the difference between the theory he is teaching and the actual practice he has previously encountered. In some instances, to be sure, this forgetfulness stems from the character of the individual teacher; he may have found practice distasteful and lacking in that certainty which he craved, so that he shifts with delight to a system in which far greater (but illusory) certainty seems to be a reality.

What I suggest, then, is not that all law professors should have had firsthand contacts with courts, lawyers and clients, but that a very large proportion of the professors should be men with such a past.

Second: The case system, so far as it is retained, should be revised so that it will in truth and fact become a case system and not a mere sham case system. A few of the current type of so-called casebooks should be retained to teach dialectic skill in brief-writing. But the study of cases which will lead to some small measure of real understanding of how suits are won, lost and decided, should be based to a very marked extent on reading and analysis of complete records of cases—beginning with the filing of the first papers, through the trial in the trial court and to and through the upper courts. A few months properly spent on one or two elaborate court records, including the briefs (and supplemented by reading of textbooks as well as upper-court opinions), will teach a student more than two years spent on going through twenty of the casebooks now in use. In medical schools, "case histories" are used for instruction. But they are far more complete than the alleged casebooks used in law schools. It is absurd that we should continue to call an upper court opinion a "case."

*Third:* Even if legal casebooks were true casebooks and as complete as medical case histories, they would be insufficient as tools for study. At best, dissection of court records would merely approximate the dissection of cadavers which first-year medical students learn. What would we think of a medical school in which students studied no more than what was to be found in printed case histories, and were deprived of all clinical experience until after they received their M.D. degrees? Our law schools must learn from our medical schools. Law students should be given the opportunity to see legal operations. Their study of cases, at the veriest minimum, should be supplemented by frequent visits, accompanied by law teachers, to both trial and appellate courts. The cooperation of many judges could easily be enlisted. . . .

*Fourth:* Now I come to a point which I consider of the first importance. I have stated that law schools could learn much from the medical schools. The parallel cannot be carried too far. But a brief scrutiny of medical education suggests the use of a device which may be employed as an adequate method of obtaining apprentice work for law students: Medical schools rely to a very large extent on the free medical clinics and dispensaries. There now exist legal clinics in the offices of the Legal Aid Society. Today, however, those offices are by no means the counterpart of the medical clinics and dispensaries. The ablest physicians devote a considerable portion of their time to medical clinics, while the Legal Aid Society is, on the whole, staffed by men who are not leaders of their profession. The Society, too, is limited in the kinds of cases it takes, and most law teachers have little, if any, direct contact with its efforts.

Suppose, however, that there were, in each law school, a legal clinic or dispensary. As before indicated, I think that a considerable part of (but not necessarily all) the teaching staff of a law school should consist of lawyers who already have varied experience in practice. Some of these men could run the law-school legal clinics, assisted by the students. The work of these clinics would be done for little or no charge. The teacher-clinicians would devote their full time to their teaching, which would include such clinical work (although they would also teach other matters). The law-school clinics, however, would not confine their activities to such as are now undertaken by the Legal Aid Society. They would take on important jobs, including trials, for governmental agencies, legislative committees, or other quasi-public bodies. Their professional work would thus comprise virtually every kind of service rendered by law offices. The teacher-clinicians would disclose to their student assistants, both in and out of "office hours," the generalized aspects of the specific doctrines pertinent to the specific cases with which they dealt. Theory and practice would thus constantly interlace. The students would learn to observe the true relation between the contents of upper-court opinions and the work of practicing lawyers and courts. The students would be made to see, among other things, the human side of the administration of justice, including the following:

(a) The hazards of a jury trial: How juries decide cases. The irrational factors that frequently count with juries. The slight effect which the judges' instructions concerning the legal rules often have on verdicts.

(b) How legal rights are affected by lost papers, missing witnesses, perjury and prejudice.

(c) The effects of fatigue, alertness, political pull, graft, laziness, conscientiousness, patience, biases and openmindedness of judges. How legal rights may vary with the judge who tries the case and with that judge's varying and often unpredictable reactions to various kinds of cases and divers kinds of witnesses.

(d) The student would learn that, except fictionally, in trials there is no such thing, for instance, as the "law of torts" as distinguished from specific decisions; and that all legal rules, including the "substantive" rules, in a fundamental sense are procedural, since, as we saw, they are only some among the many implements lawyers use in the courtroom fights we call "litigation."

Participating in the preparation of briefs, both for trial courts and on appeals, the student, with the aid of his teachers, would learn legal rules and doctrines in the exciting context of live cases. The difference is indescribable between that way of learning and that to which students are now restricted in the schools. It is like the difference between kissing a girl and reading a treatise on osculation. Abstract theory divorced from concrete practical interests is usually dull. Montessori discovered that to teach half-witted children arithmetic became easy, if they were given practical activities, interesting to them, in which adding, subtracting and multiplying were necessary aids to the desired specific achievements. They learned by "doing." If that method is good for halfwits, why not for law students (who are presumably whole wits)?

(e) Again, in a living context, the student in my sort of apprentice school would be instructed in the methods used in negotiating contracts and settlements of controversies.

(f) The nature of draftsmanship would become clearer. The student would understand how the lawyer tries to translate the wishes of a client (often inadequately expressed by the client) into wills, contracts or corporate instruments. The university law schools even now can, and some do, accomplish something in the way of teaching draftsmanship. That is, they can do something in the way of showing the students how to draft mortgages or wills or deposit agreements (or the like) which have a more or less stereotyped form. But "creative draftsmanship"—the use of novel fact-materials thrown at the lawyer by his client and sometimes worked out in negotiations with counsel representing the other party to the bargain—cannot be adequately taught in most university law schools as they are now conducted.

(g) In such a school, what I call the "enforcement approach" would soon dawn on the students. That is, they would perceive that in advising a client as to whether he should bring a suit, it may be well to begin with the projected end, to find out what the client wants, and then to ascertain whether by a lawsuit he can obtain it. For instance, if a man owes a client $5,000, but the man is hopelessly insolvent or all his assets are judgment-proof, litigation usually will be fruitless.

(h) Concern with the pressing practical affairs of clients would also induce close-up study of the legislative process in action. The student would be prodded into learning how legislation is made, would come to know the realities behind the "legislative intention" or the "purpose of the legislature."

I will be told—I have been told—that the law schools at most have but three short years to train lawyers, and that these years are already so crowded that there is no time to spend on the sort of firsthand material to which I have been referring. I am not at all impressed by such talk. For in most university law schools the major part of the three years is spent in teaching a relatively simple technique—that of analyzing upper-court opinions, "distinguishing cases," constructing, modifying or criticizing legal doctrines. Three years is much too long for that job. Intelligent men can learn that dialectical technique in about six months. Teach them the dialectic devices as applied to one or two legal topics, and they will have no trouble applying them to other topics. But in the law schools, much of the three years is squandered, by bored students, in applying that technique over and over again—and never with reference to a live client or a real lawsuit—to a variety of subject matters: torts, contracts, corporations, trusts, suretyship, negotiable instruments, evidence, pleading, and so on. Of course, it is impossible in three years, or indeed in thirty-three years, to give or take courses in all the subjects into which what is compendiously called "law" can be subdivided. If you measure the limited number of courses that can be covered in three years over against the totality of subject matters which a lawyer, when engaged in general practice, will encounter, three years seem all too brief. But the point is that the able lawyer, if he has once mastered the dialectic technique in respect of one or two subject matters, can in short order become adept in coping with a great variety of subject matters. Teach a man the use of precedent-distinguishing devices with respect to the so-called law of contracts or trusts, and he will have little trouble in applying those devices with respect to corporations, insurance, or what not.

The myopic "case system" necessarily limits the student to study of a limited portion of a very few subjects. It seems absurd to me that students should not be required to read textbooks and legal encyclopedia articles, not only on those few subjects, but on several dozen others. By that means they will attain a general nodding acquaintance with the leading concepts and peculiar vocabularies of a variety of special topics. Thus they will, for example, overcome that silly dread, experienced by many a graduate, of legal problems concerning patents, copyrights, and admiralty.

Some eighteen years ago, Judge Crane of the New York Court of Appeals characterized the typical graduate of a university law school as follows: "With the practical working of the law he has little or no familiarity. He may come to the bar almost ignorant of how the law should be applied and is applied in daily life. It is, therefore, not unusual to find the brightest student the most helpless practitioner, and the most learned surpassed in the profession by one who does not know half as much. Strange as it may seem, there were some advantages in the older methods of preparation for the bar. As you know, the law school is relatively a matter of recent growth. Formerly, a student, working in the office of a practitioner, combined the study of law with its daily application to the trouble and business of clients. He had an opportunity of hearing the story at the beginning, of noticing how it was handled by his preceptor, of reading the papers prepared to obtain a remedy; he accompanied the lawyer to court and became acquainted with the manner of the presentation of the case to the judge or to the jury. * * * You know much more law after coming out of a university [law school] than these former students ever knew, but you know less about the method of its application, and how to handle and use it."

Is not that a shocking state of affairs? Think of a medical school which would turn out graduates wholly ignorant of how medicine "should be applied and is applied in daily life." In this connection it is important, to note that, according to Flexner, in the best-equipped medical schools, the student "makes and sees made thorough physical examinations, painstaking records, varied and thoroughgoing laboratory tests, at every stage in the study of the patient; the literature of the subject is utilized; at one and the same time medicine is practiced and studied—teachers and students mingling freely and naturally in both activities." In this manner, said Flexner, there has been "effected the fusion of bedside and laboratory procedures alike in the care of patients, in teaching, and in research. * * * From the standpoint of training, fragmentariness, if stimulative and formative, is desirable rather than otherwise. * * * The student must * * * acquire a vivid sense of the existence of breaks, gaps, and problems. The clinics I am now discussing carry him from the patient in the bed to the point beyond which at the moment neither clinical observation nor laboratory investigation can carry him. There he is left, in possession, it is to be hoped, of an acute realization of the relatively narrow limits of human knowledge and human skill, and of the pressing enigmas yet to be solved by intelligence and patience." Here is much that law schools should ponder carefully. The Langdell system is their albatross. They should cast it off.

The core of the law school I propose would be a sort of sublimated law office. Those who attended it would learn by "doing," not merely by reading and talking about doings. But such a school would not limit itself to instruction in legal techniques. It would consider "strictly legal problems" in the light supplied by the other social studies (miscalled "social sciences")— history, ethics, economics, politics, psychology and anthropology. Mere pre-legal courses in those fields, unconnected with the live material of human actions with which lawyers must cope, have proved a failure. The integration ought to be achieved inside the law schools. Some of the teachers who give these courses need not have been practicing lawyers, indeed not be lawyers at all. Most of the synthesis, however, between the instruction in legal techniques and in those other wider perspectives should occur in the courses relating to legal subjects. Accordingly, all the teachers should be men who have themselves made that synthesis.

I may say that, more than twenty years ago, I was one of a group of alumni who pleaded with the University of Chicago Law School thus to widen its curriculum. Far, then, from rejecting the notion of teaching subjects not directly "legal," I would extend such teaching. I would, in addition, show (as I try to do in my own teaching) the connections between legal philosophy and other phases of philosophy. Noting that a trial judge or jury is a kind of historian, I would also show the resemblances and differences between the methods—the logics—of the natural scientists, the historians and the lawyers. I would give a first-rate course in logic and semantics. For example, apropos of the distinction between so-called "substantive law" and "procedure," I would explore the concept of "substance" in philosophy and science. I would have students study the several varieties of psychology as related to the problems of lawyers and judges, including the psychology of judges, juries, witnesses, and litigants. If I had my way I would have the schools point to the error of determinism, economic or otherwise, and severely criticize "behaviorism." I would have them indicate the lack of foundation for cyclical theories of history such as Toynbee's and Spengler's; I would show the intertwining of the legal notion of "natural law" and the notion of "laws of nature"; and I would lay much stress on legal theory.

It is a pleasure to report that many of the law schools today give marked emphasis to the role of lawyers as policy-makers or policy-advisers, and bring home to the students the need for embodying democratic ideals and values in the legal rules. But a law school which really means business about democratic ideals should interest itself mightily, as most of our schools do not, in the problem of thoroughly overhauling our trial methods, and in the problem of the inability of many litigants to obtain justice because of lack of money to meet the expense of obtaining crucial testimony.

Of course, the lawyer's interests should roam far beyond the courthouse aspect of government; yet to say that is not to say that he should submerge his interest in that aspect. Without doubt, the "full role of the lawyer in the community" compels recognition of "his impact on policy-advising and policy-making," and he should therefore give imaginative consideration" to "the whole range of institutions * * * that can be created, improved, or rearranged for community values." But, in our democracy, prominent among the vaunted community values is the right to a fair trial; and a legal education which does not vigorously stimulate the interests of the future lawyers in that direction, while they are still youthfully idealistic, although it may deserve high praise for its general educational worth, is not a democratic education for lawyers. For, I ask once more, if lawyers do not cherish the values of which courts peculiarly should be the guardians, who will or can?

The schools should also concern themselves with the problem of the effect of judicial corruption. Of that problem, law students learn little or nothing. If one inquires why, he is told that dishonest judges and purchased or "fixed" decisions are "abnormal." That answer does not content me. I share the hope that all crooks will be driven from the bench; but that hope, alas, is not yet a reality—and probably will never be if the law schools maintain their present policy of failing to discuss the subject in classrooms. What would one say of an engineering school where students heard nothing of wind pressure? Such an obstacle to engineering is deplorable from an ideal point of view. But is it to be called "abnormal" and therefore ignored? Engineering students properly study frictionless engines; but they will do injury to mankind unless they are also taught much about friction. Should not law students be taught about judicial "friction?" What would be thought of a college course in city government in which no mention was made of "graft" and "pull"? How can we afford to have men practice law who have been educated to shut their eyes to the effect of those factors on decisions? (In the case of *Root Refining Co. v. Universal Oil Products Co.*, decided in 1948, . . . the court held that, in two earlier cases, the decisions had resulted from the bribery of a judge. That judge, on the bench for many years, had decided a multitude of cases. All those decisions are now, necessarily, under suspicion of having been purchased. It would be instructive to have law students track down those decisions to see which of them became precedents that lower courts were obliged to and did follow.)

Not of course, in order that they may learn how to use bribes or political pull, but for these obvious reasons: (1) A lawyer should know which judges are corrupt, or susceptible to political influence, so that, when possible, he may keep his clients' cases from coming before those judges. (2) Lawyers should do what they can to help the public eliminate such blights on the judicial process. But lawyers engaged in practice before the courts find that a most perplexing problem: If some particular lawyers try to cause the removal of a judge they suspect of corruption, and if they fail, that judge probably will, in roundabout ways, visit his wrath on their clients. For that reason, practicing lawyers usually hesitate to initiate such removal proceedings. Moreover, most busy lawyers tend to lose a keen interest in reforms. Here is a problem which, if it is to be solved, should be discussed in the schools with the law students who, still in their formative years, are generally rife with idealism.

It is objected that public reference to any judicial dishonesty may create the incorrect and unfair belief that many judges are dishonest. The answer is to say—as I do say unequivocally—that fortunately most of the judiciary is honest, that but a very few scamps manage to get on the bench, and that the best way to avoid unfairness to the vast majority of judges is to oust the few rascals.

"Policy" teaching will be fruitless if "policy-minded" lawyers are not trained to protect policies when under fire in the trial courts. Let me give an illustration of the way such lawyer's know-how, or its lack, may vitally affect policies. In 1935–1937, the constitutionality of the PWA statute was under attack in litigation in the federal courts. When I entered that litigation for the government, I found that the cases were on appeal. They had not been tried on evidence, because my book-lawyer predecessor had "demurred" to the complaints, thereby admitting the truth of the allegations of fact made by the plaintiffs in those complaints. Those admitted allegations were to the effect that the PWA Administrator, Harold Ickes, had, in dozens of ways, shockingly misused his powers under the statute. The Solicitor General, Stanley Reed (now Mr. Justice Reed), and I agreed that, with those facts admitted, the defense of the statute's validity was in danger, since there would be such a bad "atmosphere" as to arouse marked hostility on the part of even the most liberal Justices when the cases were argued in the Supreme Court. Through considerable maneuvering, we managed to have the suits remanded, by several upper courts, to the lower courts for trial. We won those trials, obtaining findings of fact, based on the evidence, which flatly contradicted the plaintiffs' factual allegations, thus completely dissipating the bad atmosphere. Then in the Supreme Court we were victorious. I strongly suspect that, but for those trial tactics, PWA and the valuable policy it represented would have been judicially destroyed.

Although no lawyer should be unversed in the way courts function, it is true that many lawyers never get into court. They advise clients, draft their contracts and wills, attend corporate directors' meetings, help to negotiate business transactions, settle disputes without recourse to litigation, engage in arbitrations. Most university law schools do not even hint at the skills such lawyer activities demand. For instance, some of Columbia's graduates, honor men in their day at school, and now, experts in such skills, successfully practicing in New York City, have told me they would be delighted to talk about their experiences to Columbia law students. Yet Columbia never thinks of inviting them to do so. Such talks would have some slight educational value. But the only way for students really to learn those skills would be to see them in operation and to participate in those operations. Near at hand to every law school are those laboratories known as law offices, where students could learn the relation of their theoretical studies to the realities of a practicing lawyer's life. A few university law-school teachers now do take their students to look inside those laboratories. Such visits are indeed desirable. But they are pale substitutes for the real thing. The real thing would be to have such laboratories inside the law school. I do not mean the so-called "Practice Laboratory," now in vogue in some schools, where students draft documents for supposititious or paper clients. I mean, as I've said, law schools which are themselves, in part, law offices dealing with flesh-and-blood clients.

To altogether too many law teachers are applicable the comments of Anatole France: "There are bookish souls for whom the universe is but paper and ink. The man whose body is animated by such a soul spends his life before his desk, without any care for the realties whose graphic representation he studies so obstinately. He knows of the labors, sufferings, and hopes of men only what can be [found in books] sewn on to tapes and bound in morocco. * * * He has never looked out of the window. Such was the worthy Peignot, who collected other people's opinions to make books out of them. * * * He conceived of passions as subjects for monographs, and knew that nations perish in a certain number of octavo pages." Such an attitude, on the part of law teachers, means, I think, moral irresponsibility. (Their attitude recalls the story of Maxwell and Todhunter: Maxwell, having contrived an experiment which disclosed a new optical phenomenon, asked Todhunter to examine it. Todhunter refused. He explained that he had been teaching the subject of optics all his life, "and I do not want all my ideas upset by seeing it.") It induces in many a law student when he emerges from school a bitter, cynical, disillusionment. . . .

It is often said that it will do no harm to leave the law student ignorant of a large part of the facts in the legal world he will later enter, that he can learn those facts after his graduation. That argument comes to this: Have the student spend three long years being miseducated—that is, receiving erroneous impressions about the ways in which many courts and lawyers behave—because he will be able to dissipate those impressions subsequently. Dr. Brickner gave an apt reply to a similar argument: "It is a horrible thing to picture what is involved in the customary idea that * * * we have about many an adolescent, 'Oh, he is being disillusioned, he will soon be all right'— the idea that it is a customary thing for people who grow up in our society to have to go through a stage of disillusionment. That means we have been illusioned. What kind of education is it that has to be undone?" If, said Bentham, in his *Comment on the Commentaries*, "there be a case in which students stand in need of instruction, it is where the generality of books that come into their hands represent things in a different light from true ones. True it is, that after many errors and disappointments, observation and prac- tice may let a beginner into the bottom of these mysteries; but what sort of an excuse is it to give for feeding him with falsehood, that some time or other he may chance to find it out?" . . .

Professor Max Rheinstein of Chicago, . . . commenting on my notions of a revised law-school curriculum, says that I am calling for the development of the "science of administration of justice." Change the word "science" to "art," and I agree. Instruction in such an art would include firsthand observa- tion of all that courts, administrative agencies, and legislatures actually do. Such instruction would serve three purposes. First, it would aim to equip future lawyers to cope with courthouse realities, no matter how ugly and socially detrimental some of those realities are; for a lawyer cannot com- petently represent his clients if he is ignorant of the devices which his ad- versaries may utilize on behalf of their clients. Second, such instruction would stimulate the contrivance of specific practical means by which existing trial-court techniques can be improved, in order that justice may be judicially administered more in accord with democratic ideals. Third, it would train men to become trial judges.

A law school which turns its back on the observable happenings in the trial courts inevitably does what Langdell intended: It devotes itself basically to the R's. It teaches students little about those elusive characteristics of the F's on which I have been dwelling. And an F-less study of the judicial process necessarily yields a magical attitude toward the courts.

Our law schools, being principally library schools, do an admirable job of producing library-lawyers. Such lawyers function well in upper courts, since those courts are largely library-courts. A first-rate graduate of a first-rate law school, after a few years, will therefore make a first-rate upper-court judge. But our law schools do practically nothing to educate men to become trial judges. Yet, as I said, the role of the trial judge is far more important, and his task far more difficult, than that of the appellate judge. To educate a future trial judge adequately, it would be necessary to train him elaborately in the skills of fact-finding. One of the principal reasons for the backwardness of judicial fact-finding is that the law schools have shirked their obligation to teach those skills. Moreover, thanks to their disregard of the trial court, the legal profession is not sufficiently alive to the need of improving fact-finding.

In defense of much of conventional method of legal pedagogy, someone might perhaps quote Abe Martin's aphorism: "Nobuddy kin talk half as interestin' as the feller that ain't hampered by facts or infermashun"; or the comment of Ho Hum, the sage of Chinatown, that "if no man talked of that which he did not understand, the silence would be unbearable." But I think little of that defense.

However, let me say again, emphatically, that all university law schools and all their teachers do not deserve my criticism. Yale Law School, for example, is coming ever closer to grips with lawyers' realities; and all the schools have professors who are outstanding exceptions to my description of the genus "law-teacher." Bradway, at Duke University Law School, has been using clinical teaching methods for some years. Not long since, I received a letter from Professor Lon Fuller of Harvard in which he said that he, for one, had become convinced that "one of the major deficiencies in American legal education is in dealing with facts," in its overemphasis on the work of upper courts. If all legal pedagogues soon adopt that point of view, the reign of legal magic, before long, may be doomed. But, alas, that reign is still unfortunately powerful in many law schools.

*Courts on Trial* (1949)

PART 4 ❧ The Protection

of Due Process

EDITOR'S NOTE ❧ Appointed by President Roosevelt to the United States Court of Appeals for the Second Circuit in May, 1941, Judge Frank served there until his death on January 13, 1957. The eighteen judicial opinions which appear in this section were chosen from many hundreds written during his tenure in that office; I believe they best reflect his devotion to those procedures essential for the preservation of civil liberties. I made no attempt to base my choice on what is necessarily of the greatest legal interest or importance. Rather, my selections were governed by what I believe will arouse the attention of the lay reader and stimulate his own passion for judicial fair play.

In *United States v. Rubenstein* Judge Frank said: "[A]ll our complicated judicial apparatus yields but a human judgment, not at all sure to be correct, affecting the life of another human being. If we are at all imaginative, we will comprehend what that judgment will mean to him, and what a horror it will be if we wrongly decide against him. . . . [I]t seems to me that . . . if mankind's development has any significance against the background of eternity, then the dignity of each individual man is not an empty phrase." In the judicial opinions which follow the reader will encounter Judge Frank's conviction that the courts must exercise a never-ending vigilance against judicial and law-enforcement procedures which threaten the substantive rights of any individual—a judge's instructions which, confusing the jury, might prejudice the case; the "third degree"; an indigent denied a hearing "for the crime of being poor"; an appeal by a prosecutor to the passions of the jury; economic exploitation of the individual; an abridgment of the privilege

[ 289 ]

against self-incrimination; the use of trespass and unreasonable search and seizure to build the prosecution's case—indeed, any unlawful encroachment of human rights. These concerns, together with his remarkable ability to empathize with the appellant in the case before him, were, I think, the core of his greatness as a judge.

I wish to comment specifically on one case, *United States* v. *Rosenberg*, in which Judge Frank wrote the opinion for the court. Because the Rosenbergs were condemned to die, this case caused him great anguish. Unalterably opposed to capital punishment (and particularly appalled by its application here), nevertheless as a judge of the Court of Appeals he was confined to answering this question: Did the defendants receive a fair trial? Painfully, he agreed with his fellow judges that there were no grounds on which to reverse the jury's verdict as to the Rosenbergs. But, as Edmond Cahn has pointed out, in drafting his opinion, Judge Frank in effect urged the Supreme Court to consider the question of the legality of the death sentences. However, the Court declined to examine the questions which he raised.

The reader will not fail to note that Judge Frank wrote a great number of dissenting opinions, a measure of his philosophical differences with his judicial brothers. Perhaps Judge Charles Clark, with whom Judge Frank shared the bench, best summed up the nature of these differences: "[T]he most consistent of [Judge Frank's] struggles was that involving respect for the individual—personalized as against mass judicial action. If we differed, he and I, it tended to be here, where he felt that my aspirations for a uniform procedure, impartial as to all, were likely to rest heavily on some poor person not prepared therefor, and that such a person must be protected, whatever future inconsistencies might come back to trouble us." The number of cases granted review by the Supreme Court on the basis of Judge Frank's dissents was, so one scholar writes, greater than in the case of any other circuit judge.

That his concern for "the dignity of each individual man" did not go unappreciated is clear from the following letter from a prison inmate to a Yale Law School professor, the prisoner's appointed counsel: "Dear Professor, I guess you know the bad news by now. . . . One of the great Judges of the Federal Judge's [sic] for the poor man and for a man's constitutional rights, Hon. Jerome Frank, has died. He was our friend. . . . Judge Frank has all my blessing. I cannot say no more. Without him I never would have had a chance. . . ." ❧

# UNITED STATES v. ROSENBERG ❧

E ARLY IN 1952 Ethel Rosenberg, her husband, Julius, and Morton Sobell went to trial on a charge of espionage. They had been indicted for giving military secrets concerning the atomic bomb to the Soviet Union. The indictment also named Harry Gold and Ruth Greenglass (the wife of Ethel's brother David) as conspirators but not as defendants; David Greenglass and Anatoli Yakelov, both named as defendants, were tried separately. The Greenglasses and Elizabeth Bentley, a former espionage agent, presented the government's most important testimony with respect to the Rosenbergs; Max Elitcher, a Navy engineer, testified as to Sobell's involvement in the conspiracy. The prosecution contended that, in November, 1944, the Rosenbergs, via Ruth Greenglass, first received secret information from a reluctant David Greenglass, then stationed as a soldier in the Los Alamos atomic experimental station; that later, when David was on furlough, he wrote out a fuller report of the Los Alamos project for Julius, sketching a lens mold used in the experiment. At that time, Greenglass became fully embroiled in the conspiracy, meeting with certain Russian agents and helping to lay the groundwork for further espionage. According to the prosecution, Sobell, a college classmate of Rosenberg, joined Julius in involving Elitcher as a source of espionage information; the prosecution also contended that Sobell regularly delivered military secrets to Rosenberg for transmittal to Russia. The government pointed to the Rosenbergs' apparent attempt to flee the country and to Sobell's actual flight as further proof of guilt. On the stand, the Rosenbergs denied all the evidence with regard to espionage; they admitted to having a close social and business relationship with Greenglass and to knowing Sobell and Elitcher. Sobell, who also pleaded not guilty, did not take the stand. The jury returned a guilty verdict for all three defendants. The judge sentenced the Rosenbergs to death and Sobell to thirty years' imprisonment. Judge Frank, writing for the court, carefully scrutinizes the arguments made by defense counsel as to alleged errors in the conduct of the trial and the severity of the death sentence. On one issue, that of Sobell's right to a new trial, he dissents.

FRANK, *Circuit Judge*: Since two of the defendants must be put to death if the judgments stand, it goes without saying that we have scrutinized the record with extraordinary care to see whether it contains any of the errors asserted on this appeal.

1. The Supreme Court has held that the Espionage Act of 1917 makes criminal, and subject to the prescribed penalties, the communication of the prohibited information to the advantage of "any foreign nation," even if such communication does not injure this country. See *Gorin* v. *United States* . . . where the Court said: "Nor do we think it necessary to prove that the information obtained was to be used to the injury of the United States. The statute is explicit in phrasing the crime of espionage as an act of obtaining information relating to the national defense 'to be used * * * to the advantage of any foreign nation.' No distinction is made between friend or enemy. Unhappily the status of a foreign government may change. The evil which the statute punishes is the obtaining or furnishing of this guarded information, either to our hurt or another's gain." Accordingly, the trial judge, in the case at bar, properly instructed the jury as follows: "I charge you that whether the Union of Soviet Socialist Republics was an ally or friendly nation during the period of the alleged conspiracy is immaterial, and you are not to consider that at all in your deliberations."

In *United States* v. *Heine*, . . . we so interpreted the statute as to make it inapplicable to information which our armed forces had consented to have made public. The defendants now assert that the indictment, which followed the language of the statute, was fatally defective since it did not allege that the matter there described was not public. But the statutory language necessarily imported its correct judicial intepretation. Sonsequently the indictment was sufficient under Rule 7(c) of the Federal Rules of Criminal Procedure which provides: "The indictment or the information shall be a plain, concise and definite written statement of the essential facts constituting the offense charged. * * * The indictment or information shall state for each count the official or customary citation of the statute, rule, regulation or other provision of law which the defendant is alleged therein to have violated." (Rule 7[f] says: "The court for cause may direct the filing of a bill of particulars." The Rosenbergs, like Sobell, might have requested such a bill if they were really confused as to whether or not they were charged with transmitting secret information. One of the overt acts charged in the indictment covered the reception by Julius of sketches of the experiment conducted at the Los Alamos project, a good indication that the material involved was secret.) In the Gorin case, the Supreme Court rejected the contention of the unconstitutionality of the statute on the ground of its vagueness under the due process clause of the Fifth Amendment. By implication, it sustained the validity of the statute against any identical argument of vagueness, such as the one urged here, under the Sixth Amendment, since the Court's decision was primarily concerned with whether the statute set up definite enough standards of guilt to advise a citizen of what exactly was forbidden and *ipso facto* a potential defendant of what exactly he was charged with doing. The Court said: "But we find no uncertainty in this statute which deprives a person of the ability to predetermine whether a contemplated action is criminal under the provisions of this law. The obvious delimiting words in the statute are those requiring 'intent or reason to believe that the information to be obtained is to be used to the injury of the United States, or to the advantage of any foreign nation.' This requires those prosecuted to have acted in bad faith. The sanctions apply only where scienter is established. * * * Finally we are of the view that the use of the words 'national defense' has given them, as here employed, a well understood connotation. * * * National defense, the Government maintains, 'is a generic concept of broad connotations, referring to the military and naval establishments and the related activities of national preparedness.' We agree that the words 'national defense' in the Espionage Act carry that meaning. * * * The language employed appears sufficiently definite to apprise the public of prohibited activities and is consonant with due process."

We think the statute valid under the First Amendment as well. The communication to a foreign government of secret material connected with the national defense can by no far-fetched reasoning be included within the area of First-Amendment protected free speech. As interpreted in the Gorin case, the statute forbids nothing except such communication. The Court's decision that the statute was definite enough to tell citizens what was prohibited satisfies appellants' contention that many legitimate exercises of First-Amendment rights will fall within the language of the statute. The Court said, "This requires those prosecuted to have acted in bad faith. The sanctions apply only where scienter is established." Stripped down, defendants' First-Amendment argument is the same as their argument under the Fifth and Sixth—that is, vagueness—and we think the Supreme Court has answered that argument. "A criminal statute must be sufficiently definite to give notice of the required conduct to one who would avoid its penalties, and to guide the judge in its application and the lawyer in defending one charged with its violation. But few words possess the precision of mathematical symbols, most statutes must deal with untold and unforeseen variations in factual situations, and the practical necessities of discharging the business of government inevitably limit the specificity with which legislators can spell out prohibitions. Consequently, no more than a reasonable degree of certainty can be demanded. Nor is it unfair to require that one who deliberately goes perilously close to an area of proscribed conduct shall take the risk that he may cross the line." *Boyce Motor Lines v. United States.* . . .

2. The defendants, in their briefs and oral arguments in this court, have attacked the reliability of the damaging testimony given against them by the government's chief witnesses who are all self-confessed spies, and particularly the credibility of the testimony of the Greenglasses, one of whom the government has not prosecuted and the other of whom received a relatively mild sentence. Doubtless, if that testimony were disregarded, the conviction could not stand. But where trial is by jury, this court is not allowed to consider the credibility of witnesses or the reliability of testimony. Particularly in the federal judicial system, that is the jury's province.

The jury here were warned by the trial judge as follows: "As to the testimony of David Greenglass, Ruth Greenglass and Harry Gold, you must consider it carefully and act upon it with caution, for they are accused of being accomplices. An accomplice in this case is anybody that the prosecution charges agreed or confederated with any or all of the defendants in the commission of the crime charged, as alleged in the indictment. I am not saying that, because a person is a co-conspirator or an accomplice, he or she is not to be believed. If this were so, many cases in this court could not be proven. In the Federal Court a defendant can be convicted upon the uncorroborated testimony of an accomplice whose testimony satisfies the jury of the defendant's guilt beyond a reasonable doubt." So instructed, the jury found defendants guilty. Faced with such a verdict, this court is obligated to assume that the jury believed the evidence unfavorable to the defendants. On that assumption, the evidence to sustain the verdict is more than ample.

3. Defendants, however, tell us that the trial judge behaved himself so improperly as to deprive them of a fair trial. Defendants' counsel first broached this suggestion on a motion for mistrial after all the evidence had been heard, said that the judge's alleged fault had been "inadvertent," and added that the judge had "been extremely courteous to us and afforded us lawyers every privilege that a lawyer should expect in a criminal case." Soon after the denial of this motion, counsel for the Rosenbergs, summing up for the jury, stated that "we feel that the trial has been conducted * * * with that dignity and that decorum that befits an American trial." Still later, the same counsel said that "the court conducted itself as an American judge." These

remarks, by a highly competent and experienced lawyer, are not compatible with the complaints now made. Nor are those complaints deserved. We think the judge stayed well inside the discretion allowed him.

He is charged mainly with taking too active a part in the trial process by his questioning of witnesses. By this questioning he is alleged to have (1) emphasized key points of the government's case; (2) protected and rehabilitated government witnesses; (3) commented on evidence as immaterial or dismissed contradictions brought out by defense attorney as not very important or convincing; (4) examined the defendants with hostility. We have carefully examined each of the hundred or so incidents cited by defendants. . . . In general, we can find no purpose in the judge's questioning except that of clarification. If, with that purpose, he gave witnesses who had contradicted themselves a chance to resolve that conflict, and took away defendants' temporary advantage with the jury, it was an unavoidable incident of his unchallenged power to bring out the facts of the case. See, for example, *Simon v. United States*. . . . "It cannot be too often repeated or too strongly emphasized that the function of a federal trial judge is not that of an umpire or of a moderator at a town meeting. He sits to see that justice is done in the cases heard before him; and it is his duty to see that a case on trial is presented in such way as to be understood by the jury, as well as by himself. He should not hesitate to ask questions for the purpose of developing the facts; and it is no ground of complaint that the facts so developed may hurt or help one side or the other. In no case is the exercise of this power of the judge more important than in one like this, involving, as it does, lengthy circumstantial testimony, the force of which may be lost upon the jury if it is not properly presented or if its salient features are not called to the jury's attention at the time. The judge is the only disinterested lawyer connected with the proceeding. He has no interest except to see that justice is done, and he has no more important duty than to see that the facts are properly developed and that their bearing upon the question at issue are clearly understood by the jury." If some of his questions and comments indicated his opinion of the merits of counsel's attack or of the witnesses' testimony, it cannot be said that he committed reversible error, since, unlike judges in many of our state courts, a federal judge may comment outright on any portion of the evidence, telling the jury how it struck him, whom he believed, or disbelieved, and the like, provided only that he advises the jury that they are in no way bound by his expressions of such views. . . . Here the trial judge said in his charge: "No matter how careful a judge may be to avoid it, there is always the possibility that the jury or some particular juror may get an impression that the judge has some opinion with reference to the guilt or innocence of the defendants, or that he thinks that some particular phase of the case is more important than another, or that some particular witness is more credible than another, or that a certain inference of facts should not be made and so on. If you have formed any such impression you must put it out of your mind and utterly disregard it. Nothing I have said during the trial nor in these instructions was intended to give any such impression; nor were any remarks or questions addressed to any of the witnesses or to counsel so intended. On the contrary, I have been scrupulously careful to avoid any comment which might even remotely suggest that I considered the subjects of the weight of testimony, the credibility of witnesses, the inferences to be drawn or the relative importance of one segment of the evidence as against another, of the determination of the guilt or innocence of the defendants, as coming within the orbit of any of my functions as the presiding Judge in this trial. And so I tell you again, you are the sole and exclusive judges of the facts of this case; you, and you alone, will pass upon the credibility of all the witnesses, all in accordance with the instructions on that subject, which I shall give you later. Despite anything said by me or by counsel, your recollection of the testimony must prevail whenever your recollection differs from what I have said or what your counsel for either side have said in argument or otherwise; it is for you to determine what the proofs adduced by both sides disclose, regardless of anything said by me in the brief and necessarily incomplete summaries which I have given you of the contentions of the parties; and it is for you and you alone to weigh the proofs, draw such inferences of fact therefrom as you determine should be drawn and to decide each and every one of the issues of fact in the case."

4. Evidence was introduced to the effect (1) that the defendants expressed a preference for the Russian social and economic organization over ours, and (2) that they were members of the Communist Party. The defendants say this evidence was incompetent to show they would commit espionage for Russia, and that it improperly inflamed the jury against them. We think the evidence possessed relevance. An American's devotion to another country's welfare cannot of course constitute proof that he has spied for that other country. But one may reasonably infer that he is more likely to spy for it than other Americans not similarly devoted. Hence this attitude bears on a possible motive for his spying, or on a possible intent to do so when there is other evidence in the case that he did such spying. We have held such testimony admissible in a similar case involving espionage for Nazi Germany. *United States* v. *Molzahn.* . . . See also *Haupt* v. *United States.* . . .

Communist Party membership presents a somewhat more complicated problem than pro-Soviet statements. The government had to prove that the Communist Party was tied to Soviet causes in order to make membership in it meaningful as evidence of motive or intent to aid Russia. Early in the trial, the trial judge so cautioned the jury: "I want you to understand right at the outset that the fact that they were members of the Communist Party does not establish the elements necessary to prove them guilty of the crime charged in this indictment which is conspiracy to commit espionage. * * * The government will have to establish that there is some connection between communism and committing the offense charged in the indictment." To that end, the government put Elizabeth Bentley on the stand. She testified that the American Communist Party was part of, and subject to, the Communist International; that the Party received orders from Russia to propagandize, spy, and sabotage; and that Party members were bound to go along with those orders under threat of expulsion. If the jury believed her, she supplied the missing link connecting the Communist Party with the Soviet Union, and making Communist Party membership probative of motive or intent to aid Russia.

Of course, such evidence can be highly inflammatory in a jury trial. This court and others have recognized that the Communist label yields marked ill-will for its American wearer. . . . Whether and how much of that kind of evidence should come into a trial like this is a matter for carefully-exercised judicial discretion. We think the trial judge here did not abuse that discretion. Each time Party membership was alluded to, and again in his final charge, the judge cautioned the jurors "not to determine the guilt or innocence of a defendant on whether or not he is a Communist." It may be such warnings are no more than an empty ritual without any practical effect on the jurors; see Mr. Justice Jackson in *Krulewitch v. United States*. . . . If so, this danger is one of the risks run in a trial by jury; and the defendants made no effort to procure a trial by a judge alone, under Criminal Rule 23(a).

5. Early in the trial Elitcher testified that he had accompanied Sobell on a hurried ride to the Rosenbergs to deliver "valuable" information to Julius. This ride was precipitated by Elitcher's suspicion, recounted to Sobell, that he, Elitcher, was being followed. Elitcher testified about Sobell as follows: "I turned to him and said, 'Well, what does Julie think about this, my being followed?' He said, 'It is all right; don't be concerned about it; it is O.K.' He then said Rosenberg had told him that he once talked to Elizabeth Bentley on the phone but he was pretty sure she didn't know who he was and therefore everything was all right."

Defendants at the trial neither objected to this testimony nor moved to strike it. They now contend that it was inadmissible hearsay. The government contends that it was not hearsay since it was a report of a statement by Sobell, one of the Rosenbergs' fellow-conspirators, about something

Rosenberg said in furtherance of the conspiracy. If we assume that this contention is not sound, nevertheless the jury was properly allowed to consider this testimony. For, as the Supreme Court has held as to hearsay testimony: "If evidence of this kind is admitted without objection, it is to be considered, and accorded its natural probative effect, as if it were in law admissible." . . . The federal authorities are unanimous on this point. (True, we may, of our own motion, notice egregious errors to which there were no objections below if they "seriously affect the fairness, integrity or public reputation of judicial proceedings." . . . That exception might conceivably govern here if we believed the failure to object to this testimony resulted from the incompetence of defendants' counsel. But the record shows that defendants' counsel were singularly astute and conscientious. We know, too, that an able trial lawyer, for one or more of a variety of reasons, will often withhold an objection to the reception of hearsay. When he has done so, and it turns out that the jury's verdict is adverse to his client, the lawyer may not assert that reception as error.)

Greenglass also testified that Julius Rosenberg had said Miss Bentley probably knew him. The jury was therefore entitled to believe, on the basis of Elitcher's and Greenglass' testimony that Julius had spoken on the phone to Miss Bentley. In those circumstances, we see no error in permitting Miss Bentley to testify, over defendants' objections, as follows: She received several phone calls in 1943 from a man who called himself "Julius"—whose voice she did not recognize. She would then call Golos, a top Russian spy, and give him Julius' messages—acting as a go-between for "Julius" and Golos. From her talks with "Julius" and Golos, she learned that "Julius" lived in Knickerbocker Village—where, in fact, Rosenberg lived.

The testimony of Elitcher and Greenglass supplied sufficient circumstantial evidence to make it proper to allow the jury to infer that it was Julius Rosenberg, the defendant who, by phone, gave Miss Bentley the information she passed on to Golos. . . . Moreover, according to Greenglass' testimony, Julius Rosenberg told the Greenglasses that an emissary would contact them in New Mexico bearing greetings from himself, Julius; Harry Gold testified that, by command of Yakolev, another spy, he, Harry Gold, bore the greeting, "I come from Julius," when he met up with the Greenglasses, per arrangement, in Albuquerque. The trial judge, of course, told the jury that they were free to accept or reject the inference that it was Rosenberg who called Miss Bentley.

6. The trial judge instructed the jury: "Because of the development of highly destructive weapons and their highly guarded possession by nations existing in a state of tension with one another, the enforcement of the espionage laws takes on a new significance. Our national well-being requires

that we guard against spying on the secrets of our defense." Concerning this statement defendants argue: "The mandate to the jury to correlate the tensions of the times with the 'new significance' to enforce the espionage laws was not only an irrelevance, but licensed the triers of the facts to yield to their emotional bias and insinuated that it would be a reflection on their responsibility as patriotic citizens if they returned a verdict other than 'guilty.' " We do not agree. For the judge also said that he did "not mean that the mere allegation or use of the word 'espionage' should justify convicting innocent persons"; and he cautioned the jurors that it was their duty "to approach [the] task of determining the issues with * * * minds completely barren of prejudice or sympathy," to "weigh the evidence in this case calmly and dispassionately. * * * " It can hardly be seriously contended that commenting on the "new significance" of espionage law enforcement gave the jury a green light to convict on emotions rather than evidence.

7. In summing up, Rosenberg's counsel argued to the jury that the Greenglasses' testimony should not be credited because they testified as part of an understanding with the prosecutor that Ruth Greenglass would not be prosecuted and that David Greenglass would receive a relatively light sentence. When, soon after the jury heard this argument, the judge instructed the jury, he said they should consider whether the Greenglasses testified as a result of business difficulties, "or for some other unknown reason." It is urged that, as this statement inaccurately characterized defendants' argument, it constitutes error. We think not. The judge had no duty to repeat all the lawyers' arguments which the jury had heard a short time before. He explicitly told the jury that he could not cover all of the arguments made by both sides in their summations, and that his reference to some portions of evidence and not others "should not be taken as * * * any indication as to [his] opinion of the comparative importance or weight of that particular evidence." In addition, he explained (as we have already noted) that the Greenglasses were accomplices, and that their testimony must be carefully examined for that reason.

8. David Greenglass testified that Julius admitted "stealing" a proximity fuse from the Emerson Radio Company where he worked, and giving the fuse to Russia. On objection by defendants to the word "stealing," the court ordered it stricken. Defendants complain of the denial of their motions to strike all this testimony. They urge it was irrelevant since it was not shown that the proximity fuse was either secret or connected with national defense. The proximity fuse, be it noted, was an important World War II development which vastly increased the potential damage range of exploding shells. The nature of the device itself strongly suggests that it was secret, and unequivocally shows that it was connected with the national defense. At any

rate, the testimony was admissible to show an intent on Julius' part to aid Russia.

9. The Rosenbergs contend that four Government exhibits (2, 6, 7 and 8), consisting of sketches made by David Greenglass of lens molds and an atom bomb were improperly admitted in evidence. Exhibits 2 and 8 are diagrams of a clover-leaf type high explosive lens mold used in atomic bomb experiments and a cross-section of an atom bomb, respectively. David Greenglass testified that these diagrams, which he reproduced for use at the trial, were accurate replicas of sketches given by him to Julius Rosenberg in 1945, and last seen by him at that time. Greenglass further testified that Exhibits 6 and 7 were accurate representations of lens mold sketches which he turned over to Harry Gold, in conjunction with a report on atomic experimentation, in June, 1945. The original sketches were allegedly delivered to Yakolev by Gold and transmitted to the Soviet Union. Greenglass explained all four exhibits to the jury and used them to illustrate his testimonial description of the information he imparted to Rosenberg and Gold. Such sketches would ordinarily be admissible under the "map, diagram, and chart" rule which permits a witness to clarify his testimony by written illustration, so as to communicate complicated or confusing information more easily to the jury. . . . Defendants also object because David's superiors at Los Alamos were allowed to examine these sketches and to testify that they were reasonably accurate portrayals of the lens mold and atomic mechanisms used in the experimental station. We see no error here. A witness may always comment upon the substance or import of another witness' testimony; there is no reason to differentiate between verbal and nonverbal testimony in this respect. At no time were the sketches held out as those actually transmitted by Greenglass to Russia or exact replicas or copies thereof. They represented only Greenglass' recollection of what he had given the foreign agents. Hence there was no infraction of the secondary evidence rule.

10. The jury, during its deliberations, asked for a reading of that part of Ruth Greenglass' testimony covering the period from the time Rosenberg first approached her for espionage to the return of her husband to New York in 1945. Out of the jury's presence, defense counsel then asked the judge to have read to the jury the cross-examination covering the same period. The judge said he would not, without an express request from the jury. After the direct had been read to the jury, the judge asked them if they had what they wanted, and they said yes. Defense counsel, then, in the jurors' presence, again requested that the cross-examination be read. The judge at once replied that he would read only what the jury asked for. The jurors remained silent. Defense counsel objected. They now argue that the failure

to comply with their request was prejudicial error. We think not. We think the jury understood from the colloquy that the cross would be read if the jurors so desired, and that their silence meant they had no such desire. Indeed, defendants' own argument bears this out: They do not assert that the failure to read the cross was harmful because the cross contradicted or markedly differed from the direct, but, on the contrary, because it repeated the direct almost word for word, so that (say defendants) the jury, had it heard the cross, might have concluded that the testimony was a rehearsed falsehood. However, but a short time previously, Rosenberg's counsel, in summation to the jury, had made precisely that point (that is, that the cross parroted the direct). If the jurors had been impressed by this argument and, on that account, wanted Ruth's cross to check this very point, they would almost certainly have asked especially that the cross be read, particularly after defense counsel, in their presence, made this request. Accordingly, we hold that the refusal to have the cross read was within the trial judge's discretion.

11. As part of its case-in-chief, the government introduced testimony that, in 1950, after the arrest of the British atomic physicist, Dr. Klaus Fuchs, for espionage on behalf of Russia, Julius Rosenberg warned Greenglass to leave this country by way of Mexico; that Rosenberg repeated this warning after Gold's arrest; that Julius said he and his wife also intended to flee to Mexico. When the government rested, the Rosenbergs took the stand; on direct, among other things, they contradicted the foregoing testimony. On March 26, 1951, during Julius Rosenberg's cross-examination, he denied having had passport pictures taken in May or June 1950; on March 27, 1951, after the defendants had rested their case, the government called one Schneider, a professional photographer, as a rebuttal witness. Defense counsel at once objected to any testimony by Schneider, on the ground that his name was not on the list of witnesses submitted before the trial to the defendants in accordance with 18 U.S.C. sec. 3432. Thereupon, in answer to questions put by the prosecutor, Schneider testified that, on March 26, 1951, two F.B.I. agents came to see him, and that then for the first time had anyone communicated with him about the subject for which he was called as a witness. Over objection by the defense on the ground that Schneider's testimony was "not proper rebuttal," he was then allowed to testify that, in May or June 1950, at his photography shop, he had taken the photographs of the Rosenbergs and their children, and that at that time Julius Rosenberg had said the pictures were needed to enable the Rosenberg family to go abroad.

The statutory requirement concerning the list of witnesses to be supplied before trial has been held inapplicable to a rebuttal witness. Defendants argue that Schneider's testimony was inadmissible, since it served merely to corroborate evidence introduced by the government on its case-in-chief and was thus not rebuttal of new matter arising on defendants' case. A majority of this court rejects this argument. But, even if this argument is sound, the reception of this testimony was not erroneous. As it was a reasonable inference from Schneider's testimony that the government did not know of Schneider until the day before he was called as a witness, it could not have included his name in the witness-list handed defendants before the trial, which began some three weeks earlier. Consequently, the statute, properly interpreted, did not exclude Schneider's testimony altogether. See *United States v. Schneider* . . . : "The statute was never intended to preclude the United States from making use of any material testimony discovered during the progress of the trial, and all that it exacts of the prosecuting officer is that he shall in good faith furnish to the prisoner, before the trial, the names of all witnesses then known to him and intended to be used at the trial." It might well have been error to refuse a reasonable request for adjournment coupled with some showing of surprise. But defendants made no such request.

12. Sobell raises several questions affecting his conviction. The most important of these is whether or not he was proved to be a member of the Rosenberg-Greenglass-Gold conspiracy to ship information to Russia. Even accepting all of Elitcher's testimony as true, says Sobell, it showed only that he, Sobell, conspired with Julius Rosenberg to solicit Elitcher's aid in espionage activities along with that of other young engineers and to send abroad certain kinds of military engineering and fire control information, but no evidence connected him in any way with the Greenglass-Gold-Rosenberg plan to ship atomic information from Los Alamos to the Soviet Union. At the end of the government's case, Sobell's counsel moved to dismiss the indictment on the ground that not one but two separate conspiracies had been proved by the government, one involving Rosenberg, Greenglass and Gold, whose purpose was the transmission of atomic information, and the other involving Rosenberg and Sobell, aimed solely at the sending of various types of military information abroad. The motion was denied; the trial judge committing himself to the theory that the government's witnesses, if believed, proved one giant conspiracy, to send defense information abroad, of which the atomic espionage was only one "branch." Despite objection by Sobell's counsel, the judge charged the jury, on the one-conspiracy theory, as follows: "Again I want to emphasize that the conspiracy in this case is a conspiracy to obtain secret information pertaining to the national defense and then to transmit it to the Union of Soviet Socialist Republics. It is not a conspiracy to obtain information only about the atom bomb. I point that out because the Government contends that Sobell was in

the general conspiracy to obtain information of a secret nature. To determine whether Morton Sobell was a member of the conspiracy you are only to consider the testimony of Max Elitcher, William Danziger and the testimony relating to the defendant Sobell's alleged attempt to flee the country. If you do not believe the testimony of Max Elitcher as it pertains to Sobell, then you must acquit the defendant Sobell. If you find that there was a conspiracy and that Morton Sobell was a member of the conspiracy, any statements or acts of any co-conspirators are binding upon him because the law is that once you have joined a conspiracy attempting to accomplish an unlawful objective, the acts of the co-conspirators done in furtherance of the same objective, even though the co-conspirators are unknown to you, are binding upon you."

If in fact, Sobell is right that two conspiracies were proved, then prejudicial error has been committed, for Sobell was jointly tried with major atomic energy spies whose acts and declarations were held binding upon him. What distinguishes a single conspiracy from several related ones is a single unified purpose, a "common end." This "common end" is in contradistinction to the "separate ends similar in character" which characterize multiple conspiracies. *United States* v. *McConnell* . . . Thus the Supreme Court has said that defendants who separately secure fraudulent loans through banking institutions from a single governmental agency by the intermediary of a single broker have separate albeit similar ends, and lack the single unified purpose of co-conspirators. *Kotteakos* v. *United States* . . . On the other hand, salesmen who make illegal sales above ceiling price of a particular brand of whisky obtained from a particular wholesaler have a single unified purpose—to raise illegally the price of that whisky: "The whisky was the same. The agreements related alike to its disposition. They comprehended illegal sales in the guise of legal ones. * * * The scheme was in fact the same scheme. The salesmen knew or must have known that others unknown to them were sharing in so large a project." *Blumenthal* v. *United States* . . .

A majority of this court have concluded, on the following grounds, that here there was a single unified purpose: The "common end" consisted of the transmission to the Soviet Union of any kind and all information relating to the national defense; that such a single aim distinguishes this conspiracy from that in *Kotteakos*, where each defendant was interested in obtaining his own fraudulent loan only and not in the success of his fellow-borrowers. The case is closer to the *Blumenthal* situation, where all the salesmen had a united purpose to sell the shipment of whisky at an illegally high price. Sobell is confusing the particular part each conspirator played in the espionage activities with the end-all purpose of all the conspirators—the aiding of Russia by sending to it any and all kinds of secret information. It did not matter that Sobell knew nothing of the atomic episodes; he is nevertheless charged with the acts done by Greenglass, Gold and Rosenberg, in furtherance of the over-all conspiracy. The jury could and did reasonably find that Sobell consented to the dominant aim, and so became a member of the Rosenberg-Greenglass-Gold conspiracy.

The writer of this opinion disagrees. He thinks that there was error, in this respect, which requires that Sobell be given a new trial. The balance of this paragraph sets out the writer's reasons for dissenting on this issue. Even if Sobell, on Elitcher's testimony, could reasonably be held as a member of the Rosenberg-Gold-Greenglass conspiracy, the question of his membership should have been submitted to the jury. Elitcher's testimony would have supported either of two inferences that Sobell agreed only (1) to transmit certain kinds of military information to Russia or (2) that he agreed with the other conspirators to transmit "any military information of all kind." The jury should have had the opportunity to choose between the inferences and to decide whether he actually joined the larger conspiracy. See *Lefco* v. *United States* . . . "Nobody is liable in conspiracy except for the fair import of the concerted purpose or agreement as he understands it; if latecomers change that he is not liable for the change; his liability is limited to the common purposes while he remains in it." *United States* v. *Peoni* . . . The judge's instructions (quoted above) do not, I think, make it clear to the jury that Sobell in order to become a member of the larger conspiracy, had to agree to transmit all kinds of secret information, and not just certain kinds which he knew about. In effect, he charged that if the jury believed Elitcher's testimony, Sobell was a member of the larger conspiracy charged in the indictment.

13. Sobell alleges that the prosecutor's ill attempts at courtroom humor and "questions" containing inadmissible testimony deprived him of a fair trial. After examining each such incident, we cannot agree that, despite the judge's cautioning instructions to convict or acquit on the evidence alone, they were so important as to affect the jury adversely. Many of the so-called "loaded" questions were withdrawn before answering; objections to others were sustained and the prosecutor admonished; nothing in his summation concerning the defendants seems to have exceeded the liberal limits of legitimate partisanship and argumentation our courts customarily allow counsel. It is of some significance that Sobell's counsel himself, at the end of the trial, indicated that he thought the prosecutor had conducted himself fairly: "I am willing to shake his hand after a job that we both had to do." Similarly the Rosenbergs' counsel also acknowledged the good behavior of the prosecutor at the end of the trial.

14. The prosecution introduced as an entry "in the regular course of business" a card made by an Immigration Inspector at the time Sobell re-entered the United States, stating that he had been "Deported from Mexico." This evidence is attacked as both irrelevant and hearsay. But Sobell's forced return to the United States was certainly relevant to the government's theory that he had fled to Mexico to escape prosecution, for otherwise the jury might have inferred that he had returned voluntarily to stand trial. The hearsay objection is equally without merit. As an entry of this type is required in the case of every deportee from Mexico and was made by the border inspector in the course of his duties, it qualifies as a business entry under 28 U.S.C. 1732, 1733. The inspector who made the entry testified at the trial, and was available for cross-examination as to the extent of his observations and his reasons for making the entry.

15. At the end of the trial, after Sobell had been found guilty, his counsel made a motion in arrest of judgment based upon an affidavit by Sobell that he had been illegally abducted by Mexican police from his residence in Mexico City and taken across the border into the United States where he was delivered into the immediate custody of waiting United States agents. Sobell asked the trial judge to conduct a hearing on the question of whether United States officials had participated in, or instigated, his illegal kidnapping. Sobell claims that his conviction would be a nullity if it were proved that the government thus secured jurisdiction over his person in violation of United States law and international agreement.

The government answers that, even if United States officials had participated in Sobell's alleged kidnapping, the court in a criminal case, unlike a civil case, would still have jurisdiction over his person, as long as he was physically present at the trial. There appears to be authority to support this position. . . . However, there are contrary arguments. But we need not now decide that question. For we think that Sobell waived his right to challenge personal jurisdiction in this trial. Rule 12(b)(2) of the Federal Rules of Criminal Procedure says: "Defenses and objections based on defects in the institution of the prosecution or in the indictment or information other than that it fails to show jurisdiction in the court or to charge an offense may be raised only by motion before trial. The motion shall include all such defenses and objections then available to the defendant. Failure to present any such defense or objection as herein provided constitutes a waiver thereof, * * * " Yet Sobell made no such pre-trial motion challenging jurisdiction over his person, despite the fact that all the information contained in the post-trial affidavit was known to him at that time. When the government introduced evidence to show that Sobell had been legally deported from Mexico (evidence clearly contradictory to Sobell's present assertion), he made no move to bring to light the facts of his alleged illegal abduction. He preferred to take his chances on the verdict, withholding his trump card until the trial was over. The Federal Rules of Criminal Procedure allow no such tactic. Under Rule 34, motions in arrest of judgment are allowed only (1) where the indictment charges no offense and (2) where the court had no jurisdiction over the offense charged. This situation, we think, falls into neither category. . . . Personal jurisdiction can be waived in a criminal as well as a civil case. . . . *United States v. Rauscher,* . . . cited by Sobell, allowed a defendant to move in arrest of judgment on the ground that he had been tried and convicted of an offense other than the one for which he had been surrendered to the United States by Great Britain pursuant to an extradition treaty. There, however, the defendant also challenged personal jurisdiction before trial, and no question of the timeliness of his motion was involved.

16. The trial judge sentenced Julius and Ethel Rosenberg to death. The statute under which they were convicted provides that whoever violates the pertinent subsection "in time of war shall be punished by death or by imprisonment for not more than thirty years." . . . Congress had the power to prescribe the death penalty for wartime espionage. . . . This, these defendants do not deny. They claim, rather, that, even if they were properly convicted, it was unconstitutional and an abuse of discretion for the trial judge to impose the extreme penalty in their particular case, and that we must reduce their sentences. In support of that contention they assert the following: They did not act from venal or pecuniary motives; except for this conviction, their records as citizens and parents are unblemished; at the most, out of idealistic motives, they gave secret information to Soviet Russia when it was our wartime ally; for this breach, they are sentenced to die, while those who, according to the government, were their confederates, at least equally implicated in wartime espionage—Harry Gold, Emil Fuchs, Elizabeth Bentley and the Greenglasses—get off with far lighter sentences or go free altogether. Finally, they argue, the death sentence is unprecedented in a case like this: No civil court has ever imposed this penalty in an espionage case, and only twice has it been imposed by such a court in treason cases.

Unless we are to over-rule sixty years of undeviating federal precedents, we must hold that an appellate court has no power to modify a sentence. "If there is one rule in the federal criminal practice which is firmly established, it is that the appellate court has no control over a sentence which is within the limits allowed by a statute." *Gurra v. United States* . . . See also, for example, *Beckett v. United States* . . . *Scala v. United States* . . . *Peterson v. United States* . . . *Wallace v. United States* . . . *Feinberg v. United States* . . . *Carpenter v. United States* . . . *Smith v. United States* . . . *Hodgskin v.*

*United States . . . United States v. Cohen . . . United States v. Ward . . . United States v. Gottfried . . . Voege v. United States. . . .* In *Blockburger v. United States . . .* the Supreme Court said: "Under the circumstances, so far as disclosed, it is true that the imposition of the full penalty of fine and imprisonment upon each count seems unduly severe; but there may have been other facts and circumstances before the trial court properly influencing the extent of the punishment. In any event, the matter was one for that court, with whose judgment there is no warrant for interference on our part." Further discussion of this subject my colleagues think unnecessary. Consequently, the subsequent paragraphs express the views of the writer of this opinion only.

That upper courts have or should have power to reduce harsh sentences has long been urged by some commentators. . . . The existence of such power may seem the more desirable in these days when, in the recent words of the Supreme Court, "Retribution is no longer the dominant objective of the criminal law. Reformation and rehabilitation of offenders have become important goals of criminal jurisprudence." In England, Canada, and in several of our states, upper courts have held that they may revise sentences while affirming convictions. But these rulings were based on statutory authority. . . .

Some of these state courts find such authority in statutes conferring power to "affirm, modify or reverse" judgments on appeal. An identical power —to "affirm, modify or reverse"—is given to federal courts of appeal and to the Supreme Court by U.S.C.A. 28 Sec. 2106. That provision dates back to the Judiciary Act of 1789. . . . No decision by the Supreme Court or any federal court of appeals seems to have cited or considered this statute in passing on the question of the power to reduce a sentence when a conviction is affirmed. Were this question *res nova*, this court should give that section serious consideration. (The trial judge's determination of a proper sentence —no easy task—should turn on his evaluation of a host of factors, including the unique fact of the particular defendant's life, conduct and character. Where an upper court has authority to review and revise a sentence, its attempt to do so may be thwarted if the trial judge has not made public the bases of his determination—although, in some instances, a sentence may obviously be unduly harsh, no matter what the particulars of the defendant's life, etc. In the instant case, the trial judge has publicly stated the grounds on which he based the death sentence: "Citizens of this country who betray their fellow countrymen can be under none of the delusions about the benignity of Soviet power that they might have been prior to World War II. The nature of Soviet terrorism is now self-evident. Idealism as a rationale dissolves." * * * "I consider your crime worse than murder. Plain deliberate contemplated murder is dwarfed in magnitude by comparison with the crime you have committed. In committing the act of murder, the criminal kills only his victim. The immediate family is brought to grief and when justice is meted out the chapter is closed. But in your case, I believe your conduct in putting into the hands of the Russians the A-bomb years before our best scientists predicted Russia would perfect the bomb has already caused, in my opinion, the Communist aggression in Korea, with the resultant casualties exceeding 50,000 and who knows but that millions more of innocent people may pay the price of your treason. Indeed, by your betrayal you undoubtedly have altered the course of history to the disadvantage of our country. . . .") Because, however, for six decades federal decisions (including that of the Supreme Court in *Blockburger* v. *United States, supra*) have denied the existence of such authority, it is clear that the Supreme Court alone is in a position to hold that Sec. 2106 confers authority to reduce a sentence which is not outside the bounds set by a valid statute. As matters now stand, this court properly regards itself as powerless to exercise its own judgment concerning the alleged severity of the defendants' sentences.

The Rosenbergs, however, advance a different argument, that is, that, although the statute expressly and validly permits death sentences, we do have the power and the duty to order these particular death sentences reduced because they violate the Eighth Amendment of the Constitution, which forbids any "cruel and unusual punishment." Several courts have ruled that a sentence within the limits of a valid statute cannot amount to "cruel and unusual punishment," that, when a statute provides for such punishment, the statute only can be thus attacked. . . . No federal decision seems to have held cruel and unusual any sentence imposed under a statute which itself was constitutional. But let it be assumed that, even if the statute authorizing a sentence does not violate the Eighth Amendment, still a particular sentence, within the literal terms of that statute, may do so, because of the specific circumstances of the case. No such circumstances exist in this case. The test of a "cruel and unusual punishment" urged by the defendants—that is, that "it shocks the conscience and sense of justice of the people of the United States"—is not met here.

The test (unlike that applied when an upper court has discretion to modify sentences) invites the criticism that it shifts the moral responsibility for a sentence from the consciences of the judges to the "common conscience." But that criticism aside, this test counts against the defendants, for it means that this court, before it reduces a sentence as "cruel and unusual," must have reasonably good assurances that the sentence offends the "common conscience." And, in any context, such a standard—the community's attitude—is usually an unknowable. It resembles a slithery shadow, since one can seldom learn, at all accurately, what the community, or a majority, actually feels. Even a carefully-taken "public opinion poll" would be inconclusive in a case like this. Cases are conceivable where there would be little doubt of a general public antipathy to a death sentence. But (for reasons noted below) this is not such a case.

In all likelihood, it would be—if the evidence were as the Rosenbergs depict it: They say that they were sentenced to death, not for espionage, but for political unorthodoxy and adherence to the Communist Party, and that (assuming they are guilty) they had only the best of motives in giving information to Russia which, at the time, was an ally of this country, praised as such by leading patriotic Americans. But the trial judge, in sentencing the Rosenbergs, relied on record evidence which (if believed) shows a very different picture. If this evidence be accepted, the conspiracy did not end in 1945, while Russia was still a "friend," but, as the trial judge phrased it, continued "during a period when it was apparent to everybody that we were dealing with a hostile nation." For, according to government witnesses, in 1948 Julius Rosenberg was urging Elitcher to stay with the Navy Department so that he might obtain secret data; in 1948, Rosenberg received "valuable" information from Sobell; in 1950, Rosenberg gave Greenglass money to flee to Russia. This court cannot rule that the trial judge should have disbelieved those witnesses whom he saw and heard testify. And, although the indictment did not charge, and therefore the jury did not find, that the Rosenbergs intended to harm the United States, the trial judge could properly consider the injury to this country of their conduct, in exercising his discretion as to the extent of sentences within the statutory limits. Cf. Williams v. New York. . . . "It is urged, however, that we should draw a constitutional distinction as to the procedure for obtaining information where the death sentence is imposed. We cannot accept the contention. Leaving a sentencing judge free to avail himself of out-of-court information in making such a fateful choice of sentences does secure to him a broad discretionary power, one susceptible of abuse. But in considering whether a rigid constitutional barrier should be created, it must be remembered that there is possibility of abuse wherever a judge must choose between life imprisonment and death. And it is conceded that no federal constitutional objection would have been possible if the judge here had sentenced appellant to death because appellant's trial manner impressed the judge that appellant was a bad risk for society, or if the judge had sentenced him to death giving no reason at all. We cannot say that the due-process clause renders a sentence void merely because a judge gets additional out-of-court information to assist him in the exercise of this awesome power of imposing the death sentence."

We must, then, consider the case as one in which death sentences have been imposed on Americans who conspired to pass important secret information to Russia, not only during 1944–1945, but also during the "cold war." Assuming the applicability of the community-attitude test proposed by these defendants, it is impossible to say that the community is shocked and outraged by such sentences resting on such facts. In applying that test, it is necessary to treat as immaterial the sentences given (or not given) to the other conspirators, and also to disregard what sentences this court would have imposed or what other trial judges have done in other espionage or in treason cases. For such matters do not adequately reflect the prevailing mood of the public. In short, it cannot be held that these sentences are unconstitutional. (A sentence, although not "cruel and unusual," may violate the due process clause. *Townsend v. Burke* . . . There the Court held invalid a sentence imposed because of the trial judge's mistaken belief that the defendant was guilty of other crimes, and in a case where the defendant was not represented by counsel. There is nothing equivalent here. The Rosenbergs, of course, may ask the Supreme Court, considering 28 U.S.C. Section 2106, to overrule the decisions precluding federal appellate modification of a sentence not exceeding the maximum fixed by a valid statute, and to direct us accordingly to consider whether or not these sentences are excessive; or the Rosenbergs, pursuant to Federal Rule of Criminal Procedure 35, may move the trial judge for a reduction of their sentences; or, if those alternatives fail, the defendants may seek relief from the President. . . .)

AFFIRMED.

*195 F.2d 583 (1952)*

*Defense counsel requested the Supreme Court to review the case; the Court declined to do so.*

*344 U.S. 838 (1952)*

*Shortly before the date of execution, counsel on behalf of the Rosenbergs requested a stay of execution from the Supreme Court so that the Court could hear a motion bearing on the authority of trial judge to pronounce the death sentence. For that purpose, Associate Justice William O. Douglas granted the stay. The full Court then met in Special Term; the stay was vacated on the ground that the question raised on the motion lacked substance.*

*346 U.S. 273 (1953)*

*The Rosenbergs appealed to President Eisenhower for executive clemency, which he denied. On Friday, June 19, 1953, the Rosenbergs died in the electric chair.*

Malcolm P. Sharp, Was Justice Done? (1956)

# GARDELLA v. CHANDLER &

IN 1948 Daniel Gardella, a baseball player, appealed from a judgment of the District Court in which his suit for treble damages against Albert Chandler, the Commissioner of Baseball, and the top officers of the major baseball leagues, was dismissed for lack of jurisdiction. While under contract to play ball exclusively with the New York Giants, Gardella violated the terms of the so-called "reserve clause" by playing professional baseball in Mexico. As a result, he was barred from playing with any of the baseball clubs in the major leagues and, thus, deprived of his means of livelihood. He then filed suit against those responsible, charging that they were violating the antitrust laws: he claimed they were a monopoly engaged in interstate commerce. Judge Frank's concurring opinion deals with the question of whether the District Court lacked jurisdiction because of an earlier Supreme Court decision, Federal Base Ball Club v. National League. The Court of Appeals sent the case back for trial.

FRANK, Circuit Judge: 1. No one can treat as frivolous the argument that the Supreme Court's recent decisions have completely destroyed the vitality of Federal Baseball Club v. National League . . . (decided twenty-seven years ago) and have left that case but an impotent zombi. Nevertheless, it seems best that this court should not so hold. (I reach that conclusion somewhat hesitantly. For, while the Supreme Court has never explicitly overruled the Federal Baseball Club case, it has overruled the precedents upon which that decision was based; and the concept of commerce has changed enough in the last two decades so that, if that case were before the Supreme Court de novo, it seems very likely that the Court would decide the other way. This court cannot, of course, tell the Supreme Court that it was once wrong. But "one should not wait for formal retraction * * * in the face of changes plainly foreshadowed"; this court's duty is "to divine, as best it can, what would be the event of the appeal in the case before it." . . .) However, in *Ring* v. *Spina* . . . referring to that case and another similar case, this court said that, because of "the steadily expanding content of the phrase 'interstate commerce' in recent years, * * * there is no longer occasion for applying those cases beyond their exact facts." For reasons stated later, I think that, on its facts, we can properly distinguish the suit now before us from the Federal Baseball case.

I think it should be so distinguished, if possible, because (assuming, as we must, at this stage of the litigation, the truth of the statements in the complaint), we have here a monopoly which, in its effect on ballplayers like the plaintiff, possesses characteristics shockingly repugnant to moral principles that, at least since the War Between the States, have been basic in America, as shown by the Thirteenth Amendment to the Constitution, condemning "involuntary servitude," and by subsequent Congressional enactments on that subject. For the "reserve clause," as has been observed, results in something resembling peonage of the baseball player. By accepting the "reserve clause"—and all players in organized baseball must "accept" it —a player binds himself not to sign a contract with, or play for, any club other than the club which originally employs him or its assignee. Although many courts have refused to enforce the "reserve" clause, yet severe and practically efficacious extralegal penalties are imposed for violation. The most extreme of these penalties is the blacklisting of the player, so that no club in organized baseball will hire him. In effect, this clause prevents a player from ever playing with any team other than his original employer, unless that employer consents. Since the right to play with organized baseball is indispensable to the career of a professional baseball player, violations of the clause by such players are infrequent. The violator may perhaps become a judge (with a less exciting and often less remunerative occupation) or a bartender or a street-sweeper, but his chances of ever again playing baseball are exceedingly slim.

. . . [I]f [baseball] players be regarded as quasi-peons, it is of no moment that they are well paid; only the totalitarian-minded will believe that high pay excuses virtual slavery.

In what I have said about the nature of the contracts made with the players, I am not to be understood as implying that they violate the Thirteenth Amendment or the statutes enacted pursuant thereto. I mean simply to suggest that those contracts are so opposed to the public policy of the United States that, if possible, they should be deemed within the prohibitions of the Sherman Act.

2 . . . In [the Federal Baseball case], the Court held that the traveling across state lines was but an incidental means of enabling games to be played locally—that is, within particular states—and therefore insufficient to constitute interstate commerce. Here, although the playing of the games is essential to both defendants' intrastate and interstate activities, the interstate communication by radio and television is in no way a means, incidental or otherwise, of performing the intrastate activities (the local playings of the games).

True, in the Federal Baseball Club case, there was present in the record the fact that the defendants had sold the exclusive right to send "play-by-play" descriptions of the games over interstate telegraph wires. But the brief of the plaintiff filed in the Supreme Court in that case did not contend that that interstate communication was interstate commerce; it merely called attention to the telegraph service as one of several factors tending to show the popularity and national character of "organized Baseball." Moreover, the Supreme Court in its opinion in that case did not note the fact concerning the telegraph service; and it has often been held that a decision is not to be regarded as a precedent concerning a question clearly not considered by the Court, because "to make it so, there must have been an application of the judicial mind to the precise question. * * *"

Accordingly, as the Court in the Federal Baseball case, in deciding that interstate features were absent, discussed nothing but the traveling of the teams and their paraphernalia between states, as a means to the local playing of the games, I think that decision, as above indicated, should be deemed to hold no more than that such traveling does not give rise to interstate commerce for Sherman Act purposes. That such was the ruling appears from the way in which the Supreme Court there dealt with the facts: "A summary statement of the nature of the business involved will be enough to present the point. The clubs composing the Leagues are in different cities and for the most part in different States. The end of the elaborate organizations and sub-organizations that are described in the pleadings and evidence is that these clubs shall play against one another in public exhibitions for money, one or the other club crossing a state line in order to make the meeting possible. When as the result of these contests one club has won the pennant of its League and another club has won the pennant of the other League, there is a final competition for the World's championship between these two. Of course the scheme requires constantly repeated traveling on the part of the clubs, which is provided for, controlled and disciplined by the organizations, and this it is said means commerce among the States. But . . . [t]he business is giving exhibitions of baseball, which are purely state affairs. It is true that, in order to attain for these exhibitions the great popularity that they have achieved, competitions must be arranged between clubs from different cities and States. But the fact that in order to give the exhibitions the Leagues must induce free persons to cross state lines and must arrange and pay for their doing so is not enough to change the character of the business. According to the distinction insisted upon in *Hooper v. California* . . . the transport is a mere incident, not the essential thing."

I think the foregoing will serve alone to distinguish the incidental-means rationale of the Federal Baseball case: There the traveling was but a means to the end of playing games which themselves took place intrastate; here the games themselves, because of the radio and television, are, so to speak, played interstate and well as intrastate.

There is, however, another important distinction on which I think we might rely, were another distinction necessary: In that earlier case, persons in other states received, via the telegraph, mere accounts of the games as told by others, while here we have the very substantially different fact of instant and direct interstate transmission, via television, of the games as they are being played, so that audiences in other states have the experience of being virtually present at these games. That degree of difference, known to anyone who has ever sat at the receiving end of a television set, is so great as to constitute a difference in kind. To be sure, no one can draw a sharp line between differences of "degree" and "kind." However, to the question whether the difference between a difference of kind and difference of degree is itself a difference of degree, the sage answer has been given that it is a difference of degree, but a "violent" one. "Courts of justice," said an English judge some sixty years ago, "ought not to be puzzled by such old scholastic questions as to where a horse's tail begins and where it ceases. You are obliged to say, 'This is a horse's tail,' at some time."

In the Federal Baseball case, the Court assigned as a further ground of its decision that the playing of the games, although for profit, involved services, and that services were not "trade or commerce" as those words were used in the Sherman Act. But I think that such a restricted interpretation of those words has been undeniably repudiated in later Supreme Court decisions concerning medical services and motion pictures. I believe, therefore, that we will not trespass on the Supreme Court's domain if we hold that the rationale of the Federal Baseball case is now confined to the insufficiency of traveling, when employed as a means of accomplishing local activities, to establish the existence of interstate commerce.

I conclude, then, that here there is substantial interstate commerce of a sort not considered by the Court in the Federal Baseball case. These questions remain: (a) May Congress constitutionally regulate the interstate portion of such a business as that done by defendants? (b) If so, has

Congress in the Sherman Act sufficiently exercised its constitutional power to include that portion of that business? I shall consider those questions in turn.

3. Supreme Court decisions relative to the Fair Labor Standards Act leave little doubt that the Constitutional power of Congress, under the commerce clause, extends to such a situation. In *Roland Co. v. Walling . . .*, an action to enjoin an alleged violation of that Act, the defendant was engaged in commercial and industrial wiring, electrical contracting, and dealing in electrical motors and generators. One of its customers was admittedly engaged in interstate telephony, others in the repair of ships intended for movement in interstate commerce, or in the production of goods for commerce. This the Court said (in an opinion by Justice Burton) brought the defendant within the Act, which "does not require the employee to be directly 'engaged in commerce'" or even "employed in the production of an article which itself becomes the subject of commerce. * * * It is enough that the employee be employed, for example, in an occupation which is necessary to the production of a part of any other 'article or subject of commerce of any character' which are produced for trade, commerce or transportation among the several states." *Roland Co. v. Walling* was followed in *Martino v. Michigan Window Cleaning Co., . . .* where the employer was an independent contractor engaged in washing windows, painting and similar maintenance work entirely within the State of Michigan on premises used in the production of goods for commerce. This, the Court said, constituted "the production of goods for commerce," under the Fair Labor Standards Act. Several Circuit courts, including this court, have in like manner widely interpreted Congress' constitutional power under the commerce clause. . . .

Nor is Congressional exercise of the commerce power barred with respect to a particular business enterprise because its activities in or affecting interstate commerce constitute but a small percentage of its total activities. . . .

4. The Supreme Court has said that (with an exception as to labor unions not relevant here) Congress in the Sherman Act intended to use all the constitutional power conferred on it by the commerce clause. The Court (per Sutherland, J.) so stated for the first time in *Atlantic Cleaners & Dyers, Inc. v. United States. . . .* The Court (per Stone, J.) repeated that statement in *Apex Hosiery Co. v. Leader . . .* adding that the Sherman Act is aimed at restraints "comparable to restraints deemed illegal at common law, although accomplished by means other than contract and which, for constitutional reasons, are confined to transactions in or which affect interstate commerce." . . . This idea was repeated in *United States v. Frankfort Distilleries . . .* : "And with reference to commercial trade restraints such as

these, Congress in passing the Sherman Act, left no area of its Constitutional power unoccupied; it 'exercised all the power it possessed.' "

The most striking statement, however, is in the Southern case, . . . where the argument was pressed that although the Constitutional commerce power empowered it to do so, Congress in the Sherman Act did not intend to cover insurance. The court found that "all the acceptable evidence points the other way. That Congress wanted to go to the utmost extent of its Constitutional power in restraining trust and monopoly agreements such as the indictment here charges admits of little, if any, doubt. The purpose was to use that power to make of ours, so far as Congress could under our dual system, a competitive business economy."

The comprehensive sweep of the Sherman Act is also shown by the Supreme Court's reliance, in several Sherman Act cases, upon cases construing the National Labor Relations Act and other statutes. For instance, in the *Associated Press* case, . . . the Court disposed, in one sentence, of the argument that that enterprise was not subject to the Sherman Act: "We need not again pass upon the contention that trade in news carried on among the states is not interstate commerce, *Associated Press v. Labor Board.* . . ." Justice Frankfurter, concurring, agreed, saying (p. 27): "Since the Associated Press is an enterprise engaged in interstate commerce, *Associated Press v. Labor Board, supra,* these plainly are agreements in restraint of that commerce."

In the more recent case of *Mandeville Farms v. American Crystal Sugar Co.,* . . . the Court discussed the scope of the Sherman Act and of the Constitutional commerce power as if they were identical, citing *United States v. Darby* . . . (a Fair Labor Standards Act case), *Consolidated Edison Co. v. Labor Board,* 305 U.S. 197 (a National Labor Relations Act case), and *United States v. Walsh* . . . (a Food and Drug Act case). Moreover, the discussion in the *Mandeville* opinion of the effect of the *Shreveport Rate Cases* . . . goes to show that, as the Court has come to construe the commerce clause more widely in connection with the coverage of other statutes, such as the Interstate Commerce Act, it has equivalently interpreted the Sherman Act's coverage. And certainly the *Mandeville* opinion demonstrates that the Sherman Act covers activities wholly within a state but which affect interstate commerce.

5. In the light of our previous discussion . . . I think we must, for purposes of deciding the applicability of the Sherman Act, consider this case as if the only audiences for whom the games are played consist of those persons who, in other states, see, hear, or hear about, the games via television and radio. The question here is, then, I think, the same as that which we would face if a similar alleged monopoly related to the production of stage

plays in radio and television studios. I believe the producers of such plays would clearly come within the Fair Labor Standards Act. If so, they would be within the Sherman Act. And I would so hold concerning the defendants, if their conduct is as plaintiff describes it.

As the playing of the games is essential both to defendants' interstate and intrastate activities, the players' contracts relate to both. But that, as a consequence, necessary relief with respect to the interstate activities will thus unavoidably affect those which are intrastate does not preclude the granting of such relief. Nor, I venture to repeat, do I think such relief is dependent upon a showing that the illegally monopolized interstate activities, if more than trifling, represent a substantial proportion of defendants' total activities. . . .

6. Defendants suggest that "organized baseball," which supplies millions of Americans with desirable diversion, will not be able to exist without the "reserve clause." Whether that is true, no court can predict. In any event, the answer is that the public's pleasure does not authorize the courts to condone illegality, and that no court should strive ingeniously to legalize a private (even if benevolent) dictatorship.

I think we should reverse and remand.

*172 F.2d 402 (1949)*

# UNITED STATES v. RUBENSTEIN ᨶ

I n 1944 Herman Rubenstein, a lawyer, appealed from a judgment of conviction under an indictment charging him with a conspiracy to bring an alien into the country by false representations, by concealment of material facts, and by false documents. According to the government at the trial, the facts were these: A Czechoslovakian, Alice Spitz, having entered the country on a temporary visa in November, 1938, decided she wished to remain permanently. To that end, she married an American named Sandler, who agreed to terminate the marriage by divorce after Spitz had obtained her visa. After the fraudulent marriage, Spitz then consulted Rubenstein about getting her a visa. Rubenstein obtained the visa by means of various application forms which he filled in with false details and two fictitious letters bearing on Sandler's financial status, character, and the like. As a result, Spitz received her visa in December, 1940. Rubenstein then arranged the divorce by inducing someone to sign a false affidavit to the effect that he had served divorce papers on Sandler; this same man swore falsely in court that he had caught Sandler in an adulterous act. On this a divorce was granted. Rubenstein's main complaint on appeal bore on the admissibility of all the evidence concerning the divorce, particularly with regard to his suborning perjury; he claimed that it was an independent and unconnected crime, the conspiracy having ended when Spitz entered the country under the immigration visa. Judge Learned Hand, writing the majority opinion in which the conviction was affirmed, says, ". . . it is well settled law that evidence which is relevant to the proof of one crime is not incompetent because it discloses the commission of another crime." Judge Frank dissents.

Frank, Circuit Judge (dissenting): I agree, of course, that it was proper to receive evidence tending to show the sham nature of the marriage, that defendant originally arranged that there should be a divorce, and that he aided in obtaining a divorce; for that evidence went to prove defendant's complicity in a plan to violate the statute by means of a fake marriage and by concealment of a material fact.

But I cannot agree that it was proper to receive the additional testimony which (if taken as true) showed (1) that defendant in procuring the divorce used a false affidavit and suborned perjury, (2) that defendant had suggested to Sandler that he should "get a girl and go to a hotel room," and that he refused, (3) that Sandler was not served, and knew nothing of the divorce until after the entry of the divorce decree. None of that evidence was needed to show the fictitious character of the marriage or the illegal plan to conceal the intention that it was soon to be followed by a divorce. For these purposes, it sufficed to prove merely that defendant, from the first, joined in the plan for the sham marriage and divorce and that, with his assistance, Miss Spitz and Sandler were divorced not long after the marriage ceremony.

Judge Hand suggests that the "prosecutor had to prove a collusive divorce," that therefore the "precise form which the collusion took" was unimportant, and that consequently the additional testimony—as to the false affidavit and defendant's subornation of perjury, and so on—was, in effect, cumulative and did defendant no appreciable harm. I cannot agree. No doubt the prosecutor had to prove defendant's part in a prearranged divorce relating to a marriage the unreality of which defendant did not disclose to the divorce court. But it is one thing to show such misconduct—constituting a fraud on the divorce court (justifying disbarment) and perhaps some sort of crime under New York law—and quite another to add proof of the commission of the distinct and far more serious crime of suborning perjury. That added proof was by no means merely cumulative. So that while, as Judge Hand states, "it is well settled that evidence which is relevant to the proof of one crime is not incompetent because it discloses the commission of another," that doctrine cannot here warrant reception of the additional evidence, especially that tending to show the crime of subornation of perjury in the divorce proceedings. . . .

To be sure, that additional evidence might properly have been admitted for its limited bearing on defendant's credibility, since he took the witness stand; but it was not offered for that purpose and—absent a limiting instruction—should not be so accepted on appeal. . . . As this evidence was of a kind highly likely to arouse the jury's animosity against defendant, his failure to object specifically to its admission (as distinguished from his objection to the reception of any evidence concerning the divorce) or to request a limiting instruction, did not cure the error. I feel sure that if either of my colleagues had been sitting as the trial judge, he would, without prompting from defendant's counsel, either have excluded the additional evidence or given such an instruction. It has often been held (and our own rules so provide) that we should take notice of and reverse on account of a markedly serious error to which a defendant did not object at the trial.

Here we have markedly serious error. It cannot be characterized as "harmless," if the test of harmlessness be that employed by the Supreme Court and most other courts. The only conceivable remaining basis, therefore, for not reversing this judgment must be the application of the unique interpretation of the phrase "harmless error" which has unfortunately become current in this Circuit. A superficial reading of Judge Hand's opinion might make it appear that he does not employ the "harmless error" doctrine, since he says that, were it true that the additional evidence was inadmissible, "the evidence would have been so damaging that we are not sure that the verdict should stand," and adds, "We need not say, because we do not think that it was erroneous to admit the evidence" (going on in that same paragraph to assign reasons for that conclusion which, as above noted, I think untenable). But in the very next paragraph he abandons the suggestion that reversal might follow if this evidence was incompetent: He now says that, even if the additional testimony was not competent, "Rubenstein was not injured" by its admission; and, in the last paragraph of the opinion, he says, "The crime was proved beyond the faintest peradventure of a doubt. * * *" Those two remarks contain, in abbreviated form, the Second Circuit doctrine of "harmless error," that is, the test to be used in determining whether inadmissible evidence is harmless is not the probable effect of its admission on the jury but whether the Court considers the defendant guilty.

I have the very highest respect for Judge Hand. To sit with him is an inestimable privilege, a constant source of education. Consequently, I usually suspect my own tentative opinions, when they vary from his. But on this one subject I find myself recurrently and unregenerately at odds with him. In short, I cannot accept this view which my five colleagues have adopted and which he has enthusiastically endorsed: If we, sitting on a reviewing court, believe, from merely reading the record, that a defendant is guilty, then, generally, we must hold that an error, especially one of admitting evidence, even if it may seriously have prejudiced the jury against the defendant, is to be regarded as "harmless." (This rule seems to be inapplicable where the error consists of the exclusion of important evidence. . . .) Several times heretofore I have stated my reasons for opposition to that doctrine. What I shall say here is partly by way of summary and partly by way of amplification of those previous comments.

It is seldom possible with even moderate competence to conjecture solely from perusal of a written or printed record whether or not a defendant is guilty. (The ascertainment of the true facts of a case, even in the best of circumstances, is but a conjecture or guess: Since that process involves events which occurred in the past, the fact finder must rely on the narratives of other persons. That means that the "finding of facts" rests on the fact finders' guess as to whether and to what extent those narratives are accurate. . . .) As the judges of an appeal court have not heard or seen the witnesses, they have no reasonably adequate way of judging whether any of the witnesses lied or—because of unconscious bias or faulty memory—testified with inadvertent inaccuracy. (Observation of the witnesses' demeanor is by no means an infallible method of determining the accuracy of their testimony. But, no perfect method having been devised, such data are of considerable value. The printed record necessarily omits such data. The testimony of a glib liar may show up in print far more persuasively than that of a honest, cautious witness. Perhaps, if on appeals we used records consisting of talking motion pictures of the trial, this particular difficulty could be largely overcome.) On that account alone, the rule is well settled that the credibility of the witnesses is exclusively a question for the jury. When, then, an upper court, with an air of emphatic assurance, says in an opinion, as Judge Hand, speaking for the majority, says in this case, "The crime was proved beyond the faintest peradventure of a doubt," what it actually means, for all its magisterial tones, comes to no more than this: "As we were not present at the trial, we did not listen to, and observe, the witnesses and cannot determine their credibility. However, we shall make the assumption—which may not be at all correct in fact—that the government's witnesses testified honestly and with entire accuracy, and that the testimony of defendant's witnesses, in so far as it contradicted that of the government's witnesses, was wholly untrustworthy. Only by making that assumption (and, accordingly, paying no heed to the evidence offered by the defendant) do we come to the conclusion that defendant's guilt is unquestionably clear." Were that unspoken assumption explicitly stated in such an opinion, the seeming air of indubitable certainty about its pronouncement of defendant's guilt would disappear, and the weakness of this court's peculiar harmless-error doctrine would be exposed to scrutiny.

For see: My colleagues' rule is to overlook errors in admitting evidence, when (without regard to the jury's verdict) the record, in their opinion, shows that defendant is guilty. But why does the record so show? Only because of an assumption—which may easily be fictitious—that the testimony of defendant's witnesses is unreliable. Had my colleagues been present at the trial, they might have concluded that, as to pivotal items, the testimony of the government's witnesses was not worthy of belief. My colleagues employ the contrary assumption precisely because they were not present at the trial—which highlights the impropriety of their sustaining the conviction on the ground that, independent of the jury's verdict, they find the defendant guilty.

The unjustified use, in such a case, of the assumption about the government's evidence must be distinguished from its appropriate use of another context: In a case where no prejudicial evidence was erroneously received, and a defendant asks an upper court to reverse his conviction on the sole ground that the record evidence is such that no reasonable jury could have found him guilty, the judges are compelled to resort to a sort of fiction. Since they were absent from the trial and since the credibility of the witnesses is a question for the jury, the judges, perforce, must assume it to be true (whether or not it is true in fact) that all the testimony pointing to guilt was given by honest, reliable, credible witnesses and that all other testimony was not. That assumption (a fiction, an "as if") in such a case is unavoidable; therefore necessary; therefore proper. Be it noted, however, that, in such circumstances, the judges at least have before them, although in printed form, the identical evidence—neither more nor less—which had been presented to the jury. But that assumption (fiction) is not necessary and is therefore improper, when (as here) the record contains prejudicial evidence improperly admitted. For the issue on appeal is then not whether, making that assumption and on the very same record which was before the jury, the jury reasonably found against defendant. If, in a case like this, the judges conclude that defendant is guilty, they reach that conclusion by ignoring important matter which had been presented to the jury and which may well have induced its verdict. In those circumstances, the judges decide against defendant, not by affirming a jury's verdict on the record which the jury had before it, but on a strikingly different record. (. . . In all fields of thought, fictions must be cautiously employed. They are "useful lies," statements which, although contrary to truth or incapable of verification, nevertheless are immensely convenient and often necessary. But while a fiction may have such value in one context, it may be harmful in another. "Extrapolation," always tricky business, is peculiarly so when applied to fictions. . . .) For that reason, I said that the judges are deciding such a case "independent of the jury's verdict."

The important fact is that in this Circuit "harmless" error does not mean merely that the improperly admitted evidence was such that in all probability it made no difference to the jury; were that the rule, I would find it unobjectionable. (True, even with the rule thus limited, the appeal judges are conjecturing as to whether the evidence affected the jury. But the area of guessing is severely restricted.) The rule here is that, even if that evidence was such that it may well have affected the jury's verdict, yet it is no ground for reversal if my colleagues believe the defendant guilty. *The rule in this*

*Circuit thus boils down to this: If the jury, on the basis of certain evidence, has brought in a verdict of guilt, then, on quite different evidence (that is, different because the judges delete prejudicial evidence) the judges may render their own independent verdict of guilt, despite the fact that they neither saw nor heard the witnesses on whose testimony they rest their verdict.*

In so doing, the judges convert themselves into a jury. By thus substituting themselves for the legally authorized jury, I think they exercise a power beyond their legitimate—their constitutional—scope. Without warrant in statute or Constitution, the judges find the facts. I cannot believe that such a procedure satisfies the constitutional requirement of a jury trial. The defendant has been convicted by the judges, not by a jury. He has been unconstitutionally deprived of the privilege of a trial by jury fully as much as if, in the first instance, he had been compelled to go to trial before a jury-less court.

To be sure, some lawyers maintain that only through such a judge-made device can the jury system be made "workable." But such a device makes the jury system workable—by not working it. . . . If any judges happen to regard as "impractical" the constitutional obligation to give a defendant a jury trial, they should not, by indirection, amend the Constitution. They should frankly state their position and invite our citizens to bring about a constitutional amendment in the manner prescribed by the Constitution. (It is important to differentiate between specific constitutional provisions and those which deliberately employ vague phrases such as "due process." The latter, unlike the former, . . . justify—indeed compel—liberal and developing judicial interpretation. . . . The jury-trial provision does not preclude all elasticity in construction; . . . But it surely does not authorize a construction which, in effect, eliminates the function of a jury's verdict of guilt except as a preliminary to a verdict by appellate judges based upon a record significantly different from that considered by the jury.)

A jury trial unquestionably has defects. At best, such a trial, especially as now conducted—that is, as if it were a game or sporting event—is an imperfect, all-too-human, instrument for ascertaining the true facts of a case. As Borchard reported several years ago . . . occasionally it is discovered that an innocent man, after a jury trial, has been convicted and sent to jail or put to death by the government. No one can doubt that there have been undiscovered instances (no one knows how many) of convictions of the innocent. Unfortunately, some tragedies of that kind are bound to occur. I, for one, do not care to accept responsibility for any such miscarriage of justice which, with reasonable precautions, could have been avoided.

The conventions of judicial opinion-writing—the uncolloquial vocabulary, the use of phrases carrying with them an air of finality, the parade of precedents, the display of seemingly rigorous logic bedecked with "therefores" and "must-be-trues"—give an impression of certainty (which often hypnotizes the opinion-writer) concealing the uncertainties inherent in the judging process. On close examination, our legal concepts often resemble the necks of the flamingos in *Alice in Wonderland* which failed to remain sufficiently rigid to be used effectively as mallets by the croquet players. (I am here borrowing and adapting an image of Edmund Wilson used in his criticism of the verse of certain modern poets.) In a case like this, all our complicated judicial apparatus yields but a human judgment, not at all sure to be correct, affecting the life of another human being. If we are at all imaginative, we will comprehend what that judgment will mean to him, and what a horror it will be if we wrongly decide against him. To be sure, one can say that it does not pay to take too seriously the possibility that one man, more or less, may be unjustly imprisoned, considering the fact that [in World War II] millions have died and that the Atomic Age . . . may end any minute in the destruction of all this planet's inhabitants. Yet (perhaps because I am growing old or because, despite my years, I have not yet fully matured) it seems to me that, if America's part in the war was meaningful and if mankind's development has any significance against the background of eternity, then the dignity of each individual man is not an empty phrase. If it is not, then we judges, part of a human arrangement called government, should proceed with great caution when we determine whether a man is to be forcibly deprived of his liberty. Recognizing the fallibility of juries, we should, I think, be vigilant to prevent the jailing of an innocent person through an erroneous appeal to jury prejudices. In such a case as this, where seriously damaging testimony has been erroneously admitted, we should not assume that the government's witnesses necessarily reported the facts accurately, and should order a new trial.

It will not do to say that delay and expense will ensue. They are of far less importance than a fair trial. And they will be incurred infrequently because of errors, if by reversals in cases like this, we educate prosecutors and trial judges to prevent unfairness to a person on trial. Instead of so educating them, this court seems to me to invite such unfairness. For it announces that, if the district attorney succeeds, by unfair practices, in persuading a jury to say "guilty," this court will usually disregard those practices in a case in which the properly admitted evidence is compatible with guilt. That thereby such improprieties have been encouraged is suggested by the frequency with which this court has found it necessary to condone such improprieties by invoking, tacitly or openly, its unique harmless-error rule. . . .

*151 F.2d 915 (1945)*

# UNITED STATES v. ANTONELLI FIREWORKS CO. ϑ

IN THE SPRING of 1944, in the desperate hours of World War II, several officers of the corporation, Antonelli Fireworks Co., Inc., were convicted of willfully manufacturing defective war materials. They appealed from this conviction mainly on the grounds of serious errors in the conduct of the trial. Of particular concern in Judge Frank's dissenting opinion, which appears below, is the summation by the prosecuting attorney which the appellants urged was inflammatory. Judge Charles Clark, writing the majority opinion in which the conviction was affirmed, said of this, "Though the remarks were ill advised and overzealous . . ." the judge cured the possibility of error by cautioning the jury to disregard them. In his dissent, Judge Frank goes at length into details of the case.

FRANK, Circuit Judge (dissenting): 1. I have no respect for the humorless self-righteous sort of person who has a firm conviction that always he alone, of the entire regiment, is in step. Accordingly, when all my colleagues (whom I consider among the ablest of judges) repeatedly arrive at a certain conclusion, my sense of humor usually downs my doubts and nudges me into acquiescence. But on the subject of "harmless error" in criminal trials, I find myself, because of the deep seriousness of the matter, unable to follow that course. I am emboldened to persist in my disagreement by the fact that three times in the past few years the Supreme Court has reversed my colleagues for their views on that issue. . . .

2. As crucial facts have been omitted from or glossed over in the majority opinion, I must narrate them:

Some of the defendants are Italian-born and others of Italian descent. One of them, Antonelli, in his testimony spoke a decided Italian-American jargon. American soldiers were still fighting in Italy when the case was tried. The closing arguments to the jury occurred on June 8, 1944, just after our Army's invasion of Normandy had begun. In those circumstances (and perhaps bearing in mind an ancient observation, "If you want to excite prejudice you must do so at the close, so that the jurors may more easily remember what you said"), government counsel concluded his summation with this final sentence: "I cherish an overwhelming confidence * * * in the belief that * * * you will render a verdict of which you can be proudly justified in the presence of your fellowmen, those here at home who labor and have labored unceasingly in an honest effort to manufacture munitions of war as well as those of us beyond the seas who look to us for the things they need to sustain them in their hour of extreme sacrifice." Counsel for the defendants thereupon objected to these improper remarks.

At a minimum, so the Supreme Court tells us, the trial judge, in such circumstances, "without waiting for an objection," should have promptly employed a "stern rebuke and repressive measures." But here the judge was neither prompt nor stern, and uttered no rebuke. My colleagues are entirely mistaken when they say that he acted "immediately after the summation," applied "extensive corrective measures," gave a "rebuke" which "was swift and sure," and "deflated immediately" the words of the prosecutor. For it was not until the day after the summation—on the next morning when the jury reconvened after a recess—that he took any steps to correct the error. Then, for the first time (and, contrary to my colleagues' statement, not with defendants' approval) he gave but a mild cautionary instruction, devoid of anything resembling a rebuke, stern or otherwise. Thus at least some twelve hours had intervened, so that, during the jurors' overnight reflections on the case, this vicious appeal to their prejudices had had a chance to soak in, before the judge mildly counseled the jurors on the subject—and this in a case which (as I shall try to show) was by no means "strong." The inflammatory and highly prejudicial character of such a gross stimulation of such patriotic sentiments when a criminal trial is conducted in wartime has been universally recognized. . . . Never before has any court said what my colleagues say here—that such deadly remarks were "no more than an admonition to the jurors to observe their oath of office and thus to have the satisfaction of duty well done." Nor heretofore has any court deemed such remarks harmless because compressed into a single sentence, for experience teaches that a poisonous suggestion of that kind needs no elaboration. As I shall show below, the courts have frequently held that this type of error cannot be eradicated by a cautionary instruction or even by an immediate severe censuring of offending counsel. For these reasons I think this error was so markedly harmful that it requires reversal for a new and fair trial. On that ground I dissent.

A "strong" case has been defined as one in which the evidence of guilt is "overwhelming." . . . In an Appendix to this dissent I have stated in some detail some of the significant evidence to which my colleagues have but sketchily and quite inadequately referred; it will there be seen, not only that the jury could reasonably have found defendants not guilty, (that is, could reasonably have concluded that the defective work was due not to fraud but to the inexperience and incompetence of Antonelli, the other defendants, and the employees) but also that among the government's important witnesses were self-confessed accomplices and—more important—that there was considerable testimony, much of it uncontradicted, that government agents had practiced intimidation of witnesses. I therefore say that the government's case was not "strong." The courts recognize the unreliability of accomplices' testimony (while the testimony of accomplices will sustain a verdict, the fact that the judge should instruct the jury to accept it with caution . . . serves to show that a case resting on such testimony is "weak") and have often declared that a party's intimidation of witnesses is a "badge of the weakness" of his case. Wigmore . . . says: "It has always been understood—the inference, indeed, is one of the simplest in human experience—that a party's falsehood or other fraud in the preparation and presentation of his cause, his fabrication or suppression of evidence by bribery or spoliation, and all similar conduct, is receivable against him as an indication of his consciousness that his case is a weak or unfounded one, and from that consciousness may be inferred the fact itself of the cause's lack of truth and merit. The inference thus does not apply itself necessarily to any specific fact in the cause, but operates, indefinitely though strongly, against the whole mass of alleged facts constituting his cause. * * * As the general principle applies in common to all these forms of conduct, it is not necessary, nor is it usually possible, to discriminate the precedents that apply it in one or another form. Roughly classifying them, they admit all forms of personal falsification by the party in the course of the litigation; fabrication or manufacture of evidence, by forgery, bribery, subornation, and the like; suppression of evidence, by *intimidation*, eloignment, or concealment of *witnesses* or material objects. * * *" Usually in criminal cases that rule has been applied to defendants. But it applies to the government as well. . . .

3. As, of course, no court knows what influenced a particular jury's verdict of guilt in any particular case, there are three possible alternative positions with respect to "harmless error." The first is that every error is harmful; no court today takes that position. The second—which is that of the Supreme Court, of most of the circuit courts, and of the English courts—may be sum-

marized thus: An error (except as to "formal matters" that is, those which involve the "mere etiquette of trials * * * and the minutiae of procedure") is presumed to be prejudicial (that is, improperly to have induced the verdict); but this presumption is rebutted if the evidence is so "strong" that no sensible jury, had there been no error, would conceivably have acquitted, as for instance where the defendant in his testimony in effect admits his guilt. In other words, when there is substantial error the appellate court will not affirm merely because the jury, if it believed the government's witnesses and disbelieved the defendant's, could reasonably have inferred that defendant was guilty; it will affirm only if, had no error occurred, the jury could not reasonably have reached a different verdict, and will reverse "if, upon any conceivable construction of anything in the testimony, it would have been possible for a reasonable man to have reached any other verdict than the one returned by the jury."

As I have said elsewhere, this rule does not work automatically, for some limited conjecture is unavoidable; but this rule does severely restrict the area of conjecture. (Here, as in many other contexts, it is necessary, as Holmes often pointed out, to draw a line, the precise location of which, unavoidably, is arbitrary. . . .) It means that the judges do not themselves decide the issue of guilt, do not consider the credibility of the witnesses, do not invade the jury's province.

Necessarily, an upper court which does not employ either of these rules employs—either explicitly or tacitly—one which involves its own determination of the defendant's guilt or innocence, although the testimony is in conflict and the court has not heard and seen the witnesses. Such a court will hold an error "harmless" if its judges believe, from their study of the printed record, that defendant is guilty, regardless of whether those judges are convinced that the evidence is such that, absent the error, a reasonable jury which heard the witnesses would indubitably have rendered a verdict against defendant. In a court which proceeds on that doctrine of harmless error, the judges decide against the defendant, not by affirming a jury's verdict on the record which was presented to the jury, but on a markedly different record— one from which the error has been elided. The judges of such a court impliedly say in effect: "To be sure, the matter erroneously injected into the case when it was before the jury may have diverted the jury from a consideration of the properly admitted evidence and may have persuaded the jurors to find defendant guilty without regard to whether they believed the government's witnesses and disbelieved defendant's. But no one can tell that that is true, and we will not disturb a conviction on mere guesswork. So we use a different approach: We have read the record, and, while we did not observe the witnesses, and therefore lack the accepted means of determining credibility, we believe the testimony of those witnesses called by the government. We do not know, of course, whether, had we been present at the trial, we would so have believed; but we must do the best we can in dealing with such a conjectural subject. Accordingly, we hold that defendant is guilty, and consequently conclude that it is unimportant whether in actual fact (which is unknowable) the improper matter, rather than the evidence, induced the jury's verdict." The use of that doctrine means that the appellate judges are returning their own verdict, independent of (although preceded by) the jury's, and founded on a record other than that which the jury considered; for the judges are able to and do disregard the improper matter, but it is impossible to know what the jury did. Since the appellate judges' verdict rests on printed testimony, the result is a jury-less "trial by affidavits." Such a doctrine, which does indeed compel extensive judicial guesswork, is inescapable for a court which rejects both the other two positions described above.

It is this third doctrine which (with certain exceptions, noted in the Appendix hereto, but not pertinent here) has been heretofore adopted by my colleagues and which they apply here.

Their position is illuminated by their decision in a recent case, *United States* v. *Mitchell* . . . , in which the testimony was in conflict, and in which they held harmless unfairness toward the defendant on the part of the trial judge. There my colleagues refused to reverse because they concluded that the case was "strong," although that conclusion turned on my colleagues' opinion as to the credibility of the witnesses. On rehearing . . . a revised transcript of the trial court's record disclosed the inaccuracy of important "facts" on which my colleagues had previously based their views as to the "strength" of the case. My colleagues nevertheless adhered to their former decision, although no one reading the revised version of the facts . . . could possibly say that a jury would have been at all unreasonable had it acquitted. Obviously when my colleagues said that that case was "strong," they meant no more than that, without themselves observing the witnesses, they believed defendant guilty.

And so in the case at bar where, again, the testimony is in conflict: Referring to one of defendants' contentions, my colleagues say that "the jury was justified in concluding otherwise." They state that the verdict "was amply supported by the evidence," since "questions of credibility are for the jury." They conclude that "the evidence was as strong and persuasive as it is ever likely to be in a hotly disputed case," and that, "supported by the natural inferences to be drawn," the verdict was "thoroughly justified." Such expressions would be entirely appropriate if there had been no error in the course of the trial and if the issue were whether there was sufficient competent evidence to support the verdict, for then the question would be whether the court could say that no jury could rationally have found defendants guilty. But such expressions are not appropriate where (as here) the court is called on to determine whether, in a "hotly contested case," turning on "questions of credibility," it may properly hold that, if no error had occurred, no jury could rationally have found the defendants innocent.

To restate the point: In this, as in other "harmless error" cases, my colleagues have lost sight of a distinction—which I think must be made—between the function of a reviewing court when (1) the issue is whether the verdict is against the weight of the evidence and (2) when the issue is whether an error (such as, for example, erroneous admission of evidence or misconduct of counsel) is "harmless." Because they have repeatedly ignored this distinction, I think it desirable (at the cost of some repetition) to dwell on it: In a case where no prejudicial evidence has been received and where no misconduct of government counsel has occurred, if a defendant asks an upper court to reverse his conviction on the sole ground that the record evidence is such that no reasonable jury could have found him guilty, the judges are compelled to resort to a sort of fiction: Since they were absent from the trial and since the credibility of the witnesses is a question for the jury, the judges, perforce, must assume it to be true (whether or not it is true in fact) that all the testimony pointing to guilt was given by honest, reliable, credible witnesses and that all other testimony was not. That assumption (a fiction, an "as if") in such a case is unavoidable; therefore necessary; therefore proper. Be it noted, however, that, in such circumstances, the judges at least have before them, although in printed form, the identical matter—neither more nor less—which had been presented to the jury. But that assumption (fiction) is not necessary and is therefore, I think, improper, when the record contains prejudicial evidence improperly admitted, or remarks of counsel improperly made. For the issue on appeal is then not whether, making that assumption and on the very same record which was before the jury, the jury reasonably found against defendant. If, in a case like this, the judges conclude that defendant is guilty, they reach that conclusion by ignoring important matter which had been presented to the jury and which may well have led to its verdict. In those circumstances, the judges decide against defendant, not by affirming a jury's verdict on the record which the jury had before it, but on a strikingly different record.

My colleagues' doctrine runs directly contrary to the rule enunciated in an opinion delivered by Mr. Justice Miller where (answering a contention that an error in admitting evidence did no harm because "There is enough found in the record to show that the verdict was right, if it had been excluded"), he said for the Court: "The case must be such that this court is not called on to decide upon the preponderance of evidence that the verdict was right, notwithstanding the error complained of." That was a civil case; it goes without saying that the rule should be at least as favorable to a defendant in a criminal suit.

My colleagues, however, assert that such a rule is today outmoded: Recently . . . they said that there is a "modern disposition to assume that an error has been harmless. * * *" As I have pointed out elsewhere, that view is opposed to the current rulings of the Supreme Court and of the other circuits. I think that *Bollenbach v. United States* . . . confirms my position. There the Supreme Court has said that the question is not whether the appellate judges have the belief, "engendered by the dead record," that defendants are guilty, "but whether guilt has been found by a jury according to the procedure and standards appropriate for criminal trials in the federal court." When the Supreme Court . . . declared that it is wrong to presume "all errors to be 'harmless' if only the appellate court is left without doubt that one who claims its protective process is, after all, guilty," it was not speaking at large, but was engaged in reversing this court; that serves, I believe, to show that the Supreme Court thinks, as I do, that my colleagues, in cases where the testimony is in conflict, erroneously rest their decisions as to harmless error on their own belief in a defendant's guilt or innocence.

Decisions of the English courts, recently cited with approval by the Supreme Court in Bollenbach's case, are instructive. In each of the following cases thus cited, the Court was requested to affirm a conviction pursuant to a statute (§4 of the Criminal Appeals Act of 1907) much like our own "harmless error" statute. In *Maxwell v. The Director of Public Prosecutions* . . . , defendant had been improperly asked about a previous prosecution for another crime of which he had been acquitted; the court in reversing, said, "It is impossible to deny that the evidence was strong against him," as defendant had made "very damaging admissions," but it was not certain what the jury would have decided, had the question not been asked. The court concluded thus: "If in any case the evidence against a prisoner (other than that which is inadmissible) is very strong and is abundant to justify a jury in convicting, it may well seem unfortunate that a guilty man should go free because some rule of evidence has been infringed by the prosecutor. But it must be remembered that the whole policy of English criminal law has been to see that as against the prisoner every rule in his favor is observed and that no rule is broken so as to prejudice the chance of the jury fairly trying the true issues. The sanction for the observance of the rules of evidence in criminal cases is that, if they are broken in any case, the conviction may be quashed. * * * It is often better that one guilty man should escape than that the general rule evolved by the dictates of justice for the conduct of criminal prosecutions should be disregarded and discredited." In *Rex* v. *Dyson* . . . , where an improper instruction was given, the court reversed although it felt that the jury, if it had been given a proper instruction, "would in all probability have found the defendant guilty," saying that the statute (as to "substantial miscarriage of justice") was "intended to apply to a case in which the evidence is such that the jury must have found the prisoner guilty if they had been properly directed." The following English cases, in each of which the trial court erred in its directions to the jury, are also pertinent: In *Woolmington* v. *The Director of Public Prosecutions* . . . , the conclusion was, "We cannot say that if the jury had been properly directed they would inevitably have come to the same conclusion." In *Rex* v. *Lewis* . . . , the test was said to be whether "the conclusions is not to be resisted, that the jury, properly directed, would certainly have arrived at the same conclusion." In *Rex* v. *Haddy* . . . , the Court used the test that "no reasonable jury properly directed would, or could, have come to any other conclusion than that to which they did come." In *Stirland* v. *Director of Public Prosecutions* . . . , the test used was whether a "reasonable jury, after a proper summing up, could have failed to convict," or would "without doubt convict." Our Supreme Court's formulation is virtually the same.

The reason for this rule is obvious: "It is seldom possible with even moderate competence to conjecture solely from perusal of a written or printed record whether or not a defendant is guilty. As the judges of an appeal court have not heard or seen the witnesses, they have no reasonably adequate way of judging whether any of the witnesses lied or—because of unconscious bias or faulty memory—testified with inadvertent inaccuracy."

Most (not all) of the precautionary and exclusionary rules have derived from or have been perpetuated because of the recognition of the untrained capacity of jurors; for that reason, departures from those rules are usually not error when a trial judge sits without a jury (for example, reception of legally inadmissible evidence when there is other competent evidence to sustain the judgment). But if in a jury trial in a criminal suit (a) there has been a violation of any of these rules—designed to keep from the jurors matter which might improperly influence them against the defendant—and (b) the verdict is adverse to him, and (c) the evidence is not such that, had that rule not been violated, a reasonable jury would unquestionably have reached the same verdict, then, unless the verdict is set aside, the very purpose of the rule is frustrated. The point is that, if such a violation is held harmless, the rule has been abandoned, and the jury has been subjected to influences recognized, in the judicial adoption of the rule, as unfair to the defendant. In sum, unless the rule is senseless and should never have been adopted, the defendant has not received a fair trial.

4. Applying the usual "harmless error" doctrine, the courts generally hold that improper remarks (or other similar misconduct) of counsel will be deemed to have induced the verdict (*Berger* v. *United States* . . .) and to require reversal. For such remarks may affect the jury even more than erroneously admitted evidence: Close students of the subject, such as Morgan, tell us that today, unfortunately, a jury trial usually is "a game in which the contestants are not the litigants but the lawyers." An experienced trial lawyer writes: "It is a well recognized fact that in most cases the jury 'tries' the lawyers rather than the clients. * * * The personality of the lawyer is constantly before the jury and he gradually absorbs the client's cause to such an extent that unconsciously in the minds of the jury it becomes the lawyer's cause." And the courts have said that the words of the government's lawyer are likely to be exceptionally impressive, since he is an official.

Exception (as usual) is made when the evidence against the defendant is "strong," that is, the evidence of guilt is "overwhelming," so that it is all but impossible to believe that any sensible jury would have acquitted even if no improper remarks had been made; in such a case, no court will reverse, no matter how seriously the government counsel misbehaved. . . .

5. True, it is generally held that error consisting of misconduct of counsel will be deemed to have been cured if the trial court promptly gave the offending counsel a "stern rebuke," and immediately cautioned the jury to disregard the misconduct. But when (a) counsel's remarks are of an unusually inflammatory character (or he has otherwise flagrantly misbehaved) and (b) the evidence of guilt is not "overwhelming," then almost everywhere in criminal cases (except in this circuit) and virtually everywhere in civil cases, it has been held that neither a cautionary instruction nor any other action by the trial judge, by way of rebuke or otherwise, suffices to purge the error, but that he should grant a mistrial or a new trial, and that, if he does not do so, the judgment must be reversed. . . .

Indeed, the judge's cautionary instruction may do more harm than good: It may emphasize the jury's awareness of the censured remark—as in the story by Mark Twain of the boy told to stand in the corner and not think of a white elephant. . . .

6. . . . My colleagues mistakenly state, as to the "men overseas" remarks of government counsel, that the trial court "promised to take care of the matter in its charge," and that this course was "apparently completely acceptable to the defendants." As will be seen from the colloquy quoted in the note, the trial judge made no such promise, and defendants did not therefore indicate that such a course would be acceptable. True, having promptly and forcefully objected to the "men overseas" argument of counsel, defendants' lawyers did not go further and ask for a mistrial or object to the judge's

charge in that respect after it was given. But it is revelatory that their failure to do so has been treated by my colleagues as a waiver of defendants' right to assigned error now. For, even if defendants had not so much as mentioned the matter in the trial court, my colleagues would not hesitate to note it on appeal, if they regarded the error as grave enough to be a ground of reversal. . . . Since the question of the effect on the jury of government counsel's remarks can never arise unless there is a verdict of guilt, the result must be that, if my colleagues are correct (that is, that verdict of guilty is invariably to be taken as demonstrating that the evidence of guilt was so overwhelming that the misconduct did not influence the jury), in no case can such conduct be reversible error—for then every case in which a defendant appeals is a "strong" case. Surely, correct reasoning runs the other way: As the evidence of witness intimidation and the use of accomplices' testimony disclose a recognition by the government of the "weakness" of the government's case, it should be assumed that the case is not "strong" and that the verdict against the defendants resulted from the misconduct (that is, that the evidence is not such that, absent the misconduct, a reasonable jury would indubitably have found defendant guilty.) . . .

Just as [my colleagues] refuse to reverse for erroneously admitted evidence when, despite conflicting testimony, they believe a defendant guilty, so they do likewise as to counsel's improper remarks in a criminal suit.

Strangely enough, my colleagues have taken a different position as to misconduct of counsel in civil litigation. In Brown v. Walter . . . the lawyer for the successful plaintiff, in an automobile collision case, injected into the record the fact that the nominal defendant was insured by an insurance company. Although the trial judge cautioned the jury not to heed that fact, this court reversed, citing cases—including James Stewart & Co. v. Newby . . . and Brooke v. Croson . . .—to the effect that "no caution would serve to cure" such an error. Surely, if that rule is to be invoked to protect the pocketbook of an insurance company, it should be invoked in the instant case to protect natural persons from being sent to jail unjustly.

A jury trial, at best, is chancy. "Mr. Prejudice and Miss Sympathy are the names of the witnesses whose testimony is not recorded, but must nevertheless be reckoned with * * *"; and most jurors have no trained capacity for doing so. A keen observer has said that "next to perjury, prejudice is the main cause of miscarriages of justice." If government counsel in a criminal suit is allowed to inflame the jurors by irrelevantly arousing their deepest prejudices, the jury may become in his hands a lethal weapon directed against defendants who may be innocent. He should not be permitted to summon that thirteenth juror, prejudice. Lawsuits, do what we will, are hazardous: A missing witness, a lost document—these and numerous other fortuitous factors may result in a man's losing his life, liberty or property unjustly. When the government puts a citizen to the hazards of a criminal jury trial, a government attorney should not be allowed to increase those hazards unfairly. When, as here, such an attorney has done so, I, as a government servant, am unwilling to approve the result. I think it is our duty to give these defendants another trial....

8. Judges who accept what I consider the correct view of harmless error do not demand perfection in trials, or engage in fly-specking scrutiny of trial records. Also, in condemning appeals to prejudice, they have in mind the different meanings of the word "prejudice": Every society has its fundamental "value judgments," which constitute its established predilections, ideals, preconceptions—"prejudices" in that sense of the word. To the extent, then, that a government lawyer appeals to those cherished values, so far as they are relevant to the case in hand, he acts appropriately. So, too, when he urges the jury to discern the hidden motives of the defendant's witnesses. "Impartiality is not gullibility. Disinterestedness does not mean child-like innocence." But a government lawyer acts unfairly when he arouses jury prejudices that are irrelevant and distracting.

9. This court has several times used vigorous language in denouncing government counsel for such conduct as that of the United States Attorney here. But, each time, it has said that, nevertheless, it would not reverse. Such an attitude of helpless piety is, I think, undesirable. It means actual condonation of counsel's alleged offense, coupled with verbal disapprobation. If we continue to do nothing practical to prevent such conduct, we should cease to disapprove it. For otherwise it will be as if we declared in effect, "Government attorneys, without fear of reversal, may say just about what they please in addressing juries, for our rules on the subject are pretend-rules. If prosecutors win verdicts as a result of 'disapproved' remarks, we will not deprive them of their victories; we will merely go through the form of expressing displeasure. The deprecatory words we use in our opinions on such occasions are purely ceremonial." Government counsel, employing such tactics, are the kind who, eager to win victories, will gladly pay the small price of a ritualistic verbal spanking. The practice of this court—recalling the bitter tear shed by the Walrus as he ate the oysters—breeds a deplorably cynical attitude towards the judiciary.

On the other hand, a reversal in a case like this might well serve as a deterrent: If it became known that misconduct of a United States Attorney had caused the public the expense of a new trial, his resultant unpopularity might tend to make him subsequently live up to professional standards of courtroom decency. If this court really meant business about such behavior as that of government counsel in the case at bar, it would, at a minimum, announce that if, in any future case any government lawyer should thus conduct himself, it would deprive him of the right to practice in this court and would recommend that he be removed from his office as a representative of our government.

This is no light matter. In its Report on *Lawlessness in Law Enforcement*, the National Committee on Law Observance and Enforcement said, in 1931, of unfairness in prosecutions (including "the various forms of misconduct by prosecutors * * * in the courtroom," such as unfair and inflammatory comments and appeals to prejudice): "First, these unfair practices are a type of lawless enforcement of law which is especially liable to create resentment against law and government, because they are committed by district attorneys * * *—the very officials most definitely responsible for law observance. Moreover, these abuses usually occur in the publicity of a courtroom. They are not hidden away and subject to denial like the third degree. They are witnessed by spectators and may be recorded by the press, so that many members of the public may be revolted by the oppressive conduct of men chiefly responsible for the administration of justice. Such resentment easily engenders the dangerous feeling that a fair trial has been denied because the defendant belongs to an unpopular group and that for members of such a group justice through the courts is not to be expected. * * * Not to be overlooked is the effect of unfairness upon the accused. Even if he is guilty there are degrees of criminality which he may not yet have reached. It may still be possible to accomplish his readjustment to society, but hardly so if he feels deeply and justly that society in the person of its chief representatives has behaved tyrannically and brutally. The natural effect of this emotion is to alienate him still further from the community and make his regard his criminal associates as the only men who treat him decently. In consequence he may leave prison a bitter enemy of society, more willing than before to continue a criminal career. His resentments will be shared by his family and friends. The result of the unfairness upon these persons and upon the public will be a decrease in respect for law, which is a main factor in assuring its observance. Thirdly, and perhaps most seriously, unfair practices may result in the conviction of the innocent."

A legal system is not what it says, but what it does. Our "criminal law," then, cannot be described accurately in terms merely of substantive prohibitions; the description must also include the methods by which those prohibitions operate in practice—must include, therefore, not the substantive and procedural rules as they appear in words but as they actually work, or, as Llewellyn puts it, "the net operation of the whole official set-up, taken as a whole," for it "is that net operation—it is the substantive rule only as it trickles through the screen of action—which counts in life." With opinions like that in the instant case—in which my colleagues go so far as to express a fear that reversal for a new trial would be "deadening to the morale" of the prosecutor—the "official set-up," as sanctioned by this court, will surely include a disregard by government lawyers of precepts against rabble-rousing jury speeches.

I have spelled out this dissent at what may appear to be unseemly length because it deals with a subject I consider of the gravest importance for this reason: Order is a necessary condition of social existence; to attain that order, a society makes laws, the infraction of which it punishes; one of the functions of courts is to direct such punishment. But our kind of society deems it an essential principle that no court shall direct that any man be punished except after a fair trial. As no one can prove that a society rejecting that principle cannot attain order, some skeptics sneer at that principle, call it super-refined nonsense. It is, however, part of the American faith that, without that principle, a society would be inadequately civilized. That faith our courts, I think, should vindicate by a jealous insistence that trials should not only appear to be but actually be fair. In the vale of human perplexities, perfection in that endeavor is impossible. But recognition of that impossibility should not deter us from approaching as near the ideal of such fairness as we can. . . .

Lawyers may talk rhapsodically of JUSTICE. They may, in Bar Association meetings, hymn the preeminent virtues of "our Lady of the Common Law," prostrate themselves devotedly before the miracle of the common law's protection of human liberties. But, in the last analysis, there is only one practical way to test puddings: If, again and again in concrete instances, courts unnecessarily take the chance of having innocent men sent to jail or put to death by the government because they have been found guilty by juries persuaded by unfair appeals to improper prejudices, then the praises of our legal system will be but beautiful verbal garlands concealing ugly practices we have not the courage, or have grown too callous, to contemplate.

Some judges disavow responsibility for such ugliness, asserting that the judiciary has no concern with whether or not the existing legal machinery yields injustice. They agree with Lord Sumner that judges "are not now free in the twentieth century to administer the vague jurisprudence which is sometimes attractively styled 'justice as between man and man.'" Happily, that sort of "dispassionateness" does not represent the current judicial ideal. Most judges today acknowledge that administering justice constitutes at least part of their official obligations. That acknowledgment, however, remains worse than empty unless it translates itself into action.

Of course, no human contrivances for getting at the fact of guilt or innocence can be infallible. Even if the greatest care be used, some guiltless men are bound to be punished. That risk seems to many reflective thinkers greater than it should be, because we ask casually selected groups of twelve persons, most of them untrained in the difficult art of fact-finding, to make the decisions. But, since our society continues to prize the jury as a fact-finding instrument, we are committed to taking that extra risk. For that very reason, I submit, judges should be extraordinarily vigilant to prevent the unfortunate consequences of carelessly utilizing that risky instrument.

Something like our modern jury was employed by the ancient Greeks. One of the wisest of those Greeks gave his fellows some advice we would do well to follow: "It is not right to pervert the jurymen by moving them to anger or envy or pity—one might as well warp a carpenter's rule before using it."

# Appendix

## I. *Evidence showing that the government's case was not "strong"*

1. The following evidence goes to show that the defective work may well have been due, not to fraud, but to the inexperience and incompetence of Antonelli, the other defendants and the employees.

Antonelli, the sole stockholder of the company, was born in Italy and came to this country at the age of twenty-one, some thirty years ago. He is uneducated, illiterate, unable to speak English correctly. His business had been that of making fireworks. Before 1941, he had had in his employ only a few persons except for a short period each year, when sometimes he had as many as twenty. He and the other defendants had had no experience in the making of products by pressure or in mass production until he received the government contracts, involved in this litigation, which called for the rapid assembling of several millions of bombs and required the employment of about 350 persons. Antonelli was being urged by the government to speed up his work.

Colonel Zanetti, one of the government's witnesses, testified as follows: The machines used in connection with the government contracts did not supply the required pressure automatically. The uniformity of the pressure depended entirely upon the sense of touch or sight of the girls operating the machines. "It was left up to the girl." Experience taught that uniform compression could have been obtained by an automatic process; absent that process, the necessary result could be obtained only by constant inspection. Zanetti said that the type of labor available to Antonelli was not reliable.

2. The following testimony concerning *witness intimidation* is of marked significance as showing recognition by the Government of the weakness of its case:

Costanza testified that Kiefer and other FBI agents had given him to understand that "they would make things easy for him" if he "cooperated with him," and that, "while they could not promise to get me off completely, they would see to it that everything would go easy for me." Beatrice De Filippo, an employee, testified that when interviewed by FBI agents they had assured her that if she would testify in a certain way she would have nothing to fear. John DiRitis testified that he made an engagement with three employees (Lucy Sigilone, Johanna Arone, and Theresa Molinari) to come to the office of one of the defense counsel so that such counsel could interview them in connection with the preparation of the defense; but that when he (DiRitis) called for these witnesses, they refused to see the defense counsel because they had been told by Kiefer, an FBI agent, not to do so.

*After this testimony was given, Kiefer who had previously testified, was recalled to the stand by the government, but was not asked any questions concerning it, and in no way contradicted it.*

Johanna Arone, an employee and a government witness, testified, on cross-examination, that she had been questioned by representatives of the FBI, and that fear of harm that might come to her influenced her to testify against some of the defendants.

Two of the chief government witnesses were Bianchi and Pitio, self-confessed accomplices in the alleged conspiracy. Pitio had a criminal record. In his testimony he admitted that he had told a prospective witness that "if he knew what was good for him, he would get out of this lawsuit and not testify for the defense." Alice LaBrutto testified that Pitio had told her not to testify: her testimony was not contradicted.

I fail to comprehend why my colleagues refer to the testimony, above described, as "trivial stuff" that "deserved the complete ignoring which the government gave it."

## II. *Exceptions made by this Court to its "harmless-error" rule*

In fairness to my colleagues, I must say, as I have said elsewhere, that, to their working rule of harmless error, they make these exceptions: (a) when important evidence has been excluded; (b) when the trial judge has given an erroneous charge as to substantive law; (c) sometimes when the trial judge has been extravagantly unfair; (d) when defendant has been deprived of a basic constitutional right (for example, to be represented by counsel); (e) occasionally, when the sentence is excessive. But for other types of substantial error—such, for example, as erroneous admission of evidence or such as that here involved—they refuse to reverse if they think defendant guilty, although the testimony is in conflict.

## III. A judge's doubts about the wisdom of the jury system are not incompatible with his obligation to ensure fair jury trials

It has been suggested that a judge (like me) who shares the doubts about the wisdom of the jury system is inconsistent if he urges that the courts be vigilant in preserving the jury's function. I do not understand that criticism. It is the sworn duty of judges to enforce many statutes they may deem unwise. And so, when on the bench, our private views concerning the desirability of the jury system are "as irrelevant as our attitudes toward bimetalism or the transmigration of souls." Consequently, as long as jury trials are guaranteed by constitutional or statutory provisions, it is the obligation of every judge, no matter what he thinks of such trials, to see that they are fairly conducted and that the jury's province is not invaded. That does not mean that a judge may not freely express his skepticism about the system, may not seek to bring about constitutional and statutory changes which will avoid or reduce what he considers its unfortunate results as it now operates.

*155 F.2d 631 (1946)*

# UNITED STATES v. LEVITON ?❧

IN 1951 THREE DEFENDANTS, Rubin Leviton, Arthur Blumenfeld, and Martin Markowitz, were convicted under a twenty-one court indictment of violating federal regulations concerning exports of various commodities. On appeal, they objected to the form of the indictment; to the delay between their arrest and their arraignment; and to certain occurrences during trial which, they claimed, amounted to a lack of due process. The court affirmed the convictions in an opinion written by Judge Charles Clark. Judge Frank dissents.

FRANK, *Circuit Judge* (dissenting): 1. The first ground of my dissent is what I deem a flagrant violation of the so-called "McNabb rule." That rule renders a confession inadmissible in a federal trial if obtained in violation of the requirement, now set forth in Criminal Rule 5(a), that "Any officer making an arrest * * * shall take the arrested person without unnecessary delay before the nearest available commissioner or before any other nearby officer empowered to commit persons charged with offenses against the laws of the United States." The purpose of the McNabb rule is to procure for an arrested person the following protections offered by Rule 5(b) governing the arraignment procedure: "The Commissioner shall inform the defendant of the complaint against him, of his right to counsel and of his right to have a preliminary examination. He shall also inform the defendant that he is not required to make a statement and that any statement made by him may be used against him. The Commissioner shall allow the defendant reasonable time and opportunity to consult counsel and shall admit the defendant to bail as provided in these rules." As the Supreme Court said just the other day, in *United States v. Carignan*, . . . the McNabb rule rests on the idea that detention without prompt arraignment gives "opportunity for improper

[ 341 ]

pressure before the accused has the benefit of the statement by the Commissioner."

Now see how and why Leviton was deprived of that benefit: After several weeks of shadowing, four customs agents entered his office at 1:45 P.M. on Thursday, March 25. The agents announced that he was wanted for questioning at Customs headquarters, and directed him to bring along his export files. The customs agents had no warrant for his arrest. They did not warn him that anything he said would be used against him; they made no attempt to arraign him before a magistrate or judge. Once inside the building, the agents admitted that Leviton could not leave:

Q. Isn't it a fact, Mr. Linden, that Mr. Leviton could not have left the building if he desired?
A. I wouldn't have permitted him to leave the building.
Q. Why?
A. Because we wanted to talk to him and find out about the other phases of the case.
Q. You were the agent in charge of the entire investigation?
A. Yes sir.
Q. So that on the occasion in question, if Mr. Leviton wanted to leave the building you would instruct them not to permit him to leave?
A. Not until we were through; that is correct.
Q. From the moment he was there until you were through with him, with the interrogation, you would not permit Mr. Leviton to leave the building?
A. Not by himself.

Since nothing significant occurred between the time the agents entered Leviton's office and the time of his arrival at the building, plainly he would not have been allowed his freedom after 1:45 P.M. In short, he was under arrest from that moment. All afternoon and evening up to the time of his confession, he was kept under guard. The agent in charge of his case testified quite frankly that Leviton's detention was solely for the agents' convenience in interrogating him:

Q. During the course of the afternoon, you were holding Mr. Leviton in your office until you could assign an agent to question him. Is that the idea?
A. That is correct.
Q. The entire purpose of your detaining Mr. Leviton from the time he entered the building was for the purpose of interrogating him. Is that right?
A. Yes, sir.

At one point in the afternoon, around 3:00 or 3:30, Leviton made a remark, according to his guard, that "he thought he could make a fast dishonest dollar but apparently he couldn't." Soon another agent came into the room, asked Leviton a general question about flour shipments he had handled, mentioning no particular shipments or countries. Leviton told this agent to look up some files marked "Arthur Blumenfeld" in the Barr Shipping Company. The agent returned with the files at 6:30, and asked Leviton where certain declarations were; Leviton replied that he had destroyed them. Around 9:20, the interrogation began in earnest, and by midnight the defendant had signed a typewritten confession which ended thus: "I have been sitting here for nine hours. I have smoked 100 cigarettes, and I don't know whether I am coming or going." Leviton was taken then to the Federal House of Detention and arraigned the next evening at 7:00 P.M. for the crimes to which he had confessed the previous night.

So Leviton's confession came after 7½ hours in custody. Even his admission (if it can be considered as such) that he had destroyed certain declarations came only after 4½ hours of unauthorized detention. At any time between approximately 1:45 and 5:30 that afternoon, Leviton might have been arraigned before any one of a dozen magistrates or judges in the vicinity. Prompt arraignment meant a great deal to Leviton; no warrant had even been issued for his arrest; no magistrate had ever declared that there was any "probable cause" for holding him; he was denied altogether the "benefit of the statement by the Commissioner" which the Supreme Court considers so important. Because of failure to arraign, he was not informed of the charges against him; he had no counsel; he was not warned, however perfunctorily, that what he said would be used against him—all this for the sole convenience of the customs men in interrogating him—and not, mind you, at once, but when (as one of them testified) they got ready to "assign an agent to question him."

My colleagues say, nevertheless, that the delay in arraigning Leviton was a "necessary one," and that, therefore, the McNabb rule was not violated. They rely on cases saying that delays are "necessary" if caused by unavailability of an arraigning officer when arrests are made at night, on Sunday, or over a holiday, since the rule was not intended to force magistrates to work around the clock. *United States v. Walker* . . . was such a case. There the defendant was arrested on Sunday before Labor Day in a small town. We there held that the delay before his arraignment on Tuesday was *prima facie* a reasonable one, and that the defendant had the burden of proving that it was "possible to arraign" him on Sunday or Monday. This, so far as I know, is the longest time any upper court has sanctioned between arrest and arraignment, and I do not hesitate to predict (despite my colleague's insinuation that by the Walker case we have already gelded the McNabb rule) that this court or any other court would unhesitatingly call unreasonable a weekend delay, upon a showing that the arrest was deliberately made on Saturday or a holiday to prevent prompt arraignment.

Courts and commentators have conscientiously restricted the meaning of "necessary delay" to a single situation: "Reasonableness [of the delay] will probably depend upon the time required to carry the suspect to the commissioner, and not on the time desired to keep him away from the commissioner. The entire history of committal legislation leads to such an interpretation."

The idea of allowing the police whatever delay before arraignment they may deem "necessary" for interrogation fights with the basic aim of the McNabb rule: "It aims to avoid all the evil implications of secret interrogation of persons accused of crime." *McNabb v. U.S.* . . . In *Upshaw v. United States*, . . . where the Supreme Court vitiated a confession on the ground that it had been obtained during a detention which the police admitted was for the sole purpose of investigation, the Court said: "In this case we are left in no doubt as to why this petitioner was not brought promptly before a committing magistrate * * * because the officer thought there was not a 'sufficient case' for the court to hold him. * * * He admitted that petitioner was illegally detained for at least thirty hours for the very purpose of securing those challenged confessions." The Upshaw situation, in every essential respect, is duplicated here. The Customs men make no pretense that Leviton's eleven-hour "visit" was for any other purpose than to facilitate their own investigation. Since Leviton was arrested without a warrant—I note again that no judicial officer had passed on the "probable cause" for his detention—the conclusion seems inescapable that he, like Upshaw, was being held so that the agents could get a good case against him before they had to justify his arrest to a magistrate. But clearly the police, after arrest, cannot make up for their lack of probable cause at the time of arrest. That is what McNabb is for—to make sure that they can't. It should be even more "mechanically" applied in cases of arrests without warrants than in those with warrants.

My colleagues would excuse the failure to arraign here, on still another theory. They rely on cases holding that confessions which are "promptly and spontaneously" made upon arrest are admissible, even when made prior to arraignment. This exception to McNabb is a common-sense concession in the case of a willing defendant who wants to "spill" all as soon as the police finally catch up with him; in such circumstances, the police need not shut his mouth or stuff their own ears with cotton until he can be brought before a magistrate. In such cases, there is no "opportunity for improper pressure by police" to induce the confession. *United States v. Mitchell* . . . is the leading case on this point. There the defendant's confession was given at the police station before commitment, *a few minutes after* two policemen had jailed him on a charge of housebreaking and larceny. His confession was complete and detailed; he even directed the policemen to the loot. Appellate courts have followed suit where confessions were dictated and signed within an hour or so after arrival at police headquarters, *Patterson v. United States* . . . ; or where an oral confession (complete in all its details) was made immediately after arrest and merely repeated for stenographing later in the day. *Haines v. United States.* . . .

None of these cases touches Leviton's. Although there is talk in the Haines opinion about a reasonable opportunity for the police to check stories of arrested persons before arraigning them, in fact, the defendants in both that case and in Mitchell had completely implicated themselves—that is, beyond extrication—by the time the police began checking their stories. They had made confessions amply sufficient to cinch a verdict of guilt. Leviton, in contrast, dropped one meager remark about "making a dishonest dollar," a remark which, unlike a confession, could not alone possibly secure a conviction. Leviton's is not an instance of a confession begun which would have been interrupted by an arraignment. Indeed, after that remark, Leviton said nothing of significance until three hours later when he admitted destroying certain declarations. My colleagues can point to no cases permitting police to delay arraignment so that they may track down clues and leads which the defendant, consciously or unconsciously, may have revealed, but which, of themselves, do not amount to any sort of confession of a specific crime. If Leviton had been arraigned even by 5:30, the latest moment when, probably, a magistrate could have been conveniently secured, he might have shut up, leaving the puzzled customs men to speculate exactly how he "had made his dishonest dollar," and to search vainly through the files to which he had directed them for vital missing declarations.

My colleagues come up with an astonishing argument, not suggested by the government, that "if the agents had been more sophisticated in their approach, and had pressed for it," Leviton, immediately upon his arrest, would have made a full confession. He showed, my colleagues say, a "sense of guilt" from the beginning, and a desire to "cooperate throughout the period." Accordingly, so my colleagues argue, we must treat the case exactly as if, in actual fact, he had confessed at or almost immediately after the time of his arrest. Therefore, my colleagues conclude, the actual time that elapsed between his arrest and his confession must be disregarded, and the failure during that time to bring him before a commissioner or judge is irrelevant.

To my mind, this argument is itself "sophisticated"—far too much so. It rests on a nonexistent fact, a wholly fictitious "fact," that is, a pretense or make-believe that a confession occurred several hours before it actually occurred. If one could in this way fictionally date a confession back for several hours (by predating or *nunc-pro-tuncing* it) merely because a later actual confession, since it was voluntary, is to be deemed a disclosure of an initial "desire to cooperate," then the McNabb doctrine would be gutted, since never could it be violated. For that doctrine applies only when the government proves, or the defendant admits, that his confession was voluntary, that is, "cooperative"; and one could always fictionally assume (as my colleagues assume here) that more adroit officers, immediately upon his arrest, could have converted his "cooperativeness" into a confession. This is a dangerous notion. Is an officer's belief in an accused's "sense of guilt" to create an exception to McNabb? If I am not mistaken, this is a technique frequently used in police states to extort confessions: officials play upon individual's guilt-proneness by prolonged grilling and humiliating interrogation. It has proved to be an effective device in eliciting confessions—true or false—from certain types of anxious and neurotic persons who will confess their guilt-ridden fantasies under such pressure. (Redlich, Ravitz, and Dession, *Narco-analysis and Truth*, . . . conclude on the basis of experiments with drug-induced confessions that certain neurotic individuals with strong feelings of guilt, depression, and anxiety confess most easily, and that such confessions can be as easily obtained without as with the use of drugs. "Open and veiled threats" and "the feeling of inevitable doom" facilitate the development of a reactive depression in any person, but particularly in those with self-punitive tendencies and depressive moods. Such people will confess to false and true fantasies leading to punishment; false and fantastic self-accusations are a part of the depression into which they are thrown by their stimulated fears. The authors explain, on this theory, many of the public trial confessions in totalitarian regimes, and recount examples of false confessions elicited from weak persons near the breaking point without the use of "hard methods" but merely by playing upon their guilt-ridden personalities.) (It is worth adding that the trial judge here was not completely convinced of Leviton's complete "cooperativeness": The judge ruled that an illegal seizure occurred when the customs men took from Leviton a briefcase, although he apparently offered no resistance and reacted with a nod of the head.)

The McNabb rule is especially vital to the protection of just such indiscreet defendants as Leviton, for another basic reason. Despite my colleagues' dismissal of McNabb as merely a sanction or penalty for police misconduct in delaying arraignment, a much more compelling policy lies behind it— that is, the prevention, in the most effective way possible, of coerced confessions elicited by the dreaded "third degree." "For this procedural requirement checks resort to those reprehensible practices known as the 'third degree' which, though usually rejected as indefensible, still find their way into use." (*United States* v. *McNabb*.) Recognizing the difficulty of proving "torture, physical or psychological" and "the relation between illegal incommunicado detention and 'third degree' practices" (*United States* v.

*Mitchell, . . .*) the Court chose to minimize the use of coerced confessions by ruling out automatically any such statements obtained during the period and in circumstances when those police officers who are given to such practices normally apply coercion.

The cases in which defendants confess on arrest are outside the prophylactic policy, on this account: An arrested person who promptly confesses has no need to fear strong-armed police methods. But nothing is more conducive to physical brutality or psychological badgering by so-called "lawless" policeman than a situation in which the defendant, without confessing, mutters something vague about his having been dishonest, or otherwise drops a clue or two. Then undisciplined policemen are most likely to employ "torture, physical or psychological"—to break him down. This kind of susceptible defendant needs McNabb protection the most.

Since Leviton's confession, in my opinion, was inadmissible under McNabb, I think that both his conviction and Blumenfeld's (at least on counts 1–12) must be set aside. There was, my colleagues concede, no "direct proof that he (Blumenfeld) took any part in the physical preparation of these documents or even that he ever saw them." But the prosecution was allowed to read the following portion of Leviton's confession, implicating Blumenfeld, to the jury:

Q. Was Blumenfeld aware of the fact that you were using the license of the American Relief for Italy?

A. Yes, sir, because he tried to get them first, and that is how he got to me, because he knew I was the traffic manager for Barr and we handled the American Relief for Italy, and I was stupid enough to feel I could make a few easy dollars, which I see is not possible.

This excerpt from the confession was the only direct testimony that Blumenfeld knew about and sanctioned the illegal scheme. It could easily have turned the trick with the jury. Now, the admissions of one defendant implicating another are theoretically inadmissible, for obvious reasons, against the person implicated. Such accusations are hearsay—and, in the circumstances, probably ill-motivated and peculiarly untrustworthy hearsay. However, where several defendants are tried jointly, such confessions are received when necessary to prove the declarant's guilt, and a "ritualistic admonition" given to the jury to disregard the contents insofar as they implicate the other defendants. . . . But I think that such a rule does not excuse what was done here: The statements about Blumenfeld in the confession added nothing at all to the case against Leviton which was not amply proved by the remainder of his confession. The portion relating to Blumenfeld should not have been read to the jury. Blumenfeld's counsel asked for such exclusion before the reading; since he had time only to skim through the document and was not familiar with its contents, he could not point to the specific answers incriminating Blumenfeld. Apparently the judge misunderstood the nature of the objection as to the admissibility of such portions; at any rate he made it clear that he would not exclude the Blumenfeld matter, agreeing only to instruct the jury that such portions were not binding against Blumenfeld. Blumenfeld's counsel did not object further to such portions during the reading of the confessions, obviously because he considered his general objection, made before the reading, sufficient. Consequently, I think he cannot be held to have waived his objection. Nor do I think he had to request a severance previous to the reading of the confession or forever after hold his peace. For, at the time when he must have asked for severance, he had not had a fair chance to read through the confession to see whether it was so prejudicial as to require a retrial. He had earlier objected to the introduction of the entire confession as a McNabb violation, and (only because the trial judge ruled erroneously in admitting the confession) he was put in the perplexing position of having to choose, without knowledge of the confession's contents, between continuance and severance.

"It is a hard rule anyway which allows declarations to be used at all in a case where the declarant is tried along with others." L. Hand, J., in *United States* v. *Lonardo*. . . . It is a harder rule that would allow declarations which cannot be introduced against the declarant to be introduced against his confederates. That is, in effect, what would happen if Leviton's conviction were overturned and Blumenfeld's upheld. Leviton's confession is incompetent under McNabb—incompetent against not only confederates but against the declarant himself; incompetent in a much more basic way than mere hearsay. The circumstances of a McNabb confession are somewhat akin, in the Supreme Court's thinking, to those of a coerced confession to the extent that they make the evidence generally "bad" or "tainted." I think that, if the trial judge here had ruled correctly, such evidence would never have come in at all. We ought not then to extend the "ritualistic admonition" rule to cover situations where the confession should never have been admitted. To do so would be to penalize a defendant for the trial judge's error as to a co-defendant. Thus in *Anderson* v. *United States* . . . the convictions of all co-defendants tried jointly were reversed where the confessions of some implicating the others had been introduced although obtained in violation of the McNabb rule. Although the "ritualistic admonition" had been given at the time of their introduction, the Court found "There is no reason to believe * * * that the confessions which came before the jury as an organic tissue of proof can be severed and given distributive significance by holding that they had a major share in the conviction of some of the petitioners and not at all as to the others. Since it was error to admit the confessions, we see no escape from the conclusion that the convictions of all the petitioners must be set aside."

This court has already recognized a distinction between the Anderson-type case (like this one) and an ordinary situation where the declarant's confession is admissible, at least against himself. See *United States v. Gottfried . . .* where we pointed out: "In *Anderson v. United States,* the confession had itself been unlawfully obtained, and was incompetent against the declarant; for that reason its admission resulted in a mistrial of the other accused."

2. Even if the confession were admissible, I think we should reverse and remand because of events which deprived defendants of a fair trial.

(a) When the trial judge irrelevantly spoke in defense of American Relief for Italy, and indulged in a bit of what he later feared was "flag-waving," he did so by way of a rebuke to counsel for one of the defendants. The rebuke, I think, was undeserved. The question that elicited it was patently asked in the interests of the defendants. It is highly likely, then, that when the uncalled-for comment evoked applause from two jurors, those jurors were expressing enthusiastic sympathy with what they considered the judge's disapproval of the defendants.

Since the judge's indiscretion may well have induced a verdict against the defendants, it will not do, I think, to say that we will ignore the incident because the judge was only human. Of course, all judges are human, and therefore make mistakes. But as the mistake of the judge in this case may easily have harmed the defendants seriously, we should correct it by directing a new trial. We should be humane as well as human. And since the defendants and not the trial judge are languishing in jail, they, and not he, should be the objects of our humaneness.

(b) On the second day of trial, the prosecutor held a "press conference" after court. He told the newspaper reporters of matters which (so he later advised the court) they promised not to print. In the next morning's *New York Times,* there appeared a story, told with typical journalistic vigor, about "export racketeers" who "poured $500,000 of commodities into European and South African black markets." The significance of the newspaper story was this: It professed to recount the testimony of a witness that Leviton, over the phone, had offered him a $200 bribe to withdraw from customs files a fraudulent declaration. The article detailed the attempted bribe, the meeting place for its completion and the substitution of a $44 gift of shirts for the originally offered $200. This most damaging story of the $200 bribe is wholly unsupported by the evidence. Accordingly, had the prosecutor written letters to the jurors retelling this story, of course we would reverse. He did the equivalent. For it is outrightly conceded that the *Times* reporter learned this tale from the prosecutor, and that four copies of the newspaper article were found in the jury room on the third day of the trial.

My colleagues admit that "trial by newspaper" is unfortunate. But they dismiss it as an unavoidable curse of metropolitan living (like, I suppose, crowded subways). They rely on the old "ritualistic admonition" to purge the record. The futility of that sort of exorcism is notorious. . . . Justice Jackson, in his concurring opinion in *Krulewitch* v. *United States* . . . said that, "The naïve assumption that prejudicial effects can be overcome by instructions to the jury * * * all practising lawyers know to be unmitigated fiction." . . .

I think the technique particularly objectionable and ineffective here for two reasons. (1) The story was a direct result of confidential disclosure by a government officer, the prosecutor, of not-in-the-record matters, and was not merely the accidental garbling of a confused reporter. (. . . Even the most ardent advocates of freedom of the press to report and comment on trials, stress the need for curbs on press releases during trial by attorneys on either side. . . .) (2) The article was no statement of opinion or editorial, but a professed account of courtroom evidence calculated to confuse and mislead juror-readers. In such cases, courts recognize that, for all practical purposes, defendants are deprived of their constitutional rights to confront witnesses, cross-examine and contradict them, and to object to evidence as irrelevant or incompetent—in short, all the elements of a fair trial. Last year, two Supreme Court Justices advocated in a concurring opinion the reversal of a conviction upon the ground that an officer of the court had released to the local press information about confessions of the defendants never introduced at the trial. . . .

I cannot see the relevance here of cases, to which my colleagues refer, applying the "clear and present danger" test to contempts by newspapers for articles relative to pending trial (incidentally, all nonjury trials). That test has been employed only when the newspaper itself was on trial and threatened with criminal punishment. It certainly should not be carried over to a case like this one where convicted defendants may well have been prejudiced by newspaper articles. In such a case, the clear-and-present danger test would bar reversals for all but the most flagrantly scurrilous or deceptive newspaper attacks. Courts, in reversing convictions for trial-by-newspaper, have always recognized that printed matter may be prejudicial enough to require a new trial without evidencing so depraved an attitude of the publisher as to support a contempt citation. . . .

In the instant case, the newspaper and reporter, if cited for contempt, would doubtless urge as a defense that the story came from the prosecutor, an "officer of the court." That very fact, however, underscores the gravity of the error here.

(c) I think that nothing said by defendants' counsel could justify the prosecutor's statement to the jury—not supported by anything in the record —that Leviton had refused to testify before the grand jury. The statement was so perceptibly objectionable that it did not have to be called to the judge's attention. Moreover, the prosecutor, before and after this remark, told the jury of other matters not in evidence (including some of the circumstances of the alleged $200 bribe mentioned in the newspaper).

On account of item (a) or (b) or (c), standing alone, I would probably have voted for reversal. Together they leave me without doubt that justice demands a new trial.

*193 F.2d 848 (1951)*

# UNITED STATES v. ON LEE ॐ

IN 1951 A CHINESE named On Lee appealed from a conviction under a two-count indictment. Count one charged him with selling one pound of opium. Count two charged a conspiracy to sell opium. At the trial, the government produced two important witnesses: Gong Len Ying, who testified that, on January 22, 1950, On Lee sold him one pound of opium which he then delivered to Benny Gim, an undercover agent for the Bureau of Narcotics; and government Agent Lee, who overheard a conversation between On Lee and Chin Poy, a government informer, by means of a radio receiving device which was tuned to a concealed radio transmitter carried by Chin Poy. Agent Lee testified that, in this conversation, On Lee admitted being a member of a criminal syndicate which sold opium. On Lee's appeal challenged the sufficiency of the evidence and asserted errors in the conduct of the trial and in the jury charge. He particularly urged that error was committed in admitting Agent Lee's testimony, mainly on the ground that the evidence was inadmissible because it was obtained by trespass and constituted an unreasonable search and seizure in violation of the Fouth and Fifth Amendments. Judge Thomas Swan, in the opinion for the majority, affirmed the conviction. Judge Frank dissents.

FRANK, Circuit Judge (dissenting): 1. Sixty-five years ago, the case of a humble Chinese laundryman (Yick Wo v. Hopkins . . .) led to a decision involving the formulation of one of the most important constitutional principles. Today On Lee's case, as I see it, presents the violation of one of the most cherished constitutional rights, one which contributes substantially to the distinctive flavor of our democracy. This appears from the following facts:

[ 352 ]

Chin Poy, a paid informer of the Narcotic Bureau, and himself a former drug addict, paid two "friendly" visits to On Lee's four-room combined laundry and dwelling. During these visits, the two men were alone most of the time. Unknown to On Lee, Chin Poy carried, concealed inside his pocket, a 3-inch microphone which picked up everything the two men said, and transmitted it to a receiving set manned by a narcotic agent, three or four doors down the block. This government agent, almost a year later, testified at the trial to what he had thus heard. The two visits, made for the sole purpose of gathering evidence against On Lee to be used in that trial, took place after On Lee's arrest while he was at large on bail.

On Lee was convicted primarily on that agent's testimony. The informer, Chin Poy, did not testify. But the agent testified that, by means of the concealed radio, he heard On Lee admit in one of the conversations that he had conspired with one Ying to sell opium, that On Lee represented a narcotics syndicate in the sale, and that he would make a future illegal sale to Chin Poy. Aside from this indirect testimony of the conversation, the only evidence tying On Lee to the offenses was the testimony of Ying, the alleged co-conspirator, who turned "state's evidence" at the trial. Government agents testified to various meetings between On Lee and Ying, but the agent with whom Ying negotiated the only illegal sale proved at the trial had never heard On Lee's name mentioned; and no opium was found on On Lee or among his belongings. He consistently denied, after arrest and on the witness stand, any connection with dope peddling. His frequent meetings with Ying, On Lee explained by saying that he was discussing the possible purchase of a wet-wash laundry from a business friend of Ying's—a not implausible story. Except for the agent's testimony about On Lee's incriminating conversation with Chin Poy, the jury might well have believed On Lee and acquitted him. In the circumstances, then, a court must look critically at the damaging testimony of the narcotic agent to see if it warrants the conviction, for that testimony is the guts of the government's case.

The agent who, at a distance, heard the conversation by means of the hidden microphone (a method seemingly fantastic and smacking rather of lurid gangster movies or the comic strips than of American realities) was engaged, I think, in a search violative of the Fourth Amendment. My colleagues, in rejecting this conclusion, make two arguments: The first runs thus:

As nothing tangible was taken by any federal officer, no "seizure" occurred; therefore, even if there was an illegal entry on On Lee's premises, the Fourth Amendment was not violated.

That argument means this: A federal officer, without a warrant, unlawfully breaks into a man's house. While there he overhears the houseowner utter a voluntary statement of his own criminal conduct. The officer, according to my colleagues, has not violated the Fourth Amendment, since he has seized nothing, for an oral statement is an intangible, that is, as one cannot grasp sounds, one cannot seize them. Therefore, at the trial of the houseowner, the officer, over the defendant's objection, must be allowed to testify as to that oral statement.

But Chief Justice Vinson, when a circuit judge, speaking for the Court of Appeals, decided precisely to the contrary in Neuslein v. District of Columbia. . . . There officers, entering unlawfully, overheard an incriminating oral statement. "The crucial thing 'found' in this 'search,' " said the court, "was a declaration of fact by the defendant that has become decidedly incriminating. * * * The Fourth and Fifth Amendments relate to different issues, but cases can present facts which make the considerations behind these Amendments overlap. The officers violated the security of the defendant under the Fourth by unlawfully coming into his home and by placing him in custody. * * * But how did the officers find themselves in position to see and hear the defendants? The officers, in the pursuance of a general investigation, entered the home under no color of right." And so the court ruled that the "officers' testimony regarding the defendant's declaration is inadmissible," adding that, although "* * * the Fourth Amendment was written against the background of the general warrants in England and the writs of assistance in the American colonies," the Amendment "gives a protection wider than these abuses."

My colleagues criticize the Neuslein ruling as inconsistent with a statement in the nature of dictum, in Olmstead v. United States. . . . There the Court held that wiretapping did not violate the Amendment, basing its decision in large part on the fact that interception of the phone message involved no entry. The Court said: "There was no entry of the houses or offices of the defendants." This fact the Court noted five times. In passing, the Court also said, "There was no seizure. The evidence was secured by the use of the sense of hearing and that only." Citing Gouled v. United States, . . . the Court said that in that case there was actual entrance into the private quarters of the defendant and the taking away of something tangible. Here we have testimony only of voluntary conversations secretly overheard. The Amendment itself shows that the search is to be of material things—the person, the house, his papers or his effects. The description of the warrant necessary to make the proceeding lawful is that it must specify the place to be searched and the person or things to be seized." Since the Court found no entry, those remarks were, in every respect, superfluous. Doubtless for that reason, Vinson, J., twelve years later, disregarded those remarks when he wrote Neuslein. Neuslein has been cited by the Supreme Court in Harris v. United States . . . as a "case in which law-enforcement officials have invaded a private dwelling without authority and *seized evidence of crime.*" (Emphasis added.)

And the Neuslein doctrine finds support in an earlier and a later decision: Both *Silverthorne Lumber Co. v. United States* . . . and *Zap v. United States* . . . are based on the assumption that an illegal search occurs whenever government officials unlawfully gain access to a man's books in his home or office, and that it is immaterial that they get their information by reading, copying or photographing instead of by seizing the books and removing them.

In rejecting the reason of Vinson, J., in *Neuslein,* my colleagues ignore the unbroken line of decisions holding that the Fourth Amendment forbids either (*a*) illegal searches or (*b*) illegal seizures. "The things here forbidden are two—search and seizure," said Miller, J., concurring in *Boyd v. United States.* . . . For this reason, federal courts have generally excluded any kind of evidence obtained as the result of an illegal search and not merely the physical introduction in evidence of things actually seized from the defendant. In *Boyd v. United States* . . . the Court said that Lord Camden's opinion in *Entick v. Carrington* . . . was "sufficiently explanatory of what was meant by unreasonable searches and seizures" in the minds of the men who framed the Fourth Amendment. It is notable, therefore, that Lord Camden referred to the removal of papers as but an "aggravation" of the offense in unlawful search cases. . . . I think, then, that it goes against 180 years of constitutional history to say that an illegal entry, for the purposes of procuring evidence, is not a violation of the Amendment unless something "tangible" is carried away.

Our highest court has never decided that a "search" is valid merely because made by the eyes or the ears and not the hands. Indeed, so to hold would be to disregard the everyday meaning of "search," that is, the act of seeking. In everyday talk, as of 1789 or now, a man "searches" when he looks or listens. Thus we find references in the Bible to "searching" the Scriptures (John V. 39); in literature to a man "searching" his heart or conscience; in the lawbooks to "searching" a public record. None of these acts requires a manual rummaging for concealed objects. "It is not the breaking of his doors, and the rummaging of his drawers, that constitutes the essence of the offense; but it is the invasion of his indefeasible right of personal security, personal liberty and private property. * * *" *Boyd v. United States.* . . .

So, just as looking around a room is searching, listening to the sounds in a room is searching. Seeing and hearing are both reactions of a human being to the physical environment around him—to light waves in one instance, to sound waves in the other. And, accordingly, using a mechanical aid to either seeing or hearing is also a form of searching. The camera and the dictaphone both do the work of the end organs of an individual human searcher—more accurately.

True, some look-searches and listen-searches do not run up against the Fourth Amendment. If an officer stays outside the house (or other precincts protected by the Amendment), he is not engaged in an "unreasonable" search when he looks through a window or listens at a keyhole. His activity is a "search," but not an unconstitutional one—because he has not, without the owner's consent, barged in on the constitutionally protected area. Thus a searchlight beam focused on a ship's deck is not an unreasonable search (*United States* v. *Lee* . . .); nor is watching a house from an open field on which the officer is trespassing so long as his trespass does not extend to the house (*Hester* v. *United States* . . .); even peeking through a transom is apparently cricket (*McDonald* v. *United States*. . . .). Similarly, government agents may listen to conversations in a defendant's room through a detecta-phone attached to their own side of the wall. See *Goldman* v. *United States*. . . . The Goldman case (unless, as I shall later suggest, it may have been modified) teaches that men must expect official eavesdroppers, flashlight beams, spyglasses, wall-penetrating X rays, and detectaphones—in short, every sort of attempt by officials on the outside to find out what goes on in the inside of one's house.

But the Supreme Court has stood firm in protecting the inviolability of the inside from the physical presence of official outsiders, absent the in-sider's consent. The Amendment acts as a bar at the doorstep against such uninvited intruders. A man still has the right to be secure in his home, after he has drawn the shades, soundproofed the walls, and insulated the building against X rays. He does not have to keep up a twenty-four-hour watch against official invaders. If the policeman at the window opens it up to come in for a better look . . . ; if the agents have to break and enter in order to look over the transom of the owner's bedroom . . . ; if the listening device is planted inside the defendant's room rather than on the adjoining wall . . .—in all such instances a violation of the Fourth Amendment occurs. . . .

In any such case, the man is no longer secure in his house: the outsiders have moved in on him. The *Goldman* case drew this distinction prettily— almost as if the Court had anticipated this very case. There the officers, illegally entering a room of Shulman, one of the defendants, planted a "listening apparatus" (a dictaphone) in that room with wires running to the adjacent room which the officers entered lawfully. The dictaphone failed to work. The officers then resorted to a detectaphone which had no wires con-necting it with Shulman's room and which all was wholly within the adjacent room. Solely by means of this outside detectaphone, the officers heard de-fendant's incriminating conversation (carried on in Shulman's room) to which the officers testified. The defendants, said the Court, "contend that the trespass committed in Shulman's office when the listening apparatus was there installed, and what was learned as a result of the trespass, was of some assist-ance on the following day in locating the receiver of the detectaphone in the adjoining office, and this connection between the trespass and the listening resulted in a violation of the Fourth Amendment. Whatever trespass was committed was connected with the installation of the listening apparatus the dictaphone. As respects it, the trespass might be said to be continuing, and, if the apparatus had been used it might, with reason, be claimed that the con-necting trespass was a concomitant of its use."

The *Goldman* case distinction is crucial here: If the government agent, on the outside, unaided by any device smuggled into On Lee's premises, had heard what On Lee said, the agent's conduct would have been unethical (perhaps even unlawful under state law) but not unconstitutional. (Although customers may enter a man's place of business at will, it is still as immune from illegal search and seizure as his kitchen or his bedroom. Many of the leading Supreme Court cases on search and seizure have involved places of business. . . .) The microphone, however, was brought into On Lee's estab-lishment without his permission. It was just as if the agent had overheard the conversation after he had sneaked in, when On Lee's back was turned, and had then hidden himself in a closet. All the agent's subsequent evidence-gathering was a result of, a concomitant of, the unlawful invasion. As recog-nized in Goldman, such behavior is altogether different from that of an officer merely listening in an adjoining room which is no part of the de-fendant's constitutionally protected precincts. Here the agent, in effect, came inside that area, and did so without On Lee's consent.

The situation is no different than if Chin Poy had secretly installed the radio inside the house. On Lee agreed to Chin Poy's presence in his laundry; he did not agree, nor was he given the chance to disagree, to what, for all practical purposes, was the presence of someone else altogether. The invading microphone enabled a third person, about whom On Lee knew nothing, to be present at the conversations. It accomplished the same purpose as if, and should therefore be treated as if, the agent had smuggled himself into the room to listen behind closed doors, or as if the agent had been a midget and had been hidden in a bag carried by Chin Poy on to On Lee's premises.

I grant that, as long as the Goldman doctrine endures, the domain of Fourth-Amendment privacy will be rather restricted, and that it will become more so as new distance-conquering devices, for seeing, hearing, and smelling, are invented. . . . But I believe that, under the Amendment, the "sanctity of a man's house and the privacies of life" still remain protected from the unin-vited intrusion of physical means by which words within the house are secretly communicated to a person on the outside. A man can still control a small part of his environment, his house; he can retreat thence from outsiders, secure in the knowledge that they cannot get at him without disobeying the Constitution. That is still a sizable hunk of liberty—worth protecting from encroachment. A sane, decent, civilized society must provide some such oasis, some shelter from public scrutiny, some insulated enclosure, some enclave, some inviolate place which is a man's castle. Were my colleagues correct, the Fourth Amendment would be inoperative if a government agent entered a house covered with a "cloak of invisibility"—a garment which ingenuity may soon yield.

This brings me to my colleagues' second argument, which runs thus:

The introduction of the microphone, without On Lee's consent, did not render unconstitutional the act of the distant agent in listening to the conversation; for that agent was just like a spy who, gaining entrance by concealing his identity, hears and testifies to an admission made by a criminal; testimony so obtained by a spy (say my colleagues) has never been held inadmissible under the Fourth Amendment.

All else aside, this argument not only wipes out the *Goldman* case distinction but also ignores the distinction between (a) entry with the owner's consent is procured by deception, and (b) lack of any consent to the entry. This case is of the latter kind. For all practical purposes (as I have tried to show), the agent entered On Lee's premises without On Lee's knowledge and therefore minus his consent. That uninvited entry constituted just as much of a constitutional infringement as if the agent had forced his way in. To hold otherwise is to turn the Amendment into a sorry joke. It is to say to a police officer: "Take a hint. Don't bludgeon your way in. Wait till the owner is not looking, and then skulk in. The Constitution forgives a sneak's entry."

This is not at all what the courts have said when they have given a limited sanction to evidence obtained by spies who, by lies, have procured an owner's consent both to enter and to acts done by the spies after entry. Typically, in such a case, the owner, engaged in an illegal enterprise, expressly or tacitly invited prospective customers (or the like) to enter without being required to satisfy any conditions; the invitation was not conditioned on the entrant's not being a government official; the spy gained entry because the owner mistakenly trusted that this seeming customer would not disclose his observations to the government. These were the facts in *Davis* v. *United States* . . . and in *Blanchard* v. *United States*. . . . *United States* v. *Trupiano* . . . relied upon by my colleagues to support their spy analogy, involved an informer who was hired by the defendants as a workman in an illegal still and who reported his observations to the police. The workmen, like the customers, had been invited by the owner onto the premises for a specific reason; and his entrance was not illegal because of the use to which he put his observations.

It is one thing to hold that the Amendment does not safeguard a man from such errors in judging the character of those whom he lets into his house; it is another to hold that the Amendment does not protect him from officers who get in when he does not know it. We shudder at the nocturnal "knock at the door" by searchers armed with no warrants. How much worse is a secret search by a knockless, sneaky, unknown entrant. In the first case, the citizen has the opportunity to question the searcher's authority, perhaps to dissuade or resist. In the second, he is powerless against an unseen snooper.

The spy cases are, at best, difficult to reconcile with *Gouled. v. United States* . . . where it was held that a government agent, paying defendant a "friendly visit," conducted an illegal search when he went through defendant's papers without defendant's knowledge. Assuming, however, that *Gouled* has been virtually overruled, the spy cases must, I think, be deemed to go to the very edge of unconstitutionality. No upper court, up to today, has gone further. In *Fraternal Order of Eagles* . . .—overruling in effect *United States v. Warner* . . . cited by my colleagues—entrance was limited to a special class possessing credentials, and the government spies used stolen credentials which gave them the false appearance of members of that special class. The court held inadmissible the evidence they procured.

The practice of broadcasting private inside-the-house conversations through concealed radios is singularly terrifying when one considers how this snide device has already been used in totalitarian lands. Under Hitler, when it became known that the secret police planted dictaphones in houses, members of families often gathered in bathrooms to conduct whispered discussions of intimate affairs, hoping thus to escape the reach of the sending apparatus. Orwell, depicting the horrors of a future completely regimented society, could think of no more frightening instrument there to be employed than the "telescreen" compulsorily installed in every house. "The telescreen," he writes, "received and transmitted simultaneously. Any sound that Winston made, above the level of a very low whisper, would be picked up by it; moreover, so long as he remained in the field of vision which the metal plaque commanded, he could be seen as well as heard. There was of course no way of knowing whether you were being watched at any given moment. How often, or on what system, the Thought Police plugged in on any individual wire was guesswork. It was even conceivable that they watched everybody all the time. But at any rate they could plug in your wire whenever they wanted to. You had to live, did live, from habit that became instinct, in the assumption that every sound you heard was overheard, and, except in darkness, every movement scrutinized." Such a mechanical horror may soon be the dubious gift of applied science. My colleagues' decision, by legitimizing the use of such a future horror, invites it. I think that the decision is wrong and that the invitation should not be issued.

2. I consider the decision wrong because of the Fourth Amendment. I am not sure it is correct even aside from the Amendment. I have in mind the post-Olmstead doctrine of *McNabb* v. *United States* . . . and *Anderson* v. *United States* . . . , that is, that the federal courts will not receive evidence obtained by federal officers through violation of federal or state laws.

3. Apart from the radio evidence, I think the conviction should be reversed on still other grounds. Early in the trial, a detective was allowed to repeat the accusatory statement of Ying (On Lee's alleged co-conspirator) made against On Lee after his arrest, when he was present. The judge received this evidence on the theory that, since On Lee had not denied the statement, he had thus admitted by silence what he had not denied. The judge was wrong. In *United States* v. *Lo Biondo* . . . we held that a defendant need not deny any accusations made to his face after his arrest, and that his silence in such circumstances cannot be construed as an admission of his guilt. The trial judge in the instant case later partly realized his mistake, and, by his charge to the jury, sought to correct the misimpression. In a case where the evidence against the defendant was particularly substantial or convincing, I might agree that such an error is harmless, if thus subsequently corrected. But in this case, the evidence was anything but overwhelming, and a misimpression of this sort might easily sway the jury toward conviction. To make matters worse, the judge here, in seeking to correct his error, positively harmed the defendant's case in the jury's eyes: The judge announced that, if the defendant had denied his guilt *before arrest*, he did not have to repeat his denials later after arrest. In the charge, this was the only exception to the general rule of guilt by silence. Since the record contained no evidence that On Lee had denied guilt *before* arrest, the jury might well have believed that On Lee did not come within any exception and must therefore have admitted his guilt by remaining mute.

Such an error should be deemed harmless, if at all, only when the government's case against the defendant is "strong." But here it was not. As already noted, the pivotal evidence was the agent's testimony about conversations he overheard. The following is therefore important: Chin Poy, the informer, was not called by the government and therefore did not himself testify to those conversations. Had the agent attempted to testify to what Chin Poy told him of these conversations, his testimony would have been excluded as hearsay—weak hearsay, at that, since no reason was given for not calling Chin Poy. The sole basis of receiving the agent's testimony was that he stated he had heard the conversations, that is, was not merely retelling what

Chin Poy had told the agent out of court. Yet, in the course of cross-examination of the agent, it came out that he had to rely on Chin Poy's out-of-court statements about the conversations. Consider these facts: (a) The agent's receiving set, on at least one occasion, was supposed to have been hooked up with a recording device in a nearby truck which could have made a record that could have been played to the jury. But the agent testified that he had made no such record because "the recorder was not working that evening." (b) He also testified that the kind of radio device he utilized often failed to work properly because of noisy surroundings or transmitted unintelligible noises. (c) He further testified that he did not take notes of all the conversations while they were going on. (d) Only an hour or so later, did he make notes and memoranda concerning what he had heard. And the memo was made after comparing his notes with those of Chin Poy, so that the agent's memo was, at best, a collaborative product. (e) To make matters far worse, the agent did not use his notes and memoranda to refresh or prompt his recollection, although he deliberately tried to give the appearance of doing so. For, during his direct testimony, he kept referring to a written statement. On cross, however, he confessed that this statement was not his own—since his own notes and memos, he said, had been "destroyed" or "filed away." The paper he used to refresh his recollection in testifying was a written statement made by Chin Poy of his recollection of the conversations. So that, in order to testify, the agent had to use out-of-court statements of Chin Poy, a man never seen or heard by the jury and never subjected to cross-examination. Surely a case resting on the agent's testimony is not "strong."

*193 F.2d 306 (1951)*

*The case was reviewed by the Supreme Court, which affirmed the conviction.*

*343 U.S. 747 (1952)*

# IN RE FRIED 🐦

O N JUNE 7, 1946, special agents of the FBI arrested six men who, according to the Bureau, had in their possession 256 bales of crude rubber which they knew to be stolen goods. Prior to a grand-jury investigation, the prisoners appealed from a ruling of the district court which denied their application for an order (1) suppressing certain evidence and (2) to return to them books and other documents which, they claimed, were seized in a search made without their consent and (3) to suppress confessions made by them which, they said, were elicited by illegal, coercive methods. After a hearing in which he heard witnesses on both sides, the judge presiding in the district court ruled that the search and seizure was legal since it was freely consented to by one of the prisoners; no evidence was heard regarding the confessions, as the judge dismissed this part of the petition on the ground that the court lacked all power, before indictment, to suppress them. Judge Frank wrote the opinion for the court, adding a partial dissent.

FRANK, Circuit Judge: (1,2) 1. Substantial testimony, the credibility of which was, of course, for the district judge to determine, sustains his conclusion that such authorized voluntary consent was given to the searches as to validate them and the seizures.

2. The district judge refused to consider any evidence whatever concerning the confessions. He ruled, in effect, as follows: Even if government officers were to use the most brutal, coercive methods in obtaining a man's confession to the commission of a crime, a district court would be powerless to prevent the government from presenting that confession to a grand jury in order to bring about that man's indictment for that crime. We cannot agree, and we therefore reverse and remand on this issue.

[ 362 ]

(3) If an article has been illegally seized by a federal official, its potential use as evidence will be restrained by a district court, although no indictment is pending. The reason, as suggested by Judge Sibley (*Foley* v. *United States*, . . .), is that the court "may reach forward" to control the presentation, in a case which may come before it, of evidence acquired by unlawful conduct of federal officers. The government, however, argues as follows: (a) This doctrine rests on—is inseparably tied up with—the "property right" of the person from whom the article was taken, to have it returned to him. (b) A confession, even if written and signed, is an intangible which cannot be returned to the confessant; memory of its contents cannot be eradicated from the memories of the officials; the confessant therefore has no "property right in the confession." (c) Consequently, as it cannot be returned to him, an essential condition of its judicial suppression is lacking.

This contention necessarily includes a mistaken assertion: When an article illegally seized by the government is "contraband," so that the petitioner has no "property right" in it, its return to him will be denied, yet its use as evidence will be restrained. Rule 41(e) of the Federal Rules of Criminal Procedure . . . provides: "If the motion is granted the property shall be restored *unless otherwise subject to lawful detention* (emphasis added) and it shall not be admissible at any hearing or trial." The Advisory Committee's notes report that Rule 41 (e) "is a restatement of existing law and practice" (with one exception not here relevant).

The following argument is also made: The suppression, in advance of an indictment, of an illegally obtained confession must rest on the fact that, if there be an indictment, the confession will be excluded at the ensuing trial because of its incompetence or presumed untruthfulness; therefore, if such a confession is thus suppressed, in advance of indictment, it must logically, but absurdly, follow that the court will similarly prevent the possible use before a grand jury of any evidence which for any reason would be incompetent at a trial or which is shown to be untruthful. Not at all. The courts refuse to receive in evidence an unlawfully acquired confession, not because of its presumptive untruthfulness or unreliability or because it is irrelevant, but because of the illegality of the means by which it was acquired.

The government further argues that an indictment founded upon such illicit evidence will do the applicant no harm, since such evidence will not be admitted at the trial which follows the indictment. That is an astonishingly callous argument which ignores the obvious. For a wrongful indictment is no laughing matter; often it works a grievous, irreparable injury to the person indicted. The stigma cannot be easily erased. In the public mind, the blot on a man's escutcheon, resulting from such a public accusation of wrongdoing, is seldom wiped out by a subsequent judgment of not guilty.

Frequently, the public remembers the accusation, and still suspects guilt, even after an acquittal. Prosecutors have an immense discretion in instituting criminal proceedings which may lastingly besmirch reputations. That discretion is almost completely unfettered. It should surely not extend so far as to preclude judicial interference with a prosecutor's aim to induce an indictment by offering to a grand jury evidence which is the product of illegal acts of federal officers.

The "third degree" and cognate devices alarmingly persist in this country. The reports of the United States Supreme Court alone disclose eight cases in the six years 1940–1945 in which convictions were reversed because of the use of coerced confessions. The indications are that the following statement, made in 1930 by a Committee of the American Bar Association, could be made today: "It is conservative to say that for every one of the cases which do by a long chance find a place in the official reports, there are many hundreds, and probably thousands of instances of the use of the third degree in some form or other." We have cause for shame as a nation that such foul exploits by government officials are designated the "American method." Until such miserable misbehavior is stamped out, it will remain an empty boast that we have, and that we respect, a Constitution which guarantees civil liberties, blocks representatives of government from lawless incursions on the rights of the individual. As possible prosecution of offending officers and civil actions for damages against them seem to have no practical value, the courts, unfortunately, can do little to eliminate these evils; but what slight powers they have to do so they should vigorously exercise. Among those powers is the issuance of orders that screen from scrutiny by grand juries evidence derived from such official illegality.

It is urged that, if motions to suppress confessions before indictment are entertained, the courts and prosecutors will be unduly burdened and decisions of such motions will be made by judges unable to consider the issues as intelligently as the judges presiding at trials. But that argument is equally applicable to motions for suppression, in advance of indictment, of unlawfully seized documents; and, as to them, it has been rejected by the Supreme Court.

(4) We do not now decide that there was any official abuse. We reverse and remand in order that the district court may pass on that issue of fact. Judge A. N. Hand would affirm the district court's order as to the confessions. Judge Learned Hand would suppress any of the confessions shown to have resulted from constitutional violations; to that extent he and I agree; such, therefore, is the decision of this court.

3. I, however, would go further than Judge Learned Hand. The following is thus a partial dissent from that decision:

Even if a confession follows a lawful arrest and does not result from coercive measures violative of the confessant's constitutional privileges, I think a federal district court should suppress it before indictment when—should it not be suppressed and should indictment and trial ensue—the confession would be inadmissible at the trial because federal officers obtained it by means of a violation of federal statute governing their authority. . . . For, as above stated, the reason for suppressing a confesion procured by a violation of a constitutional privilege is solely the illegality of the means used in procuring it; and the means are just as illegal if they consist of official transgression of a federal statute. The FBI and the office of the United States Attorney are but two different branches of the Department of Justice. I think it irrational that one branch of the Department should be allowed to bring about an indictment through evidence which has come into its possession through any illegal acts of another branch. Nor should it be forgotten that the federal judges, too, are part of the federal government. The privileges and immunities of citizens created by the Fourth and Fifth Amendments to the Constitution undoubtedly, at times impede the apprehension and conviction of criminals. Further obstacles of that kind have been erected by the FBI statute, . . . which, by imposing limits on the investigatory methods lawfully available to the FBI, extends the citizens' immunities. Since Congress is the constitutional agency empowered to create such new immunities by enacting statutes, I think the restrictions put on official behavior by that statute deserve as much respect from the courts as the constitutionally imposed restrictions.

Opposition to pretrial suppression of illegally acquired confessions, and even a limited opposition to such suppression when no constitutional but only statutory immunities have been invaded, seem to me to imply criticism of those Supreme Court decisions holding inadmissible any evidence which federal officers obtain unlawfully. I do not join in that criticism. Particularly are those decisions valuable in the case of confessions, since they do something to guard against that most grievous kind of wrong—the conviction of innocent persons. . . .

I am puzzled by the attitude of those who, although sincerely believing in democracy, characterize such decisions as the "coddling of the criminal classes" and "misguided sentimentality." That attitude, I think, reflects a failure to recognize that, in its criminal procedure, a democratic society perforce pursues conflicting aims—to convict the guilty without endangering the innocent. Continental Europe once widely proclaimed the first aim and neglected the second, acting on the principle that, for "the public good," it is "better that a hundred innocent persons should suffer than that one culprit should escape," a principle which encouraged the use of torture (including fatigue resulting from sleeplessness). In modern pre-Hitler days, that principle had been generally disavowed in those countries. In our own we have, in theory at least, adopted something like its opposite, aware that, as Jerome Hall puts it, "the easier it is made to prove guilt, the more difficult does it become to establish innocence." For any criminal procedure constructed solely "with professional offenders in mind, or on the supposition that 'the rogues have too many chances to escape' * * * would result in a ritual whose efficiency would be equaled only by its terror." Hall remarks, "There is wisdom in the observation that the *substantive criminal law should be designed for criminals, the procedural for honest people.*"

That observation suggests that the problem before us here cannot be explored adequately without some consideration of a deeper problem which is obscured (1) by the distinction between "substantive law" and "procedure," and (2) by the relative neglect, on the part of most of those interested in "procedure," of its most important component, that is, judicial fact-finding. The "substantive" legal rules, civil or criminal, embody social policies ("social value judgments"). To enforce, and thus give effect to, such policies is considered one of the principal duties of the courts. They discharge that duty, however, not at wholesale but at retail, by applying those rules in specific lawsuits to the particular facts of those respective suits as "found" by the courts. As a "substantive" rule merely declares that specified legal consequences will be attached to a specified state of facts, the rule should be operative only in particular instances where those facts actually occurred. Accordingly, the social policy embodied in any such rule is not actually enforced when, in deciding a case, a court, through misapprehension of what actually occurred, applies that rule to facts which in truth never existed. The whole job then miscarries: Mistakenly to apply a rule to nonexistent facts—to facts mistakenly "found"—is no less unjust, no less a defective operation of judicial administration, than to apply an erroneous "substantive" legal rule to the actual facts. Either way, the policy expressed in the correct rule is frustrated. An error in "finding" the facts thus yields what might be called "injustice according to law."

. . . Fact-finding is today the soft spot in the administration of justice. In considerable measure that is true because the reformers have largely disregarded the actual fact-finding methods used by the trial courts which, as they are the chief fact finders, and for other reasons, constitute the most important part of our judicial system; even the procedural reformers have restricted their attention chiefly to those phases of trial-court "procedure" which manifest themselves in upper-court and occasional trial-court opinions.

It has been too little noticed that a "substantive legal right"—an "interest" said to be "legally protected" by a "substantive" legal rule—has no practical value when a court by mistakenly mis-finding the facts—because of missing witnesses or documents, or because it believes the testimony of witnesses who in truth are inaccurate, and so on—decides that the claimant has no such "right" or "interest." Doubtless, for analytic purposes, there is often much utility in formally differentiating between "substantive" and "procedural" rights (or "primary" and "secondary," or "antecedent" and "remedial," or "telic" and "instrumental" rights). Once, however, it is stated, in terms of this formal analysis, that a judicial decision is the "result of the application of the (substantive) rule of law to the *facts procedurally established*," it becomes clear that a mistaken "procedural establishment" of the facts destroys, for courtroom purposes, the asserted "substantive right," from which it follows that, so far as courts are concerned, the effective assertion of any "substantive right" depends entirely on the claimant's ability to maintain his so-called "procedural right." The Roman lawyers perhaps sensed this truth when they spoke of the "procedural consumption" of a "right of action" by which it was transformed into a "right to judgment." In other words, for practical court purposes, no "substantive" right exists— whether it be a right asserted by a private person or by the government in its role of vindicator of a "substantive" criminal rule—unless a court gives an enforceable judgment in favor of the alleged right-holder; and, ordinarily, a court will not give such a judgment, even when it uses a seemingly "correct" rule, if it goes wrong on the facts. Of course, similarly a mistake in fact-finding may cause an erroneous judgment adverse to one who defends against an asserted claim.

. . . To ensure . . . that "the substantive criminal law" is "designed for criminals," and the "procedural for honest people," it is essential that in criminal prosecutions the courts untiringly seek to eliminate practically avoidable defects in fact-finding, as well as in other aspects of "procedure." (To be sure, mistaken decisions in civil suits, due to mistakes in fact-finding, may have consequences virtually as grave as those which stem from mistaken convictions in criminal suits: By a wrongful defeat in a civil suit, a man may be ruined and his children may become delinquent, through loss of his livelihood, his savings, or his investments.) In our democratic society, only a hardened cynic will assert that to convict an innocent man, through mistaken fact-finding induced by his coerced confession, should be a matter of no great concern, since the conviction will help to create or preserve public respect for the "substantive" criminal rule which the court applied— although erroneously—fully as much as if the man were guilty, provided only that the mistake is never publicly disclosed. And only such a cynic will say that the public welfare is similarly served by indictment of the innocent, induced by grand-jury mis-finding of the facts, when an indictment is fol-

lowed by an acquittal of which the public never learns. As a wrongful indictment inflicts a substantial harm on the indicted person, infringing his
"substantive right" to be exempt from such harm, the courts should actively
repudiate the cynic's view. (One wonders whether statutes should not
provide governmental compensation for persons wrongfully indicted.) Since
preventive justice is usually the best sort of justice, the courts, I think, should
try, by all feasible means, to forestall such harms. It is not feasible to enjoin
the presentation to grand juries of all untrue, irrelevant, or incompetent
evidence. I think it entirely feasible, however, and eminently desirable, to
order preindictment suppression of any confession obtained by means of an
infraction either of the Constitution or of a statute regulating the federal
police.

Affirmed as to the seizures; reversed and remanded as to the confessions.

*161 F.2d 453 (1947)*

# UNITED STATES ex rel. CAMINITO v. MURPHY ८३

IN 1941 SANTO CAMINITO, *together with two other men, was indicted by a New York Grand Jury for a murder which took place during an attempted holdup. At the trial, the state offered in evidence Caminito's signed confession that he had participated in the holdup of a man named Hameroff as a result of which Hameroff was killed. The jury brought in a guilty verdict; the three men were sentenced to life imprisonment. Caminito, claiming that his confession had been forced and that therefore he had been denied due process, instituted habeas corpus proceedings in the United States Court of Appeals. Judge Frank writes the opinion for the court.*

FRANK, *Circuit Judge:* The sole evidence of Caminito's guilt consisted of his signed pretrial confessions. At the trial, his counsel timely objected to their admission, and moved to strike them on the ground that they had been unconstitutionally procured; he also moved to dismiss the indictment on the ground that the State had not proved Caminito guilty. Caminito testified that the police had coerced the confessions. The trial judge left to the jury the question whether the confessions had been thus induced. The jury, by returning a verdict of guilt, found that they were voluntary.

Caminito testified that, before giving the confessions, the police had beaten him. As the police testified to the contrary, we shall ignore that part of his testimony. But the following facts are not disputed:

(1) Caminito was taken into custody by the police on Sunday, May 11, 1941 at 6:00 P.M.

(2) Commencing about 9:00 P.M. Sunday, he was continuously interrogated by five or six police officers for a period of approximately five hours, until 2:00 A.M. the following morning, Monday, May 12th.

(3) At 3:00 A.M. on Monday, May 12th, he was locked in a cell in which there were no bed, blankets, spring or mattress, but only a wooden bench. (He testified that the cell was unheated. A witness for the State testified that the cell was equipped with a radiator but that he "did not know if the heat was on" during the time Caminito was there confined.)

(4) At 10:00 A.M. on Monday, May 12th, the questioning was resumed. The interrogation continued all day, with several detectives taking turns.

(5) Members of Caminito's family, his friends, and an attorney retained by the family called at the station house where he was detained and tried to get information concerning his whereabouts. The police officers knew these facts, but kept him incommunicado. Other than the police and the district attorney, no one was permitted to see him until he was arraigned forty hours after being taken into custody.

(6) During the afternoon of Monday, May 12th, two women and a man were brought in to face Caminito. He was not told that they were detectives. Each falsely pretended to identify him as the person who was sitting at the wheel of the automobile at the time of the shooting, which occurred in connection with the holdup.

(7) About 9:00 P.M., Monday, May 12th, twenty-seven hours after having been taken into custody, he signed a confession. He gave a second confession to a district attorney a short time later.

(8) About 2:30 or 3:00 A.M. the following morning, Tuesday, May 13th, he was first placed under arrest.

(9) He was brought before a magistrate later that same day, more than forty hours after having first been taken into custody. The arraignment could and should have been held long before that time. The police officers knew that the courts were open for that purpose.

(10) Caminito had never been previously arrested or convicted.

(1–3) These facts make it clear that the trial did not measure up to the standards prescribed by the due-process clause of the Fourteenth Amendment. The confessions obtained by these loathsome means were no more evidence than if they had been forged. Absent, then, any admissible evidence of guilt, the trial judge should have dismissed the indictment or directed a verdict of acquittal. To jail a man convicted without evidence of guilt is to impose "involuntary servitude" which, "except as a punishment for crime," the Thirteenth Amendment forbids. Only in *Erewhon*, which recognized "the crime of being maligned unjustly," could this conviction be justified.

(4) Alone or together, neither the unlawful detention for many hours nor the deceit in confronting Caminito with disguised police officers who lied in identifying him would suffice to vitiate the confessions as unconstitutionally obtained. But those factors did aggravate the following unconsti-

tutional practices which—even in the absence of those factors—rendered the confessions inadmissible: (a) The police interrogated him almost continuously for twenty-seven hours, with but a brief interval for rest in a cell so badly equipped as to make sleep virtually impossible for a man already harried by the questioning. (b) During this long period, the police, in effect, kidnapped him: They kept him incommunicado, refusing to allow his lawyer, his family, and his friends to consult with him.

Accordingly, the writ of habeas corpus must issue. . . .

All decent Americans soundly condemn satanic practices, like those described above, when employed in totalitarian regimes. It should shock us when American police resort to them, for they do not comport with the barest minimum of civilized principles of justice. It has no significance that in this case we must assume there was no physical brutality. For psychological torture may be far more cruel, far more symptomatic of sadism. Many a man who can endure beatings will yield to fatigue. To keep a man awake beyond the point of exhaustion, while constantly pummeling him with questions, is to degrade him, to strip him of human dignity, to deprive him of the will to resist, to make him a pitiable creature mastered by the single desire—at all costs to be free of torment. Any member of this or any other court, to escape such anguish, would admit to almost any crime. Indeed, the infliction of such psychological punishment is more reprehensible than a physical attack: It leaves no discernible marks on the victim. (Perhaps it is inaccurate to describe such punishment as not "physical," since pronounced fatigue may have hidden physiological consequences.) Because it is thus concealed, it has, under the brutalitarian regimes, become the favorite weapon of the secret police, bent on procuring confessions as a means of convicting the innocent.

Caminito testified as follows as to why he confessed: At 10:30 P.M. on Monday, May 12th, the police allowed him to talk to Noia [a co-defendant] who had been similarly subjected to prolonged questioning. "He said, 'Let us give them [the police] the same story they gave us.' He says, 'It would not mean anything. * * * We can see a lawyer this way. We will tell the lawyer what happened, and they cannot do us nothing. We did not do it. You don't have to worry. You can prove where you were, and I can prove also.' I said, 'No it is not right.' He said, 'How long can I stand this? * * * Let us make up the story they gave us and give them the same story and get it over with.' * * * So I told him the story that the detectives had told me of what happened, as I had heard maybe fifty times, so he said, 'That is the story they told me.'" Then they agreed to confess. While confessing, when Caminito did not know the desired answer, the police captain told him what to say and he said it. "They put the words right in his mouth." He "gave those answers for fear." We do not rest our decision on that testimony: (The State makes much of the fact that, as to one single item of the confession, he testified that he had made it up without prompting.) Even without it, we are bound to infer, on the undisputed facts, that something of the sort actually happened. For his testimony in this respect closely resembles many reports of those who, behind the Iron Curtain, after like treatment, confessed to crimes they had not committed.

Aristotle, thousands of years ago, wrote of torture "that people under its compulsion tell lies quite as often as they tell the truth, sometimes persistently refusing to tell the truth, sometimes recklessly making a false charge in order to be let off sooner. We ought to be able to quote cases, familiar to the judges, in which this sort of thing has actually happened. We must say that evidence under torture is not trustworthy, the fact being that many men whether thickwitted, tough-skinned, or stout of heart endure their ordeal nobly, while cowards and timid men are full of boldness till they see the ordeal of these others; so that no trust can be placed in evidence under torture." In the sixteenth century, Montaigne said that tortures "seem to be a test of endurance rather than of truth. For why should pain rather make me say what is, rather than force me to say what is not? * * * The effect is that the man whom the judge has put to the torture, that he may not die innocent, is made to die both innocent and tortured."

It is imperative that our courts severely condemn confession by torture, the so-called "third degree." To treat it lightly, to condone it, encourages its continued use, with evil effects on the police: The official who utilizes the third degree, since he violates statutes and the Constitution, is himself a criminal; and his infliction of torture on others brutalizes him.

Hall remarks on the "startling fact that there is hardly a single physical act of brutality inflicted by the * * * N.K.V.D. which American policemen have not at some time perpetrated" (but adds that our police are less "scientific" about torture). The important difference is that in Russia the coercion of confessions is (at least with respect to some subjects) legal and avowed, while with us it is always illegal and secret. That difference is basic: It means that we have a principle of justice on which we can rely to bring such coercion into disrepute and disuse.

That principle the police traduce when they act on the theory that, to discharge their duty, they have the authority to dispense with a suspect's constitutional privileges because they believe him guilty. For it is not the function of the police in our democracy to determine a man's guilt.

Trials fairly conducted have, alas, led to the conviction of some innocent men. All such tragedies cannot be avoided even in the best contrived of legal systems. But surely we dare not permit tragedies of that sort to result from confessions by torture. One shudders to think what happens to an innocent man sent to jail. Bitter, resentful, he may become an apt student of the hardened professional criminals he meets in jail, and thereby be converted from innocence into real criminality. If he withstands such a conversion, he will, as a marked man, when released, have a hard struggle to earn an honest living. If again charged with crime, he will encounter a serious difficulty at a trial: If he takes the witness stand, his previous conviction will count against him; if, on that account, he does not testify, his silence will adversely affect him. And let it not be forgotten that police zeal to convict an innocent man means often that the guilty man escapes punishment.

We have here at some length expressed our abhorrence of confession by torture for this reason: That practice is unknown in England where, to our shame, they call it the "American method." There are those who say that American conditions compel such official resort to crime to catch and convict criminals. The absurdity of such a view is evidenced by the fact that our most effective American police force, the FBI, abjures this execrable method and, in its school for state and city police, teaches that the "third degree" is both detestable and inefficient. Because proof, in court, of its use is most difficult, the only real hope for its eradication lies in the educative influence of such police as the FBI, so that all our American policemen will be trained to detest it. Repeated and emphatic judicial denunciations of that barbarism—whenever it is exposed, as in this case—can help to that end. Until that end is realized, the many decent police officers, in a police force generally addicted to that practice, will find themselves at so grave a disadvantage that sooner or later, they may, if they do not themselves indulge in it, at least acquiesce in it. For the accustomed ways of any group usually come to seem the right ways. As Chesterton said, "The horrible thing about all legal officials, even the best, about all judges, magistrates, detectives and policemen, is not that they are wicked (some of them are good), not that they are stupid (several of them are quite intelligent); it is simply that they have got used to it."

At any rate, as long as many policemen third-degree the helpless, the public will tend to believe that all police officers do likewise, that police brutality, although unfortunate, is normal. (That such a belief is widespread, anyone can see who reads the hundreds of popular, hard-boiled, detective novels.) As a consequence, the public suspects that almost all policemen deal brutally with suspects. Accordingly, the citizenry do not regard the police with respect, and fail adequately to cooperate with the police, a cooperation without which the police in a democracy cannot efficiently perform their lawful functions. Worst of all, public cynicism develops concerning the basic ideals expressed in our constitution. . . .

Recently many outstanding Americans have been much concerned—and justifiably—with inroads on the constitutional privileges of persons questioned about subversive activities. But concern with such problems, usually those of fairly prominent persons, should not blind one to the less dramatic, less publicized plight of humble, inconspicuous men (like Caminito) when unconstitutionally victimized by officialdom. It will not do to say—as some do—that deep concern with such problems of the humble is the mark of an "old-fashioned liberal." For repeated and unredressed attacks on the constitutional liberties of the humble will tend to destroy the foundations supporting the constitutional liberties of everyone. The test of the moral quality of a civilization is its treatment of the weak and powerless.

Reversed.

222 F.2d 698 (1955)

# UNITED STATES ex rel. LEYRA v. DENNO ८৯

I N 1953 Camilo Leyra, sentenced to death for the murder of his parents, appealed from a denial of his petition for a writ of habeas corpus, asserting a lack of due process at the trial in which he had been convicted. He had been tried twice; his conviction in the first proceeding was reversed because of the improper admission of a statement of guilt, made shortly after his arrest, to Dr. Helfand, a psychiatrist called in by the District Attorney's office. Dr. Helfand elicited the statement by threats and by an authorized promise of leniency from the district attorney if Leyra confessed. Later he confessed again, to others. In the second trial, the judge charged the jury that they must decide whether these later confessions had been the result of Dr. Helfand's illegal coercion or whether they had been made voluntarily, free from the doctor's influence. Two other doctors testified with regard to this question: the physician called by the government thought that Dr. Helfand's threats and promises had had no continuing effect; and the doctor for the defense testified that the later confessions had, in effect, been elicited by Dr. Helfand. The court on appeal is asked to decide whether the question of the validity of the later confessions should, in fact, have been left to the jury or whether, as Leyra contended, the trial judge should have decided the issue of their admissibility. Judge Charles Clark wrote the majority opinion in which the denial of the writ of habeas corpus was affirmed. Judge Frank dissents.

Frank, Circuit Judge (dissenting): 1. Defendant's position is this: (1) Dr. Helfand, acting on behalf and with the approval of the district attorney, promised defendant that, if he would confess, he would not be prosecuted for first-degree murder; (2) these promises induced defendant's confession, made a few hours later on the same day, to two assistant district attorneys. Defendant contends that the State had the resultant burden of overcoming, by evidence, a powerful inference that the promises had such a continuing effect.

The trial judge so charged, saying: "I charge you that you are bound to consider the established fact that Dr. Helfand practiced illegal coercion upon the defendant and made authorized promises of leniency to him. The presumption is that coercion and promise of leniency continued to affect the defendant's later confessions." And the judge added that those confessions must not be considered as evidence of guilt "unless the prosecution has convinced you, beyond a reasonable doubt, that such coercion and promise of leniency did not extend over and affect" the later confessions.

I think that charge was correct. (Except that I would substitute the word "inference" for "presumption.") But I think the State introduced no evidence whatever to support a finding that the effect of the promises—as distinguished from the effect of the coercion—had worn off when the defendant made the later confession to the assistant district attorneys. In short, there was a complete failure to overcome the inference of a persisting influence of the promises, and, absent countervailing evidence, neither the jury nor anyone else could rationally disregard that inference. It seems to me, therefore, that the confession to these officials was vitiated, and that to allow the jury to consider it amounted to a lack of due process. (See *Lisenba* v. *California* . . . : "The concept of due process would void a trial in which, by threats or promises in the presence of court and jury, a defendant was induced to testify against himself. The case can stand no better if, by resort to the same means, the defendant is induced to confess and his confession is given in evidence." . . .) For that reason, I think habeas corpus should be granted (with power in the State, of course, to try defendant again).

2. My colleagues reach a contrary conclusion. They rest it on an assertion of fact which I think the record flatly contradicts: They say that the two doctors so disagreed in their testimony about the subject of the promises' lasting effect as to "create a conflict in the evidence justifying submission * * * to the jury" of this crucial issue of fact. In other words, my colleagues assert that one of the doctors testified that Dr. Helfand's promises did not influence the confessions to the assistant district attorneys. But here is what the State-court record shows:

(a) Dr. Bellinger, the expert called by the defendant, testified that the promises had "carried over" to the confessions made to those officials.

(b) Dr. Murphy, the expert called by the prosecutor, testified at length that the coercion exercised by Dr. Helfand had no effect on his confessions to the Police Captain Meenahan and to the defendant's partner Herrschaft.

He was then asked about the effect of the promises on the confession to the police captain. He answered, hesitatingly and confusedly, as follows:

A. It is impossible to give a definite answer to that, I feel. The promises were made in the line of persuasion, just as promises were made to a little kid to be good in school, things like that. It has the same effect, but they would not be effective sufficient to incriminate a person who is trying to survive, trying to keep his skin, as it were.

Q. In other words, the defendants—

A. It would have to be—I don't think that the effect of that would carry over, no, I don't.

Subsequently he was recalled by the State, on rebuttal, and, in response to a question from the prosecutor, stated that the confession to Herrschaft was "free of any influence caused by any promises of immunity." Immediately thereafter questions were put to him by the prosecutor and the judge with reference to the effect of the coercion and the promises on the confession to the assistant district attorneys. This entire colloquy reads as follows:

By Mr. Cone (the prosecutor):

Q. Now, Doctor, this break having occurred through the effects of the defendant's meeting with William Herrschaft, would the resultant freedom from mental coercion and from the effects, if any, of the promise of immunity, continue to the time when the defendant made his statements to the district attorney, which I read to you a few minutes ago, so that his answers to the district attorney's questions, and statements made by the defendant, without specific question from the district attorney, were voluntary, free from mental coercion, free of any influence caused by any promise of immunity. Can you render an opinion regarding that question with a reasonable degree of certainty?

A. I can.

The Court: Can you state that with reasonable certainty?

Mr. Cone: I just said that.

Mr. Scholem: I object to the question.

The Court: The objection is overruled.

Mr. Scholem: As to that particular question.

The Court: Overruled; that is one of the specific issues in this case that is being litigated.

Mr. Scholem: Exception.

Mr. Cone: I think, with the interruption, I had better perhaps put the question to the doctor again.

The Court: Did the doctor answer the question?

The Witness: Yes, I believe that the subsequent interrogation by the district attorney, following the confession to Herrschaft, was given out of his free will, voluntarily, with no evidence or coercion involved. Does that take care of that?

*The Court: What about the promise?*

*The Witness: I don't know what effect the promise had. It is a thing which is something I cannot pass judgment on.*

*The Court: In that particular instance?*
*The Witness: That is right.*
The Court: Anything else, Counsel?
Mr. Cone: I think that will be all.

This is the last testimony of Dr. Murphy on that subject.

I submit that—with Dr. Bellinger testifying that the promises did carry over and Dr. Murphy, the State's expert, specifically saying he did not "know what effect the promises had"—there was no testimony to rebut the inference of the continuing influence of the promise or promises on the confession made to the assistant district attorneys. This, then, is not a case where there is a conflict in the evidence and a State-court determination of fact resolving the conflict, a determination to which (to say the least) we would have to give heed. (See, for example, *Lisenba v. California,* . . . "Where the claim is that the prisoner's statement has been procured by such means" [that is, threats or promises] "we are bound to make an independent examination of the record to determine the validity of the claim. The performance of this duty cannot be foreclosed by the finding of a court, or the verdict of a jury, or both. *If the evidence bearing upon the question is uncontradicted, the application of the constitutional provision is unembarrassed by a finding or a verdict in a state court; even though, in ruling that the confession was admissible, the very tests were applied in the state court to which we resort to answer the constitutional question.*" . . . [Emphasis added.]

3. My colleagues, however, advance another alternative suggestion which, as I understand it, is this:

Dr. Helfand's statements to defendant consisted of an intermixture of wheedling and threats; consequently, he gave no promise which properly can be differentiated or separated from the threats. The foregoing (my colleagues say or imply) has these consequences: (1) If it be true (as I think it clearly is) that the trial judge, the two expert witnesses, the prosecutor and defense counsel, all dealt with Dr. Helfand's statements as including a promise or promises which should be regarded as separate from the threats, then all those persons erred. (2) The jury had before it Dr. Murphy's testimony that the threats did not carry over to the confession to the district attorneys, and the jury so found. Therefore (my colleagues say or imply), in order to sustain the jury's finding that the promises thus did not continue to be effective, there was needed no evidence to that effect, since Dr. Murphy's testimony of the carryover of the threats sufficed for that purpose, despite the fact that he unequivocally testified he could not say whether or not the promises carried over to the confession to the district attorneys.

I think this suggestion untenable in the light of the following:

(a) Judge Leibowitz, the trial judge, no novice in a trial court, repeatedly —while the testimony was being received as well as in his charge—treated Dr. Helfand's statements as involving promises not comprised in, or merely a subordinate aspect of, the threats. See the Appendix to this dissenting opinion.

(b) That Appendix also contains excerpts from Dr. Helfand's statements to the defendant. I think they demonstrate that Judge Leibowitz correctly interpreted them as including promises distinct from, and not merged in, the threats.

(c) The highest New York Court, in its opinion on the first and second appeals . . . has hinted at nothing to the contrary. My colleagues quote a portion of the opinion on the first appeal. But that opinion . . . also contains the following:

> Another alleged infirmity in defendant's statement to the doctor is urged upon us. It is said that this statement contained promises of leniency which might be attributed, under the circumstances, to the District Attorney. . . . The court at first instructed the jury that "There is no claim here that the District Attorney induced this defendant to make a confession upon the promise that he will not be prosecuted therefor." Defendant's counsel duly excepted, and requested an appropriate charge from the court, which might eliminate premeditated murder. After some colloquy the court agreed, withdrew its original instructions in this respect, and then charged the jury in effect that they had to find a promise of complete immunity by the doctor or none at all, and only if the jury found that the former induced the confession might they acquit. While this may have been inadvertent on the part of the trial court, this instruction, to say the least, was misleading and did not cure the original instruction excepted to by defendants and which the court agreed to correct, and may well have been detrimental to defendant, particularly in the light of the doctor's statement to him that "unless you can show that in a fit of temper you got so angry that you did it * * * it's premeditation. See?" . . . Moreover, here again the jury should have been instructed to consider separately the later confessions, in the light of any promise that may have been made during the defendant's statement to the doctor. . . .

The opinion on the second trial . . . contains the following, which clearly does not indicate that the promises were engulfed in or were but an aspect of the threats:

> The trial judge did not stop there but dealt with it in his main charge and we believe fully and adequately by pointing out again and again that as a matter of law the confession made to Dr. Helfand was not to be considered on the issue of guilt. Moreover, he was careful to instruct the jury as to the defendant's contention leaving them to say with what force and effect the "coercion and promise * * * did in fact carry over and into each of the subsequent confessions," at the same time giving like instruction as to the People's contention, leaving it for the jury to say whether the later confessions made to other persons "were entirely voluntary and not induced by any promise of leniency." In this manner and by this means the defendant's statement to Dr. Helfand was effectively insulated from the jury for consideration on the issue of guilt and was made available to them for the sole and limited purpose of saying whether or not the

later statements made to others were dependent in any way on coercion or inducement, coupled with the clear and positive instruction that if so found to be, it was "worthless as evidence." Such submission for separate consideration was in obedience to our specific ruling at the prior trial.

(d) The prosecutor and the State's attorney general—in their briefs in the State courts, in their answer to defendant's petition for certiorari, in their brief and oral argument in this court—have never even whispered this notion that no promises were made except as part of the threats.

(e) Federal District Judge Ryan, when denying habeas corpus, said nothing remotely of the sort in his opinion.

That threats accompanied the promises did not serve to swallow up the promises, but rather to underscore them. Every parent of a young child, every owner of a pet animal, combines assurances of penalties for undesired conduct and of rewards for desired behavior; the child or pet animal recognizes the difference. Jeremy Bentham in his book, *The Rationale of Reward* (first published in 1811), has a chapter entitled "Of Reward and Punishment Combined," in which he notes that, when such a combination is used by a government, each has its effect. If a school announces that it will flunk any student with an average grade of less than sixty and will graduate any student who betters that average, one whose average is sixty or over will be astonished if told that the second part of the school's announcement was subsidiary to the first and therefore not to be taken seriously as a promise.

4. Relying on the testimony of Dr. Murphy and on the smooth and easy flow of the later confessions, the prosecutor convincingly argued to the jury that Dr. Helfand's coercive efforts had worn off and that defendant, during those subsequent confessions was calm, undisturbed by emotions which the threats had stimulated. But the very fact that defendant was thus calm and collected in no way negates, but is entirely consistent with, the inference that he had the promises very much in mind, and, free of coercion, voluntarily confessed to the officials because of the promises. The more cool and collected he was, the more influential they became.

5. I thoroughly agree with my colleagues that a federal court has a most unpleasant duty when, in a case like this, it must pass on the constitutional validity of a decision rendered by the highest court of a State, particularly in a murder case. That duty is indeed unpleasant, since past experience shows that its exercise may stir up intense local resentment. Nevertheless, obedient to our sworn obligation, as frequently construed by the United States Supreme Court, we must ignore the possibility of such resentment. In discharging that obligation, I think we should not be singularly astute to avoid interference with a State judgment, ordering that a human being be put to death, by resort to a determination of fact (favorable to that judgment) which the State

Courts and the State officials have themselves not ventured to so much as even intimate. Moreover, to repeat, the record here does not sustain such a determination.

## Appendix

### 1. Excerpts from statements by Dr. Helfand to defendant

*Q.* If you tell us the details and come across like a good man, then we can help you. We know that morally you were just in anger. Morally you are not to be condemned. Right?

*A.* Right.

*Q.* But you have to tell us the details, then we will know that you are above board and on the level. Otherwise, we just don't do nothing to you and you will get the worst of it. * * *

*Q.* You may as well tell us and we'll work with you. We'll play ball with you. We'll help you if we can. * * *

Don't be afraid. We're all with you. We want to help you. * * *

* * * [S]o you may as well tell us and get our help. If you don't tell us and get our help, I'll wash my hands of you.

I'll help you Buddy, I am with you one hundred percent but you got to play ball with me. * * *

These people are going to throw the book at you unless you can show that in a fit of temper you got so angry that you did it. Otherwise they toss premeditation in and it's premeditation. See.

### 2. Judge Leibowitz's references to promises by Dr. Helfand

*By the Court:*

*Q.* Dr. Bellinger, during the examination of the defendant by Dr. Helfand, Dr. Helfand on numerous occasions said to him, "We will help you. We will help you. Play ball with us. They will throw the book at you. Premeditation." Do you recall all of that, which was repeated by counsel?

*A.* Yes, sir.

*Q.* In other words, Dr. Bellinger, they made a certain promise to the defendant, promise of leniency?

*A.* Yes.

*Q.* Now what I want to ask you is this: In your opinion, did that carry over to subsequent confessions?

*A.* Yes, I think it did.

*Q.* You say it did?

*A.* I say in my opinion, it did.

*Q.* It carried over, you say, to the confession made to Captain Meenahan?

*A.* Yes, Judge. * * *

*Q.* And did the promise also carry over to the district attorney's confession?

A. Yes, in my opinion, it did. It was all done the same night, and in the same room."

In his charge, the judge included the following:

I charge you also, as a matter of law, that this so-called Helfand confession is invalid and may not be considered by you as evidence of guilt, on the further ground that Dr. Helfand, who was then acting for the district attorney, made a promise to the defendant in order to induce him to confess, and, thus, did induce him to confess by reason of such promise; the said promise being, in effect, that if he made such confession, he, the defendant, would not be prosecuted for the capital offense of murder in the first degree, but, possibly, for a lesser crime. * * *

In arriving at a solution of these problems, I charge you that you are bound to consider the established fact that Dr. Helfand practiced illegal coercion upon the defendant and made authorized promises of leniency to him. The presumption is that such coercion and promise of leniency continued to affect the defendant's later confessions; unless the prosecution has convinced you, beyond a reasonable doubt, from all the credible evidence in the case, that such coercion and promise of leniency did not extend over and affect the later confession made to Meenahan. Unless you are so convinced, the later confession made to Meenahan must be entirely disregarded and not considered by you as evidence of guilt.

Let us now turn our attention to the so-called Herrschaft confession. Gentlemen, the same elements must be considered by the jury, to wit: Was the confession made? Was it voluntary? Did the Helfand coercion and the promises extend over and affect this confession? Did the prosecution sustain the burden of establishing, beyond a reasonable doubt, that the coercion and promises did not carry over and affect the Herrschaft confession? * * *

You must also be satisfied, beyond a reasonable doubt, that the promise of leniency made by Dr. Helfand did not carry over and induce and influence the making of this confession to the assistant district attorneys. * * *

The defendant contends, with what force and effect, of course, it is for you to say, that the coercion and promise referred to did in fact carry over and into each of the subsequent confessions.

The prosecution, on the other hand, contends that the coercion and promise by Dr. Helfand did not in anywise extend over into any of the confessions made to Meenahan, then to Herrschaft, and then to the assistant district attorneys; that the confessions so made to these persons were entirely voluntary and not induced by any promise of leniency.

*208 F.2d 605 (1953)*

The case reviewed by the Supreme Court, which reversed the decision of the lower court.

*347 U.S. 556 (1954)*

# UNITED STATES v. ST. PIERRE ⮞

IN 1942 ROSARIO ST. PIERRE, summoned before a grand jury, confessed to having embezzled money entrusted to him by appropriating it instead of delivering it to the person to whom it belonged. When asked for what person the money was intended, St. Pierre refused to answer on the ground that the information would tend to incriminate him, since that person would then be called as a corroborating witness without whose testimony he could not be brought to trial. The district court sentenced him for criminal contempt. St. Pierre appealed the order of that court on the ground that he was exercising his privilege against self-incrimination under the Fifth Amendment. Judge Learned Hand, in the opinion for the court, held that, in confessing to the crime, St. Pierre had waived his privilege. Said Hand, ". . . after a witness has confessed all the elements of the crime, he may not withhold the details; . . . even in the narrowest sense the disclosure of the identity of the respondent's victim was only a detail of what he had already confessed." Judge Frank dissents.

FRANK, Circuit Judge (dissenting): 1. St. Pierre, not as a voluntary witness but under subpoena, confessed before a federal grand jury that he had embezzled money from a person not known to the government, and whose name he did not divulge, and also that he had carried that money across state lines. When asked, before the grand jury, for the name of that person, he refused to answer, asserting his constitutional privilege. Unless St. Pierre is compelled to answer that question, the government, if he is tried for violating the National Stolen Property Act, cannot make out a case against him which will go to the jury, and he cannot, therefore, be convicted and punished for that crime. But, if he is compelled to answer the question, he will put the government in possession of evidence which will enable the government, in such a proceeding, to go to the jury. So it appears that to compel him to answer that question is to compel him to give evidence without which his punishment for that crime is impossible and with which it becomes possible.

2. To make it clear that such is the situation here, it is well to note the following: (a) A confession before the grand jury is not a "judicial" confession. (b) Therefore, the confession cannot, without extrinsic corroboration, be used against St. Pierre. The corroborative evidence may be slight in weight, but there must be some such evidence, even if "circumstantial," as to the *corpus delicti*. . . . (c) Here the government, on the record before us, has no such corroborative evidence. For its evidence, other than the confession, will show merely that St. Pierre traveled from New York to Canada, and returned, accompanied by a woman, and with $5,000 in cash in his possession. Such evidence, standing alone, can give rise to no reasonable inference, however slight, of the violation of the National Stolen Property Act. (d) If, however, St. Pierre is compelled to disclose the name of the person from whom he embezzled, the government, in all likelihood, will then have sufficient evidence to go to the jury; for then, by calling the embezzlee as a witness, either (1) it can go to the jury without the use of the confession or (2) it can go to the jury by obtaining from the witness the corroborative evidence necessary to make the confession admissible.

3. Accordingly, the question here is this: Can a witness, under subpoena before a grand jury, be compelled against his objection, based on the constitutional privilege against self-incrimination, to answer a question when (a) without the answer to that question it is not possible for the government to convict and punish him for the commission of a crime and (b) the answer to that question will probably make possible such conviction and punishment? I think that the answer is clearly No.

My colleagues here arrive at the contrary conclusion. They do so by saying that St. Pierre, because of his confession, "waived" the privilege. The character of an effective waiver or surrender of the privilege thus becomes important.

In discussing the doctrine of waiver or surrender of the privilege, one of two positions must be adopted: (a) The first position is that there is a rational relation between the nature of the privilege and what constitutes a waiver or surrender of the privilege; the conduct by a witness amounting to abandonment of the privilege must be plainly inconsistent with his assertion of the privilege. (b) The alternative position is that what amounts to a surrender or waiver has no rational relation to the privilege.

The latter position, of course, is so arbitrary that we should not adopt it unless the precedents leave us no other choice. There are no authoritative precedents calling for such an arbitrary and irrational attitude. And, as my colleagues nowhere so state that they have adopted it, I assume that they have not.

Accordingly, I read the majority opinion here as based on the position that there must be a rational and not an arbitrary relation between (1) the character and purpose of the privilege and (2) the conduct of the witness which constitutes a surrender or waiver. On that basis, the discussion in my colleagues' opinion of what constitutes a surrender or waiver of the privilege must be taken as implying their conception of the nature of the privilege itself. And, since they hold that there is a waiver when a witness gives evidence involving the disgrace of admitting the commission of a crime, even when that evidence does not make possible his punishment, the necessary implication of my colleagues' opinion is this: The privilege is not that of freedom from compulsion to give testimony which will lead to one's punishment for crime; the privilege is that of freedom from compulsion to give testimony which will involve the disgrace of admitting to criminal conduct although that testimony does not put one in danger of punishment.

The decisions concerning the privilege, and its history, demonstrate the contrary. Not mere disgrace but punishment is the key concept. The existence of a likelihood of punishment is indispensable to the existence of the privilege, is its basic rationale. Again and again, in describing the privilege, the courts use such expressions as "protection [to the witness] against being brought by means of his own evidence within the penalties of the law," or "he might be convicted, when otherwise, and if he had refused to answer, he could not possibly have been convicted." Where the possibility of punishment is absent, the privilege vanishes—as where, for instance, a statute affords "absolute immunity against future prosecutions for the offence to which the question relates," or a pardon or the running of the statute of limitations completely shelters the witness from punishment for the crime.

History also shows that not the disgrace of admitting criminal conduct but the danger of punishment is at the heart of the privilege. As we know, that privilege was a consequence of the struggles of the Puritans, in seventeenth century England, with the ecclesiastical court, the High Commission, which sought to punish them for violations of the law against heresy. The Puritans at that time never denied that that law was valid. But they resisted the efforts of the High Commission which was using the oath ex officio to compel them to give evidence against themselves of that crime, evidence indispensable to their conviction and punishment as lawbreakers. The Puritans, who insisted that the oath ex officio was unlawful, considered it no disgrace to commit the crime of heresy; they were proud of their heresy; if, without fear of punishment, they could have confessed to what the law denounced as heretical acts, they would have been glad to do so. What they sought to avoid in their attacks on the procedures of the High Commission was punishment for violation of a substantive law which they considered abhorrent. No one in those days dreamed of saying that self-incrimination was wrongful at common law. But the beginning of the Puritan Revolution brought about the destruction by statute, in 1641, of the High Commission and, with it, of the offensive oath. The sentiment against the oath spread far, and, before long, the privilege against self-incrimination was recognized at common law.

When, in 1789, that privilege was incorporated, through the Fifth Amendment, in our Constitution, it was still aimed at prevention of punishment of a witness on the basis of his own compelled testimony. Eighteen years later, in 1807, Marshall, C. J., in the trial of Aaron Burr, using language not inapposite in the case at bar, said, "It would seem then that the court ought never to compel a witness to give an answer which discloses a fact that would form a necessary and essential part of a crime which is punishable by the laws"; speaking of facts which may not be elicited, he went on to say, "That fact of itself might be unavailing, but all other facts without it would be insufficient. While that remains concealed within his bosom, he is safe, but draw it from thence and he is exposed to prosecution."

4. It is, then, well settled that the object of the privilege is protection against punishment, not prevention of compulsory disclosure of criminal conduct involving disgrace but without punishment. Accordingly, testimony by a witness, given without objection, leading to disgrace by an admission of criminal conduct, cannot alone constitute a waiver of the privilege. Before there is such a waiver, the witness must go further, and, without objection, testify to facts which put him in danger of punishment. If the witness has merely gone to the point of disgracing himself by the admission of criminal conduct, then a compulsory disclosure of further facts which will put him in danger of punishment cannot reasonably be said to be the disclosure of mere "details."

5. All the cases center about the punishment factor. It would seem that the not-too-well disguised criticism, in my colleagues' opinion of the remarks of the Supreme Court in Brown v. Walker, . . . in Arndstein v. McCarthy, . . . and in McCarthy v. Arndstein . . . stems from my colleagues' failure to keep their eye on that pivotal factor of punishment. And it is, I think, because of their disregard of that factor that they hold that a decision for St. Pierre here would be an "irrational refinement of the privilege," and that an answer, without which his punishment is impossible, and with which he will be put in jeopardy, would be the disclosure of "only a detail of what he has already confessed."

6. Only if that pivotal punishment factor is borne in mind do the Supreme Court decisions dealing with the so-called "waiver" of the privilege become intelligible. In Arndstein v. McCarthy . . . and McCarthy v. Arndstein, . . . the Supreme Court, when deciding that there had been no such waiver, twice cited with approval (to the annoyance of my colleagues) the case of Foster v. The People. . . . There Judge Campbell said that the test of whether there has been a "waiver" is whether the witness "has or has not furnished sufficient evidence to criminate himself," and that the waiver is effective and the privilege gone when and only when the witness "has once made a decisive disclosure." What "criminate" and "decisive" mean in that context seems to puzzle my colleagues. But there is no puzzle if punishment is recognized as the key factor. Judge Campbell, indeed, made clear his meaning, for, in the same context, he uses, interchangeably with "criminate," the phrases "convicted himself" and exposing himself "to a criminal charge." "Criminate" (as the seventeenth century Puritans and our successful eighteenth century Bill of Rights advocates well knew) means to be in danger of punishment. A witness has not "criminated" himself and has not made a "decisive" disclosure unless and until he has, without his objection, given evidence, bearing on his commission of a crime, which will make it possible for the government to punish him for that crime through the use of that evidence.

7. The nature of "decisive" testimony constituting a "waiver" is illuminated by the decisions relating to the so-called immunity statutes. It has often been held that the privilege is not, by such a statute, removed one inch beyond the precise extent of the immunity from punishment granted by the statute. The witness is required to give evidence which bears on his commission of the crime for which, under the immunity statute, he cannot be punished; but he cannot be constitutionally compelled to give any evidence which will tend to lead to his conviction and punishment for a crime from which the immunity statute does not completely exculpate him.

To highlight the issue here, let us suppose that a section of the National Stolen Property Act provided substantially as follows: "No one can be convicted of the crime of transporting embezzled property in interstate commerce on the basis of his own evidence admitting the commission of that crime unless he also testifies to the name of the person from whom the property was embezzled." Clearly, under such a statutory provision, a witness who gave exactly the testimony given by St. Pierre here could not be compelled, against his objection, to reveal the name of the person whose money he had unlawfully withheld, because, absent his evidence as to the name of that person, he could not be punished, while his "decisive" testimony, as to that name, would make possible his punishment. And so here, there is no "waiver" because St. Pierre has not yet "criminated" himself. Unless the doctrine of "waiver" is utterly arbitrary and irrational—unless, that is, it is unrelated rationally to the nature of the privilege—the waiver, surrender, or self-removal of the privilege by the witness, must, like the removal resulting from an immunity statute, directly affect the punishment. An immunity statute cancels the privilege because it removes the punishment; a "waiver" cancels the privilege because the witness creates the danger of punishment by giving testimony, without his objection, which can be used against him to convict him.

8. It is well settled, and this court has recently held, that a witness may properly refuse to answer a question on the ground that the answer will incriminate him, even though the question on its face is harmless, where the setting is such that the answer would be "a positive step in the disclosure of a crime." A witness may, therefore, at the beginning of a series of dangerous questions, perceiving where they may lead, assert the privilege. If, however, he fails to do so early in the course of questioning and, although he might then have objected, answers some questions which may have a tendency to incriminate him, those answers do not deprive him of the privilege of later refusing to answer further questions which more clearly put him in danger of punishment. That plainly is the doctrine of McCarthy v. Arndstein. . . . There, in an examination of a bankrupt, he had answered some questions which made "partial disclosures" and which presumably he might have refused to answer because they tended in the direction of subjecting him to danger of punishment. The court held that the fact of his failure to object to those questions and of his having made "partial disclosures" did not deprive him of the right to answer subsequent questions which went still further and more directly into the danger zone. In the instant case, St. Pierre doubtless could successfully have asserted his privilege long before he admitted that he had embezzled property and transported it in interstate commerce. But his failure to do so cannot deprive him of the privilege of stopping at that point when it became obvious that an answer to the further question as to the name of the embezzlee would put him in danger of punishment, since his previous answers had not yet created a situation where the government could, on the basis of his earlier answers and other evidence available to it, procure his conviction and punishment.

9. The majority opinion, in support of its conclusion that St. Pierre waived or surrendered the privilege, cites cases (several of which are dicta) which are, and have been recognized to be, significantly different from the instant case. The facts in those cases may be summarized as follows: In a suit to which the witness is not a party, he is called to testify by one of the parties and, without objection, gives testimony which obviously will aid the

party who called him; his testimony, thus given without objection, tends to show his own participation in a crime. It is held in some of the cited cases that, in those circumstances, in fairness to the other party to the suit, the witness can then be required, over his objection, to go further and give the "details" of the criminal transaction, but cannot be required to go into matters not germane to those concerning which he had previously testified. In most of such cases there are two elements: (a) The witness, without objection, has given testimony in a suit between two other persons and knowingly in aid of one of those persons; accordingly, he is not permitted by his conduct, to create injustice to the other party which would result if that party were unable to examine the witness further in order to show his lack of credibility or that the full story, if told, would not weigh against that party. As it is sometimes put, "A witness has no right, under a pretense of a claim or privilege, to prejudice a party by a one-sided garbled narrative," and "should not be allowed by any arbitrary use of his privilege, to make a partial statement of facts to the prejudice of either party." And stress is sometimes laid on the fact that the witness, when thus giving testimony favorable to one party "knows in the beginning that his testimony in the case must expose him to a criminal charge." (b) Even in such cases, it must first be shown that the witness has, to some extent, crossed the line to the point where he has already put himself in danger of punishment through the use of his own testimony.

The leading English case, *Regina v. Garbett*, . . . although contrary to the American cases to which I have just referred, is nevertheless illuminating. There Garbett, in a civil action between Bragdon and Booth, to which Garbett was not a party, appeared as a witness and gave evidence favorable to Booth, the defendant. In the course of his testimony, he disclosed facts which tended to show that he was a party to a forgery. The court then compelled him over his objection, on cross-examination by counsel for the plaintiff, to answer the direct question whether he had committed a forgery. Subsequently he was put on trial for that crime, and, in that criminal trial, the question arose as to the admissibility against him of his compelled answer in the earlier civil suit. The sole argument made by the government for admissibility of that evidence was that Garbett, in the civil action, had waived his privilege because he had knowingly given testimony which favored one side." Lord Denman, who apparently favored the admission of the evidence, in a colloquy, asked: "Where a witness states, in general terms, what will entitle his friend to a verdict, and is then asked as to the particulars of the transaction, can he, by claiming this privilege, prevent the other side from knowing those particulars, which may have a very important effect in contradicting or explaining the general evidence he had previously given?"

*Regina* v. *Garbett* has been twice cited with approval by our Supreme Court. That does not necessarily mean that the rule of that case has, without qualification, been adopted by the Supreme Court, although it does go to show that that court is not inclined to narrow the privilege or broaden the doctrine of waiver. But, even assuming that the *Garbett* case is wholly wrong, and that contrary American decisions state the correct rule, those cases have no application here. For, as my colleagues themselves recognize, the factor of unfairness to one party to the suit is not here present; as they themselves note, the instant case is not one in which it can possibly be said that St. Pierre's testimony thus far given was (to quote the majority opinion) such as "to furnish one side with what may be false evidence and deprive the other of any means of detecting the imposition." Even if we were to ignore the fact that St. Pierre's testimony was not given in adversary suit, but in an investigatory grand jury proceeding, there is nothing in the record before us to show that his testimony, as thus far given, is favorable to anyone, or that his failure to answer the question here under consideration, would prejudice the government in its efforts to prosecute anyone other than St. Pierre himself.

I agree with my colleagues that, in cases like *Regina* v. *Garbett*, there is room for saying that, where a witness testifies knowingly in aid of one party to a suit, a right to assert the privilege to bar further questioning by the other party may put at the disposal of the witness a "mischievous instrument." But in the case now before us there is no such mischief. The sole mischief here, if there is any, inheres in the constitutional privilege itself. And it should not be forgotten that the privilege arose out of Puritan opposition to compulsory disclosures not in adversary suits but in preliminary inquisitional proceedings, and that, in the instant case, the question was put in a grand jury room where the witness is not permitted to have his counsel present.

*Buckeye Powder Co.* v. *Hazzard Power Co.*, . . . cited in the majority opinion, is, I think, not in point. There, in a treble damage suit under the Sherman Act, a witness, in answer to a question, stated, without objection, that he had written an article (which was in evidence) adversely reflecting upon the plaintiff. He then objected to answering further questions concerning his having written the article, on the ground that the answers might expose him to criminal prosecution for libel. The court held that, as he had already admitted writing the article, he had waived his privilege.

Of course there is no need to consider those cases in which a person himself on trial in a criminal proceeding voluntarily becomes a witness; for it is well settled that (to state the rule generally) by taking the witness stand the defendant in a criminal suit abandons his privilege as to any matters in issue.

10. In the proceedings below St. Pierre was denied access to the grand jury minutes. . . . It was therefore necessary for him, in order to raise the question of his privilege, to show, in some other way, that he might be charged with a federal offense. To make that proof, he took the stand before the trial judge; his testimony was there considered as a narrative of his testimony before the grand jury. In those circumstances, it cannot fairly be said that, by thus testifying before the trial judge, he waived his privilege. . . .

11. Up to now I had been discussing "waiver." There is, however, the following phase of this case, not at all considered in the majority opinion, as to which waiver is irrelevant. Since, as above noted, a grand jury proceeding is not "judicial," St. Pierre's confession cannot, under the due process clause, be used in a criminal proceeding against him unless it was voluntary. The burden of showing that it was voluntary is on the government, and it has made no such showing here. We should, therefore, deal with this case on the assumption that the confession cannot be used against St. Pierre. But we can take the facts disclosed in the confession into account in examining the "setting" to see whether his disclosure of the embezzlee's name will tend to incriminate him. If we do so, it is apparent that the answer will have that forbidden effect, for it will give the government such leads that, without using the confession, it can make out a case against him. Accordingly, on that basis alone, under the authority of our recent decision in *United States v. Cusson,* . . . we should reverse.

12. To avoid misunderstanding, I think it desirable to disclose the springs of my dissent. The following remarks are not to be taken as at all directed against my colleagues, to whom they do not apply, but as designed to make clear my own approach to the problem and to indicate why I disagree with certain critics of the privilege.

(a) Those critics, regarding that privilege as pernicious and knowing that it is difficult to procure the repeal of the constitutional provision which confers it, urge the courts to eliminate it by emasculating interpretations. Any judges who do not readily comply with that suggestion they call "reactionary."

It is easy to caricature the privilege. I recall the case of a witness who, when asked by the judge why he refused to answer a question, replied, "Because my lawyers tell me I'm a crook." I have no quarrel with those who assert that the constitutional guaranty of freedom from unreasonable searches and seizures is, at least today, far more important for the preservation of democracy, and far more justifiable on rational grounds, that the constitutional privilege against self-incrimination. But it is not, I think, the business of judges, when deciding cases, to consider the desirability of constitutional provisions. Those who urge judges to gut the privilege by narrowing constructions, saying that it is based on a foolish sentimental desire to protect criminals, forget that the seventeenth century Puritans whose efforts gave rise to it wanted to protect themselves from the effective enforcement against them, through their own testimony, of then valid criminal laws, and that the Americans who wrote the privilege into our constitution were not stupid men but, with knowledge of what they were doing, unquestionably intended to afford just that protection to persons whom the government might seek to punish for crimes.

The privilege is still in our Constitution whether we like it or not, and whether or not we call it a foolish sentimental safeguard of criminals. I happen to think that there is more to be said for the reasonableness of the privilege than its harshest critics will admit, but this is not the place to come to its defense on rational grounds. For, reasonable or unreasonable, it is part of the Constitution which we, as judges, took an oath to enforce. Of course, there is need for differentiation in judicial attitudes toward the specific and the general clauses of the Constitution; with respect to the latter, it has been wisely recognized, beginning with John Marshall, that pliancy in interpretation is necessary if the Constitution is not to act as a strait-jacket; and the Supreme Court, accordingly, has been unwilling, in interpreting such clauses, to be bound by its own precedents to the same extent as in other legal provinces. That differentiation is pertinent here. For, as the Federalist shows, a majority of the Constitutional Convention opposed the inclusion in the Constitution of specific provisions along the lines of a Bill of Rights, in part because they wanted the Constitution, in general, to be vague in its requirements. What Judge Hough has called the "convenient vagueness" of phrases like "due process," "interstate commerce," or "impairment of the obligation of contracts," has been regarded as wisely permitting "adaptive" interpretations to meet changing national needs. In *Home Building & Loan Association* v. *Blaisdell*, . . . Chief Justice Hughes said, in speaking of the contracts clause, "If by the statement that what the Constitution meant at the time of its adoption it means today, it is intended to say that the great clauses of the Constitution must be confined to the interpretation which the framers, with the conditions and outlook of their time, would have placed upon them, the statement carries its own refutation." Where, however, a constitutional provision, like the one here under consideration, had a fairly clear and precise meaning when it was adapted, and was not intended to be vague, then the Supreme Court has given it an "historical interpretation."

It is possible to argue that the literal language of the Fifth Amendment shows an intention to make the privilege operative only when a question is asked in a criminal proceeding against the witness; but the Supreme Court long ago decided that the intention of those words was to incorporate the entire common law privilege, and, consequently, it is not open to this court to say that the Amendment has a narrower meaning. Taking the constitutional provision, then (as we must), as having been designed to include the common law privilege, I think that judges are dangerously and unwisely going beyond their legitimate functions if, because of their personal beliefs that that provision was originally unfortunate or is now outmoded, they take it on themselves to frustrate its meaning and purpose by crippling interpretations.

It is our sworn obligation not to cut into this privilege by decisions which will allow government prosecutors to circumvent it and to defeat the plain purpose of those who lawfully inserted it in the Constitution. Judges should not convert themselves into constitutional conventions. They may properly, within appropriate limits, avail themselves (as the Supreme Court Justices often have done) of the elasticity of these constitutional phrases purposely left elastic, but they should not tamper with those phrases not designed to be flexible. Strangely enough, often those who are most opposed to any changes in judicial constructions of those designedly elastic clauses of the Constitution are often the most vigorous in their demands that the courts should eviscerate the specific and relatively inelastic self-incrimination clause.

(b) Since I think that the fullest practicable disclosure to the courts of all important evidence bearing on the facts of cases is essential to the administration of justice, I agree heartily with critics of all privileges accorded witnesses that each of those privileges needs periodic examination to determine whether the policy which prompted it is sufficient to outweigh its interference with access to such evidence. Indeed, I take far more seriously than do many of those critics the idea that, if courts of justice are to do justice, it is imperative that the courts come closer than they do today to the actual facts, and exercise more care in the art of fact-finding. The several privileges and the out-of-date exclusionary rules of evidence (including notably the rule against hearsay) doubtless need reconsideration by our legislatures. But they are the least of the impediments to adequate fact-finding—which, while it is the most difficult and perhaps the most important part of the judicial process, receives the least study. As long as we continue to employ the jury's general verdict, instead of using special verdicts, it is pretty much a waste of time to bother about the niceties of the evidence which juries are permitted and not permitted to hear. For there is much reason to believe that juries frequently bring in inscrutable general verdicts which have little relation to the evidence and little or nothing to do with any purported findings of fact made by them. And, if that is true, then the abolition of the hearsay rule and of all the privileges, coupled with the greatest improvements in pretrial discovery, will often merely mean that juries will hear more evidence which they will disregard. Courtroom fact-finding, since it is a human undertaking, can never be perfect, but it can and should be improved as far as possible. And the greatest single obstacle to that improvement is the devotion of much of our legal profession to the thesis that a lawsuit is essentially a sporting event, a thesis which, when limited to an espousal of the preservation of an appropriately supplemented contentious procedure, is intelligent, but, which, when carried to excess, as it often is, flies in the face of common sense and would shock all of us lawyers and judges if custom had not made us callous to the injustices it all too frequently produces.

I am, then, not moved in this dissent by any sentimental desire to protect criminals or by a desire to prevent as full judicial scrutiny as is practicable of the facts of cases. I am moved by fear of the consequences to democratic government in general, and to the courts in particular, of judicial disregard of specific unrepealed sections of the Constitution. Courts, when they conduct themselves in that manner, invite popular rejection of our established legal institutions by unlawful means.

*132 F.2d 837 (1942)*

# UNITED STATES v. FIELD ❧

T HE APPEAL *discussed below came as an aftermath of Dennis et al. v. United States (1951), in which eleven members of the Communist Party were convicted in the district court for violation of the Smith Act, which makes it a crime to conspire to advocate the overthrow of the United States government by force and violence. The defendants in the Dennis case, after their arrest, were released on bail furnished by the Bail Fund of the Civil Rights Congress of New York. After trial, the judge ordered the surrender of the defendants to begin their prison terms. Seven appeared but four did not; and when bench warrants did not produce them the next day, the judge declared their bail forfeited. The court then ordered the appearance of certain officers of the Bail Fund for an inquiry regarding the missing defendants. Three of the five trustees of the Fund, Frederick Field, Dashiell Hammett, and W. Alpheus Hunton, appeared separately; all refused to answer certain questions and to produce certain books and records of the Fund. The court cited them for contempt and sentenced them to prison, with a provision for release should they decide to purge themselves. They appealed on two basic arguments: That the district court had no jurisdiction to conduct the inquiry; and that, in their refusal to answer questions and produce books and records, they were protected by their privilege against self-incrimination under the Fifth Amendment. Judge Charles Clark, writing for the court, affirmed the order of the district court. Judge Frank concurs, dissenting as to one ruling of the court.*

FRANK, *Circuit Judge* (concurring as to affirmance but dissenting as to one ruling: 1. I entirely agree that we must affirm the convictions on the grounds that the court had jurisdiction, and that the defendants had no constitutional privilege either with reference to producing the Bail Fund's records or as to oral testimony concerning matters "auxiliary to the production" of those records.

2. But I disagree on one point decided in the last few paragraphs of my colleagues' opinion: The defendants were asked to testify orally in answer to some other questions which—so my colleagues concede—(1) would tend to self-incrimination, (2) were not at all "auxiliary" to the production of the records, and (3) would ordinarily be covered by the anti-self-incrimination constitutional privilege. Peculiarly within that category were questions about when the defendants last saw, or about their acquaintance with, the Dennis-case refugees. This is precisely the kind of question the reply to which the Supreme Court, earlier this year, held privileged as tending to self-incrimination, in a case much like this. See *Hoffman* v. *United States*. . . . There the witness Hoffman refused, when asked, to give testimony as to his connections with fugitives for whom bench warrants had been issued. The questions to which the privilege applied were . . . :

Q. Do you know Mr. William Weisberg?
A. I do.
Q. When did you last see him?
A. I refuse to answer.
Q. Have you seen him this week?
A. I refuse to answer.
Q. Do you know where Mr. William Weisberg is now?
A. I refuse to answer.

The following, almost identical questions asked the defendant Hunton in the present case, are held today by my colleagues to be without the privilege:

Q. Do you know Henry Winston?
A. I cannot answer the question on the ground that the answer may tend to incriminate me.
Q. Do you know where Robert G. Thompson, Gilbert Green, Gus Hall or Henry Winston are presently located?
A. I do not.
Q. When did you last see Robert G. Thompson?
A. I decline to answer on the ground that the answer might tend to incriminate me.
Q. When did you last see Gilbert Green?
A. I decline to answer on the ground that the answer might tend to incriminate me.
Q. Have you seen Robert G. Thompson since Thursday of last week?
A. I decline to answer on the ground that the answer might tend to incriminate me.
Q. Have you seen the defendant Gilbert Green since July 5?

A. I decline to answer on the ground that the answer might tend to incriminate me.

My colleagues' position as to those questions is this: The defendants bargained away the privilege many months before any judicial inquiry arose, when they voluntarily became sureties and thereby impliedly promised to disclose to the government any information which might aid in bringing into custody the convicted persons for whom the defendants had gone bail. I have no doubt that the defendants did assume that obligation. Doubtless, too, the effective assertion of the privilege would be flatly inconsistent with that obligation and would be a breach of it. But I do not accept my colleagues' thesis that a court may criminally punish a man who breaks such a contract by which he agrees, long in advance, to surrender his anti-self-incrimination privilege. In short, I think that no such advance (pre-inquiry) contract can validly destroy the privilege (not to give oral self-incriminating testimony) when asserted by a witness in response to questions during a proceeding, if that privilege would otherwise apply.

No case relating to bail sureties, or other persons, has been cited by my colleagues in support of their position. Nothing in any of the previous decisions relative to this Bail Fund bears on the subject. My colleagues' ruling is a startling innovation; it marks the deepest inroad on the privilege to this date. In this particular case, that ruling may seem to have relatively little consequence; for, even if my view prevailed, it would mean only that the defendants would be entitled to urge the trial judge to use his discretion to reduce their sentences. When, however, the defendants have served their sentences, they may again be asked the same questions and again be held in contempt, if they repeat their refusals to answer. Moreover, the majority ruling on this point may have wide precedential consequences. All this explains why I shall spell out my reasons for disagreeing on this issue.

I think that, as I shall try to show, my colleagues have erroneously applied (1) cases admittedly having nothing to do with oral testimony, and (2) cases holding that civil remedies (that is, remedies other than criminal punishment) may be used, where one who asserts the privilege thereby breaks an obligation, voluntarily assumed, to testify orally.

I begin with the latest federal case on which my colleagues rely, *Shapiro v. United States.* . . . I think that it plainly demonstrates that an advance voluntary assumption of an obligation to testify orally does not destroy the privilege. In the Shapiro case the Court was construing an OPA statute which required those engaged in a business regulated by that Act both (a) to make and keep records open to inspection and subject to subpoena and (b) to "appear and testify" orally under oath at administrative inquiries. The Court held that the defendant, by engaging voluntarily in such a business, assumed the obligation of compliance with these requirements. It also held that the statute made "public records" of the required records; that therefore the defendant had no constitutional privilege with respect to their production; and that, accordingly, on compulsorily producing them, he was not entitled to immunity from prosecution on the basis of the facts disclosed therein, despite the statutory immunity provision in §202(g) of the OPA statute. The immunity thus conferred, said the Court, was only "co-terminous with what otherwise would have been the constitutional privilege." But, significantly, the Court carefully differentiated the lack of effect on the privilege of the obligation to testify assumed by the defendant. The Court said . . . , "Of course all *oral* testimony * * * can properly be compelled only by exchange of immunity for waiver of privilege."

To summarize: The defendant Shapiro took on two obligations—(1) to keep and produce records and (2) to testify orally. The first was not at odds with the privilege, because the records had been made "public records." But the Supreme Court said that the second was within the privilege, which means that the privilege not to testify orally could not be destroyed by Shapiro's previous voluntary assumption of an obligation so to testify. As a result, Shapiro could have been compelled to testify orally as to matters tending to self-incrimination only because of the correlative statutory grant of immunity. But, in the case on appeal before us here, as there was no grant of immunity to the defendants, their privilege remained, notwithstanding their implied promise to make disclosure.

The distinction, laid down in the Shapiro case, between production of required records and compulsion of oral testimony has been reaffirmed in our own court: "We recognize that if Daisart had been required to submit reports pursuant to OPA's record-keeping requirements, then Smith could not claim immunity if compelled to produce them. . . . We think, though, the production of records must be distinguished from oral testimony as to what the records would contain, had they been produced. * * * [T]he very matter that would incriminate had to be forced from the lips of the defendant himself, rather than obtained from the records or books." *United States* v. *Daisart Sportswear*, . . . reversed on other grounds, *Smith* v. *United States*. . . .

My colleagues in now wiping out this distinction rely on (1) state court cases which, like the Shapiro case, sustained, as valid, in the face of the privilege, statutes requiring druggists or others to keep records open to public or official inspection and to produce them in court, or (2) cases requiring certain kinds of oral reports to be made to the police. But in these cases the state courts themselves have carefully pointed out, as a basis of sustaining those statutes, that the statutes made no attempt to compel the reporter, against an assertion of his privilege, to testify in court as to the contents of such reports. I think that not the slightest intimation in those cases justifies my colleagues' interpretation of them as holding that one required by statute to make such reports loses his privilege, in a judicial inquiry to which the contents of the report are relevant, to refuse to give self-incriminating oral testimony. Such a result is, I believe, without precedent in this country. The Supreme Court, in fact, took all these state court reporting statutes into consideration in *Shapiro v. United States*. . . . Yet it was adamant in insisting that the privilege still applied to all oral testimony.

My colleagues consider it an "anomaly" to differentiate the production of documents from "questions concerning their contents." Even had the questions asked of the defendants here been thus restricted, I would not regard the distinction as anomalous; more to the point, the Supreme Court does not. But whatever there may be of anomaly in applying the privilege to questions concerning the books' contents vanishes with respect to the questions asked here which were utterly unrelated to these contents, that is, questions about when the defendants had last seen the fugitives, and the like.

My colleagues do not cite, and I have been unable to discover, a single American case deciding that a statute can validly abolish the privilege with respect to giving oral testimony. Moreover, in the instant case, no statute required the defendants to report or make disclosures. Their obligation to disclose is wholly contractual, deriving by implication from their contract as sureties. No American case has been cited, and I can find none, to the effect that, by any advance contractual promise, the privilege can be abrogated. All the pertinent decisions hold the other way. Consider the case of a fiduciary. He patently owes an obligation, assumed when he becomes a fiduciary—an obligation which is at least as important as if embodied in an express contractual promise—to disclose to his beneficiary all dealings with the beneficiary's money or other property. Yet when a beneficiary has sued his fiduciary, it has been uniformly held in this country that the fiduciary may refuse to give self-incriminating oral testimony about such dealings, although the result may be seriously to impede or frustrate the obligation he unquestionably undertook voluntarily. . . .

Very much in point are the cases relative to policemen and other public officers, for they involve contractual obligations owed to a government. A policeman, when he takes office, contracts in the most solemn manner conceivable—as signalized by his oath of office—to aid in the detection and apprehension of criminals. His solemn promise obviously includes a promise to give information to the government about the deeds of suspected criminals. Yet the courts, whenever the issue has arisen, have said, with no exception, that such an officer, if called in an inquiry concerned with facts squarely within the scope of the officer's sworn official duty, may efficaciously assert the privilege. . . . The courts, in such cases, fully acknowledging the official's obligation to testify orally, hold that the remedy for the breach is not criminal punishment, but removal from office. "We are not unmindful of the constitutional privilege * * * which may be exercised by all persons, including police officers, in any proceeding, civil or criminal [citations]. As we view the situation when pertinent questions were propounded to appellants before the grand jury, the answers to which questions would tend to incriminate them, they were put to a choice which they voluntarily made. *Duty required them to answer. Privilege permitted them to refuse to answer. They chose to exercise the privilege but the exercise of such privilege was wholly inconsistent with their duty as police officers.* They claim they had a constitutional right not to answer under the circumstances, but * * * *they had no constitutional right to remain police officers in the face of their clear violation of the duty imposed upon them.*" *Christal v. Pol. Com. of San Francisco.* . . .

Suppose a policeman who had been assigned to arresting the Dennis-case fugitive Thompson had been asked, just as one of the defendants here was asked: "When did you last see Thompson?" Suppose the officer, on the basis of the privilege, had refused to answer. The precedents all teach that he could not have been adjudged in contempt.

In short, on the assertion of the privilege, the courts will not use criminal punishment as a means of compelling specific performance of a policeman's contractual obligation, but will approve other remedies for the policeman's breach of that obligation. So here: The defendants, because they have broken their contractual disclosure-obligation, may be rejected as sureties in future cases. . . . And if money damages can be proved, they can be held civilly liable. But I think that, no more than the privilege-asserting policeman, can they be jailed or fined for the breach.

My colleagues, I think, betray the weakness of their position by citing, as "apposite," *Canteline v. McClellan*, . . . Was anyone there held in contempt for refusal to answer questions? Not at all. The court there quoted with approval the passage from the *Christal* case which I quoted above. That alone should serve to show how inapposite is *Canteline*. But we have better proof of its irrelevance: There was before the court in that case an amendment to the New York constitution which, so far as New York proceedings were concerned, could have wiped out the privilege for public officials, or, indeed, for everyone. But that amendment did not modify the privilege; it did not provide that an official could be jailed if he refused to answer self-incriminating questions; it provided merely that an official exercising the privilege should lose his office. In *Canteline*, the court applied that amendment.

The weakness of my colleagues' position further appears from their citation of *Hickman v. London Assur. Corp.* . . . and *Swedish-American Tel.*

Co. v. *Fidelity & Casualty Co.* . . . . In the *Hickman* case, the plaintiff, insured by the defendant, agreed in his policy to submit to an examination under oath in matters concerning the loss. Plaintiff brought suit on the policy, although, setting up his privilege, he had previously refused to disclose the required information to defendant. The court found that, as he had breached it, he could not recover on the policy. The court did not, however, attempt, by punishing the plaintiff, to coerce him into specifically performing his contractual promise. The Swedish-American Tel. Co. case seems singularly inapposite, since it did not in any way involve the privilege against self-incrimination. In that case, the defendant company, insured by the plaintiff, had agreed that, in order to enable the plaintiff to check on the premiums earned, the defendant's books should be open to inspection by the plaintiff. In a suit, about the premiums, brought by the plaintiff, the court ordered defendant to produce for plaintiff's inspection the pertinent books of the defendant. The company was fined for civil contempt when it refused. It asserted that the discovery order was an unreasonable search and seizure. The Supreme Court of Illinois held that it was not. Nothing in that case relates to oral testimony.

All the precedents say that the self-incrimination privilege relative to oral testimony cannot be abolished constitutionally by advance contracts between private persons or even between a government and its crime-detecting officials. My colleagues are either ignoring those precedents or announcing a new doctrine which, for these purposes, puts contracts between governments and bail-sureties in a special class. But why such a special class? Why should a policeman, suspected of conspiracy with criminals whom he owes a duty to detect and arrest, have the benefit of the privilege despite his contractual duty, while a private bail-surety does not, although the harm such a surety, if allowed to keep silent, does to society and public morals is far less grave than that done by such a silent policeman? The fact that a policeman wears a uniform, advertising his status as a public servant, certainly does not mean that discharge of his obligation—a part of his "due performance of accepted office"—is not at least as "close and direct" as that of a private citizen acting as a surety. Nor is the surety's assumption of his obligation one iota more "voluntary" than is that of a policeman. In truth, one might plausibly argue that, in a practical sense, the surety's is less "voluntary"; for every man entering the police force thoroughly understands—more, he is told at length—that he is agreeing to detect and disclose crimes, whereas the implied disclosure-obligation of a private bail-surety is not generally well understood.

Since then, my colleagues' decision cannot reasonably rest on the notion of a special class, it must be taken as overruling the precedents, that is, as holding that any advance contractual promise inconsistent with the exercise of the privilege extinguishes the privilege. If my colleagues' remarks about the need for a "close and direct" relation between promise and privilege leave any lingering doubts on this score, those doubts can be easily dispelled in this way: insert in a contract an express provision that one of the parties promises to divulge, to the other, information of a designated kind, and that the promissor surrenders his privilege with reference to oral testimony in so far as it would interfere with performance of that promise. Then, presto chango, up the chimney goes the privilege. Thus, if my colleagues' decision is generally accepted, the sole practical effect of the constitutional privilege will be to add a few words to a contract. So the high hopes of Madison and his fellows, expressed in this Fifth Amendment privilege, will end up in a rubber-stamp contractual clause. Especially will all government employees be stripped of the privilege—by contract. Before long, rubber-stamped out of existence, the privilege will be but a quaint item of antiquarian lore.

At any rate, my colleagues are today ruling that, by a contract with the government, any man can validly surrender that constitutional privilege long before there arises a judicial inquiry in which he is asked to give self-incriminating oral testimony under oath. I regard that ruling as at odds with the rationale of Supreme Court decisions in respect of other constitutional privileges. Thus, for example, no one thinks an official or private person can validly contract away his right to trial by jury in any or all future criminal proceedings; he can, however, waive that right after indictment if then fully aware of what he is doing. Advance abandonment is forbidden to prevent the right being thoughtlessly foregone. And, for like reasons, the same rule governs the advance abandonment of the privilege against oral testimony which tends to incriminate. Nevertheless, it might be suggested that, since the privilege is personal and may be relinquished by not asserting it when one is judicially questioned, it must be capable of disposition by a contract made long in advance of the questioning. The answer is that the courts hold that, because of public policy considerations, many important rights or privileges cannot be bartered away before the happening of events calling them into operation, but may be abandoned after such happening. "A promise not to plead the statute of limitations as a defense, or a promise to 'waive' the benefit of it, has generally been held to be contrary to the public interest if it is made at the time of the contract the enforcement of which is involved"; but such a promise "is valid if made after the accrual of the cause of action to be affected by it." A contractor cannot in advance bargain away such defenses as fraud and duress, and yet he can * * * validate a previous bargain that was induced by fraud or duress." So with the disposition of a mortgagor's "equity of redemption." Similarly, a worker cannot, in advance of their accrual, "contract out" his rights under a workmen's compensation statute. A licensee under a patent may not lawfully agree in advance not to plead the invalidity of any patent if sued for infringement. A provision of a contract is invalid by which one party agrees not to bring suit in or remove a suit to a federal court, although the right thus to sue or remove may be abandoned lawfully when the cause of action arises. In the same way, to this extent, the self-incrimination privilege is inalienable—not to be yielded up—in advance.

It seems to me that my colleagues have forgotten or have undervalued the stirring words uttered by the Supreme Court years ago: "* * * [A]ny compulsory discovery by extorting the party's oath, * * * to convict him of crime, or to forfeit his property, is contrary to the principles of a free government. * * * [I]t is abhorrent to the instincts of an American. It may suit the purposes of despotic power; but it cannot abide the pure atmosphere of political liberty and personal freedom." . . . Perhaps I am too old-fashioned, but I confess to being thrilled by those words. If we take them lightly, if by one after another encroachment we keep diminishing this constitutional privilege, a bit here and a bit there, I fear that we are likely to move rapidly, although unwittingly, in the direction of the unfree, authoritarian, kind of government whose principles have long seemed unprincipled to Americans. Eastern European history is proving once more the value of this privilege—proving that a law-enforcement system habitually trusting to compulsory self-incriminating disclosures cannot long escape recourse to bullying and torture. It is noteworthy, too, that those American officials who, deplorably, use the brutalitarian third degree manifest unusually strong hostility to this privilege. So that if, at times, this privilege protects the guilty, yet often it serves as a shield to the innocent. I think my colleagues have left little of that shield.

To be sure, some persons—Wigmore is typical—who are by no means brutalitarian look upon the privilege as largely one which fosters foolish sentimentality toward criminals, and wish that it were not incorporated in the Constitution. But even if that wish were warranted (which I gravely doubt) the way to realize it would be by amending the Constitution, not by judicial decisions which erase it.

*193 F.2d 92 (1951)*

# UNITED STATES v. LISS 🦆

IN THE EARLY 1940's, twenty defendants were convicted for the crime of conspiring to violate the laws regulating the sale and dispensing of narcotic drugs. In their appeal, they complained of various errors committed during the course of the trial; the chief objection common to all was that the conspiracy as defined in the indictment embraced several different crimes which should not have been tried as one. Judge Learned Hand wrote the opinion for the court in the which the convictions of three appellants, Palmer, Geffner and Jaffe, were upset, and those of the remaining appellants, affirmed. Judge Frank dissents in part.

FRANK, Circuit Judge (dissenting in part): For the following reasons, I dissent as to the conviction of the defendants other than Liss and Conte.

There are some persons (and I am one of them) who have come to doubt the virtues of jury trials in civil actions. However, even of those who entertain such doubts, most agree that in criminal actions the right to a jury trial should be preserved—that is, the accused should be tried by jury if he so elects (although it is perhaps less certain than is generally supposed that defendants fare better with the average jury than with the average trial judge sitting without a jury). But whatever may be the views of judges about the jury system, until the jury is abolished by legislation and constitutional amendment, it is their duty to maintain the function of the jury in all jury trials. And that means that, in a criminal action tried before a jury, a defendant should not be convicted unless the jury finds him guilty—after a fair trial. Perhaps I am old-fashioned in saying that I believe that the doctrine of "harmless error" does not dispense with the necessity of a fair trial of a defendant whom the appellate judges believe to be guilty. I still believe that the guilt of the accused is not enough, that no matter how guilty he may be, he is, under the Constitution, entitled to a fair jury trial. A jury trial does not seem to me to be fair when it plainly appears that the jury has not been well informed as to the facts. As I understand the fundamental principle of the jury system, we appellate judges do not sit as a jury. It surely follows that we ought not to sustain a verdict of guilty after an unfair trial merely because, upon reading the printed record, we believe that, had we been the jury, we would have convicted. Any other rule has the result that the presence of the jury will often become a mere formality; for then, if only the jury finds guilt, no matter by what unfair tactics it was persuaded to do so, we judges, in actual fact, decide the case.

I cannot subscribe to a rule that what is substantial reversible error depends not on whether it probably affected the jury to the substantial prejudice of the defendant but on whether we appellate judges think the defendant guilty or innocent. If that is to be [the] rule, I would urge that criminal jury trials be abolished as expensive and time-consuming shams. . . .

At a minimum, if that is to be the rule, we should make it unmistakably clear, so that the public will thoroughly understand what a jury trial now really is—and is not. The "principle of publicity," which governs in the American judicial process, calls not only for trials held in public but also for the publication of judicial opinions that disclose the grounds of decisions; that publicity is illusory if the true grounds are not stated. (There Holmes is our guide; he taught that it is wholesome for courts to spell out their mental processes and frankly to acknowledge just what they are doing. . . .) To adopt a rule of decision concerning jury trials without publicizing it prevents the public from knowing how its government operates. That is unwise in a democracy where the workings of all branches of government should be plain to the citizens. There can be no true democracy when citizens are treated like infants who must not be told the facts of life; mysteries as to the workings of government impair one of the most important features of democratic participation—the capacity of citizens intelligently to criticize and seek changes in those aspects of government which they consider undesirable—and breed a sense of frustration and a cynicism which may pave the way to the destruction of democracy. If we are to apply a rule by which we, who do not see or hear the witnesses, are, in many cases, to decide the facts, we should so announce. We ought not to become fact finders while appearing not to be. Moreover, if we are to find the facts, we ought at least to impose on ourselves the obligation we now impose on trial judges when they sit without a jury— that of publishing the findings.

In the case at bar there was the greatest likelihood that the jury was confused. The indictment, as my colleagues concede, was misleading in that it charged twenty defendants with engaging in one conspiracy when, as the evidence disclosed, there were in fact three distinct alleged conspiracies. One of these conspiracies was not unlawful. Conte and Liss were parties to the other two conspiracies. But, as my colleagues say, there was no evidence whatever that Rudy was a party to the third, and no evidence that the other defendants, except Liss, Conte, and Rudy, were in any way involved in the second. It is difficult for me to believe that the jury, at the end of this long trial, was able to keep in mind the distinction between the second and third conspiracies and to comprehend, with any degree of clarity, that evidence relevant to the second should not be considered in determining whether there was guilty participation in the third, or vice versa.

The jury may well, then, have erroneously combined the evidence and found guilt when it would not have done so had it observed the distinction. In those circumstances, the least that the trial judge should have done was to aid the jury in his charge by differentiating the conspiracies. Not only did he not do so but, as my colleagues point out, his charge was not too enlightening. Moreover, he expressly refused, when requested by Rudy's counsel, to instruct the jury that there was no testimony showing Rudy's connection with the third conspiracy—and that, too, after a trial which consumed eight days in which testimony was taken that fills more than seven hundred and fifty printed pages. (The trial judge refused Rudy's request to charge the jury that there was "no testimony in the case that the defendant Rudy had any part in the purchase, sale, distribution, extraction or diversion of lead and opium-wash." The trial judge gave as his reason for this refusal that the request was made too late under the Rules. In this he was mistaken. At one time there had been a Rule in the Southern District of New York that, when requests were not submitted before summing up, the judge, in his discretion, could refuse to consider them. But this Rule was abolished in 1938. The taking of the testimony was concluded on April 20, 1940, at about 4:00 P.M. Counsel for Liss then delivered his summation to the jury which he concluded at about 5:15 P.M. Counsel for Rudy was then instructed by the court to deliver his summation and did so only after the court had denied his application to adjourn until the following morning. The next day, at 2:30 P.M., Rudy's counsel submitted to the court his written request to charge while counsel for other defendants were still in the process of addressing the jury and when the prosecutor had not yet delivered his summation. The court commenced its charge to the jury at 3:40 P.M. At the conclusion of this charge, Rudy's counsel asked the court to charge on his written request. In the circumstances, the refusal to charge as requested was, I think, an abuse of discretion.)

My colleagues concede that there may have been confusion, but they conclude that this jury, in fact, was not misled. That, I submit, is unverified and unverifiable guessing. It is well settled that, generally, it is improper for the court to be affected by anything it may learn, even from the jurymen themselves, as to how the jury arrived at its verdict. Unable as we are, therefore, to interrogate the jurors, any effort on our part to determine that they were or were not confused is an undertaking which most psychologists would regard as hopeless. Who are we judges that we should so confidently probe the mental interiors of the jurors? The best that can be said is that the chances are as good that the jurors were bewildered as that they were not. Where such chances are anywhere near equal, there has been substantial error. We judges ought to take judicial notice of what every ordinary person knows about juries, and therefore to recognize that the twelve citizens, casually summoned to serve as jurors, are not trained fact finders and can be easily bewildered. Our experience shows that even trial judges, experienced in finding facts, when sitting without a jury, sometimes do not avoid confusion as to the evidence when, as here, there are many defendants and the trial is not brief. The need for safeguarding defendants from misunderstanding by the jury is peculiarly acute in conspiracy trials which lend themselves to unfairness, since, at best, they often permit the jury to hear evidence as to some of the defendants which the jurymen may easily but mistakenly believe has a bearing on the guilt of others.

It is true that a variance between the indictment and the proof is not invariably fatal error. Whether or not it constitutes such error depends upon whether the record in the particular case does or does not show a likelihood of substantial prejudice. My colleagues suggest that the issue is similar to that of the propriety or impropriety of joining separate crimes in a single indictment or of consolidating separate indictments for trial. Yet in all the cases which they cite, and in which such joinders or consolidations have been held proper, the courts have pointed out either that the separate crimes were closely related (in some of them, the proof of the one being necessary for the proof of the other) or that, as in our decision in United States v. Lotsch, . . . "the evidence as to each was short and simple; there was no reasonable ground for thinking that the jury could not keep separate what was relevant to each." That factor of shortness and simplicity—and of consequent ease of comprehension by the jury—is absent here. McElroy v. United States . . . condemned the consolidation of an indictment against one defendant with an indictment against another when the charges were "not provable by the same evidence, and in no sense resulting from the same series of acts." It has been thought that the full rigor of the McElroy doctrine has been somewhat mitigated. But in the cases where it has been so held, the several charges were very closely connected. My colleagues' ruling here is the farthest north of the McElroy case to be found in the books.

Of course I agree that upper courts should not, by demanding perfection . . . obstruct "the criminal prosecution of complicated crimes" unavoidably involving large numbers of defendants. But a trial even for a single conspiracy is complicated. The complexity of such a trial should not be increased by needlessly injecting into it the trial of another conspiracy. More ought to be done, I think, to prevent prosecutors from employing the excuse of need for "expedition" to use, unnecessarily, conspiracy trials, in which large numbers of defendants are herded into one suit, instead of bringing several actions. The trial dockets are not so congested as to compel such omnibus trials. . . . At any rate, aware of the potential dangers of injustice involved in all conspiracy actions, we ought to be singularly insistent that they be conducted with exceptional fairness. "Expedition" and "efficiency" in the prosecution of crimes ought not to be purchased at the expense of justice. The recent expansion of the activities of so-called "administrative agencies" has centered attention upon their conduct with a result which, on net balance, is beneficent: the demand that dispatch in administration must not infringe on the rights of citizens. Because courts and prosecuting attorneys have a far older history, it is often forgotten that they, too, are engaged in administration, a truth which, strangely enough, has been obscured by burying it in a revealing phrase, "the administration of justice." That phrase should bring to mind the fact that courts and district attorneys, no less than administrative agencies, are administrators; their task is to "administer" what we call 'justice." No more than administrative agencies should they emphasize dispatch in administration to the neglect of their primary function—justice. Here, as elsewhere, the major problem of our times is to reconcile the Expert State and the Free State. . . .

*137 F.2d 995 (1943)*

# IN RE J. P. LINAHAN, INC. ❧

IN 1943 CERTAIN CREDITORS and stockholders of J. P. Linahan, Inc., which
was being reorganized in involuntary bankruptcy proceedings, appealed
from an order of the district court which denied their application to remove
the Special Master in charge of the reorganization. Their grounds for appeal
are stated in the opinion for the court by Judge Frank.

FRANK, Circuit Judge: [1.] 1. Appellants complain that the district court,
having appointed Referee Olney as Special Master in Chapter X proceedings
begun by involuntary petition and contested by appellants, denied appellants'
application to remove that Special Master because of bias. Appellants pointed
to matters alleged to show such bias, most of which are so frivolous as to
deserve no discussion. Special emphasis is put on these facts. The Master
has heretofore entered orders, accompanied by findings, adverse to appellants;
the district court's orders, approving these orders of the Master, were, in some
instances, reversed by this court on previous appeals; some of the findings of
the Special Master are alleged to have been, at least by inference, disapproved
on these appeals and, in one instance, to have been based on hearsay. These
facts do not call for removal of the Special Master. Appellants entertain a
fundamentally false conception of the prejudice which disqualifies a judicial
officer.

Democracy must, indeed, fail unless our courts try cases fairly, and there
can be no fair trial before a judge lacking in impartiality and disinterestedness.
If, however, "bias" and "partiality" be defined to mean the total absence of
preconceptions in the mind of the judge, then no one has ever had a fair
trial and no one ever will. The human mind, even at infancy, is no blank piece
of paper. We are born with predispositions; and the process of education,

formal and informal, creates attitudes in all men which affect them in judging situations, attitudes which precede reasoning in particular instances and where, therefore, by definition, are pre-judices. Without acquired "slants," preconceptions, life could not go on. Every habit constitutes a pre-judgment; were those pre-judgments which we call habits absent in any person, were he obliged to treat every event as an unprecedented crisis presenting a wholly new problem, he would go mad. Interests, points of view, preferences, are the essence of living. Only death yields complete dispassionateness, for such dispassionateness signifies utter indifference. "To live is to have a vocation, and to have a vocation is to have an ethic or scheme of values, and to have a scheme of values is to have a point of view, and to have a point of view is to have a prejudice or bias. * * *" (Kenneth Burke, Permanence and Change.) An "open mind," in the sense of a mind containing no preconceptions whatever, would be a mind incapable of learning anything, would be that of an utterly emotionless human being, corresponding roughly to the psychiatrist's descriptions of the feebleminded. More directly to the point, every human society has a multitude of established attitudes, unquestioned postulates. Cosmically, they may seem parochial prejudices, but many of them represent the community's most cherished values and ideals. (To those devoted to "natural law" philosophy, the basic "preconceptions" in any particular legal system, to the extent that they are valid, represent specific local applications of universal principles. "Natural law" philosophy, however, recognizes not only that those universal principles are few and highly general but that their applications vary with time, place, and circumstance.) Such social preconceptions, the "value judgments" which members of any given society take for granted and use as the unspoken axioms of thinking, find their way into that society's legal system, become what has been termed the "valuation system of the law." The judge in our society owes a duty to act in accordance with those basic predilections inhering in our legal system (although, of course, he has the right, at times, to urge that some of them be modified or abandoned). The standard of dispassionateness obviously does not require the judge to rid himself of the unconscious influence of such social attitudes. (A word of caution is needed here. These social value judgments are often said to be a product of the "spirit of the times." One may doubt, however, whether, in any period, there is a single time spirit or, to use a common phrase, a single "climate of opinion.")

In addition to those acquired social value judgments, every judge, however, unavoidably has many idiosyncratic "learnings of the mind," uniquely personal prejudices, which may interfere with his fairness at a trial. He may be stimulated by unconscious sympathies for, or antipathies to, some of the witnesses, lawyers, or parties in a case before him. As Josiah Royce observed,

"Oddities of feature or of complexion, slight physical variations from the customary, a strange dress, a scar, a too-steady look, a limp, a loud or deep voice, any of these peculiarities * * * may be, to one, an object of fascinated curiosity; to another * * *, an intense irritation, an object of violent antipathy." In *Ex parte* Chase . . . Judge Peters said he had "known a popular judicial officer grow quite angry with a suitor in his court, and threaten him with imprisonment, for no ostensible reason, save the fact, that he wore an overcoat made of wolf skins," and spoke of "prejudice, which may be swayed and controlled by the merest trifles—such as the toothache, the rheumatism, the gout, or a fit of indigestion, or even through the very means by which indigestion is frequently sought to be avoided." "Trifles," he added, "however ridiculous, cease to be trifles when they may interfere with a safe administration of the law." Frankly to recognize the existence of such prejudices is the part of wisdom. The conscientious judge will, as far as possible, make himself aware of his biases of this character, and, by that very self-knowledge, nullify their effect. (One of the subtlest tendencies which a conscientious judge must learn to overcome is that of "leaning over backward" in favor of persons against whom his prejudices incline him.) Much harm is done by the myth that, merely by putting on a black robe and taking the oath of office as a judge, a man ceases to be human and strips himself of all predilections, becomes a passionless thinking machine. The concealment of the human element in the judicial process allows that element to operate in an exaggerated manner; the sunlight of awareness has an antiseptic effect on prejudices. Freely avowing that he is a human being, the judge can and should, through self-scrutiny, prevent the operation of this class of biases. This self-knowledge is needed in a judge because he is peculiarly exposed to emotional influences; the "court room is a place of surging emotions * * *; the parties are keyed up to the contest, often in open defiance; and the topics at issue are often calculated to stir up the sympathy, prejudice, or ridicule of the tribunal" (Wigmore, *Principles of Judicial Proof* . . . .). The judge's decision turns, often, on what he believes to be the facts of the case. As a fact finder, he is himself a witness—a witness of the witnesses; he should, therefore, learn to avoid the errors which, because of prejudice, often affect those witnesses.

But, just because his fact-finding is based on his estimates of the witnesses, of their reliability as reporters of what they saw and heard, it is his duty, while listening to and watching them, to form attitudes toward them. He must do his best to ascertain their motives, their biases, their dominating passions and interests, for only so can he judge of the accuracy of their narrations. He must also shrewdly observe the stratagems of the opposing lawyers, perceive their efforts to sway him by appeals to his predilections. . . . He must cannily penetrate through the surface of their remarks to their real purposes and motives. He has an official obligation to become prejudiced in that sense. Impartiality is not gullibility. Disinterestedness does not mean childlike innocence. If the judge did not form judgments of the actors in those courthouse dramas called trials, he could never render decisions.

His findings of fact may be erroneous, for, being human, he is not infallible; indeed, a judge who purports to be superhuman is likely to be dominated by improper prejudices. When upper-court judges on an appeal decide that the findings of a trial judge are at fault because they—correctly or incorrectly—think those findings insufficiently supported by relevant and competent evidence, that appellate decision does not brand him as partial and unfair. When, his decision reversed because of errors in his findings of fact or conclusions of law, the case comes back to his court for a further hearing, he will not, if he is the kind of person entitled to hold office as a judge, permit his previous decision in the case to control him.

These comments dispose of the issue here. Referee Olney has honorably discharged the duties of his office for many years. Nothing in his official career or in the record of this case justifies the suggestion that he did not and will not conform to the judical standards of fairness as we have defined them. Judge Coxe, one of our ablest and most experienced trial judges, has refused to remove Referee Olney as Master in these proceedings. We see nothing to warrant us in interfering with Judge Coxe's discretion. Indeed, had he ruled otherwise, we would have been strongly inclined to reverse him.

*138 F.2d 650 (1943)*

# KELLER v. BROOKLYN BUS CORP. ॐ

IN APRIL, 1939, Mrs. Leona May Hudson was killed by a bus from which she had just alighted. Her daughter, Mrs. Keller, sued the bus company for damages, claiming negligence. The jury found for the bus company. Mrs. Keller appealed from that judgment, her major claim being that the judge erred when he instructed the jury regarding which side must bear the burden of proof. Judge Thomas Swan, writing the opinion for the majority, ruled to uphold the trial court's verdict. Judge Frank dissents.

FRANK, *Circuit Judge* (dissenting): As I am far less experienced in deciding jury cases on appeal than my very wise colleagues, for whose views I entertain the sincerest respect, I have hesitated to disagree with them in this case. But this seems to me an instance of Homer nodding. I think the majority opinion unwisely overrules former decisions of this court, disregards rulings of other Circuit Courts of Appeals, and has the effect of improperly substituting— contrary to the Seventh Amendment as construed recently by the Supreme Court—a judicial for a jury verdict in a case in which, as my colleagues say, the evidence is conflicting. My reasons for that conclusion are as follows:

The trial judge in his charge gave two conflicting versions of the burden-of-proof rule. The first was wrong, sufficiently so that, if not retracted, the majority opinion concedes it would compel reversal; the second was correct. If it were clear that the jury understood that the judge meant to substitute the second for the first, then the error would be harmless. But I perceive no basis for the belief that the jury understood that he had changed his mind, since he did not so state or imply. See what he did: Immediately after he uttered his earlier mistaken version, he ignored an exception thereto, made by appellant's counsel. Then he went on to give instructions on other matters. After a considerable interval—five folios later in the transcript—he was requested to and did state the correct rule. But he did not then say or imply: "This is in place of what I previously said on this subject, which was mistaken and which you must ignore." How, then, can we say that the jury knew that the second was a retraction?

For reasons noted below, we are obliged to assume that they listened intently to all his remarks. If they accepted him—which again we are obliged to assume—as the infallible source of all legal learning relevant to the case, they must have thought that his legal dissertation was intended to be logical and self-consistent. It would, indeed, have been presumptuous for them to have decided, without advice from the judge to do so, that part of his legal discourse was wrong. And, if they did not, then, if they were conscientious, and worked as juries are supposed to do, they must have been baffled. To illustrate: Suppose that my two brother judges and I read a paper by an eminent physicist on radioactivity. If we found what appeared to us to be inconsistent statements, we would, in all likelihood, reject the suggestion that the savant had at any point been in error; we would reason that the appearance of inconsistency was due to our limited knowledge of a subject as to which we were but amateurs, and we would try, in some way, to reconcile his seemingly discrepant remarks. In similar fashion, the jury here—if, I say, they acted as juries are supposed to act, heeding the legal instructions from an expert and according to him appropriate respect for his superior legal wisdom—must have tried to harmonize the discrepant parts of his charge. On that assumption, they were asked to achieve the impossible.

As an alternative, we might conjecture that the jury thought (a) that the judge was merely, in new verbiage, repeating what he had said before or (b) that they were at liberty to choose either rule. On any of these hypotheses, the defendant was deprived of a fair trial by jury.

Of course, we should not be fly-specking in our examination of what goes on in a trial. Perfection is no more to be sought in courtroom conduct than in any other human activity. I agree that we should never engage in "an overzealous scrutiny of every word that may fall from the judge's mouth" (*United States* v. *Warren* . . .), else there would be few unreversed judgments. . . . The harmless-error doctrine is so eminently sensible that it should freely be used. But its use in connection with jury trials, where, as here, the jury brings in merely a general verdict, often presents a troublesome problem.

Some State courts have been exceedingly liberal in their application of that doctrine even in jury cases. But State courts are not bound by the Seventh Amendment. Doubtless because the federal courts are subject to that Amendment, the Supreme Court has been more strict—despite the enactment in 1919 of the "harmless error statute" . . . in federal jury cases, *especially with respect to erroneous instructions to the jury.* . . . [R]ecently . . . the court said that that Act was intended merely "to prevent matters concerned with the mere etiquette of trials and minutiae of procedure from affecting the merits of a verdict." That case involved an erroneous instruction. There were many earlier similar decisions. In *Fillippon v. Albion Vein Slate Co.*, . . . in a case which arose before that Act went into effect, it was said: "And of course in jury trials erroneous rulings are presumptively injurious, especially those embodied in instructions to the jury; and they furnish ground for reversal unless it affirmatively appears that they were harmless." In *McCandless v. United States*, . . . where the Act was applicable, the court, while so recognizing, nevertheless substantially repeated that statement.

Wigmore deplores such rulings. But our master's voice is that of the Supreme Court, not Wigmore's. For a time, the Eighth Circuit Court of Appeals, in a series of decisions, held that the statute had changed the earlier rule so that, it said, the burden is on the complaining party to show that an error was harmful. Those decisions won the applause of Wigmore. But in 1941, in *Fort Dodge Hotel Co. v. Bartlett*, . . . (a case involving an erroneous instruction) that same court reversed those rulings in obedience to the intervening decisions of the Supreme Court. Our court, too, I think, must fall in line. Heretofore, it has done so. Several times it has recognized that, where there is a general verdict, it is frequently impossible to ascertain, with any sufficient degree of assurance, what errors did or did not harmfully affect the jury's verdict. Cf. *Christian v. Boston & M. R. R.*, . . . , *Schilling v. D. & R. H. Corp.* . . .

That problem is particularly difficult of solution where the judge's charge is confusing and contradictory. . . .

The judge's charge is a markedly important component of the postulate underlying the general-verdict-jury system, which postulate may be briefly described thus: The jury listens with strict attention to what the judge tells them concerning any particular applicable legal rule; they understand thoroughly the meaning of that rule; they accept it as a major premise and, with nice logic, "apply" it to the minor premise (that is, the "facts" as the jury "finds" them after careful deliberation); they thus arrive at their verdict. A serious error in the judge's instructions, likely to confuse the jury, can be regarded as harmless only if one rejects that basic postulate.

There are many who are skeptical about its correspondence with the actualities of jury behavior. Whether or not that skepticism is justified, we, while acting in our judicial capacity, are forbidden, as a matter of "law," to inquire: It is well settled that, generally, it is improper, after the trial is concluded, for a court to learn, even from the jurymen themselves, how any jury went about its business. As a consequence, the manner in which any particular jury discharged its functions is, for us, an unknowable, when that jury was permitted to return a general verdict unaccompanied by special findings of fact. As Sunderland (one of the ablest students of trial procedure) says:

> In a vast majority of cases, the general verdict is a complete mystery, throwing a mantle of impenetrable darkness over the operations of the jury. * * * No one but the jurors can tell what was put into it, and the jurors will not be heard to say. * * * The court protects the jury from all investigation and inquiry. * * * The peculiarity of the general verdict is the merger into a single indivisible residuum of all matters, however numerous, whether of law or fact. It is a compound made by the jury which is incapable of being broken up into its constituent parts. No judicial reagents exist for either a qualitative or quantitative analysis. The law supplies the means for determining neither what facts were found, nor what principles of law were applied, nor how the application was made. There are, therefore, three unknown elements which enter into the general verdict: (a) the facts; (b) the law; (c) the application of the law to the facts. And it is clear that the verdict is liable to three sources of error, corresponding to these three elements. It is also clear that, if error does occur in any of these matters, it cannot be discovered, for the constituents of the compound cannot be ascertained. * * *

Such is the situation here. Had there been a special or fact verdict, or if the general verdict had been coupled with answers to fact interrogatories, we would almost surely know whether the mistaken portion of the judge's charge contributed to the jury's conclusions. As it is, we are unable so to determine. Not that special or fact verdicts (or jury answers to fact interrogatories) can be cure-alls. But they can do much to bring the behavior of juries as fact finders into line with that fortunately increasing tendency to improve fact-finding manifested in the requirement that the orders of administrative agencies, and of judges sitting without juries, must be accompanied by adequate findings of fact. . . .

The adequate determination of the "facts" in law suits is the weak spot in the judicial process. Many thousands of dollars and years of effort have been spent in devising "Restatements" of the legal rules; but, even if they were faultless, they would be of little worth in the administration of justice, if courthouse fact-finding were not substantially bettered. As an important step in that direction, Rule 49 of the new Federal Rules of Civil Procedure was designed to encourage the use of the special verdict or, in the alternative, the general verdict accompanied by the jury's answers to interrogatories as to issues of fact. It is strange to insist on niceties in fact-finding by administrative officials and trial judges, all men trained in the art of sifting evidence, and, at the same time, to fail to do what is possible to require jurors, untrained in that art, to disclose more accurately their reactions to the evidence. But, sitting in an appellate court, we have no power to direct the trial judges to call for fact verdicts. When, however, a trial judge fails to do so, we ought to be singularly careful to see to it that the resultant unexplained lump verdict of the jury does not cover up substantial errors at the trial.

Although some judges (and I am one) may be highly doubtful as to the value of the jury in most noncriminal cases, especially when the verdicts are general, and although it is entirely appropriate that we should inform the public and Congress of our doubts, we must, until Congress more drastically alters the jury system, accept the general verdict as one of the facts of life. We have no right, because of our doubts, to disregard, either consciously or unconsciously, what I have called its basic postulate. That postulate must govern us, no matter how lacking in reality we may think it. While performing our judicial duties, we must often enforce rules we deem unwise. And so, when on the bench, our private views concerning the wisdom of the general verdict and its necessary implications are as irrelevant as our attitudes toward bimetalism or the transmigration of souls. (Indeed, if we were to reject the basic postulate, then the elaborate ritual of the judge's charge would become, confessedly, a ridiculous ceremonial, and many of the hours spent by us and other upper courts on appeals in jury cases, would, concededly, be wasted.) Cf. Holmes, J., in *Aikens* v. *Wisconsin* ... : "It was urged farther that to make a right depend upon motives is to make it depend upon the whim of a jury and to deny the right. But it *must be assumed that the constitutional tribunal does its duty.* * * *"

If, as I believe we are required to do, we adhere to the basic postulate of the general verdict system, then, where there is a conflict in the evidence, this, I think, follows: (1) Substantial errors in the judge's instructions as to the legal rules must be assumed to have resulted in an erroneous verdict unless those errors were so adequately corrected by the judge that we can say that, without doubt, the jury knew that they were to be ignored. (2) If the instructions are confusing and contradictory on a material issue, the jury must be assumed to have been confused and unable to reach a proper verdict. The application of some such rules of thumb to the instant case induces my dissent.

For I see no basis for the belief that, in some unexplained way, the jury penetrated the judge's mind and thus learned that, in the last sentence of his charge, he meant to withdraw his former faulty advice. Not that there is no place for repentance; there is room for a more or less unequivocal correction by the judge of a previous mistake, of course; but here the fact of any intention to correct was, to say the least, highly equivocal.

My colleagues, to be sure, stress the fact that the proper statement of the "law" came at the very end of the judge's charge. But what justification is there for believing that the last words in a speech are invariably the ones most heeded by an audience? I take it that that is not an irrebuttable presumption, a "rule of law," that is, a generalization about facts—founded on observation and experience—no longer open to debate. Nor is it, I believe, an established cannon of psychology (an art which, as yet, is far from becoming a science and is possessed of very few generally accepted canons).

I find it impossible, therefore, to decide that the jury were correctly guided. To say that the jurymen were not misled is to indulge in unverified and unverifiable guessing. I fail to perceive any foundation for my colleague's statement that they "entertain no doubt" that the second correct instruction "removed any misconception which may have been engendered in the jury's mind by the preceding" erroneous instruction. Who are we that we should so confidently probe the mental interiors of the jurors? A sagacious English judge, almost five centuries ago, observed that the devil himself knoweth not the mind of man. Unable, as we are, to interrogate the jurors, any effort on our part to determine, merely from their general verdict, which of the two conflicting instructions influenced them, is an undertaking which would be regarded as hopeless by all psychologists—except perhaps those devoted to that crude type of "behaviorism" which might be called "veterinary psychology" in the light of the following story told by Wigmore: "It is said that Prince von Bismark was once ruffled by the number of questions put to him by his medical attendant, an eminent physician of no less individuality and self-possession than the Chancellor. The latter intimated that the physician could do his duty without putting so many intrusive questions. 'Very well, Highness,' said the other, 'but, if you wish to be cured, without questions asked, you had better send for a veterinary surgeon.'"

The best that can be said is that the chances that the jury were not misled are as good as the chances that they were. In such circumstances, it does not seem to me that we should conclude that the error was without substantial harm to plaintiff and that she received a fair trial. The majority opinion says, "Whether a subsequent correct charge is sufficient to cure a prior inadvertent error is necessarily a matter to be determined in the sound judgment of the appellate court." I agree, where it is clear that the second charge could have left "no doubt in the minds of the jury as to what the court ultimately declares the law to be." But this is not at all such a case. To say here that the jury's mind was cleared of all doubt is to indulge in pure conjecture. And such conjecturing is not a matter for the appellate court.

There are possible two extreme and opposing positions concerning such a case as this: (1) Nothing in the judge's charge makes any difference to the jury; therefore even the grossest errors or the most pronounced inconsistencies in the charge are harmless. (2) Everything in the charge must be assumed to be of importance; therefore, even the slightest error is prejudicial. Common sense suggests a middle category: If the evidence is such that all doubts as to the "facts" of the case are negligible and it is fairly apparent that no other verdict than that which was rendered could have been reached by a jury in its senses, then the verdict should not be disturbed except for the grossest inconsistencies in the charge. But that is not this case, for here the evidence was in conflict.

Indeed, my colleagues say, "There were matters for the jury." Of course there were, since the witnesses flatly disagreed with one another as to the pivotal facts in the case. Accordingly, had the jury brought in a verdict for the plaintiff, I cannot believe that my colleagues would have reversed the judgment on the ground that such a verdict was against the weight of the evidence. I fail, therefore, to understand what they mean when they say "it is difficult to see how" the jury "could properly have reached any other verdict" than that rendered for the defendant. If there had been no prejudicial error, of course that verdict would have to stand. But where, because of misleading instructions, there has been substantial error in a jury trial, it is not, I think, for upper-court judges to say that that error should be overlooked because, reading the record, they think that the testimony of one witness is more credible than that of another, especially when the witnesses testified not by deposition but wholly in open court. The Supreme Court decisions, cited above, show that, in jury cases, federal courts must not thus apply the harmless-error doctrine.

Consequently, if we affirm here, we will be substituting our findings for a jury's. This appears from the following analysis: The verdict occurred after the jury had heard a confusing charge. *As no jury has considered the evidence in the light of a proper charge, our determination that the verdict rendered should stand will mean, in practical effect, that we are deciding, in a case where the evidence is in conflict, what verdict should be rendered by a properly instructed jury. And that means, in effect, that the court is bringing in a verdict. But, where, as here, there is conflicting evidence, the Seventh Amendment forbids judicial verdicts in jury cases.* . . .

The previous decisions of this court as to the prejudicial effect of confusing instructions are, I think, in accord with my conclusion. There are, in other federal courts and in state courts, dozens of similar decisions, but it would be tedious to cite them. The majority opinion cites two cases said to be contra: (a) The opinion of Judge Aldrich, in 1911, in *Taxi Service Co.* v. *Phillips* . . . , which is distinguishable on its facts; if not, it gives no persuasive reasons for its contrary conclusion. (b) *People* v. *Goldstein* . . . lays down no legal rule but turns on its peculiar facts and does not purport to overrule earlier New York cases . . . which state the rule I think applicable here. Moreover, as I read *Berry* v. *United States*, . . . and related cases, we are not required, on the issue in the instant case, to follow New York decisions pursuant to *Erie* v. *Tompkins* . . . since we, unlike the State courts, are controlled by the Seventh Amendment.

*128 F.2d 510 (1942)*

# UNITED STATES v. FARINA ॐ

THREE DEFENDANTS, Joseph Farina, Peter DiPalermo, and Daniel Sperdutto, in 1949 appealed from a conviction for a conspiracy to sell counterfeit money. Judge Augustus Hand, writing the majority opinion, considered that the only grounds for reversal worthy of serious consideration were the contentions of the defendants that the trial judge erred in his charge to the jury with regard to statements about "the presumption of innocence" and his definition of "reasonable doubt." After quoting at length from the judge's charge, Judge Hand said, "No objection was taken to any part of the charge, and we are satisfied that nothing said in the course of it calls for reversal." Judge Frank dissents.

FRANK, *Circuit Judge* (dissenting): What influences juries, courts seldom know. Indeed, most courts (including the federal courts) not only do not diligently seek such knowledge but have a general policy of deliberate unwillingness to learn—and usually seal up the only possible sources from which they could learn—what occurred in the jury room. As we recently said, per Judge Learned Hand, this policy stems from awareness that, were the truth disclosed, probably not more than 1 percent of verdicts could stand.

This self-imposed judicial ignorance—preventing the courts from knowing how a particular jury behaved and from attaining moderately well-educated guesses as to how juries in general probably conduct themselves—has had some strange corollaries: (1) In spite of—or perhaps because of—this ignorance, upper courts make this remarkable assumption: A very substantial mistake by the trial judge in the wording of a highly intricate substantive rule is assumed to have affected the jury and therefore (necessarily and logically) to have led to a wrong verdict—even when the difference between the correct and the mistaken wording of the rule is one that only a lawyer, after careful study, can detect, so that very probably the mistake could not actually have had any effect on the jury. (As Judge Rossman observed, lawyers engaged in a jury trial frequently say they are not sure of the meaning of a substantive-rule instruction, until it has been written up, after the jury has been discharged. . . .) In such a case, thanks to the unverified and usually unreal assumption, the upper court notes the error—although it was not called to the trial judge's notice—and orders a new trial. (2) Yet, para-doxically, many an upper court will refuse to reverse for a mistake in the charge, unrelated to any intricate substantive rule largely unintelligible to the jury, but dealing with matters far more comprehensible by the jury and therefore far more likely to have influenced their verdict. Such errors, the very kind most to be suspected of working harm, are, I think, too often dis-missed as harmless.

My colleagues' opinion in this case illustrates, I think, the second point. For the faulty "presumption of innocence" instruction—that the presumption was "designed for the protection of the innocent" and was "not intended as a bulwark behind which the guilty might hide"—may easily have misled the jury, to the grave prejudice of the accused. We do not know whether or not it did. But we do know that that "presumption" is much discussed popularly, out of court. Consequently, there prevails a belief, probably well founded, that jurors listen attentively to, and take with peculiar seriousness, the par-ticular part of the judge's instructions defining that "presumption." On that account, I think the Fifth Circuit, in Gomila v. United States . . . wisely held such an instruction reversible error, although, there, as here, the defendant had not objected when the charge was delivered.

My colleagues, however, differentiate the charge in the Gomila case because it contained a "cumulation of errors." (The "presumption of inno-cence" error, however, was the first error discussed in the Gomila opinion.) But so, too, here. (Were it necessary, I would hold that the "presumption of innocence" error alone warranted reversal.) The trial judge, far from curing his "presumption of innocence" error by his comments on "reasonable doubt," aggravated that error when he told the jury that such a doubt is one which a juror "can give a reason for entertaining." This again was matter to which the jurors probably paid close attention, since the important "reason-able doubt" principle is also often popularly discussed out of court. The judge's definition of that principle, therefore, most probably impressed the jury.

Now, this very sort of instruction was severely criticized, and made the basis of reversals, by Judge Walter H. Sanborn of the Eighth Circuit. He, one of our greatest judges, was no soft "sentimentalist," eager to absolve criminals, but he was sensitive to the possible tragic impact on men's civil liberties of verdicts due to carelessly phrased statements by trial judges to juries. As he pointed out, the instruction he condemned means that the jurors must not consider any doubt about guilt unless they can articulate, at least to themselves a sound "reason" for doing so.

Our own judicial experience teaches that sometimes even trial judges have difficulty in rationally explaining the grounds of their decisions. Some trial judges resent any obligation in jury-less cases, where the oral testimony is conflicting, to go beyond publishing laconic, unexplained, judgments, even to the extent of filing special findings of fact. Some of those judges complain that the formulation of fact-findings is too arduous and, more, bound to be artificial. I share the view that, on net balance, that complaint is unjustified. There would be more justification for complaint if a trial judge were required to reveal, or even to disclose, that he himself knew, the "reasons" for his special findings. But there is no such requirement.

Surely, then, we ought not ask a juror, who has nothing like a trial judge's experience and training, not merely to find facts but also to be able to recognize, and to make explicit to himself and the other jurors, the "reason" for joining in a finding of fact or for any intermediate step in his mental processes. Mr. Justice Holmes, speaking for the Supreme Court, said the reasoning of an administrative body need not be thus articulate, since its decision expresses "an intuition of experience which outruns analysis and sums up many unnamed and tangled impressions * * * which may lie beneath consciousness without losing their worth." We should not exact more of a jury. Accordingly, the jurors were badly misinstructed when told they must ignore any doubt which they could "give no reason for entertaining."

My colleagues assume, in effect, that the jurors construed that instruction as would an intelligent law student or lawyer, well versed in the traditional meaning of "reasonable doubt." I cannot go along with that assumption. Far more probably, the jurors thought the judge meant just what he said. One can, then, well imagine that one of the jurors, when in the jury room, impressively remarked to his fellow jurors: "Remember that the judge especially warned us we must discard any doubt about guilt unless we can 'give a reason' for holding it." So it seems to me not at all improbable that the jurors, acting under this erroneous instruction, and incapable of formulating a rational explanation of a doubt they entertained, concluded that they had the duty to discard a doubt which, had they been properly instructed, would legitimately have yielded an acquittal. The defendants ought not bear the risk that the verdict derived from such an error. . . .

184 F.2d 18 (1950)

# UNITED STATES v. FORNESS ౭ఄ

IN 1941 THE United States appealed from a judgment of the district court which had dismissed their suit brought on behalf of the Seneca Nation of Indians to enforce the Nation's cancellation of a lease upon lands in the City of Salamanca, New York. Judge Frank writes the opinion for the court.

FRANK, C.J.: This appeal presents the issue of whether the Seneca Nation of Indians, as lessor to the appellees of lands located within the City of Salamanca, New York, may cancel the ninety-nine year lease because of default in the payment of rent. Although there is directly before us only one lease, on which the annual rent is but $4.00, the question is of greater importance because the Nation, by resolution, has canceled hundreds of similar leases. The Salamanca Trust Company, which holds a $15,000 mortgage on the property here involved, and three other financial institutions intervened as parties defendant because of their interest as mortgagees of similar plots. The City of Salamanca, which has acquired by tax sales a number of properties under lease from the Seneca Nation, has also intervened. These lands are part of the Allegany Reservation, which, with several others, was set aside by the United States, pursuant to treaties, for the Seneca Nation. . . . During the railroad-building era beginning about 1850, railroad companies and settlers leased reservation lands from the Senecas, and these leases were purportedly ratified by the State of New York. When this ratification was invalidated by the New York Supreme Court, Congress passed the Act of February 19, 1875, 18 Stat. 330, which ratified existing leases and authorized their renewal for terms of twelve years. This was enlarged to ninety-nine years by the Act of September 30, 1890, 26 Stat. 558.

Pursuant to this authority, the lease here involved was made on February

[ 423 ]

19, 1892 (as a renewal of an earlier lease) for ninety-nine years to Hector G. Forbes, who, in 1919, assigned it to Frank A. Forness and his wife, appellees here. The lease provided for the payment of $4.00 rent annually in advance, on or before the nineteenth day of February, and stipulated that, if the rent was not paid as provided, the Nation "may re-enter the premises, or resort to any lawful remedy, to remove all persons therefrom." The appellees have erected upon the plot a building costing $63,000.00 and in 1934 the property was mortgaged to the Salamanca Trust Company for $15,000.00. Appellees last paid rent on April 11, 1930, and since then they have been in default. Between January 1, 1939 and February 19, 1931, they received the usual notice, showing rent due in the amount of $36.00 (that is, overdue rent for eight previous years and rent for the ensuing year) plus interest of $8.64 on the overdue rent. On March 4, 1939, the Council of the Seneca Nation passed a resolution canceling all leases then in arrears. On learning of this resolution, Forness promptly tendered by check to the Indian agent the amount of $44.64, his obligation as indicated in the notice. The check was deposited by the agent, with others, in a special account. No payment has been made by the agent to the Senecas.

Cancellation of these leases, although obviously unexpected by Forness or his neighbors, was not prompted by caprice. There is overwhelming evidence that lessees of these lands were customarily lax about paying their rent. In 1911, for example, 1,095 leases were in default; in 1915, 494; in 1931, 529. An attempt was made in 1911 by the Senecas to retain an attorney to collect the arrears, but the Department of Interior ruled that the 1901 Act, which allocated the disposition of the rentals, prevented use of the funds for this purpose. In 1915, the Nation adopted a resolution canceling defaulted leases; the cancellation, however, was not enforced. The present action by the Nation, then, represents the culmination of a long struggle by the Indians to enforce their economic rights. In spite of this undenied provocation, they coupled with their cancellation of the leases an offer to re-rent the affected plots on generous terms (at an annual rental of 2½ percent of the appraised value of the property, less the value of the improvement). Thus computed, the annual rent on appellees' plot will be $115. Any such lease was to be subjected to all encumbrances which had attached to the canceled lease.

Appellees argue first that this suit, brought by the United States on behalf of the Seneca Nation to enforce the cancellation, is in effect an action of ejectment, and that the action is barred by Sections 997–999 of the New York Civil Practice Act, which provide that upon a tender of the arrears before judgment, the court shall dismiss the complaint. But state law cannot be invoked to limit the rights in lands granted by the United States to the Indians, because, as the court below recognized, state law does not apply to the Indians except so far as the United States has given its consent. . . . But, it is argued, such consent to the application of state law was granted by Congress, by the Act of February 19, 1875, which authorized this lease and permitted the laying out of villages on the Cattaraugus and Allegany reservations of the Seneca Nation. Section 8 of that Act provided:

That all laws of the State of New York now in force concerning the laying out, altering, discontinuing and repairing highways and bridges shall be in force within said villages, and may, with the consent of said Seneca Nation in council, extend to, and be in force beyond, said villages in said reservations, or in either of them; and all municipal laws and regulations of said State may extend over and be in force within said villages; *Provided, nevertheless,* that nothing in this section shall be construed to authorize the taxation of any Indian, or the property of any Indian not a citizen of the United States.

Appellees assert, and correctly, that the words "municipal laws" often are used to refer to the laws of a country dealing with intramural matters as distinguished from "international laws" dealing with its extramural affairs. Appellees then go on to insist that the symbol "municipal laws" has only that single referent, regardless of context. Such an argument involves the "one-word-one-meaning" fallacy. Similar reasoning would compel the conclusion that a clotheshorse is an animal of the equine species, and make it impossible to speak of drinking a toast. When, as in the statute, the "laws" of a state of the Union are under discussion, there can be no intelligent reference to its international or extramural laws, for it has none under our federal Constitution. Appellees' construction would, in effect, read the word "municipal" out of the statute. "Municipal laws" of such a state can have but one referent, that is, the laws of its municipalities. The meaning is the same as when we speak of the "Municipal Building" of the City of New York. When confronted, as we are here, with a word having two meanings, we should, of course, not select that meaning which gives it the least possible sense in the context in which it is used. In addition to the objection just indicated to appellees' construction, we can find no reason for the specific mention in the statute of state highway and bridge laws if, as appellees contend, all state laws were comprehended in the generic term "municipal laws." We conclude, then, that the statute did not make the "laws"—statutory or decisional—of the State of New York applicable to the reservation. The provisions of the New York Civil Practice Act, therefore, do not bar the result asked by the Indians. And *Erie R. Co. v. Tompkins* . . . is inapplicable.

Appellees argue that if the tender does not prevent cancellation by virtue of the provisions of the Civil Practice Act, it nevertheless has resulted in a waiver of any right to a cancellation of the lease by the Indian agent, as agent of the Seneca Nation, since he accepted appellees' check for the amount of rent due, deposited it to the credit of the Treasurer of the United States, and failed to return the proceeds to them. They point to the Act of February 28, 1901, which provides that all rents due on leases of lands within this reservation "shall be paid to and be recoverable to the United States Indian Agent for the New York Indian Agency for and in the name of the said Seneca Nation," as proof of his authority thus to bind the Senecas, and they urge that this agency has been recognized and ratified by subsequent conduct. We need not pass on the doubtful proposition that the agent was the agent of the Senecas, for it is clear that his authority, at most, was only that of a collecting and disbursing agent. As such he had no implied power to make or break leases, nor to waive the Seneca's power to do so. For the same reason the evidence that the Senecas had ratified his actions is irrelevant; at best, it might show that he was accepted as a collection agent, but it falls far short of indicating that the Senecas have ever accepted him as a proper person to waive their right of cancellation. The findings that they have regarded him as having broader powers were plainly unsupported by any evidence; the most that was shown was a custom to accept overdue payments, and no Seneca Indian was called to show that the Nation knew or ratified even this. Even if the agent had authority to make—or if the Nation ratified—a waiver, his action was insufficient to constitute one. He caused the money to be deposited in a special account; none of it has been paid to the Nation, and it is, in effect, being held in escrow.

Another ground urged by appellees in support of their theory that there has been a waiver of the right to cancel the lease, needs only brief mention. It is that the notice sent to appellees by the agent said that rent, though due on February 19, might be paid on or before April 20. In the case before us the appellees paid the overdue rent to the agent before April 20. We will assume arguendo that the terms of this notice were sufficiently acquiesced in by the Seneca Nation to prevent cancellation unless default in any particular installment continued beyond April 20. But whatever its effect as to rent due for the current year, the notice did not purport to extend the time for payment of rents due for previous years. Here appellees were in default for nine years; they are in no position to rely, as to the rent not paid in any of the previous eight years, on the two-month-grace period with reference to the currently due installment.

It is urged that the lease cannot be canceled because no proper "demand" was made for the rent. Appellees refer to the ancient common law requisite of a demand, as reported by Coke, viz., that the landlord must ask for "the precise sum due, at a convenient time before sunset upon the day when the rent is due, upon the land, at the most notorious place of it, though there be no person on the land to pay" . . . citing and relying on *Coke on Littleton*

(Coke's First Institute) . . . ; cf. 2 Tiffany, *Landlord and Tenant* . . . ; Taylor, *Landlord and Tenant*. . . . The details must be strictly observed by the landlord; thus, we are told, "he cannot demand it at the back door of the house but at the fore door." Coke, *ibid*. The requirement was based on the feudal idea that "the land is the debtor" and that "the rent issueth out of the land" (Coke, *ibid*; 2 Pollock and Maitland, *History of English Law* . . . ; 7 Holdsworth, *History of English Law* . . . , a notion of dubious applicability to a modern office building. The idea that the purpose of requiring a demand is to render forfeiture more difficult was not articulated until recent times. It would be a rash man who would say that no notions of avoidance of forfeiture were involved even in the feudal doctrine; for, at any period, among lawyers as well as among others, there are fashions in the expressions of ideas, and an idea which does not comport with the linguistic fashion may remain unexpressed although actually operative. It is possible, for example, that Coke's insistence on the common law requirement of a demand was a competitive device to attract lessee litigants from the equity courts, which were relieving against forfeiture. But whether or not Littleton and Coke were thinking at all of relief from forfeiture in connection with the strict demand doctrine, they did not phrase the doctrine in those terms. The transvaluation of that doctrine to make it patently a part of the doctrine of avoidance of forfeiture is a more modern development; today it has, in effect, become merged in the equitable attitude of unfriendliness, generally, to forfeitures, an attitude which we shall discuss presently in its application to the facts of the instant case.

At any rate, the lack of such a demand on the due date was not alleged, nor did the defendants tender this issue at the trial. More important, to require such a demand here would be to insist upon an empty gesture, since the defendants knew that the rent was due.

The rigid doctrine as to demand on the due date is a product of the medieval era. It has been called a period of "strict law," the salient characteristics of which are formalism, inflexibility, and indifference to the moral aspects of conduct. Ceremonialism is of its essence: "Estates in land begin in ceremony and end in ceremony," said Coke. Scholars have assigned many reasons for this excessive formalism. Chief among them, it is said, is the distrust of judicial discretion. "Form," wrote Jhering, "is the sworn enemy of caprice, the twin sister of liberty * * *. Fixed forms are the school of discipline and order, and thereby of liberty itself. They are a bulwark against external attack, since they will only break, not bend, and where a people has truly understood the service of freedom, it has also instinctively discovered the value of form and has felt instinctively that, in its forms, it did not possess and hold to something purely external, but to the palladium of liberty." It has been said:

In an epoch of inferior civilization, a rigidly enforced adherence to form serves a two-fold purpose. On the one hand, it is an effectual means of curbing the passions of the litigants, of preventing tumultuous conduct and un- necessary harangues, as well as of compelling the parties to look at the facts calmly and make their statements with care. On the other hand, it acts as a check upon the premature tendency to exercise what seems natural justice * * *. A detailed consideration of the facts of the particular case, furthermore, is only compatible with the idea that that determination of the judge, because he is trained and unprejudiced, possesses a higher value than the untrained and preju- diced determination of the party, and that, therefore, in matters affecting his own interest, the party must bow to the decision of the judge. This idea was opposed, and could not but be opposed, to the then-prevailing self-consciousness of the individual. For, so far as experience, judicial capacity and training were concerned, the persons who were called upon to render judgment offered no better guaranty than the persons whose legal affairs were the subject of adjudication.

Writing of the strict procedure of medieval English law, Pollock and Mait- land tell us that one of its best qualities

was that in theory it left little or nothing, at least within the sphere of procedure, to the discretion of the justices. They themselves desired that this should be so and took care that it was or seemed to be so. They would be responsible for nothing beyond an application of iron rules * * *. For good or ill they made their choice. The ill is but too easily seen by anyone who glances at the *disorderly mass of crabbed pedantry that Coke poured forth as "institutes" of English law;* the good may escape us * * *. As time goes on, there is always a larger room for discre- tion in the law of procedure; but discretionary powers can only safely be entrusted to judges whose impartiality is above suspicion and whose every act is exposed to public and professional criticism.

Bowman describes the attitude behind this early formalism thus: "From the despotism of rulers men sought refuge in the despotism of rules. Under the influence of this idea, the rules of law became wholly inelastic and inflexi- ble." In such an era, says Maine, "substantive law has * * * the look of being gradually secreted in the interstices of procedure; and the early lawyer can only see law through the envelope of its technical forms." In much of the medieval period in England, says Holdsworth, "a strict and literal accuracy was required in the pleadings. A mistake in a name, or syllable, or letter was fatal." The same kind of coercion of form, or "form-rigorism," is found in medieval German procedure, where there was required an "observance, pain- ful to the utmost, of a multitude of unimportant externalities * * *. This phenomenon * * * has drawn from Siegel * * * the observation that 'it seems as if the formalities in question had been expressly contrived for the purpose of bringing the litigant to grief, so subtle and insidious was their design, so difficult their execution.' " Winfield remarks that "formalism in procedure is not a disease of early law, but is the life blood of it."

So far at any rate as English medieval law is concerned, this picture of a period of "strict law" has perhaps been overdrawn. Too much should not be made of such historical periodizations. Too often that kind of history-writing, as Aldous Huxley somewhere suggests, results from the ignorance or prejudices of historians. The case for the excessive "strictness" of medieval English law is made out by concentrating attention almost entirely on the activities of the centralized common law courts and, too, in a limited span of years. Thanks to the researches of Bolland, Barbour and others, we know that up to the fourteenth century, and to some extent thereafter, even into the fifteenth, a kind of equity was administered in those common law courts; when this common law equity decayed, when the equitable principles thereto-fore recognized at common law evaporated, when common law ossified into a rigid technical system, then equity came to be administered by the Chancery and other non-common law courts.

Nevertheless, if we regard primarily the common law courts, the period when there arose the rigid rule of demand for rent on the due date may, with some justification, be called a period of "strict law." Such rules "devised for purposes now forgotten, survive their occasion in the shape of formal re-quirements * * *. The rules which make up the traditional element of a legal system often grow up with reference to quite different ends from those we now seek and before the ends we now seek had been recognized * * *. Today, when interest and rights are defined and remedies exist only for securing them within defined limits, there are better means of controlling judicial action than hard and fast formal procedure."

The strict doctrine for which appellees contend derives from the status of landlord and tenant. But here another status or relation is also involved —that of the Indians with reference to our other citizens. And that other status, which has a special significance founded in current facts, should operate to abate and modify the rigidities of the landlord tenant status inso-far as they have a basis solely in past history and not in present realities. There was some need, in the medieval period, to protect with marked zealousness, the economic position of the tenant from harsh and oppressive treatment at the hands of the landlord. There is little need to afford such protection to the tenants of the Indian landlord in the instant case. The reason for the rule being non-existent here, the rule itself should here be ignored. We may re-call Holmes's comment: "It is revolting to have no better reason for a rule of law than that so it was laid down in the time of Henry IV. It is still more revolting if the grounds upon which it was laid down have vanished long since, and the rule simply persists from blind imitation of the past." Today there is no slavish adherence to such views as those expressed by Thirning some five centuries ago: "*Hornby*—This defendant will be undone and impoverished forever if this action is maintained against him for then twenty suits will be brought against him on the same ground. *Thirning*—What is that to us? *It is better that he be ruined than that the law be changed for him* * * *." . . . We should, rather, act in the spirit of Marshall, C. J., who described Lord Mansfield as "one of the greatest judges who ever sat on any bench," because he did "more than any other, *to remove those technical impediments* which grew out of a different state of society and too long continued to obstruct the course of substantial justice * * *." *Livingston* v. *Jefferson*. . . .

Fortunately, we are not trammelled by the ancient doctrine. No legal rules of any particular State are here controlling. Accordingly we are in the same position as federal courts often were during the ninety-six years before *Erie R. Co.* v. *Tompkins* . . . came to bury *Swift* v. *Tyson*, . . . that of making an independent judgment as to the appropriate legal rules. We must look to the "common law" for a determination of this case. But as Holmes has forcefully pointed out, there is no "transcendental body" of common law uniform and unchanging for all jurisdictions having an Anglo-American legal system, nor are courts prohibited "from refusing to follow the English decisions upon a matter where the local conditions are different." It should be noted, also, that where the federal courts are applying "federal law"—as, for instance, in the application of federal statutes—the Supreme Court has held that they are not, "in the face of changed conditions * * * still chained to the ancient formulae * * *." It follows that we are here at liberty to apply legal rules as to landlord and tenant which comport with the Congressional intent concerning the Senecas.

We cannot believe that Congress intended that, in our times, the rights of American Indians as landlords should be determined by the early seventeenth century views of Coke—an antique dealer in obsolescent medieval ideas— commenting enthusiastically on the fifteenth century writings of Littleton, a medieval lawyer. Indeed if we were to emulate Coke, we would not take too seriously any precedent which we found undesirable. For although Coke relished antiquities, he was "no case lawyer, if by that we mean one who regarded a past decision as quite conclusive. On the contrary, he was more than ready to argue that a case decided in past time was wrong, and he very definitely believed in selecting from the number of past decisions those with which he agreed." (In truth, eminent legal historians have said that Coke had no hesitation in unscrupulously distorting or even fabricating precedents to suit his purposes.)

Moreover, in deviating from Coke, we are not without precedent. As early as 1730, Parliament, recognizing that the requirement of demand for rent on the due date was unduly ritualistic, abolished it when the lessee is in default for more than six months. Statute of 4 Geo. II, c. 28. A number of states have enacted similar or more liberal statutes. Much might be said for the position—accepted in one State—that the English statute, adopted prior to Independence is part of the "common law." . . . We do not say that there is a federal "common law" which includes the 1731 English statute as such. It is enough that, in construing the federal statute relating to the Senecas, Coke's learning on the requirement of a demand need not be regarded as the last word, since it has been recognized in England and America as long outmoded. The unprotected position of the Indians clearly suggests that the Congressional purpose was that Indians' leases should be governed by a rule of "property law" at least as favorable to them as that which is followed in our more progressive states, particularly when that issue involved is a requirement which, in the case at bar, would have been without any useful function.

There is this further fact: According to Coke, demand must ordinarily be made on the land, "because the land is the debtor, and that is the place of demand appointed by law," but the rule was otherwise if some other place was designated at which the rent was to be paid. *Coke on Littleton*, . . . *Van Rennselaer v. Jewett*. . . . We think it a fair inference from the terms of the Act of February 28, 1901, 31 Stat. 819, that the rent was payable at the office of the Indian agent. Appellees do not contend that he was not there to receive it, and we assume that they do not intend to urge that the Indian agent should have stood on the steps of his office and mouthed an oral demand to the bystanders, as was done in *Van Rennselaer v. Jewett*. . . .

We turn, then, to the argument based upon the tender made by appellees, which they assert will stimulate a court of equity to overturn the cancellation of the lease. It is well established that, as a general rule, equity will relieve against a forfeiture cause by nonpayment of rent on the due date. . . . But it is equally well established that that rule, being equitable, is not inflexible, and that such relief will be granted only to an innocent suitor, that is, one with clean hands. This requirement bars relief to one who has been negligent —or at least grossly so—or who has inexcusably or deliberately gone into default. . . . We think the defendants fall in the category of persons whose own conduct makes relief inequitable. . . . There is not here a mere technical delay caused by an oversight; defendants, on the other hand, cavalierly ignored their modest obligation for eight years. Rents were allowed to fall into arrears, not only on this property, but on four others owned by one of the appellees. Perhaps because they knew the amounts were so small that suit would not be brought by the Indians, perhaps out of sheer defiance of a historically maltreated people, perhaps out of complacency born of past experience that the Indians were patient—the defendants chose of their own accord to let many years slip by without payment.

Circumstances like these cannot be excused by the lame apology that others were doing likewise, and that the Senecas were known to be long-suffering. Even if such an excuse were not tantamount to an astonishing claim of a vested right in wrongdoing, preventing any correction of an evil condition, it would still fall far short of proving laches on the part of the Indians. It would be both impractical and unfair to require the Indians to bring suit each year for the paltry sum owed on this plot, a suit costing more than the amount which it would yield, and it would be equally impractical and unfair to hold that they must expend part of the rent for badgering defendants and their neighbors into prompt payment. To hold that the Senecas cannot cancel this lease because they have treated defendants and others generously in the past would, in these circumstances, be a miscarriage of justice. We do not say that complacency by a landlord may never amount to a waiver of the right to strict enforcement of his lease, but under the circumstances disclosed here, where there has been shown a flagrant abuse of a landlord, helpless because of the small amounts involved, if not for other reasons as well, the conduct does not amount to a waiver. The very difficulty of enforcing the payment of rent due on this and similar leases creates some possible doubt as to the application of the doctrine against forfeiture, upon which appellees build their case. The common sense behind the granting of relief is that the primary object of the parties is the payment of rent, for which the right to reentry is only security; on this reasoning, landlords are denied the use of their power of reentry where the rent payment, to which that power is only incidental, is made. We may question, though we need not decide, whether the doctrine should be applied when experience indicates that lessees are so recalcitrant that only a vigorous enforcement by the landlord of all its rights will be effective.

When a defendant asserts an equitable defense he is, negatively, seeking equitable relief. Then—at least to some although perhaps to a lesser extent —factors are pertinent which would be apposite if he were a plaintiff asking the affirmative aid of equity. If the defendants here were, as plaintiffs, asking specific performance of a contract to execute the lease now before us, it is doubtful whether they would succeed. The consideration—$4.00 a year —comes close to being unconscionably small. True, an unconscionably small consideration may not always be alone sufficient to bar a negative or even an affirmative equitable remedy. But here the consideration consists of annual future installments of rent so small in amount that, as we have noted, the expense of suits for their recovery makes their collection impractical; the consequence is that, for practical purposes, the lease is the equivalent of one which explicitly denies the landlord any right to sue for the rent, leaving him the cancellation of the lease as his sole remedy for nonpayment. That the tenant, under such a lease, can unfairly take advantage of the landlord is amply demonstrated in this case. A lease of that kind may shock even a calloused conscience. It would seem that the defendants' assignor, as tenants, in making such a lease with the Indians, as landlord, for a term of 99 years, drove a hard bargain. In those circumstances, the conscience of the chancellor, which must be stimulated if the tenants are to receive even negative equitable relief, will not be easily aroused on their behalf. And it should not be stimulated in this case, all the facts considered.

There is another reason why such relief is not proper here. Defendants, at least, are entitled only to relief against a "forfeiture." The Indians, as we have said, offer to enter into a new lease upon most equitable terms, and, on oral argument, the United States, on their behalf, expressed complete willingness to have those terms embodied in our decree. No doubt the loss of an advantageous bargain can be a forfeiture, and if the defendants here have to pay $115 annually instead of $4, they will suffer a financial loss which will be diminished neither in amount nor in intensity by our refusal to call it a "forfeiture." But equity will not relieve against any and all losses; we must first find some shocking or clearly unfair feature. Suppose, in the case at bar, the parties by agreement had provided that on a default in the payment of the $4 rent, the landlord could not retake possession, but would be privileged to charge thereafter rent computed as the appellants here have offered to compute it. Would we have them relieved against the provision for increased rent on the ground that it worked a forfeiture? We think not, and we think that this answer is decisive of the argument made by appellees. . . .

Our refusal to exercise our equity powers in these circumstances is reinforced by an unhappy realization that the dealings of certain of our citizens with the Indians have often been far from praiseworthy. The federal courts usually, unless precluded by complete want of power, have done what they could to prevent unfairness to Indians. . . .

Under seriously adverse conditions, guardianship of the American Indians by the federal government has been necessary; they have accordingly been considered the nation's "wards." Of recent years (extending over three presidencies) a program has been developed by the federal government to restore the Indians as soon as possible to a position of self-reliance. See F. S. Cohen, *Handbook of Federal Indian Law* (1941) v, 83ff. That they are inherently able, in proper circumstances, to attain such a position is apparent from the character of the Indian civilization on this continent prior to the advent of the white man and from the nature of the civilization of those

Latin-American countries—now cooperating with us in a war against fascism —where a large part of the population is Indian. But certainly in 1892, when the lease in suit was made, the Seneca Indians were still subject to exploitation.

It is of interest that, after the decision in Worcester v. Georgia was rendered, Mr. Justice Story wrote to his wife, on March 4, 1832, "Thanks be to God, the Court can wash their hands of the iniquity of oppressing the Indians and disregarding their rights."

There were included in the record proposed findings and objections thereto. This was improper. . . . Although we cannot condone this practice, it happens that in this case the inclusion of this material in the record seems to show that the appellant's objections were made not to the findings listed in the record as defendants' requests to find, but rather to other proposed findings with which the findings of the district court are apparently identical. We have recently asked for "brief and pertinent findings of contested matters * * * rather than the delayed, argumentative, over-detailed documents prepared by winning counsel." . . . Otherwise, we lose the benefit of the judge's own consideration. In the instant case, a comparison of the findings with the opinion seems to show that the findings proposed by the defendants were mechanically adopted, with the consequence that some of the findings made by the district court are not supported by the evidence and not substantially in accord with the opinion. Such a result can usually be avoided by following what we believe is the better practice of filing findings with the opinion, when the evidence is still fresh in the mind of the trial judge, and permitting the parties to file objections under F. R. C. P. 52(b). . . .

We stress this matter because of the grave importance of fact-finding. The correct finding, as near as may be, of the facts of a lawsuit is fully as important as the application of the correct legal rules to the facts as found. An impeccably "right" legal rule applied to the "wrong" facts yields a decision which is as faulty as one which results from the application of the "wrong" legal rule to the "right" facts. The latter type of error, indeed, can be corrected on appeal. But the former is not subject to such correction unless the appellant overcomes the heavy burden of showing that the findings of fact are "clearly erroneous." Chief Justice Hughes once remarked, "An unscrupulous administrator might be tempted to say 'Let me find the facts for the people of my country, and I care little who lays down the general principles.'" That comment should be extended to include facts found without due care as well as unscrupulous fact-finding; for such lack of due care is less likely to reveal itself than lack of scruples, which, we trust, seldom exists. And Chief Justice Hughes's comment is just as applicable to the careless fact-finding of a judge as to that of an administrative officer. The judiciary properly holds administrative officers to high standards in the discharge of the fact-finding function. The judiciary should at least measure up to the same standard.

It is sometimes said that the requirement that the trial judge file findings of fact is for the convenience of the upper courts. While it does serve that end, it has a far more important purpose—that of evoking care on the part of the trial judge in ascertaining the facts. For, as every judge knows, to set down in precise words the facts as he finds them is the best way to avoid carelessness in the discharge of that duty: Often a strong impression that, on the basis of the evidence; the facts are thus-and-so gives way when it comes to expressing that impression on paper. The trial court is the most important agency of the judicial branch of the government precisely because on it rests the responsibility of ascertaining the facts. When a federal trial judge sits without a jury, that responsibility is his. And it is not a light responsibility since, unless his findings are "clearly erroneous," no upper court may disturb them. To ascertain the facts is not a mechanical act. It is a difficult art, not a science. It involves skill and judgment. As fact-finding is a human undertaking, it can, of course, never be perfect and infallible. For that very reason every effort should be made to render it as adequate as it humanly can be.

The judgment dismissing the complaint is reversed, and the case is remanded for entry of a judgment for the plaintiff, on condition that the offer of the new lease, as set forth in plaintiff's affidavits, be kept open for sixty days following the entry of the judgment.

*125 F.2d 928 (1942)*

# UNITED STATES v. JOHNSON ⅋

IN 1956 GEORGE JOHNSON, convicted of a federal crime and sentenced to a three-year prison term, tried to appeal his case. Since he lacked funds to pay for the transcript of his trial, and since that transcript was necessary for the appellate judges to review his case, he requested that the district court permit him to appeal in forma pauperis—that is, he asked the government to furnish the transcript without charge, and to provide counsel. The district-court judge who had presided at his trial turned down this request, certifying that the appeal was frivolous and not taken in good faith. Johnson then asked the United States Court of Appeals to review this decision. Judge Caroll Hincks, writing the majority opinion, said, "Court dockets crowded with meritorious appeals should not be further burdened by frivolous appeals. . . . Such a determination [of bad faith] is final, absent a showing that the trial judge acted without warrant. . . . Motion is wholly denied." Judge Frank dissents.

FRANK, Circuit Judge (dissenting): 1. Before 1956 when the Supreme Court decided Griffin v. Illinois . . . the courts, in cases cited by my colleagues, had held in effect that no constitutional question arose when there existed a discrimination against a man, solely because of his poverty, seeking to appeal from a judgment of conviction; the courts reasoned that no one had a right to appeal and therefore such a discrimination did not affect any constitutional rights. But in Griffin the Supreme Court declared that, once a state provides for appeals from convictions, such a discrimination against the poor violates the Fourteenth Amendment's guaranty of due process and equal protection of the laws. It would seem clear that the Griffin doctrine, via the due process provision of the Fifth Amendment, applies as well to a poor man's appeal from a federal conviction.

The *Griffin* doctrine therefore brings sharply into focus the correct interpretation and effect of that part of 28 U.S.C. *Section 1915*(a) which reads, "An appeal may not be taken *in forma pauperis* if the trial court certifies that it is not taken in good faith." Were that language interpreted literally—so that the trial judge's certificate, his mere fiat, would not be reviewable—the statute, I think would fall foul of the *Griffin* doctrine, for it would mean this:

(1) If a convicted man has the money to pay the docket fee and for a transcript of the proceedings at his trial, the upper federal court, by at least reading the transcript, will ascertain whether or not there was reversible error at the trial, or whether or not there was such a lack of evidence that the defendant is entitled to a new trial or a dismissal of the indictment.

(2) If, however, the defendant is so destitute that he cannot pay the docket fee, and if the trial judge has signed a certificate of "bad faith," then although a reading of the transcript shows clear reversible errors, the federal appellate court is powerless to hear the appeal and thus to rectify the errors; and even if the defendant has money enough to pay the docket fee but not enough for a transcript, the upper court usually has no way of determining whether there were such errors, must therefore assume there were none, and must accordingly refuse to consider his appeal. As a consequence, a poor man erroneously convicted—for example, where there was insufficient proof of his guilt—must go to prison and stay there. In such a situation— that is, where the upper court, if it had the transcript before it, would surely reverse for insufficiency of the evidence or on some other ground, but cannot do so solely because the defendant cannot pay for a transcript—the result is this: *He is punished because he is guilty of the crime of being poor* (more or less on the principle, openly avowed in *Erewhon* . . . that one who suffers misfortunes deserves criminal punishment).

This must be the consequence if the trial judge's certificate is not reviewable. It is no answer to say, as my colleagues do, that "the deprivation of aid to prosecute a frivolous appeal is not 'punishment.'" For such a literal interpretation of the statute will prevent the upper court from ascertaining whether or not the appeal is frivolous; if, in truth, it is not frivolous but the defendant, due to his poverty, is not permitted so to demonstrate, then, I think, he is punished for the crime of poverty.

Were the literal interpretation adopted, the statute would plainly discriminate against the poor. For then a trial judge who had committed grave errors could usually, by a "bad faith" certificate, (a) block an appeal by an indigent defendant as (b) the judge could not do in the case of a well-to-do defendant. Doubtless, seldom would a trial judge seek thus to prevent an indigent's appeal when the judge had some doubt whether there were reversible errors. But a trial judge, in all honesty, may believe the trial free of error. In the instant case the trial judge stated, "The jury was adequately and properly instructed as to the law"; but experience teaches that not too infrequently a trial judge mistakenly entertains such a view of his instructions to the jury.

Fortunately, cases cited by my colleagues go to show that, even before *Griffin*, the courts had rejected the harsh literal interpretation of the statute. Those cases hold that the trial judge's "bad faith" certificate is not final if the defendant shows the upper court that the trial judge, in making his certificate, acted "without warrant or not in good faith." In other words, those cases hold, in effect, that the trial judge's certificate of "bad faith" enjoys no unqualified finality, that the execution of such a certificate is discretionary, and that it will be disregarded if it is made to appear to the appellate court that the trial judge "abused" his discretion. This I interpret to mean that if it is made to appear to the appeal court that there is merit in a poor man's claims of errors at the trial, an appeal *in forma pauperis* will be allowed, notwithstanding the trial judge's adverse certificate.

But how can the existence of such a meritorious appeal be shown unless the defendant has access to a transcript of the events at the trial? My colleagues' opinion fails to answer that question. The pre-*Griffin* cases seem, at first glance, to have left this problem unsolved. They seem to say, what I think my colleagues say: "Yes, we will give you permission to appeal *in forma pauperis*—if you can prove what we will prevent you from proving." For suppose that, in fact, a trial judge, in uttering a "bad faith" certificate, did "abuse" his discretion: nevertheless, absent a transcript (which the indigent defendant is unable to buy) it would seem that, usually the defendant cannot show that there was such an "abuse," that is, that the appeal has merit (in that, for example, the evidence included a coerced confession or inadmissible and prejudicial testimony, or the prosecutor indulged in highly inflammatory and improper remarks to the jury). . . .

But such a result is not necessary: In the federal courts, a destitue defendant, to whom a transcript is not available, can obtain the equivalent, in the manner described in *Miller* v. *U.S.* . . . and *U.S.* v. *Sevilla* . . . :

If competently advised by counsel, the defendant will present to the trial judge a statement of the proceedings at the trial, "made up from the best sources available." The judge then will have the duty to assist in amplifying, correcting, and perfecting that statement from the best sources available to him. To that end, the judge may and should interrogate the witnesses, the counsel who represented the government and the defendant at the trial, and any other persons having reliable information. Outstanding among such other persons is the official reporter who took stenographic notes during the trial. The judge may require the reporter to read to the judge from those notes. However, in order to avoid so laborious a task, the judge may avail himself of 28 U.S.C. Section 753(b) by directing the official reporter to transcribe the notes and, free of charge, deliver a transcript to the judge.

With the statement (consisting of the transcript or otherwise prepared) approved by the trial judge, the upper court will be able to decide whether the judge's certificate of "bad faith" is justified. In that way the *Griffin* doctrine will be satisfied. In order, however, adequately to procure such a statement, and also adequately to point out in a petition to the upper court that (if it be a fact) the judge's certificate was mistaken, the ordinary indigent defendant will need the assistance of counsel. Without such lawyer-assistance, such a defendant will be at a marked disadvantage as compared with a nonindigent defendant. Accordingly, I think the *Griffin* doctrine requires that an indigent defendant have such legal assistance; I think the spirit of the Sixth Amendment, taken together with Criminal Rules 39(a) and 44, reinforces that requirement.

In the instant case, defendant, who had had a court-appointed lawyer up to the time of his conviction, had none thereafter. His need for one is reflected in the crude character of his application *in forma pauperis*. In *U.S. v. Sevilla* . . . we appointed a lawyer to aid the defendant in preparing a statement of the trial proceedings, although there the defendant, an alien, could not, under the statute, appeal *in forma pauperis*. A fortiori, here, where defendant is not an alien, we should appoint a lawyer to guide defendant (a) in procuring a statement of the trial proceedings and (b) in drafting and presenting to us a revised motion for relief *in forma pauperis*.

I conclude then that, although we should now deny defendant's motion, we should do so with leave to file a revised motion after the defendant—with the aid of counsel designated by us to assist him—has obtained a statement of the proceedings at the trial; such counsel should also aid defendant in preparing and presenting the revised motion. We can then, on that basis, informedly consider whether to grant leave to appeal *in forma pauperis*.

2. Because of my colleagues' approach to the problem, I think it desirable to add the following:

(a) As my colleagues say, the courts should discourage frivolous appeals. However, judicial denials of *forma pauperis* appeals cannot discourage appeals by defendants who are financially well off; and the fact that a defendant—for example, a wealthy professional criminal or a member of a wealthy criminal gang—can afford to pay for his appeal is no assurance that it is not frivolous. But let us arbitrarily assume, *arguendo*, that the appeals of poor men in

prison are much more likely to be frivolous than those of the financially well
heeled. Even so, the fact remains that usually, without a transcript or the
equivalent, an appellate court cannot tell whether or not a particular man's
appeal has substance. Here, then, is an apparent dilemma: In order to know
whether to grant a forma pauperis appeal, which carries with it a right to a
transcript supplied gratis, usually the upper court must have before it a
transcript or its equivalent.

The way out of this apparent dilemma is to consult the interest of justice:
Surely, even if but one out of a hundred attempted appeals by indigents has
merit, justice compels the conclusion that that appeal shall be heard. It is
no answer that so many appeals will result as to "crowd the docket." If so,
more judges should be appointed. True, the cost of running the government
will somewhat increase. But I, for one, cannot sleep well if I think that, due
to any judicial decisions in which I join, innocent destitute men may be
behind bars solely because it will cost the government something to have
their appeals considered.

The American Bar Foundation noted in 1955: "Although the right of
counsel may be clearly expressed in law, the exercise of the right to counsel
may be impaired substantially by the imposition of costs and fees. In some
jurisdictions a defendant, without resources to provide for his own defense,
may have a completely adequate defense, from preliminary hearing to final
appeal, entirely free of costs or fees. In others, court costs, the cost of transcripts, * * * and the like may operate to deprive him of the opportunity
which the law purports to give him." In the light of Griffin v. Illinois, I think
(contrary to my colleagues) that the federal courts are not in the second
category.

(b) The Griffin doctrine represents an important step forward in the
direction of democratic justice. My colleagues, regarding it as a bold step,
shudder away from applying that doctrine to a case like that at bar (indeed
are reluctant to apply pre-Griffin decisions like U.S. v. Sevilla . . .).

Yet Griffin, splendid though it is, is not exceptionally bold. We still have
a long way to go to fulfill what Chief Justice Warren has called our "mission"
to achieve "equal justice under the law," in respect of those afflicted with
poverty. In our federal courts, and in most state courts, there is no provision
by which a poor man can get funds to pay for a pretrial search for evidence
which may be vital to his defense and without which he may be deprived
of a truly fair trial. Furnishing him with a lawyer is not enough: The best
lawyer in the world cannot competently defend an accused person if the
lawyer cannot obtain existing evidence crucial to the defense, for example,
if the defendant cannot pay the fee of an investigator to find a pivotal missing witness or a necessary document, or that of an expert accountant or

mining engineer or chemist. It might, indeed, reasonably be argued that for the government to defray such expenses, which the indigent accused cannot meet, is essential to that assistance by counsel which the Sixth Amendment guarantees. Legal Aid has no money available for that purpose, nor, in most jurisdictions, does the Public Defender (if there is one). In such circumstances, if the government does not supply the funds, justice is denied the poor—and represents but an upper-bracket privilege.

Sixteen centuries ago, Lactantius wrote, "Nobody is poor unless he stands in need of justice." It should give us pause not only that Magna Carta forced the king to agree, "To no one will we sell, to no one will we refuse, * * * justice," but also that, in ancient predemocratic days, many a Bill in Eyre or Bill in Chancery succesfully asked the aid of the court because the petitioner was poor and needed help against a wealthy and powerful opponent. Surely our democracy should follow and enlarge upon those examples. Most of our state constitutions, echoing Magna Carta, proclaim that "every person ought to obtain justice freely without being obliged to purchase it"; yet, as matters now stand, men are often "obliged to purchase justice" or go without it if they have not the wherewithal. Such are the coercions of poverty that a decent, sensible lawyer may well advise an innocent man, too poor to obtain essential defense evidence, to bargain with the prosecutor to accept a plea of guilty to a lesser crime than that with which the defendant is charged.

For thirteen years, I have been calling attention to this problem and urging a solution. I was most agreeably surprised, therefore, to learn, just the other day, that in Scandinavia it has been the practice, for upward of seventy years, not only to allow every accused a defense counsel of his choice at government expense, but to place the police department and the office of the prosecutor equally at the service of the defense and the prosecution; defense counsel may have these agencies, at government expense, make all necessary investigations . . . ; and the prosecution is responsible for producing at trial the witnesses called by the accused as well as all other evidence he wishes introduced—again at government expense.

The federal government and all the states in this country, the richest on the globe, will, I hope, soon emulate the less opulent Scandinavian countries. Pending the time when they do so, considerations of expense should not stand in the way of the far more modest undertaking which I think necessary in the instant case, that is, governmental assistance to a poor man necessary to enable him, as well as a rich defendant, to appeal his conviction if his appeal is meritorious. If my colleagues' decision, which denies such assistance, were compelled by the statute and the precedents, I would concur, contenting myself with urging reform by legislation. I think, however, the statute and the precedents have no such compulsion but, on the contrary, authorize us to do justice (as above described).

Although the courts can do and have done something to protect the poor (or relatively poor) from the consequences of gross inequalities in economic bargaining power, of course the courts cannot and should not try to do away with the effects of all or most economic differences. But they can and should wipe out all the litigious disadvantages of poverty whenever a man is charged with, or convicted of, a crime.

My colleagues seem to have a fear—of a sort often voiced in the past by other judges when liberalization of doctrines has been urged—that dire consequences will follow. So, when in 1731 an English Act was enacted providing that all judicial proceedings should be in English, "some wise men predicted it would ruin England, some still wiser men seized on minor inconveniences that resulted from it as quite sufficient to damn it, and succeeding generations wondered why it had not passed a century earlier."

We would do well to listen carefully to those recent remarks of Lord Justice Denning: "But * * * when I see how the lawyers [of England and America] have withstood despotism and tyranny from without, I sometimes think that within the law they have not been as vigilant as they should. Freedom has on occasions been abused even within the law itself. * * *" The decision in this case should not be one of those occasions. For a man is free only if, among other things, "he is not liable to be * * * imprisoned without redress under an equal and impartial law * * *. Freedom is not something which has to be safeguarded, but rather something to be extended." Freedom confined to the status quo cannot grow; and freedom which does not grow tends to wither. Danger to democratic freedom lurks in the sentiment, "Come weal, come woe, my status is quo."

238 F.2d 565 (1956)

*The case was reviewed by the Supreme Court. The Court vacated the judgment of the Court of Appeals and ordered that court to hear the appeal.*

352 U.S. 565 (1957)

# AERO SPARK PLUG CO. v. B. G. CORPORATION ❧

I N 1941 AERO SPARK PLUG CO., INC., and *Mosler Ignition Corporation*
*appealed from a decree of the district court dismissing their complaint in*
*which they alleged that B. G. Corporation had infringed a patent held by*
*them. The district court also held that one of the claims in their patent was*
*invalid. Judge Harrie Chase, in writing the opinion for the court which*
*affirmed the decree, said, "Since there is no infringement even if the patent*
*be valid, we do not decide the question of validity." Judge Frank, concurring,*
*believes the court should go further and hold the patent invalid. The first*
*part of his concurrence, omitted here, discusses this question in great technical*
*detail.*

FRANK, *Circuit Judge* (concurring): . . . It is true that where a case
presents both a constitutional and another ground of decision, courts often
(and properly) prefer to avoid the constitutional issue if they can. That
practice is far from crystallized into a rule that it is reversible error to rely
on unconstitutionality alone, or to rely both on unconstitutionality and on a
nonconstitutional ground. And even as a practice, it is plainly inapplicable
to patent cases: A finding of unconstitutionality is a grave step because it
involves a nullification of the action of the legislative branch of the government; wherefore courts should shrink from facing that issue, and should
sidestep it so far as possible. In this it is comparable with Supreme Court
jurisdiction over state decisions alleged to invade a federal right; the federal
issue must be necessarily presented. There is no such sanctity attached to a
patent's validity. The presumption arising from its issuance by the Patent
Office is a faint one. An invalid patent masquerading as a valid one is a
public menace, and should be fair game.

It is no adequate answer to say that courts should not concern themselves with the protection of persons not parties to suits pending before them. The fact is that courts daily do so concern themselves, and in circumstances where the desirability of doing so is far less obvious than here and the means far less effective. Because I think that to hold invalid a patent which is obviously void is a matter of major public importance, I think it desirable to elaborate that point:

Perhaps the central theme in most discussions of the judicial process is the obligation of judges to consider the future consequences of their specific decisions. Such discussions usually stress the "rule" or precedent aspect of decisions. Thus Dickinson, in 1927, paraphrasing (it may be unconsciously) Aristotle's remarks made almost twenty-two hundred years earlier, writes, "One danger in the administration of justice is that the necessities of the future and the interest of parties not before the court may be sacrificed in favor of present litigants"; he thinks it imperative that judges should "raise their minds above the immediate case before them and subordinate their feelings and impressions to a practice of intricate abstract reasoning, * * * centering their attention on a mass of considerations which lie outside the color of the case at bar."

Although much can be said for that attitude—of considering a decision primarily with reference to its significance in future cases—it is sometimes given too much weight. Excessive concentration of attention, by some upper-court judges, on the formulation in their opinions of so-called legal rules, with an eye chiefly to the impact of those rules on hypothetical future cases not yet before the court, sometimes results in their allotting inadequate attention to the interests of the actual parties in the specific existing cases which it is the duty of courts to decide. Such judges never quite catch up with themselves; for, in cases which actually occur, they are deciding future cases that may never occur. Legal history shows that such an attitude leads to judicial pronouncements which, at times, are none too happy in their effects on future cases. For the future develops unanticipated happenings; moreover, it does not stay put; it refuses to be trapped.

The intended consequences of efforts to govern the future often fail; the actual consequences—which may be good or evil—are, frequently, utterly different. Results are miscalculated; there is an "illusion of purpose." Of course, present problems will be clarified by reference to future ends, but, as I have elsewhere suggested, such ends, although they have a future bearing, must obtain their significance in present consequences, otherwise those ends lose their significance. For it is the nature of the future that it never arrives. "Tomorrow today will be yesterday." Any future, when it becomes the present, is sure to bring new and unexpected problems. There is much wisdom in Valéry's reference to the "anachronism of the future."

And the paradox is that when judges become unduly interested in the future consequences of their rulings, they are (as Walter Bingham pointed out years ago) doing precisely what they say they must avoid—they are deciding not real but hypothetical cases, with no one present to speak for the imaginary contestants. The interests of the parties to cases actually before the court are thus sacrificed to the shadowy unvoiced claims of supposititious litigants in future litigation which may never arise; and the judicial process becomes the pursuit of an elusive horizon which is never reached. No one —except perhaps those judges—is satisfied, since the interests of the parties to real present cases are overlooked, and the interests of the parties in subsequent cases are often inadequately determined in their absence. No doubt it expands the ego of a judge to look upon himself as the guardian of the general future. But his more humble yet more important and immediate task is to decide individual, actual, present cases. The exaggerated respect paid today to upper-court judges, as distinguished from trial-court judges, is both a cause and a result of this over-emphasis on the rule-aspect of decisions. Such judicial legislation as inheres in formulating legal rules is inescapable. But courts should be modest in their legislative efforts to control the future, since they cannot function democratically, as legislative committees and administrative agencies can, by inviting the views of all who may be affected by their prospective rules. And, because they do not learn those views, and must largely rely on their own imaginations, they should be cautious about attempting, in present cases, to project their formulations too far and too firmly into the days yet to come. To cope with the present is none too easy, in part because the present is only a moving line dividing yesterdays and tomorrows, so that reflections on what will happen are unavoidable elements of current problems. But, although continuity, both backward and forward, is to some extent a necessity, judges should not shirk the present aspect of today's problems in favor of too much illusory tinkering with tomorrows. (It is noteworthy that in constitutional cases, where there is a peculiar necessity of regarding the interests of those who are not parties to the suits which raise constitutional questions, the Supreme Court has increasingly given less and less weight to *stare decisis*, recognizing the need for adaptation to changing circumstances. . . .) The future can become as perniciously tyrannical as the past. Posterity worship can be as bad as ancestor worship.

Dean Leon Green's tentative analysis of the factors which affect upper-court decisions helps to reveal the extent to which the judges of those courts, when deciding cases, often interest themselves in the future at the expense of the present. He refers to (1) the "administrative" factor, (2) the "ethical or moral" factor, (3) the "economic" factor, (4) the "prophylactic or preventive" factor, and (5) the "justice" factor (the "merits" of the particular case). The "administrative" factor, for instance, relates to "the workability" of a rule, its "ease and certainty of performance" in the future. Thus we find courts saying that, if recovery were allowed "in this class of cases, it would *naturally* result in a flood of litigation in cases where the injury complained of may be easily feigned without detection"; or that "in practice it is *impossible* to administer any other rule"; or that a rule "is an arbitrary exception based upon a notion of what is practicable." The "prophylactic" factor, bred of a desire of judges "to fashion rules for a healthy future," is frequently operative, for "judges are inveterate prophets and legislators"; they "scale their penalties, they impose damages, both punitive and exemplary, not merely for the individual offender's lesson, but as a preventive of future harms"; they "spend much time fashioning prophylactic rules both of substantive and procedural design in their efforts to purify the social stream through the judicial process." Those and similar factors are undeniably important. But it is not always fortunate when judges tend first to consider such factors before turning their attention to the parties to the particular actual cases which they are called upon to decide.

The elaborate (and sometimes fatuous) concern with the future potentialities of expressions in judicial opinions, which accompany and justify specific decisions is, in considerable measure, due to uncritical veneration of the doctrine of "standing by the precedents"; for, if an opinion does, in truth, lay down rules which must thereafter be followed by the courts themselves in later cases, the responsibility in deciding existing controversies is far greater than that of being fair to the parties to those controversies, for then a judge is playing the important role of legislator. That responsibility, however, can be too much underscored.

*Stare decisis*, within limits, has undeniable worth. As we said recently, "Of course, courts should be exceedingly cautious in disturbing (at least retrospectively) precedents in reliance on which men have importantly changed their positions." As I have said elsewhere, "Undoubtedly, in order to achieve impartial administration of justice, 'equality before the law,' and legal certainty, as far as it is practicable, it is important, generally, that a court should not deviate, except prospectively, from its own decision in a prior case, even if that decision was in error, especially where such deviation will harm persons who acted in reliance upon that decision—as, for instance, a decision assigning specific legal consequences to specific words in a deed or lease." But precedent worship has been so unreflective that there has been insufficient inquiry into its practical workings. There is need to apply to it more of that constructive skepticism voiced by Wigmore twenty-five years

ago. We have paid too little heed to the way in which John Chipman Gray
—a successful practicing lawyer in the field of real property where, above
all, precedent has been traditionally sanctified—challenged the fundamental
thesis of *stare decisis* when he said that few men, in the conduct of their
practical affairs, actually rely on past judicial rulings. Perhaps his skepticism
went too far. Yet, in the twenty years which have elapsed since he issued
that challenge, few persons have met it, and most lawyers and many judges
go on declaiming that life would be unbearably uncertain if courts did not
adhere to their earlier formulations of "rules" and "principles." We know
virtually nothing of the extent to which men do, in fact, rely on past judicial
utterances. If, as is often said, *stare decisis* is bottomed on something like
estoppel, courts should not be too hesitant about changing their previous
formulations when change is highly desirable, in the absence of proof of
actual reliance by the litigant who opposes such a change. It might be well
to hold that such reliance will be presumed but that that presumption is
rebuttable. And, in any event, such changes, as Wigmore suggested, can
be made prospective, and not retroactive, where there is any likelihood that
there was reliance. If the sanctity of *stare decisis* were thus moderately
diminished, and if authorities were employed as they were by the much
abused scholastics, that is, only when shown to be reasonable, upper-court
judges might lose some of their prestige, but they could, by reducing their
Jovian aloofness, devote more time to the interests of litigants in specific
actual cases and less to the possible future harm of "just" decisions of those
actual controversies.

Fortunately, wise judges have devised escapes from improvidently formulated rulings. For instance, the courts have recognized the fact that chance
circumstances—such as the peculiar interests of the parties to a suit or the
laziness or incompetence of their lawyers—may prevent the adequate presentation of all the aspects of a case and thus induce judicial neglect of those
aspects, with resultant inadequacy in the judicial generalizations. So the
Supreme Court has wisely said, "Questions which merely lurk in the record,
neither brought to the attention of the court nor ruled upon, are not to be
considered as having been so decided as to constitute precedents."

But, no matter what is done, the problem of deciding cases so that
decisions will not be hurtful, as precedents, to future litigants, is not too easy
of solution. It is surprising, then, that my colleagues, who like all judges,
seek, every day, as they must, to solve that difficult problem, refuse, in the
case at bar, to tackle a problem the solution of which is far simpler and with
results far more easily foreseeable: Here the question is not of the future
consequences, on litigants in possible future suits, of a general rule articulated
in an opinion accompanying a decision, but of how a decision as to the

specific rights of a particular person before the court may affect others not in court against whom that same person may, in the future, attempt to assert those very rights. It resembles the question of revoking the license to drive an automobile of a man who has been proved to be an incompetent driver: In deciding whether that specific man should be permitted to drive in the future, it is necessary to consider those who may be injured by his future conduct if his license is not revoked, and the precedental effect of the decision on future similar litigation, not relating in any way to the specific man, is, relatively, unimportant. The public interest in that specific man's later activities should be a paramount consideration. His potential future victims are not present, and, for that very reason, their interests should be a major concern of the tribunal called upon to render decision.

Consequently, if we must here choose between deciding that the patent is not valid or is not infringed—a choice I think we are not required to make—our choice should be the former. By such a choice, we will do no harm to the patent system. It is under fire today, and may not survive attack unless its major abuses are removed. Among such abuses is the persistence of cancerous "spurious" patents. To shift the metaphor, they are vicious Zombis. Their attacks on the public interest bring the patent system into disrepute.

*130 F.2d 290 (1942)*

# BIBLIOGRAPHY

## Part 1. The Democratic Spirit

1. "On Holding Abe Lincoln's Hat," talk before the Lawyer's Division, Joint Defense Appeal, New York City, June, 1953.

2. "The Place of the Expert in a Democratic Society," 16 *Philosophy of Science* (1949) 3.

3. "The Speech of Judges: A Dissenting Opinion," 29 *Virginia Law Review* (1943) 625.

4. "Judge Learned Hand," excerpts from a manuscript based on lectures delivered at Yale Law School, November, 1955. A different version, 24 *University of Chicago Law Review* (1957) 666.

## Part 2. The Conflict Between Freedom and Authority

1. *If Men Were Angels* (Chapters I, II, X, XII, XVIII), Harper & Brothers, 1942.

2. *United States v. Roth*, 237 F.2d 796 (1956). Concurring opinion.

3. Book review (of George Calhoun's *Introduction to Greek Legal Science*), 57 *Harvard Law Review* (1944) 1120.

## Part 3. What Courts Do in Fact

1. *Law and the Modern Mind* (Chapters I, II, IV, V from Part One; Chapter I from Part Three), Brentano's, 1930; Coward McCann, 1949; Anchor Books, 1963.

2. *Courts on Trial* (Chapters III, IV, VI, XII, XV, XVI), Princeton University Press, 1949; Atheneum Paperback 27, 1963.

3. *Not Guilty* (excerpt from Chapter Eight), Doubleday, 1957; Popular Library, 1962.

4. *Skidmore v. Baltimore & Ohio R. Co.*, 167 F.2d 54 (1948). Opinion for the court.

[ 449 ]

## Part 4. The Protection of Due Process

1. *United States v. Rosenberg*, 195 F.2d 583 (1952). Opinion for the court.
2. *Gardella v. Chandler*, 172 F.2d 402 (1949). Concurring opinion.
3. *United States v. Rubenstein*, 151 F.2d 915 (1945). Dissenting opinion.
4. *United States v. Antonelli Fireworks Co.*, 155 F.2d 631 (1946). Dissenting opinion.
5. *United States v. Leviton*, 193 F.2d 848 (1951). Dissenting opinion.
6. *United States v. On Lee*, 193 F.2d 306 (1951). Dissenting opinion.
7. *In re Fried*, 161 F.2d 453 (1947). Opinion for the court.
8. *United States ex rel. Caminito v. Murphy*, 222 F.2d 698 (1955). Opinion for the court.
9. *United States ex rel. Leyra v. Denno*, 208 F.2d 605 (1953). Dissenting opinion.
10. *United States v. St. Pierre*, 132 F.2d 837 (1942). Dissenting opinion.
11. *United States v. Field*, 193 F.2d 92 (1951). Concurring opinion.
12. *United States v. Liss*, 137 F.2d 995 (1943). Dissenting opinion.
13. *In re J. P. Linahan, Inc.*, 138 F.2d 650 (1943). Opinion for the court.
14. *Keller v. Brooklyn Bus Corp.*, 128 F.2d 510 (1942). Dissenting opinion.
15. *United States v. Farina*, 184 F.2d 18 (1950). Dissenting opinion.
16. *United States v. Forness*, 125 F.2d 928 (1942). Opinion for the court.
17. *United States v. Johnson*, 238 F.2d 565 (1956). Dissenting opinion.
18. *Aero Spark Plug Co. v. B. G. Corporation*, 130 F.2d 290 (1942). Concurring opinion.